Export Management

Export Management

D C Kapoor

Director

National Institute of Careers in
Export and Marketing (NICEM)
New Delhi

VIKAS®

VIKAS® PUBLISHING HOUSE PVT LTD

VIKAS® PUBLISHING HOUSE PRIVATE LIMITED
E-28, Sector-8, Noida-201301 (UP), India
Phone: +91-120-4078900 • Fax: +91-120-4078999
VIKAS® Registered Office: A-27, 2nd Floor, Mohan Co-operative Industrial Estate, New Delhi-110044
E-mail: helpline@vikaspublishing.com • Website: www.vikaspublishing.com

SALES AND BRANCH OFFICES OF VIKAS® AND S CHAND AND COMPANY LIMITED

Chennai : Ph: 044-2363 2120, chennai@schandpublishing.com
Guwahati : Ph: 0361-2738 811, 2735 640, guwahati@schandpublishing.com
Hyderabad : Ph: 040-4018 6018, hyderabad@schandpublishing.com
Jalandhar : Ph: 0181-4645 630, jalandhar@schandpublishing.com
Kolkata : Ph: 033-2335 7458, 2335 3914, kolkata@schandpublishing.com
Lucknow : Ph: 0522-4003 633, lucknow@schandpublishing.com
Mumbai : Ph: 022-2500 0297, mumbai@schandpublishing.com
Patna : Ph: 0612-2260 011, patna@schandpublishing.com

Export Management
ISBN: 978-81259-0939-2 Product Code: V8EXM60BMGT10ENAA02O

First Published 2002
Reprinted several times between 2002 and 2018
Reprint 2022

PRINTED IN INDIA
By Vikas Publishing House Private Limited, Plot 20/4, Site-IV, Industrial Area Sahibabad, Ghaziabad-201010 and Published by Vikas Publishing House Private Limited, E-28, Sector-8, Noida-201301

Preface

I do not claim that this book is the only or the last word on the Export Management Series. Neither is it absolute, except in terms of arrangement, sequence and manner of presentation.

The world is forever changing, but the events that have taken place since 1989 have been particularly dramatic. There have been border changes country name changes and technological innovations all of which have contributed to, altering the traditional depiction of countries in both shape and size. Our trading environment in terms of market structure and buyer knowledge, power and expectations has changed materially and so we need new tools to deal with these new market dynamics.

In this changing environment, instead of just developing managers, executives and exporters, we need to develop them to become good competitors. I am trying to provide a simple, verbiage – free and, above all, holistic compendium of principles and concepts pertaining to one of the most important areas of modern Business Management.

I hope this study material will be helpful to all everyone whether you are a student, entrepreneur, exporter, importer or marketers.

D C Kapoor

ACKNOWLEDGEMENTS

I acknowledge with all sincerity and gratefulness, the following organisations and their publications.

Government of India –Ministry of Commerce, Ministry of Textiles; Director General of Foreign Trade; Central Silk Board; Indian Silk Export Promotion Council (ISEPC); Apparel Export Promotion Council (AEPC); Export Promotion Council for Handicrafts; Handlooms Export Promotion Council; Council for Leather Exports; Gem & Jewellery Export Promotion Council; National Institute of Fashion Technology (NIFT); Indian Trade Promotion Organisation (ITPO); EAN India, etc.

Federation of Indian Chambers of Commerce and Industry (FICCI); Federation of Indian Export Organisations (FIEO); and International Chamber of Commerce (ICC).

International Organisations: WTO; ITC, FORUM, GATI, UNCTAD, CBI News Bulletins, Protrade; IGEP and others.

References: Philip Kotler, Cundiff & Still; Peter Drucker, G.B. Giles, Simon Majaro, William J. Santon, Rustom S. Davar, Impex Times, Exim Times, Anupam, Nabhi, Stanley Vance; James Culliton, M.E. Herley, Cuaude Cellich, Terry Mc Culliton, Tony Fletcher, Neil Russel Jones, Wendell Simth and others.

D C Kapoor

CONTENTS

// CHAPTER 1 //

WHY EXPORT

Exporting is merely trading – but the customer lives in another country. Exporting is only an extension of the need to trade. Man's economic and social progress has developed because of the increasing specialisation of labour. For example, one man found it inconvenient both to be a hunter and to raise crops. The solution was for one man to specialise in hunting and another in farming. Each would produce enough for himself and for the other. They would then exchange their surplus.

INCREASING SPECIALISATION

The technology of tool-making resulted in further specialization and interfamily exchange developed into intercommunity exchange. Subsequent tribal groups specialised in particular activities and exchanged their surplus with other tribes. The ultimate extension was trade between nations, that is, international trade.

We are now going to know about a particular trader who specialises in making shoes and sells them from his market stall. (During the course of the present project, we shall hear a lot more about this Ruralian businessman, named Mr. Trader.)

Trader Meets the Tourists

Mr. Trader is a busy market stallholder in Ruralia. One day, he notices that a group of tourists from Industria are particularly interested in a new kind of shoes he has introduced. Every tourist buys two or three pairs.

Mr. Trader converses with the tourists who explain that they are attracted by the shoes because the level of craftsmanship is higher than that of shoes made in factories in Industria. Ruralia leather is also more comfortable and supple than that of Industrian shoes. Mr.Trader is pleased to learn that his shoes have these advantages over Industrian shoes.

Exports and the Balance of Payments

As we shall see, there are several good reasons why it is important for countries and for individual companies to export and to keep expanding their exports.

From the national point of view, the most important reason is that unless a country *exports* it will not have the foreign currency it must have to *import* the things it needs but cannot supply itself. Without foreign currency, a developing country cannot import the materials, equipment and technology it needs for development—even the basic necessities of life. It is clear why this is so if you think about the balance of payments.

What is the 'balance of payments' The balance of payment is a statement of accounts which shows the difference between the amount of money that has come into a country and the amount that has gone out of the country within a particular period of time.

If the inflow of money into a country is more than the outflow, the balance of payments would be in *surplus*.

If more money has gone out of the country and is more than the inflow, then it has a *deficit* in its balance of payments. In other words, the balance of payments is the difference between the total value of the country's *inflow* and *outflow*.

Inflow

On the inflow side, there is the money that flows in from other countries for:

Visible exports The export of goods. Goods are called 'visible' because they are easily seen.

Invisible exports Tourism, shipping, and royalties that foreign companies pay to extract your minerals, the servicing of foreign ships and planes in the harbours and airports, and so on.

In addition to these inflow from visible and invisible exports, there are the capital inflows—foreign investment, loans and grants.

Other inflows include money sent back to a country by its people working abroad as well as the interest earned on investments abroad.

Outflow

The outflows in a balance of payment statement are broken down the same way. Money goes out of the country for:

Visible imports Imports of goods.

Invisible imports Such as payments for foreign technology, travel abroad, shipping your goods on foreign ships, insurance paid to foreign countries. The inflows and outflows for services such as tourism and insurance are less easy to see and so they are called 'invisible.'

These are also the capital outflows. For example, interest payments on foreign loans and dividends paid to parent companies by subsidiaries in your own country.

Most developing countries face a problem on the balance of payments. The need is to increase foreign exchange earning and help solve balance of payments problems on a more permanent basis. Cutting imports instead of increasing exports is a poor solution because it can lead to stagnation and it prevents the purchase of capital goods and materials from abroad.

A country must export in order to be able to import. But how can it find out how *much* it needs to export? How can it *plan* its export? The hunter and farmer were hungry for crops or meat and knew that they had to produce a surplus of their own products in order to exchange it for what they needed. They had a good idea of how much surplus to produce.

A nation needs an information system in the same way as a company needs an accounting system. A company's accounts show the money that has come in and the money that has gone out. A country has to have a similar statement to describe the flow of money between itself and the rest of the world. This is called the balance of payments statement. If a country has more outflow of cash than inflow in a specified period, it must make up the difference by paying out of its reserves or by borrowing money.

The balance of payments is the overall balance between a country's outward flow of cash and its inwards flow from the rest of the world.

The balance of payments is not concerned with the movement of money inside a country. The balance of payments shows the difference between the amount of money that has come into the country and the amount of money that has gone out of it.

International trade in goods is known as *visible* imports and exports. International trade in services such as shipping, insurance, consultancy, financial services and tourism is known as *invisible* imports and exports. Other important parts of the balance of payments are capital flows such as investment, loans, grant and repatriation of capital. Finally, there are remittances from workers living abroad, dividends and loan interest.

Most developing countries are heavily in deficit. What can be done to correct the position? The following syndicate exercise will show that there is no easy solution.

Country X: Student Groups A, B, C, D

In the centre, H1 is the balance of payments situation of a typical developing country. Total outflow exceed inflow by $30 million. How can the balance be put right?

Various courses of actions are suggested to deal with the deficit. The ways of reducing the outflow are listed on the left. Ways of increasing inflow are listed on the right.

Each Student Group considers the problem from a different viewpoint:

Student Group A	Student Group B	Student Group C	Student Group D
Government View	Shipping & Tourism Company	Small Trading Company	Large Industrial Company view

Each Student Group represents its findings to the full seminar, detailing the ways in which its strategy will affect each item in the balance of payments.

We have considered ways of overcoming an unfavourable balance of payments in Country X. The two most obvious ways are by reducing the visible imports or increasing visible exports. But exporting more goods also helps to increase the economic activity and provides more and better jobs.

Imports can be limited by import quotas and import tariffs. But, in order to export, a developing country needs to import raw materials, machinery and consumer goods for foreign exports. It also needs to use the transportation services and know-how of other countries and spend money on travel and advertising to export markets. So, all cash outflow must be carefully controlled – but in a way that does not prevent imports which are essential for the development of export trade and the economy in general.

We have seen how exporting is very good from a national viewpoint. But, what attractions does exporting have from a company and personal viewpoint.

Importance of Balance of Payment

Sometimes a country can buy goods and services from abroad on a barter basis – by paying for them with goods instead of money.

But, barter trade is never enough to meet a country's import needs. Most foreign suppliers want to be paid in currency—either in the currency of their own country or some other currency with which they can purchase whatever they need. If a country's balance of payments is in deficit, it means that not enough foreign currency is coming into the country to pay for its purchases from abroad. If the deficit continues, sooner or later, the country will find that it cannot pay for its imports and it will have to cut them down.

The purpose of the following exercise is to show that it is not easy to solve problems relating to the balance of payments.

> Balance of Payments Exercise H1 shows the situation relating to the balance of payments of a typical developing country. The total outflow exceeds the inflow by $30 million. How can this serious situation be rectified?
>
> You consider the problem and then describe how you think the balance of payments could be improved, detailing the ways in which your proposed strategy will affect each item in the balance of payments. You should be able to defend your arguments against criticism.
>
> In the centre of H2, is the balance of payments situation shown in H1. Various courses of action are suggested to deal with the deficit. The ways of reducing the outflow are listed on the left. The ways of increasing the inflow are listed on the right. You consider these two types of possible action and then discuss the particular actions which can be recommended.
>
> Comment on the views expressed. Indicate the realistic limits of savings against each item in the balance of payments, and point strongly to the need for more visible exports.

It may be possible for a country to reduce imports by cutting down on purchases of foreign luxury items and other goods which the country really does not need. But, the scope for doing so is often already very limited. Substantial cuts in imports are often painful; they can reduce the standard of living and hold back economic growth. For example:

★ People may have to go without goods they need and which are not produced locally.
★ Factories may have to shut down or cut production because they cannot import necessary parts or materials.
★ Development projects can be stopped or slowed down.

Comparative Advantage

The idea of exporting and of nations exchanging surplus of products may be easy enough to accept. It certainly made good sense to Mr. Trader. But why did one particular *Nation* begin to specialise in one particular activity? *Because they had particular advantages which made it easy for them*. For example, these comparative advantages might be soil, climate, mineral deposits, special mental or physical aptitudes, geographical position, labour costs, etc.

Many countries buy from abroad because the products are cheaper or better or more readily available than at home. That is why many European countries and the United States buy so many electronic goods from Japan.

Most countries in the world, especially the busy, densely populated ones, have to buy some goods from abroad or else go without them. Many countries also have to buy raw materials from abroad, especially metals and other minerals, because they are not available at home. All countries need to import products and pay another country for them. To pay for imports, a country must get money from the rest of the world. Otherwise it could go bankrupt.

Import-substitution Problems

Developing countries often do not make the maximum use of the productive capacity they already have. This is particularly true in countries which have concentrated on import-substitution, to encourage home industries to produce goods that would otherwise have to be imported.

This emphasis on meeting the needs of the home market means that production is limited and it also varies with fluctuations in home demand. So, producing goods for import-substitution reasons is often inefficient and costly.

Short-term Solutions

Over a limited period of time—and this can be a matter of many years – a country can make up for a deficit in its balance of payments by:

- ★ Borrowing from other countries or from international institutions
- ★ Soliciting outright grants from other countries
- ★ Drawing in its reserves of gold or foreign currency, if it has any.

But these are not short-term solutions because:

- ★ Loans must be repaid, and the interest payments can themselves become a burdensome outflow and reduce even further the amount of foreign exchange that is available for imports.
- ★ Dependence on grants from other countries can have undesirable political consequences. The availability of such grants is very limited anyway.
- ★ A country's reserves of gold and foreign currency are bound to be limited. Even if they were large, they could not cover a deficit forever.

It is clear that sooner or later a country has to get its foreign currency outflow and inflow more or less in balance. It can do this by reducing the outflow, or increasing the inflow, or by doing a bit of both.

Long-term Solutions

Over the longer term, a country can put its balance of payments on a healthier footing by becoming self-sufficient in many goods. Many developing countries try to achieve this by following a policy of import substitution.

This involves encouraging the local production of imported products through means such as direct government investment or investment incentives, coupled with high tariffs or other trade barriers to protect the home industries from import competition.

It is good if countries can reach a point where they do not have to rely on foreign suppliers for critical goods.

But import substitution cannot really solve a country's balance of payments problems because:

- ★ No country can produce everything that it needs or that its people would like to have.
- ★ As a country develops, its import requirements actually increases, even if it does become self-sufficient in many products.

If carried too far, an import substitution policy can actually hold back a country's economic development:

- ★ If companies are protected by export barriers from competition, they may have no incentive to operate efficiently.

If they are geared to serve only the limited local market, they may not be able to operate on an efficient scale of production.

- ★ Investment capital may be diverted to protected, inefficient industries, instead of being invested in ways that would be more productive.
- ★ By erecting high trade barriers to protect its import-substitution industries, a country can invite retaliation by other countries, with the result that its exports suffer.

HOW EXPORTS BENEFIT A COUNTRY

Export Expansion

A better answer instead of putting so much emphasis on import substitution, it makes more sense for governments to balance it with a policy of export expansion.

The idea is to join in what has been called the *international division of labour*, where each country makes the best use of its resources by concentrating on producing and exporting products in which it has a competitive advantage, while buying from other countries the products they produce more efficiently.

By increasing their export earning, countries are better able to pay for their imports. But there are other reasons why developing countries should try to expand their exports, develop new, export-oriented industries and seek new markets.

Governments take a keen interest in exports because they speed economic development and improve the standard of living of the people. Success means increasing the total amount of exports. It also means diversifying those exports – not only in terms of products but also in terms of exports markets. This spreads both the risk and the benefits.

Increased scale By exporting, industries can increase the scale of their production, thus increasing efficiency and lowering costs.

Better usage of national resources Many developing countries concentrate on their traditional export products – even when the demand for at least some of these products in world markets is declining. It is clearly in their interest to allocate some of these resources to products for which the demand is increasing.

Diversification of products and markets It is all the more important that diversification of products and markets should be there because some developing countries see only limited growth prospects for their traditional exports. The reasons for this include:

- Declining growth of demand in world markets for many primary products
- Technological changes that economise on raw materials
- Competition for artificial substitute

Widening beyond the home market, an important objective of exports is to seek a wider market than the limited home market. Many developing countries with a small population and very low per capita income find that they have the natural resources to produce a particular product. But the home market is often too small to justify a factory of even the minimum efficient size.

This type of problem was faced by the Government of Somalia earlier when trying to establish a Gypsum factory. In spite of the fact that the country has big deposits of Gypsum, the amount of the finished product that could be sold on the home market did not justify setting up a factory. This situation, which is fairly common, can often be dealt with successfully if production is aimed towards foreign markets.

Reducing unemployment The effects on employment of export expansion can be very significant. This is particularly true if the exporting is by labour-intensive industries, and if the industries are located in rural areas where there is a serious shortage of jobs.

Technological advance Expansion and diversification into exports also lead to improvement in the level of technological 'know-how'. Competition in international markets stimultes the exporters to adapt their products to the needs of the market, often leading to the use of more modern technological processes and production methods. This has a dynamic effect on industry in the developing country.

These beneficial effects are not confined to production aspects. Greater knowledge is gained about marketing research, export costing and pricing, management of marketing channels, personal selling and publicity. This can have a very beneficial effect on business efficiency in general.

Better products Another argument for export expansion is that competition in world markets stimulates your own industries to produce better quality goods, a development which is also of benefit to people buying the same goods at home.

In producing better quality goods, your factories also demand a higher level of skills, so that the impact of export expansion is to increase the level of jobs as well as the number of them.

Everyone knows that exports are good for the country as a whole. But, businessmen will only enter the export field, if they know that exporting is going to increase their business and produce profits.

Foreign exchange benefits A country must achieve a surplus from the export of products that it is good at producing – so that it may import goods for which it has no comparative advantage.

The hunter exchanged his surplus with the farmer – and some international trade is still done on a better basis. Most trade is now carried out using money, both within a country and internationally.

If we need US Dollars to buy the goods we need, what is the use of earning German Marks? Because there is a market for currencies in the same way as there is for products—we can buy Dollars with German Marks.

Export is Good for Business

We are going to hear of the experiences of a typical manufacturer, Mr. Trader. You will be hearing a lot more about him during this project.

Introducing Mr. Trader

Mr. Trader is a shoe manufacturer in Ruralia. He began his life making and selling shoes from a market stall. At first he only sold to the local people; he then began selling to tourists from Industria. The tourists were impressed by the quality and craftsmanship of his shoes.

Through hard work and his own ability, Mr. Trader builds up a lively and growing business, selling shoes in the home market through a network of wholesalers and retail outlets. His company reaches a critical stage. Mr.Trader wants to expand his sales but the market is too small. Because he is confined to the small home market, his production is low and therefore his unit costs are high – and so are his prices. Although he has no competition, this means that many people cannot afford to buy his shoes.

There is another problem, too. Mr. Trader finds that the home market is very seasonal. People tend to buy shoes only during particular time-slots of the year. This makes production and stock control very difficult. Mr.Trader's Sales Manager, John Green, is worried about the way sales is going and they discuss the problem together.

How a Company Benefits

Individual businessmen may be patriotic, but they must also be interested in the survival and prosperity of their own businesses. Why should a company want to export, regardless of trying to help the nation as a whole?

1. In single markets, many products are very seasonal, for reasons of climate (example: umbrellas), religion (example: gifts) or economics (people may only be able to afford some things once a year). Sales to export markets will often fill in the seasonal 'troughs' in demand, so that factories can be kept busy all the year through and cash flow problems can be eased.
2. Businessmen often believe that exports will be unprofitable because goods will have to be sold at lower prices. This is not always the case,

but even if it is so, the higher volume will often mean a lower cost per unit of production yielding overall greater profits.

3. If a company is exposed to new ideas from other markets, and if its products have to compete without any protection in the world markets, the experience will improve every aspect of the company's operations.
4. In many countries, only those companies which export are allowed foreign exchange to buy imported machinery, and they are given preference in the allocation of licence to build new premises or to import raw materials.
5. Opportunity to expand the market share.
6. Increase production if capacity is underutilized in the domestic market.
7. Decrease dependence on domestic sales or compensate for stagnating the domestic market.
8. Diffuse domestic competition by expanding into less competitive foreign markets.
9. Follow domestic leaders into foreign markets to reduce foreign market research costs.
10. Competition in international markets stimulates the exporters to adapt their products to the needs of the market, leading to an improvement in their level of technological know-how.
11. From a personal point of view, it is more challenging, more interesting and more enjoyable to travel and work in the international business environment rather than to be 'stuck' in the often narrow and unstimulating activities of a well-known home market.

WHY SHOULD A BUSINESSMAN EXPORT

The government may be convinced that export expansion is in the national interest, but it has to convince businessmen like Mr.Trader that it is in *their* interest as well – they are the ones who must do the exporting. This may be especially difficult if businessmen have been protected in the home market.

Here are some reasons why exporting makes sense from the businessman's point of view:

Exporting offers a firm numerous advantages but unfortunately, many firms have not seized the incredible opportunities that exist in the worldwide market place. The massive restructuring of political boundaries, the opening and globalisation of new consumer markets, the increasing market orientation of the States of the former Soviet Union, and the Uruguay Round Agreements have generated unprecedented export opportunities. Ours is a global economy, influenced by the worldwide access to manufacturing technology which has created competitive manufacturers who are able to produce cheaper, faster and better. Many developing countries have become serious rivals to developed economies because of their links to global communication systems and the explosion of their television, print and electronic access to information. There has been a more opportune time for Indian firms to capitalise on these market shifts and to export for the reasons listed here.

Increase sales and profits If the firm is performing well domestically, expansion into foreign markets is likely to improve its profitability.

Gain global market share By exporting, the firm will learn from its competitors, their strategies and what they have done to gain a share in the foreign markets.

Reduce dependence on existing domestic markets By expanding into foreign markets, the firm will increase its marketing base and reduce its dependence on local customers.

Acquire stability in the face of domestic market fluctuations By tapping global markets, firms are no longer held captive to economic changes, varying consumer demand and seasonal fluctuations in the domestic economy.

Make use of excess production capacity Exporting could increase the utilisation of production capacity and the length of production runs, thereby reducing average unit costs and raising the economies of scale.

Enhance competitiveness Exporting enhances a firm's and a country's competitive advantage. While the firm will benefit from exposure to new technologies, methods and processes, the country will benefit from an improved balance of trade. India's share in the world trade is currently only 0% and is expected to rise to 1% by the turn of the century.

Create domestic jobs In 1996/97, Indian exports of goods and services from small-scale industry alone supported a total of 158.91 lakh jobs it the country.

Find excellent no-cost or low-cost experts in export For many firms, the decision not to export is based on fear of the unknown. Trade promotion organisations throughout the country have been established to assist companies that are strong domestically but have not contemplated venturing into export markets. These organisations help businesses in every step of the export process.

More stability In single markets, demand for many products is very seasonal, for reasons of climate (example: umbrellas), religion (example: gifts) or economics (people may only be able to afford some things once a year).

Sales to export markets will often fill in the seasonal 'troughs' in demand, so that factories can be kept busy all the year and cash flow problems can be eased.

Lower unit costs Businessmen often believe that exports will be unprofitable because they will have to be sold at lower prices. This is not always the case, but even if it is so, the higher volume will often mean lower cost per unit of production – yielding overall greater profits.

New ideas If a company is exposed to new ideas from other markets, and its products have to compete in world markets, the experience will improve every aspect of the company's operations.

Access to foreign exchange In many countries, only those companies that export are allowed foreign exchange to buy imported machinery, and they are given preference in the allocation of licence to import raw materials.

It is important to note that many of the risks of exporting are similar to those faced in the domestic market.

Risks of expanding into domestic or foreign markets

- ★ Sales may not meet projections
- ★ Competition may be greater than anticipated
- ★ Customers may be slow to pay or not pay at all

Risks unique to exporting Repatriation of profits from the target country may be constrained or forbidden.

- ★ Fluctuations in exchange rates may decrease or eliminate profits, or even result in losses.
- ★ In cases of non-payment or other contractual problems, there may be questions of jurisdiction i.e., Indian courts may not be able to enforce contracts between parties in different countries.
- ★ Instability in the target country can lead to losses from war or civil strife or nationalization by the foreign government.
- ★ The product may not be accepted in the foreign market.

// CHAPTER 2 //

WHAT IS EXPORTING

As we discussed earlier, the purpose of this project is to make the reader familiar with the several aspects of exporting. Before we start looking at them in detail, let's look at the overall picture to see how all these aspects fit in.

A DEFINITION OF EXPORTING

What is Exporting? In the briefest terms, it is the process of earning money by selling products (or services) in foreign markets. It is finding customers and enterprise which can serve better than these customers' current suppliers. It is in serving these customers successfully that the enterprise grows and prospers, simultaneously increasing direct and indirect employment. At this point, "selling" and "marketing" applies to a product that the market needs.

Who said exporting is easy Perhaps not the first time. That is why thorough preparation and hard work are required. Subsequent efforts will benefit from experience. Furthermore, exporting can be very profitable and – if you like, a challenge – very exciting.

In order to accomplish this, an exporter must do what any seller must do, whether he is marketing his products in his own country or abroad.

He must provide the right product:

★ in the right place
★ at the right time
★ at the right price
★ he must make sure that he gets paid for it.

The basic principles are the same for doing business at home or abroad. But, it is generally more complicated to market products abroad, and much easier to make mistakes which can be fatal to success.

Finding Markets

Often companies have a very good idea of where they can export their products. This may be because they already have been selling to particular countries successfully, or because they know where other suppliers of similar products have been successful. But often the problem of finding markets is not so simple. An exporter may be missing opportunities to increase his sales and profits if he exports to particular markets without investigating others which might hold better prospects. Or a company may never have exported before and not know which countries to approach first.

Market research is necessary to find out which are the most promising markets, and how to go about selling to them and meeting their requirements. The importance of conducting a market research – or of having someone to do it is overlooked by may potential exporters, and even by companies which actually are exporting. Why market research is so important will become more apparent as we look in some detail at what is involved in export marketing and the procedures related to it.

The Marketing Concept

In fact, the need for a market research will be immediately apparent to anyone who appreciates how important it is to offer prospective customers, products they need or would like to have. Research can reveal to the exporter these needs or wants.

No one would argue with the idea that the man who offers people a product they need or like, is likely to be more successful than the man who offers a product that people do not need or do not like. But many businessmen do not grasp the implication of this idea. Let us study the case about one such businessman.

Introducing Mr. Vague

Like Mr. Trader, Mr. Vague is a businessman in Ruralia who has become interested in exporting. He participates in a government-sponsored Trade Fair showing his clothing items – and is disappointed with the results. He is not prepared to adapt his product to suit the tastes of the market.

Discussion

Students should give their opinions about Mr. Vague's approach in selling his products. Can they cite similar cases from real life? What is wrong with Mr. Vague's attitude? What should he do? What should he have done even before going to the Trade Fair?

Mr. Vague is a typical example of the businessman who is used to getting by – or even flourishing – because enough customers are willing to buy what he happens to be producing. It does not occur to him that he might be able to do better if he were willing to find out what people really wanted and adapt his product to suit their tastes.

Like Mr. Vague, many businessmen get by with this self-centred approach because they do not have much competition. But, in today's world, competition is bound to increase, and trying to overcome it by merely cutting prices is not a very satisfactory answer – and could lead to disaster. Mr. Vague would be wise to consider how he might change his products to make them more attractive to people in comparison with those of his competitors, so that they might be willing to pay a higher price for them. Moving into export markets could be the way for Mr. Vague to expand his business and overcome the impact of greater competition at home. But, he stands a much greater chance of succeeding, if he tries to adapt his product to suit the tastes of the buyers. He certainly should not expect prospective customers to change their tastes to suit his product.

If he has taken the trouble to find out about the tastes of people in Industria – about the kind of shirts that are popular – he might have been able to make some suitable samples to show at the Fair, and perhaps he would have achieved happier results!

We have been speaking about the tastes of customers. But that is only one aspect of market requirements. As we shall see, there are many others. And the businessman who takes the trouble to find out what those requirements are, and who tries to meet them, stands the greatest chance of success. This is what is meant by the **Marketing approach**.

Marketing is important even when selling some basic commodity that everyone needs. If you are in a market supplying products which people do not necessarily need or can buy from other sources, then the proper marketing approach became even more important.

Let us consider some typical cases from developing countries to see how this approach applies.

Discussion

Evaluate the attitude behind the following examples of some developing countries exporting policies.

- ★ *Country A* refused to consider supplying coffee in sacks in any other material except sisal because country A produced sisal as well as coffee.
- ★ *Country B* served goat meat rather than lamb meat in its tourist hotels because goat was its own traditional food.
- ★ *Country C* sent leaflets to its customers in the language of country C although this was not spoken by its customers.
- ★ *Country D* refused to answer export customer's enquiries cabled on Fridays because Friday was a traditional holiday in country D.

These are examples of failure to think from the customer's point of view and they resulted in reduced exports.

The Marketing Mix

Successful export marketing (or marketing at home for that matter) involves using a variety of techniques in a suitable way and making a series of right decisions about the many options that one has, always keeping in mind the requirements and characteristics of the market itself. It all adds up to what is called the marketing mix—the particular combination of techniques used and choices made in order to market products in a specific situation.

Product	Price	Place	Promotion	Presentation

Fig 2.1 The P's of the marketing process

Here are some of the variables in the marketing mix.

- ★ ***Product*** Its function, its basic design, its qualities... what it is.
- ★ ***Price*** This depends on the costs, where the product is sold; who it is sold to and competitors' costs.

★ ***Place (Marketing channels)*** The intermediaries through which the end-user is reached (physical distribution). How the product is transported and stored.
★ ***Promotion (Marketing communications)*** Stimulating demand through a variety of techniques, including advertising, publicity, trade fairs and personal selling.
★ ***Presentation*** Its styling (colours, detailing – design elements that affect a product looks rather than how it works), its packaging.

Let us look a bit more closely at the major elements of the marketing mix.

Product

There are often many basic characteristics of products which are within the power of the producer to change – at least to some degree – in order to meet the requirements of the market. These include the quality of the product, the material from which it is made, and how well it works.

Even more basic than that is the concept of the product itself. In many cases, manufacturers have the option to produce *different products* with the same equipment and even the same materials. For example, a producer of hand-tools can decide to go into the toy market and produce miniature tools for children. Or he may move even further away from his original product line to produce, for example, castings for toy trains. So, the product itself is one variable of the marketing mix.

Pricing

But a good product that is well-designed and well-presented can still fail if the pricing is wrong. What price to charge for a product is difficult to decide. The price to the customer has to take many costs into account.

There is, of course, the cost of the materials that go into the product. Then, there are the costs of production – factory overheads, wages, distribution etc. As we shall see, the true costs may be quite different from what they seem.

And there is the danger of a product being *priced too high* in comparison with competitive goods as well as the danger of *underpricing*.

An exporter must take into account conditions in distant markets – which can be very different from those he is familiar with at home.

Place (Marketing Channels)

It is rare that a producer can sell his product directly to the user. Usually be must sell to the middlemen, such as importers, distributors and wholesalers. If his product is ultimately bought by consumers, it must also be handled by retailers. Each trade in each country has its own pattern of sales channels, and the exporter must try to select the best from a range of possibilities.

Physical distribution Exporting involves the obvious problem of getting the product transported from the factory or other production facility to the buyer.

Promotion (Marketing Communications)

Exporters, or companies that would like to export, must bring their product to the attention of the people who would handle it – their prospective trade channels – as well as to the ultimate buyer. More than that, they may have to persuade them that there is some advantage in handling or buying this product instead of the product of a competitor. The exporter must select from a variety of possible advertising and publicity media which are available for marketing communications.

Presentation

The presentation of a product is closely related in a marketing sense to the product itself, and in many cases, it really is part of the product in the mind of the buyer. Styling details of a product – such as its colour or the different sizes offered or its shape – can greatly influence its success in the market.

Another important aspect of presentation is packaging, especially for consumer products. Good packaging not only make a product more attractive, but also more convenient to use.

Besides choosing the best mode of transport, the exporter may have to provide for warehousing in the market, so that long shipping times do not interrupt the flow of products to the customer. He may also have to take steps to ensure that his distributors or other middlemen carry adequate stocks of spare parts. All this is part of physical distribution, one more vital element in the marketing mix.

The Original 4ps of the marketing mix, were product, price, place and promotion. These have seen additions – position, packaging, people, as the boundaries of marketing spread beyond selling to encompass more of the organisation. Says Abraham Koshy, Professor of marketing at IIM Ahmedabad, "They are seen by some as the be-all and end-all of marketing and by others as an outdated concept, but they are only classifications of decisions in marketing."

Water Viera, President, marketing Advisory Services Group, subscribes to the outdated view that "**The four Ps** are really talking from inside the Manufacturer's Office, looking inward". In his opinion, there will be other sets of letters that better outline the new marketing. He suggests **the 4Cs**.

- ★ ***Customer*** Begin with the customer, then develop the product.
- ★ ***Cost*** Look at cost, see if its suits for that customer at the cost, and from the cost, derive the price rather than expect the customer to buy at cost-plus pricing.
- ★ ***Convenience*** Where will the customer buy it most conveniently, a Catalogue, the Internet, directly?
- ★ ***Communication*** Don't look at promotion, look at communication with a customer who is a partner in the business.

Helping the C-sighted marketer will be **the 4Rs**

- ★ ***Relevance*** the product or service has to be relevant, and it has to be relevant to that customer that you're thinking of.
- ★ **Resources** Do you have the resources to make it available to that customer at the right price?

★ ***Relationship*** marketers will have to work at relationships, not just conduct a transaction, but have to look at profit and customer value over a lifetime.

★ ***Returns*** What are we getting out of it, what are customers and shareholders getting out of it?

While the scope of the marketing mix will definitely go beyond just one letter, there's at least one P that will remain. For companies, as somebody rightly said only the "Paranoid will survive."

Discussion

Emphasise that the relative importance of each element in the marketing mix will vary with the type of the product and specific situation. Give examples of how the mix varies in different cases.

For example, with a product like petrol, the most important element might be *physical distribution*. But soap powder may be bought because of heavy *advertising*. So publicity is the most important element. With unbranded consumer products such as fresh fruits the most important element may be success in getting the product on the store shelves – establishing good marketing channels.

SPECIAL EXPORTING PROBLEMS

Although export marketing is basically no different from marketing at home, it is more complicated. The reasons for this are the greater distance and risk involved, the rules and regulations of other countries in addition to the exporter's own, the established practices of international trade, and such complications as differences in language and culture. To deal with these problems, exporters should learn a whole set of special procedures and practices.

Quoting a Price

As soon as a manufacturer receives an enquiry about his product, he quotes a price to the customer. Quoting for orders in the home market is relatively simple. The manufacturer knows how much he can produce his goods for. He knows also how much his costs are – factors like rent for his factory, wages for his staff, delivery costs etc. So he can quickly calculate a selling price that will give him his necessary profit. But when he is quoting a price for an export order, the exporter must take into account a whole set of extra costs, and he must know which of these the buyer will take care of, and which ones he himself will have to cover.

Terms of Delivery

When an exporter quotes a price for a product, he is making an offer. If this offer is accepted by the customer, then a contract is formed – an export contract. This contract includes the terms under which the goods are to be delivered. These terms define which costs will be paid by the exporter and which by his customer. They also make it clear who owns the responsibility for the goods if anything happens to them. So, it is vital for the exporter to know what the terms of delivery used in international trade actually mean.

Terms of Payment

Many a businessman has found out too late that he has made a loss on a price he thought would give him a fair profit – and his mistake was simply in quoting the wrong terms of payments.

An exporter must ascertain that he will get his money and that payment is not delayed beyond the terms which have been agreed upon.

There are several safe measures an exporter can take. He can make sure that his customer is credit-worthy. Next, he can insist that payment be made through such safe means as a *Letter of Credit*. Using such safeguards means that the exporter can obtain protection from defaulters. A variety of terms of payment are available to suit different circumstances.

Financing the Export Order

But it is of no use if an exporter obtains a large order and does not fulfill it. He must check that he has the necessary cash to finance the contract – bearing in mind that he may not receive payment for the goods until a certain point in the future. The exporter must be able to time his cash inflow so that he remains solvent while fulfilling the order. He may have to arrange special financing which is available to exporters. He will probably have to produce the goods and deliver them to the market before being paid.

Summary

To summarise, to a great extent, successful exporting means following the basic rules of marketing, analysing the needs of the market and getting all the elements of the marketing mix right. But exporting abroad can be a lot more complicated than marketing at home because of the great distance involved and such factors as having to observe different laws, or to deal with people the exporter may never have met and who speak different languages, and to ensure he gets paid when so much can go wrong.

ASSESSING EXPORT POTENTIAL

Before you start exporting, you have to do many things. The first and perhaps the most crucial step is to assess the export potential of your enterprise.

You may ask yourself why you need to examine you export potential when you are already familiar with your domestic market. Succeeding in your local market is a necessity but not a sufficient condition for entering foreign markets. You should, therefore, begin with an internal audit of your export potential.

What is export potential? It is the company's ability to take advantage of its business opportunities abroad.

Export potential is derived from a set of enterprise characteristics such as domestic marketing performance, resources and products. It is, therefore, measurable at the enterprise level. We shall suggest what *internal characteristics* make up a successful exporter. There are also *external factors* which we shall discuss first. A characteristic of the external factors is that you cannot influence them as an individual exporter. Some important external factors are as shown in the following figure.

Comparative advantages of Your country	Export promotion policy of your government	Exchange rate	Opportunities in specific export market

Fig 2.2 External Factors

The inherent strengths *or comparative advantages* of your company, e.g. its resources, location, climate and cost structure of the economy will set the stage for your enterprise's export efforts.

Government Policy on taxes, financing schemes, information and incentive programmes, and other matters plays a significant role in aiding export efforts. It may also hinder exporting through bureaucratic red-tape and restrictions on imports, foreign travel, advertising abroad and other means.

The relationship between your currency and that of your export customer (exchange rate) floats, e.g. changes continually. As your currency weakens, it gives you a competitive edge in export markets. As it strengthens, you may lose competitiveness.

Exporting succeeds when there is a good fit between your product and your market. A good fit exists when you can respond to an *export opportunity* with exactly the product benefits the export customer wants. It is up to your company to capitalise on the opportunities that always develop in specific export markets.

INTERNAL ASSESSMENT OF READINESS TO EXPORT

Having developed an understanding of the environmental factors that contribute to export potential, let us concentrate on the individual enterprise's own readiness to export.

An individual enterprise's export potential can be summed up under two independent dimensions: its **organisational readiness to export** and **product readiness.**

Organisational Readiness to Export (ORE)

A number of factors internal to the organisation determine how well-equipped it is to engage in export transactions. These factors are listed here.

Manufacturing capacity There should be sufficient plant and equipment availability to supply the home market plus additional capacity to meet demands from abroad.

Management and organisation Exporting requires additional management time, especially in the early stages of market development. If your existing management structure is already thinly stretched by the domestic business, it will be difficult to take on the new commitments resulting from exporting. Similarly, the existing organisation may not be suitable for handling export sales.

Financial resources Marketing abroad requires additional working capital, and capital for market investigations, promotion, product adaptation, and so on. It would be unwise to begin exporting if your company's financial base is barely sufficient for your domestic business.

Technical knowledge An enterprise that has the technical workforce capable of product development and adaptation is likely to have a greater potential than one without such capabilities.

Marketing know-how Although marketing expertise gained in the home market is not always directly applicable abroad, we find that enterprises with a substantial home market experience are better able to adapt to the requirements of export business.

Export experience An enterprise's export performance to date and the lessons learned from successes or failures have a bearing on its export potential.

Management's goals and priorities Management's current plans for its domestic business, e.g. investment, product launches expansion of sales force have a direct relationship to its export potential. These require resources and management effort that may limit the enterprise's ability to develop its export business.

Product Readiness for Export (PRE)

Product advantages carry over to the export market as well. If the enterprise's products are successful in the domestic market, competitively priced, up-to-date in design and engineering and appealing to the selected customer segment, marketing opportunities abroad are likely.

To assess your product readiness for export, you must look at each of your products critically, and identify their strengths and weaknesses. You must also do this analysis in the context of the targeted export markets.

Overall Assessment of Export Potential

After doing the series of exercises given below, you should be able to summarise your major findings and conclusions about both ORE and PRE.

It is strongly recommended that you should carry out this analysis in collaboration with someone outside the company, e.g. an officer responsible for export promotion in your national enterprise agency.

By using a scoring procedure, or by making a subjective assessment, you can classify your enterprise under one of the three categories (low, moderate or high) in each of the two dimensions. Its position in the matrix given below is dictated, then, by its relative strengths in the ORE and PRE areas. Depending on where your company lies in this matrix, a different set of recommendations will apply. You should not consider entering the exporting business unless you reach at least a moderate level in both areas.

Product and Organisational Readiness of an Enterprise				
		Product Readiness Report		
		High	Moderate	Low
Organisational	High	1	2	3
Readiness to	Moderate	4	5	6
Export	Low	7	8	9

ASSESSING EXPORT MARKETS

If the evaluation of your export readiness is positive, you should now assess the attractiveness of the export markets.

Marketing Attractiveness

Market attractiveness can be assessed very crudely without a detailed market research by a preliminary examination of whether:

- ★ Export markets for your product(s) are growing.
- ★ Export markets are dominated by very large companies and multinationals that supply all market needs at competitive prices.
- ★ Export markets respond primarily to price in the marketing mix.
- ★ Export markets are regulated and/or protected by the governments and their policies.

Exercise 1

Reflect a few minutes on how the above mentioned factors can influence market attractiveness. Write down your ideas.

If the export markets for your enterprise's type of product are growing, then, it is likely to be easier to enter those markets and capture a market share without meeting a fierce competition from those already supplying the markets. Those fighting for survival in mature markets that are not growing, or that have begun to decline, will normally offer a strong resistance to any newcomer.

When export markets are supplied by very large or multinational companies with products that cover the full range of customer needs such as in consumer electronics, it is very difficult to find a way to compete. Multinationals provide the customer with products not only of high quality but also at low costs as a result of their high production volumes.

Consider a small enterprise entering such an export market on the basis of high levels of customer service for specialised products that are too small for the large multinationals to handle. Examples are Electronic control systems customer-designed for certain industries, sophisticated tool-making and production of specialised components and parts.

If the export markets for your enterprise's product respond primarily to price, you must ask whether it is worthwhile to become involved. Marketing a product that competes only on price is seldom profitable. So what you want to find is an export market where you can compete on quality, service or specialist design, i.e. on non-price issues as some fashion clothing firms have been doing.

Despite all that has been said about supporting free trade, some markets are still protected against imports by tariffs and quotas, or by regulations on product standards, import procedures, and other measures in favour of the domestic producers. The implementation of the results of the Uruguay Round will weaken these tendencies. Market access will generally be made easier. This may also mean increased competition for you in your domestic market.

Let us do a small Exercise:

Exercise 2

Evaluate, by circling one number in each line, your enterprise's standing in terms of your kind of product and what you know in general about your export market. Check the extent to which the market is:

Growing	2	1	0	−1	−2	Declining
Not dominated by large firms	2	1	0	−1	−2	Dominated by large firms
Responsive to many non-price factors	2	1	0	−1	−2	Responsive only to price
Not regulated by Government	2	1	0	−1	−2	Regulated by Government

Let us try to interpret your possible results.

If three or four of your "circles" are around 2 and 1, export market attraction for you is "strong".

If most of your "circles" are on 0, your position appears rather doubtful.

If two or more of your "circles" are on −1 and −2, exporting on the strength of your current technology does not look like a good prospect. This does not mean that you will never be able to export, though it only means you may have to rethink your product strategy before you consider exporting seriously.

To explore export marketing seriously and analytically a company has to:

- ★ Select export markets
- ★ Build an export marketing mix
- ★ Develop an export marketing plan
- ★ Consult a professional trade promotion agency about its analysis and the assistance the agency can given in implementing the plan

Market Selection

Exercise 3

Consider a moment the possible advantages of undertaking a market selection. Write down your ideas.

Market research is necessary to identify the most promising markets and to find out how to go about marketing in these markets and how to meet their requirements. The importance of conducting a market research or of having someone to do it, is overlooked by many potential exporters and even by companies that are actually exporting.

The whole process of market selection is rather like the prospectors' search for gold. They start by studying general geological data. Then, they pinpoint particular areas and survey these areas perhaps from the air. They then narrow down their research to areas on the ground and finally after more investigations, they study the mineral-bearing ore to determine exactly where to start mining operations. At every stage, possibilities are eliminated, until the choice is narrowed down to one.

Similarly, exporters start with the whole world, and with overall statistical analysis. As they narrow down their search, they look more closely at the details and if they are successful, they find the countries or the groups within parts of countries, to which they can profitably sell their products.

At each stage, the research costs more, so that it is essential to eliminate as quickly as possible the markets that will not repay the research effort.

Import/Export Statistics

The first requirement is, therefore, to find the markets that will repay further research. The best initial indicator of a market's likelihood of buying a product is whether or not it currently imports that type of products. Fortunately, this information is usually available, because nearly every country records the flow of goods across its boundaries, to levy import duties and to determine the value of its own exports.

Most countries publish their import/export figures. In addition, these figures are summarised, converted into dollars, and published by international agencies. It should, therefore, be easy for you to find out what countries are now importing your type of product and from what sources.

You may judge the amount of business and the rate of growth or decline. When volume and value figures are given, you should also be able to calculate the average FOB (Free on Board) prices.

To do this, you must know

- ★ Which data are essential
- ★ Where to find the data
- ★ How to use them

Exercise 4

Reflect on the data you should try to look for and where to find them. Write down your ideas.

Did you have any ideas on where to look for the data? Some possible answers are now discussed.

National data are usually published and are available from government ministries or libraries; collected data for the whole world are published by the United Nations and by the Organisation for Economic Cooperation and Development (OECD). OECD world trade statistics are probably the most commonly available, but they deal only with the trade of member countries of OECD, i.e. the major industrialised countries. They, therefore, do not give figures on trade among developing countries, among economies in transition and trade between these two groups of countries.

Data published by individual countries are the most detailed. The problem of language can usually be overcome by working on the basis of the **SITC** (Standard International Trade Classification) or **HS Code** numbers so that a detailed search for a particular product's performance or that of a class of products is possible. Isolated figures are less useful than a series of figures which can show the growth or decline and relative size of markets. It is necessary to have figures for several years to obtain useful information on trends, as year-to-year changes can be misleading.

Let us do an Exercise to understand the use of such statistics:

Exercise 5

Imagine you are a market researcher for your country's Machine Tools export Corporation. The Corporation is responsible for all your country's exports of metal-working machinery. Large volumes of the machinery are exported to the United State of America, Japan, France and Germany. It is late 199.. and the Corporation is planning a major sales drive in one or two countries to extend market coverage in Europe. The management considers the following countries: France, the United Kingdom, Spain, Italy, Germany and Turkey.

You have been asked to recommend an order of priority for introducing your product into these countries. Promotion resources are limited, although production can be easily expanded.

The Corporation wishes to enter markets that are large and growing.

The information on priorities is required quickly so that further research in the selected market or markets can be initiated by the Managing Director of the Corporation on a business trip to Europe which he is undertaking next week.

You first have to choose the SITC classification that will best cover your range of products. You look at the SITC list at the front of your copy of the OECD publication Foreign Trade by Commodities: Series C, and study the relevant section.

73 Metal-working machinery

73 Metal-working machinery (other than machine-tools) and parts thereof, n.e.s.

Having selected classification 73, the following figures might have been obtained on total imports from OECD statistics:

Data on Total Imports	1	2	3	4
Country	1997 ($'000)	1998 ($'000)	1999 ($'000)	1999 (units)
France	401,000	402,000	417,000	53,373
Italy	266,000	418,000	280,000	29,386
Spain	198,000	219,000	377,000	18,416

Turkey	62,000	94,000	73,000	5,040
United Kingdom	402,000	357,000	392,000	23,660
Germany	530,000	617,000	626,000	57,568

Problem: a. How will you rank the six countries in order of priority?

b. Why have you chosen this order?

Support your argumentation by making use of the data.

Once you have finished this exercise (not before), you may turn the page and look at our suggestions for possible answers.

Your calculations may be as follows:

Country	Market Size	Market growth 1998–99		Value per unit		Total ranking	Final
	Col 3 a	Col 3+2 b	Rank c	Col 3+4 d	Rank e	f = a+c+e	g
France	2	4%	3	7.81	6	11	4
Italy	5	–33%	6	9.52	5	16	6
Spain	4	71%	1	20.47	1	6	1
Turkey	6	–23%	5	14.48	3	14	5
United Kingdom	3	9%	2	16.57	2	7	2
Germany	1	1%	4	10.87	4	9	3

Explanation:

a. Ranking by market size = 1999 imports (column 3)

b. Market growth $= \frac{1999 - 1998 \text{ imports}}{1998 \text{ imports}} \times 100$

c. Ranking by marketing growth

d. Value per unit $= \frac{1999 \text{ imports (value)}}{1998 \text{ imports (number)}}$

e. Ranking by value per unit

f. Total ranking = Sum of individual rankings

g. Final ranking = Ranking of f. above

As you can see, knowledge of simple mathematics and accuracy in placing decimal points are needed when interpreting the market data. Speedy calculation can be made easier by rounding. We have developed some basic criteria using market size, market growth and value per unit. Each criterion has been given the same weight. This, however, may give rise to objections since some criteria may be more important than others. One could also argue for taking into account absolute increases, not just percentages of growth over a two-year period. This would place France in a better position than the United Kingdom. It could also be advisable to consider other factors such as the availability and quality of supplies, distance and availability of freight services, and the established position of other related products from your country in the market. There are other important shortcomings of the presented data: lack of figures for the years before 1997 because a longer time span would be necessary to judge the market growth; trend of unit values is missing as well as data on more specific products.

Anyway, on the basis of the available data, there is no doubt that three most promising markets are Spain, the United Kingdom and Germany. The Corporation should concentrate its efforts on additional market research on these three markets.

BUILDING UP A MARKET PROFILE

Once you have your short list of export markets, you should build up a short profile of each market. For this, more accurate information should be collected. The questions that have to be answered can be assigned to three areas: the **market, competition** and **technology**.

The Market

You must distinguish between the total market and the segment of it you hope to serve. For instance, if you were considering exporting instant coffee to Japan, you would be well advised to find the total size of the Japanese coffee market and also the size of the instant coffee segment. The second would be much smaller than the first, but quite probably growing, while the other is declining.

Next, check the growth rate. You are unlikely to enter a declining market. In stable markets, competitors will react fiercely when you enter, because the only way you will get business is by taking it from them. If the market is growing, entry may be easier, provided you have the product that the customers want.

The important questions you must answer are:

* Is the market or the market segment big enough?
* Does it have a future?

Then, study the channel of distribution for your product. If it is too long, it could squeeze out your profits.

Competition

Who will you have to out-perform to be profitable in each of your short-listed markets? If the main suppliers to the market are large powerful firms, competing head-on will be a disaster. However, if such companies do not cover certain segments of the market, then you may have found a real market opportunity, but which is probably small in size.

If there are many relatively small competitors chasing the same customers, you may be able to compete with them. However, competition will tend to revolve around pricing tactics, so your expected profits will be low.

You should consider yourself lucky, if you have identified a market segment or niche where there are few direct competitors. There, you could have the opportunity to build up long-term customer loyalty to a specialised product or service.

Technology

You need to know where you stand in regard to the prevailing technology levels for your kind of products.

You can now use the scoring procedure outlined below to determine priority among the short-listed markets. Depending on the resources available to you, one or more markets can thus be identified. Note that each question has a factor according to its relative importance.

1. The Market		**Weighing factor**
a. Sales trend		3
Declining market	–2	
Static market	–1	
Growth in line with population growth	0	
Growth faster than population growth	+1	
Growth much faster than population growth	+2	
b. Volume trend		4
Declining unit sales	–2	
Static unit sales	–1	
Growth in line with population growth	0	
Growth faster than population growth	+1	
Growth much faster than population growth	+2	
c. Long-term prospects		6
Will almost certainly decline	–2	
Will probably decline	–1	
Likely to be static	0	
Will probably grow	+1	
Will almost certainly grow	+2	
d. Current market size		3
Less than US$ 500,000	–2	
US$ 500,000 – US$ 1 million	–1	
US$ 1 million – US$ 2.5 million	0	
US$ 2.5 million – US$ 50 million	+1	
Over US$ 50 million	+2	
e. Buyer's characteristics		2
Concentration on old persons	–2	
Strong bias towards older age groups	–1	
Little difference by age	0	
Some bias towards young age groups	+1	
Strong bias towards young age groups	+2	
f. Area profile		1
Concentration in one or two areas	–2	
Strong regional differences	–1	
National appeal with bias towards the rural areas	0	
Uniform appeal nationally	+1	
National appeal	+2	
g. Economic factors		5
Very sensitive to economic conditions	–2	
Fairly sensitive	–1	

Some sensitivity	0	
Should be reasonably sensitive	+1	
Strong continuous demand	+2	
h. Seasonality		3
Sales concentrated in one month of the year	–2	
Strong seasonality in one part of the year	–1	
Two peaks during the year	0	
Some seasonality	+1	
No seasonality	+2	
i. Distribution		5
Long marketing channel	–2	
Only one intermediary	0	
Direct selling	+2	
2. Competition		
a. Penetration of branding		3
Dominated by two or three major brands	–2	
One dominating brand with own-brand-element	–1	
Fragmentation among many brands	0	
Two or three brands with strong own-brand-element	+1	
Commodity market moving towards branding	+2	
b. Companies in the market		5
Three or more major marketing companies in the market	–1	
Market divided between two major marketing companies	–1	
One major company in the market	0	
Market divided among two or three unsophisticated companies	+1	
Market fragmented among a number of unsophisticated companies	+2	
c. Marked expenditure		3
Very high expenditure	–2	
High expenditure	–1	
Average for product category	0	
Low expenditure	+1	
Very low expenditure	+2	
d. Product differentiation		5
Little prospect of product advantage	–2	
Uncertain prospect of product advantage	–1	
Some prospects for a slight advantage	0	
Some prospects for important product advantages	+1	
Good prospects for important advantages	+2	

e. Brand images		**4**
Cannot use your brand names	–2	
Unlikely to use brand names	–1	
Can possibly use brand names	0	
Your brand names would be sensible	+1	
Brand names would be positively helpful	+2	
3. Technology		
a. Technology		**5**
Very different technology unfamiliar to your company required	–2	
Fairly different technology unfamiliar to your company required	–1	
Different technology but familiar to your company	0	
Similar technology	+1	
Similar technology, some capacity available	+2	
b. Buying resources		**3**
Severe buying disadvantages compared with the competition	–2	
Some disadvantages	–1	
No difference from competition	0	
Competitive advantages	+1	
Strong buying advantages	+2	

Once you have answered the questions, obtain the score by multiplying each answer with the corresponding factor and sum up the results. For instance, for topic, 1 a sales trend, if you find yourself in a market with "growth much faster than population growth," you would have a score of 6 points (+2 multiplied by factor).

If you have achieved a total positive score and do not have more than three single scores of "–2", you have the minimum requirements for further considering that market. A score above "+30" should mean a fairly promising market. Remember, however, that you should compare several markets and that the market profile is only one step in preparing for exporting.

Export Market Information

To prepare the final answers to all the questions you have been asked in "Market selection" and "Building up a market profile," you will need much more information. Do you know how to obtain that information? This matter is so important that we will devote more time to it in a subsequent module. Here we give a few suggestions.

- ★ Contact your chamber of commerce which will give you advice and access to the information you need.
- ★ Talk with other exporters about the markets of interest to you. What do they know that may be valuable to you?
- ★ Talk to other companies exporting products similar to, or compatible with your product, but not directly competing with it. Can you perhaps

find a way to enter export markets together?

★ Professional marketing research can be commissioned as the export project advances.

As soon as you can, *visit the International market* and obtain a personal feel for the reality of customer needs.

Now let us try another Exercise.

Exercise 6

Complete the following sentences by choosing one or more of the options given.

1. The first thing to do to obtain export market information is to:
   a. Visit the market.
   b. Contact the Trade Promotion Organisation (TPO) or Chamber of Commerce and obtain the basic information available on the market.
   c. Commission a market research study.
2. Other SMEs exporting to the country of interest to you.
   a. Will have nothing useful to tell.
   b. Will confuse you because their products and marketing problems are likely to be different from yours.
   c. Will give you basic guidelines on how to do business in the market and on regulations and procedures.
3. Professional marketing research is
   a. A costly luxury for your company when entering a new market.
   b. An important step in assessing the feasibility of entering an export market.
   c. Too difficult to arrange because you do not know any marketing research firms or practitioners.
   d. Is quite arranged.

Solutions to the exercise : 1b., 2c., and 3b.

// CHAPTER 3 //

TRENDS IN INDIA'S FOREIGN TRADE

During the current year, as per provisional estimates, exports amounted to Rs 1,01,850 crores in April to December, 1998 as compared to Rs 91,192 crores during April to December, 1997, registering a growth of 11.7% in terms of rupees. Imports have registered an increase of 23.36% in rupee terms having increased to Rs 1.32,447 crores in April to December, 1998, from Rs 1,07,523 crores during April to December 1997. The trade deficit during April to December, 1998, is estimated at Rs 30,597 crores. The details of foreign trade in rupee terms and dollar terms for the period April to December, 1998-99 are given in Table 3.1 and 3.2 respectively.

TRENDS IN EXPORTS

The trends in India's export of principal products/groups during 1996-97, 1997-98 and April to November, 1997 and April to November, 1998 are given in Table 3.3.

Commodity Trends

During April to November, 1998, the principal commodities which registered a significant increase in exports over the corresponding period of the previous year include tea, guargum meal, rice, leather manufactures excluding footwear, castor oil, coal, gems and jewellery, garments, natural silk textiles, coir and coir manufactures, floriculture products, mica and handicrafts. Commodities that witnessed the moderate growth upto 15% include spices, coffee, tobacco (manufactured), cashew, fruits and vegetables, processed fruits and juices, miscellaneous processed items, shellac, basic chemicals, pharmaceuticals and cosmetics, man-made textiles, made-ups, etc., plastic and linoleum, rubber, glass and other products, jute manufactures and sports goods. Exports of other cereals, pulses, unmanufactured tobacco, sesame and niger seeds, groundnut, oil meal, marine products, sugar and molasses, meat and meat products, spirit and beverages, iron ore, processed minerals, other ores and minerals, leather footwear, residual chemicals and allied products, engineering goods, electronic goods, project goods, cotton yarn, fabrics, made-ups, etc., wool and woollen manufactures, carpets, cotton raw including waste and petroleum products declined during the period.

Export Commodities

The export performance of principal commodities/groups during 1997-98 and April to November, 1998 and April to November, 1998 are reviewed in the following paragraphs.

Plantations Plantation crops primarily comprise tea and coffee. Exports of plantation crops increased during April to November, 1998 by 31.8% in rupee terms. Exports of coffee increased by 15.3% during this period to Rs 1,225 crores from 1,062 crores during the same period of last year. Exports of tea increased from Rs 971 crores during April to November, 1997 to Rs 1,454 crores during April to November, 1998 registering a positive growth of 49.7%.

Agriculture and allied products This group comprises a wide variety of agricultural products covering cereals, pulses, tobacco, spices, nuts and seeds, oil meals, guar gum meals, castor oil, shellac, sugar and molasses, processed food, meat and meat products, etc. Share of items under the group 'agricultural and allied products' was 11.3% in total exports during April to November, 1998. During April to November, 1998, the exports of agricultural and allied products showed an increase of 13.8% from Rs 8,919 crores during April to November, 1997 to Rs 10,151 crores during April to November, 1998. The items which have indicated a significant increase during this period as compared to the corresponding period of the previous year are rice, guar gum meal, castor oil and miscellaneous processed items. The items which recorded decline in exports are other cereals, tobacco (unmanufactured), sesame and niger seed, groundnut, oil meals, sugar and molasses, meat and meat products, spirit and beverages and pulses.

Marine products The exports of Marine products are Rs 2,973 crores during April to November, 1998, as against Rs 2,990 crores during April to November, 1997, indicating a decrease of 0.6%.

Ores and minerals Ores and minerals are traditional items of exports. Their contribution in the total exports is about 2.4% during April to November, 1998. The main items of exports in this category are iron ore, manganese ore, chrome ore, aluminium, mica and coal. During April to November, 1998, the exports of ores and minerals were valued at Rs 2,183 crores registering a decline of 10.8% over the same period of last year. Iron ore and processed minerals have shown a sharp decline during this period and mica has registered a positive growth of 20% during April to November, 1998, as compared to the corresponding period of the previous year.

Leather and leather manufactures The value of exports of leather manufactures has increased from Rs 3,694 crores during April to November, 1997 to Rs 4,269 crores during April to November, 1998, showing a positive growth of 15.6%. Leather goods account for 4.1% share in the total exports during April to November, 1998. 'Footwear' exports constitutes 29% of the exports of leather and leather products and exports of leather footwear declined by 19.4% during April to November, 1998, as compared with the corresponding period of the previous year. Most of the leather products are exported to developed countries like Germany, France, US, UK, Italy, Japan and CIS countries.

Gems and jewellery Gems and jewellery are major export items accounting for about 17.3% of our total exports during April to November, 1998. The export of gems and jewellery during April to November, 1998, amounted to Rs 15,583 crores as compared to Rs 17,672 crores during the corresponding period of last year, showing a positive growth rate of 33.5%.

Chemical and allied products Chemical and allied products have a positive growth of 1.8% during April to November, 1998, over the same period of the pervious year in rupee terms. Plastic and linoleum products in the international market are very competitive and stringent environmental and public health controls need to be maintained. Quality control in terms of packaging standards and delivery schedules require further attention, if a continuous increase is to be maintained.

Engineering goods The share of engineering goods contributes 10.9% to the total exports during April to November, 1998. The main items under the group 'Engineering Goods' are ferro alloys, non-ferrous metals, machine tools, machinery and instruments, transport equipments, residual engineering items, etc. Exports of engineering goods amounted to Rs 9,834 crores during April to November, 1998, as against Rs 10,139 crores during April to November, 1997, showing a decline of 3%. Other products covered under this group are capital goods and consumer durables.

Electronic and computer software In the event of technological advancement and breakthrough in industrial infrastructure, electronics and computer software industry has been identified as a thrust sector for export. The non-traditional sector consists broadly of consumer electronics, control instrumentation and industrial electronics, computer systems, communication equipment, components and software.

Electronic goods excluding software has a share of 1.4% of India's exports during the period April to November, 1998. Exports of electronic goods excluding software during April to November, 1998, are valued at Rs 1,220 crores as compared to Rs 1,886 crores during April to November, 1997, showing a decline of 35.3%.

Textiles Textiles including carpets, handicrafts and raw cotton are the major traditional export items accounting for nearly 27.7% share in the total exports during April to November, 1998. Total value of Indian textiles exports during April to November, 1998, increased to Rs 21,588 crores from Rs 20,039 crores during the corresponding period of the previous year showing a positive growth rate of 7.7%. Coir and coir manufactures recorded the highest growth in this sector of about 33.3% followed by natural silk textiles (30.1%), readymade garments (24.9%), jute manufactures (8.3%) and manmade textile made-ups, etc. (0.7%). Cotton yarn fabrics, made-ups, etc. and wool and woolen manufactures recorded a negative growth of 10% respectively. Handicrafts recorded a positive growth of 36.3% during April to November 1998, compared to the corresponding period of the previous year. Raw cotton including waste and carpets showed a decline of 78.6% and 8.3% respectively during April to November 1998.

Handicrafts The main items of exports of handicrafts are various types of handmade carpets and works of art, such as metal artware, textiles (handprinted), woodwares and zari goods. Exports of carpets declined during April to November, 1998, to Rs 1,278 crores from Rs 1,394 crores during April to November, 1997, indicating a negative growth of 8.3% during April to November, 1998. Handicrafts exports increased to Rs 1,865 crores from Rs 13,678 crores during the corresponding period of the last year showing a positive growth of 36.3%.

TRENDS IN INDIA'S IMPORTS

The trends in India's imports during the year 1997-98 as compared to 1996-97 and April to November, 1998, and April to November, 1997 are shown in Table 3.4.

India's total imports amounted to Rs 1,17,948 crores during April to November, 1998, as compared to Rs 92,989 crores during the same period of the last year showing a positive growth rate of 26.8% in rupee terms.

Imports of items under bulk category inter-alia, POL, fertilizers, edible oils, sugar, newsprint, paper board and manufactures, etc. registered an increase to Rs 37,708 crores during April to November, 1998, from Rs 36,613 crores during April to November, 1997, reflecting a growth of 3%. The imports of sugar increased to Rs 768 crores during April to November, 1998, showing an increase of 477.4%. The other major items which witnessed an increase are wheat (62%), edible oil (132.8%), fertiliser crude (46.8%), sulphur and unroasted pyrites (12.7%) and paper board and manufactures (9.6%).

Items which recorded a negative growth are cereal preparations (68.9%), fertilizer manufactured (12.6%), petroleum crude and products (10.9%), newsprint (6.5%), metali-ferrous ores and scrap (4%), non-ferrous metals (9.4%), pulp and waste paper (10%), iron and steel (0.5%) and crude rubber including synthetic (2.3%).

In other items, a major growth has been recorded during April to November, 1998, over the same period of the last year in such items as project goods, (99%), non-metal mineral manufactures (59.4%), other raw minerals (38.3%), pearls, precious and semi-precious stones (24.4%), dyeing and tanning materials (20.8%), raw hides and skins (27.3%), textiles yarn fabric, etc. (31.5%), professional instruments, etc. (32.8%), electronic goods including computer software (23.6%) and leather (9%).

A high decline has been recorded in items such as pulses (62.7%), raw wool (24.8%), transport equipment (17.3%), raw silk (2.9%) synthetic and regenerated fibres (28.8%) and fruits and nuts (16.2%).

Imports of major products are reviewed in the following paragraphs.

Crude oil and petroleum products The imports of crude petroleum and products during April to November, 1998, were valued at Rs 18,431 crores as against Rs 20,686 crores during April to November, 1997, showing a decline of 10.9%.

Fertilisers The total imports of fertilisers have declined from Rs 3,281 crores during April to November, 1997, to Rs 3,161 crores during April to November,

1998, showing a negative growth of (3.6%). This includes crude fertiliser as well as those manufactured, sulphur and unroasted pyrites.

Pearls, precious and semi-precious stones The diamond industry in the country draws heavily on imports of rough precious and semi-precious stones. Imports of pearls and precious and semi-precious stones amounted to Rs 9,813 crores during April to November, 1998, as compared to Rs 7,890 crores during the corresponding period of the previous year showing a positive growth of 24.4%.

Capital goods Imports of capital goods largely represented by machinery, including transport equipment, project goods and professional instruments have shown an increase from Rs 16,449 crores during April to November, 1997, to Rs 20,404 crores during April to November, 1998, showing a growth of 24%. In this category, project goods have shown a higher growth of (99%) followed by professional instruments (32.8%), electrical machinery (47.7%) and non-electrical machinery (3.7%) during April to November, 1998, as compared to the corresponding period of the pervious year. A decline has been registered in transport equipment (17.3%).

Chemicals and chemical materials Organic and inorganic chemical materials and medicinal and pharmaceutical products constituted the major components of imports under this category. The import of organic and inorganic chemicals rose to Rs 7,660 crores during April to November, 1998, from Rs 6,982 crores during April to November, 1997, showing a positive growth of 9.7%.

Medicinal and pharmaceutical products have registered an increase from Rs 898 crores during April to November, 1997, to Rs 986 crores during April to November, 1998, showing a positive growth of 9.8%.

Direction of India's Foreign Trade

The trends of India's export to and import from different regions are given in Table 3.5 and 3.6 respectively. The exports figures in respect of regions and sub-regions shown in Table 3.5 do not include the export of crude oil from Mumbai high and petroleum products to respective countries of consignment, but these are included in the aggregate of exports. During April to November, 1998, Asia and Oceania accounted for 34.8% of India's total exports, West Europe (27.4%), America (25.6%), Africa (6.4%) and East Europe (3.1%).

During April to November, 1998, Asia and Oceania were the largest supplier of goods which accounted for 45.2% of our imports, followed by West Europe 32.2%, America 11%, Africa 8.5% and East Europe 2%.

A comparison of respective shares of sources of our imports reveals that regions whose shares have increased during April to November, 1998, as compared to the corresponding period of the last year include West Europe from 29.9% to 32.2%, Africa from 7% to 8.5%. Imports have declined from Asia and Oceania i.e. from 48.1% to 45.2%, America 11.9% to 11% and East Europe from 3.1% to 2%.

Table 3.1 Details of India's Foreign Trade — 1998-99 Imports and Exports (Provisional)

(Rs in crores)

	April	*Apr-May*	*Apr-June*	*Apr-Jul*	*Apr-Aug*	*Apr-Sep*	*Apr-Oct*	*Apr-Nov*	*Apr-Dec*	*Apr-Jan*	*Apr-Feb*	*Apr-Mar*
Imports												
1996-97	10205.44	21750.97	31777.17	41641.12	52449.17	63181.94	74686.67	85526.57	97111.17	111068.69	124334.53	136844.35
1997-98	10860.36	22362.07	34137.77	46029.22	58900.04	69388.58	81141.28	92956.03	107523.00	122355.00	136662.14	151553.52
1998-99	**13701.47**	**27445.76**	**40339.04**	**57388.21**	**72132.03**	**88642.33**	**103088.45**	**117947.93**	**132446.84**	-	-	-
% Growth 96-97	43.76	36.00	26.59	17.87	16.84	16.69	16.78	13.89	12.84	13.80	14.61	12.49
% Growth 97-98	6.42	2.81	7.43	10.54	9.84	9.82	8.64	8.69	10.72	10.16	9.91	10.75
% Growth 98-99	26.16	22.73	18.17	24.68	22.47	27.75	27.05	26.89	23.18	-	-	-
Exports												
1996-97	9604.36	19079.52	28534.22	37860.19	47392.50	56800.81	66664.78	75544.49	85623.12	95875.98	105690.68	117524.98
1997-98	9033.41	19344.70	29133.09	39492.86	49765.55	60422.80	71515.02	80784.58	91191.88	101848.25	113018.39	126285.76
1998-99	**10224.32**	**30009.37**	**30546.45**	**43766.70**	**56054.88**	**67833.57**	**78866.51**	**89897.25**	**101850.15**	-	-	-

	April	*Apr-May*	*Apr-June*	*Apr-July*	*Apr-Aug*	*Apr-Sep*	*Apr-Oct*	*Apr-Nov*	*Apr-Dec*	*Apr-Jan*	*Apr-Feb*	*Apr-Mar*
% Growth												
96-97	23.94	26.12	26.74	23.98	22.54	21.91	20.59	17.31	14.94	13.27	12.27	10.39
% Growth												
97-98	–5.94	1.39	2.10	4.31	5.01	6.38	7.28	6.94	6.50	6.23	6.93	7.45
% Growth												
98-99	13.18	3.44	4.85	10.82	12.64	12.26	10.28	11.28	11.69	-	-	-
Trade Balance												
1996-97	–601.08	–2671.45	–3242.95	–3780.93	–5056.67	–6381.13	–8021.91	–9982.01	–11488.05	–15192.71	-18643.85	–19319.37
1997-98	–1826.95	–3017.37	–5004.68	–6536.36	–9134.49	–8965.78	–9626.26	–12171.45	–16331.12	–20506.75	-23643.75	–25267.76
1998-99	–3477.15	–7436.39	–9792.59	–13621.51	–16077.15	–20808.76	–24221.94	–28050.68	–30596.69	-	-	-

Note: During December 98, exports valued at Rs 11952.90 crores were reported (including late returns of previous months) and gives a growth rate of 14.9% over the values of exports (Rs 10407.30 crores) in December 1997.

Table 3.2 Details of India's Foreign Trade – 1998-99
Imports and Exports (Provisional)

(US $ million)

	April	*Apr-May*	*Apr-June*	*Apr-July*	*Apr-Aug*	*Apr-Sep*	*Apr-Oct*	*Apr-Nov*	*Apr-Dec*	*Apr-Jan*	*Apr-Feb*	*Apr-Mar*
Imports												
1996-97	2980.64	6281.90	9146.27	11920.04	14948.70	17952.93	21183.51	24216.96	27452.39	31354.08	35057.09	38547.81
1997-98	3032.44	6243.91	9532.30	12859.55	16443.80	19316.89	22561.37	25732.77	29484.77	33285.73	36983.29	40778.78
1998-99	**3454.98**	**6850.48**	**9889.42**	**13922.38**	**17369.74**	**21260.67**	**24671.40**	**2817.30**	**31582.86**	-	-	-
% Growth												
96-97	31.89	23.39	14.45	5.95	4.69	5.20	6.42	4.66	4.41	6.13	7.81	5.99
% Growth												
97-98	1.74	-0.60	4.22	7.88	7.59	7.60	6.50	6.26	7.40	6.16	5.49	5.79
% Growth												
98-99	13.93	9.71	3.75	8.26	5.63	10.06	9.35	9.50	7.12	-	-	-
Exports												
1996-97	2805.09	5510.36	8212.87	10837.73	13507.49	16139.76	18908.24	21390.53	24204.83	27065.26	29800.31	33105.72
1997-98	2522.32	5401.41	8134.85	11033.44	13893.62	16820.93	19884.78	22363.38	25006.48	27707.02	30584.86	33979.94
1998-99	**2578.17**	**4994.35**	**7488.69**	**10617.81**	**13498.29**	**16269.74**	**18874.54**	**21476.10**	**24286.87**	-	-	-

	April	Apr-May	Apr-June	Apr-July	Apr-Aug	Apr-Sep	Apr-Oct	Apr-Nov	Apr-Dec	Apr-Jan	Apr-Feb	Apr-Mar
% Growth												
96-97	13.17	14.43	14.58	11.45	9.80	9.91	9.91	7.81	6.36	6.19	5.61	4.01
% Growth												
97-98	–10.08	–1.98	–0.95	1.81	2.86	4.22	5.16	4.55	3.31	2.37	2.63	2.64
% Growth												
98-99	2.21	–7.54	–7.94	–3.77	–2.85	–3.28	–5.08	–3.97	–2.88	-	-	-
Trade Balance												
1996-97	–175.55	–771.54	–933.40	–1082.31	–1441.21	–1813.17	–2275.27	–2826.44	–3247.56	–4288.82	–5256.78	–5442.09
1997-98	–510.12	–842.51	–1397.45	–1826.11	–2550.18	–2495.96	–2676.59	–3369.39	–4478.29	–5578.70	–6398.43	–6798.84
1998-99	–876.80	–1856.13	–2400.73	–3304.58	–3871.46	–4990.94	–5796.86	–6701.20	–7295.99	-	-	-

Note: During December 98, exports valued at US $2810.77 million were reported (including late returns of previous months) and gives a growth rate of 6.34% over the values of exports (US $2643.10 million) in December 1997.

Table 3.3 Export of Principal Commodities

(Rs in crores)

Sl. No.	Commodities	April - March 1997	April - March 1998	% change Mar'97 to Mar '98	April Nov. 97	April- Nov 98(P)	% change Apr-Nov '97 Apr-Nov '98
I.	**Plantations**	**2464**	**3127**	**26.9**	**2033**	**2679**	**31.8**
	1. Tea	1037	1505	45.1	971	1454	49.7
	2. Coffee	1427	1622	13.7	1062	1225	15.3
II.	**Agri & Allied Products**	**16147**	**15356**	**–4.9**	**8919**	**10151**	**13.8**
	1. Cereals	1879	3791	101.8	3919	3287	–16.1
	(a) Rice	3172	3214	3.2	1869	3784	102.5
	(b) Wheat	698	-	-	-	3	-
	(c) Others	49	13	–73.5	10	4	–60.0
	2. Pulses	132	355	168.9	179	161	–10.0
	3. Tobacco	756	1058	39.9	703	522	–25.7
	(a) Unmanufactured	660	910	31.9	589	403	–31.6
	(b) Manufactured	96	148	54.2	114	119	4.4
	4. Spices	1202	1408	17.1	895	1025	14.5
	5. Nuts and Seeds	1889	2283	20.9	1491	1243	–16.6
	(a) Cashew incl. CNSL	1288	1392	8.1	978	1045	6.9
	(b) Sesame and Niger Seed	275	334	21.5	193	143	–25.9
	(c) Groundnut	326	557	70.9	320	55	–82.8
	6. Oil Meals	3495	3404	–2.6	1416	922	–34.9
	7. Guar gum Meal	356	545	53.1	304	495	62.8
	8. Castor Oil	627	575	–8.3	373	498	33.5
	9. Shellac	52	29	–44.2	26	29	11.5
	10. Sugar and Molasses	1018	248	–77.0	230	7	–96.9
	11. Processed Food	1668	1210	–27.5	761	809	6.3
	(a) Fruits and Vegetables	695	674	–3.0	432	434	0.5
	(b) Processed Fruits & Juices	209	282	34.9	189	209	13.0
	(c) Misc. Processed Items	764	254	66.8	144	166	15.3
	12. Meat and Meat Products	709	883	13.3	553	536	–3.1
	13. Floriculture Products	63	78	23.8	55	65	18.2
	14. Spirit and Beverages	201	73	–63.7	54	48	–11.1
III.	**Marine Products**	**4008**	**4313**	**7.6**	**2990**	**2973**	**–0.6**

Sl. No.	Commodities	April-March 1997	April-March 1998	% Change Mar'98-Mar '97	April-Nov. 97	April-Nov 98(P)	% Change Apr-Nov '98 Apr-Nov '97
IV.	**Ores & Minerals**	**4161**	**3962**	**–4.8**	**2441**	**2183**	**–10.8**
	1. Iron Ore	1706	1763	3.3	1086	936	–13.8
	2. Mica	25	25	0.0	20	24	20.0
	3. Processed Minerals	1203	1228	2.1	798	674	–15.5
	4. Other Ores and Minerals	1144	883	–22.8	517	411	–8.9
	5. Coal	83	63	–24.1	26	78	200.0
V.	**Leather & Mfrs.**	**5609**	**5362**	**–4.4**	**3694**	**4269**	**15.6**
	1. Footwear	1989	1895	–4.7	672	541	–19.4
	2. Leather and Mfrs.	3620	3467	–4.2	3015	3722	23.4
VI.	**Gems & Jewellery**	**16872**	**19014**	**12.7**	**11672**	**15583**	**33.5**
VII.	**Sports Goods**	**277**	**289**	**4.3**	**195**	**196**	**0.5**
VIII.	**Chemicals & related Products**	**13891**	**16126**	**16.1**	**10175**	**10363**	**1.8**
	1. Basic cheml., Pharma & Cosmetics	8866	10263	15.8	6484	6940	7.0
	2. Plastics and Linoleum	1915	1904	–0.6	1226	1242	1.3
	3. Rubber, Glass and other Products*	2425	2626	8.3	1594	1598	0.3
	4. Residual Chemicals & Allied Products	685	1333	94.6	871	583	–33.1
IX.	**Engineering Goods**	**14396**	**15585**	**8.3**	**10139**	**9834**	**–3.0**
X.	**Electronics Goods**	**2782**	**2600**	**–6.5**	**1886**	**1220**	**–35.3**
XI.	**Project Goods**	**187**	**161**	**–13.9**	**225**	**124**	**–44.9**
XII.	**Textiles**	**28493**	**30523**	**7.1**	**20039**	**21588**	**7.7**
	1. Readymade Garments	13324	14034	5.3	8877	11083	24.9
	2. Cotton Yarn, Fabrics, Made-ups, etc.	11082	12094	9.1	8242	7417	–10.0
	3. Manmade Textiles Made-ups, etc.	2494	2854	14.4	1894	1851	0.1
	4. Natural Silk Textiles	457	554	21.2	348	454	30.1
	5. Wool and Woollen Mfrs.	368	310	0.5	244	214	–12.3
	6. Coir and Coir mfrs.	217	254	71.1	159	212	33.3
	7. Jute Mfrs.	551	363	–34.1	315	341	8.3

Sl. No.	Commodities	April - March 1997	April - March 1998	% Change Mar'98 - Mar '97	April- Nov. 97	April- Nov 98(P)	% Change Apr-Nov '98 Apr-Nov '97
XIII.	**Handicrafts**	**1689**	**1928**	**14.2**	**1368**	**1865**	**36.5**
XIV.	**Carpets**	**2097**	**1984**	**–5.4**	**1394**	**1278**	**–8.3**
	1. Hand-made (excl. Silk)	1549	1506	–2.8	1052	963	–8.5
	2. Mill made (excl. Silk)	479	390	–18.6	279	263	–5.7
	3. Silk Carpet	69	88	27.5	63	52	–17.5
XV.	**Cotton Raw incl. Waste**	**1575**	**840**	**–46.7**	**746**	**160**	**–78.6**
XVI.	**Petroleum Products**	**1710**	**1311**	**–23.3**	**1032**	**363**	**–64.8**
XVII.	**Unclassified Items**	**2459**	**3805**	**54.7**	**1619**	**5068**	**213.0**
	Grand Total	**118817**	**126286**	**6.3**	**80573**	**89897**	**11.6**

Note:
* Includes Paints, Enamels, Varnish
(P) – Provisional

Table 3.4 Imports of Principal Commodities

(Rs in crores)

Sl. No.	Commodities	Apr.-Mar. '97	Apr.-Mar. '98 (P)	% Change	Apr.-Nov. '97	Apr.-Nov. '98 (P)	% Change
I.	***Total Imports***	***138919***	***151554***	***+9.1***	***92989***	***117948***	***+26.8***
II.	**Bulk Imports**	**57205**	**53638**	**–6.2**	**36613**	**37708**	**+3.0**
	1. Cereals & Preparations	487	1061	+117.9	558	829	+48.5
	(a) Rice	-	-	-	-5	-	
	(b) Wheat	404	971	+140.3	497	805	62.0
	(c) Other Cereals	-	-	-	-	-	-
	(d) C. Preparations	83	90	+8.4	61	19	–68.9
	2. Fertilisers	3235	4104	+26.9	3281	3163	–3.6
	(a) Crude	478	690	+27.2	403	592	–46.8
	(b) Sulphur & Unroasted Pyrites	323	349	+8.0	221	249	+12.7
	(c) Manufactured	2434	3065	+25.9	2657	2322	–12.6
	3. Edible Oil	2929	2733	–6.7	2214	5155	+132.8
	4. Sugar	3	443	+14666.7	133	768	+477.4
	5. Pulp & Waste Paper	823	1046	+27.1	698	628	–10.0
	6. Paper Board & Manufactures	674	845	+25.4	520	570	+9.6
	7. Newsprint	1096	1000	–8.8	739	691	–6.5
	8. Crude Rubber incl. Synthetic	629	594	–5.6	396	387	–2.3

Sl. No.	*Commodities*	*Apr.-Mar. '97*	*Apr.-Mar. '98 (P)*	*% change*	*Apr.-Nov. '97*	*Apr.-Nov. '98 (P)*	*% change*
9.	Non-ferrous Metals	3925	3377	–14.0	2266	2053	–9.4
10.	Metalliferrous Ore & Scrap	2910	2296	–21.1	1843	1769	–4.0
11.	Iron & Steel	4865	5601	–15.1	3279	3264	–0.5
12.	Petroleum Crude & Products	35629	30538	–14.3	20686	18431	–10.9
III.	**Pearls, Precious, Semi-precious Stones**	**10384**	**11680**	**+12.5**	**7890**	**9813**	**+24.4**
IV.	**Machinery**	**21225**	**19441**	**–8.4**	**11732**	**12107**	**+3.2**
1.	Machine Tools	1864	1556	–16.5	954	978	+2.5
2.	Non-electrical Machinery[@]	12937	13160	+1.7	7913	8204	+3.7
3.	Electrical Machinery[@]	1155	1357	+17.5	856	1264	+47.7
4.	Transport Equipment	5269	3368	–36.1	2009	1661	–17.3
V.	**Project Goods**	**7520**	**5879**	**–21.8**	**3068**	**6107**	**+99.0**
VI.	**Others 42585**	**60916**	**+43.0**	**33686**	**52213**	**+55.0**	
1.	Cashew Nuts	688	744	+8.1	350	348	–0.6
2.	Fruits & Nuts	456	454	–0.4	314	263	–16.2
3.	RawWool	581	593	+2.1	431	324	–24.8
4.	Raw Silk	215	223	+3.7	140	136	–2.9
5.	Synth. & Reg. Fibres	423	459	+8.5	316	225	–28.8
6.	Pulses	890	834	–6.3	735	274	–62.7
7.	Raw Hides & Skins	184	182	–1.1	110	140	+27.3
8.	Leather	274	351	+28.1	243	265	+9.0
9.	Coal, Coke & Briquettes	3532	4348	+23.1	2787	2626	–5.8
10.	Non-metal Mineral Mfrs.	429	531	+23.8	271	432	+59.4
11.	Other Raw Minerals	308	303	–1.6	193	267	+38.3
12.	Organic & Inorganic Chemicals	9446	11120	+17.7	6982	7660	+9.7
13.	Dyeing, Tanning Material	600	659	+9.8	419	506	+20.8
14.	Medicinal & Pharma Products	1089	1301	+19.5	898	986	+9.8
15.	Artificial Resins etc.	2826	2565	–9.2	1823	1815	–0.4
16.	Chemical Products	936	1009	+7.8	700	1176	+68.0

Sl. No.	*Commodities*	*Apr-Mar '97*	*Apr-Mar '98 (P)*	*% Change*	*Apr-Nov '97*	*Apr-Nov '98 (P)*	*% Change*
17.	Textile Yarn, Fabrics etc.	1273	1492	+17.2	939	1235	+31.5
18.	Metal Manufactures	1123	1210	+7.7	693	1121	+61.8
19.	Professional Instruments etc.[@]	1962	2652	+35.2	1649	2190	+32.8
20.	Electronic Goods incl. Computer Software	5354	7611	+42.2	4894	6048	+23.6

Note:

@ Other than electronic

(P)– Provisional

Other of which for Apr-Nov '98 inclusive of Errors & Omissions.

Table 3.5 India's Exports by Regions/Sub-regions

(Rs in crores)

Sl. No.	*Region/Sub-region*	*1996-97*	*1997-98 (P)*	*% Change 1997-98 1996-97*	*Apr-Nov 1997*	*Apr-Nov 1998(P)*	*% Change Apr-Nov 1997-98*
I.	**West Europe**	**32892**	**35562**	**8.1**	**22415**	**24637**	**9.9**
		(28.1)	**(28.4)**		**(28.2)**	**(28.2)**	
1.	ECM Countries	29660	32909	11.0	20780	23014	10.7
		(25.3)	(26.3)		(26.1)	(26.3)	
2.	EFTA Countries	2412	1623	-32.7	951	1036	8.9
		(2.1)	(1.3)		(1.2)	(1.2)	
3.	Rest of Europe	820	1030	25.6	684	587	–14.2
		(0.7)	(0.8)		(0.9)	(0.7)	
II.	**Asia and Oceania**	**48354**	**49083**	**1.5**	**31239**	**31287**	**0.2**
		(41.3)	**(39.3)**		**(39.3)**	**(35.8)**	
1.	ESCAP	36457	35379	–3.0	23065	20697	–10.3
		(31.1)	(28.3)		(29.0)	(23.7)	
2.	Rest of Asia & Oceania	11897	13704	15.2	8174	10590	29.6
		(10.2)	(11.0)		(10.3)	(12.1)	
III.	**Africa 5722**	**6999**	**22.3**	**4496**	**5751**	**27.9**	
		(4.9)	**(5.6)**		**(5.6)**	**(6.5)**	
IV.	**America**	**26236**	**28846**	**9.9**	**18588**	**22985**	**23.7**
		(22.4)	**(23.1)**		**(23.4)**	**(26.3)**	
1.	North America	24525	26191	6.8	16934	21186	25.1
		(20.9)	(21.0)		(21.3)	(24.2)	

Sl. No.	Region/Sub-region	1996-97	1997-98 (P)	% Change 1997-98 1996-97	April - Nov 1997	April - Nov 1998 (P)	% Change Apr-Nov 1997-98
2.	South America	1192	1892	58.7	1190	1189	–0.1
		(1.0)	(1.5)		(1.5)	(1.4)	
3.	Other American Countries	519	763	47.0	464	610	31.5
		(0.4)	(0.6)		(0.6)	(0.7)	
V.	**East Europe**	**3903**	**4485**	**14.9**	**2803**	**2791**	**(–)0.4**
		(3.3)	**(3.6)**		**(3.5)**	**(3.2)**	
1.	Former RPA Countries	3336	3860	15.7	2477	2337	–5.6
		(2.8)	(3.1)		(3.1)	(2.7)	
2.	Other East European Countries	567	625	10.2	326	454	39.3
		(0.5)	(0.5)		(0.4)	(0.5)	
	Total of the above*	117107	124975		79541	87451	
	Grand Total	**118817**	**126286**		**80573**	**89897**	**11.6**

Note:

1. The total exports figures of regions and sub-regions do not include exports of crude oil and petroleum products.
2. Figures in brackets indicate percentage share of individual region/sub-region with respect to total of all regions at (*).
3. (P) – Provisional.

Table 3.6 India's Imports by Regions Sub-regions

(Rs in crores)

Sl. No.	Regions & Principal Countries	Apr-Mar '97	Apr-Mar '98	% change in 1997-98 Over 1996-97	Apr-Nov '97	Apr-Nov '98(P)	% Change in 1998 Over1997-98
I.	***West Europe***	***42153***	***48242***	***14.4***	***27830***	***38005***	***+36.6***
		(30.3)	**(31.9)**		**(29.9)**	**(32.6)**	
1.	ECM Countries	35192	36251	3.0	23961	29578	+23.4
		(25.3)	(24.0)		(25.8)	(25.4)	
2.	EFTA Countries	6710	11689	74.2	3630	8290	+128.4
		(4.8)	(7.7)		(3.8)	(7.1)	
3.	Rest of Europe	251	302	20.3	239	137	–42.7
		(0.2)	(0.2)		(0.3)	(0.1)	

Sl. No.	*Regions & Principal Countries*	*Apr-Mar '97*	*Apr-Mar '98*	*% change in 1997-98 Over 1996-97*	*Apr-Nov '97*	*Apr-Nov '98(P)*	*% Change in 1998 Over1997-98*
II.	**Asia and Oceania**	**66318 (47.7)**	**70691 (46.7)**	**6.6**	**44698 (48.1)**	**53344 (45.7)**	**+19.3**
1.	ESCAP	34897 (25.1)	39198 (25.9)	12.3	24054 (25.9)	34390 (29.5)	+43.0
2.	Rest of Asia & Oceania	31421 (22.6)	31493 (20.8)	0.2	20644 (22.2)	18954 (16.2)	–8.2
III.	**Africa**	**10230 (7.4)**	**11013 (7.3)**	**7.7**	**6530 (7.0)**	**9994 (8.6)**	**+53.0**
IV.	**America**	**16304 (11.7)**	**17284 (11.4)**	**6.0**	**11073 (11.9)**	**13001 (11.2)**	**+17.4**
1.	North America	14197 (10.2)	15095 (10.0)	6.3	9703 (10.4)	11057 (9.5)	+14.0
2.	South America	1853 (1.3)	1781 (1.2)	–3.9	1131 (1.2)	1583 (1.4)	+40.0
3.	Other American and Caribbean Countries	254 (0.2)	408 (0.2)	60.6	239 (0.3)	361 (0.3)	+51.0
V.	**East Europe**	**3914 (2.8)**	**4088 (2.7)**	**4.4**	**2858 (3.1)**	**2300 (1.9)**	**–19.5**
1.	Former RPA Countries	3228 (2.3)	3523 (2.3)	9.1	2570 (2.8)	1997 (1.7)	+22.3
2.	Other East European Countries	686 (0.5)	565 (0.4)	–17.6	288 (0.3)	303 (0.2)	+5.2
	Total of Above*	138919	151318	-	92989	116644	25.4
	Grand Total	**138919**	**151554**	**9.1**	**92989**	**117948**	-

Note: P – Provisional

(*) Grand Total for Apr.-Nov. '98 inclusive Errors & Omission.

1. Figures in brackets relate to percentages of Grand Total.

WORLD TRADE

The rate of growth in the volume of world merchandise exports slowed to 3.5 per cent in 1998, from over 10 per cent in 1997, largely due to the continuing economic contraction in much of Asia.

SCENARIO OF WORLD TRADE

World output growth slipped to 2 per cent in 1998, as compared to 3 per cent in 1997. Although trade growth still exceeded the output growth in 1998, it was by a smaller margin than the average for the 1990s.

Export growth in 1999 is expected to match that of 1998, but for this projection to be realised, trade growth will have to accelerate during the course of 1999. This projection also assumes that slowing output growth in the United States and Western Europe will be offset somewhat by recovery in Asia. A faster than expected slowdown in the United States or Western Europe, or slower recovery in Asia, would clearly imply export volume growth below 3.5 per cent in 1999.

These are among the findings of the WTO's first report on trade development last year and the outlook for this year. Other highlights are explained in the subsequent paragraphs.

- ★ Trade contraction in Asia has been the biggest factor in the global trade slowdown. But there has been a marked slowdown in global export expansion throughout 1998, reflected in the performance of all major regions.
- ★ Trade performance measured in volume terms differed widely among regions in 1998, particularly on the import side. Imports into Asia fell by 8.5 per cent, stagnated or fell slightly in Africa and the Middle East, and expanded by 7.5 per cent in Western Europe and by some 10 per cent in North America, Latin America, at 10 per cent and 6.5 per cent respectively, and increased marginally in Asia (1 per cent). Western Europe's export growth was slightly above the global average, at 4.5 per cent, and that of North America was below the average, at 3 per cent.
- ★ Export of merchandise and commercial services amounted to US$ 56.5 trillion in 1998. In value terms, merchandise exports amounted to US$ 5.2 trillion and commercial services to US $1.3 trillion. This represents a fall of almost 2 per cent in dollar terms over exports in 1997, but still exceeds the level attained in 1996. This is the steepest decrease since 1982. Exports of commercial services recorded the first annual decline in value terms since comprehensive statistics became available in the mid-1980's.
- ★ Commodity prices fell sharply in 1998, pushing the share of primary products in world exports below 20 per cent in current price terms for the first time during the postwar period. Oil prices fell by 30 per cent in 1998, or 40 per cent from a year-end to year-end basis. This picture has been mitigated by increased oil prices in the first quarter of 1999. Non-oil primary commodity prices fell by 15 per cent on a yearly average basis in 1998, and by some 10 per cent on a year-end basis. Prices of internationally traded manufactured goods and services also declined in 1998, but by considerably less than those of primary products.
- ★ Reduced commodity prices have particularly affected the export earnings of African and Middle Eastern countries. In addition to the 11 member countries of OPEC, some eight other countries depend on fuel exports for more than 50 per cent of their export earnings. Over twenty, mostly developing countries, depend on agricultural exports

for 35 per cent or more of their export earnings, but these countries are generally not as severely affected as the oil exporters by commodity price falls.

MAIN FEATURES OF WORLD TRADE IN 1998

World GDP and trade growth slowed in 1998 as the Asian crisis deepened and its repercussions were felt increasingly outside Asia. The volume of world merchandise exports grew by 3.5 per cent in 1998 after an outstanding growth rate of 10.5 per cent in 1997. This export volume growth rate compares with an average growth rate of 6.0 per cent in the period 1990-95. The deceleration in global output growth was less pronounced than for international trade in 1998, as world GDP rose by 2 per cent, or by 1 percentage point less than in 1997 (Chart I).

The deceleration of global merchandise trade growth continued throughout the year, leaving the global trade level in the fourth quarter of 1998 only slightly above the level reached at the end of 1997. All major regions experienced a marked slowdown of their trade growth in the course of 1998.

The recent cyclical fall in commodity prices, which started in early 1997, continued unabated throughout 1998. Oil prices fell by 30 per cent and non-oil commodity prices by 20 per cent in 1998, with very different implications for various countries and regions of the world. While the share of primary commodities (including processed food) in world merchandise trade was only slightly above one-fifth in 1997, it was more than two-thirds for the Middle East, Africa, and Latin America (excluding Mexico). In a sample of 91 developing countries, 67 of them recorded a share of primary products in total merchandise exports above 50 per cent, reaching as high as 95 per cent in some cases.

Prices of internationally traded manufactured goods and services also have declined in 1998, though considerably less than those of primary products. Exchange rate variations, which were large in the course of 1998, can have a major impact on the dollar prices of internationally traded goods. However, as the dollar's average annual appreciation vis-a-vis the ECU (now the Euro) was considerably smaller in 1998 than in 1997, West European export prices measured in dollar terms, decreased far less last year than in 1997. This smaller decrease in Europe's export prices more than offset the steeper price declines in all other regions. Therefore, despite the accelerated fall in commodity prices in 1998, the global price decline for all merchandise exports was 5.5 per cent, which was somewhat less pronounced than in 1997.

Trade performance in 1998 differed widely among regions. While oil-exporting regions recorded the steepest annual decline in merchandise exports, countries directly affected by the Asian financial crisis reported the steepest import decline. The contractionary forces of the Asian crisis and falling commodity prices were, however, attenuated by the robustness of continued economic growth in the United States and strengthened demand in Western Europe. The reversal of private capital flows away from the emerging markets contributed to low interest rates in North America and Western Europe. In addition, the falling fuel prices led to weaker import prices and real income gains for net-fuel importing countries.

Table 3.7 World Exports of Merchandise and Commercial Services, 1996-98

(billion dollars and percentage)

	Value			*Annual change*		
	1996	1997	1998	1996	1997	1998
Merchandise	5150	5325	5225	4.5	3.5	–2.0
Commercial Services	1275	1320	1290	6.7	3.5	–2.0

All major regions experienced a market slowdown of their trade growth in the course of 1998....

Western Europe, the world's largest regional trader, was the only region not to record a deceleration in import growth in 1998 as compared to 1997. Western Europe's import growth rate of 7.5 per cent was, however, less than the 10 per cent rate recorded by North America, Latin America and the transition economies. In sharp contrast, imports into Asia fell by nearly 8.5 per cent, and a stagnation or a decrease in import volumes is estimated for Africa and the Middle East.

Regional differences in the volume growth of exports are far less pronounced than for imports. All regions recorded a lower export expansion in 1998 than in the preceding year. The transition economies and Latin America recorded the strongest volume growth. Asia's export volume increased marginally, as the strong contraction of inter-Asian trade was only just offset by a sharp rise in extra-regional flows. Western Europe's export growth remained somewhat above the global average of 3.5 per cent, while that of North America fell below the average.

The dollar value of world merchandise trade declined by 2 per cent, the steepest decrease since 1982. The export value of manufactured goods continued to rise slightly while that of agricultural products, metals and fuels declined. These divergent developments, byproduct category in 1998 pushed the share of primary products below 20 per cent in current price terms for the first time in the post-World War II period.

Exports of commercial services recorded the first annual decline in dollar value since 1983. All the three major services categories (i.e., transport, travel and other commercial services) saw a decrease. Both exports of goods and commercial services decreased slightly but at $5225 and $1290 billion respectively, but were still above the levels reached in 1996 (Table 3.7).

In its seventh year of expansion, the United States' economy experienced an acceleration in private consumption and continued double-digit investment growth. GDP growth was almost 4 per cent, unchanged from 1997. The booming US economy stimulated intra-NAFTA trade, and sustained exports and output in other regions. North America's merchandise import volume rose by 10.5 per cent in 1998, which was the strongest growth of all Regions. (Table 3.8).

Table 3.8 Growth in the Volume of World Merchandise Trade by Selected Regions, 1990-98

(Annual percentage change)

Exports					*Imports*			
Ave. 1990-95	*1996*	*1997*	*1998*		*Ave. 1990-95*	*1996*	*1997*	*1998*
6.0	5.5	10.5	3.5	World	6.5	6.0	9.5	4.0
7.0	6.0	11.0	3.0	North America	7.0	5.5	13.0	10.5
8.0	11.0	11.0	6.5	Latin America	12.0	8.5	22.0	9.5
5.5	5.5	9.5	4.5	Western Europe	4.5	5.5	7.5	7.5
5.0	6.5	12.5	10.0	Transition Economies	2.5	16.0	17.0	10.0
7.5	5.0	13.0	1.0	Asia	10.5	6.0	6.0	–8.5
1.5	1.0	12.0	–1.5	Japan	6.5	5.5	1.5	–5.5
11.5	7.5	11.5	2.0	Asian Traders	12.0	4.5	6.5	–16.0

In value terms, North America's merchandise exports decreased slightly in 1998, as volume growth decelerated and prices declined. North America's mercandise imports, however, increased by 4.5 per cent in value terms, leading to a widening of the region's merchandise trade deficit to $253 billion (Table 3.9). The evolution in North America's commercial services trade mirrored that of merchandise trade, with export increasing only very slightly and imports rising by 4.5 per cent, reducing further the region's surplus in services trade.

INTERNATIONAL TRADE

Table 3.9 Growth in the Value of World Merchandise Trade by Region, 1990-98.

(Billion dollars and percentage)

Exports (FOB)						Imports (CIF)				
Value	Annual Percentage Change					Value	Annual Percentage Change			
1998	1990-95	1996	1997	1998		1998	1990-95	1996	1997	1998
5225	7.5	4.5	3.5	–2.0	World	5410	7.5	5.0	3.0	–1.0
898	8.5	6.5	9.5	–1.0	North America	1151	8.0	6.0	10.5	4.5
274	9.0	32.5	10.0	–2.0	Latin America	339	14.5	9.5	19.0	5.0
118	14.0	20.5	15.0	6.5	Mexico	129	12.5	25.5	23.5	14.0
157	7.0	8.0	7.0	–7.0	Other Latin America	211	15.5	2.5	16.5	0.5

2338	6.0	3.5	–0.5	2.5	Western Europe	2359	5.5	3.5	–1.5	5.0
2171	6.5	3.5	–0.5	3.0	European Union (15)	2163	5.5	3.0	–2.0	5.5
178	7.0	6.5	5.0	–1.0	Transition Economies	207	5.0	17.0	9.5	3.0
99	7.5	6.0	8.0	9.0	Central/Eastern Europe	133	11.5	17.0	7.0	11.5
106	0.5	16.5	2.0	–16.0	Africa	129	5.5	–1.0	6.0	–1.5
26	3.5	5.5	6.0	–15.0	South Africa	29	10.5	–1.5	9.5	–11.0
138	1.5	17.0	4.0	–21.0	Middle East	139	5.5	7.0	6.5	–6.0
1294	12.0	0.5	5.5	–6.0	Asia	1090	12.0	4.5	0.5	–17.5
388	9.0	–7.5	2.5	–8.0	Japan	281	7.5	4.5	–3.0	–17.0
184	19.0	1.5	21.0	0.5	China	140	20.0	5.0	2.5	–1.5
504	14.0	3.0	2.5	–7.5	Six East Asian Traders*	438	15.0	3.0	0.5	–25.0

* Chinese Taipei; Hong Kong; China; Malaysia; Korea; Singapore; and Thailand

The Import Pattern

The downward trend in petroleum and its products ($5.8 billion) continued, as imports fell by 23.7%. Gold and silver ($4.4 billion) remained the second most important commodity in imports, and imports rose by 67.6%. Imports of food and related items rose by 44.2% and those of export related goods by 4.4%. However, imports of capital goods fell by 2.3%. Among food and related items, imports of edible vegetable oils and sugar increased by more than 100% each. In export related goods, a decline of about 15% was registered by cashew nuts and organic chemicals, while others registered an increase. Imports of project goods rose sharply by 40.2%, while those of transport equipment fell by 36.8%. Most other commodities, for instance, raw wool (33%), non-ferrous metals (26.8% and pulp and waste paper (21.4%) registered a decline. However, a sharp increase was recorded by raw cotton and waste (350%) and chemical material and products (39.8%). Overall, imports rose by 2.9% from $37.1 billion to $38.2 billion.

How Things Came In

(In $million)

Commodities	*Apr-Feb'99*	*Apr-Feb'98*	*% Change*
Petroleum, Crude and Products	5803.0	7606.0	–23.7
Gold and Silver	4421.0	2680.0	67.6
Pearls and Precious Stones	3311.0	2873.0	15.3
Non-electrical Machinery	2799.0	3250.0	13.9
Electronic Goods	1913.0	1820.0	5.2
Project Goods	1851.0	1320.0	40.2
Vegetable Oils (edible)	1625.0	719.0	126.0
Organic Chemicals	1352.0	1604.0	–15.7
Inorganic Chemicals	1155.0	1072.0	7.7
Iron and Steel	1042.0	1261.0	–17.4

Commodities	*Apr-Feb'99*	*Apr-Feb'98*	*% Change*
Coal, Coke and Briquettes	870.0	1080.0	–19.5
Fertilisers Manufactured	751.0	837.0	–10.3
Professional Instruments and Optical Goods	727.0	649.0	11.9
Non-ferrous Metals	624.0	851.0	–26.8
Artificial Resins and Plastic Materials	604.0	6453.0	-6.4
Metalliferous ores and Metal Scrap	574.0	666.0	–13.9
Transport Equipment	527.0	835.0	–36.8
Electrical Machinery	399.0	337.0	18.5
Textiles Yarn Fabrics Made-up Articles	398.0	369.0	7.79
Chemical Materials and Products	371.0	265.0	39.8
Manufactures of Metals	365.0	282.0	29.6
Wood and Wooden Products	329.0	378.0	–13.1
Medicinal and Pharma Products	316.0	355.0	–11.1
Machine Tools	312.0	379.0	–17.9
Sugar	238.0	100.0	137.0
Newsprint	215.0	259.0	–17.1
Wheat	214.0	263.0	–18.8
Pulp and Waste Paper	211.0	269.0	–21.4
Paper Board and Manufactures	182.0	201.0	–9.4
Crude Fertilizers	174.0	162.0	7.5
Dyeing Tanning and Colouring Materials	166.0	164.0	1.3
Cashew nuts	160.0	190.0	–15.8
Non-metalic Minerals mnfs excl. pearls	138.0	125.0	10.5
Other Food and Related Items	126.0	362.0	–65.1
Printed Books, Newspapers	123.0	136.0	–9.2
Synthetic and Reclaimed Rubber	107.0	110.0	–7.9
Raw Wool	101.0	150.0	–32.9
Fruits and Nuts	92.0	146.0	–37.5
Cotton Raw and Waste	82.0	18.0	355.6
Leather	81.0	91.0	–11.1
Sulphur and Unroasted Iron Pirates	73.0	88.0	–16.9
Other Commodities	2539.0	1527.0	66.3
Total	**38,163.0**	**37,077.0**	**2.9**

The Export Pattern

The decline in exports continues, though its magnitude seems to be decreasing. During April-February this year, exports dropped by a small 1.7% to $30 billion. There was a decline in all major categories, as exports of agricultural and allied products fell by 7.6%, ores and minerals by 16.6% and manufactured goods by 1.6%. Most agro-commodities registered a steep fall, but there were some good performers too. Exports of non-basmati rice rose by 168.8% tea by 27.2% and guargum meal by 29.2%. In the case of ores and minerals, while exports of coal and mica increased by 123.9% and 43.2% respectively, those of iron ore and processed minerals dropped by 19.2% and 305 respectively. In manufactured goods, gems and jewellery continued to be the top FOREX earner to be followed by readymade garments and textiles, yarn and fabric made-ups, though the latter declined by 15.6%. Other performers in this category were manufactures of metals and handicrafts, which recorded an increase of 11% and 20% respectively.

How Things Went Out

(In $million)

Commodities	*Apr-Feb'99*	*Apr-Feb'98*	*% Change*
Gems and Jewellery	5048.0	4450.0	13.4
Readymade Garments	3954.0	3445.0	14.8
Textiles Yarn Fabrics, Made-ups	3342.0	3957.0	–15.6
Leather and Leather Manufactures	1425.0	1360.0	4.8
Drugs, Pharmaceuticals and Fine Chemicals	1322.0	1282.0	3.1
Machinery and Instruments	1022.0	1039.0	–1.7
Manufactures of Metals	966.0	870.0	10.9
Marine Products	958.0	1090.0	–12.2
Non-basmati Rice	951.0	354.0	168.8
Other Manufactured Goods	662.0	884.0	–25.2
Transport Equipment	630.0	766.0	–17.8
Paper/wood Products	141.0	141.0	0.4
Handicrafts	573.0	478.0	19.9
Tea	482.0	379.0	27.2
Inorganic and Organic Chemicals	471.0	526.0	–10.4
Other Agricultural and Allied Products	468.0	856.0	–45.4
Electronic Goods	446.0	664.0	–32.6
Primary Iron and Steel	438.0	655.0	–33.1
Dyes and Intermediates	424.0	544.0	–22.0
Plastic and Linoleum Products	423.0	456.0	–7.2
Oil Meals	407.0	860.0	-52.7
Basmati Rice	399.0	395.0	0.8
Carpet Handmade	369.0	381.0	–3.2
Coffee	351.0	395.0	–11.3
Iron Ore	349.0	432.0	–19.2
Cashew	344.0	358.0	–3.8
Petroleum, Crude and Products	90.0	332.0	–72.9
Spices	329.0	335.0	–1.6
Rubber Manufactured Products	256.0	300.0	–14.6
Processed Minerals	216.0	308.0	–30.0
Other Ores and Minerals	189.0	190.0	–0.4
Meat and Preparations	168.0	206.0	–18.5
Guargum Meal	157.0	121.0	29.2
Cosmetics/toiletries	147.0	153.0	–3.9
Castor Oil	147.0	147.0	0.1
Glass/glassware/ceramics/refractories	140.0	166.0	–15.3
Paints/enamels/varnishes	139.0	137.0	–0.2

Commodities	*Apr-Feb'99*	*Apr-Feb'98*	*%Change*
Tobacco unmfrs.	120.0	219.0	−45.2
Carpet Millmade	91.0	97.0	−6.3
Jute mfrs excl. floor coverings	91.0	93.0	−1.5
Ferro alloys	78.0	92.0	−15.9
Iron and Steel Bar and Rods	76.0	109.0	−30.3
Sesame and Niger Seed	66.0	75.0	−12.1
Processed Fruits and Juices	66.0	67.0	−1.3
Coal	28.0	12.0	123.9
Mica	9.0	6.0	43.2
Other Commodities	699.0	368.0	69.9
Total	**30.020**	**30.547**	**−1.7**

India's Major Partners

During April-February this year, the US ($6.5 billion) continued to be the top buyer and even improved its performance by 9.4%. Exports to Germany ($1.7 billion) declined marginally, but it jumped two positions to end at No 2. Japan lost three positions to finish at No 6 as exports to that country declined by 13%. The biggest losers in this period were Russia, Singapore and China, while Russia lost ($629 million four positions and dropped to No 13, Singapore ($459 million) dropped three positions to No 14 and China ($371.1 million) five positions to No 18. The Netherlands ($690 million) also lost two positions to finish at No 12. The gainers in this period included Bangladesh ($839.1 million) which gained five positions to enter the top 10 at No 9. Similarly, France ($741.8 million)gained two positions to finish at no 19, while Saudi Arabia ($007.5 million) gained four positions to reach No 11 from No 15. The new entrants in this period were Spain ($437.4 million), Canada ($417.6 million) and South Africa ($351.4 million) at Nos 15, 16 and 19 respectively. The latter managed to enter the top 20 even though exports dropped marginally.

Top 20 Buyers

(April-February 1999)

Rank	*Rank (Apr-Feb'99)*	*Countries*	*India's Exports (in $million)*	*% Change*
1	1	USA	6520.9	9.4
2	4	Germany	1655.0	−0.3
3	2	UK	1646.2	−11.1
4	6	UAE	1628.6	13.8
5	5	Hong Kong	1601.6	−3.6
6	3	Japan	1481.9	−13.2
7	7	Belgium	1152.4	11.2
8	8	Italy	914.7	−5.1
9	14	Bangladesh	839.1	34.2
10	12	France	741.8	11.8
11	15	Saudi Arabia	697.5	18.0
12	10	Netherlands	690.0	−2.3
13	9	Russia	629.0	−24.1

14	11	Singapore	459.0	–32.0
15	-	Spain	437.4	15.0
16	-	Canada	417.6	9.9
17	17	Sri Lanka	396.9	–10.7
18	13	China	371.1	–43.9
19	-	South Africa	351.4	–0.7
20	20	Australia	348.0	–10.4

The US ($3.3 billion) was India's top trading partner in this period, and it topped the list of sellers too. With a 15.2% improvement in its performance, Switzerland ($2.6 billion) replaced Saudi Arabia ($1.7 billion) at No 2. The latter became one of the losers in this period, finishing at No 7 with a drop of 26.1% in imports. The shake-ups continue down the list as both Belgium ($2.4 billion) and UK ($2.3 billion) gained two positions each to reach No 3 and No 4 respectively. Japan ($2.1 billion) gained three positions to reach No 5, while Germany ($1.9 billion) slipped by two positions to finish at No 6. Australia ($1.4 billion) dropped out of the top 10, though its performance improved marginally by 0.4%. Malaysia entered the top 10, though its performance improved marginally by 0.4%. Malaysia entered the top 10 at No 9 as imports rose by 34.8%. Amidst all these ups and downs, Singapore ($1.3 billion), Italy ($1 billion) and Indonesia ($742.8 million) managed to hold on to their positions by registering an increase of 19.5%, 21.4% and 9.8% respectively. The only new entrant during this period was South Africa ($1.1 billion) at No 13 as imports from that country increased by a phenomenal 182.9%.

Top 20 Sellers

(April-February 1999)

Rank	*Rank (Apr-Feb'99)*	*Countries*	*India's Exports (in $million)*	*% Change*
1	1	USA	3284.1	–2.3
2	3	Switzerland	2631.5	15.2
3	5	Belgium	2407.2	6.8
4	8	UK	2367.8	9.6
5	8	Japan	1225.2	12.6
6	4	Germany	1920.8	–15.7
7	2	Saudi Arabia	1711.4	–26.1
8	9	UAE	1567.6	-2.2
9	11	Malaysia	1476.6	34.8
10	7	Kuwait	1390.4	–35.4
11	10	Australia	1389.9	0.4
12	12	Singapore	1255.5	19.5
13	-	South Africa	1144.0	182.9
14	15	South Korea	1072.2	26.6
15	14	Nigeria	1014.0	0.8
16	16	Italy	1010.4	21.4
17	13	China	966.8	–6.8
18	18	Indonesia	742.8	9.8
19	17	France	644.4	–6.4
20	19	Russia	477.6	–25.5

THE INDIAN TEXTILE INDUSTRY

The Indian textile industry is both important and complex. Twenty per cent of the value addition in the manufacturing sector is con tributed by the Textile sector. Contribution to GDP is 4 to 5 per cent and export earning is more than 30% of the total export of the country. It has the potential for the generation of a large employment. The complexity of this sector is on account of its complex sectoral dispersal matrix with the organised sector, the disorganised sector and down the line, are the weavers, artisans and farmers. In respect of fiber specific configuration, there is a wide range in the textile sector from cotton, jute, wool, silk blends, man-made fiber and hundred per cent cotton. For the production of textiles, there is an intricate interplay of the processes, which include ginning, reeling, spinning, weaving, and garment manufacture.

TEXTILE INDUSTRY

The textile sector has witnessed a phenomenal growth during the last decade and a half in terms of installed spindleage, yarn production and output of cloth. The spindleage capacity has moved up from about 28.09 million in 1992-93 to 33.93 million by the end of December 1998. A noticeable feature in this growth process has been the installation of a large number of open-end rotors in 1990s and the tendency to set up 100% export oriented units in the field of weaving. The production of spun yarn is anticipated to touch the figure of 2,860 mn.kgs. During the current financial year 1998-99, registering an annual growth of 6% during the last five years it is worth noting that the production of blended yarn and 100% non-cotton yarn has shown an upward trend in recent years. The production of blended yarn is anticipated to touch the figure of 630 mn.kgs during 1998-99, registering an annual growth of 15.6% during the last five years. The production of 100% non-cotton yarn is anticipated to touch the figure of 185 mn.kg. during 1998-99, registering an annual growth of 5.6% during the last five years. The total production of cloth by all sectors i.e. mill, powerloom, handloom, and khadi, wool and silk has also shown an upward trend in recent years. The total production of cloth is anticipated to touch the figure of 37,450 mn.sq. mtrs during 1998-99, shownig an annual growth of 6.1% during the last five years. The cloth production from the decentralised hosiery sector has shown a significantly higher annual growth rate of 12.3% during the last five years.

The satisfactory performance in cloth production has resulted in a favorable per capita domestic availability of cloth in the country. Despite the growth in population and exports, the per capita availability has risen to about 30.61 sq.mtrs.in 1998-99 (provisional) from around 24.50 sq.mtrs. in 1992-93.

Modernisation A Technology Upgradation Fund Scheme for textile and jute industries to provide for interest incentive on loan from financial institutions has been approved by the government with a view to modernisation, technological and quality upgradation of these industries so as to enhance their productivity, quality and competitiveness. This scheme will be operative for five years commencing from 1st April, 1999.

Textile policy In keeping with the changing scenario in the textile industry and global trade, it was felt necessary to re-focus our textile policy to facilitate improving our competitiveness both internationally and domestically. Accordingly, an Expert Committee under the Chairmanship of S.R. Sathyam has been set up in July, 1998, to analyse the presentstatus of the industry, its competitiveness, the impact of the existing textile policy of 1985 and to suggest policy measures to improve the productivity and competitive edge of the Indian textile industry in a holistic manner. The Committee is expected to submit its report during, 1999.

Export With a view to reversing the downtrend in cotton tarn exports, the government has announced a number of measures, which include the delinking of cotton yarn exports from hand yarn obligation, although the obligation continues without reduction of level, operational flexibility to 100% EOUs producing cotton yarn to export cotton yarn without any count/domestic cotton use restriction upt 31st December, 1999, and the announcement of a higher ceiling of 200 million kgs for the export of cotton yarn of 40s and below counts.

The government has succeeded in getting a favourable verdict from the textile monitoring body under the WTO in the matter relating to Colombia's preventive action against import of denim fabrics inter-alia from India. Antidumping proceedings on import of unbleached cotton fabrics from India were also dropped by the European Union.

NIFT An international conference of leading fashion schools of the world was held in New Delhi in November 1998. The objective of the conference was global networking of the fashion schools for providing integrated fashion education facilities to students all over the world besides faculty exchange, sharing of industry experience, etc. The conference decided on the establishment of IFFTI (International Foundation of Fashion Technology Institutes) with its headquarters at New Delhi in the NIFT campus.

The Computer Department of NIFT has been strengthened during this year to cover NIFT students all over the country.

Handlooms The MDA Scheme was reintroduced in a modified form for the next two years. All India Handloom Ministers' Conference was held to deliberate upon the problems being faced by the handloom industry and to suggest ways and means to take corrective measures for the industry. Reintroducing the market development assistance, formation of state level monitoring committees, system of evaluation and monitoring in place, and providing employment opportunities to weavers were major issues of concern which were discussd and acted upon.

Special emphasis and focus was on the North-Eastern region. The share of North-Eastern states in the release of funds for developmental activities of handlooms has gone up from 16% to 21%. A separate conference of all the ministers and secretaries of the north-eastern states was organised. The conference deliberated upon the unique problems facing the North-East region like the low level of technology, lack of availability of raw materials, transportation of finished goods, etc.

Handicrafts A new scheme for the setting up of urban haats in metropolitan cities on the lines of Dilli haat has been introduced during 1998-99. It is proposed to sanction 4-5 such haats. These haats would provide permanent marketing outlets to the artisans.

Exports of handicrafts during 1998-99 have been Rs 5431.56 crores till December 1998, as against Rs 4737.45 crores in the corresponding period last year, signifying a growth of 14.65%.

With a view to enhancing exports of handicrafts products, the indian handicrafts and gifts fair, which was initially held once, a year is being held twice a year. The scope of the fair has also been enlarged by including carpets and jute products.

Jute As a result of research, IJIRA developed an alternative fibre lubricant which can be used for making hydrocarbon free jute packaging. Since this would result in environment friendly packaging, it is expected to have an easy access to the international market in cocoa and coffee. A large number of jute mills are now in the process of using this alternative fibre lubricant on a commercial scale.

Cotton Given the importance of cotton in the Indian cotton economy, a cotton technology mission is proposed to be launched aimed at improving production, productivity and quality of cotton. The mission will focus on resarch for improving seed and farm level technology, extension of technology to the farmer supported by an efficient delivery system for inputs, especially by way of Seed Integrated Pest Management (IPM), credit and irrigation, apart from impriving marketing, infrastructure, facilitating marketing arrangements and contamination free efficient cotton processing by way of ginning and pressing.

Sericulture The third International Conference on wild silk moths was held in Bhubaneswar, Orissa (11-14 November, 1998) which was attended by reputed Scientists from India and abroad.

To make available superior quality of mulberry raw silk to domestic weavers, import of raw silk grade 2A and above has been allowed under SIL with the condition that the value of the surrendered SIL should be three times the value of the imported items.

An integrated Eri and Muga project for the North-Eastern states has been finalised in consultation with Ministry of Rural Area and Employment and will be implemented from 1999-2000 for three years.

Under the aegis of the UNDP Country Cooperation framework I (CCF-I) a project under fibre and handicrafts programme is being undertaken with UNDP assistance. The programmes will cover non-mulberry silk, jute, angora wool, carpets and cane and bamboo. The programme will be launched during 1999-2000 and will be operative for a period of three years.

Powerloom A scheme for the upgradation of Powerloom Service Centres (PSCs) has been approved by the government to enable the PSCs to provide better consultancy services and training facilities to the powerlooms sector. The expenditure on this scheme, which would cover 21 PSCs initially is expected to be approximately Rs 16 crores, during the remaining years of the IX Five Year Plan period.

Research and developement The programme for providing facilities to the felt testing needs of the industry was continued during 1998-99, 13 laboratories were taken up for upgradation and 2 new laboratories were proposed to be set up at the estimated cost of Rs 14.9 crores. Besides 15 laboratories from the ongoing upgradation programme from the previous years were completed and made operational. Cumulatively, so far, 40 laboratories have been upgraded including 20 eco-laboratories set up in 1995-96 has also been completed, which indicates a growing awareness about the nèed for maintaining quality and testing samples.

Information technology An Economic Research and Market Intelligence Unit (ERMIU) has been set up in the ministry with its headquarters in the textile commissioner's office at mumbai having an online connectivity with the ministry and textile committee. Equipped with the latest computers and V-SAT facilities, the ERMIU is designed to source data from national and international sources, compile, analyse and interpret the same and also provide periodic issue-based inputs and research results by way of policy inputs to the government. In course of time, it is also proposed to provide online connectivity to other textile related organisations and industry associations for feeding and souring information from the ERMIU.

Industrial survey The textile committee has conducted an industrial survey in Surat (Gujarat) and Ichalakaranji (Maharashtra) to assess the quality level of the powerloom fabrics produced in these two major decentralised powerloom and textile processing centres. The surveys have thrown light on the present quality level and the scope for further improvement therein. These reports were well received by the industry.

Consumer protection The Standing Committee on consumer matters set up by the government under the chairmanship of the Textile Commissioner has made commendable efforts to create an awareness among the textile consumers about various quality parameters. The regional offices of the textile commissioner and the textile committee, in close coordination with local NGO's, state government officials and consumer groups have conducted 33 consumer awareness seminars/workshops in various part of the country. This has created a tremendous enthusiasm among the NGOs about Textile related consumer activities.

TEXTILE EXPORTS

Profile of Textile Exports (Including Jute, Handicrafts and Coir)

The export of Indian textile plays a pivotal role in the Indian economy. Textile exports account for about 30% of Indian exports of all commodities, making Indian textiles the largest single net foreign exchange earner for the country.

Indian exports of all textiles in 1997-98 including jute, coir and handicrafts were of the order of Rs 46278.81 crore as against Rs 41828.15 crore in 1996-97, which represented an increase of 10.6%. In dollar terms, the same has increased from US$ 11839.13 million in 1996-97 to US$ 12389.91 million in 1997-98 representing an increase of 4.6%. The exports during the current financial year for April-December 1998, are of the order of Rs 38458.8 crore as against Rs 33962.8 crore during the corresponding period of the previous year. The major chunk in export has taken place in the field of apparel and cotton textiles. Sector-wise break up of Export performance during April-December 1997, and April-December 1998, is given hereunder.

Cotton yarn The export of cotton yarn, including sewing thread had shown an increase in 1997-98 over the previous year with exports being Rs 5865.64 crore (US$ 1596.79 million) in 1996-97. The exports during the current financial year (April-December 1998) have, however, registered a marginal increase to Rs 4476 crores as against Rs 4448.7 crore during the corresponding period of the preceding year. It amounts to a 13.2% fall in $ terms mainly during to the currency and financial crisis in the South East Asian region which accounts for almost half of our cotton yarn exports.

The export of cotton yarn of below 40s counts is subject to a specific ceiling keeping in view the interest of the decentralised sectors of Handlooms and Powerlooms.

In addition, the export of yarn of counts above 40s is freely allowed except the quantity covered under a bilateral agreement, where there is a quantitative limit.

Cotton mill made / powerloom textiles The export of mill made/powerloom, cotton fabrics and made-ups amounted to Rs 7,251.50 crore in 1997-98 registering an increase of 11.1% as compared to the achievement of Rs 6,526.12 crore in 1996-97. The export during (April-December 98) amounted to Rs 6313.8 crore as compared to Rs 5224.5 crore during the corresponding period of the previous year. The main markets for cotton textiles remain the same as in the previouos year, such as US, EU, and the Middle East.

Cotton handlooms The export of handloom textiles increased from Rs 1758.89 crore in 1996-97 to Rs 1859.53 crore in 1997-98. In terms of US dollars, the exports increased to a level of 505.93 million US$ during 1997-98 from 495.48 million US$ during 1996-97. The exports during the current exercises and day-to-day supervision overmatters relating to the allocation of export entitlements. There is a quota coordination committee under the Chairmanship of the Textile Commissioner with representatives of Export Promotion Councils as members, to review the operation of the policy periodically. Under the export quota policy the available quota is distributed under different systems of allocation, such as Past Performance Entitlement (PPE), First Come First Served (FCFS), Manufacturer Exporters Entitlement (MEE), Non-quota Entitlement (NQE), Powerloom Exporters Entitlement (PEE), New Investors Entitlement (NIE), etc. The garment export entitlement policy is implemented by the Apparel Export Promotion Council (AEPC), whereas the textile export entitlement policy is implemented by the Cotton Textiles Export Promotion Council (TEXPROCIL).

Non-tariff Barriers

The Indian textile sector also faces non-tariff barriers by importing countries.

Columbia had initiated safeguard action against the imports of denim fabrics inter-alia from india on 20th april 1998, invoking the agreement on textiles and clothing. The matter was immediately taken up by India before the textile monitoring body under the WTO. The TMB recommended on 31st July, 1998, that colombia should rescind the safeguard measures. The colombian government accepted the recommendations of the TMB on August 5, 1998.

The European Union (EU) had imposed provisional antidumping duties on importers of unbleached cotton fabrics from India. This was the third back-to-back measure initiated on this item. India took up the case bilaterally with the European Commission (EC). The Ministerial Councils of the EU decided on 5th October, 1998 to drop the proceedings.

The European Commission has initiated two parallel investigations, namely, antisubsidy and antidumping proceeding concerning the import of Polyester Texturised Filament Yarn (PTFY) originating inter-alia from India. The Synthetic and Rayon Textiles Export Promotion Council is coordinating the defence of producers and exporters in the PTFY anti-dumping case. However, the antisubsidy proceedings are being contested by the government of India also, besides the producers and exporters.

The EC had initiated antidumping investigations in September 1996, concerning the import of cotton type bed linen items originating inter-alia, from India. Subsequently, the EC imposed definitive antidumping duty on imports of cotton type bed linen originating from india. The government of India has had one round of consultations with the EC's on the subject and the process in on.

Steps to Boost Textile Exports

The government has been operating several schemes and has undertaken some new initiatives with a view to helping the textile exporting industry to overcome some inherent disadvantages and to facilitate the growth in exports of textile and textile products from the country. The central objective of most of the schemes is to ensure the availability of capital goods and raw materials to the manufacturers at globally competitive rates.

Table 3.10 Production of Fabrics in Different Sectors

(Million Sq. Mtr.)

	1992-93	*1993-94 (Revised)*	*1994-95*	*1995-96*	*1996-97*	*1997-98*	*1998-99 (Apr.Dec.) (P)*	*1998-99 (A)*
Mill sector								
Cotton	1407	1356	1252	1159	1222	1238	868	1220
Blended	532	575	745	602	488	466	351	460
100% Non-cotton	61	59	263	258	247	244	175	240
Total	**2000**	**1990**	**2271**	**2019**	**1957**	**1948**	**1394**	**1920**
						(1476)		
Handloom Sector								
Cotton	4686	5241	5429	6239	6441	6699	4471	6295
Blended	8	2	13	18	52	69	90	65
100% Non-cotton	525	608	738	945	963	835	612	810
Total	**5219**	**5851**	**6180**	**7202**	**7456**	**7603**	**5173**	**7170**
Decentralised							**(5857)**	
Powerloom Sector								
Cotton	7306	7836	7021	7014	7238	6652	4380	6200
Blended	1996	2524	2640	3137	3948	4481	3338	4465
100% Non-cotton	5342	5733	6315	7050	8166	9818	7672	10655
Total	**14644**	**15994**	**15976**	**17201**	**19352**	**20951**	**15390**	**21320**
Decentralised							(15635)	
Hosiery Sector								
Cotton	2944	3357	3307	4488	4940	5403	3874	5270
Blended	148	153	262	268	400	735	604	970
100% Non-cotton	90	127	179	282	193	256	416	260
Total	**3182**	**3637**	**3748**	**5038**	**5533**	**6394**	**4894**	**6500**
All Sectors							**(4834)**	
Cotton	16343	17790	17019	18900	19841	19992	13593	18985
Blended	2684	3155	3661	4025	4888	5751	4383	5960
100% Non-cotton	6018	6527	7495	8535	9569	11153	8875	11965
Total	25045	27472	28175	31460	34298	36896	26851	36910
					(27802)			
Khadi, Wool & Silk	430	426	431(P)	431	515	540	405	540
Grand Total	**25475**	**27898**	**28606**	**31891**	**34813**	**37436**	**27256**	**37450**
					(28207)			

(P) Provisional (A) Anticipated

(Figures in bracket refers to corresponding period of previous year.)

Table 3.11 Export of Textiles 1998-99

(Rs in crores and $ million)

Sl. No. Item	Target 1998-99		*Export during the months* April-Dec 1997		April-Dec 1998		% increase		Target Achieved
	% share	US$	Rs	US$	Rs	US$	Rs	US$	US$
1. Ready-made garments	41	5900	13024.7	3543.6	15469.0	3680.4	18.8	3.9	62.4
2. Cotton Textiles (a+b+c)	30	4175	11075.6	3066.0	12281.0	2933.8	10.9	–4.3	70.3
a) Cotton fabrics & Made ups (MM/PL)	14	1975	5224.5	1446.3	6313.8	1508.3	20.9	4.3	76.4
b) Cotton fabrics & Made ups (HL)	4	600	1402.4	388.2	1491.2	356.2	6.3	–8.2	59.4
c) Cotton Yarn	12	1600	4448.7	1231.5	4476.0	1069.3	0.6	–13.2	66.8
3. Man-made Textiles	8	1200	2737.7	751.3	2960.3	705.5	8.1	–6.1	58.8
4. Silk	2	300	641.9	177.7	746.5	178.3	16.3	0.3	59.4
5. Wool & Woollens	3	365	887.0	243.0	887.6	219.2	0.1	–9.8	60.1
Total (1-5)	**84**	**11940**	**28366.9**	**7781.6**	**32344.4**	**7717.2**	**14.0**	**–0.8**	**64.6**
6. Handicrafts (a+b)	14	2035	4737.4	1311.5	5431.6	1297.5	14.7	–1.1	63.8
a) Carpet & other Floor coverings			1316.8	364.5	1423.4	340.0	8.1	–6.7	
b) Other Handicrafts			3420.6	947.0	4008.2	957.5	17.2	1.1	
7. Coir	0.5	70	173.0	47.9	200.7	47.9	16.0	0.0	68.4
8. Jute	1.5	230	685.5	189.8	482.1	115.2	–29.7	39.3	50.1
Grand Total	**100**	**14275**	**33962.8**	**9330.8**	**38458.8**	**9177.8**	**13.2**	**–1.6**	**64.9**

Note:

1. Source: Export Promotion Council & Commodity Boards.
2. Export figures are provisional.

// CHAPTER 4 //

INSTITUTIONAL FRAMEWORK AND EXPORT PROMOTION MEASURES IN INDIA

The Department of Commerce in the Ministry of Commerce is headed by the Secretary. This Department is responsible for the country's external trade and all matters connected with it, such as commercial relations with other countries, state trading, export promotional measures and the development, and regulation of certain export oriented industries and commodities. The Department of Commerce formulates policies in the sphere of foreign trade, in particular, the import and export policy of the country.

DEPARTMENT OF COMMERCE

Functional Divisions

The Department of Commerce consists of eight principal functional divisions as mentioned below.

- (i) Administrative and General Division
- (ii) Finance Division
- (iii) Economic Division
- (iv) Trade Policy Division
- (v) Foreign Trade Territorial Division
- (vi) Export Products Divisions
- (vii) Export Industries Division
- (viii) Export Services Division

Autonomous Bodies

1. Commodity boards There are five statutory Commodity Boards under the Department of Commerce. These Boards are responsible for production, development and export of tea, coffee, rubber, spices and tobacco respectively. The names and addresses of these Commodity Boards are given in Appendix II.

2. Export Inspection Council, New Delhi The Export Inspection Council, a statutory body, is responsible for the enforcement of quality control and compulsory pre-shipment inspection of various exportable commodities covered under the Export (Quality Control and Inspection), Act, 1963.

3. Indian Institute of Foreign Trade, New Delhi The Indian Institute of Foreign Trade, registered under the Societies Registration Act, is engaged in the following activities:

(i) Training of personnel in modern techniques of international trade.
(ii) Organisation of research in problems of foreign trade.
(iii) Organisation of marketing research, area surveys, commodity surveys and market surveys.
(iv) Dissemination of information arising from its activities relating to research and market studies.

4. Indian Institute of Packaging, Mumbai The Indian Institute of Packaging is registered under the Societies Registration Act. The main aims of the Institute are to undertake research of raw materials for the packaging industry, to organise training programmes on packaging technology, to stimulate consciousness of the need for good packaging etc.

5. Indian Diamond Institute The Indian Diamond Institute (IDI) is registered under the Societies Registration Act. It was established in 1978 with the objective of strengthening and improving the availability of trained manpower for the gems and jewellery industry by conducting various diploma/post diploma level courses in this field. Some of the important courses conducted by IDI for the gems and jewellery sector include:

(i) Diploma in diamond processing
(ii) Diploma in diamond trade management
(iii) Diploma in gemology
(iv) PG Diploma in diamond technology
(v) PG Diploma in gemology
(vi) PG Diploma in jewellery designing, manufacturing and appraising

The Institute is financed by the Government of India. Ministry of Commerce and the Gem and Jewellery Export Promotion Council. The Institute has been striving to augment its resources by undertaking consultancy and job works.

6. Export Promotion Councils There are at present eleven Export Promotion Councils under the administrative control of the Ministry of Commerce as given in Appendix-III. These Councils are registered as non-profit organisations under the Companies Act/Societies Registration Act. The Export Promotion Councils perform both advisory and executive functions. These Councils are also the registering authorities under the Export and Import Policy, 1997-2002. These Councils have been assigned the role and functions under the said Policy.

7. Federation of Indian Export Organisations, New Delhi The Federation of Indian Export Organisations (FIEO), New Delhi, is an apex body of various export promotion organisations and institutions. It also functions as a primary servicing agency to provide integrated assistance to the government recognised export houses/trading houses and as a central coordinating agency in respect of export promotional efforts in the field of consultancy services in the country. FIEO organises seminars and arranges participation in various exhibitions in India and abroad. FIEO is also involved in dissemination of awareness on modern information technology through the internet and home page of EDI and Electronic commerce among the exporters.

8. Indian Council of Arbitration, New Delhi The Indian Council of Arbitration, set up under the Societies Registration Act, promotes arbitration as a means of settling commercial disputes and popularises the concept of arbitration among the traders, particularly those engaged in international trade. The Council, a non-profit service organisation, is a grantee institution of the Ministry. The main objectives of the council are to promote the knowledge and use of arbitration and provide arbitration facilities for amicable and quick settlement of commercial disputes with a view to maintaining the smooth flow of trade, particularly, our export trade on a sustained and enduring basis.

9. Marine Products Export Development Authority, Cochin The Marine Products Export Development Authority, a statutory body, is responsible for the development of the marine products industry with special reference to exports.

10. Agricultural and Processed Food Products Export Development Authority, New Delhi The Agricultural and Processed Food Products Export Development Authority is also a statutory body which serves as the focal point for agricultural exports, particularly the marketing of processed foods in value added form.

11. Public Sector Undertakings The following trading/service corporations function under the administrative control of the Ministry of Commerce:

(i) State Trading Corporation of India Ltd. (Cashew Corporation of India Ltd. being merged as a division in STC).
(ii) Mineral and Metal Trading Corporation of India Ltd. and its subsidiary Mica Trading Corporation of India Ltd.
(iii) Projects and Equipment Corporation of India Ltd..
(iv) Spices Trading Corporation of India Ltd..
(v) Export Credit Guarantee Corporation of India Ltd..
(vi) Indian Trade Promotion Organisation (ITPO).

Advisory Bodies

1. Board of Trade There is a Board of Trade under the Ministry of Commerce which was constituted on May 5, 1989, to provide a forum for ensuring a continuous dialogue with trade and industry in respect of major developments in the field of international trade. The Chairman of the Board of Trade is the Commerce Minister and Director General of Foreign Trade is the Member Secretary. The membership of the Board includes the Governor, the Reserve Bank of India, Secretaries of the Ministries of Commerce, Industry, Finance and Textiles, Special Secretary, Prime Minister's Office; President of FICCI, ASSOCHAM, CII, FIEO, FASSI; representative of trade and industry and a few specialists.

2. Export Promotion Board There is an Export Promotion Board under the Chairmanship of the Cabinet Secretary to provide policy and infrastructural support through greater coordination among the concerned Ministries for boosting the growth of exports.

The representation received from various Chambers of Commerce, organisations and experts are examined by the various divisions of the Ministry and the emerging issues are taken up with the concerned Ministries. In case of disagreement, the matter is placed before the Export Promotion Board for a final decision. The Export Promotion Board takes important decisions regarding electronics, textiles and garments, plastic and gems and jewellery, telecommunications, infrastructure, toys and engineering exports sectors, etc.

Attached and Subordinate Offices

1. Directorate General of Foreign Trade, New Delhi This Directorate is headed by the Director General of Foreign Trade and is responsible for execution of the Exim Policy announced by the government from time to time for the promotion of exports. In addition, work relating to issue of licences and monitoring of export obligations etc. is also looked after by this organisation. The Directorate has its headquarters at New Delhi and there are 31 regional offices in the field formations. These Offices are located at the following stations:-

1. Ahmedabad	2. Amritsar	3. Bangalore
4. Baroda	5. Bhopal	6. Calcutta
7. Chandigarh	8. Chennai	9. Coimbatore
10. Cuttack	11. Ernakulam	12. Guwahati
13. Hyderabad	14. Jaipur	15. Kanpur
16. Ludhiana	17. Madurai	18. Moradabad
19. Mumbai	20. CLA, New Delhi	21. Panipat
22. Panaji	23. Patna	24. Pondicherry
25. Pune	26. Rajkot	27. Shillong
28. Srinagar (Functioning at Jammu)		29. Surat
30. Varanasi	31. Visakhapatnam.	

2. Directorate General of Antidumping and Allied Duties The Directorate General of Antidumping and Allied Duties was inaugurated in April 1998 with a view to institutionalising the system of investigation of dumping as well as subsidies cases. The Directorate is headed by an Additional Secretary in the Ministry of Commerce and also has a facilitation cell which advises all interested parties of information required, procedures and time frames involved, besides assisting the industry with regard to technical issues.

3. Directorate General of Commercial Intelligence and Statistics, Calcutta (DGCI & S) This Directorate is the primary government agency for the collection, compilation and the publication of the foreign, inland and ancillary trade statistics and dissemination of various types of commercial information. The Directorate brings out a number of publications particularly on trade statistics, which are utilised in framing economic policies, formulating trade agreements with foreign countries and monitoring these agreements. These publications are also used by the trading public and research scholars. It maintains a commercial library which is used by the exporters, importers, research scholars and others.

4. Export Processing Zones The Ministry of Commerce has set up seven export processing zones at various locations as below.

(i) Kandla Free Trade Zone, Gandhidham.
(ii) Santacruz Electronics Export Processing Zone, Mumbai.
(iii) Falta Export Processing Zone, Falta (West Bengal).
(iv) Madras Export Processing Zone, Chennai.
(v) Cochin Export Processing Zone, Cochin.
(vi) Noida Export Processing Zone, Noida, (UP).
(vii) Visakhapatnam Export Processing Zone, Visakhapatnam.

The above export processing zones are responsible for the administration of free trade zones and in setting up 100% export-oriented multi-product industrial units.

MINISTRY OF TEXTILES

Functions and Organisational Setup of the Ministry of Textiles

The Ministry of Textiles is responsible for policy formulation, regulation, development and export promotion in respect of the textile sector including cotton, wool, silk, jute and other fibres, and handicrafts. However, it does not deal with non-celluloic synthetic fibres such as nylon and polyester acrylic.

The developmental activities of the Ministry are oriented towards making adequate quantities of raw material available to all sectors of the textile industry and augmenting the production of fabrics at reasonable prices from the organised and decentralised sectors of the industry. Towards this objective, the Ministry lays down the guidelines for a planned and harmonious growth of various sectors of the industry. Special emphasis is given to the development of handlooms in view of its large employment potential. The Ministry monitors the techno-economic status of the industry and provides the required policy framework for modernisation and rehabilitation. The Ministry coordinates the activities of the Textile Research Association and lends financial support to them for undertaking research and development.

A Secretary who is assisted in discharge of his duties by 4 officers of Joint Secretary status and the Development Commissioners for Handlooms and Handicrafts, Textile Commissioner and the Jute Commissioner heads the Ministry of Textiles.

The principal functions of the Ministry are:

(i) Textile Policy and Coordination
(ii) Man-made Fibre
(iii) Cotton Textile Industry
(iv) Jute
(v) Silk
(vi) Wool and Woollen Industry
(vii) Powerloom Industry
(viii) Export Promotion
(ix) Planning and Economic Analysis
(x) Integrated Finance Matters
(xi) Computerisation.

List of Organisations/Bodies Under the Ministry of Textiles (Except Attached/Subordinate Offices)

Public Sector Undertakings	*Statutory Bodies*	*Export Promotion Councils*	*Advisory Bodies*	*Autonomous*	*Textiles Research Associations*
National Textiles Corporation Ltd.	Jute Manufacturers Development Council	Handloom Export Promotion Council	Cotton Advisory Board	Central Wool Development Board	Ahmedabad Textile Industry Research Association
British India Corporation: (a) The Elgin Mills Company	Central Silk Board	Apparel Export Promotion Council	Jute Advisory Board	National Institute of Fashion Technology (NIFT)	Bombay Textile Research Association
			Coordination Council		
(b) Cawnpore Textiles Limited	Textiles Committee	Cotton Textile Export Promotion Council	Textile Research Association	National Centre for Jute Diversification	South India Textile Research Association
Cotton Corp. of India Ltd.	Commissioner of Payments	The Synthetic and Rayon textile Export Promotion Council	All India Handloom Board		Northern Indian Textile Research Association
Jute Corporation of India Ltd.		Indian Silk-Export Promotion Council	All India Handicrafts Board		Silk and Art Silk Mills Research Association
Birds Jute Exports Ltd.		Wool and Woollen Export Promotion Council	All India Powerloom Board		Man-made Textile Research Associaion
National Jute Manufacturers Corporation					Indian Jute Industries Research Association

Public Sector Undertakings	*Statutory Bodies*	*Export Promotion Councils*	*Advisory Bodies*	*Autonomous*	*Textiles Research Associations*
Handlooms Export Corporation		Carpet Export Promotion Council			Wool research Association
Central Cottage Industries Corporation		Export Promotion Council for Handicrafts			
North-Eastern Handicrafts and Handlooms Development Corporation		Powerloom Development and Export Promotion council			
National Handlooms Development Corporation.					

Boards

1. All India Handicrafts Board The All India Handicrafts Board has been constituted under the Chairmanship of the Minister of Textile with the Development Commissioner (Handicrafts) as Member Secretary. The Board advises the government in matters pertaining to the development of the handicraft sector.

2. All India Powerloom Board The All India Powerloom Board was constituted as an Advisory Body under the Chairmanship of the Ministry of Textiles. It has representatives of Central and State governments and Powerloom Federation/Associations of Powerloom Industry as its members. The functions of the Board are to advise the government on matters concerning the growth and development of the powerloom sector. The Board was reconstituted vide resolution dated 28.10.1998. It has 29 members.

3. Central Wool Development Board The Board has been constituted with a view to promote the growth and overall development of the wool and woollen industry. Various developments schemes are implemented through the state governments concerned. Facilities for testing are also provided. The Board has its headquarters at Jodhpur and has 19 members.

4. All India Handloom Board The All India Handloom Board has been constituted under the Chairmanship of the Minister of Textiles. The Board advises the government on various aspects of handloom development.

5. Cotton Advisory Board The Cotton Advisory Board is a representative body of Government/Growers/Industries/Traders. It advises the government generally on matters pertaining to production, consumption and marketing of cotton, and also provides a forum for liaison among the cotton textile mill industry, the cotton growers, the cotton trade and the government. It was reconstituted on 21.4.1997.

6. Central Silk Board The Central Silk Board was constituted with the objective of promoting the growth and development of sericulture in the country. The programmes for development of the sericulture industry are primarily formulated and implemented by the State Sericulture Departments. However, the Central Silk Board supplements the efforts of the states by providing the necessary support for research and development and extension and training through its countrywide network of units. Besides, the Central Silk Board organises the production and supply of quality silkworm thread, mulberry cuttings, etc. and also undertake directly as well as jointly with the State Sericulture Departments, the implementation of various sericulture projects.

7. Jute Advisory Board The Jute Advisory Board advises the government generally on matters pertaining to jute falling within the purview of jute (Licensing and control) Order, 1961 including production estimates of jute and mesta. The Jute Commissioner is the Chairman. The Board is constituted for a period of 2 years. The Board was reconstituted in December, 1997. It has 20 members.

Attached Offices

Office of the Development Commissioner for Handlooms The Development Commissioner heads this office for handlooms. It implements various schemes for the promotion and development of the handloom sector and has been providing assistance to handloom weavers in a variety of ways. Its subordinate offices are Weavers' Service Centres, Indian Institute of Handloom Technology and the Enforcement Machinery for Implementation of Handloom (Research of Articles for Production) Act, 1985.

Office of the Development Commissioner for Handicrafts The Office of the Development Commissioner for Handicrafts functions under the Ministry of Textiles for the promotion and export of handicrafts. The Development Commissioner heads it and assists the state governments in planning and executing development schemes for handicrafts. It has 6 regional offices at Mumbai, Calcutta, Lucknow, Chennai, Guwahati and New Delhi.

Subordinate Offices

Office of the Textile Commissioner The Office of the Textile Commissioner has it headquarters at Mumbai with 8 regional offices throughout the country. The office is headed by the Textile Commissioner. The Textile Commissioner acts as the principal Technical Advisor to the Ministry. This office is entrusted with the responsibility of implementation of various control orders. Through the network of regional offices, the Textile Commissioner carries out techno-economic surveys and advises the government about the general economic health of the textile units.

The development activities of the Office of the Textile commissioner centres around planning the growth and overall development of the textile sector. Thirteen powerloom service centres are functioning under the administrative control of the Textile Commissioner.

Office of the Jute Commissioner Located at Calcutta, this office is entrusted with the responsibility for implementation of the policies of the government on jute, as the Textile Commissioner acts as the principal Technical Adviser to the Ministry on all matters relating to the jute industry including the jute machinery industry.

Development Councils

Jute Manufactures Development Council The Jute Manufactures Development Council was constituted as a statutory body under the Chairmanship of the Secretary (Textiles) with effect from 1.5.1984 with the objective of increasing the efficiency and productivity in the jute industry, the financing of activity for such development and for matters connected therewith. JMDC has been delegated all functions relating to export promotion in the jute sector and to perform other activities on the domestic market of jute sector as are performed by a Commodity Board. The activities of the Council are funded from the grants made available by the Central Government from the proceeds of Cess on the production of jute levied under the Jute Manufactures Cess Act, 1983.

APPENDIX I

List of subjects under the control of the department of commerce.

DEPARTMENT OF COMMERCE (VANIJYA VIBHAG)

General International Trade Policy

1. International commercial policy.
2. International agencies connected with commercial policy (e.g. UNCTAD, ESCAP, ECA, ECLA, EEC, EFTA, GATT, WTO and related bodies, ITCB).
3. International commodity agreements other than agreements relating to wheat.
4. All matters relating to international trade policy including tariff and non-tariff barriers; preferential trading arrangements, regional trade blocks and economic groupings.
5. All matters relating to antidumping investigations and duties faced by the Indian exporters abroad and all work relating to the designated authority under the antidumping provisions of the Customs Tariff Act.

Foreign Trade

6. All matters relating to foreign trade including the monitoring of trade performance, trade negotiations and agreements (including all matters and agreements under General Agreement on Tariffs and Trade/ WTO, Commonwealth Tariff Preferences and other preferential trading arrangements viz. Bangkok Agreement, SAPTA, GSTP, etc.), trade missions and delegations, trade cooperation and promotion and protection of interests of Indian traders abroad.
7. Import and Export Trade Policy and Control excluding the matters relating to:
   i) Import of feature films.
   ii) Export of Indian films - both feature films and short films.
   iii) Import and distribution of cine-film (unexposed) and other goods required by the film industry.
8. Directorate General of Foreign Trade

State Trading

9. Policies of state trading and performance of organisations established for the purpose, including:
   i) State Trading Corporation and its subsidiaries excluding Handicrafts and Handlooms Export Corporation and Central Cottage Industries corporation.
   ii) MMTC Limited and its subsidiaries.

Trading with the Enemy: Enemy Property

10. Trading with the enemy; enemy firms and enemy property reparations (other than German industrial equipment); Controller of Enemy Trading; Controller of Enemy firms; Custodian of Enemy Property for India.

11. International Customs Tariff Bureau including residuary work relating to Tariff Commission.
12. Development and expansion of export production in relation to all commodities, products, manufacturers and semi-manufacturers, and projects including the following:
    (a) Agricultural produce within the meaning of the Agricultural produce (Grading and Marking) Act, 1937 (1 of 1937).
    (b) Marine products.
    (c) Industrial products (engineering goods, chemicals, plastics, leather products, etc.).
    (d) Fuels, minerals and mineral products.
    (e) Specific export oriented products (including plantation crops etc. but excluding jute products and handicrafts which are directly under the charge of this department).
    (f) Consultancy, civil construction and turn-key projects.
13. All organisations and institutions connected with the provision of services relating to the export effort including:
    (a) Export Credit and Guarantee Corporation.
    (b) Export Inspection Council.
    (c) Directorate General of Commercial Intelligence and Statistics.
    (d) India Trade Promotion Organisation.
    (e) Free Trade Zones.
    (f) Indian Institute of Foreign Trade.
14. Projects and programmes for stimulating and assisting the export efforts.
15. Production, distribution (for domestic consumption and exports) and development of plantation crops such as tea, coffee, rubber and cardamom.
16. Processing and distribution for domestic consumption and exports of Instant tea and Instant coffee.
17. i) Tea Board.
    ii) Coffee Board.
    iii) Rubber Board.
    iv) Spices Board.
    v) Tobacco Board.

APPENDIX II

1. RUBBER BOARD,
Shastri Road,
P.B. No. 280,
Kottayam - 686001.

2. COFFEE BOARD,
1-Dr. Ambedkar Veedhi,
Bangalore - 560001.

3. TEA BOARD,
14 - BTM Sarani,
Brabourne Road,
P.B. No. 2172,
Calcutta - 700001.

4. TOBACCO BOARD,
P.B. No. 322,
G.T. Road,
Guntur - 522004.

5. SPICES BOARD,
Sugandha Bhavan,
P.B. No. 2277,
Palarivattam P.O.,
Cochin - 682025.

APPENDIX III

List of Export Promotion Councils Under the Ministry of Commerce

1. ENGINEERING EXPORT PROMOTION COUNCIL,
   World Trade Centre,
   3rd floor, Vandhana Building,
   4th floor, 11, Tolstoy Marg,
   New Delhi-110001.
2. OVERSEAS CONSTRUCTION COUNCIL OF INDIA,
   H - 118 Himalaya House,
   Kasturba Gandhi Marg,
   New Delhi - 110001.
3. BASIC CHEMICALS, PHARMACEUTICALS
   AND COSMETICS EXPORT PROMOTION COUNCIL,
   Jhansi Castle,
   4th floor, 7 Cooperage Road,
   Mumbai-400039.
4. CHEMICALS AND ALLIED PRODUCTS
   EXPORT PROMOTION COUNCIL,
   World Trade Centre, 14/1B, Ezra Street,
   Calcutta - 700001.
5. PLASTICS EXPORT PROMOTION COUNCIL,
   Centre-1, 11th floor,
   World Trade Centre,
   Cuffee Parade, Colaba,
   Mumbai - 400005.
6. COUNCIL FOR LEATHER EXPORTS,
   Leather Centre,
   (3rd floor and 4th floor),
   53, Sydenhams Road, Periamet,
   Chennai - 600003.
7. SPORTS GOODS EXPORT PROMOTION COUNCIL,
   1-E/6, Swami Ram Tirth Nagar,
   Jhandewalan Extn.,
   New Delhi - 110055.
8. GEM AND JEWELLERY EXPORT PROMOTION COUNCIL,
   Diamond Bazar, 5th floor,
   391-A, Dr. D. Bhadkamkar Marg,
   Mumbai - 400003.
9. SHELLAC EXPORT PROMOTION COUNCIL,
   World Trade Centre, 14/B Ezra Street,
   Calcutta - 700001.
10. CASHEW EXPORT PROMOTION COUNCIL,
    Post Box No. 1709,
    Chittoor Road, Ernakulam South,
    Cochin - 682016.
11. ELECTRONICS AND COMPUTER SOFTWARE
    EXPORT PROMOTION COUNCIL,
    PHD House, Phase II, 3rd floor,
    Opp. Asian Games Village,
    New Delhi - 110016.

// *Chapter 5* //

Export Promotion Measures

The Ministry of Commerce is responsible for the external trade and related matters such as export promotion measures, commercial relations with other countries, development and regulation of export oriented industries and commodities and State trading. The Ministry formulates and implements policies in the sphere of foreign trade, reflected in the export-import policy of the country. In addition, the Ministry also undertakes promotional measures to promote exports.

Trade policy liberalisation began in June, 1991, and focused on liberalisation, openness, transparency and globalisation. The reform package focused on outward orientation in the economy from import regulating-activity to export promotion activity, moving away from quantitative restrictions to tariff protection and improving the competitiveness of the Indian industry to meet the global market requirements.

Trade policy reforms have provided an export-friendly environment conducive to accelerated export performance with simplified procedures. Trade reforms revised continuously since 1991 have helped to strengthen the export production base, remove procedural irritants, facilitate input availability besides focusing on quality and technological upgradation and improve competitive edge.

After a setback during 1991–92, when exports declined by 1.5% in terms of dollars, revival of exports started during 1992-93. Indian exports registered an average growth of 20% in dollar terms during 1993-94 to 1995-96. However, this high growth could not be sustained and export growth rate declined to 5.3% in 1996–97 and to 1.55 during 1997-98. During April-December, 1998–99, India's exports were valued at US $24,287 million registering a decline of 2.88% in dollar terms, though in terms of rupees, the growth was positive and high at 11.69%.

EXPORT PERFORMANCE

Export performance is influenced inter-alia by international market conditions, supportive infrastructure, credit availability and policy framework. Export promotion measures are continuously being taken through changes in policies and procedures for providing export promotion and also consultation with trade and industry.

Highlights of Trade Performance

India's exports during April-December, 1998–99, was US $24,286.87 million compared to the export level of US $25, 006.48 million for the corresponding period of the previous year registering a decline of 2.88%.

Imports during April-December, 1998-99, was US $31,582.86 million, which is higher than the deficit at US $29,484.77 million during the same period last year.

The trade deficit for April-December, 1998-99, was US $7,295.99 million, which is higher than the deficit at US $4,478.29 million during the same period last year.

The principal commodities in respect of which India's exports registered an increase during April-December, 1998-99, in dollar terms are tea, guargum meals, castor oil, coal, gems and jewellery, ready-made garments, natural silk textiles, coir and coir manufactures, handicrafts, processed fruits and juices, floriculture products and mica.

SECTORAL PERFORMANCE

Plantations

Export of plantations crops increased from Rs 2,464 crores in April-March, 1996-97, to Rs 3,127 crores in 1997-98 registering a growth of 26.9%. During April-November, 1998-99, these exports increased by 31.7% in rupee terms. Export of coffee increased by 15.3% during the period while that of tea increased by 49.7%.

Agriculture and Allied Products

The export growth of this category of products has been negative at 4.9% decreasing from Rs 16,317 crores in April-March, 1996-97, to Rs 15,519 crores in April-March, 1997-98. During April-November, 1998-99, however, exports of agri and allied products increased from Rs 9,017 crores to Rs 10,243 crores mainly due to the improved export of rice. The items registering a significant increase during this period include rice, spices, guargum meal, castor oil, shellac, processed fruits and juices, miscellaneous processed items and floriculture products. Items recording a decrease in exports are pulses, tobacco, sesame and niger seeds, groundnut, oil meals, sugar and molasses, meat and meat products and spirit and beverages.

Marine Products

The exports of marine products were valued at Rs 4,313 crores in April-March, 1997-98, which is 7.6% higher than the exports valued at Rs 4,008 crores during April-March, 1996-97. During April-November, 1998, these exports declined to Rs 2,973 crores from Rs 2,990 crores achieved during April-November, 1997, showing a fall of 0.6%.

Ores and Minerals

This category of items registered a decline of 4.8% during April-March, 1997-98, when exports fell from Rs 4,162 crores achieved in 1996-97 to Rs 3,962 crores. During April-November, 1998, there was a decline of 10.8%, when exports declined from the level of Rs 2,337 crores in April-November 1997 to Rs 2,184 crore in April-November, 1998.

Leather and Leather Manufactures

The export of leather and leather manufactures also registered a decline of 4% during 1997-98, the value of exports declining from Rs 5,701 crores to Rs 5,462 crores over the period. However, during April-November, 1998, these exports have registered a significant increase of 15.6%, increasing from a level of Rs 3,694 crores in April-November, 1997, to Rs 4,270 crores in April-November, 1998. Most of the leather products are exported to developed countries like Germany, France, US, UK, Italy and Japan and CIS countries.

Gems and Jewellery

Gems and jewellery sector is a major item of India's exports. This sector registered a 12.7% export growth during 1997-98, when exports increased from Rs 16,872 crores in April-March, 1996-97, to Rs 19,014 crores in April-March, 1997-98. During the current year (1998), a higher growth of 33.5% has been witnessed, when exports increased to Rs 15,583 crores during April-November, 1998, from a level of Rs 11,763 crores achieved during the corresponding period last year.

Chemicals and Allied Products

Chemicals and allied products registered a positive export growth of 14.7% during April-March, 1997-98, when its value increased to Rs 16,702 crores from a level of Rs 14,564 crores achieved during the corresponding period of the previous year. In April-November, 1998, the export growth was only 2.3%, the value of exports increasing from Rs 10,563 crores in April-November, 1997, to Rs 10,809 crores in April-November, 1998.

Engineering Goods

The exports of engineering goods registered a 8.3% growth during 1997-98. The value of such exports increased to Rs 15,585 crores as compared to Rs 14,396 crores achieved during 1996-97. However, disappointingly during April-November, 1998, engineering exports witnessed a decline of 3%, its value falling to Rs 9,835 crores from Rs 10,140 crores during April-November, 1997.

Textiles

Textiles, a major in India's export basket witnessed a positive growth of 7.2% last year, when its export value increased form Rs 28,561 crores achieved during 1996-97, to Rs 30,618 crores during 1997-98. Textile exports registered a positive growth of 7.9% during April-November, 1998 over the corresponding period of the previous year, with its value increasing from Rs 20,073 crores to Rs 21,653 crores. Ready-made garments (24.9%, natural silk textiles (30.7%) and coir and coir manufactures (33.6%) were the high growth items under this category during April-November, 1998.

Handicrafts

Export of handicrafts registered a high growth during 1997 and 1998. During 1998-98, its export value increased to Rs 1,927 crores from Rs 1,689 crores during 1997-97, registering a growth of 14.1%. During the April-November, 1998, the growth rate has been 36.3%, with its value increasing to Rs 1,865 crores from a level of Rs 1,368 crores achieved during April-November, 1997.

EXIM POLICY MEASURES

India's external trade sector was further liberalised with the changes introduced in the new Exim Policy for 1997-2002. The highlights of the Exim Policy (1998-99) are as under:

(1) Interest rates on export credits have been lowered from 11% to 9%. Bank guarantees have been dispensed with and a reduction in transaction cost has been effected through decentralisation and simplification of procedures.

(2) DEPB rates for more than 2000 items have been announced and the DEPB has been made a more effective instrument of export promotion by seeking to neutralise the incidence of special Customs Duty of 5%.

(3) Licence on production programme basis has been allowed with flexibility like the change in description of an export product. Advance licence with actual user condition have been allowed based on positive value addition only. Advance licences to export houses/trading houses/star trading houses/super star trading houses are now being issued automatically.

(4) Value addition of goods manufactured through capital goods imported under EPCG licence has been permitted. A fluctuation of 10% of CIF value of imports under EPCG Scheme has been permitted automatically. Additional SIL is being given on the basis of incremental exports.

(5) Transferability of DEPB and advance licence have been allowed without waiting for realisation in respect of exports made against an irrevocable letter of credit.

(6) A manufacturing company or an industrial house with an annual manufacturing turnover of Rs 300 crores and Rs 1000 crores have been made eligible for the status of star trading house and super star trading house respectively.

(7) Debonding under Zero Duty EPCG Scheme has been allowed.

(8) Hotel and Tourism sectors have been made eligible for TH/STH/SSTH status.

Details of Important Export Promotion Measures

The details for important export promotion measures undertaken by the government from time to time are listed here.

Export houses, trading houses and star trading houses The objective of the scheme of export houses, Trading houses and star trading houses is to give recognition to the established exporters and large export houses to build up the marketing infrastructure and expertise required for export promotion. The registered exporters having a record of export performance over a number of years are granted the status of export houses/trading houses/star trading houses/super star trading houses subject to the fulfilment of annual average export performance in terms of FOB value or Net Foreign Exchange earnings on physical exports prescribed in the Exim Policy.

The export houses, trading houses, star trading houses and super star trading houses scheme allows registered exporters certain additional benefits available to them under this policy. The exports made, both in Free Foreign Exchange and in Indian rupee are taken into account for the purpose of recognition only. The FOB and NFE criteria for the purpose of recognition has been reduced to 50% during 1997-98 as a transitional arrangement.

Table 5.1 Eligibility Criteria

(Rs in crore)

Category	*Average FOB Value of Exports Made During the Preceding Three Licensing Year*	*FOB Value of Exports Made During the Preceding Year in Rs*	*Average net Foreign Exchange Value of Exports Made During the Prededing Three Licensing Years*	*Net Foreign Exchange Value of Exports Made During the Preceding Licensing Years*
Export House	12.5	18.75	10	15
Trading House	62.5	93.75	50	75
Star Trading House	312.5	468.75	250	375
Super Star Trading Houses	925	1387.5	740	1110

Table 5.2 The Rate of Entitlement of SIL

Category of Exporters	*Entitlement Rate on Value of Exports Realised in the Preceding Licensing Year*	*Entitlement Rate on NFE*
Export Houses	6%	7.5%
Trading House	8%	10%
Star Trading House	10%	12%
Super Star Trading House	12%	15%

Quality

In accordance with the provisions of paragraph 14.4 of Chapter 14 of the Exim Policy, the manufacturers/processors who have acquired the quality status of ISO 9000 (series) of IS/ISO 9000 (series) or ISO 14000 (series) or HACCP Certification or WH – GMP Certification have been made eligible for the grant of Special Import Licences (SIL) at the rate of 5% of the FOB value of export of goods and services with the aforesaid Quality Certification.

Deemed Exports

Under the Exim Policy 1997-2002, certain transactions in which the goods supplied do not leave the country and payment of such goods are made in

India by the recipient of the goods have been treated as Deemed Exports. These supplies include (i) supply of goods against licences issued under the Duty Exemption Scheme (ii) supply of goods to units located in Export Processing Zones (EPZs) or Software Technology Parks (STPs) or to Export Oriented Units (EUOs) or Electronic Hardware Technology Parks (EHTPs) (iii) supply of capital goods to holders of licence under the EPCG Scheme, subject to the condition that such suppliers will be eligible for benefits only under paragraphs 6.9 of the Policy (iv) supply of goods to projects financed by multilateral or bilateral agencies/funds as notified by the Department of Economic Affairs, Ministry of Finance under International Competitive Bidding (ICB) or under limited tender system in accordance with the procedure of these agencies/funds, where the legal agreements provide for tender evaluation without including custom duty (v) supply of capital goods and spares to the extent of 10% of FOR value to fertiliser plants if the supply is made under procedure of ICB (vi) supply of goods to any project or purpose in respect of which the Ministry of Finance by a notification permits the import of such goods at zero customs duty coupled with the extension of benefits under this chapter to domestic supplies (vii) supply of goods to the power, oil and gas sectors including refineries (viii) supply of marine freight containers by 1005 EOU (domestic freight container-manufacturers) provided the said containers are exported out of India within six months or such further period as permitted by the Customs.

Such supplies (deemed exports) are eligible for the following four benefits in respect of manufacture and supply of goods qualifying as deemed exports: (a) Special Imprest Licence/Advance Intermediate Licence (b) Deemed Exports Drawback Scheme (c) Refund of Terminal Excise Duty and (d) Special Import Licence at the rate of 6% of FOR value (including all taxes and levies).

EXPORT PROMOTION—CAPITAL GOODS SCHEME

Capital goods, both new and second-hand, jigs, fixtures, dies and moulds may be imported under this scheme. The import of computer systems may also be allowed under this scheme.

Spares up to 20% of CIF value may also be imported under the scheme subject to export obligation prescribed therein.

The scheme offers two windows. Under the first window, the capital goods may be imported at a concessional rate of customs duty of 10% and in such cases, the importer is under obligation to export 4 times of the CIF value of capital goods over a period of 5 years.

The second window offers zero duty imports in case the CIF value of capital goods is 20 crores or above. The export obligation in such cases is 6 times of the CIF value of capital goods on FOB basis and 5 times the CIF value of such capital goods on NFE basis and the period over which this obligation is to be completed is 8 years. However, for the following sectors the threshold limit has been kept at Rs 1 crore for eligibility under Zero Duty EPCG Scheme (a) electronics (b) food processing (c) garments (d) leather (e) sports goods (f) gem and jewellery sectors (g) produce and product of agriculture, acquaculture, animal husbandary, floriculture, horticulture, pisciculture, viticulture, poultry, sericulture (h) biotechnology sector and the following subsectors of engineering sector: machine tools, parts and accessories thereof, automotive components and accessories; bicycle parts and accessories, hand tools cutting and small tools; casting and forgings (ferrous and non-ferrous) all sorts; pumps, electric motors and parts thereof, fasteners, all types (ferrous and non-ferrous); bright bars and shafting; scientific and surgical instruments.

For the software sector, the threshold limit for eligibility under Zero Duty DPCG has been kept at Rs 10 lakhs or more. The export obligation in such cases is 6 times of the CIF value of capital goods on FOB basis and 5 times of the CIF value of capital goods on NFE basis and the period over which this obligation is to be completed is 6 years.

Under the scheme, the import of capital goods in SKD/CKD condition is also allowed. The sourcing of such capital goods from domestic suppliers is also permitted and such domestic suppliers can import components for the manufacture of such capital goods.

The scheme is provided under Chapter 6 of the Exim Policy and Handbook of Procedure (Vol.I).

Duty Exemption Scheme

The Duty Exemption Scheme is an important instrument for boosting exports. The scheme consists of duty free licence and duty entitlement pass book as contained in Chapter 7 of the Exim Policy and Handbook of Procedures 1997-2002.

Duty-free licence The duty-free licence consists of advance licence, advance intermediate licence and special imprest licence.

Advance licence Advance licence is granted to merchant exporters or manufacturer exporters for the import of inputs required for the manufacture of goods without payment of basic customs duty with a corresponding export obligation based on the value and quantity of the export product. Such inputs are however, subject to the payment of additional customs duty at the time of import. However, exemption from payment of additional customs duty is also allowed in regard to advance licence issued with actual user condition to the following categories.

(a) Manufacturer exporter
(b) Merchant exporter

Merchant exporter agrees to the endorsement of name(s) of supporting manufacturer(s) on the relevant Duty Exemption Entitlement Certificate.

The Advance licence where exemption is admissible in respect of the additional customs duty as well shall not be transferable even after the completion of export obligation, whereas the Licence where exemption is admissible only in respect of the basic customs duty are transferable after the completion of export obligation subject to laid down conditions.

Advance intermediate licence An advance intermediate licence is granted to the manufacturer exporter for the import of inputs required in the manufacture of goods to be supplied to the ultimate exporter holding an advance licence/special imprest licence.

Special imprest licence The special imprest licence is granted to a manufacturer exporter for the import of inputs required in the manufacture of goods to be supplied to EOUs/EPZs/STPs/EHTPs, supply of capital goods to holders of licence under Zero Duty DPCG Scheme, supply of goods to projects financed by multilateral or bilateral agencies/funds as notified by the Department of Economic Affairs under the international competitive bidding or under the limited tender system, supply of capital goods and spares to the extent of 10% of FOR value to fertiliser plants, if the supply is made under the procedure of the international competitive bidding and supply of goods to refineries and supply of goods to any project or purpose, in respect of which the Ministry of Finance by a notification permits the import of such goods at zero customs duty. A special imprest licence is also granted for supplies made to United Nations Organisations or under the Aid Programme of The United Nations or other multilateral agencies and paid for in foreign exchange.

The duty free licence/relevant DEEC Books shall specify the following details:

(a) The name and description of items to be imported and exported/supplied.
(b) The quantity of each item to be imported or wherever the quantity cannot be indicated, the value of the item shall be indicated. However, if in standard input output norms, the quantity and value of individual inputs is a limiting factor, the same shall be applicable.
(c) The aggregate CIF value of imports.
(d) The FOB/FOR value and quantity of exports/supplies.

Duty entitlement passbook Duty Entitlement Pass Book Scheme is to neutralise the incidence of basic and special duty on the import content of the export product. The neutralisation shall be provided by way of grant of duty credit against the export product.

Exporters are eligible for benefits under this scheme both on pre-export as well as post-export basis. DEPB on post-export basis is granted against exports already made and item imported against it are freely transferable upon realisation of the export proceeds. Under the DEPB on pre-export basis, exporters tied with the supporting manufacturer and having export performance in the preceding three licensing years are eligible. The entitlement under this Scheme is 5% of the average export performance of the applicant during the preceding three licensing years. It also carries export obligations which have to be off-set within a period of 12 months and they are non-transferable and subject to actual user condition even after off-setting of their obligation against such DEPB.

EOUs/EPZs/EHTP/STP Export Processing Zones (EPZs), set up as special enclaves, separated from the Domestic Tariff Area by fiscal barriers, are intended to provide an internationally competitive duty free environment for export production at a low cost. The Export Oriented Units (EOUs) Scheme is complementary to the EPZ Scheme in that it adopts the same production regime but offers a wide option in locations with reference to factors like source of raw materials, ports of exports, availability of technological skills, etc.

These units may import all types of goods which are duty free, including capital goods and restricted items required by such units for manufacture, production and processing. However, prohibited items in the negative list of imports are not permitted. That apart, import of basmati, paddy and brown rice is also not permitted. Second hand capital goods with a minimum residual life of 5 years are also permitted to be imported by these units.

These units are required to earn a minimum Net Foreign Exchange earning of 20% except in certain specified sectors where individual value addition norms have been prescribed. This minimum value addition stipulation is, however, not applicable to units in the electronic hardware sector. Biotechnology units can be set up with the positive Net Foreign Exchange earning. The details of the scheme are given in Chapter 9 of the Exim Policy and Handbook of Procedures (Vol. I) 1997-2002.

SECTOR SPECIFIC MEASURES

The benefits of Export Promition Capital Scheme has been extended to a number of such sectors of the engineering section. During 1998-99, standard input output norms for an additional 156 items of the engineering products were fixed. Import of computer drawn designs/drawings has been made freely importable.

The seven-phase project under the Commonwealth Fund for Technical Cooperation (CFTC) named "Integrated Marketing Programme of Indian Herbal Medicines in West Europe" with the objective of promoting awareness and recognition of Indian herbal medicines and to identify export opportunities was completed.

A special task force to consider the credit needs of the seafood industries has been constituted. An interest subsidy scheme to subsidise a portion of interest on the bank loans obtained for the purpose of modernisation/ upgradation of the marine product industry has been introduced.

Value addition norms and wastage norms for gold/platinum/silver jewellery and articles have been rationalised. Value addition will be calculated after the deduction of the agency commission. Personal carriage of samples of jewellery up to $1,00,000 has been allowed for export promotion tours. Personal carriage by foreign buyers from EPZs/EOUs has also been allowed. Legal Undertaking (LUT/Joint LUT) Limits for different categories of exporters have been modified. Under the loan scheme, the period for the fulfilment of export obligation has been increased from 90 to 120 days.

Trade Finance

In the interest of export promition and to make exports competitive, credit facilities are provided by the commercial banks to the export sector at pre-shipment and post-shipment stages both in rupees and in foreign currency, at interest rates lower than the commercial rates under various schemes of RBI. Exports have the option to select the export credit route more favourable to them between the rupee route with the benefit of forward premium or the foreign currency route at LIBOR linked interest rates.

The interest rates applicable on rupee credit both at pre and post shipment stages are regularly reviewed by the RBI and are adjusted from time, taking into account various factors including developments in the financial markets, exchange rate differential etc. The interest rate on pre-shipment rupee credit for a period up to 180 days was reduced from 12 to 11% w.e.f. 30.4.1998. Further, with a view to step up the rate of growth of exports, it has been decided, that as a special temporary facility, rupee export credit will be made available to exporters at lower rates by making a 2% cut in interest rates on pre and post-shipment credits i.e. at 9% against 11% w.e.f. 6th August, 1998. This facility will be available up to 31st March, 1999. Banks have also been authorised by RBI to grant export credit in foreign currency at rates linked to LIBOR (London Inter Bank Offer Rate). With a view to enabling exporters to access export credit in foreign currency more effectively at internationally competitive rates, it has been decided that w.e.f. 12.6.1998, banks should charge a spread of not more than 1.5% over LIBOR (excluding withholding Tax) as against 2 to 2.5% over LIBOR being charged earlier.

To ensure an adequate availability of credit to the export sector, RBI is closely monitoring the flow of credit to the export sector, both under the rupee scheme as well as foreign currency schemes viz. Pre-shipment Credit in Foreign Currency (PCFC) and Rediscounting of Export Bills abroad (EBR). Export credit refinance has been restored to 10% (instead of 50%) of the increase in outstanding export credit eligible for refinance over the level of such credit as on February 16, 1996 w.e.f. the fortnight beginning May 9, 1998.

To ensure the timely availability of funds to the exporters, RBI has prescribed time limits for banks for sanction of fresh/enhanced/adhoc credit limits and also for the renewal of existing credit limits. Banks have been instructed to sanction fresh/enhanced credit limits to finance exports within 45 days from the date of receipt of application with complete data and financial accounts. In the case of renewal of credit limits and sanction of adhoc credit facilities, banks are required to act within a period of 30 days and 15 days respectively from the date of application with relevant particulars. All cases of rejection of export credit are to be brought to the notice of the chief executive of the banks with reasons for such rejections. Banks have been further advised to see that no export order suffers for want of banks finance.

The Ministry of Commerce constantly interacts with the RBI to ensure adequate availability of credit to the exporters both in foreign currency and rupee terms at an internationally competitive rate.

MARKET DEVELOPMENT ASSISTANCE (MDA)

The Government of India established the MDA Fund in 1963 with a view to stimulating and diversifying the export trade along with the development of the marketing of Indian products and commodities abroad. It is utilised for the following purposes:-

(a) Market Research, commodity research, area survey and research.

(b) Product promotion and commodity development.
(c) Export publicity and dissemination of information.
(d) Participation in trade fairs and exhibitions.
(e) Trade delegations and study teams.
(f) Establishment of offices and branches and godowns in countries abroad.
(g) Grant-in-aid to Export Promotion Councils and other approved organisations for the development of exports and the promotion of foreign trade.
(h) Any other scheme which is calculated generally to promote the development of markets for Indian products and commodities abroad.

The expenditure is controlled by the MDA Committee. The Marketing Development Assistance is provided under the following sub-heads:-

Grant-in-Aid to Export Promotion and Market Development Organisation

MDA grant is available to 20 Export Promotion Councils, grantee Institutions/approved organisations such as Federation of Indian Organisations, Indian Institute of Foreign Trade, Indian Institute of Packing, Indian Council of Arbitration and Indian Diamond Institute and export houses, trading houses and star trading houses, etc. The budget provision for MDA for all these organisations are approved by the MDA Committee. The actual expenditure under this head during the last five years was as under:

Table 5.3

Year	*Expenditure (Rs in Crores)*
1994-95	12.94
1995-96	16.00
1996-97	19.91
1997-98	20.95
1998-99 (Up to November 1998)	9.95

DIRECTORATE GENERAL OF FOREIGN TRADE

The Directorate General of Foreign Trade has its headquarters at New Delhi and has 31 administrative offices located at Mumbai, Calcutta, Chennai, CLA New Delhi, Kanpur, Bangalore, Ahemedabad, Pune, Ludhiana, Moradabad, Ernakulam (Cochin), Jaipur, Varanasi, Hyderabad, Guwahati, Coimbatore, Panipat, Jammu, Rajkot, Patna, Madurai, Shilong, Amritsar, Bhopal, Panjim (Goa), Chandigarh, Surat, Cuttak, Baroda, Pondicherry and Vishakapatnam for the benefit of trade and industry. The export promotion offices at Mumbai, Calcutta, Chennai, Cochin, Nagpur and Pune are also functioning under the administrative control of the concerned Joint Director Generals of Foreign Trade at respective stations. The office of export promotion at Nagpur has been merged with JDG, Mumbai.

The main function of the organisation is to assist and advise the government in the formulation of the Exim Policy and to implement the policy through the mechanism of licensing. After the trade reforms and changes in the Exim Policy, the principal function of the organisation at present is the promotion of exports and facilitation of imports to promote export trade. The new Act, namely, The Foreign Trade (Development and Regulation) Act has come into existence w.e.f. 7.8.1992 and Rules thereunder have also been finalised and notified. Keeping in view the special thrust in export efforts and the resolution of the government to resolve exporters' problems in a coordinated manner and on immediate basis, all the field offices of DGFT Organisation also act as export facilitation centres, in addition to being nodal agencies to attend to the problems and grievances of the exporters. They also liaise and coordinate with the field functionaries of other departments i.e. department of revenue, banking, railways, shipping and power, etc. to resolve all the trade and export related problems faced by the exporters pertaining to these departments.

Trade Data Collection and Dissemination

Special efforts were made to streamline the data dissemination of foreign trade. Special efforts were also made to ensure that the aggregate data on imports, exports and balance of trade are released within one month after the reference month and the data on principal commodities and countries are released within 55-60 days. The method of compiling a bilateral index on trade was reviewed and efforts made to identify major trade partners and specific commodities for compiling the bilateral trade index for imports and exports. An initiative was also taken to attempt the collection of trade data to reflect states' contribution to exports by indicating the place of origin/manufacture of export products. An experimental effort was made to collect the data from Delhi port with the introduction of EDI at the Delhi Customs. Efforts are in progress to arrive at the methodology for compiling the state level data based on inter-ministerial consultations. Efforts are being made to provide a value added service using the DGCI&S data to help exporters locate new markets and products in the increasingly, competitive international trading environment. Special efforts are also being made to upgrade and modernise the data processing facilities at the DGCI&S in tune with the general switch to EDI by the Customs who provide the source of trade data and compile data on company-wise exports/imports for specific purposes.

Directorate General of Anti-dumping and Allied Duties

The Directorate General of Anti-dumping and Allied Duties was created on 13th April, 1998. The Directorate would investigate allegations of dumping and subsidies and recommend suitable duties to the Central Government. The number of cases recommended for imposition of Anti-Dumping Duties by the designated authority in the Ministry of Commerce increased to a total of 23 products by 30.9.1998. Recommendations have been made for the imposition of provisional duties in another 3 cases, while 13 cases are under investigation, including 6 review cases as on 30.9.1998 for imposition of duties or otherwise.

Electronic Commerce (EC) and Electronic Data Interchange (EDI)

EDI is a modern concept aimed at promoting an efficient and paperless trading which is increasingly being adopted in many countries around the world. The Ministry of Commerce is striving to promote the use of EC/EDI in the area of international trade in India.

In the wake of liberalisation of the Indian economy and the consequential emphasis on exports, it has become necessary to modernise the logistical edge to the extent possible. The government has therefore identified the use of EDI and EC as one of high priority in trade facilitation.

Sectoral EDI implementation review meetings with all the trade regulating and facilitating agencies like banks, customs, airports, ports, VAN's service providers and education and awareness spreading institutions are regularly being organised to ensure the switching over to electronic commerce and integration of these agencies with their associated community partners. The various technical and management issues raised during these meeting are taken up with concerned departments.

The report of the committee for process reengineering constituted to study the current processes as well as work flow and information flow of trade processes so as to streamline the procedures to reduce the time in international trade transactions by simplifying the procedures, has been finalised and being adopted by the concerned departments.

In order to highlight the capabilities of electronic commercc and electronic data interchange, the Ministry of Commerce organised EDICON '98, a conference and exhibition on EDI/EC during May 28-30, 1998. The theme of EDICON '98 was "Trade Facilitation through Electronic Commerce." A similar conference is planned to be held every year. The event was a great success and was attended by around 500 participants. During the EDICON'98, a special session was organised for CEO's of top Indian companies to stress the urgent need for adoption of EC/EDI tools by Indian companies to be competitive. The session was well received by industries and was attended by around 150 CEO's.

In order to create an awareness and education on EDI, four organisations have been selected by the Ministry of Commerce—National Informatics Centre (NIC), Indian Institute of Foreign Trade (IIFT), All India Management Association (AIMA), and Federation of Indian Export Organisations (FIEO). These organisations have standardised course contents for short-term as well as long-term programmes for different levels.

In order to overcome the constraints of legal barriers like admissibility of EDI/EC generated documents/contracts and its acceptability as primary evidence in a Court, it has been decided to formalise the amendments required in various Acts of Indian Laws. A legal committee was formed to suggest changes needed in various Acts of Indian Laws. A draft model law has since been sent to the Legislative Department for examination and adoption.

India Trade Promotion Organisation

India Trade Promotion Organisation (ITPO) is the premier trade promotion agency of the country. Its mission is to organise trade fairs/exhibitions in

India and abroad, buyer seller meets, trade promotion and product development programmes apart from information dissemination on products and markets.

ETPO's exhibition at Pragati Maidan, New Delhi, and in other parts of the country effectively mirror the latest development in various sectors of industry and cater to both export and import requirements. Events which over the years have been developed and institutionalised include International Shoe Fair, Shoe Camp, India International Trade Fair and Delhi Book Fair. About 36 events are to be organised by other organisers during the financial year 1998-99 in Pragati Maidan. Important events among them are Petrotech, Water Asia, International garments Fair, 13th India Engineering Trade Fair/Microtech'99, India Handicrafts and Gifts Fair Spring '99, and Carpet Fair '99.

During April to December, 1998, ITPO has organised participation in 32 fairs/exhibitions, abroad which include 13 general international fairs, 17 specialised commodity fairs and two exclusive Indian exhibitions in Egypt and Azerbaijan. Out of 32 events, 10 have been organised in Europe, 7 in South East Asia, 7 in American countries and 8 in WANA region. The participants in these events have reported business booked to the tune of Rs 11,217.82 lakhs and business under negotiation amounting to Rs 1,03,693.79 lakhs. ITPO, on behalf of the Government of India, organised India's participation at Expo'98, Lisbon (Portugal), May 22 to September 30, 1998.

During the period from April-December, 1998, two buyer-seller meets were organised in Japan, one for home furnishings and another for garments and fashion accessories which have resulted in export orders valued at US $6.28 million and enquiries of US $14.72 million. A total of 3 Contact Promotion Programme (CPP) are scheduled during 1998-00, of which the CPP for home furnishings in Spain and Portugal has been implemented and other covering auto parts in Singapore, Philippines and Sri Lanka are being taken up in the first quarter of 1999.

During April-December, 1998, ITPO organised 4 product catalogue shows in Egypt, Azrbaijan, Iraq and Peru. During the year, ITPO has organised Product Promotion Programme (PPP) for leather products in US and Canada, home furnishings, carpet and floor coverings in Australia and New Zealand and for computer software and services in US and Canada. Two market surveys on trade and investment opportunities are proposed to be conducted in the coming months in Peru and South Africa.

Indian Institute of Foreign Trade

The Indian Institute of Foreign Trade (IIFT) was set up in 1964 by the Government of India with a view to impart training to junior, middle and senior level executives in different areas of foreign trade management; for undertaking policy-oriented research, market surveys, commodity and country studies, disseminating foreign trade information through its publications, research reports and offering consultancy services.

The Institute continues to enlarge its training and research activities keeping in view the paramount needs of the external sector. It has also restructured its programmes to bring in tune with the changing International business environment. During 1998-99, the Institute has conducted a number of educational and management development training programmes.

Testing and U.N. certification Nearly 900 items were tested for UN Certification and 7000 other samples were tested by the Institute at its facilities at Mumbai, Calcutta, Delhi and Chennai. Four certificates were issued by the Eastern Regional Centre as per Australian Wool Corporation/New Zealand specifications for the testing of wool samples for exports.

Training programmes/seminars The Institute continued to pass on its expertise to the industry personnel by way of conducting seminars and training programmes at all the four centres of the Institute. Under the intensive training course at Mumbai and Calcutta, during the year, as many as 47 participants including 14 overseas participants from developing countries under India's International Assistance Scheme, such as the Colombo Plan, the SCAAP and the ITEC were benefited.

As many as 24 executive development programmes were conducted by the head office and three regional centres of IIP. The programmes were spread over various industry/commercial centres all over India. The number of centres covered are 18 and a total of 860 industry delegates benefited from such programmes.

National Centre for Trade Information

The thrust of NCTI's activities has been in terms of use of the electronic media and dissemination of information using the same for the purpose of promotion of India's exports.

Functioning as the Trade Point-India under the Trade Efficiency Programme of UNCTAD, NCTI performs the function of dissemination of trade opportunities, using the electronic media for the benefit of its members.

Trade leads, tender notifications, joint venture offers are also posted on NCT's website: Hyperlink **http://www.nctindia.com** for the same purpose.

NCTI has compiled a CD-ROM of its kind in India titled "CD-ROM of Overseas Imports and Product-wise HS Directory." This CD-ROM has been compiled from lakhs of ETOs downloaded from across the globe for the past few years. Finally, 35,000 overseas importers as well as Directory of Harmonised Classification (HS ITS Code) group-wise have been incorporated in the CD-ROM for the benefit of the trading community. Periodic updates of the CD-ROM are on the cards. As the next step, NCTI is involved in the compilation of a CD-ROM of country profiles.

NCTI has the competence of compiling value added reports on the basis of raw data, both Indian trade statistics as well as international/global trade statistics. A recent example of this has been in terms of the following three reports submitted to MOC:-

(i). "Sport Goods"
Global Imports (1992-1196)
Exports from India (1990-91 to 1996-97)
Statistical analysis and trends for top 15 countries

(ii) "Leather Goods"
Global Imports (1992-1996)
Exports from India (1990-91 to 1996-97)
Statistical analysis and trends for top 15 countries

(iii) "Sports Goods"
Analysis of Basket of Sports Goods
Exported from India to USA (1996-97) and
Imported into USA from rest of the World (1996)

In respect of point no. 1 above, NCTI attempts to reach the small and medium enterprise for doing international business, without having to invest in any elaborated infrastructure abroad. In this respect, NCTI is also pursing a proposal with the Ministry of Commerce, to implement the benefits of EDI, electronic commerce and the internet for the small and medium enterprises in the State of UP for the leather exporting industry. This would be a pilot project, which after completion, would be replicated across other key sectors and regions of the country.

NCTI also compiles a quarterly journal, "Trade Connect" meant for overseas circulation. This Journal tries to assimilate all the positive aspects of the Indian economy for the benefit of India's partners abroad.

Indian Institute of Package, Mumbai

The Indian Institute of Package (IIP), Mumbai, a Research and Development, Training and Education Organisation set up in 1996, under the Ministry of Commerce, has been entrusted with the responsibility of bringing about improvements in the standards of packing in the country, particularly for exports. IIP has been registered under the societies' Registration Act, 1860.

It has on its roll, 1000 numbers, representing industries of a heterogeneous nature. It undertakes technical consultancy, testing services on packaging development, training and educational programmes, promotional awards contests, information services, international affiliations with APF/WPO etc. and other important activities. The Institute has its regional branches at Calcutta, Chennai and New Delhi.

The packaging scenario all over the world is vast changing, and in this context, the domestic Industries are expected to adopt the changes rapidly. The Institute gaining inspiration from the vast development and anticipated further needs has centered its activities with a view to propagate scientific packaging and upgradation of technology and endeavour its resources towards environmental causes as well.

Testing and UN Certification

Nearly 5500 samples were tested and UN Certification was done for 750 items by the Institute at its facilities at Mumbai, Calcutta, Delhi and Chennai. Four certificates were issued by the Eastern Regional Centre as per Australian Wool Corporation/New Zealand specifications for the testing of wool samples for exports. It is envisaged that approximately 2000 samples will be tested and 200 UN Certificates will be issued in the remaining period.

// CHAPTER 6 //

PROFILE OF THE EUROPEAN UNION

The European Union (EU) has been founded on the European Communities, supplemented by the policies and forms of cooperation established by the Treaty of the European Union (TEU) in 1993. The European Communities is the collective name for three international organisations:

- ★ The European Coal and Steel Community (ECSC) formed in 1951
- ★ The European Atomic Energy Community (Euratom) formed in 1951
- ★ The European Community (EC) formed in 1958

The intensification of efforts towards the European unification after the Second World War sprang from the realisation that there was no other way to end Europe's destruction. The desire for peace left its mark on the Treaties establishing the Community and the Union. The principal aims were namely to preserve and strengthen peace, to achieve economic integration for the benefit of all the citizens of the Union through the creation of a single internal market, to work towards a political union and to strengthen and promote social cohesion within the Union.

OBJECTIVES

The Treaty of the Economic European Community was amended in 1987 by the signing of the Single European Act (SEA) which especially mentions the internal market as an important objective. For example, the SEA set out the EC's goal as establishing the internal market by December 31, 1992, introduced qualified majority voting in the Council of Ministers for the majority of measures required to achieve this, and provided the European Parliament, through the 'cooperation procedure,' with a significant role in the adoption of single market legislation.

In 1993, the member states of the Community signed the Treaty of the European Union (TEU) with ambitious objective concerning developing cooperation and environmental policy. Since that moment, the EU has set itself several new objectives.

Goal of the European Union Since 1993 (TEU)

To promote economic and social progress which is balanced and sustainable, particulary in the creation of an area without internal frontiers; through the strengthening of economic and social cohesion and through the establishment of economic and Monetary Union, ultimately including a single currency.

- ★ To implement a common foreign and security policy including the eventual framing of a common defence policy, which might in time lead to a common defence.
- ★ To develop close cooperation on justice and home affairs.
- ★ To strengthen the protection of the right and interests of the National member states through the introduction of a citizenship of the Union.

The European parliament Although the Parliament is the first mentioned institution, it is in many ways less esteemed and influential than most of the National Parliaments of the member states. The representatives in the European Parliament of the people in the member states are elected by direct universal suffrage (every five years). The European Parliament consists of 626 members and the number of members per country is weighed by population which includes legislation (decision-making), scrutiny and control of the Executive and recruitment and socialisation. The legislative and decision-making role of the European Parliament has been enhanced by the TEU. The Council however, continues (usually) to make the key decisions.

The council of Ministers Composed of ministerial level representatives from the National Governments of the member states, the Council is the principal lawmaker of the EC and deciders on legislative proposals originating from the Commission (sometimes in cooperation with the European Parliament). The Presidency of the Council, rotating between the member states at six monthly intervals, provides the direction and momentum for EC activities, including completing the common European market. Council decisions can be adopted on the basis of unanimity, straightforward majority voting or qualified majority voting. The Council of Ministers is the institution which defends the national interests of the member states.

The commission The Commission consists of 20 members, who are chosen on the grounds of their general competence and whose independence is beyond doubt. They are appointed for a period of 5 years. The governments of the member states shall nominate by common accord, after consulting the European Parliament, the person they intend to appoint as the President of the Commission.

The European Court of Justice (ECJ) The European Court of Justice (ECJ) ensures that in the interpretation and application of the TEU., the law is observed. The ECJ consists of 15 judges and 8 advocates-general. Persons are chosen whose independence is beyond doubt and who possess the highest judicial qualifications and they are appointed by a common accord of the governments of the member states for a term of six years.

The ECJ has both a judicial and an enforcement role, deciding on interpretation and overseeing the way National Courts actually apply the rules. The Court of Justice has become an activist body with an influence on policy.

It also gained authority from the Single European Act (SEA) which created a subordinate Court of First Instance (also 15 judges, one of whom can be appointed as an advocate-general for a period of six years).

The Court of Auditors The Court of Auditors is an internal working institution to control the finance of the other EU institutions. As an institution, it is therefore not very important for exporters to the EU.

The customs union and the single market The main purpose of the European Community is the establishment of a common market. For that purpose, the activities of the Community shall include for example, a customs union, a common commercial policy and an internal market, characterised by the abolition of obstacles between the member states, to the free movement of goods, persons, services and capital. Therefore, the common market is more challenging than the internal market. To set up an internal market is an activity to realise a component of the common market. The terms 'Internal market' and 'single market' are used interchangeably to indicate the efforts of the Community to realise the free movements.

The focal point of economic integration is the single internal market setup by the member states to create a unified economic territory, undivided by either customs or trade barriers. This single market rests on the pillars of four fundamental freedoms—the free movements of goods, persons, services and capital. First and foremost, it allows capital and labour, the basic factors of production, to develop their potential, untrammelled and unhindered. Workers can move freely to seek jobs, where demand is higher, and where wages and working conditions are therefore better. They can settle with their families and work anywhere in the EU. Firms can produce, sell and compete freely wherever it suits them best. No member state may treat its own National more favourably than Nationals from its EU partners.

Nature of a customs union The essential nature of a customs union is free trade between the Union's members and the establishment of a common external tariff on trade with non-member states. The creation of a customs union involves the abolition of all import and export duties, and of quantitative restriction on trade between the member states. In addition, it involves the harmonisation of national tariffs on trade with third countries and their subsequent replacement by an external tariff common to all member states. In the Treaty of Rome, the customs union is supplemented by provisions for the free movement of persons, services and capital. Furthermore, the effective functioning of the customs union is promoted internally through a common competition policy, and externally through a common commercial policy.

Not only economic and financial issues, but also political issues have resulted in the amendment of the Treaty of Rome by the Single European Act (SEA), so that the completion of the internal market could become an explicit aim of the EU. The essential aim of completing the single market was the realisation of the four freedoms—the free movement of goods, persons, services and capital.

SINGLE MARKET AND OBJECTIVES

Freedom of the Movement of

- ★ Goods
- ★ Persons

- ★ Services
- ★ Capital

Removal of Quantitative Restrictions

Creating a single market where all goods can be freely traded requires not only the removal of Customs barriers, but also the lifting of quantitative restrictions. These are designed to protect a country's industries, warding off foreign competition on the domestic market, either by a temporary or indefinite ban on certain imports or alternatively by restrictions in terms of value of volume (quotas). Measures of this kind are forbidden by the Treaties and this prohibition has, in the main, been respected by the members states since the expiry of the prescribed transition periods. Thus, inter-EU Trade is now free of all quota restrictions.

Consequences of the New Approach for Exporters in Developing Countries

The above solution avoids unnecessary harmonisation and even manages to bridge apparently irreconcilable conflicts of interest. Consumers are given the widest possible choice of products from across the entire Community as well as from third countries and those products are guaranteed to meet certain minimum health and safety standards. On the other hand, manufacturers can market their products anywhere in the single European market. This generates cost savings, greater freedom of competition and lower production costs, leading in turn to lower prices, a wider range of products and greater innovation.

Free mobility Freedom of movement for workers is already largely a reality. The right was enshrined in the Treaties and comprehensively implemented by a Council Regulation in 1968, assuring all EU Nationals of equal treatment in terms of employment, wages and other working conditions throughout the EU. Individuals are guaranteed geographical and occupational mobility and a minimum level of social integration in any member state where they choose to work.

Geographical mobility Geographical mobility is a person's right to go and stay in another member state in order to seek employment or take up and pursue an occupation. Originally, only workers and those seeking work enjoyed a guaranteed right of residence under the EU law. But, several Directives were adopted in 1990, extending this right to students, pensioners and non-employed people provided that they had sufficient means to support themselves and adequate health insurance cover.

National immigration authorities cannot refuse to grant someone the right of residence guaranteed under the EU law (in particular, on grounds of public policy, security or health) except in very serious cases, and any such refusal can be challenged before a Court of Justice.

Occupational mobility Occupational mobility covers people's right to pursue whatever occupation they wish and their terms of employment and working conditions. Here again, nationals of other member states may not be treated differently from local workers. For instance, they are entitled to equal pay, occupational reintegration, access to training or re-training centres and re-employment in the event of redundancy.

Social integration Social integration refers to a worker's right to all the general welfare benefits available in the host country. In other words, workers from other member states, are entitled to the same rights and privileges as local people in terms of accommodation (including Council housing), for example, Trade Union activities or social security.

Lastly, the EU rules on social security guarantee employees and the self-employed as well as their families, not only family allowances but also adequate coverage in the event of illness, disability, occupational accident or disease, unemployment, death of a close relative, and old age. The essential point is to ensure that no one loses social security entitlements or is penalised, simply because they exercise their right to move freely within the EU.

Freedom of establishment Broadly speaking, freedom of establishment concerns people's right to take up and pursue independent occupations. Therefore, it covers doctors, lawyers, architects, estate agents, brokers, advertising agencies and the like, as well as technical, artistic and craft activities. It also expressly covers the establishment and running of businesses, in particular companies and company agencies, branches or subsidiaries. On the other hand, it does not cover activities connected with the permanent or occasional exercise of public authority. The member states are free to decide for themselves which occupations are to be entrusted with such authority.

Freedom to provide services The freedom to provide Services covers the same activities as the freedom of establishment, but in the case of Services, the activities are limited in time and must in some way involve crossing an internal EU frontier. As with the right of establishment, activities connected with the exercise of public authority are excluded.

There are three different cases where a cross-frontier element may be involved:

- ★ The provider of a service may temporarily go to the recipient, crossing the border himself to perform the service in another member state. This is the typical case which the freedom to provide Services is intended to cover. It represents a necessary corollary to the right of establishment, which is designed to help those wishing to establish themselves in another member state and integrate permanently into the working life there.
- ★ Going beyond that, the Court of Justice has also recognised that the freedom extends to the case where the recipient goes to the country of the provider to obtain the service. Thus, the Court has held in particular, that tourists and people undergoing medical treatment, must also be regarded as recipients of Services, as must those travelling for the purposes of education or business.
- ★ The rules on freedom to provide Services also apply where the service provider and recipient remain in their own countries and only the

service crosses the border. A typical case of this kind is radio and television broadcasting.

POLITICAL UNION

Peace and reconciliation are central to the process of European integration. Not once since the Second World War has Europe tried to impose its ideas on the rest of the world, other than by setting an example of how to solve problems by negotiation. Nevertheless, because Europe emerged as an important economic and trading power, the European Union is increasingly called upon to act as a mediator and a stabilising force in world affairs.

Until the Treaty on European Union, political cooperation between the member states was carried out under European Political Cooperation (EPC). The EPC was established in 1970 and was improved and extended by the Single European Act. The aim of the EPC was to improve communication between member states on all major foreign policy issues. Therefore, regular consultations between foreign ministers and constant contacts between their officials would take place to discuss their points of view and attempt to arrive at a common approach. European Union institutions such as the European Committee and the Parliament were only indirectly involved.

Because of the geopolitical changes in Europe since 1989, for example, the collapse of the Warsaw Pact, the unification of Germany, the disintegration of the Soviet Union and the break-up of Yugoslavia - the member states decided to make a major move towards political cooperation.

Cooperation in Justice and Home Affairs

The problems of immigration and asylum, drug trafficking and other aspects of international crime are matters of increasing concern to the citizens of Europe. The Treaty on European Union provides for extensive cooperation in justice and home affairs and its gradual extension to form a Community policy. The main aim of cooperation in home affairs is policy towards non-member countries as regards immigration and asylum.

The following areas are to be harmonised and involve all the member states:

- ★ Common Policy on asylum
- ★ Immigration of citizens of non-Union countries
- ★ Illegal immigration, illegal residents and illegal workers

Cooperation in the field of justice mainly involves coordinate measures to combat drug trafficking, uncover large-scale international fraud, pursue other forms of international crime and deal with matters relating to civil disputes and customs offences.

Common foreign and security policy The Treaty on European Union forms the basis of a political Union built around a common foreign and security policy. The objectives of the Union are:

- ★ To safeguard the common values, fundamental interests and independence of the Union
- ★ To strengthen the security of the Union and its member states in all ways

- To preserve peace and strengthen international security
- To develop and consolidate democracy and the rule of law, and respect for human rights and fundamental freedom

Article A of the Treaty of Maastricht establishes a Union 'founded on the European Communities, supplemented by the policies and forms of cooperation established by this Treaty.' This means that community and intergovernmental procedures will exist side-by-side in a single institutional framework.

European citizenship The Treaty of Maastricht also established the citizenship of EU. Every person holding the nationality of a member state shall be a citizen of the EU. Citizens of the EU shall enjoy the rights conferred by the Treaty and shall be subject to the duties imposed thereby.

In short, the concept of citizenship implies the free movement of citizens and their political rights. The essential reason for including the citizenship is an attempt to make the EU more democratic. On the other hand, in the Treaty, there are some links made with the European Convention on Human Rights and Fundamental Freedom (ECHIR). This Convention is not a convention based on the EU Treaty. The ECHR was established (in 1950) by more European countries than the EU member states. Nevertheless, the EU will respect fundamental rights, as guaranteed by the ECHIR, as a general principle of Community law.

ECONOMIC AND MONETARY UNION

One of the main objectives of the EU is to promote economic and social progress which is balanced and sustainable, in particular, through the establishment of an Economic and Monetary Union, ultimately culminating in a single currency. First, attention is paid to the Monetary system as it has existed since 1979. Second, the Monetary Union will be dealt with. It depends on the political progress in this case.

Monetary system In July 1978, the heads of state or government decided to establish the European Monetary System (EMS), which came into force in March 1979. After a difficult beginning, the EMS has provided a base for stable exchange rates and better informed Economic and Monetary Policy. The EMS has created a zone of monetary stability in Europea, encouraging growth and investment.

The EMS has the following two main components:

- The European currency unit (now renamed EURO)
- The exchange rate

ECU The ECU is seen as the key element in the system. It is a basket of the currencies of the member states, except the new members who joined in 1995, with four basic functions.

- A unit of account in the exchange rate mechanism
- A base for determining divergence indicators
- A unit of account for operations under the intervention and credit mechanism
- A means of settlement between the monetary authorities of the member states

The exchange rate Each currency has a central exchange rate linked to the ECU. This is used to determine central rates for each pair of currencies. Until August 1993, bilateral exchange rates were allowed to fluctuate within a band of 2.25% or up to 6% in exceptional cases, around the central rate. Since then, the band has been increased to 15%, following serious upsets on the currency markets. In the event of bilateral exchange rates approaching the 15% threshold, central banks have unlimited liability to intervene to ensure that the threshold is not crossed.

The EMS has succeeded in creating a zone of increasing monetary stability, but it has still to achieve its true potential. Several currencies remain outside the exchange rate mechanism or are allowed to fluctuate within the wider bands. Insufficient convergence of national budgetary policies has created tensions, and the planned transition to the second stage is still awaited.

Monetary union The European Monetary Union (EMU) is a part of the programme for the completion of the common market within the European Community. The EMU is to be achieved in three stages, in accordance with the procedure and timetable set out in the Treaty.

The first stage began on 1st July, 1990, and the deadline of 31st December, 1993, was successfully met. During this period, the following measures were implemented.

- ★ The liberalisation of currency and capital movements
- ★ Introduction of closer coordination and common supervision of the member states' economic policies
- ★ Strengthening of the cooperation between central banks
- ★ The adoption of the Maastricht Treaty
- ★ The freezing of the composition of the ECU (1st November, 1993)

The second stage, which began on 1st January, 1994, and will end some time before 31st December, 1999, has one principal goal: to secure a broad convergence between the economic policies of the member states. To this end, the European Council formulated economic policy guidelines and the member states were required to submit 'medium-term programmes' setting out all the economic policy measures planned to ensure their full participation in the final stage of the EMU. At this stage, the European Monetary Institute (EMI) was established. It is responsible for strengthening the coordination of the member states' monetary policies, monitoring the European exchange rate mechanism, promote the use of ground for the creation of a European Central Bank in stage three. At the beginning of the third stage, a European Central Bank will be set up. The bank will be independent of national governments and will manage the monetary policies of the member states that have progressed in stage III. Transition to the third period will take place some time between 1 January, 1997, and 1st January, 1999, but the EMU will come into effect on this latter date.

From ECU to EURO At a summit meeting in December 1995, the 15 EU heads of states voted to attempt to introduce the new European currency, the EURO from 1st January, 1999. According to the plan, member states eligible to join the EMU were selected based on the economic figures of 1997.

On 1st January, 1999, the exchange rates of the participating countries are irreversibly fixed. Another decision was that the government would issue new obligations and loans in EUROs, as from 1999. In 2002, the national currencies will lose their status as a legal tender and the EMU will then be a fact physically.

Indistinctness The December 1995 summit has not answered all the important questions about the transition to the EMU. No decisions have been made on the interpretation of the Maastricht Treaty criteria. At the moment, the EMU leading group will most probably consist of Germany, Luxembourg, the Netherlands and France, and probably Belgium, Ireland, Austria and Finland. Sweden, Spain, Portugal, Italy, Denmark (because of political reasons) and the United Kingdom are less likely to be among the leaders. For most of these countries, entry into the EMU will occur some years later. Important criteria are the national debt as a percentage of the GDP and the financing deficit of a country.

One of the greatest problems of the transition to the EMU is that not every country is able to participate. Nonparticipating countries will most probably be confronted with higher interest, making it more difficult to catch up with the leading group. Besides this, these countries could devaluate their currency, which would not just have a negative effect on the EMU business community on a short-term but also on the internal market. To prevent these developments, it is of the utmost importance that the relation between participants and nonparticipants is handled properly, so that the nonparticipating countries will be able enter the EMU sooner.

TRADE POLICY OF THE EUROPEAN UNION

The trade policy of the EU has often been criticised by outsiders because of protectionist measures. Since the EU is the most important trade bloc in the world, the fact that the trade liberalisation process is guided by the Uruguay Round has profound implications for trade partners of the EU.

Apart from complying with the international liberalisation process, the EU also operates preferential trade policies with Central and Eastern Europe and developing countries. Apart from the generalised system of preferences, the EU has trade and development agreements with the so-called ACP countries (70 African, Caribbean and Pacific states), Mediterranean countries and Central and East European countries.

GATT–Uruguay Round and Trade Liberalisation

The main aim of the General Agreement on Tariffs and Trade (GATT) was to stimulate a liberal, transparent and stable trading atmosphere. The most recent negotiations, the Uruguay Round, were concluded in 1994. The outcome was a first step in the direction of a liberalised global trade regime. The EU has committed itself to lower import tariffs between 1995 and 2000 for manufactured products by an average of 37%, as compared to 1994. The average weighted tariff will then only be 3.8%. Tariffs will be eliminated completely for the following product groups: construction materials, farm equipment, medical equipment, steel, beers, liquor, pharmaceuticals, paper, toys and furniture.

Tariffication of non-tariff barriers has been agreed upon for agricultural goods. Then, the average of all the tariffs is to be reduced by 36% over a six-year period, starting July 1995. Some conditions apply. First of all, no individual tariff may be reduced by less than 10% over the period. Secondly, a minimum access is required: import opportunities must be opened for the equivalent for 3% of internal consumption rising to 5% by the end to tropical products by 100% for tropical raw materials; 35% for semi-processed tropical products. Besides that, the quota under the Multi-Fibre Arrangement will be phased out over a period of 10 years.

Multi-fibre Arrangement (MFA)

The MFA has regulated a large percentage of all the trade in textiles and clothing up until the present. However, it will be phased out between 1995 and 2005. This means that a very, comprehensive and discriminatory agreement, consisting of voluntary export restrictions limiting the volume of exports from developing countries, will become history.

By gradually scaling down the MFA, the textiles and clothing sector will be subjected to the normal WTO regulations. The scaling down process is taking place in four phases, with the emphasis on the final years. Every importing country may choose which textile products it wants to integrate in each phase, provided that the products are selected from each category: yearns, fabrics, processed textile products, clothing. At the same time, the remaining quota for products which are not yet integrated should automatically be liberalised by a certain percentage in every phase (respectively 16%, 25%, 27% and 32%). During the transition period, selective safeguarding measures may be applied when serious disadvantage is inflicted on the domestic industry. These safeguarding measures can only apply to those products which are not yet integrated and may not last longer than a period of three years or until the product is integrated in the WTO regulations.

Table 6.1

To Take Effect On:	*Liberalisation of the Import Volume of 1990 by:*
1-1-1995	16%
1-1-1998	17%
1-1-2000	18%
1-1-2005	49%

By and large, the outcome of the Uruguay Round can be applauded. Trade liberalisation will benefit all trading nations worldwide. However, some countries may benefit more than others. Some will benefit in the short-term, others in the long-term. As for developing countries, some of the consequences in the short-term may be less positive, due to an erosion of trade preferences. For example, ACP countries and least developed countries were already excluded from the quota scheme under the MFA. Their comparative preferential status will therefore be eroded. The various trade agreements with the developing countries and countries in transition are described in more detail in the following section.

Generalised System of Preferences (GSP)

Developing countries are generally exempted from the main GATT/WTO principles of reciprocity and nondiscrimination. They receive trade privileges through preferential tariffs, often equal to a zero tariff. These preferences are laid down in the GSP.

A reminder: the nondiscrimination principle stipulates that any tariff concession granted to one country must also apply to other trading partners which are members of the WTO. The principle of reciprocity stipulates that any country, which grants a trade partner a concession, can demand some concession in return.

The GSP as applied by the EU grants almost all industrial products duty-free access. Preferential access is given to about 400 agricultural products, often at reduced rather than zero-duty rates.

Based on the outcome of the Uruguay Round and the general trend towards liberalisation of world trade, a need was felt to reconsider the GSP. A general lowering of trade barriers would mean that the relative advantage of the preferences received by developing countries would erode. A renewed GSP (also referred to as the RGSP) was the result. The new preferential scheme was introduced on January 1, 1995. The differences between the two preferential schemes were introduced on January 1, 1995. The differences between the two preferential schemes are listed below:

- ★ The tariff preferences for industrial products from developing countries are rendered in terms of a deduction of the General Customs Tariff (GCT) without quantitative restrictions. This means that the system of tariff contingents and ceilings is abolished.
- ★ Moreover, the renewed GSP contains two new mechanisms (the gradation mechanism and solidarity mechanism) which are used to make distinctions between developing countries (favoured nations). That means, that for certain favoured nations, which can be regarded as very or sufficiently competitive, the tariff preference can be considered no longer necessary. In those cases, the preference can be abolished and the normal GCT will be applicable.
- ★ The renewed GSP has a duration of four years instead of one year.

New Tariffs under the Renewed GSP

Under the renewed GSP, basic tariffs are set for four different categories of industrial products.

Textiles and clothing are among the highly 'sensitive' goods. The categories, 'sensitive,' and 'semi-sensitive' include certain chemical products, fertilisers, dyes, rubber products, electrical appliances, optical and precision instruments, ceramics, glassware and precious stones. However, it does not mean that all chemical, wood, rubber products etc. are classified as semi-sensitive. It depends very much on the specifications of the product whether, it is classified as semi-sensitive or nonsensitive. Each individual product needs to be checked as to which tariff applies.The following table explains new tariffs under the renewed GSP.

Table 6.2

Product category	*Tariff*	*Preferential Margin*
Highly sensitive products	85% of GCT	15%
Sensitive products	70% of GCT	30%
Semi-sensitive products	35% of GCT	65%
Non-sensitive products	0% of GCT	100%

Maximum Preference for Least-developed Countries

A tariff of 0% on all industrial products will be maintained for the least developed favoured nations (as in the old GSP). The same goes for industrial products originating in five Andean countries (Bolivia, Colombia, Ecuador, Peru and Venezuela). In these cases, the maximum preferential margin of 100% will be applicable. The Andean countries receive super GSP treatment, as a stimulus in the fight against production and trade in cocaine.

Basic Products Excluded

Just as in the old GSP, basic products (primarily raw materials and non-ferrous alloys) are exempted from tariff preference which are mentioned in a separate list. Other products, which for certain reasons did not have a tariff preference in the old GSP, are also excluded from the renewed GSP. Furthermore, there is a number of products for which, in the old GSP, there were relatively low tariff contingents, which were exhausted quite rapidly. In the renewed GSP, these products are subject to full import duties.

Correction mechanisms The effect of these mechanisms is that the preferential margins may be reduced or abolished for certain countries and certain products. Fundamental differences between the two mechanisms are the criteria used.

Taxes All products sold in the EU are subject to Value Added Tax (VAT). Generally, there is a low tariff for basic necessities and high tariff for luxury goods. Although the original objective was harmonisation of the tariffs, ranges have been narrowed, but considerable differences still exist between the EU member states. Since the European Commission recently concluded that the existing VAT regime functions satisfactorily and there are no significant distortions of competition resulting from disparities in rates, no major changes are expected in the current VAT regime in the EU member states in the short-term. However, harmonisation of the tariffs is still on the agenda and may therefore be realised at a later stage.

Import licensing Import licence may be required for sensitive and strategic goods, amongst which are textiles (under the rules of the MFA), steel products, coal and coke, and weaponry. Import licences are normally granted without too much difficulty and the importer is responsible for applying for licence. If the product falls under the MFA and is subject to an import quorum, the exporter has to supply the importer with an export licence or certificate, in order for the importer to obtain an import licence (double-control system).

Quota The most common quota is the quantitative quota which fall under the MFA. This quota clearly indicates the maximum volume of goods which can be traded. Once the quota is filled, there are no more opportunities to continue trading, not even against higher tariffs. This is not the case for tariff quota. Once this quota is filled, trade can still continue, although full tariffs come into force. As described earlier, the MFA is being phased out. Consequently, the quota system is being dismantled in a number of steps. However, it will go up to the year 2005 before all the quota have been abandoned.

Bans There is a ban on some products, which means that import is forbidden or only allowed under certain conditions. The ban is mainly applied to trade in dangerous products, such as chemical waste, medicines, pesticides, plants and foodstuff, electrical products and exotic animal and plants can also be subject to a ban, based on safety and health considerations. Important laws regarding these products are the law on chemical waste and the CITIES Law on endangered animal and plant species. The most recent example of a ban imposed on the import of a specific product is the ban on the import of beef from UK following the growing concern surrounding the so-called mad cow disease. This ban has been implemented EU-wide. Another recent example of an import ban, although not implemented EU-wide, is the ban on the AZO dyes. The ban has been imposed by Germany and The Netherlands and Sweden is likely to follow.

NEW GENERATION REGULATIONS

The trade liberalisation process, which accelerated with the conclusion of the Uruguay Round, means that non-tariff barriers like quota will be abandoned, and that tariff barriers will be reduced. In other words, the traditional projectionist measures will diminish.

Although in the short-term, the relative advantage of developing countries, which accrues to them through the preferential trade schemes, is lowered due to the general lowering of trade barriers, in the long-term, developing countries will also benefit from a more liberalised global trade regime.

However, despite the trade liberalisation, access to the European market by exporters in developing countries and countries in transition may well become more difficult, due to the fast increasing regulations in the field of safety, health, quality and environment. The focus is on the well-being of the consumer, now and in the future. In the past, tariff and non-tariff barriers generally emerged as a concern for producers. Consumer and environment protection has replaced the producer and employment protection.

The new generation regulations bear a relevant significance to the marketability of goods, from developing countries and countries in transition, on the EU market. Generally, EU-wide minimum levels of requirements have been set or will be set in the years ahead. Individual member states are allowed to set additional requirements. In practice, this means that any product that conforms to the minimum requirements is allowed free movement within the EU. If any national government sets higher requirements, the local producers will have to satisfy them. Imports which satisfy the minimum EU levels will not face the higher demands. Still, as consumer consciousness increases, quality becomes more important and consumers may prefer those products which satisfy the higher standards. Overall, it is advisable to fulfill the highest requirements.

In this respect, one also has to realise that it is not the only superimposed legislation by governments which determines the high standards for safety, health and the environment. The consumer is becoming more and more critical towards products and their potential harmful effects. As referred to earlier, the 'green' and 'healthy' consumer, with an appeal to 'light'; and responsible products constitutes an increasingly important market segment.

CE Marking

The CE marking has been introduced in order to show whether or not a product conforms to the European applicable and legal demands, in terms of safety, health, environment and consumer protection. The CE marking is not a guarantee for quality. The CE marking is obligatory for all products which come under 'New Approach' Directives, (see the directives in the box). This approach is called 'New Approach' because legislation and normalisation are separated and it is different from the 'Old Approach' where detailed requirements were put down in the legislation too. The directives are translated into national legislation.

There are CE laws applicable to the following products.

Foodstuffs There are European lists and norms drawn up for hygiene, establishing which additives are permitted in the production of foodstuffs.

Presentation and description The European Union has drawn up a directive for establishing how the composition of foodstuffs, their shelf storage life and exact content shall be clearly stated on the package. Another directive concerns information about special diet Foodstuffs. There is also an EC directive for the composition, production and description of certain products, for packaging materials, which come into contact with foodstuffs and for the trade in fresh meat.

Cosmetic products The European Union has drawn up a directive regulating the composition, description and packaging of cosmetic products and also forbids the use of certain substances and provides for condition and restrictions for other substances.

Textile There are several European directives related to the description, composition and certain analysing methods for establishing the composition of these products.

Dangerous substances There are many directives for classification, assessment tests, marketing, description and application of many poisonous substances, such as insecticides and solvents, paints, lacquers, printing ink, glue and asbestos.

Pharmaceuticals There are uniform EC directives for testing, assessing, approving, describing and patent rights in this field. There is also a directive aimed at a better insight into pricing.

Industrial products There is a whole series of directives aimed at increasing the safety of passenger cars, two-wheeled vehicles and haulers. Machines and most electrical equipment also come under new directives.

Misleading advertising This directive forbids 'misleading advertising', implying all advertising, which 'in a dishonest manner misleads its target group or attempts to mislead it.' If the consumer is of the opinion that he has been deceived by an advertising text or presentation, he can take legal action against the producer. Reverse burden of proof now applies in Europe, so that the producer has to prove that he is innocent.

Product liability This is a uniform regulation by which a producer is held liable for damage caused by his product to the consumer. The producer is also liable without being guilty. The burden of proof lies with the producer. Suppliers and anybody presenting himself as a producer are jointly liable.

Peddling An increasing number of complaints, related to false promises in advertising, intimidation and similar practices connected with purchase agreements made during door-to-door sales, has resulted in the EU Commission proposing a directive to strengthen the consumer's rights in this sector. The proposal establishes two far-reaching stipulations: on the one hand, the purchaser has one week's reflection time regarding business entered into with a salesman who, at the time, was outside the boundaries of his company premises. The purchaser can, without any problem within the one week limit, withdraw from the sales contract. On the other hand, the salesman is under the obligation to inform the consumer in writing that he has the right to withdraw from the sales contract.

Payments There is a non-binding recommendation regarding payments effected without the use of cash, in particular with regard to credit card systems. The bodies which issue this sort of credit cards are strongly advised to do all they can to limit the responsibility of the card owner in cases of loss, theft and fraud.

Information systems In each EU member state, there is a 'communal system for the rapid exchange of information concerning the danger of consumer and durable goods', whenever the authorities of one EU member state establish the fact that a particular product has led or could lead to serious, direct damage to health and considers to communicate their position to the EC Commission immediately. Brussels passes this on to the relevant authorities in the other member states, so that the latter can take suitable measures. This early warning system applies to foodstuffs, industrial products, electrical equipment and children's toys.

Safety of toys The essential safety demands are being harmonised and toys put on sale in the EU member states have to conform to these demands. Toys can only be circulated if, when used in conformity with their purpose or when used in a manner, which can be expected bearing in mind the normal child behaviour, they present no danger to the safety and/or health of the users or of third parties.

Consumer credit Credit institutions must inform whoever takes out a loan of the annual cost percentage. Furthermore, the information supplied to the consumer in a written agreement shall be more extensive than it has been up until now.

This list is by no means complete.

The use of CE marking indicates conformity of the product related to the EU's Essential Demands' on safety, health and the environment.

The conditions for applying the marking are the following:

The marking is reserved exclusively for indicating conformity to EC directives which are comprehensive in nature and which therefore go beyond all national legislation on the matter.
The marking signifies that the product complies with the provisions of these directives and that the manufacturer, importer or a third party has carried out the relevant conformity assessment operations.
The marking must be affixed to the product, unless specific EC directives allow to be placed on packaging or the accompany documentation.
The marking should relate to all of these requirements which concern the given product. If the product is covered by several directives, the use of the marking signifies conformity to all of the directives involved.
The marking should not indicate the directives and/or standards to which the product conforms. Such information should instead be included in the test reports and certificates accompanying the product, the construction manual/file.

A quality system such as ISO 9000 can sometimes be a way of avoiding the strict tests. Instead of the finished product being tested, the notified body accepts the production process and the company management certificate.

The directives are issued by the European Commission and are transposed into national legislation of the EU member states within a set timeframe. The importance of the CE marking will increase, with 40% of the tradable products expected to be subject to directives in the coming years, the intention being to upgrade the safety of the European citizens and the environment.

The necessity and value of a conformity certificate is self-evident. Without such a qualification marking, one may lose out in the future. As for the existing quality labels in the various EU countries, it is expected that these will remain, parallel to the CE marking, with the latter gaining in importance, as it will function as a passport of transborder traffic to and in the EU.

Product Liability

Product liability has moved in the direction of better protection of consumer interests. A reversal of the burden of proof has taken place. The consumer no longer has to prove that a product has caused an accident or damage. Instead, the manufacturer has to prove that his product has not been the cause. The importer is held responsible for imported products. To reduce his own risks, the importer should be very careful in selecting a supplier of goods. Those exporters with a good reputation, able to deliver goods of a high and consistent quality and preferably in possession of an ISO 9000 series certificate, will have better chances in the European market than less qualified exporters.

ISO 9000

The International Organisation for Standardisation (ISO) was developed by the ISO 9000 standards for quality management and quality assurance. Today, more than 70 countries have adopted the ISO 9000 series as national standards. The ISO 9000 standards represent an international consensus on the essential features of a quality system. Manufacturers or service providers which have obtained an ISO 9000 series certificate possess a valuable asset. It is an important selling point when doing a business in the competitive EU market and contributes strongly to confidence in a trade partner. The ISO 9000 series consists of five standards ISO 9000 to ISO 9004.

ENVIRONMENTAL REGULATIONS

The rising concern for environmental preservation and protection has forced the EU to set new standards in this area. In some EU countries, this has already led to legislation and/or voluntary agreements between the government and procedures. The agreements do not only apply to products but to the packaging as well. In this respect, it is interesting to note that, for example, manufacturers in Germany have set up the so-called Dual System. It is a waste recycling system through which manufacturers of packaging material contribute to a fund, which is used to finance recycling of the packaging material. Now, the government and manufacturers of household appliances in The Netherlands have started a dialogue on the reuse of electrical appliances. The concept is similar to the Dual System. Manufacturers and, in the case of imported products, the importers will be held responsible for the collection and recycling of used appliances. This means that when consumers buy a new product, they can deliver the old product to the retailer, who will subsequently carry the responsibility of channelling it into the recycling chain, which is funded by the manufacturers.

EU Policy

The emphasis in the EU's 'Fifth Action Programme on the Environment' (1993-2000), is on dealing with the root causes of environmental problems, rather than responding to the problems as they occur which refers to tackling pollution and problems at early stages.

The implications are that products will increasingly be audited on their environmental impact. That means not only by looking at the product itself, but also by scrutinising the raw materials used, the production process, maintenance, transportation, storage, use, waste disposal and treatment, in other words the entire product life cycle.

Packaging Waste Management

Major waste management related programmes are:

- ★ To minimise the generation of waste
- ★ To maximise the reuse and recycling of waste
- ★ To promote environmentally sound waste disposal and treatment

The EU has issued a directive on packaging and packaging waste (94/62/EEC). Among other measures, the directive sets maximum levels of concentrations of heavy metals in packaging and describes requirements specific to manufacturing and composition of packaging. These include the following.

- ★ Packaging shall be manufactured in such a way that the volume and weight be limited to the minimum amount to maintain the necessary level of safety, hygiene and acceptance for the packed product and for the consumer.

★ Packaging shall be designed, produced and commercialised in such a way as to permit its reuse or recovery, including recycling, and to minimise the environmental impact when packaging waste or residues.

★ Packaging shall be manufactured in such a way that the presence of noxious and other hazardous substances and materials is minimised with regard to the presence in emissions, ash or latched, when packaging or residues from waste management are incinerated or landfilled.

Green Dot

In Germany, trade and industry are obliged to take back packaging materials, in order to reuse or recycle them. The regulation also applies to imported goods. Foreign companies have to conform to this just as much as German companies. The Green Dot has become the symbol of the German packing waste reuse and recycling system. The symbol shows the consumer that the sales packaging can be reused or recycled. It is important to note that the Green Dot can not be printed on the packaging just like that. It symbolises a packaging waste recycling system that needs to be financed by the parties involved. There is a change for permission to affix a Green Dot on the packaging and a contract has to be entered into. The financial contribution of the companies is used for the financing of the waste recycling system. The amount of the financial contribution is dependent on the volume of packaging waste.

A wholesaler, importer or manufacturer who refuses to take back packaging is not allowed to use the green dot. Apart from the legal consequences this may have, he may be regarded as environmentally irresponsible in the eyes of the consumer. It is likely that the consumer will be less willing to buy such a product.

ENVIRONMENTAL MANAGEMENT SYSTEM

There are three main tools which can and should be used by manufacturers to make an assessment of the environmental impact of their products and to consider improvements for more environmentally sound products and production processes.

Life Cycle Assessment (LCA)

LCA is also called the "Cradle to Grave" approach. As mentioned earlier, manufacturers have to look at the environmental aspects of their product in the different stage of the life cycle.

A material which is very environmentally sound when the product is used could be very polluting, energy-consuming or difficult to break down in the excavation, refining, production or discarding stage of the life cycle.

On the other hand, the use of a material which is less environmentally sound when the product is used, could be justified because the impact on the environment is less in another stage of the life cycle. The European Commission has decided that the LCA method will be the technique used to decide whether or not a product can be referred to as an environmentally sound product.

Cleaner Production

Cleaner production is the conscious use and production of products and processes to prevent the pollution of air, water and land. This means that a careful look is taken at the overall processes and waste materials. A lot can often be improved, for example, a processliquid (often water) could be reused instead of being discarded: toxic process liquids could be replaced by non-toxic liquids; simple measures could increase the efficiency of machine, etc.

Eco-design

Eco-design is basically a matter of giving the environment a place in product development. This means that during product design, efforts are made to reduce the use of raw materials, minimise the generation of waste, minimise the use of (fossil) energy and reduce toxic emission. This will ultimately lead to a reduction of material and energy used.

Although these tools are used by manufacturers to reduce the impact of their product(ion) costs in fact, manufacturers can gain a competitive advantage when the environmental assessment and management tools are properly used.

They will be able to supply more environmentally sound products to a market where demand for these products is increasing.

Eco-labelling

Eco-labelling schemes are being developed in the EU for specific product groups. They are often introduced without the participation of foreign suppliers. This implies that the criteria adopted for the granting of eco-labels may fail to take account of the characteristics of products from developing countries and conditions prevailing in them. However, it is important to be well-informed about developments in these fields. The use of eco-lables will have considerable marketing implications.

Eco-labelling schemes aim at providing consumers with a choice in buying products which have been designed, produced and packaged, and which can be disposed of at the end of the useful life, in an environmentally sound way. The use of such labels also encourages producing and processing industries to make a more sustainable use of natural resources. The eco-labelling schemes are generally based on the aforementioned Life Cycle Assessment, The environmental impact of the product is assessed throughout the entire life cycle of the product.

The Fundamental Rights of the Consumer

The individual consumer is no match, all on his own, for many of the companies, which sell him their goods and services. The EU member states have therefore drawn up legislation and instigated initiated procedures to protest the rights of the consumer. The introduction of the internal market, 'Project 1992', necessitated the development of a consumer policy with european dimensions. 1975 saw the 'first programme of the European Economics Union concerning the protection of and information to the consumer' being adopted. The Union has based its consumer policy on the protection of the five Fundamental Rights, which are central in the member states' policy. These are:

Protection of the health and safety of the consumer Only products which entail no danger for health and safety regulations must be established, that complete information must be provided regarding potential dangers and that the consumer must be protected against physical injury.

Protection of the customer's economic interests There is, for instance, a general ban on misleading advertising and dishonest provisions in contracts with consumers.

The consumer's right to information and education It must be made possible for the consumer to make a choice, based on clear information, from among the products and services offered. This implies objective information regarding the characteristics and price of the available products. The consumer must also be reliably informed regarding the efficient and safe use of these products.

The right to compensation for damage The consumer has the right to advice and assistance when seeking compensation for faulty products or for injury or damage resulting from the use of goods and services. He must be able to make use of simple, affordable and speedy procedures, in order to settle complaints and claims. (Refer to the new product Liability Legislation.)

Consumer representation and involvement Consumer representatives must be able to make their voice heard regarding decision-making procedures on matters which concern them, at the local, national and EU level. As far as the Union level is concerned, this not only applies to specific consumer issues but also to other relevant policy fields, such as legislation on foodstuffs/provisions, transport, competition policy, financial services, the environment and other matters.

Consequences for exporters in developing countries It is very important that an exporter to the EU is aware of the fact, that within the EU it is common that safety and health issues have a central role in the product-related decision-making process.

It is important that exporters in developing countries wishing to export to the EU know that they are confronted with a general ruling. This ruling describes the controls related to the compliance of products imported from third countries (i.e. non-EU countries), concerning regulations on the product safety.

In general terms, the ruling says:

- ★ If a product show(s) certain characteristics which, when used under normal circumstances, result in direct danger to health and/or safety, this product/these products shall not be admitted to the EU member states.

It also says, that, when exporting to the EU, the correct documents or markings can be discussed with the Customs authorities, in order to obtain admission to the EU. Another important factor for third countries exporting to the EU is that, in the case of possible threats to health and/or safety, the importer of these products is the one who will be held responsible for the ensuing damage(s).

// CHAPTER 7 //

INTERNATIONAL ECONOMIC ORGANISATIONS

The World Trade Organisation (WTO) is the legal and institutional foundation of the multilateral trading system. It provides the principal contractual obligations determining how governments frame and implement domestic trade legislation and regulations. It is also the platform on which trade relations among countries evolve through collective debate, negotiation and a judication. WTO is the only international body dealing with the rules of trade between nations.

The WTO was established on 1st January, 1995. Governments had concluded the Uruguay Round negotiations on 15 December, 1993 and ministers had given their political backing to the results by signing the Final Act at a meeting in Marrakesh, Morocco, in April 1994. The 'Marrakesh Declaration' of 15 April, 1994, affirmed that the results of the Uruguay Round would "strengthen the world economy and lead to more trade, investment, employment and income growth throughout the world". The WTO is the embodiment of the Uruguay Round results and the successor to the General Agreement on Tariffs and Trade (GATT). Those documents are essentially contracts binding the governments to keep their trade policies within agreed limits.

Out of the potential membership of 152 countries and territories, 76 governments became members of the WTO on its first day, with some 50 other governments at various stage of completion of their domestic ratification procedures and their terms of entry. India was one of the founder members of WTO (1995).

Not only does the WTO have a potentially larger membership than GATT (129 by the end of 1996), it also has a much broader scope in terms of the commercial activity and trade policies to which it applies. The GATT applied only to trade in merchandise goods. The WTO covers trade in goods, services and "trade in ideas" or intellectual property. The system's overriding purpose is to help trade flow as freely as possible.

The WTO is based in Geneva, Switzerland. Its essential functions are

- ★ Administering and implementing the multilateral and plurilateral trade agreements which together make up the WTO
- ★ Acting as a forum for multilateral trade negotiations
- ★ Seeking to resolve trade disputes
- ★ Overseeing national trade policies
- ★ Cooperating with other international institutions involved in global economic policy-making

THE PRINCIPLES OF THE TRADING SYSTEM

The WTO Agreement contains some 29 individual legal texts—covering everything from agriculture to textiles and clothing, and from services to government procurement, rules of origin and intellectual property. Added to these are more than 25 additional ministerial declarations, decisions and understandings which spell out further obligations and commitments for WTO members. However, a number of simple and fundamental principles run throughout all of these instruments which, together, make up the multilateral trading system.

Trade Without Discrimination

For almost fifty years, key provisions of GATT outlawed discrimination among members and between imparted and domestically produced merchandise. According to Article I, the famous "most-favoured-nation" (MFN) clause, members are bound to grant to the products of the other members, treatment no less favourable than that accorded to the products of any other country. Thus, no country is to give special trading advantages to another or to discriminate against it: all are on an equal basis and all share the benefits of any moves towards lower trade barriers.

Apart from the revised GATT (known as "GATT 1994"), several other WTO agreements contain important provisions relating to MFN and national treatment. That on Trade-Related Aspect of Intellectual Property Rights (TRIPS) contains, with some exceptions, MFN and national treatment requirements relating to the provision of intellectual property protection by WTO members. The General Agreement on Trade in Services (GATS) requires members to offer MFN treatment to services and service suppliers of other members. However, it permits listed exemptions to be MFN obligation covering specific measures for which WTO members are unable to offer such treatment initially. Where such exemptions are taken, they are to be reviewed after 5 years and should not be maintained for more than 10 years. On the other hand, national treatment is only an obligation in the GATS where members explicitly undertake to accord it for particular services or service activities. This means that national treatment is often the result of negotiations among members.

The Principles

The trading system should be

- ★ without discrimination—a country should not discriminate between its trading partners (they are all, equally, granted "most-favoured-nation" or MFN status); and it should not discriminate between its own and foreign products, services or nationals (they are given "national treatment")
- ★ freer—with barriers coming down through negotiation
- ★ predictable—foreign companies, investors and governments should be confident that trade barriers (including tariffs, non-tariff barriers and other measures) should not be raised arbitrarily; more and more tariff rates and market-opening commitments are "bound" in WTO

- ★ more competitive—by discouraging "unfair" practices such as export subsidies and dumping products as below cost to gain market share
- ★ more beneficial for less developed countries—by giving them more time to adjust, greater flexibility and special privileges

Why is it called "most-favoured" The name sounds like a contradiction. It suggests some kind of special treatment for one particular country, but in the WTO, it actually means nondiscrimination—treating virtually everyone equal.

What happens under the WTO is this. Each member treats all the other members equally as "most-favoured" trading partners. If a country improves the benefits that it gives to one trading partner, it has to give the same "best" treatment to all the other WTO members, so that they all remain "most-favoured".

Most-favoured nation (MFN) status did not always mean equal treatment. In the 19th Century, when a number of early bilateral MFN treaties were signed, being in an exclusive club because only a few countries enjoyed the privilege. Now, when most countries are in the WTO, the MFN club is no longer exclusive. The MFN principle ensures that each country treats its over-100 fellow-members equally.

But there are some exceptions....

Other WTO agreements with non-discrimination provisions include those on rules of origin, pre-shipment inspection, trade-related investment measures and the application of sanitary and phytol sanitary measures.

The Uruguay Round

The agenda – The 15 original Uruguay Round subjects are (1) Tariffs (2) Non-tariff barriers (3) Natural resource products (4) Textiles and clothing (5) Agriculture (6) Tropical products (7) GATT articles (8) Tokyo Round codes (9) Antidumping (10) Subsidies (11) Intellectual property (12) Investment measures (13) Dispute settlement (14) The GATT system (15) Services.

It took seven-and-a half years, almost twice the original schedule. By the end, 125 countries were taking part. It covered almost all trade, from toothbrushes to pleasure boats, from banking to telecommunications, from the genes of wild rice to AIDS treatments. It was quite simply the largest trade negotiation ever, and most probably the largest negotiation of any kind in history.

At times, it seemed doomed to fail. But in the end, the Uruguay Round brought about the biggest reform of the world's trading system, since GATT was created at the end of the Second World War. And yet, despite its troubled progress, the Uruguay Round did see some early results. Within only two years, participants had agreed on a package of cuts in import duties on tropical products which are mainly exported by developing countries. They had also revised the rules for settling disputes, with some measures implemented on the spot. And they called for regular reports on GATT members' trade policies, a move considered important for making trade regimes transparent around the world.

A round to end all rounds The seeds of the Uruguay Round were sown in November 1982 at a ministerial meeting of GATT members in Geneva.

Textiles—Back in the Mainstream

Textiles, like agriculture, is one of the hardest – fought issues in the WTO, as it was in the former GATT system. It is now going through a fundamental change under a 10-year schedule agreed in the Uruguay Round. The system of import quotas that has dominated the trade since the early 1960s is being phased out.

From 1974, until the end of the Uruguay Round, the trade was governed by the Multifibre Arrangement (MFA) a framework for bilateral agreements or unilateral actions that established quotas limiting imports into countries whose domestic industries were facing a serious damage from rapidly increasing imports.

The quotas were the most visible feature. They conflicted with GATT's general preference for customs tariffs instead of measures that restrict quantities. They were also exceptions to the GATT principle of treating all trading partners equally because they specified how much the importing country was going to accept from individual exporting countries.

Since 1995, the WTO's Agreement on Textiles and Clothing (ATC) has taken over from the Multifibre Arrangement. By 2005, the sector is to be fully integrated into normal GATT rules. In particular, the quotas will come to an end, and importing countries will no longer be able to discriminate between exporters. The Agreement on Textiles and Clothing will itself no longer exist. It is the only WTO agreement that has self-destruction built in.

Integration—Returning products gradually to GATT rules Textiles and clothing products are being returned to GATT rules over the 10-year period. This is happening gradually, in four steps, to allow time for both importers and exporters to adjust to the new situation. Some of these products were previously under quotas. Any quotas that were in place on 31 December, 1994, were carried over into the new agreement. For products which had quotas, the result of integration into GATT will be the removal of these quotas.

Other WTO agreements with nondiscrimination provisions including those rules of origin, reshipment of inspection, trade-related investment measures the application of sanitary, phytol sanitary measures, Tariffs: more bindings and closer to zero, Agriculture: Fairer markets for farmers, Textiles: back in mainstream, Services: rules for growth and investment, Intellectual property: protection and enforcement, Antidumping; subsidies, safeguards, contingencies, etc., Non-tariff barriers: Technicalities, red tape etc., Multilaterals of minority interest, and Trade Policy Reviews ensuring transparency.

Four Steps Over 10 Years

The schedule for freeing textiles and garment products from import quotas (and returning them to GATT rules), and how fast remaining quotas should expand.

The example is based on the commonly-used 6% annual expansion rate of the old Multifibre Arrangement. In practice, the rates used under the MFA varied from product to product.

Steps	Percentage of Products to be Bought Under Gatt (Including Removal of Any Quota)	How Fast Remaining Quotas Should Open Up, If 1994 Rate was 6%
Step 1 (1 Jan 1995 to 31 Dec. 1997)	16% (minimum, taking 1990 imports as base)	6.96% per year
Step 2 (1 Jan 1998 to 31 Dec. 2001)	17%	8.7% per year
Step 3 (1 Jan 2002 to 31 Dec. 2005)	18%	11.05% per year
Step 4 (1 Jan 2005 and final elimination of quotas) Agreement of Textiles and Clothing terminates.	49% (maximum)	No quotas left

The actual formula for import growth under quotas is by 0.1 × pre-1995 growth rate in the first step; 0.25 × step 1 growth rate in the second step; and 0.27 × step 2 growth rate in the third step.

The WTO's Most Individual Contribution

No review of the achievements of the WTO would be complete without mentioning the Dispute Settlement system, in many ways the central pillar of the multilateral trading system and the WTO's most individual contribution to the stability of the global economy. The new WTO system is at once stronger, more automatic and more credible than its GATT predecessor. This is reflected in the increased diversity of countries using it and in the tendency to resolve cases 'out of court' before they get to the final decision—19 out of 71 cases so far. The system is working as intended—as a means above all for conciliation and for encouraging resolution of disputes, rather than just for making judgements. By reducing the scope for unilateral actions, it is also an important guarantee of fair trade for less powerful countries.

Without a means of settling disputes, the rules-based system would be worthless, because the rules could be worthless and could not be enforced. The WTO's procedure underscores the rule of law, and it makes the trading system more secure and predictable. The system is based on clearly-defined rules, with timetables for completing a case. First rulings are made by a panel and endorsed (or rejected) by the WTO's full membership. Appeals based on points of law are possible.

Principles—Equitable, fast, effective, mutually acceptable WTO members have agreed, that if they believe fellow – members are violating trade rules, they will use the multilateral system of settling disputes instead of taking action unilaterally. That means abiding by the agreed procedures and respecting judgements.

How are disputes settled Settling disputes is the responsibility of the Dispute Settlement Body (the General Council in another guise). The Disputes Settlement Body has the sole authority to establish "panels" of experts to consider the case, and to accept or reject the panels' findings or the results of an appeal. It monitors the implementation of the rulings and recommendations, and has the power to authorise retaliation when a country does not comply with a ruling.

How Long to Settle A Dispute

These approximate periods for each stage of dispute settlement procedure are target figures—the agreement is flexible. In addition, the countries can settle the dispute themselves at any stage.

Totals are also approximate

60 days	Consultations, mediation, etc.
45 days	Panel set up and panelists appointment
6 months	Final panel report to parties
3 weeks	Final panel report to WTO members
60 days	Dispute Settlement Body adopts report (if no appeal)
Total: 1 year	(without appeal)
60-90 days	Appeals report
30 days	Dispute Settlement Body adopts appeals report
Total: 1 year 3 months	(with appeal)

Panels Panels are like tribunals. But, unlike in a normal tribunal, the panelists are usually chosen in consultation with the countries in dispute. Only if the two sides cannot agree does the WTO Director-General appoint them. This only happens rarely.

Panels consist of three (occasionally five) experts from different countries who examine the evidence and decide who is right and who is wrong. The panel's report is passed to the Dispute Settlement Body, which can only reject the report by consensus.

Appeals Either side can appeal a panel's ruling. Sometimes, both sides do so. Appeals have to be based on points of law such as legal interpretation they cannot re-examine existing evidence or examine new evidence.

Each appeal is heard by three members of a permanent seven-member Appellate Body set up by the Dispute Settlement Body and broadly representing the range of WTO membership. Members of the Appellate Body have four year terms. They have to be individuals with recognised standing in the field of law and international trade, not affiliated with any government.

The appeal can uphold, modify or reverse the panel's legal findings and conclusions. Normally, appeals should not last for more than 60 days, with an absolute maximum of 90 days.

The Dispute Settlement Body has to accept or reject the appeals report within 30 days and rejections are is only possible by consensus.

GENERAL AGREEMENT ON TARIFFS AND TRADE (GATT)

The WTO's predecessor, the GATT, was established on a provisional basis after the Second World War in the wake of other new multilateral institutions dedicated to international economic cooperation—notably, the "Bretton woods" institutions, now known as the World Bank and the International Monetary Fund.

The original 23 GATT countries were among 50 countries which agreed a draft Charter for an International Trade Organization (ITO)—a new specialized agency of the United Nations. The Charter was intended to provide not only world trade disciplines but also contained rules relating to employment, commodity agreements, restrictive business practices, international investment and services. India was one of the founder members of GATT (1947).

In an effort to give an early boost to trade liberalisation after the Second World War and to begin to correct the large overhand of projectionist measures which remained in place from the early 1930s, tariff negotiations were opened among the 23 founding GATT "contracting parties" in 1946. This first round of negotiations resulted in 45,000 tariff concessions affecting $10 billion or about one-fifth-of the world trade. It was also agreed that the value of these concessions should be protected by early and largely "provisional" acceptance of some of the trade rules in the draft ITO Charter. The tariff concessions and rules together became known as the General Agreement on Tariffs and Trade (GATT) and entered into force in January 1948.

Although the ITO Charter was finally agreed at a UN Conference on Trade and Employment in Hanvana in March 1948, ratification in national legislatures proved impossible in some cases. When the United States government announced, in 1950, that it would not seek Congressional ratification of the Havana Charter, the ITO was effectively dead. Despite its provisional nature, the GATT remained the only multilateral instrument governing international trade from 1948, until the establishment of the WTO in 1995.

Although, in its 47 years, the basic legal text of the GATT remained much as it was in 1948, there were additions in the form of "plurilateral"—voluntary membership, agreements and continual efforts to reduce tariffs. Much of this was achieved through a series of "trade rounds."

Trade Rounds — The Package Route to Progress

The biggest leaps forward in international trade liberalisation have come through multilateral trade negotiations, or "trade rounds" under the auspices of GATT, the Uruguay Round was the latest and most extensive.

Although often lengthy, trade rounds offer a package approach to trade negotiations — an approach with a number of advantages over issue-by-issue negotiations. For a start, a trade round allows participants to seek and secure advantages across a wide range of issues. Second, concessions which are necessary but would otherwise be difficult to defend in domestic political terms, can be made more easily in the context of package which also contains politically and economically attractive benefits. Third, developing countries and other less powerful participants have a greater chance of influencing the multilateral system in the context of a round than if bilateral relationships between major trading nations are allowed to dominate. Finally, overall reform in politically-sensitive sectors of world trade can be more feasible in the context of global package — reform of agricultural trade was a good example in the Uruguay Round.

Most of GATT's early trade rounds were devoted to continuing the process of reducing tariffs. The results of the Kennedy Round in the mid-sixties, however, included a new GATT Antidumping Agreement. The Tokyo Round during the seventies was a more sweeping attempt to extend and improve the system.

The Tokyo round — A first try at reforming the trading system Conducted between 1973 and 1979 and with 102 participating countries, the Tokyo Round continued GATT's efforts to progressively reduce tariffs. The results included an average one-third cut in customs duties in the world's nine major industrial markets, bringing the average tariff on manufactured products down to 4.7% at the time of GATT's creation. The tariff reductions, phased in over a period of eight years, involved an element of harmonisation, bringing the highest tariffs down proportionately more than the lowest.

How is the WTO different from GATT The World Trade Organisation (WTO) is not a simple extension of GATT. On the contrary, it completely replaces its predecessor and has a very different character. Among the principal differences are the following.

- ★ The GATT was a set of rules, a multilateral agreement, with no institutional foundation, only a small associated secretariat which had its origins in the attempt to establish an International Trade Organisation in the 1940s. The WTO is a permanent institution with its own secretariat.
- ★ The GATT was applied on a "provisional basis", even if, after more than forty years, governments chose to treat it as a permanent commitment. The WTO commitments are full and permanent.
- ★ The GATT rules applied to trade in merchandise goods. In addition to goods, the WTO covers trade in service and trade-related aspects of intellectual property.
- ★ While GATT was a multilateral instrument, by the 1980s, many new agreements which constitute the WTO are almost all multilateral and, thus, involve commitments for the entire membership.
- ★ The WTO dispute settlement system is faster, more automatic, and thus much less susceptible to blockages, than the old GATT system.

The implementation of WTO dispute findings will also be more easily assured.

The "GATT 1947" continued to exist until the end of 1995, thereby allowing time for all GATT member countries to accede to the WTO and permitting an overlap of activity in areas like dispute settlement. Moreover, GATT lived on as "GATT 1994," the amended and updated version of GATT 1947, which is an integral part of the WTO Agreement and which continues to provide the key disciplines affecting international trade in goods.

THE GENERAL AGREEMENT ON TRADE IN SERVICES (GATS)

The General Agreement On Trade in Services (GATS), negotiated during the Uruguay Round, is the first set of multilateral-agreed and legally-enforceable rules and disciplines ever negotiated to cover international trade in services. The agreement contains three elements, a framework of general rules and disciplines, annexes addressing special conditions relating to individual sectors, and national schedules of market access commitments. These schedules-like tariff schedules under the GATT are an integral part of the agreement.

A Council for Trade in Service oversees the operation of the agreement.

The Framework

The framework consists of 29 articles including a series of basic obligations:

Total coverage The scope of the agreement is all internationally traded service, however they are delivered. The agreement defines four modes of delivery—services supplied from one member country to another (e.g. international telephone calls); services supplied in the territory of one member to the consumers of any other (e.g. tourism); services provided through the presence of a commercial entity of one member in the territory of any other (e.g. banking); and services provided by individuals of one member in the territory of any other (e.g. fashion models or consultants).

National treatment In the sectors recorded in its schedule and subject to any conditions indicated there, each government must treat services and service suppliers of other members no less favourably than its own like services and service suppliers.

Most favoured nation treatment A government must not discriminate between services or service suppliers of other members, but must accord *all* of them treatment no less favourable than that it accords to like services and service providers of *any*.

Transparency Requirements include publication of all relevant laws and regulations. Since domestic regulations, in the absence of tariffs, provide the most significant means of influence or control over services trade, the agreement requires that all such measures should be administered in a reasonable objective and impartial manner. Governments are also required to establish the means for a prompt review of administrative decisions relating to the supply of services.

Recognition The agreement requires that bilateral agreements between governments on the recognition of qualifications (for example, the licensing or certification of service suppliers) should be open to other members who wish to negotiate accession to them or to negotiate comparable agreements. Recognition must not be accorded in a discriminatory manner, or operate as a disguised restriction on trade.

International payments and transfers For current transactions relating to specific commitments under the agreement shall not be restricted, except in the event of balance-of-payments difficulties, where such restrictions will be limited, temporary and subject to conditions.

Market access and national treatment Commitments are recorded in national schedules. These schedules identify those services and service activities for which market access is guaranteed, and specify any conditions to which that access is subjected.

Any limitations on the commitments to give equal access to foreign service suppliers, and to accord them treatment no less favourable than that given to domestic suppliers, must be entered in the schedules. These commitments are bound, like bound tariffs, they can only be modified or withdrawn after negotiation of compensation with affected countries. They thus provide guaranteed conditions under which foreign investors and exporters and importers of services can do business.

Progressive liberalisation The agreement requires successive rounds of further negotiations, the first to begin within five years, in order to take the process of liberalisation further, both by increasing the level of commitments in schedules and by reducing the adverse effects on trade of government measures.

THE INTERNATIONAL TRADE CENTRE (ITC)

The international Trade Centre (ITC) is the focal point in the United Nations system for technical cooperation with developing countries in trade promotion. ITC was created by the General Agreement on Tariffs and Trade (GATT) in 1964 and since 1968 has been operated jointly by GATT (now by the WTO) and by the UN, the latter acting through the United Nations Conference on Trade and Development (UNCTAD). As an executing agency of the United Nations Development Programme (UNDP), ITC is directly responsible for implementing UNDP-financed projects in developing countries and economies in transition related to trade promotion.

Main Programme Areas

ITC works with developing countries and economies in transition to set up effective trade promotion programmes for expanding their exports and improving their import operations. This covers six key areas.

Product and market development Direct export marketing support to the business community through advice on product development, product adaptation and international marketing for commodities, manufactures and service. The aim is to develop and market internationally competitive products and services to expand and diversify these countries' exports.

Development of trade support services Creation and enhancement of foreign trade support services for the business community provided by public and private institutions at the national and regional levels. The objective is to ensure that enterprises have the facilities to export and import effectively.

Trade information Establishment of sustainable national trade information services and dissemination of information on products, services, market and functions to enterprises and trade organizations. The purpose is to lay a foundation for sound international business decisions and for appropriate trade promotion programmes.

Human resource development Strengthening of national institutional capacities for foreign trade training and organisation of direct training for enterprises in importing and exporting. The goal is to achieve efficient foreign trade operations based on relevant knowledge and skills.

International purchasing and supply management Application of cost-effective import systems and practices in enterprises and public trading entities by strengthening and advisory services provided by national purchasing organisations, both public and private. The aim is to optimise foreign exchange resources expended on imports.

Needs assessment and programme design for trade promotion Conception of effective national and regional trade promotion programmes based on an analysis of supply potential and constraints, and identification of related technical cooperation requirements. The objective is to reinforce the link between trade policy and the implementation of trade promotion activities.

In all of these services, ITC gives particular attention to activities with the least developed countries (LDCs).

UNITED NATIONS CONFERENCE ON TRADE AND DEVELOPMENT (UNCTAD)

UNCTAD was established by the UN General Assembly in December 1964 to promote international trade, particularly that of developing countries, with a view to accelerating economic development. It has now become a principal instrument of the General Assembly for deliberation and negotiations in the field of international trade and related issues of international economic cooperation. UNCTAD covers the entire spectrum of politics, both in developed and developing countries which influence the external trade and economic development, particularly those of developing countries.

UNCTAD-IX was held in Midland, South Africa from 27th April to 11th May, 1996. The Indian delegation was led by the Commerce Secretary. The period from 1992 to 1996 witnessed drastic changes in the international trade scenario, particularly, the emergence of WTO and changes in the global economic context. These changes and the financial crisis being faced by the UN system had generated an apprehension before UNCTAD-IX, that UNCTAD's mandate, role and work programme may undergo substantial purning and downsizing. Some of the developed countries had also felt that UNCTAD should confine its activities to the least developed countries. The Indian delegation made a strong plea for retaining UNCTAD's broad mandate for promoting trade and development on a global basis and stated that globalisation and liberalisation cannot be accepted as a panacea for resolving developmental problems of developing countries. The latter must develop their own natural resources, human resources and infrastructure to the maximum extent.

The intergovernmental machinery of UNCTAD has been restructured to make it more focused so that it concentrates on the areas of its strength. The intergovernmental machinery with Trade and Development Board (TDB) at the apex, will have three Commissions viz.,

(a) Commission on trade in goods and services and commodities.
(b) Commission on investment, technology and related financial issues.
(c) Commission on enterprise, business facilitation and development.

The Commission will convene expert meetings on specific issues. The total number of expert meetings will not exceed 10 in an year, of which, up to 4 may be convened by the Commission on trade and up to three each by the other two.

THE ECONOMIC AND SOCIAL COMMISSION FOR ASIA AND THE PACIFIC (ESCAP)

ESCAP is the regional arm of the United Nations dealing with economic and social development of the Asia-pacific region. India is one of its founding members. The main activities of ESCAP include the evolution and execution of projects in the socioeconomic fields, with the aim of improving national capabilities to deliver effective social services and develop the requisite infrastructure and environmental capabilities.

The ESCAP's major work during the year focused on:

(a) Regional economic cooperation
(b) Poverty alleviation through economic growth and social development
(c) Environment and sustainable development
(d) Transport and communications
(e) Statistics

Apart from the intergovernmental meetings, the Government of India representatives and experts participated in various other activities of ESCAP, such as expert group meetings, workshops, seminars, trainings, etc., organised by the ESCAP secretariat in Bangkok and other places.

India had a very fruitful cooperation with ESCAP during the year with its active participation in various projects, activities including meetings organised by ESCAP. The following are some of the important activities of ESCAP held in India.

(1) Ministerial conference on infrastructure and world infrastructure forum.
(2) EDI and trade facilitation.
(3) An ESCAP workshop on women in local government in South-Asia
(4) ESCAP funded pilot project for creation on barrier-free environment for disabled and elderly persons.

THE CENTRE FOR THE PROMOTION OF IMPORTS FROM DEVELOPMENT COUNTRIES

CBI is the centre for the promotion of imports from developing countries, operating since 1971 within the policy framework set by the Netherlands Minister of Foreign Affairs and the Minister for Development Cooperation. SBI supports Small and Medium-sized Enterprises (SMEs) and Trade Promotion Organisations (TPOs) in developing countries in their promotion of exports to the European Union.

CBI Offers Export Marketing Services

Based on up-to date market information and training and are organized in the form for Integrated Export Promotion Programmes for SME exporters and Bilateral Cooperation with TPOs. Those seeking CBI marketing services should fill in CBIs exporter's company profile form and provide all relevant information, such as prices, terms and product information.

CBI market information includes CBI News Bulletin (11 times a year), containing market news and publication of offers.

- ★ CBI guide Exporting to the EU, The Netherlands as the gateway to Europe
- ★ Product market surveys for 85 product groups
- ★ Trade documentation centre
- ★ Brochures and manuals on EU and environmental regulations
- ★ Green Buss (R) database on European trade-related environmental policy and technology

CBI training includes orientation seminars on export planning/management, trade promotion/marketing, and trade fair participation.

- ★ Management seminars for TPO staff on the organisation of collective trade fair participation

CBI integrated export promotion programmes for six product groups/year consists of product market testing (special promotions) in the CBI Product Display Centre in Rotterdam

- ★ Product adaptation advice at the exporter's factory
- ★ Export marketing seminar
- ★ International trade fair participation in the EU

Market entry services for International trade fair participation in the EU (for selected fairs other than those which are part of Integrated Export Promotion Programmes).

- ★ Consultancy for incoming missions
- ★ Support to outgoing buying missions
- ★ Individual assistance to visitors
- ★ Assistance to trade and marketing centres

CBI bilateral trade cooperation includes trade cooperation agreements with TPOs in developing countries on integrated export promotion.

- ★ Trade promotion
- ★ Business information and communication

★ Training
★ Market entry services

CBI multilateral cooperation with multilateral organizations (ITC/WTO) and European import promoting organisations (FORUM) to globalise trade promotion.

HOW THE INTEGRATED EXPORT PROMOTION PROGRAMMES WORKS

CBI offers a package of assistance to manufacturers and exporters in developing countries, to help them secure better chances of obtaining a foothold on the West-European market for this purpose, a number of CBI services has been combined into

Integrated Export Promotion Programme (IEPPs)

It consists of three phases.

★ a special promotion and, for these selected.
★ a product adaptation Mission D and participation in the Expro seminar.
★ trade fair participation, preceded by a briefing.

Selection for CBI-sponsored participation in a trade fair depends on results and performance in the previous phases.

The CBI Integrated Export Promotion Programme (IEPPs) are phased as to support and instruct participants step by step, beginning with market orientation and product testing. For those who reach the third and final phase, the programmes end with assistance in establishing personal contacts with importers in the West-European markets through CBI-sponsored trade fair participation.

Countries which have already achieved a structurally competitive position on the EU market in certain sectors may be excluded from participation in specific SBI export promotion programmes. Check with SBI for all certainty.

Phase 1 Special Promotion

During Phase 1, products are displayed in the CBI showroom and market tested by CBI product exports and at the same time are viewed by importers and wholesalers (potential buyers). Immediately after Phase 1, participating companies are informed by CBI as to test results, including adjustments, and are supplied with the addresses of interested buyers.

Phase 2 Product Adaptation

Phase 2 is intermixed. It consists of visits by the CBI product experts to selected exporter/manufacturers in their home countries, to help implement adaptation to EU market requirements and regulations. Based on these visits, candidates are selected for participation in Phase 3, an international trade fair.

EXPRO Seminar

Also part of Phase 2 of the IEPP, a two-week marketing and management seminar, focused on the EU market and containing product-specific modules is held by SBI in Rotterdam. This EXPRO seminar is compulsory for participants selected for the last phase of the IEPP.

Phase 3 Trade Fair Participation

In phase 3, exporters are offered the opportunity of CBI-sponsored participation in an international trade fair in Europe. The fair is preceded by a briefing, preparing exhibitors to meet and negotiate with trade visitors during the fair. The main objective of fair participation is to establish personal contacts with buyers.

Having completed Phase 3, the exporter is equipped to expand export activities, using newly-acquired product and marketing knowledge having gained contacts in the EU market. Nevertheless, CBI remains in the background, as a source of expertise and advice.

Follow-up

Six to eight weeks after the trade fair, the most promising contracts/visitors registered are followed up by the CBI. Ten to twelve months after the fair, all the exporters who exhibited and the importers registered as visiting the CBI stands are again contacted by the CBI, to solve possible problems and to evaluate the results of the Integrated Export Promotion Programme.

Condition for participation An exporter should not have regular exports to the Netherlands of the products(s) he/she wants to promote.

INTERNATIONAL TRADE ASPECTS

Countries all over the world are increasingly engaging in international trade. In order to prevent international disputes, regulation of this trade to a certain extent – can help to improve efficiency and effectiveness of international transactions.

This module deals with tariff barrier reduction on an international level. More specifically, attention will be paid to the working of the World Trade Organisation (WTO) as this organisation is the only International Trade Organisation which aims at the reduction of (tariff) barriers to trade on a world-wide scale. The WTO was recently set up as a successor to GATT. GATT now forms a part of the WTO, which also covers GATS, the General Agreement on Trade in Service, and Intellectual Property Rights (IPRs).

GLOBAL RELATIONS (WTO)

Countries use all kinds of methods to protect their own production from competition from outside. One of those methods consists of imposing tariffs and duties that have to be paid when a product is imported. The price of products is thereby raised, the demand then generally slacks off and imports fall. The Netherlands and other European countries' external trade condition are mostly determined by EC Regulations. Special agreements between the EU and EFTA countries (the earlier mentioned EEA) also exist. On an international scale, the member states of the European Union are bound as a block to the agreements of the WTO.

The WTO is the most important Organisation for regulating global trade, replacing the General Agreement on Tariffs and Trade (GATT). The European Commission acts as the single spokesman for the 15 EU member states in a WTO context. Already widely publicised, agriculture and service included for the first time as sectors in the context of GATT/WTO - have turned out to be the stumbling block on the path to concluding the Uruguay Round of GATT/WTO negotiations. The EU also plays a not-unimportant role in the framework of the United Nations.

Twenty-three countries signed the General Agreement on Tariffs and Trade (GATT), established in 1947. The organisation was meant to be the forerunner of the International Trade Organisation (ITO), but the latter was later renamed, when installed, and is called the World Trade Organisation (WTO), of which, GATT now only forms one part. The WTO is the one and only Global Body which aims at the liberalisation of global trade on a multilateral basis.

Uruguay Round

The Uruguay Round discussions began in 1986 (Punta del Este, Uruguay) and were supposed to be concluded at the end of December 1990. However, because of stumbling blocks along the road, negotiations lasted until April 1994. The final act embodying its results came into force on January 1, 1995.

Broadly speaking, three developments made several GATT member countries feel that there was a need to hold a new round of negotiations. Firstly, it had become evident that, although as a result of the adoption of associate agreements, the rules of GATT in a number of areas had been strengthened, its rules were not being applied in two important trade sectors, viz. agriculture and textiles. In the agricultural sector, most of the developed countries had taken an advantage of the loophole to establish policies that were not always consistent with GATT principles (the EU's Common Agricultural Policy is a clear example of this). In the textile sector, a number of countries imposed restrictions on imports, particularly those originating in developing countries. They did this under the so called Multi-fiber Arrangement (MFA) which provided a legal cover for derogation from the GATT rules against the use of quotas.

Secondly, by the same time, it has become evident that trade in service has grown into an important component of international trade. The rules of GATT applied only to trade in goods and there were no international rules on measures taken by countries to protect their service. Industrial opinion was growing, therefore, both for the efficient development of the service industries in different countries and to develop trade in service, it was time to bring this trade under international discipline.

Thirdly, industries and trading organisations were complaining that, because of different national standards for the protection of Intellectual Property Rights (IPRs), such as patents and trademarks and ineffective enforcement by governments of the national rules providing for such rights, trade in counterfeit goods was on the increase. The absence of adequate protection was also considered as a deterrent to foreign investment in the production of patented goods and a reason for the reluctance of industries in developed countries to sell or license technology to industries in developing countries.

In many ways, the launching of the negotiations coincided with the decision of a number of developing countries to reorient their trade and economic policies away from import substitution to export-oriented growth. The measures they were taking to reduce tariffs, to liberalise their import control system and to open their doors to foreign investment were consistent with GATT principles. Though these measures were unilateral and not influenced by the launching of negotiations, they enabled developing countries - including those, which were originally skeptical - to take a constructive attitude to the issues being discussed and to agree to integrate them more fully into the legal system which was being formulated.

This shift in trade policies and the adoption of market - oriented reforms also led a number of developing countries to seek GATT membership.

Simultaneously, with the breakdown of Communism, policies favouring privatisation and market oriented reform in the countries, that are now called 'transitional economies' prompted most of them to apply for GATT membership.

WORLD TRADE ORGANISATION (WTO)

One of the major achievements of the Uruguay Round has been the establishment of the World Trade Organisation (WTO). GATT has ceased to be a separate Institution and has become part of the WTO. In the following sections, a closer look at the WTO, its structure and its councils — for regulation of trade in goods and service and dealing with the issue of Intellectual Property Rights (IPRs) - is discussed in detail.

Objectives of the WTO

The WTO was officially established through the Marrakesh Agreement establishing the World Trade Organisation (WTO) which entered into force on January 1, 1995. The WTO is the umbrella Organisation responsible for overseeing the implementation of all the multilateral Agreements, which have been negotiated in the Uruguay Round, and those Agreements, which will be negotiated in the future. Its basic objectives are similar to the 'old' GATT which has ceased to exist as a separate Institution and has become part of the WTO. These objectives have been expanded to give the WTO a mandate to deal with trade in service. Furthermore, in promoting economic development through the expansion of trade, adequate attention has to be given to protecting and preserving the environment. In this respect, WTO adopts the principle of 'sustainable development' as agreed on in Rio de Janeiro during the United Nations Conference on Environment and Development (UNCED, June 1992).

Functions of the WTO

The Agreement establishing the WTO distinguishes four different function of the WTO, viz:

★ It shall facilitate the implementation, administration and operation if the Uruguay Round legal instruments, as well as any new agreements that may be negotiated in the future.
★ It shall provide a forum for further negotiations among member countries on matters covered by the Agreements, as well as on new issues falling within its mandate.
★ It shall be responsible for the settlement of differences and disputes among its member countries.
★ It shall be responsible for carrying out periodic reviews of the trade policies of its member countries.

Structure of the WTO

The main WTO Body responsible for decision-making is the Ministerial Conference which is expected to meet every two years. The first of such meetings was held in December, 1996 in Singapore. During the two years between the meetings, the functions of the conference are performed by the General Council, which meets as a dispute settlement body when it considers complaints and takes necessary steps to settle disputes between member countries. It is also responsible for carrying out reviews of the trade policies of individual countries, on the basis of the reports prepared by the WTO Secretariat.

The General Council is assisted in its work by the:

★ Council for trade in goods, which oversees the implementation and operation of GATT 1994, and its associate agreements;
★ Council for trade in service, which oversees the implementation of GATS.
★ Council for trade-related aspects of Intellectual Property Rights (TRIPS) which oversees the operation of the Agreement on TRIPS.

WTO Membership

By the end of 1996, 129 countries had joined WTO. Former GATT members that have not so far acceded to WTO could do so until the end of 1997 (the end of the transition period).

Countries, which are at present not GATT members can become members of WTO by negotiating for accession.

When negotiating, they have to agree to take steps to align their national legislation with the rules of the multilateral agreements. In addition, they have to make commitments to reduce tariffs and modify their regulations, so as to prove improved access for foreign goods and service. These commitments are often referred to as the price of the 'entry ticket' entitling the acceding country to benefit on a Most Favoured Nation (MFN) basis from all tariff reductions and other commitments undertaken by member countries in the past.

The WTO Councils

As stated, the WTO covers goods, service and trade-related intellectual property rights. A description of these three groups follows below. Note that these, councils came into existence in their current shape only in 1995, after the official establishment of the WTO (a result of the Uruguay Round).

GATT—The Trade in Goods

The objective of the multilateral system for the trade in goods created by GATT is to provide industries and business enterprises in different countries, a stable and predictable environment, in which they can trade with one another, under conditions of fair and equitable competition. This system should promote trade, investment, production and employment and should thereby facilitate the economic development of all countries.

The GATT's open and liberal multilateral trading system is built on four basic and simple rules.

The first rule, while recognising that it is important for member countries to follow open and liberal trade polices, permits them to protect domestic production from foreign competition, provided that such protection is extended only through tariffs and is kept at low levels. To this end, it prohibits countries from using quotas, except in specified cases. The rule against the use of quotas has been strengthened in the Uruguay Round.

The second rule provides for the reduction and elimination of tariffs and other barriers to trade through multilateral negotiations. The tariffs thereby reduced are listed on a tariff-line basis in each country's schedule of concessions. The rates given in these schedules are known as bound (fixed) rates. Member countries are under an obligation not to increase tariffs above the bound rates.

The third rule requires countries to conduct their trade without discriminating against countries from which goods are imported or to which goods are exported. This rule is laid down in the Most Favoured Nation (MFN) principle. An important exception to this rule is permitted in the case of Regional Preferential Arrangements. (The EU uses this exception for maintaining the Lome Convention, the Maghreb and the Mashraq Agreements).

The fourth rule is known as the national treatment rule. It requires countries not to impose on an imported product, after it has entered their domestic markets on paying customs duties at the border, and internal taxes such as sales, or value added tax rates higher than those levied on a similar domestic product.

In short, GATT works on the basis of nondiscrimination and reciprocity. The first implies that if one trade partner is granted favourable import terms, this should automatically apply to other GATT members, even though exceptions are possible. The reciprocity means that when one country lowers import duties, it can demand a reciprocal lowering. In all, there have been seven negotiating rounds since GATT was established.

The success of GATT is illustrated by the increase in the number of member countries ($110) and the considerable reductions in trade tariffs, which have been achieved. They have been reduced from an average of 40% to 5%. It has to be observed that pressure from the International Monetary Fund (IMF) has bought about tariff reduction in many countries.

During the Uruguay Round, the new agreement related mainly to the following topics:

- ★ Valuation of goods for customs purposes
- ★ Pre-shipment inspection of goods
- ★ Mandatory and voluntary product standards and sanitary and phytosanitary regulations
- ★ Import licensing procedures
- ★ Rules applicable to exports
- ★ Subsidies on industrial exports
- ★ Dumping practices
- ★ Trade-related Investment Measures (TRIMs)
- ★ Opening of markets for agricultural goods

GATS—The Trade in Service

Prior to the Uruguay Round, trade in service was not subject to any discipline at the international level. The GATS, which was negotiated in the Round, takes a first major step towards bringing the trade gradually under international discipline. The objectives of GATS are similar to those of GATT. It aims at 'promoting the economic growth of all trading partners and the development of developing countries' through the expansion of trade in service.

The term 'service' covers a wide range of economic activities. The WTO has divided the numerous activities in the following 12 sectors.

- ★ Business (including professional and computing) service
- ★ Communication service
- ★ Construction and engineering service
- ★ Distribution service
- ★ Educational service
- ★ Environmental service
- ★ Financial (banking and insurance) service
- ★ Health service
- ★ Tourism and travel service
- ★ Recreational, cultural and sporting service
- ★ Transport service
- ★ Other services not included elsewhere

These 12 sectors have been further divided into 155 subsectors. The trade in service is growing and currently accounts for over 20% of all international trade. The General Agreement on Trade in Service (GATS) applies the basic rules on trade in goods to trade in service. However, the rules have been suitably modified to take into account the differences between goods and service and the four modes in which international trade in service take place.

The GATS consists of a framework of rules and liberalisation commitments specific to the service sectors and subsectors listed in each country's schedule.

The framework of rules requires countries to apply Most Favoured Nation (MFN) treatment by not discriminating between service products and service providers of different countries. However, it may be possible for a country to maintain measures for a transitional period of 10 years, which are inconsistent with the MFN principle. The national treatment principle visualises that the countries should not treat foreign service and service providers less favourable than their own service products or service providers. While the framework does not impose a binding obligation, it requires countries to indicate in their schedule of concessions, the sectors in which and the conditions subject to which, such national treatment is to be extended.

Among the other important provisions of the framework of rules are those which require member countries to ensure transparency in the regulations applicable to service industries and activities, as well as rules which aim at ensuring the increasing participation of developing countries in trade in service.

Trade-related Aspects of Intellectual Property Rights (TRIPS)

The development of international trade can be adversely affected, if the standards adopted by countries to protect Intellectual Property Rights (IPRs) vary widely from one country to another. Furthermore, the ineffective enforcement of such rights can encourage trade in counterfeit and pirated goods, thereby damaging the legitimate commercial interests of manufacturers who hold or have acquired these Rights. The TRIPS Agreement, negotiated in the Uruguay Round, therefore lays down the minimum standards for the protection of OPRs as well as procedures and remedies for their enforcement. It establishes a mechanism for consolation and surveillance at the international level to ensure compliance with these standards by member countries at the national level.

The obligations of the World Trade Organisation (WTO) Agreement on Trade-Related Aspects of Intellectual Property Rights (TRIPs) came into effect for developed countries on 1 January, 1996.

The Agreement provides a transitional period of five years (up to 1 January, 2000) for developing countries to bring their IPR legislation in conformity with the provisions of the Agreement. The transitional period for the least developed countries is 11 years (up to 1 January, 2006).

Developing countries which do not at present provide product patent protection in an area of technology have up to 10 years to introduce such protection. However, in the case of pharmaceutical and agricultural chemical products, they must accept the filing of patent applications from the beginning of the transitional period, though these applications need not be granted until the end of this period.

If authorisation for the marketing of the relevant pharmaceutical or agricultural chemical is obtained during the transition period, the developing country concerned must, subject to certain conditions, provide an exclusive marketing right for the product for five years, or until a product patent is granted, whichever is shorter. During any transitional period, a standstill clause applies which forbids members to reduce the levels of protection for Intellectual Property such as exist in their territory. Subject to certain exceptions, the general rule is the obligations in the Agreement apply to existing as well as to new Intellectual Property Rights.

The objects of Intellectual Properties are the creations of the human mind, the human intellect. Intellectual Properties include copyright, patents industrial designs and trademarks. Copyright relates to the rights of creators of literary, scientific, and artistic works. Patents give exclusive rights to inventors. However, inventions can be patented only if they are new, non-obvious and are capable of industrial applications. Industrial designs are new or original aesthetic creations determining the appearance of industrial products. These three rights are available for a limited duration. A trademark distinguishes a product or a service from those of others; they also assist consumers in making informed choices on the basis of the information provided by manufacturers about the quality of the product.

Intellectual Property Rights (IPRs) are, for many companies, as much a commercial commodity as a manufactured product is for the innovator, and his invention is as important as the automobiles are for a car manufacturer. If everybody can freely use the invention, the innovator would be 'out of business' in a short time.

Implications of IPRs for Trade

Any unauthorised use of Intellectual Property constitutes an infringement of the right of the owner. Until about two decades ago, such infringements had implications largely for domestic trade. They were further considered posing problems mainly at the national level, which - apart from affecting the interests of the owners of rights - impinged on scientific progress and cultural life.

In recent years, however, there has been an increasing realisation that the standards adopted by countries to protect their IPRs, as well as the effectiveness with which they are enforced, have implications for the development of international trade. There are many reasons for this, of which three are especially worth noting.

Firstly, industrial production in most industrialised countries is increasingly becoming research and technology intensive. As a result, their export products both traditional (such as chemicals, fertilisers and pharmaceuticals) and comparatively new (telecommunications equipment, computers, televisions videos) now contain more patented high technology and creative inputs.

Manufacturers are therefore keen to ensure that, wherever they market their products, their patent rights are adequately protected to enable them terrace up their research and development expenditure.

Secondly, due to the removal of restrictions on foreign investment by a large number of developing countries, new opportunities are emerging for the manufacture in these countries of patented products under license or within joint ventures. The willingness of industries in industrialised countries to enter into such arrangements and to make their technology available, however, depends on how far the IPR system of the host country provides them with an assurance that their property rights to technology will be adequately protected and not taken possession of by local partners, making use of reverse engineering.

Thirdly, technological advances that have made reproduction and imitation simple and cheap have matched the technological improvements in products entering international trade. In countries where Laws on IPRs are not strictly enforced, this has resulted in an increased production of counterfeit and pirated goods, not only for sale in the domestic markets but also for export.

Counterfeit and Pirated Goods

Estimates of revenue foregone by industries as a result of counterfeiting, pirating and other infringement of Intellectual Property Rights vary widely, but there is no doubt that the value involved is significant. Goods are particularly treated as counterfeit when they are offered for sale under well-known trademarks, which the seller has no authority to use. These are generally labour intensive products which, because of the reputation of the brand name, can be sold at high prices. They include clothing, shoes, watches, cosmetics, leather goods, and household and sporting goods. Pirated goods are those that infringe on copyright and related rights. Book publishers, producers of records, discs, films, tapes and cassettes are often the victims of violation of copyright and related rights. The Technological progressive software industry is the leading victim of the speed with which Intellectual Property can be illegally copied and distributed on an international scale.

WIPO Convention on IPRs

Efforts to develop rules providing adequate protection to Intellectual Property Rights at the International level have been made for over a century, mainly under the auspices of the World Intellectual Property Organisation (WIPO) and its predecessor organisations. As a result, a number of conventional laying down of international obligations to protect the rights of owners of IPRs have been adopted.

The value of goods and service entering international trade increasingly resides in their Intellectual Property component. For example, the purchaser who buys a compact disc is not interested in the actual CD as such, but in the music or the computer software recorded on it.

Similarly, the value of a pharmaceutical resides mainly in the knowledge that has been gained about the therapeutic qualities and safety of the chemical entity in question.

Thus, the protection of Intellectual Property has become increasingly important to the international competitive positions of companies. This helps to explain why Intellectual Property protection has progressed to the forefront of international trade issues and why the Agreement of Trade-Related Aspect of Intellectual Property Rights (TRIPS), negotiated in the Uruguay Round, establishes the minimum international standards for the protection and enforcement of each of the main areas of Intellectual Property. The Agreement lays down the procedures for consultations between governments when one party has reason to believe that the licensing practices or conditions of an enterprise from another member country constitute an abuse of the Agreement, or have adverse effects on competition.

Type of Property Rights Covered by TRIPS

Under Intellectual Properties, we classify in particular:

- ★ Patents
- ★ Industrial designs
- ★ Trade marks
- ★ Copyrights and related rights
- ★ Layout-designs of intellectual circuits

All these Intellectual Properties can be protected in one way or another.

Patents Inventions are protected if they are new, non-obvious and industrially applicable. The TRIPS Agreement requires, that at least 20-year patent protection be available for all inventions, whether of products or processes, in almost all fields of technology.

Inventions may be excluded from patent ability, if their commercial exploitation is prohibited for reasons of public order or morality. Otherwise, the permitted exclusions are for diagnostic, therapeutic and surgical methods, and for plants (other than microorganism's processes). Plant varieties, however, must be protectable either by patents or by an effective *sui* generis system (such as the breeder's rights provided in the conventions of UPOV, the Intellectual Union for the Protection on New Varieties of Plants). Compulsory licensing and governmental use of patents without the authorisation of the patent owner are subject to detailed conditions.

Rights conferred in respect of patents for processes must extend to the products directly obtained by the process. Under certain conditions, alleged infringes may be ordered by a Court to prove that they have not used a patented process.

Industrial designs Industrial designs are, for example, applicable in the field of textiles, motor cars and electronics. The designs are ornamental. Industrial designs are protected, under the Agreements, for a period of not less than 10 years.

Owners of protected designs must be able to prevent the manufacture, sale or importation of articles bearing or embodying a design, which is a copy of the protected design.

Copyright The TRIPS Agreement ensures that computer programmes are protected as literary words and outlines as how databases should be protected. An important addition to existing international rules in the area of copyright and related rights is the provision on rental rights. Authors of computer programmes and producers of sound recordings have the right to authorise or prohibit the commercial rental of their words to the public. A similar exclusive right applies to films, where commercial rental has led to widespread copying, which is materially impairing the right of reproduction. Performers are protected from unauthorised recording, reproduction and broadcast of live performances (bootlegging) for no less than 50 years. Producers of sound recordings must have the right to prevent the reproduction of recordings for a period of 50 years. The Berne Convention of 1978 covers all the above groups, as well as books and publications and has made a distinction for the protection of the copyright between works (books, recordings and so forth) before 1978, and works after 1978. For works before 1978, the following applies:

- ★ Those works which have no copyright should be protected.
- ★ Private individual at least up to 50 years after the death of the author.
- ★ Commercial works (by companies); either 75 years after publication or 100 years after creation (the longer one applies).
- ★ Works, which are copyright protected, 28 years of protection and 47 years' extension.

For works after 1978, the following is valid:

- ★ Private works are protected at least up to 50 years after the death of the author.
- ★ Commercial works (by companies), either 75 years after publication or 100 years after creation (the longer one applies).

Trademarks The Agreement defines what types of signs and logos must be eligible for protection as trade marks or service marks and what the minimum rights conferred on their owners must be. Marks that have become well-known in a particular country enjoy additional protection. More attention is paid to trade marks, particularly in the EU market, in the module about the European Union.

Consequences for Exporters in Developing Countries

The Uruguay Round has made some exceptions with regard to enforcement for developing countries. The rule of full reciprocity of preferential treatment does not apply to business dealings between developed and developing countries. The system of relative reciprocity, applicable to developing countries, takes into account, that developing countries may not be able to make concessions on the same basis as developed countries. The rule, however, recognises that developing countries are not all at the same level of development; some of them, particularly the Newly Industrialising Countries (NICs) have reached higher stages of growth. These countries are required to make larger concessions in the form of tariff reductions than those at lower levels of economic growth.

Because of the rule of relative reciprocity, only a few developing countries had made tariff concessions in earlier GATT Rounds. These concessions mainly applied to only a few products. This changed considerably in the Uruguay Round. Almost all the developing countries have agreed to make concessions (although at lower percentages than developed nations).

What is the relevance of the Uruguay Round to the decisions that industries and business enterprises make in their international trade activities? When considering this question, one must bear in mind that governments have negotiated improved market access to enable business enterprises to convert trade concessions into new trade opportunities. The objective behind the strengthened rules of the Uruguay Round is to ensure that the markets remain open and that an exporter's access is not disrupted by the sudden and arbitrary imposition of import restrictions.

Business communities are, however, not fully aware at present of the advantages which the multilateral trading system resulting from the Uruguay Round can generate for them.

The main reason for this is the immense complexity of the system, which has so far prevented these communities from taking an interest in, and getting acquainted with, its, rules. It is, for example, not widely known that the legal system not only confers benefits on producing industries and business enterprises, but also creates rights in their favour.

In trade of goods, almost all tariffs of developed countries and a high proportion of those in developing countries have been bound against further increases by the Uruguay Round. This ensures that sudden increases or the imposition of other restrictions will not disrupt the improved market access resulting from the tariff reductions by importing countries. This security of access enables exporting industries to make investment and production plans under greater conditions of certainty. Stability of access is provided through the requirement for all countries to apply at the border, the uniform set of rules negotiated in the Uruguay-and previous-Round. Countries are obliged to ensure that their rules for determining dutiable value for customs purposes, for inspecting products to ascertain conformity to standards or for the issue of import licenses and conform to the provisions of the Round's agreements. This helps exporters, since dissimilarities in the requirements of different markets are (slowly) eliminated.

The primary responsibility for taking advantage of the liberalisation measures now falls on enterprises. Trade clearly does not expand automatically in the wake of tariff reductions and the removal of trade barriers. This will happen only if business enterprises adopt appropriate export development strategies to take into account the impact of the liberalisation measures on the products they export. The implementation of the Uruguay Round's results, creates both opportunities and challenges for developing countries. The challenge will come from the increased competition in both domestic and foreign markets, which follows the removal of tariffs and other (non-tariff) barriers. The establishment of the WTO and the new (legal) system, which has emerged, should ensure that this increased competition remains fair.

It should be noted for clarity's sake that WTO Agreements have been negotiated on an international level by governments and that it is now up to governments to implement these negotiated measures. Business communities should have full access to a country's governmental efforts in implementing these provisions.

// CHAPTER 8 //

COMMERCIAL RELATIONS AND TRADE AGREEMENTS

There are 66 commercial offices functioning in the Indian Missions/ Posts Abroad which are funded by the Ministry of Commerce. These commercial offices working as units are attached to the Indian Missions. It includes the Office of the Ambassador of India to WTO in Geneva.

The commercial offices abroad provide the institutional framework and are meant to promote India's trade and economic exchanges with the world. Their primary task is to assist the government in the formulation of its trade and economic policies, through regular feedbacks on the prevailing global market trends, trade activities, etc.

In keeping with the requirement of quick dissemination of information, data and bilateral/multilateral exchanges, a computer database reporting system has been introduced in the Ministry, for monitoring the activities of the commercial offices abroad. The commercial representatives posted abroad are kept informed of the important developments in the Indian economy, by means of quarterly news letters. Most of the commercial wings are now linked to e-mail, Internet, Home-page, etc.

The international trade scenario is expanding and changing fast. In the wake of the liberalisation process, which was initiated in the mid-1991 for gearing up the Indian Economy, a review has been initiated in this Ministry, in consultation with the Ministry of External Affairs for restructuring and streamlining the Indian commercial wings with the view to equip them to discharge their function efficiently and effectively.

SOUTH ASIA AND SAARC

The South Asia comprises of Afghanistan, Bangladesh, Bhutan, India, Maldives, Nepal, Pakistan and Sri Lanka. With the exception of Afghanistan, all these are members of the South Asian Association for Regional Cooperation (SAARC).

In 1997-98, the total trade turnover with these countries touched the level of Rs 6,872 crores against Rs 6,990 crores achieved in the previous year, reflecting a marginal decline of 1.7%. While India's exports to these countries stood at Rs 5,898 crores in 1997-98 against Rs 6,122 crores in 1996-97, registering a fall of 3.75% imports from these countries reached Rs 974 crores in 1997-98, as compared to Rs 868 crores in 1996-97, registering a growth of 12.2%. Our trade with these countries amounted to just 2.5% of our global trade.

During April-October 1998, our total trade with the South Asian neighbours amounted to Rs 4,697.43 crores against Rs 3,448.44 crores in the same period during the previous year, i.e. a growth of 36.2%. While Indian exports to these countries touched Rs 3,505.33 crores in April-October 1998, as compared to Rs 3,023.76 crores in the same period last year, i.e. an increase of 15.9%, our imports from these countries were to the tune of Rs 1,192.10 crores as compared to Rs 424.49 crores during April-October 1997. The spectacular increase in import was mainly due to increased imports from Pakistan, Nepal and Afghanistan in the current year.

Afghanistan

During 1997-98, our exports to Afghanistan amounted to Rs 74.47 crores as compared to Rs 80.73 crores in 1996-97. Import rose from Rs 10.84 crores in 1996-97 to Rs 45.24 crores in 1997-98. During the period April-October 1998, exports touched Rs 31.48 crores as compared to Rs 41.21 crores during the same period in the previous year. Imports increased from Rs 8.36 crores during April-October 1997 to Rs 56.30 crores during the corresponding period in 1998-99.

The main items exported to Afghanistan include tyre and tubes, tea, drugs and pharmaceuticals and main imports from Afghanistan are fruits and nuts, excluding cashew nuts.

(Rs in crores)

	1996-97	*1997-98*	*1997-98 (Apr-Oct)*	*1998-99 (Apr-Oct)*
Exports	80.73	74.47	41.21	31.48
Imports	10.84	45.24	8.36	56.30

Bangladesh

Bangladesh is our largest trading partner in the region. During 1997-98, both exports to and imports from Bangladesh declined mainly due to market conditions in the country. Our exports came down to Rs 2,839.39 crores in 1997-98, as compared to Rs 3,084.80 crores during the previous year. Similarly, imports during 1997-98 declined to Rs 190.05 crores from 220.91 crores during 1996-97.

During April-October 1998, India's exports to Bangladesh amounted to Rs 1,902.80 crores as compared to Rs 1,382.31 crores in the same period in the previous year which reflected an increase of 37.7%.

(Rs in Crores)

	1996-97	*1997-98*	*1997-98 (Apr-Oct)*	*1998-99 (Apr-Oct)*
Exports	3084.80	2839.39	1382.31	1902.80
Imports	220.91	190.05	103.11	133.96

Imports from Bangladesh amounted to Rs 133.96 crores during April-October 1998, as compared to Rs 103.11 crores in the same period in the previous year, registering an increase of 29.9%.

The bilateral trade is carried out within the framework provided by the India-Bangladesh Trade Agreement, with mutually Most Favoured Nation (MFN) treatment accorded to each other.

Major items of export to Bangladesh are textiles, machinery and instruments, transport equipment, rubber products, chemical and pharmaceuticals, minerals and ores, etc.

Major imports from Bangladesh are fertilisers, raw jute and organic chemicals.

Important issues relating to bilateral trade were discussed in the Trade Review Talks held in Dhaka in December, 1998.

Bhutan

There is a traditional free trade and commerce between India and Bhutan. Commercial transactions are carried out in Indian rupees and Bhutanese Ngultrums. India provides unhindered transit facilities to landlocked Bhutan to facilitate its trade with third countries.

(Rs in Crores)

	1996-97	*1997-98*	*1997-98 (Apr-Oct)*	*1998-99 (Apr-Oct)*
Exports	78.03	52.88	21.84	22.63
Imports	119.93	125.15	32.47	24.96

Maldives

India-Maldives trade is regulated by the bilateral Trade Agreement signed in 1981. Exports from India to Maldives amounted to Rs 28.11 crores in 1997-98, while imports were only Rs 0.84 crores. Exports touched Rs 16.53 crores during April-October 1998, and imports amounted to Rs 0.05 crores during the same period.

(Rs in Crores)

	1996-97	*1997-98*	*1997-98 (Apr-Oct)*	*1998-99 (Apr-Oct)*
Exports	36.80	28.11	18.19	16.53
Imports	0.61	0.84	0.24	0.06

Nepal

Indo-Nepal relations on trade and other related matters are governed by the bilateral Treaties of Trade and Transit and Agreement for Cooperation to Control Unauthorised Trade. The Trade of Transit was renewed on 5th January, 1999, for a period of seven years and will hereafter, be automatically extended for further periods of seven years at a time, unless either party gives to the other a written notice, six months in advance, of its intention to terminate the Treaty. The modalities of transit routes, conditions of transit and customs arrangements as contained in the Protocol and Memorandum to the Treaty will be reviewed and modified every year, or earlier if warranted, to meet the changing conditions before the automatic renewal. Such changes made would be an integral part of the Treaty. The Treaty of Trade is valid upto December 5, 2001 and shall be automatically extended for a further period of five years at a time, unless either contracting party gives a notice for its termination. The Agreement for Cooperation to Control Unauthorised Trade is also valid upto December 5, 2001.

Though under the international conventions, Nepal being a landlocked country, India is obliged to provide only one transit route to facilitate Nepal's trade with third countries, 15 transit routes have been provided through the Indian territory and more such routes can be added to the list with mutual agreement. In addition, facilities have also been provided for Nepalese trade with Bangladesh and Bhutan. On the request of the Government of Nepal, an additional transit route was opened during 1997 through Phulbari-Banglaband, to facilitate trade between Nepal and Bangladesh for the movement of Nepalese cargo, on two days a week under escort. This was renewed at the Commerce Secretary level in March 1998, and it has been decided to increase the number of days of movement of the transit cargo from two to four days a week and also to waive the requirement of insurance. An undertaking is given by an Agency nominated by HMGN, that they will compensate for any loss to the Government of India in the event of deflection of the goods in transit.

(Rs in Crores)

	1996-97	*1997-98*	*1997-98 (Apr-Oct)*	*1998-99 (Apr-Oct)*
Exports	588.30	594.17	339.03	336.69
Imports	227.45	351.56	170.62	347.73

Pakistan

India's trade with Pakistan is constrained by the discriminatory policy adopted by Pakistan against imports from India. While we accord MFN treatment to imports from Pakistan, they allow their private sector to import only out of a list of 594 items from India. Despite bilateral discussions and our diplomatic demarches in this regard, Pakistan is yet to allow its trade with India on a free and MFN basis.

As a part of the composite and integrated dialogue process between India and Pakistan, talks at the Commerce Secretary level were held between the two countries on economic and commercial cooperation in New Delhi on 10th November, 1998. The two countries exchanged views on various aspects of economic and commercial cooperation. On this issue of granting MFN status to India, Pakistan conveyed that this would be done in due course.

During 1997-98, exports from India amounted to Rs 594.17 crores as compared to Rs 558.12 crores in the previous year. Imports from Pakistan in 1997-98 touched Rs 139.68 crores against Rs 128.36 crores in the previous year.

During April-October 1998, exports declined to Rs 221.58 as compared to Rs 312.82 crores in the same period in the previous year. Pakistan was forced to import sugar in 1997-98, due to a shortage of the commodity in the country. During April-October 1997, Pakistan imported sugar worth Rs 132.70 crores from India, whereas there is no import in the current year. Following vastly improved domestic availability, Pakistan has exported sugar worth Rs 435.53 crores to India during April-October 1998, thereby contributing to a total export of Rs 528.77 crores to India during this period as compared to Rs 41.33 crores in the same period last year.

(Rs in Crores)

	1996-97	*1997-98*	*1997-98 (Apr-Oct)*	*1998-99 (Apr-Oct)*
Exports	558.12	594.17	312.82	221.58
Imports	128.36	139.68	41.33	528.77

Sri Lanka

Sri Lanka has traditionally been an important export market for India and is the second largest importer of Indian goods in the region after Bangladesh. The bilateral trade is carried out in accordance with the Trade Agreement signed in 1961. The trade is in free convertible currencies and on a MFN basis. The trade has grown strongly in recent years, with India enjoying a big trade balance in her favour. Both countries are parties to WTO, SAPTA (SAARC Agreement for Preferential Trading Arrangement) and the Bangkok agreement, within the framework of which, mutual preferential trade concessions are extended to each other.

India and Sri Lanka have signed a Free Trade Agreement on 28th December, 1998, under which tariff a large number of items would be phased out within a time frame. While India would reduce the tariff to zero in three years, Sri Lanka would do so in eight years. India will immediately eliminate import duty on around 1000 items when the agreement comes into force upon entering. Tariff on all other products will be reduced, barring those in the negative list of imports and textiles to 25%. Garments will be retained in the negative list. The items in the negative list number less than 400 and it includes mainly garments, petrochemicals, alcoholic spirits, coconut and coconut oil. Sri Lanka will reduce the import duty of around 900 items to zero immediately, while a 50% cut in tariffs will be effected on around 600 items as soon as the agreement comes into force.

The issues regarding bilateral trade and commercial cooperation were discussed in the 4th Session of the India-Sri Lanka Sub-commission on Trade, Finance and Investment held in New Delhi on 14-15 December, 1998.

(Rs in Crores)

	1996-97	*1997-98*	*1997-98 (Apr-Oct)*	*1998-99 (Apr-Oct)*
Exports	1694.79	1771.57	908.36	973.62
Imports	160.33	121.48	68.37	100.34

SAARC

In recognition of the fact that our geographical proximity, cultural and religious affinity and economic synergies can be used to our mutual benefit, the seven countries of South Asia, viz. India, Nepal, Pakistan, Bangladesh, Sri Lanka, Bhutan and Maldives have organised themselves into an association called The South Asian Association for Regional Cooperation (SAARC). The SAARC countries celebrated the completion of the first decade of their existence on 7th December 1995. The major achievement in the first decade was the operationalisation of the SAARC Agreement for Preferential Trading Arrangement (SAPTA). As a result, concessions have been exchanged between the members. India is the major participating economy in the region and has given deeper cuts (upto 50%) in the MFN tariff rates on imports of maximum number of commodities (106) from the countries in the region, followed by Pakistan — 10 to 20% in 35 commodities, Bangladesh — 10% in 12 commodities and Bhutan — 15% in 11 commodities. The completion of the second round of SAPTA negotiations has resulted in the exchange of tariff concessions on 1972 lines. Out of this, India has offered concessions on 911 Tariff lines and received concessions on 456 tariff lines at the six-digit level. The third Round of SAPTA negotiations has also been completed to further deepen and enlarge the exchange of tariff concessions and removal of non-tariff barriers. The ultimate objective, as mandated by the leaders of the SAARC member-countries is to establish a Free Trade Area in the region (SAFTA) by 2001 A.D. Special bodies have been constituted by the SAARC administration for the timely achievement of this objective.

Steps have been taken to facilitate the movement of the trading community within the region by improving the visa procedures. Customs procedures are also being simplified through regular interaction of the participating members. Harmonisation of standards of export manufactures and their quality control are also under active consideration of the SAARC forum. Steps are being taken to create a congenial environment for the promotion and protection of intra-regional investment. India has liberalised the procedures for promoting Indian investments in the SAARC region by raising the ceiling for approvals under the fast track channel from US $4 million to US $8 million and then to US $15 million. For investments in rupees in Nepal, this ceiling is Rs 60 crores.

In addition to the meetings of SAARC bodies constituted in the SAARC Charter, the Commerce Ministers of SAARC member-states also hold meetings in order to monitor the progress of SAARC intra-regional trade and other economic activities. The first meeting of the SAARC Commerce Ministers was held in New Delhi in January 1996. The second meeting was held in Islamabad on April 29-30, 1998. The third meeting of the SAARC Commerce Ministers was held at Dhaka during February 2-3, 1999. With a view to display the potential for the exchange of commodities within the region, the first SAARC trade fair was held in New Delhi in January 1996 and the second SAARC trade fair was held in Colombo between 8-15 September, 1998. At the 10th SAARC Summit held at Colombo during July 21-31, 1998, India opened its market for entry of about 2000 products from the SAARC member countries which are restricted for imports for the reasons of balance of payment.

NORTH-EAST ASIA

The North-East Asia region comprises of China, Japan, Republic of Korea, Hong Kong, Taiwan, Democratic People's Republic of Korea and Mongolia. The financial crisis faced by East and South Asia region in 1997 has adversely affected the economic conditions of some countries in the region, particularly Japan and South Korea.

During April 1997 to March 1998, India's exports to countries in the region which stood at Rs 19,87,712.4 lakhs were 2.59% higher than the exports of Rs 19,37,461.61 lakhs during the previous year. Imports from the region in the financial year (1997-98) stood at Rs 18,33,447.2 lakhs as compared to Rs 16,34,153.5 lakhs in April-March 1996-97, thereby registering an increase of 12.19%, which is the growth in the total volume of trade during April-March 1996-97. Japan, China, Hong Kong and Republic of Korea are the major trading partners of India in this region.

The pattern of trade with the countries in North-East Asia over the past five years has been as follows:-

(Rs in Crore)

Year	*Exports*	*Imports*	*Total*	*Balance of Trade*
1992-93	788274.74	689173.59	1477448.33	(+) 99101.15
1993-94	1195925.9	878302.82	2074228.72	(+) 317623.1
1994-95	1387807.9	1266124.1	2653932.0	(+) 121683.8
1995-96	1708598.1	1643485.2	3352083.3	(+) 65112.9
1996-97	1909397.4	1626613.1	3536010.5	(+) 282784.3
1997-98	1987712.4	1833447.2	3821159.6	(+) 154265.2
1998-99 (Apr-Sep)	861469.25	1116084.6	1977553.8	(-) 254615.4

(Source: DGCI&S, Calcutta)

Commodity analysis of exports Production-wise export analysis for 1997-98 shows that:

- ★ Exports of gems and jewellery form the most important component of our export basket to this region constituting about 28.2% of our total exports to countries in North-East Asia, the major destinations being Hong Kong and Japan. About 29.6% of India's total exports of gems and jewellery during 1997-98 were exported to countries in this region.
- ★ Iron ore is another significant commodity exported to this region with 78.5% of India's total iron ore exports moving to destinations in North-East Asia. China and Japan together accounted for about 68% of India's total exports of iron ore in 1997-98.
- ★ Japan is a major market for our marine products, being the destination for about 46% of India's total marine products during 1997-98. China is another growing market for India's marine products. Fifty-eight per cent of India's total exports during 1997-98 were to countries in North-East Asia.

★ Exports of Cotton yarn, fabrics, made-ups, etc. iron and other ores, iron and steel bars/rods, manufactures of metals, leather, oil, meals and spices are some other important exports to this region. Significant beginnings have been made in exports to North-East Asia during 1996-97 and 1997-98 in respect of some other export items like tobacco, groundnut, floriculture products, guar gum meal, seasame and niger seeds, some dyes and dye intermediates and processed minerals.

Commodity analysis of imports The major items of import from this region include machinery (except electric and electronic), organic and inorganic chemicals, electronic goods, project goods, transport equipments, professional instruments, textiles, yarn and raw silk. Other prominent import items include pearls and semi-precious stones, artificial resins and plastics, coal, coke, iron and steel, non-ferrous metals, manufactures of metals and synthetic and reclaimed rubber.

SOUTH-EAST ASIA

India's trade with South-East Asia region comprising the ASEAN countries (viz. Indonesia, Malaysia, Singapore, Thailand, Philippines, Brunei, Vietnam, Myanmar and Laos), Kampuchea, Australia, New Zealand and countries of Oceania registered a normal growth of about 3% during 1997-98 in the wake of financial and currency turmoil faced by some of the countries in the region, viz., Indonesia, Malaysia, Philippines, Thailand, etc. While India's trade with Australia, New Zealand, Myanmar, Philippines, Vietnam and Malaysia witnessed a growth, the trade with Indonesia, Singapore, Thailand and Brunei registered a decline. Imports from this region registered an increase of about 15%, while exports declined by about 14% during 1997-98. Singapore, Malaysia, Indonesia, Thailand, Philippines, Australia and Vietnam were our major export destinations in the region, whereas for imports, Singapore, Malaysia, Indonesia and Australia continued to be the forerunners.

During April-August 1998, India's trade with the countries in the region at US $3,281.47 million was less by 0.20% of the trade at US $3,287.95 million during the corresponding period in the previous year.

While India's exports at US $768.24 million during April-August 1998 to the countries in the region have gone down by 40%, imports have registered a growth of 25.9%.

Our trade with this region during the past five years is as under:

(US $ million)

Year	*Exports*	*Imports*	*Total*	*Balance of Trade*
1993-94	1981.71	1950.00	3931.71	(+)31.71
1994-95	2326.27	3059.50	5385.76	(–)733.23
1995-96	3177.77	3881.88	7059.65	(–)704.11
1996-97	3353.43	4492.58	7846.04	(–)1139.12
1997-98(P)	2895.42	5165.48	8060.90	(–)2270.06
1998-99(P) (Apr-Sept)	923.76	3134.02	4057.78	(–)2210.26

(DGCI&S data converted to US $) (P-Provisional)

The principal commodities for export to this region during the period 1997-98 include oil meals, cotton/fabrics, made-ups, machinery, and instruments, primary and semi-finished iron and steel, drugs and pharmaceuticals, meat, etc.

The major commodities imported from this region were coal/coke/briquettes, vegetable oils, electronic goods, organic chemicals, machinery except electrical machinery, wood and wooden products, non-ferrous metals, raw wool, pulses, wheat, electrical machinery etc.

In consonance with India's 'Look East Policy' and after having become a full dialogue partner with ASEAN, ASEAN-India Working Group on Trade and Investment (ASEAN-India WGTI) has been established under the aegis of the ASEAN-India Joint Cooperation Committee to give a major fillip to India's relationship with ASEAN in trade and investment, which are major areas of focused cooperation with ASEAN. The first meeting of the ASEAN-India WGTI was inaugurated by the Commerce Secretary and attended by 25 delegates from 9 ASEAN countries. The meeting acknowledged the need for enhancing the interaction between the private sectors on both the sides and evolving ways and means for information exchange by involving private sectors. The ASEAN also recognised the need for enhancing cooperation in core infrastructure projects in India.

There has been a regular exchange of business delegation with countries in this region, as also in participation in trade fairs of mutual interest.

The Embassy of India, Hanoi had organised the 'Pride of India' Exhibition in Hanoi from 14-17 January, 1998, to commemorate the 50th anniversary of India's independence. The exhibition which had about 30 participants from both public and private sectors in India was well-received by the Vietnamese business community as well as government circles. To sustain the success of the first exhibition, the second 'Pride of India' was also held at Vietnam from 23-26 October, 1998.

EUROPE

Europe presently comprises of 12 countries of erstwhile East Europe, i.e. Bulgaria, Macedonia, Albania, Federal Republic of Yugoslavia, Bosnia and Herzegovina, Croatia, Slovenia, Hungary, Slovakia, Czech Republic, Poland and Romania and the countries of West Europe. East Europe comprises of countries in the European Union (EU) (Austria, Belgium, Denmark, Finland, France, FRG, Greece, Ireland, Italy, Luxembourg, The Netherlands, UK, Spain, Sweden, Portugal) and Norway, Switzerland, Iceland, Liechtenstein, Turkey, Malta, and Cyprus.

Indo-Europe Trade

India's exports to europe have increased by 61.13% from US $6,057.19 million in 1992-93 to US $9,759.71 million in 1997-98. However, imports from the European countries have also registered a growth of 70.97% from US $7,717.38 million in 1992-93 to US $13,194.37 million in 1997-98. European countries accounted for about 30% of India's total trade during this period.

Data on bilateral trade with Europe (both East and West) during the last 5 years is as under:-

(US $ million)

Year	*Exports*	*Percentage*	*Imports*	*Percentage*	*Balance of Trade*
1994-95	7896.72	+19.14	8572.43	+6.58	–675.71
1995-96	9448.18	+19.65	11845.06	+38.18	–2396.88
1996-97	9448.93	+0.01	12241.47	+3.35	–2792.54
1997-98 (P)	9759.71	+3.29	13194.37	+7.78	–3434.66
1997-98 (P)	4842.76	-	5970.39	-	–1127.63
1998-99 (P) (Apr-Sept)	4596.99	-5.07	6957.66	+16.54	–2360.67

(Source: DGCI&S, Calcutta) (P - provisional)

The group of erstwhile 'Rupee Payment Area (RPA) Countries' have always occupied an important place in India's foreign trade. The political and economic changes in East Europe and the USSR from the late 1980s onwards naturally had profound implications, on India's trade with the erstwhile RPA countries. As a result of various circumstances trade has been adversely affected, and in order to revive trade, it was decided to terminate the rupee trade arrangement and move to a situation of trade based on hard currency with all former RPA countries.

Trade with Hungary, Bulgaria and Poland switched to hard currency trading in 1970s and 1980s. The process of finalisation of fresh Trade Agreement with Federal Republic of Yugoslavia has also been initiated and is expected to be concluded soon.

Steps taken to boost trade with East European countries With the disintegration of the COMECON countries, India's trade with the erstwhile East Europe declined severely. Various factors can be attributed to it like the collapse of a well-established trade organisation, dismantling of rupee payment system, severe liquidity constraints, internal socio-economic disarray due to a rapid shift from command and control economy to liberal and market economy. India had to compete in an open market with improved quality and intense competition on costing, changing habits of the population, etc.

West Europe

The main items of exports to West Europe during 1997-98 comprised of textiles, yarn, fabrics, garments, leather and leather goods, gems and jewellery, carpets, engineering goods, besides agricultural and marine products. Major imports by India from this region are manufactured goods, machinery, transport equipment and other capital goods.

The European Union is India's largest trading partner and provides for a quarter of its exports and a third of its imports. With 15 member states and 367.8 million citizens with a very high purchasing power, it is our largest market and one which has shown an increasing trend in imports from India as a percentage of its total imports. A new Indo-EU Cooperation Agreement on Partnership and Development was signed on 20th December, 1993, in Brussels which has come into force with effect from 1st August, 1994. It broadens the scope of cooperation to cover a whole range of new sectors and also reflects the communities, interest in India becoming an effective partner.

Status Note on Trade Regime in the Countries of European Union

EU and its member countries are members of WTO and hence bilateral trade between India and EU is in conformity with WTO regulations. While on the one hand Indian goods and products enjoy EU's GSP benefits, on the other some Indian products are subjected to EU's stringent Anti-Dumping and subsidy investigations. Such actions and other non-tariff barriers including, enlargement of EU/Quota Regime/Trade Preference Agreements, etc. are kept under a constant watch and timely actions are initiated in coordination with the trade and industry to meet such challenges.

In recent year, India's exports to the community have increased substantially from US $3,413 million in 1988-89 to US $8,854 million in 1997-98 thereby registering on increasing of 159.42%. Similarly, imports grew by 70.69% from US $6,012 million in 1988-89 to US $10,262 million in 1997-98.

To periodically review the bilateral, commercial and economic relations, institutional arrangements in the shape of Joint Commissions/Committees exist with most of the countries in the region and meetings are held alternately in New Delhi and the respective capitals of the countries concerned.

Meeting of the Indo-EC Joint Commissions headed by the Commerce Secretary on the Indian side and Shri Enncho Ekoffi on the EC side were held in Brussels on 14th and 15th January, 1998. The Ministry of Commerce is the nodal agency for most of the Joint Commissions. There are, however, Joint Commissions with certain other European countries for which other Ministries are the nodal agency. These countries include Germany, Sweden, Poland, Bulgaria and Hungary.

Programmes on Trade and Economic Cooperation

In order to augment Indian exports to the West European region, some trade promotion programmes are in operation with the European Union.

Indo-German Export Promotion Project (IGEP) In Indo-German Export Promotion Project (IGEP) was established in 1998 with German assistance, for project development and market development for selected Indian products. The project has been extended upto 1999. The German assistance for the present three year phase (1997-99) is to the tune of DM 12 million. The sectors being covered by IGEP's current activities include (i) silk/textiles (ii) leather shoes/apparel/articles (iii) gold/silver jewellery (iv) arts and crafts (v) bicycle/auto parts (vi) engineering goods/castings and forgings (vii) computer software and IT products, etc.

Indo-British Partnership Initiative (IBPI) In 1997-98, the important outcome of the visit of British Prime Minister Mr John Major to India in January 1993, was the launching of the Indo-British Partnership Initiative

(IBPI). This is an industry driven initiative, sponsored by CII on the Indian side and CBI on the British side. This initiative envisages action to be taken on both sides, to increase awareness of investment opportunities in selected sectors, achieving a quantum jump in bilateral trade and providing better access to the british industry for establishing manufacturing units in India for export to third countries. A core group of 24 CEOs was set up to identify and initiate activities under the initiative. IBPI has now become the mascot of the Indo-British economic cooperation.

Indian International Marketing Centre (IIMC), Rotterdam In tune with the ongoing liberalisation programmes in India, private enterprises are now being encouraged and assisted to provide marketing logistics support to Indian exporters. The Indian International Marketing Centre Limited (IIMC) was thus established at Rotterdam in the private sector, with financial subsidy and backing of the Government of the Netherlands. It is supported mainly by a group of Indian entrepreneurs. The objectives of IIMC are (a) to promote export of Indian goods and products (b) to establish offices, marketing centres, distribution centres, warehousing facilities, and processing activities in India and abroad (c) to act as a nodal agency to bring buyers, sellers, exporters and importers together by undertaking export promotional activities (d) to source technologies for the Indian industry and trade. The main activity of the centre which has commenced operation in November, 1995, is to provide marketing services to Indian exporters and to strengthen their export effort to Europe from its strategic location in Rotterdam, the biggest port in Europe.

Indo-EU Economic Cross Cultural Programme (IECCP) A six year multi-dimensional cooperation project entitled Indo-EU Economic Cross Cultural Programme (IECCP) has been launched in November 1996, with EU financial assistance to the tune of Euro 30 million (roughly equivalent to US $40 million).

Activities to be implemented under the programme, centres around the three broad sectors viz., (i) media and communication (ii) university and studies and (iii) entrepreneurial dimensions. The programme aims to encourage and develop links between European and Indian cultural organisations/research centres/universities/professionals/decision makers/opinion formers and industry. It would raise the profile of European Union in India and vice-versa and strengthen a two way dynamic economic / cultural presence in the regions. Institutions/agencies doing work in these sectors have been called upon to propose suitable projects for being financed out of the above project funds.

The project would be advised and managed by a scientific committee consisting of three members each from India and EU and a management agency contracted by the EC. A total number of 29 projects have been approved for EU financing to the tune of Euro 9.45 million, after the first call for proposals.

Indo-EU partenariat The concept of Indo-EU Partenariat is a model cooperation project for enhancing industrial and business cooperation between India and EU. Under this, match-making between Indian and EUSMEs would be firmed up, benefitting both sides. Both India and EU are interested in the successful implementation of this project and its follow up, upto March 2000. Groundwork for this programme is already on, both in India and in EU.

The programme was inaugurated on 14th March, 1999 and the match-making exercises were held on 15th and 16th of March 1999. A high level steering committee under the chairmanship of the secretary, IPP has been constituted for the implementation of the Partenariat. The committee has the EU Ambassador in India and FICCI, ASSOCHAM and CII as its members. The total budget for the programme would come to Rs 5.36 crores, which is to be equally shared by both the sides. EU funding comes out of the Asia-Invest contributions.

The sectors to be covered by the Partenariat include:

- ★ Chemicals and Plastic Processing
- ★ Electronics and Information Technology (Hardware)
- ★ Environmental Technology
- ★ Food Processing and Packaging
- ★ Light Engineering
- ★ Software and Other Services

Asia-Invest An EU funded "Asia-Invest Programme" is under implementation for industry organisations and individual enterprises for seeking EU's financial grants. Two calls seeking proposals under this programme, have been issued so far.

India is an important partner country for implementation of this regional project, aimed at enhanced investment cooperation between the two regions. EU is providing Euro 45 million (roughly equivalent to US $ 50 million) as co-finance for implementation of the project, to facilitate direct cooperation between Small and Medium sized Enterprises (SMEs) of the two regions. Proposals could be submitted for market research/monitoring activities, tie up for possible cooperation projects, upgradiation of language and business culture, skills to conduct business in new markets, upgradation and adaptation of standards, etc. The priority sectors identified for funding are automotive, building machinery/equipments, processed foods, transport, environment, energy and service sector industries. Proposals need to be preferably supported by counterpart European companies or organisations. Different instruments under the Asia-Invest could be tapped by strategies, and also used to identify suitable cooperating partners. The programme would also provide information to make right decisions on partnerships, markets, investments, etc. Apex Organisations like FICCI, CII, SIDBI, NSIC etc. coordinate the participation of Indian SMEs in this programme.

COMMONWEALTH OF INDEPENDENT STATES AND BALTIC STATES (CIS & B)

The CIS region comprises of 15 independent nations namely, Russia, Armenia, Azerbaijan, Belarus, Georgia, Moldova, Ukraine, Kazakhstan, Kyrghyzstan, Tajikistan, Turkmenistan, Uzbekistan, Latvia, Lithuania and Estonia. Russia, Armenia, Azerbaijan, Belarus, Georgia, Moldova and Ukraine have been grouped under CIS. Kazakhstan, Kyrghyzstan, Tajikistan, and

Uzbekistan constitute the Central Asian Republics. Latvia, Lithuania and Estonia are the Baltic States. While Russia occupies an important position in India's foreign trade, the Central Asian Republics have been identified as a 'thrust area' for our trade.

Bilateral trade with these countries has been as under:

(Rs in Crores)

Years	*Export*	*Import*	*Total*	*Percentage Growth*
1993-94	2490	1200	3690	
1994-95	2830	2352	5182	(+)40.4
1995-96	3829	4091	7920	(+)52.8
1996-97	3238	2557	5995	(–)26.4
1997-98	3749	3293	7042	(+)17.4
1997-98 (Apr-Sep)	1462	1242	2704	
1998-99 (Apr-Sep)	1511	931	2442	(-)9

(Disaggregated data has been made available by DGCI&S) with effect from 1st April 1993)

Out of India's global exports and global imports, India's share of Exports and Imports to this Region during the year 1997-98 was, 3% and 2.2% respectively.

The principal commodities of our export to this region include tea, coffee, tobacco, cashew, leather, footwear of leather, drugs, pharmaceuticals, fine chemicals, spices (rice other than basmati), processed minerals, cosmetics and toiletries and cotton yarn, fabric, RMG and cotton including accessories. Pulp and waster paper, cotton raw and waste, metali-ferrous ores and metal scrap, organic chemicals, fertilizers, newsprint, iron and steel, non-ferrous metals, machinery except electricals and electronics, transport equipments, project goods, etc. are the important items of our import from this region.

Bilateral framework Agreements on Trade and Economic Cooperation have already been concluded with all the countries except with Azerbaijan. Negotiations are already on with Azerbaijan about signing the agreement. Mutual Most-Favoured-Nation (MFN) treatment is accorded in respect of trade with these countries.

Bilateral trade and economic cooperation between India and the CIS countries is kept under regular review through the bilateral Joint Commissions/Working Groups and Joint Business Councils.

RUSSIA

The Russian Federation which represents the major portion of the former USSR, continues to be India's most important economic partner in the region.

The bilateral framework Agreement on Trade and Economic Cooperation with Russian Federation, signed on 22nd May, 1992, provides that all transactions between the two countries would be undertaken in hard currency, unless otherwise specified by Intergovernmental Agreements. The only exception with Russia is that trade is also carried on through debt repayment route and escrow accounts. The bulk of our export to Russian Federation is moving through these routes.

During the year 1998-99, the following meetings have been held to discuss various matters regarding bilateral cooperation:-

(a) The Fifth session of the Indo-Russian Joint Commission for which, the Ministry of External Affairs is the nodal agency, was held in Moscow in November 1998.

(b) The Fifth meeting of the Working Group on TEC under the banner of Indo-Russian Joint Commission was held in November 1998, in Moscow.

(c) Under the aegis of the Indo-Russian IGC, the Third meeting of the Indo-Russian Working Group on pharmaceuticals was held at Moscow in November 1998.

(d) Under the aegis of the Indo-Russian Working Group on Financial Matters a meeting was held at New Delhi in November 1998, to sort out the various issues concerning finance and banking in the Indo-Russian bilateral trade.

(e) Under the aegis of the Indo-Russian Working Group on TEC, the Fifth Meeting of the Sub-group on Transport was held in Moscow in November 1998.

During the Fifth Session of the Indo-Russian Working Group on Trade and Economic Cooperation held in Moscow on 24 and 25th November 1998, both the sides had taken a frank and constructive approach to resolve the various issues, i.e. consignment sale, pending claims, opening of banks and broad basing the trade basket. In this connection, the addendum to the arrangements between Vneshecono bank and RBI, providing for consignment of exports under debt repayment route has been signed. The Joint Document on promotion of Trade, Economic, Industrial, Financial and S and T cooperation between Russia and India was also finalised. It was also agreed by both sides to take concrete steps is making long-term arrangements for expansion of trade.

UNITED STATES

US is India's largest trading partner accounting nearly for 20% of the country's exports and 10% of its imports. Thus, US plays a dominant role in India's trade. On the other hand, India accounts for only 0.6% of US's total exports and 0.8% of its Imports. The pattern of Trade since last few years has been as follows:

(Rs in crore)

Year	*Exports*	*Imports*	*Bilateral Trade*	*Balance of Trade*
1991-92	7201.69	4919.38	12121.07	(+)2282.31
1992.93	10106.07	6147.20	16253.27	(+)3958.87
1993.94	12543.88	8599.85	21143.73	(+)3944.03
1994-95	15764.32	9123.61	24887.93	(+)6640.71
1995-96	18465.66	12915.72	31381.38	(+)5549.94
1996-97	23271.68	13084.90	36356.58	(+)10186.78

1997-98	24640.68	13509.66	38150.34	(+)11131.20
1997-98 Apr-Aug 1997	9831.37	53454.44	15185.81	(+)4476.93
1998-99 Apr-Aug 1998	12602.36	5932.83	18535.19	(+)6669.53

The bilateral trade had been more or less stagnant in the 1980s, but increased significantly thereafter. During 1997-98, our exports to the US have registered a growth of about 6%, and imports have grown by about 3% between 1996-97. During April-August 1998, India's exports to US have grown up by 28% and the imports from US have grown up by 11%. India has been having a favourable balance of trade for the last one decade.

Composition of India's exports to US Composition of Indian exports to US over the years has undergone a significant change. The share of non-traditional items and value-added products which have increased India's exports to US in recent years, have risen mainly on account of significant increase in the exports of textiles and clothing, gems and jewellery, leather and leather products, engineering goods, computer items, etc. At present, major items of exports to US are textiles and apparels, diamonds, jewellery and precious stones, engineering goods, shrimps and prawns, cashewnuts, carpets, handicrafts, naphtha, dye stuffs, auto tyres, computer software. During 1997-98, gems and jewellery sector constituted the highest share of about 29% in our total exports to US, followed closely by textiles with 26% share. Other product groups have been Engineering Products (8.6%), carpets and handicrafts (6.9%), chemical products (6.7%) and agricultural products (6.7%). These six product groups contributed for more than 84% of our total exports to US.

Composition of India's imports from US As in the case of exports, the composition of imports from US have also undergone a change. The major items imported from US, at present, are fertilisers, aircrafts, turbo jets, aircraft parts, machinery parts, malt extracts, soya bean oil, automatic data processing machines, electronic goods, wood pulp, parts of railway locomotive, etc. During 1997-98, engineering products had a maximum share of about 47%. The share of chemical products is at about 24%.

Trade promotional activities India and US embarked on a renewed initiative in mutual economic cooperation, as a result of Indian Prime Minister's successful visit to US in May, 1994. In January, 1995, during the visit of the US Commerce Secretary, the Indo-US Commercial Alliance was launched initially for 2 years. The Alliance focuses on four sectors viz., agri-business, information technology, power and transportation and infrastructure. The Commercial Alliance has done notable work in the direction of improving trade and investment relations, particularly in the thrust sectors. The second and third joint board meetings of the alliance were held in New Delhi in March, 1996 and Washington DC in October, 1996 respectively. At the Washington DC meeting, the Board of the Alliance decided to extend the commercial alliance by another two years, upto January, 1999. During this meeting, the two sides resolved to include environment sector as another thrust area. It was also agreed to encourage participation of small and medium Enterprises. The Indo-US Economic and Commercial Sub-commission which was revived in 1995, met in Washington DC in December, 1996. The 19th meeting of the Indo-US Joint Business Council was also held in New Delhi in December, 1996.

CANADA

India's bilateral trade with Canada is not commensurate with the size and potential of the two countries. During 1997-98, Canada accounted for 1.23% of India's total exports and 1.05% of its total imports. The pattern of trade in the last few years has been given.

Indo-Canadian bilateral trade has been characterised by an adverse trade balance to India, except for the year, 1994-95 and 1996-97. However, our exports to Canada during the last few years have been growing significantly. During 1997-98, our exports to Canada grew by about 24% and the imports from Canada grew by about 43% over 1996-97. During April-August 1998, India's exports to Canada have grown up by 21%, whereas the imports from Canada have declined by about 8%, leaving the balance of trade in favour of India by Rs 137.82 Crores.

(Rs in Crores)

Year	*Exports*	*Imports*	*Bilateral Trade*	*Balance of Trade*
1991-92	464.79	690.40	1155.19	(–)225.61
1992-93	552.51	1138.23	1690.74	(–)585.72
1993-94	714.65	735.68	1450.33	(–)21.03
1994-95	837.79	833.50	1671.29	(+)4.29
1995-96	1021.68	1275.15	2296.83	(–)253.47
1996-97	1253.12	1112.44	2365.56	(+)140.68
1997-98	1548.88	1585.76	3134.64	(–)36.88
1997-98 (Apr-Aug 1997)	671.69	738.30	1409.99	(–)66.61
1998-99 (Apr-Aug 1998)	815.03	677.21	1492.24	(+)137.82

Composition of India's exports to Canada Major items of export to Canada include garments, textiles, yarns, carpets, leather goods, minerals, bulk drugs, chemicals and allied products, handicrafts, engineering products, gems and jewellery, coffee, spices, etc.

Product-wise export analysis of the year 1997-98 shows that, textile items constituted more than 57% of our total exports to Canada. Other significant product groups were engineering products (9%), agricultural products (9%), chemical products (8%) and gems and jewellery (7%). These five product groups constituted more than 89% of our total exports to Canada.

Composition of India's imports from Canada Major items of imports from Canada include rubber, paper, miscellaneous wooden products, pulses, crude minerals, leather, metal scraps, fertilisers, plastic material, newsprint, iron and steel, non-ferrous metals, project goods and electrical machinery.

During 1997-98, engineering products had a maximum share of about 33% in India's imports from Canada. The other items accounting for large shares are newsprint/journals (19%) and agricultural products (14%). These three products constituted about 66% of the total imports from Canada.

Banking institutions in both the countries are also providing institutional linkages for potential investors and traders. The State Bank of India has three branches in Canada (Toronto, Vancouver and Surrey). The Canadian Banks now present in India include, four branches of Bank of Nava Scotia (New Delhi, Mumbai, Coimbatore and Bangalore) and one branch of Toronto Dominion Bank (Mumbai).

INDO-LATIN AMERICAN BILATERAL TRADE

The Latin American and Carribbean (LAC) region, comprising 43 countries, accounts for about 5% of the world trade. India's share in the global trade of Latin America has traditionally been low. Distance, language barriers and inadequacy of information about business opportunities are some of the factors affecting trade.

Position from 1991-92 to 1997-98 In spite of various constraints, India's trade with the region grew rapidly between 1991-92 to 1997-98. Our trade with the region has increased from Rs 1,159 crores in 1991-92 to Rs 4,843 crores in 1997-98, an increase of about 31.8% in six years. Our exports increased from Rs 304 crores to Rs 2,654 crores, whereas our imports from the region increased from Rs 855 crores to Rs 2,189 crores during the same period.

Launching of New Programmes — "Focus: Lac"

Considering the potential that the Latin American and Caribbean region offers and India's insignificant presence in the region, an activity based integrated programme, namely "Focus: LAC - a programme for enhancing India's trade with Latin America" was formally launched by the Commerce Minister in November 1997, at a function held at ITPO, New Delhi. The programme is an integrated effort of the Government of India, Indian Trade Promotion Organisation, Export Promotion Councils, Chambers of Commerce and Industry and institutions such as EXIM Bank, ECGC, etc. The product groups, i.e. textiles, engineering products and chemical products, have been identified as the focus product groups of the programme. The significant aspects of the programme are as follows:

Special Import Licence (SIL) Earlier, 1% extra SIL was granted to export houses, trading houses, star trading houses and super star trading houses. Over and above, their entitlement for export of products to LAC region, provided exports to such countries were more than 10% of their total exports. This has been raised to 2% and the condition of 10% export criteria has been removed.

Textile quota policy The textile exports to certain Latin American countries have been accorded double weightage for the purpose of determining entitlements under the non-quota exports entitlements system in the Textiles Quota Policy.

Double weightage For the purpose of recognition to the export houses, trading houses, star trading houses and super star trading houses, double weightage shall be given on FOB or NFE basis on exports to the Latin American countries, provided such exports are made in freely convertible currency.

Support for sale tours Earlier, there was a provision for granting market development assistance to export houses etc., for two sales-cum-study tours and one additional tour to the Latin American region in a calendar year. The number of additional sales tours to the Latin American region has been increased to two. The condition of 5% increase in exports for a second tour will not be applicable.

Support for participation in fairs/exhibitions Earlier, there was a provision for granting market development assistance to export houses etc. for participation in three fairs/exhibitions abroad and one additional participation in fairs/exhibitions in the Latin American region in a calendar year. The additional participation in fairs in LAC region has been raised to two, and the condition of 5% increase in exports for the second participation will not be applicable.

Support for market surveys The EPCs would be given 80% support, instead of 60%, on the expenses incurred on market surveys conducted by them in the LAC Region.

ECGC cover Earlier, most of the Latin American countries had been put in "C" or "D" category for grant of ECGC cover. The grading has been revised for some of the countries.

Impact of "Focus: LAC" Programme

The implementation of the "Focus: LAC" has started showing results. It has renewed interest among the business communities of both the sides to enhance trade with each other. Our trade with the region has increased from Rs 3,807 crores in 1996-97 to Rs 4,843 crores in 1997-98 which is an increase of about 27%. During 1997-98, India's exports to the region at Rs 2,654 crores have shown a growth of more than 56%, whereas the imports from the region at Rs 2,189 crores have shown a growth of about 4% over the previous year. The balance of trade with the region, which has traditionally been adverse to India, has gone in favour of India for the first time during 1997-98.

India's trade with the Region during last few years has been as follows:

(Rs in Crores)

Year	*Exports*	*Imports*	*Total Trade*	*Balance of Trade*
1991-92	304.41	854.63	1159.04	(–)550.22
1992-93	480.44	915.84	1396.28	(–)435.40
1993-94	757.58	1001.04	1758.62	(–)248.46
1994-95	1125.48	2449.73	3575.21	(–)1324.25

1995-96	1231.19	1981.48	3212.67	(–)750.29
1996-97	1699.53	2107.68	3807.21	(–)408.15
1997-98	2653.75	2188.93	4842.68	(+)464.82
1997-98(Apr-Aug 97)	878.33	791.45	1669.78	(+)86.88
1998-99(Apr-Aug 98)	1101.23	969.95	2071.18	(+)131.28

During April-August 1998, India's exports to the region have grown by about 25% and the imports from the region have grown by about 23%. The balance of trade remained in favour of India by Rs 131.28 crores.

Major exports and imports and important markets in the region India's major exports to the region are textiles and readymade garments, engineering goods such as bicycles and their components, automotive components, hand tools, tyres and tubes, chemicals and allied items. India's major imports from the Region are iron and steel and their products, non-ferrous metals, crude minerals, chemicals, PVC products, pulp and paper waste, raw wool, etc.

The major nine countries accounting for nearly 93% of Indian exports to the region are Chile, Brazil, Mexico, Argentina, Panama, Columbia, Venezuela, Peru and Trinidad and Tobago, out of which four countries, viz., Chile, Brazil, Mexico and Argentina, account for about 70% of our exports to the region.

Activities of 1998-99

1. A comprehensive Action Plan for 1998-99 including various activities, viz., participation in trade fairs/exhibitions, organisation of buyer-seller meets, market surveys, sales-tours, etc., has been prepared under the "Focus: LAC" programme in consultation with the EPCs and Apex Chambers for promotion of Exports to its Latin American Regions.
2. An Interministerial Advisory Committee on Trade with Latin America has been set up to review the progress of implementation of the "Focus: LAC" programme and to advise future strategy in order to sustain and intensify the momentum already gained.
3. The Indian Trade Promotion Organisation (ITPO) in consultation with the Ministry of Commerce has decided to institute the following seven Export Awards for 1998-99, for promoting India's exports to Latin American countries:
   - ★ One award for overall highest exports by any Indian company to the Latin American region
   - ★ Five individual awards for the exporting companies which achieve the highest Export turnover in each of the following categories
     - (a) Agricultural, Allied and Plantation Products
     - (b) Textiles, Textile Products, Leather and Leather Manufactures
     - (c) Engineering, Metallurgical and Electronic Products
     - (d) Chemical and Allied Products
     - (e) All Other Manufacturers, Minerals and Ores
   - ★ One special award for innovative marketing efforts

4. Guidelines have been issued that from 1998-99 onwards, a minimum of 10% of Market Development Assistance (MDA) grant shall be spent by Export Promotion Councils (EPCs) and FIEO for export efforts to the Latin American region.
5. The India-Latin America Interest Group has been set up under the aegis of FICCI to explore strategies and discuss possibilities for enhancing trade relations between India and Latin America. The first meeting of the group was held in July 1997, which was also addressed by the Commerce Secretary.
6. An exclusive Committee on Latin America has been set up under the aegis of CII, with the view of enhancing trade with the Latin American region.
7. Separate funds would be earmarked under the India Brand Equity Fund to finance industry specification promotion programmes in the Latin American region.
8. Separate delegations would be sent by the Ministry of Commerce, FIEO, FICCI and CII to the countries of Latin America during 1998-99 for promotion of trade with the region.

BILATERAL TRADE BETWEEN INDIA AND WEST ASIA AND NORTH AFRICA (WANA)

West Asia and North Africa (WANA) region comprises of 19 countries, divided into three groups namely, (i) 6 GCC countries (Bahrain, Kuwait, Oman, Qatar, Saudi Arabia, UAE) (ii) 7 West Asian countries (Iraq, Iran, Israel, Jordan, Lebanon, Yemen, Syria) and (iii) 6 North African countries (Algeria, Egypt, Libya, Morocco, Sudan, Tunisia). The WANA region occupies an important position in India's foreign trade.

India's trade with the countries in this region is conducted in free foreign exchange. Mutual Most-Favoured-Nation (MFN) treatment is accorded in respect to trade with most of these countries. Some of these countries, particularly Gulf countries, have largely free economies, while in countries like Iraq, Libya, Jordan, Morocco and Syria, imports are regulated by state-owned organisations, to differing extents.

Our principle export products to this region are tea, spices, fruits and vegetables, tobacco meat, oil-cakes, chemicals, drugs and pharmaceuticals, engineering goods and textiles. On account of large imports of our essential requirements of crude oil, POL products and fertilisers, there is a large adverse balance of trade with the region as a whole.

During 1997-98, India's exports to WANA region showed an increase of 17.7% over 1996-97. In absolute terms, our exports increased from Rs 11,874 crores in 1996-97 to Rs 13,975 crores in 1997-98. On the import side, the increase was not significant in 1997-98 when compared to 1996-97. In absolute terms, our imports from WANA region countries increased from Rs 35,086 crores in 1996-97 to Rs 35,262 crores in 1997-98.

The growth in exports was the result of various export promotion efforts undertaken both at the government and at the business level. In short, our total trade with WANA region registered a growth of 5% during 1997-98, as compared to 1996-97. UAE and Saudi Arabia are our largest trading partners in the WANA regions. While UAE accounted for about 42% of our total exports and 18% of our total imports in the WANA region, Saudi Arabia's share was 18% of our exports and 27% of our imports in this region.

The upward trend in exports has continued in the first half of 1998-99 too. A perusal of trade figures for 1998-99 (April-September) shows that India's exports to WANA region countries, have increased by 33% in rupee terms and 15% in dollar terms, when compared with the corresponding period of previous year 1997-98. In absolute terms, the figures stand at Rs 5,967 crores and Rs 7,917 crores during April-September periods of 1997-98 and 1998-99 respectively. The Gulf region continues to occupy the top position in the whole region, with UAE and Saudi Arabia being the top two destinations of Indian exports in the region. However, the imports, during the same period, have shown a declining trend, depicting a negative growth of (–) 9% in rupee terms and (–)21% in dollar terms. This development is interesting to note vis-vis India's global exports and imports both of which have shown positive growth of 13% and 28% respectively, during the first six months of the current financial year 1998-99.

In recent years, Dubai has rapidly emerged as a major entrepot. India's exports invoiced to Dubai, find their destination in a multitude of markets in the Gulf, Iran, Central Asian Republics, Russia and North East Africa. Similarly, India has become, after Iran, the second largest destination of re-exports from Dubai. Our trade and economic linkages with UAE in general, and Dubai in particular, have commanded a special focus in our cooperation effects.

Prior to the Iran-Iraq war, India and Iraq had diversified on intensive trade relations. However, the Iran-Iraq War, followed by the Gulf crisis of 1990 and consequent imposition of UN sanctions against Iraq, have almost halted the trade flow between India and Iraq. Only essential items like food, medicines, etc. are permissible for export from India to Iraq, with the approval of the UN Sanctions Committee. As a special measure on humanitarian ground, UNO launched the "Oil for Food" programme. Currently, the fifth phase of the "Oil for Food" programme for 6 months is in operation which has commenced from 25th November 1998. Under this programme, Indian companies have bagged export orders worth about US $ 50 million for various items which includes tea, pharmaceuticals, poly propylene bags, school/ stationery items, etc.

The first Joint Business Council (JBC) meeting between India and Iran, under the aegis of Federation of Indian Chambers of Commerce and Industry (FICCI) and the Chambers of Commerce, Industry and Mines from Iranian side, was held in Tehran in May 1998. The two sides identified new areas of cooperation such as computer software, power sector, agro products, etc.

India's export growth to WANA region which increased by 18% has become possible, due to the joint efforts put in by our Ministry, our missions abroad and the private sector. With our relentless efforts, India's bilateral trade with these countries is poised to grow further.

Africa

Sub-Saharan Africa consists of 51 countries. However, South Africa, Kenya, Mauritius, Nigeria, Tanzania, Uganda, Ethiopia, Ghana and Senegal are the largest trading partners of India, in the sub-Saharan African region. Mutual Most-Favoured-Nation treatment is accorded in respect of trade, to most sub-Saharan African countries.

India's principal export products to this region are rice (other than basmati), transport equipments, machines and instruments, cotton manufacturers, drugs and pharmaceuticals, fine chemicals, allied products and iron and steel manufactures.

During 1997-98, India's exports to the sub-Saharan Africa region, showed an increase of 15.76% over 1996-97. In absolute terms, Indian exports increased from Rs 4,787.66 crores during 1996-97 to Rs 5,542.21 crores during 1997-98. On the import side, the decrease is about 1.84% in 1997-98 as compared to 1996-97. In absolute terms, Indian imports from the sub-Saharan African region decreased from Rs 8,063.04 crores during 1996-97 to Rs 7,914.55 crores during 1997-98.

With a view to boost trade relations with the various countries in the sub-Saharan region India has already signed trade agreements with 17 sub-Saharan African countries, which includes Cameroon, Senegal, Zambia, Kenya, Zimbabwe, Ghana, Mozambique, Liberia, Uganda, Nigeria, Angola, Rwanda, Ivory Coast, South Africa, Bourkina Faso, Namibia and Ethiopia. During 1998-99, a formal trade agreement between India and Seychelles, was signed on 18th September, 1998. The draft trade agreements with Gambia and Swaziland, have been approved by the Government of India and the Governments of Gambia and Swaziland.

A major industrial technology exhibition, "India Tech '98" jointly organised by Engineering Export Promotion Council, Electronics and Software Export Promotion Council and Department of Telecommunications was held in Nairobi (Kenya) from September 1–4, 1998. It covered four sectors: engineering, electronics, telecommunications and computer software. Fifty-seven Indian companies including HMT, TATA, ITI, Maruti, TCIL, Eicher, SIDBI, Exim Bank, MTNI, etc. took part from India. Inquiries worth US $10 million were generated. Exim Bank and the Industrial Development Bank of Kenya signed an agreement on a new line of credit worth US $4.5 million.

A statement containing trade data for 1997-98, actual bilateral trade statistics from April-September 1998, and also for the period January-December 1998 (on pro-rata basis) is given below:

India's Trade with Sub-Saharan African Countries

Sl. No	Country	Export-Import 1997-98		Export-Import Apr-Sep 98		Export-Import Apr-Dec 98 (On Pro-rata basis)	
1.	Angola	39.95	0.00	26.83	0.00	40.24	0.00
2.	Benin	72.58	44.56	34.64	47.72	51.96	71.57
3.	Botswana	10.88	0.00	4.46	0.00	6.69	0.00
4.	Burundi	5.75	0.00	2.14	0.00	3.21	0.00
5.	Burkina Faso	3.39	0.20	4.74	7.34	7.11	11.01
6.	Cameroon	24.83	62.11	18.09	17.20	27.14	25.80
7.	Canary Is.	74.74	0.00	22.73	0.00	31.10	0.00
8.	Cape Verde Is.	0.08	0.00	0.32	0.00	0.48	0.00
9.	Cen. Atr. Rep.	1.40	0.00	1.49	0.00	2.24	0.00
10.	Chad	30.00	0.90	5.63	0.00	8.45	0.00
11.	Comoros Is.	4.24	2.78	11.42	0.00	17.13	0.00
12.	Congo	53.13	22.91	51.67	9.47	77.51	14.21
13.	Djibouti	33.36	0.69	28.37	0.05	42.56	0.08
14.	Ethiopia	244.93	2.43	163.36	1.26	245.04	1.89
15.	Equitorial Guin	0.38	0.53	0.01	0.00	0.02	0.00
16.	Gabon	12.47	39.69	8.00	9.13	12.00	13.70
17.	Gambia	56.27	0.00	25.65	0.00	38.48	0.00
18.	Ghana	179.47	220.51	111.27	9.85	166.91	14.77
19.	Guinea	23.79	0.21	15.14	0.12	22.71	0.18
20.	Guinea Bissau	4.01	127.22	3.31	57.14	4.97	85.71
21.	Ivory Coast	47.08	187.11	184.92	95.37	277.38	143.06
22.	Kenya	449.72	78.44	290.35	47.02	435.53	70.53
23.	Lesotho	0.59	0.00	0.23	0.00	0.35	0.00
24.	Liberia	11.40	13.95	5.43	0.00	8.15	0.00
25.	Madagascar	26.96	11.70	18.44	8.61	27.66	12.92
26.	Malawi	25.54	1.28	25.41	0.00	38.12	0.00
27.	Mali	56.24	7.39	85.88	0.00	128.82	0.00
28.	Mauritius	664.15	22.76	320.40	4.54	480.60	6.81
29.	Mauritania	12.92	0.52	10.34	0.00	15.51	0.00
30.	Mozambique	111.29	49.63	38.56	35.81	57.84	53.72
31.	Niger	20.39	0.30	29.10	0.00	43.65	0.00
32.	Migeria	794.23	4151.00	423.78	2078.56	635.67	3117.84
33.	Namibia	6.16	0.21	6.03	0.04	9.05	0.06
34.	Reunion	7.09	0.00	5.93	0.00	8.90	0.00
35.	Rwanda	25.35	0.00	7.91	0.37	11.87	0.56
36.	Sao Thome and Pri	1.20	0.00	0.11	0.00	0.17	0.00
37.	Senegal	107.38	177.83	96.80	200.16	145.20	300.24
38.	Seychelles	22.32	0.00	29.27	0.00	43.91	0.00
39.	Sierra Leone	4.64	0.00	2.41	0.00	3.62	0.00
40.	Somalia	74.62	6.53	66.07	1.78	99.10	2.67
41.	Soma	0.00	0.00	0.00	0.00	0.00	0.00
42.	South Africa	1426.81	1794.01	796.76	2331.37	1195.14	3497.06
43.	Spanish Sahara	0.00	0.00	0.00	0.00	0.00	0.00
44.	St. Helena	1.41	0.15	0.70	0.00	1.05	0.00
45.	Swaziland	3.62	66.37	1.87	0.10	2.81	0.15
46.	Tanzania	247.77	247.17	154.21	83.53	231.32	125.30
47.	Togoland	103.10	18.50	33.47	2.23	50.21	3.35

48. Uganda	159.11	1.28	94.05	0.25	141.07	0.38
49. Zaire	82.72	127.71	24.60	24.49	36.90	36.74
50. Zambia	86.80	357.83	35.52	133.00	53.28	199.50
51. Zimbabwe	85.95	68.14	41.17	30.61	61.76	45.92
Total	5542.21	7914.55	3368.99	5237.12	5053.48	7855.67

INTERNATIONAL TRADE CONFERENCES

The Economic and Social Commission for Asia and the Pacific (ESCAP)

The Economic and Social Commission for Asia and the Pacific (ESCAP) is the regional arm of the United Nations dealing with economic and social development of the Asia-Pacific region. India is one of its founding members. The main activities of ESCAP include evolution and execution of projects in the socio-economic fields, for improving national capabilities to deliver effective social services and develop requisite infrastructural and environmental capabilities.

ESCAP's major work during the year is focused on:

(a) Regional Economic Cooperation
(b) Poverty Alleviation through Economic Growth and Social Development
(c) Environment and Sustainable Development
(d) Development of Transport and Communications in the region
(e) Enhancing capabilities of National Statistical Organisations.

The 54th Annual Session of the Economic and Social Commission for Asia and the Pacific which was held at Bangkok during 16th to 22nd April, 1998, deliberated on the theme topic "Asia and Pacific into the Twenty-first Century: Prospects for Social Development." Issues relating to South-East Asian financial crisis, regional economic cooperation, pro-active trade agenda for 2000 and beyond, regional cooperation on environment and sustainable development, transport and tourism, infrastructure, rural poverty alleviation, etc. were discussed.

The Commission endorsed India's suggestions on:-

(i) Preparation of a proactive positive agenda for future trade negotiations under the WTO
(ii) Priority consideration for routing of Trans-Asian Railway southern corridor linkages through the North-Eastern Sector of India
(iii) Hosting of the second Ministerial conference on Space Applications in New Delhi, in 1999

India also cosponsored five resolutions on enhancing social developments in the region which were adopted during the above session.

During the year 1998-99 (till November 1998), the Government of India was represented in many important ESCAP Intergovernmental Meetings.

Apart from the Intergovernmental Meetings, the Government of India representatives and exporters participated in various other activities of ESCAP, such as expert group meetings, workshops, seminars, trainings, etc., organised by the ESCAP Secretariat in Bangkok and other places. India worked in close cooperation with ESCAP during the year, with active participation in various projects/activities and meetings.

Under the New Delhi Action Plan (NDAP), ESCAP had identified 64 projects for implementation. During the 53rd Annual Session of ESCAP held in April 1997, 20 projects were prioritised, (15 as top priority projects and 5 as top most priority projects) for implementation in India. One of these projects of interest to India is the Asian Land Transport Infrastructure Development Project (ALTID).

This project has three components:

(a) Asian Highway Project
(b) Trans-Asian Railway Project
(c) Accession to Seven International Conventions on Land Transport Facilitation.

To evaluate the progress in the implementation of the ESCAP sponsored programmes/initiatives, a National Coordination Committee (NCC) has been set up under the Chairmanship of the Commerce Secretary. The Committee is being assisted by four Technical Working Groups, one in the Ministry of Commerce to oversee the implementation of NDAP and the other three on (i) Asian Highway Project and Asian Infrastructure Development Alliance (ii) Trans-Asian Railway Project (iii) Accession to Seven International Conventions on Land Transport Facilitation in the Ministries of Surface Transport, Railways and Department of Revenue respectively. The National Coordination Committee in its first meeting held during April 1998, evaluated the progress in the implementation of various ESCAP sponsored programmes.

ESCAP had during its 54th Annual Session, agreed that the issues of connectivity with Myanmar through the North-Eastern region of India as part of the TAR southern corridor, should also be given priority. For this purpose a national consultant who had been nominated on an export group set up by ESCAP to study the potential TAR linkages. He has submitted his report to the ESCAP Secretariat suggesting three TAR routes which have been proposed to traverse the North-Eastern region of India.

The 55th annual session of ESCAP was held in Bangkok in April, 1999. The commission focussed its deliberations on implications of recent Economic and social developments in the region. The theme topic for this Session was "Asia and the Pacific into the Twenty-first Century: Information Technology, Globalisation, Economic Security and Development."

WORLD TRADE ORGANISATION

Organisational Structure

The World Trade Organisation (WTO) is the successor organisation to the GATT. It came into effect on 1.1.1995 after the conclusion of the Uruguay Round of Multilateral Trade Negotiations. India was a founder member of both GATT, in 1947, and the WTO in 1995. As on 31st August 1998, the membership of the WTO stood at 132. The mandate of the WTO covers Trade in Goods, Trade in Services, Trade-related Investment Measures and Trade-related Intellectual Property Rights (TRIPS).

The WTO is headed by a Ministerial Conference consisting of the Trade Ministers of all the members. This is the highest policy making body of the WTO and is required to meet once every two years. In the interregnum, its functions are carried out by the General Council, consisting of the representatives of all the members. The General Council is assisted in its work by three Sectoral Councils, viz, (i) the Council for Trade in Goods (ii) The Council for Trade in Services (iii) and the Council for Trade Related Aspects of Intellectual Property Rights (TRIPs) and by large number of Committees, Working Groups/ Parties and other bodies dealing with specific agreements or subjects. All these bodies are serviced by the Secretariat headed by the Director General of the WTO. In addition to such functions as may be assigned to the General Council under various agreements, the General Council also acts as the Dispute Settlement Body (DSB).

Trade in Services

The General Agreement on Trade in Services (GATS), negotiated during the Uruguay Round, is the first set of multilaterally agreed and legally enforceable rules and disciplines ever negotiated to cover international trade in service to oversee the operation of the agreement.

The negotiations on basic telecommunications were resumed after the Singapore Ministerial Conference and were concluded on 15th February, 1997. The negotiations resulted in the tabling of 55 offers, covering 69 participating governments and submission of MFN exemption lists by 9 participating governments. This represented a substantial improvement over the April 1996 results, which produced 34 offers covering 48 governments. India also participated in these negotiations and filed a schedule of specific commitments and list of MFN exemptions.

As decided in the Singapore Ministerial Conference, the financial services negotiations resumed in Geneva from 10th April 1997 and were concluded on 12th December 1997. During the current round of negotiations, 56 offers representing 70 countries were filed. India also filed an improved offer during these negotiations. India withdrew MFN exemptions relating to banking services and other financial services, including insurance. In case of foreign bank branches, the annual limit per year (both for new entrants and existing banks) has been increased from 8 to 12.

The Working Party on Professional Services finalised guidelines for Mutual Recognition Agreements of Arrangements in the accountancy sector, on 15th May 1997. The objective of these guidelines, is to make it easier for the parties to negotiate Recognition Agreements and for third parties to negotiate their accession to such agreements or to negotiate comparable ones. The Working Party is presently involved in the process of finalising the multilateral disciplines on domestic regulation in the accountancy sector, to ensure that domestic regulatory requirements are based on objective and transparent criteria and are not more burdensome than necessary.

The Working Party on GATS rules is working on the following areas:-

(i) Negotiations on Safeguards under Article X of GATS
(ii) Negotiations on Subsidies under Article XV of GATS
(iii) Negotiations on Government Procurement under Article XIII of GATS

The Working Party has taken the work relating to negotiations on safeguards under Article X of GATS as its priority work. These negotiations were scheduled to be completed before the end of the year (1997), deadline as specified in Article X of GATS. As it was not possible to conclude the negotiations by the specified target date, the deadline for conclusion of these negotiations had been extended till the end of June, 1999.

Article XIX of GATS stipulates that members shall enter into successive rounds of negotiations, beginning not later than five years from the date in which the WTO agreement comes into force and periodically thereafter, with a view to achieve a progressively higher level of liberalisation. Thus the deadline for the next round for service negotiations is 01.01.2000. In the Singapore Ministerial Declaration, the Ministers agreed to a process of analysis and exchange of information in the Service sector, to better understand the issues involved and identify their interest before commencing the negotiations in the years 2000. The Geneva Ministerial Conference has merely reiterated the decisions taken at the SMC.

It is in this perspective that the Information Exchange Programme (IEP) has been started in the Council for Trade in Services (CTS) as a preparatory work to the forthcoming negotiations. Under this, individual sectors as per the sectoral classification followed in the WTO, are being taken up for detailed discussion in the CTS.

A number of meetings of the CTS have been held so far. India has been highlighting certain general points regarding the IEP.

(a) IEP should cover all the services sectors to the extent feasible. This has largely been followed.

(b) The WTO Secretariat should be actively involved in this exercise.

(c) The developing countries have specific interests in movement of natural persons, i.e. mode 4 delivery of Services. India's position has been that, apart from sectors, modes of delivery must be an integral part of the IEP.

India has repeatedly held that the developed countries had not provided adequate market access in the area of movement of natural persons. Whatever specific commitments have been undertaken by the developing countries have not been of great benefit to the developed countries. The system needs to be corrected.

(d) IEP should not pre-judge the scope of future negotiations. However, at the same time availability of relevant information would be essential, for undertaking preparatory work in connection with these negotiations.

(e) India has reiterated that there is a need to analyse the impact of the existing liberalisation in the services on developing countries, especially in the sectors where further negotiations have taken place since the Uruguay Round like Financial services and Basic telecommunications.

Dispute Settlement Body

The state of play of the Dispute Settlement Body reveals that, the WTO received over two hundred trade disputes for resolution in just a little more than four years of its existence, that is over 55 (fifty-five) disputes a year, in contrast to about six disputes a year under WTO's predecessor, the GATT 1947. The record so far would suggest, that about twenty five percent of the disputes are resolved by the parties themselves at the initial, consultations stage, and that the appellate procedure is being used with respect to all panel reports issued so far for a final ruling.

India has filed eight complaints and has been the subject of twelve complaints. In respect to India's dispute with Poland on the import regime of Poland for automobiles, a bilateral solution was reached in July, 1996. Similarly the dispute between India and the United States of America on the import restrictions introduced by the United States of America on imports from India of women's and girl's wool coats, was resolved with the removal of these measures by US in April, 1996. Following the adoption by the Dispute Settlement Body in May 1997, that the safeguard measures imposed by US on imports from India of woven wool shirts and blouses violated the provisions of the WTO agreement of textiles of clothing, and so US removed this measure thereby concluding this dispute between India and US. The dispute between India and Turkey with regards to the restrictions on imports by Turkey on Textiles and clothing products, is underway. Regarding the dispute between India (along with Malaysia, Thailand and Pakistan) and US regarding the prohibition on import by US of certain shrimp and other shrimp products from India and other countries mentioned above, the Dispute Settlement Panel as well as the Appellate Body of the WTO have made a ruling against the US in favour of India and the other complainants.

US and the European Community, in separate requests, have alleged that India's patent protection for pharmaceutical and agricultural chemical products is inconsistent with India's obligations under the Agreement on TRIPS. As regards the dispute raised by the US, India had filed an appeal against the ruling of the panel to the Appellate Body. The Appellate Body upheld the major findings of the panel. The panel report, as modified by the Appellate Body Report have been adopted by the Dispute Settlement Body of the WTO. It has now been mutually agreed between India and the US that India will implement the DSB decision by 19th April, 1999. In respect of the complaint by the EC, the panel has made a similar ruling as in the case of India's dispute with US on patents.

In the matter of six separate disputes initiated against India by Australia, Canada, the EC, New Zealand, Switzerland and US, as regards the Quantitative Restrictions on imports maintained by India for balance of payments purpose, mutually agreed solutions were reached with Australia, Canada, the EC, New Zealand and Switzerland in November, 1997 and with Japan also which was a third party in these disputes. Since no mutually agreed solution could be reached with the US, on the basis of a request by the US, a Dispute Settlement Panel was established to examine the US allegation that the continued maintenance of Quantitative Restrictions on imports for balance of payments purpose by India is inconsistent with India's obligations under the WTO Agreement. The panel has sent its interim report and the final report will be made available shortly. In November, 1997, the EC has also initiated Dispute Settlement proceedings against India as regards the negative list for the export of several commodities and in particular raw hides and skins, in India's Exim Policy (1997-2002), alleging that the restrictions violate the obligation of India under GATT 1994. The first round of consultation has taken place. The EC requested proceedings against India regarding India's Auto Policy, India's Import Restrictions under Article XX and XXI of GATT and India's measures affecting customs duties—Special Additional Duties (SAD). The first round of consultation with the EC, with regard to all the three disputes has been held recently in Geneva.

Safeguard Measures

The Agreement on Safeguards permits restrictions on import for a temporary period, by either increasing tariffs or imposing QRs (Quantitative Restrictions). Safeguard action can be taken only when it is established by a properly conducted investigation, that there is a sudden increase in imposed Quantitative Restrictions (both absolute and relative to domestic production) which has caused or threatens to cause serious injury to the domestic Industry.

Safeguard measures are designed basically to give preparatory time to the domestic Industry, to adjust and to prepare for increased competition impending removal of such temporary restrictions on import of a particular product.

Under Indian Customs Tariff Act, 1975, a new Section 8B was introduced by Finance Act, 1997, giving power to Central Government to impose the Safeguard Duty. The duty chargeable under this section is in addition to any other duty imposed under this act or under any other law which is in force at that time.

India has imposed Safeguard Duty on import of acetylene black (including conductive carbons), propylene glycol and flexible slabstock foam of molecular weight 3000-4000.

(i) The rate of Safeguard Duty on import of acetylene black (including conductive carbons) as imposed is (a) 18% subject to a maximum of Rs 12,950 PMT, when imported upto and inclusive of 9th day of December, 1999 and (b) 5% subject to a maximum of Rs 8,830 PMT when imported from 10th December 1999 to 9th December 2000 (both days inclusive).

(ii) The rate of Safeguard Duty on Propylene Glycol as imposed is 16% when imported upto and inclusive of 23rd day of December, 1999 and 11% when imported from 24th of December, 1999 and 23rd of day of June, 2000 (both days inclusive).

(iii) On flexible slabstock foam the rate of Safeguard Duty is 20% when imported upto and inclusive of 23rd day of December, 1999 and 5%

when imported from 24th day of December, 1999 and 23rd day of June, 2000 (both days inclusive).

Trade-related Aspects of Intellectual Property Rights (TRIPS)

The Council of Trade Related Aspects of Intellectual Property Rights (TRIPs) has held several meetings during the years 1997-98, to review Intellectual Property Rights laws of the developed countries and their enforcement. India has actively participated in these meetings and asked questions on these laws to understand their implications for India's trade interests. Separately, India is also in the process of examining the need for updating or amending India's Intellectual Property Rights Laws to meet its obligations under the agreement. The Indian Copyright Law already meets the TRIPs standards. For examining the need for updating or amending the other laws, the Ministry of Industry has constituted an Inter-Ministerial Committee. The committee, through its sub-groups, is examining the existing laws with a view to recommend whether any changes are required in them to meet India's obligations under the TRIPs agreement. A bill proposing some limited amendments to the Indian Patents Act 1970, has been passed in the Rajya Sabha in December, 1998. These amendments provide for filing of applications for patents on inventions which are not patentable under the law at present and for grant of exclusive marketing rights, subject to certain conditions providing safeguards in public interest. The Ministry of Commerce is separately processing a draft bill for enacting a law on protection of geographical indications. This bill, when enacted, would protect India's export products with geographical indications such as Darjeeling tea and basmati rice. Currently such marks can be protected as certification under common law, under passing off action.

Technical Barriers to Trade (TBT)

The WTO Agreement on Technical Barriers to Trade held its first triennial review of the implementation of the agreement during the year 1997. The triennial review has recommended, inter-alia, that the provisions relating to technical assistance and special and differential treatment for developing countries should be more effectively implemented and has drawn-up a plan for this purpose. The plan would be implemented in the next three years and the progress reviewed in the next triennial review, in the year 2000. In 1998, the Bureau of Indian Standards (BIS) presented a paper on country experience in the Committee of Technical Barriers to Trade, on implementing voluntary Quality Standards.

Investment and Competition Policy

Taking into account the existing WTO provisions on matters related to investment and competition policy and the built-in agenda in these areas included under the TRIMS Agreement and on the understanding that the work undertaken shall not pre-judge whether negotiations will be initiated in the future, the SMC agreed to establish a Working Group to study issues relating to the interaction between trade and competition policy, including anticompetitive practices, in order to identify any areas that may merit further consideration in the WTO framework. Both the Working Groups have drawn up check lists of issues to be discussed. Some of the issues in these check lists have been discussed extensively and papers have been submitted by various WTO Members, including India, on these issues. In addition, International Intergovernmental Organisations like UNCTAD, OECD, IMF and the World Bank have also given their contributions to this educative process. While this educative process is continuing in the WTO Working Groups, an expert group was set up to study on both the Trade in Investment and Trade in Competition Policy in depth and to give a report to the government, along with recommendations on the stand that should be taken by India in the WTO to defend the national interest. The reports of the expert group on Trade and Investment has been received, while that of the expert Group on Trade and Competition Policy is awaited.

Geneva Ministerial Conference of the WTO and Later Developments

The second Ministerial Conference of the World Trade Organisations (WTO) was held in Geneva between 18-20 May 1998. The conference concluded with the adoption of the Ministerial Declaration and a Declaration on Electronic Commerce on 20th May, 1998. India's concerns relating to the Multilateral Trading System as reflected through the statements of our Commerce Minister, are adequately reflected in the Ministerial Declaration and the Declaration on Electronic Commerce.

On further work in the WTO, based on the built-in agenda, India emphasised the need for improved market access to professionals from developing countries, for removal of non-tariff barriers provided under the TRIPs Agreement for higher level of protection available currently only to wines and spirits, to also extend to products of developing countries, like basmati rice, and for equitable sharing of benefits reaped from Intellectual Property protection, for products based on indigenous knowledge and biodiversity of developing countries. The need to transfer environmentally sound technologies and products, in specific cases at fair and reasonable terms to developing countries was also stressed.

The conference endorsed India's view that existing agreements arising out of the Uruguay Round should be effectively implemented, so as to ensure that the benefits of the Multilateral Trading System flow to all countries, especially developing countries like India. The Ministerial Declaration clearly and unambiguously states that 'Full and faithful implementation of the WTO Agreement and Ministerial Decisions is imperative for the credibility of the Multilateral Trading System and indispensable for maintaining the momentum for expanding global trade, fostering job creation and raising standards of living in all parts of the world'.

In a separate Declaration on Electronic Commerce, the Ministerial Conference has agreed on the need for a work programme on this important subject.

The Geneva Ministerial Conference (which was the second Ministerial Conference of WTO Trade Ministers) decided to initiate a process in the General Council, to discuss and deliberate on various multilateral trade issues raised by members. The objective of the process is to make recommendations on these issues to the next Ministerial Conference, "Fully respecting the principles of decision making by consensus". The recommendations to be made will include implementation issues, issues in the built-in-agenda, possible future work on the basis of the work programme initiated at Singapore, follow-up to the high-level meeting on least developed countries and other matters proposed and agreed to by members concerning their Multilateral Trade Relations.

Interaction with Industry

Trade policy division of the Ministry of Commerce, in formulating its stance on various WTO issues, especially those being brought up before the General Council in the process leading up to the next Ministerial Conference, has been in close touch with industry associations, expert bodies and concerned Ministries. On the basis of the consultations held, 13 issue papers prepared by the Ministry were presented by India in different WTO forum.

The major industry associations involved in consultations include the CII, FICCI, ASSOCHAM, PHDCCI and FIEO. As many as eleven meetings have been held with them during April to December, 1998. Concerned industry associations have been consulted before taking major decisions, such as joining the Information Technology Agreement. The professional Institutes such as ICAI and ICWAI have also been consulted and fully involved in matters relating to professional services.

Interaction with Academic Institutions and Experts

Studies have been entrusted to RIS (Research in Information Systems for Non-aligned Countries), ICIER (Indian Council for International Economic Relations) and NCAER (National Council of Applied Economic Research) and the Rajiv Gandhi Centre for Contemporary Studies on a range of issues, including the positions to be developed for mandated negotiations stated under the Agreement on Agriculture and that on Services in the year 2000, on the "new" subject of electronic commerce, on reviewing the Agreement on Technical Barriers to Trade, on examining the post-Uruguay Round structure of industrial tariffs and the question of adequacy of our BOP position in the context of Article XVIII:B of GATT. A proposal for setting up an independent Centre for Trade issues under the IIFT has been approved by the government. Recognising the need for developing legal expertise or Multination Trade Laws within the country, the Ministry of Commerce has created a corpus fund in the National Law School of India University, Bangalore, for instituting a new chair in International Trade Law and Negotiations. The National Law School is not only assisting the Ministry in legal aspects relating to negotiations, but will over a period of time, produce a generation of young lawyers with sound expertise in Multilateral Trade Law. This will greatly enhance our negotiating capacity and skills in the years to come.

Global System of Trade Preferences (GSTP) Among Developing Countries

The Agreement establishing the Global System of Trade Preferences (GSTP) among the developing countries was signed on 13th April 1988 at Belgrade, following conclusion of the first round of negotiations. The Agreement was signed by 48 countries which exchanged concessions in the course of that round. The Agreement came into force on 19th April 1989 and 40 countries including India have ratified it so for.

The GSTP establishes a framework for the exchange of trade concessions among the members of the group of 77. It provides a mechanism for negotiations in successive stages for establishing, trade preferences with a view to promoting trade and economic cooperation among developing countries. It lays down rules, principles and procedures for conduct of negotiations and for implementation of the results of the negotiations. The coverage of the GSTP extends to arrangements in the area of tariffs, para-tariff, non-tariff measures, direct trade measures including medium and long-term contracts and sectoral agreements.

The negotiations in the first round were confined almost exclusively to the exchange of tariff concessions on products, covering a small share of the foreign trade of participating countries. Agreed preferences covered a small number of tariff lines and in many instances, modest tariff reductions and bindings. It was, however, not entirely unexpected, considering that this was the first round. More importantly, the focus was on the adoption of the GSTP agreement so that an instrument was available to developing countries to undertake measures to deepen and extend trade relations among themselves.

During the first round, India exchanged tariff concessions with 14 countries. The concessions were offered on 31 products, by establishing Tariff margins ranging between 10% to 50% over the basic duty components. In return, India received direct tariff concessions from these 14 countries. Concessions offered by the participants covered products of export interest to India which include traditional products like tea, shellac, jute and cashew nuts and non-traditional products like pharmaceuticals, engineering goods and rubber tyres. In addition, India benefited from the multilateralisation of concessions exchanged amongst other participants.

One of the basic principles of the agreement on the GSTP is that, it is to be negotiated step-by-step, improved and extended in successive stages. Accordingly, the Ministerial Meeting on GSTP held in Tehran on 21st November, 1991, adopted the Tehran Declaration on the launching of the second round of GSTP negotiations. The aim of the second round is to facilitate the process of accession to the GSTP agreement and to carry forward the exchange of trade concessions.

In the second round of GSTP negotiations, a number of sessions of bilateral consultations for exchange of concessions on a product-by-product basis have been held. During the first two sessions of bilateral negotiations held in Geneva during 15-26 May, 1995 and 25-29 September, 1995, there were consultations with 16 participating countries and during these sessions participating countries could identify items of mutual interest for the exchange of tariff concessions. During the third and forth session of bilateral negotiations which were held from 4-8 March, 1996 and 24-28 June, 1996, India held consultations/negotiations with 20 and 17 GSTP participating countries respectively.

During these sessions of bilateral negotiations, we have agreed to exchange concessions with 12 countries viz., Cuba, Indonesia, DPR Korea, Republic of Korea, Egypt, Libya, Iran, Nigeria, Romania, Columbia, Thailand, and Morocco. In all, India has offered tariff concessions on 27 tariff lines at the six digit level, in consultation with the administrative ministries/departments with preference margins ranging between 10% to 100%. In return, India will receive concessions on 43 tariff lines from these 12 countries, with preference margins ranging between 5% to 70%.

The second round of GSTP negotiations were formally concluded in the 12th session of the Committee of Participants held in Geneva on 8-10th December, 1998. The draft of the 1998 protocol to the agreement of GSTP was adopted in this session. The protocol will be open for signature until 31st December, 2000. The schedule of concessions annexed to the protocol will be finalised, after carrying out technical verification of the schedules by the participants.

Generalised System of Preferences (GSP)

The Generalised System of Preferences (GSP) is a non-contractual instrument by which industrialised countries unilaterally extend tariff concessions to developing countries. The Generalised System of Preferences (GSP) formally accepted in 1968, by the members of the UN at the second UNCTAD Conference in New Delhi, was first implemented by the European Community, through the framework of the community's Generalised Scheme of Preferences which came into effect on 1st July, 1971.

The GSP offers developing countries tariff reductions or in some cases duty-free concessions, for their manufactured exports and certain agricultural exports as well. It is a tariff instrument, which is automonous and also complementary to GATT.

Its aim is to grant the developing countries tariff preferences over the developed countries, thus allowing them preferences over the developed countries, and thereby allowing their exports easier access to the Market of the developed countries. GSP is being offered by the following countries:

United States	Japan	Hungary
European Union	Norway	Belarus
Canada	Switzerland	Slovakia
Australia	Bulgaria	Russian Federation
New Zealand	Poland	

Czech Republic GSP Schemes of these countries detail the tariff lines under which these benefits are available, besides the conditions and the procedures governing the benefits. These schemes are renewed and modified from time to time.

Normally, the customs of GSP offering countries require information in Form 'A' (prescribed for GSP Rules of Origin) duly filled by the exporters of the beneficiary countries and certified by authorised agencies. The Ministry of Commerce is the Administrative Ministry for such authorisation. Currently, the following nine organisations have been authorized to issue Certificate of Origin under GSP.

S.No	*Name of the Organisation*	*Authorised for*
1	Export Inspection Council through their field Offices known as Export Inspection Agencies with 57 Offices all over India.	All products
2	Directorate General of Foreign Trade through Regional Offices known as Joint Director General/Deputy Director General of Foreign Trade	All products
3	Development Commissioner, Export Processing Zone at Santa Cruz (Bombay), Cochin, Madras, Falta, Vishakhapatnam, Kandla and Noida.	All products manufactured by EOU's/ Units in EPZ within respective jurisdiction of the Development Commissioner.
4	Development Commissioner for Handicrafts through their 14 Regional Offices all over India	Authorised for handicrafts
5	Marine Products Export Development Authority through their 12 Regional Offices all over India	Marine products
6	Textile Committee through 28 Regional Offices all over India.	Textiles and made-ups
7	Central Silk Board through 8 Regional Offices all over India	Silk products
8	Coir Board, Cochin	Coir and Coir products
9	Tobacco Board, Guntur	Tobacco and Tobacco products

SAARC Agreement for Preferential Trading Arrangement (SAPTA)

The SAARC Agreement fot Preferential Trading Arrangement (SAPTA) was signed on 11th April 1993, at the Seventh SAARC Summit held in Dhaka. The agreement was signed by all the seven SAARC countries namely, India, Pakistan, Nepal, Bhutan, Bangladesh, Sri Lanka and the Maldives (hereafter referred to as "The contracting states"). The agreement has entered into force after completion of the formalities by all the contracting states on 7.12.1995.

SAPTA establishes a framework for the exchange of trade concessions among the member countries of SAARC. It provides a mechanism for negotiations in successive stages, for establishing trade preferences, with a view to promot trade and economic Cooperation among the member countries of SAARC. It lays down principles and procedures for conduct of negotiations and for implementation of the results of the negotiations. The coverage of

SAPTA extends to arrangements in the area of tariffs, para-tariff and non-tariff measures, direct trade measures including medium and long-term contract and sectoral Agreements.

In the first round negotiations of SAPTA, member countries exchanged tariff concessions on 226 items, India gave concessions ranging from 10% to 100% on 106 tariff lines. The second round, which was more comprehensive, concluded in November, 1996. In this round, 1975 tariff lines were covered, with India giving concessions on 911 tariff lines. The third round concluded on November 23, 1998. In this round, the member States exchanged concessions on 3456 tariff lines, out of which India offered concessions on 1917 tariff lines. Out of the concessions offered by India, only 43 tariff lines are available for non-IDC member countries (Sri Lanka and Pakistan).

The final objective of the negotiations under SAPTA is the achievement of the South Asian Free Trade Area or SAPTA. At the SAARC Summit at Male in May 1997, the goal of establishing a South Asian Free Trade Area had been accepted and the importance of achieving this goal by the year 2001 underlined. The tenth SAARC Summit at Colombo in July 1998, took a concrete decision to transform this goal into a reality. It was decided that a group of experts from all the seven SAARC countries will commence negotiations on an Agreement or Treaty for a South Asian Free Trade Area. This agreement will spell out binding schedules for freeing trade and is expected to be finalised and put in place by 2001.

During the SAARC summit at Colombo in July 1998, an offer was made to all the SAARC member countries, that India would be willing to enter into bilateral Free Trade Agreements with them, to accelerate the pace of economic integration in the region. A positive response was received from Sri Lanka. After two round of negotiations, a Free Trade Agreement was signed on December 28, 1998, by our Prime Minister and the President of Sri Lanka in New Delhi. Further, during the Summit, the Prime Minister also announced that import restrictions maintained by India for BOP reasons on 2307 items, shall be removed for imports from the SAARC countries. This has come into effect from August 1, 1998. These measures are expected to promote trade and economic cooperation between the SAARC member countries.

United Nations Conference on Trade and Development (UNCTAD)

UNCTAD was established by the UN General Assembly in December 1964, to promote international trade, particularly that of developing countries, with a view to accelerating economic development. It has now become a principal instrument of the General Assembly for deliberation and negotiations in the field of international trade and related issues of international economic cooperation. UNCTAD covers the entire spectrum of policies in both developed and developing countries, which influence the external trade and economic development, particularly in those of developing countries.

UNCTAD-IX was held in Midrand, South Africa from 27th April to 11th May, 1996. The period of four years from 1992 to 1996 witnessed drastic changes in the international trade scenario, particularly the emergence of WTO, and changes in the global economic context. These changes and the financial crisis faced by the UN system, had generated an apprehension before UNCTAD-IX that UNCTAD's mandate role and work programme may undergo substantial pruning and downsizing. Some of the developed countries had also felt that UNCTAD should confine its activities to the least developed countries. The Indian Delegation made a strong plea for retaining UNCTAD's broad mandate for promoting trade and development on a global basis and stated that globalisation and liberalisation cannot be accepted as a panacea for resolving developmental problems of developing countries. The latter must develop their own natural resources, human resources and infrastructure to the maximum extent.

Outcome of UNCTAD-IX

The UNCTAD-IX Conference adopted two documents viz., "The Midrand Declaration" and a report "A Partnership for Growth and Development: Final Document for the Ninth Session of UNCTAD." The final documents of UNCTAD-IX provide for the following main features:

(i) The "Midrand Declaration" reiterates UNCTAD's mandate as the focal point for dealing with trade and related issues of the development. It emphasizes that UNCTAD's policy research and analytical work must illuminate the global economic changes as they relate to trade, investment, technology, services and development. It should also provide a forum for policy dialogue among the member States, to enable developing countries to enhance benefits of trade and participate in the world economy on a more equitable basis.

(ii) There is a need for close cooperation between UNCTAD and other International Institutions particularly WTO in view of the complementarity of their role. UNCTAD should respond to the development needs of developing countries, to enable them to participate more equitably in the rule based Multilateral Trading System.

(iii) The Intergovernment machinery of UNCTAD has been restructured to make it more focussed so that it concentrates on the areas of its strength. The Intergovernment machinery with Trade and Development Board (TDB) at the Apex, will have three Commissions, viz.

(1) Commission on Trade in Goods and Services and Commodities
(2) Commission on Investment, Technology and Related Financial Issues
(3) Commission on Enterprise, Business Facilitation and Development

The commission will convene expert meetings on specific issues. The total number of expert meetings will not exceed ten in a year, of which upto four may be convened by the Commission on Trade and upto three each on the other two.

Trade and Development Board and other Commission Meetings

The Trade and Development Board held the Forty-fifth Session from 12-23 October, 1998. The highlights of the session were a high level segment on the impact of financial crisis on trade, investment and development regional perspectives and "Interdependence and global economic issues from a trade and development perspectives: the causes, Management and prevention of financial crisis: Regional perspectives."

As mandated at Midrand, the new Inter-Governmental machinery of UNCTAD is fully functional and the three commissions have already held three sessions each so far. India hosted a regional symposium on "International Countries" in New Delhi during 15-16 July, 1998. This symposium was attended by participants from 16 developing countries in Asia, including India. The purpose of the symposium was to familiarise government officials from Asian countries, with existing international investment arrangements, from a development perspective. It therefore, contributed to a better understanding of the development implications, of key issues and concepts relevant to these arrangements.

As was expected, after the Midrand conference, UNCTAD has emerged as a lean and focussed institution. Its capacity to make meaningful interventions in trade and development related issues has been strengthened due to greater organisational focus.

Indian Council of Arbitration

The Indian Council of Arbitration, set-up under the Societies Registration Act, 1860, is a grantee Institution of the Ministry of Commerce. The main objectives of the Council are, to promote the knowledge and use of arbitration and to provide alternative dispute resolution facilities, such as arbitration/ conciliation for amicable and quick settlement of commercial maritime disputes, with a view to maintain a smooth flow of trade, particularly export trade on a sustained and enduring basis. The Council has evolved its Rules of Arbitration and Conciliation on International Standards based on the Arbitration and Conciliation Act, 1996, for economical and expeditious arbitration and conciliation procedures on international, commercial and maritime disputes. It has entered into Arbitration Service Agreement with important foreign arbitral institutions to provide arbitration services under their respective rules, if the arbitration is held in India.

// *Chapter 9* //

Organising Export

Most enterprises entering the export trade begin with modes, objectives and budgets. It is advisable for the company to pick one or two safe markets, for its initial experiments with exporting. When the management has built up some confidence and gained some experience, it can re-evaluate the effort required to go into a full-scale export venture.

There are several ways of organising exports. The alternative ways described below are listed in order of increasing complexity and risk.

SUBCONTRACTING FOR A FOREIGN COMPANY

A foreign company may find it useful to subcontract part of its production operations to enterprises. The subcontract may cover either, phases of production process or a certain volume of the product being manufactured. Under this arrangement, the foreign company generally benefits from the enterprise's lower labour costs, while maintaining control of its marketing operations. The enterprise's principal advantage is that, it does not need to be involved in marketing its output. Its main disadvantages are that, the bulk of the profits goes to the foreign company and the enterprise does not gain marketing knowledge and experience.

EXPORTING THROUGH DOMESTIC INTERMEDIARIES

This is the simplest form of exporting. The enterprise sells to an export intermediary in the domestic market, who then sends the products to market overseas. In this case, the commercial risks are hardly different from those of selling at home. These intermediaries include export houses, export trading companies, and other export merchants. They work primarily with companies with little or no exporting experience.

JOINT EXPORTING

This involves the creation of a joint exporting scheme for a group of enterprises with economic constraints, which do not allow them to engage in individual export efforts. The enterprises are often in the same industry and produce complementary products. The group of enterprises may form a new entity, or join an existing agency such as a trade or industry association. It may be established entirely on the initiative of the membership, or with the sponsorship of the public sector.

The importance of joint exporting is likely to increase, as the implementation of the Uruguay Round will open up access to new markets. If this way of exporting is chosen, a collaboration agreement will be needed.

The enterprises or the Chamber of Commerce should draft this agreement and ascertain that its provisions comply with the Uruguay Round Regulations.

EXPORTING THROUGH AN INHOUSE EXPORT CELL

When the enterprise exports reach a threshold level, it can invest in an internal export cell. Initially the cell may consist of a single staff member and operate on a modest export budget. However, it is likely to pay-off handsomely because, exporting as a new activity requires separate and full attention.

A major advantage of creating an internal export cell is the experience gained in managing export operations. When exporting is delegated to outside parties, no such benefit accrues. The in-house capabilities for carrying out export operations are also increased, when an internal export call is set up.

JOINT VENTURES ABROAD

This involves a joint undertaking with a local partner in the target country. Under one form of joint undertaking, the enterprise establishes a new company abroad, with the financial participation of a local marketing firm, a local financing firm, a local manufacturing firm or a combination of all these. Under a joint manufacturing arrangement, the enterprise could supply raw materials, intermediate materials, technology or labour to the joint venture. A joint marketing venture could obtain export orders for the enterprise. In addition to reducing the political and economic risks of exporting, joint ventures offer the following advantages.

★ They enable the enterprise to utilise the specialised skills of its partner in the target market.

★ They give the enterprise more rapid access to the local distribution system.

★ They facilitate the enterprise's entry into markets where operations wholly owned by foreigners are discouraged.

★ They offer the enterprise the additional capital and personnel it requires for its international operations.

JOINT EXPORT SCHEMES OR CONSORTIA

Joint export schemes are an attractive choice for enterprises with limited resources. A joint export marketing group is a formal association of companies which combine their export efforts, although they may remain competitors in the home market.

Joint export schemes offer advantages of size. By pooling their resources, individual members may venture into operations that are impossible for each of them individually. Together, they may be able to enter new markets or take fuller advantage of the potential of their existing markets.

The increase in production makes it possible for the group, to supply a major market that is not interested in handling the small output of individual companies. Furthermore, with bigger volumes involved, a marketing group can obtain quantity discounts on shipping rates, packaging materials, advertising space, etc.

They have greater capacity than individual companies, to increase production to meet demands. Furthermore, since members of consortia are often widely distributed throughout the country, joint export marketing schemes spread employment opportunities nationwide.

Joint export marketing groups often result in improved communications and cooperation between the government and the industry. It is easier and more cost-effective for the government to aid companies, if they are re-linked in a joint export marketing group. The plans of these groups can also be integrated more effectively with the government's own development plans.

From the national point of view, the benefits of joint export marketing can be summarised as follows:

★ Results in a rapid rise in foreign exchange earnings.
★ Develops export marketing know-how.
★ Upgrades production skills and product quality.
★ Facilitates the development of more sophisticated products.
★ Assists in the implementation of government development plans.
★ Offers advantages of scale.
★ Generates employment opportunities.
★ Acts as a communication channel between the government and the industry.
★ Offers a good example to other groups and industries.
★ Enhances goodwill for the country.

A major difference between export marketing consortia in developed countries and those in developing countries lies in, the extent to which government organisations play a role in their establishment and operations.

In the developed countries, consortia have largely resulted from the joint efforts of privately owned companies to take advantage of existing services and opportunities. There have been outstanding examples of this in Denmark, Finland, Ireland, Sweden and United Kingdom.

In developing countries, there is a basic need for the government to support the expansion of the export trade. This places a heavy responsibility on government agencies, to facilitate the creation of joint export marketing groups.

Governments offer joint export marketing groups on the following services to encourage or supplement the groups' activities

★ Supplying technical information on international standards and specifications.
★ Organising overseas promotion including, participation in joint stands at trade fairs and exhibitions.
★ Providing credit facilities and credit insurance facilities on terms competitive with those available in other countries.
★ Providing quality control facilities and market research services.
★ Organising joint transportation arrangements to reduce freight costs.

Enterprises help consortia by making sure that they do not suffer under the laws of their country. This might happen under some taxation systems.

For instance, if consortia are classified as trading organisations instead of manufacturing organizations, they would not qualify for certain export rebates.

Can you think of joint groups that have succeeded?

THE ROLE OF THE ENTERPRISES' AGENCIES

Enterprises, generally government-run, have an important role to play in creating joint export marketing groups and in helping them to overcome their problems. In some instances, they even participate as partners in the consortium.

The agencies' marketing advisers, work closely with the enterprises and are in a good position to act as go-between's in the creation of marketing groups. These advisers can spot opportunities for exporting particular products, know the capabilities and weaknesses of the enterprises, and can facilitate the negotiations involved in getting the groups started.

For all their advantages, joint groups are not a cure-all for export problems. Infact, a significant number of them have failed. Here are some of the aspects that the Enterprises' agencies should be concerned with, when organising or joining exporting groups.

A main problem is the enterprises' need for financial assistance. This is one of the biggest obstacles faced by the enterprises in joint export marketing groups. Governments have been able to help in the following three ways

- ★ Making direct grants to groups and providing sufficient working capital.
- ★ Giving financial assistance as an export incentive.
- ★ Covering the cost of special group facilities.

Enterprises' agencies provide funds and advise to the export consortia on various aspects of fixed investments, working capital, publicity budgets, special projects, development funds, share capital, member's contributions, commissions and mark-ups.

The enterprises' agencies also mediate during disputes between members of joint export marketing groups. Unless there is a mechanism for settling such disputes impartially, it could affect the effectiveness of a group that should be contributing to the growth of the national economy.

Another potential problem is that, prospective members may fear the loss of their identity in the consortium. This can be resolved if the member can be satisfied that, membership will enable it to earn export profits but will not result in a loss of identity in the home market.

Prospective members may fear that joining a group will mean disclosing confidential information about their own activities. Enterprises' agencies can help to remove such suspicions by the manner in which they guide the negotiations.

Prospective members may be reluctant to cooperate with their competitors, or fear that they may be swamped by bigger firms. They may also have misgivings about future changes in membership, shortages of management and marketing expertise, and about technical developments, product design and adaptation, licensing agreements and transportation arrangements.

// CHAPTER 10 //

STARTING AN EXPORT BUSINESS

Foreign Trade is attractive, prestigious and interesting. The exporter is exposed to the international market in which there are numer-ous avenues open to him. An imaginative exporter with a firm determination will have ample scope for extensive trade expansion.

Exporting is a scientific activity requiring, knowledge of the rules and regulations relating to export control and promotional measures, procedural formalities and documentation required not only in India, but also in the countries of importation. All the stages right from the selection of products, location of overseas markets/customers, export pricing and contracts, production/procurement of goods, packing, labelling and shipment formalities, to realisation of export proceeds, assistance and facilities, sales promotion activities, etc. are systematically explained in various modules. In addition to this, the essential steps in exporting are also discussed briefly. These steps help to make the exporters' day-to-day task easier.

It is not necessary to strictly follow the steps detailed below, in the same sequence. Registration formalities can also be completed simultaneously.

ORGANISING

To start an export business it is first imperative to create the necessary infrastructure, however modest it may be. It might involve starting a complete new organisation and/or adding new activities to an existing one.

NAMING THE CONCERN

Where there is already some sort of an organisation, including a manufacturing concern, exporting can be started under the same name and style. To set up a new firm, the first essential task is to name the firm. The name and style should be 'attractive', 'short' and 'meaningful'. For example, addition of the word "International" or "Overseas" to some name of a person or flower tends to lend a new meaning to the firm, whereby it is explicit that the latter deals in export/import business.

TRADE NAME AND LOGO

Moreover, the name, symbol or logo chosen should reinforce the company's name and create an image in the customers' mind when they see the letter-head and business cards. The design of the trade name or logo could be prepared by an artist.

STYLE

The style under which a firm will work, is also known as the form of constitution of the firm under different enactments. It may be constituted as:

(1) a proprietary concern (2) a partnership firm (3) a company.

A Proprietory Concern

This is the easiest to constitute without much expense and legal formalities. Just a decision to set up a firm must be taken. It is owned and controlled by an individual, under a name of his choice without seeking any clarification whatsoever from anywhere. There is no formal registration or permission to be sought for from any organisations, except in cases where the exporter wishes to export textiles under the Quota System. In such cases, clearance of the name (and not style) is to be obtained from the Apparel Export Promotion Council.

If the size of business is small, it would be advantageous to form a sole proprietory business organisation without much expense and legal formalities. However, the biggest disadvantage of a sole proprietorship business is the limited liability to raise funds which restricts its growth. Besides, the owner has unlimited personal liability. In order to avoid this disadvantage, it is advisable to form a partnership firm.

A Partnership Firm

This is almost as easy as a proprietory concern and can be set up with ease and economy. It may or may not involve registration with the Registrar of Firms. Obviously, a partnership firm involves more than one partner. The number of partners may be any, but it is better to limit the number of partners from 2 to 3 upto 5. It is not advisable to have many partners as, too many cooks spoil the broth. A partnership firm is better than a proprietory concern because, it brings in more money, varied experience and the expertise of the partners. There can be a division of work and, hence specialisation can be achieved in different segments of business activities. It is simple to constitute a partnership firm by writing a partnership deed on non-judicial stamp paper of specified value, signed by every partner and witnessed by two persons/firms. It is advisable that the Partnership Deed may be got registered with the Registrar of Firms under the Partnership Act, 1932.

The liability of the partners though joint and several, is practically distributed amongst the various partners, despite the fact that personal liability of the partner is unlimited. The major disadvantage of a partnership form of business organisation is that, conflict amongst the partners is a potential threat to the business.

A Company

A company is another form of business organisation, which has the advantage of distinct identity and limited liability to the share holders. It can be constituted either as a private or public limited company under the Indian Companies Act. In a private limited company, there can be a minimum of two shareholders, with a maximum 50% share each and the public cannot be invited to subscribe to its capital. Under a public limited company, there can be a minimum number of 7 partners with no upper limit. The public limited company can be a closely-held-company or a widely-held company. In a closely-held company, the funds cannot be raised from the public, whereas in a widely-held company, the shares or the debentures of the company can be floated in the market. The constitution of a firm such as a company, either private or public limited, confers a status in business, in comparison to a proprietory or partnership firm. But it involves certain additional formalities to be completed, which involve money and time. A public limited company offers enormous potential for growth, because of access to substantial funds. The liquidity of investment is high because of easiness of transfer of shares. However, its formation can be recommended only when the size of the business is large. For a small business, a sole proprietory concern or a partnership firm will be the most suitable form of business organisation.

In case it is decided to incorporate a private or public limited company, the same is to be registered with the Registrar of Companies. Hence, one has to take judicious decision according to the need and requirements of the exporting firm.

CATEGORIES OF EXPORTERS

The proprietor or a partner of a firm, director of a private or public limited company or an executive or manager of a small or large company may wish to enter into the overseas market for selling their products. If a manufacturer would like to sell his products overseas, he may act as a manufacturer exporter. If a person wishes to buy products from other manufacturers and sell them in the overseas market, he then becomes a merchant exporter. If a manufacturer would like to sell products of other manufacturers along with his own products, he may act as a manufacturer and merchant exporter at the same time.

The exporter can choose from any one of the following modes of operations.

(i) Merchant exporter i.e. buying the goods from the market or from a manufacturer and then selling them to foreign buyers.

(ii) Manufacturer exporter i.e. manufacturing the goods needed for export.

(iii) Sales agent/commission agent/indenting agent i.e. acting on behalf of the seller and charging commission.

(iv) Buying agent i.e. acting on behalf of the buyer and charging commission.

The first and the foremost question that a prospective exporter has to decide, is about the kind of business organisation needed for the purpose. A crucial decision has to be taken, as to whether the business will be run as a sole proprietory concern or a partnership firm or a company. The proper selection of organisation depends upon (i) the exporters' ability to raise finance, (ii) his capacity to bear the risk, (iii) his desire to exercise control over the business (iv) the nature of regulatory framework applicable to the exporter.

LOCATION

As far as possible, the exporter should locate the company in a well known business are of the city/town. To operate in some of the metropolitan cities, it is better to locate the export firm in and around Connaught Place or Nehru Place in New Delhi, Fort or Nariman Point in Bombay, Mount Road or Anna Salai in Chennai (Madras), Chowringhee in Calcutta and MG Road or Airport Road in Bangalore, to cite a few places. A good location always lends business credibility to the status of a firm.

LETTERHEAD

After naming and locating the concern, other details like printing of good letterheads, envelopes and obtaining telephone, fax, e-mail, etc. should be dealt with. The information to be given in the letterhead should essentially include (i) complete name and address including the country's name (ii) telephone nos., fax no. and e-mail address (iii) some outstanding achievement like having got an Export Award, etc. The banker's name and address can also be given. But details of the items in which the company deals in need not be given.

BUSINESS CARD

The most important marketing tool is the business card. It is what others will keep to remember the company by and even more importantly, it represents the quality of service offered to a potential client. It would help to look at the business card to see the kind of impression it makes to notice if it looks professional to make sure that the address information is clear and complete, and also to check the electronic access information such as the e-mail address and an Internet address for easy accessibility.

When potential customers look at a business card, they make unconscious assumptions about factors like whether the firm is willing to invest the resources to do a good job (professionally designed and typeset business card), whether it is well qualified (the presence or absence of credentials), whether the firm thinks internationally (the presence or absence of your country in your address), whether it would be easy to contact the company (the presence or absence of electronic addresses), and so on.

Another factor that needs to be thought about is the matter of accommodating other languages. One practical approach is to use the back of the business card for the language of the market that is targeted. To maintain a professional image, that side of the business card will have to be properly printed along with the logo.

EXPORT PERSONNEL/STAFF

Depending upon the financial position and the scale on which a firm intends to carry on its export business, it should appoint personnel for handling various export marketing operations. However, it may in the beginning, give added responsibility of handling export business to the existing sales personnel, if any. This arrangement seems simple and economical and it usually works well, especially if a company's export sales are largely concentrated in one or two areas where the documents demanded are not complicated and credit or shipping problems are few. Such personnel to whom an added responsibility is given for export sales may be got trained in export marketing techniques. Training programmes are organised by various institutions like universities and other public and private import export institutes, viz., Indian Institute of Foreign Trade (IIFT), New Delhi, National Institute of Careers in Export and Marketing (NICEM), Bangalore, etc.

BANK ACCOUNT

A current account has to be opened in the name of the organisation in whose name it is intended to export, in a branch of a commercial bank which is authorised to deal in foreign exchange.

PERMANENT INCOME-TAX ACCOUNT NUMBER

It is necessary to apply to the Income Tax Officer having jurisdiction over the organisation for the allotment of a permanent account number, in case the firm does not have one. The exporter's code number has to be cited in the form of allotment. In case, this number has not been allotted it is still possible to apply.

EFFECTIVE BUSINESS CORRESPONDENCE

The importance of business correspondence is great, as it is an introduction with the buyer in proxy, which may clinch his response according to the impression created by the correspondence. For creating a very favourable and excellent impression, it is necessary to use a beautiful letter head and a good envelope which is nicely printed. The language should be polite, soft, brief and to the point, giving a very clear picture of the subject to be put before the customer. Letters should be typed/computer typed set, preferably in the language of the importing country. Also it is better to make sure that the full and correct address is written and that the envelope is duly stamped. It should also be borne in mind that the aim of the business correspondence is not only to clinch the buyer's order but also to obtain certain information which is needed for exporting.

EXPORT DECISION

Before taking any decision regarding exporting, it is important to act on the following points.

1. Selecting a quality product.
2. Selecting a particular overseas market.
3. Beginners should concentrate only on few products and a minimum of three countries.
4. Ensuring that the selected products can be manufactured or procured from other sources at the competitive prices and in sufficient quantity that will enable the delivery schedule to be met
5. Getting the full information of similar products of other manufacturers if already available in selected markets, their prices, marketing techniques, terms of business etc. so as to offer the

product(s) to foreign buyers with a bargaining edge in order to capture the market.

6. Assessing the degree of competition of product(s) which is to be exported in a particular market.

SELECTING THE MARKETS

Target markets should be selected after careful consideration of various factors like political embargo, scope of exporter's selected product, demand stability, preference to products from developing countries, market penetration by competitive countries and products, distance of potential market, transport problems, language problems, tariff and non-tariff barriers, distribution infrastructure, size of demand in the market, expected life span of market and product requirements, sales and distribution channels.

For this purpose, adequate market information should be collected before selecting one or more target markets. The information can be collected from various sources like Export Promotion Councils (EPCs) Commodity Boards, Federation of India Export Organisation, (FIEO), Indian Institute of Foreign Trade (IIFT), Indian Trade Promotion Organisation (ITPO), Indian Embassies abroad, Foreign Embassies in India, Import Promotion Institutions abroad, Overseas Chambers of Commerce and Industries, various directors, journals, market survey report, etc.

EXPORT COMMODITY SELECTION

While selecting the commodity for exports, following points have to be taken into consideration:

1. The Exporter's manufacturing capacity, if he is a manufacturer of a particular commodity.
2. The availability of commodity from other manufacturers when the exporters desire to act as a merchant exporter.
3. The demand for the commodity in the importing country.
4. The Government of India's Policy and Regulations in respect of export of various commodities.
5. The Foreign Government's Policy and Regulations in respect of import of various commodities.
6. Total profitability of such commodities considering cash incentives available, if any.
7. The import replenishment available, if any.
8. Quota fixation, if any, in respect of such commodities in both the countries.
9. Knowledge and experience of similar exporters in respect of the export of such commodities in various countries.

The product to be exported has to be carefully selected. For proper selection of a product, it is necessary to study the trends of export of different items from India. The selected product must be in demand in the countries where it is to be exported. It should be possible to procure or manufacture the selected products at most economic cost, so that it can be competitively priced. It should also be available in sufficient quantity and it should be possible to supply it repeatedly and regularly. Besides, while selecting the product, it has to be ensured that the exporter is conversant with Government Policy and Regulations in respect of the product selected for export. The import regulations in respect of such commodities by the importing countries, should also be known. It would be preferable if the exporter has previous knowledge and experience of the commodities selected for export.

OBTAINING PARTICULARS OF FOREIGN BUYERS/FINDING PROSPECTIVE BUYERS

The exporter may obtain the particulars of foreign buyers from either one of the following sources:

1. Trade representatives of foreign governments in India as well as the indian trade representatives abroad.
2. Various Export Promotion Councils and Commodity Boards and other Government and Semi-government Agencies.
3. International Trade Directories and International Yellow Pages.
4. Participating/visiting International Trade Fairs and Exhibitions in India and abroad.
5. Reading material i.e. various newspapers, weekly, fortnightly, monthly trade bulletins, magazines, journals published by various agencies like FIEO, ITPO, EP Councils, Commodity Boards and Chambers of Commerce.
6. Advertising in Indian as well as foreign newspapers, magazines and journals.
7. Relatives, friends and other contacts in foreign countries.

Once the competition is assessed, the exporter will know his position regarding

a) the price which he can offer to the overseas buyer,
b) the terms of credit which he can offer,
c) the packaging, transportation, storage, distribution and after-sales-service methods he can adopt,
d) the promotional efforts which he can offer in terms of publicity literature, visual publicity, advertisements, gifts, etc. depending on the product.

SELECTING CHANNELS OF DISTRIBUTION

The following channels of distribution are generally utilised while exporting to overseas markets:

1. Export through Export Consortia.
2. Export through Canalising Agencies.
3. Export through other Established Merchant Exporters or Export Houses, or Trading Houses.
4. Direct exports.
5. Export through Overseas Sales Agencies.

NEGOTIATING WITH PROSPECTIVE BUYERS

Whatever channel of distribution for exporting to the overseas countries is proposed to be utilized, it is essential that the exporters should possess necessary skill for negotiating with the overseas channels of distribution. The ability to negotiate effectively is needed for discussion with importers or trade agents. While conducting business negotiations, the prospective exporter should avoid conflict, controversy and criticism vis-à-vis the other party. During conversation, the attitude should be to communicated effectively. There should be coherence, creative compromise, concessions, commonality, consesus, commitment and compensation in business negotiations.

PROCESSING AN EXPORT ORDER

The exporter should not be happy merely on receiving an export order. He should first acknowldege the export order, and then proceed to examine carefully the items, specification, pre-shipment inspection, payment conditions, special packaging, labelling and marketing requirements, shipment and delivery date, marine insurance, documentation, etc. If he is satisfied about these aspects, a formal confirmation should then be sent to the buyer, otherwise a clarification should be sought from the buyer before confirming the order.

After confirmation of the export order immediate steps should be taken for procurement/manufacture of the export goods. In the meanwhile, the exporter should proceed to enter into a formal export contract with the overseas buyer.

ENTERING INTO EXPORT CONTRACT

In order to avoid disputes, it is necessary to enter into an export contract with the overseas buyer. The export contract should be carefully drafted incorporating incomprehensive but precise terms, all the relevant and important conditions of the trade deal. There should not be any ambiguity regarding the exact specifications of goods and terms of sale including export price, mode of payment, storage and distribution methods, type of packaging, port of shipment, delivery schedule, etc.

EXPORT PRICING AND COSTING

Export pricing should be differentiated from export costing. Price is what is offered to the customer. Cost is the price that is payed/incured for the product. Price includes the profit margin, whereas cost includes only that expenses that the exporter has incurred.

Export pricing is the most important tool for promoting sales and facing international competition. The price has to be realistically worked out, taking into consideration all export benefits and expenses. However, there is no fixed formula for successful export pricing. It differs from exporter to exporter depending upon whether the exporter is a merchant exporter or a manufacturer exporter or exporting through a canalising agency.

The exporter should also assess the strength of his competitor and anticipate the move of the competitor in the market. Pricing strategies will depend on various circumstantial situations. It is still possible to be competitive with higher prices, when a better delivery package or other advantages are offered. The prices will be determined by the following factors:

1. Range of products offered
2. Prompt deliveries and continuity in supply

3. After-sales service in products like machine tools and consumer durables
4. Product differentiation and brand image
5. Frequency of purchase
6. Presumed relationship between quality and price
7. Speciality of value goods and gift items
8. Credit offered
9. Preference or prejudice for products originating from a particular source
10. Aggressive marketing and sales promotion
11. Prompt acceptance and settlement of claims
12. Unique value goods and gift items

As regards quoting the prices to the overseas buyer, the same are quoted in the internationally accepted terms called Incoterms. A full module has been added about Incoterms in this book.

UNDERSTANDING RISKS IN INTERNATIONAL TRADE

While selling abroad, the exporter may undergo the following risks:

1. Credit risk
2. Currency risk
3. Carriage risk
4. Country risk

These risks can be insured to a great extent by taking appropriate steps. Credit risk against the buyer can be covered by insisting upon an irrevocable Letter of Credit from the Overseas buyer. An appropriate Policy from Export Credit and Guarantee Corporation of India Ltd (ECGC) can also be obtained for this purpose. Country risks are also covered by the ECGC. As regards currency risk, i.e. possible loss due to adverse fluctuation in Exchange Rate, the exporter should obtain forward cover from his bank, which is authorised to deal in foreign exchange. Alternatively, he could obtain the export order in Indian Rupees. Carriage risk, i.e. possible loss of cargo in transit can be covered by taking a Marine Insurance policy from the General Insurance Corporation's Companies.

ARBITRATION

The arbitration clause recommended by the Indian Council of Arbitration reads as follows: "All disputes or differences whatsoever arising between the parties out of relating to the construction, meaning and operation of effect of this contract or the breach thereof shall be settled by Arbitration in accordance with the Rules of Arbitration of the Indian Council of Arbitration and the Award made in pursuance thereof shall be binding on the parties" (or any other arbitration clause may be agreed upon between the parties).

Any other special condition, prevalent in or relevant to the particular line of trade or transaction, can also be specified.

IMPORTER-EXPORTER CODE NUMBER (IEC NUMBER)

Every person whether an individual or a firm or a company importing or exporting goods (other than for the personal use and not connected with trade or manufacture or agriculture) is required to obtain an Importer-Exporter Code Number from the Regional Import/Export Licensing Authority. Apply in the prescribed form, in duplicate, to the concerned authority alongwith-

1. Profile of applicant exporter/importer in Annexure 1A.
2. Bank Certificate in Annexure 1 to Appendix 2A
3. Bank Receipt (in duplicate)/Demand draft for Rs 1000 evidencing payment of fee. Where fee is not paid by Demand Draft., it is to be deposited in such a branch of the Central Bank, which is authorised to accept ITC deposits. The fee is to be deposited in prescribed form (Annexure 4) in the specified branch of the Central Bank.
4. Photograph (two copies) of the proprietor/partner/director/trustee, duly attested by the banker.
5. Where the application is signed by an authorised signatory, a copy of the legal authority letter.
6. Declaration about the applicant's non-association with a firm caution-listed by RBI, as detailed below.
   "The ---------------proprietor/partners/ directors (as the case may be) of the firm/company is/are not associated as proprietor/partners or directors in any other firm/company which has been caution-listed by the RBI."
7. If there is NRI investment without repatriation benefits, a declaration on the applicant's letterhead should indicate whether it is held with the general/specific permission of RBI. In case of specific approval, a copy may also be furnished.
   or
   If the NRI investment is with repatriation benefit, full particulars should be given thereof, with a photocopy of the RBI approval.

IEC Certificate

The IEC certificate will be issued in the prescribed form at Annexure.

Validity

The IEC number allotted to a firm/company will be valid for import/export of any commodity, by that firm/company.

REGISTRATION WITH EXPORT PROMOTION COUNCILS (EPCs)

Any person applying for (1) a licence to import/export or (2) any other benefit or concession under the Exim Policy, is required to furnish a RCMC (Registration-cum-Membership Certificate) Number granted to him by the authorities like Export Promotion Councils, Commodity Boards, Federation of Indian Export Organisation (FIEO) and Agricultural and Processed Food Products Export Development Authorities (APEDA), Marine Product Export Development Authority (MPEDA), unless specifically exempted under the policy.

Registered Exporters

The firms after registeration and obtaining RCMC from concerned registering authorities are known as a Registered Exporters. Hence, the term "Registered

Exporters" has special connotation. The Registered Exporters can be (1) Manufacturer-Exporters (2) Merchant-Exporters.

Export houses, trading houses, star trading houses or a super star trading house may fall in any of the two categories or in both categories i.e. they can be Manufacturer-Exporters and also merchant exporters. The procedure for registration of Export Houses, etc. is explained later on.

One Registration

An exporter registered as Manufacturer-Exporter or Merchant Exporter may export any number of product without obtaining more than one registration. Hence, one registration is sufficient to obtain the export benefits, even though one may export more than one product including those not falling within the purview of the Registering Authority with whom the exporter has registered and obtained RCMC.

Therefore only one registration is required and no registration with more than one EPC etc. is necessary even if the exporter is engaged in exporting products falling in more than one product group and, hence, within the purview of different EPCs/Commodity Boards (CBs) etc.

Registering Authorities

The RCMC is issued by the following organisations known as the Registering Authorities:

1. An EPC from the total of 22 EPCs existing at present and 6 Commodity Boards out of 7, Agricultural & Processed Food Products Export Development Authority (APEDA), Marine Products Export Development Authority (MPEDA), etc. Central Silk Board is not the Registering Authority. Jute Manufactures Development Council (JMDC) is not a registering authority under the Exim policy 5. However, registration with this Organisation is necessary for taking benefit of the External Marketing Assistance Scheme for jute products.
2. FIEO, Federation of Indian Export Organisations in case of Export Houses, Trading House, Star Trading Houses and Super Star Trading Houses. Alternatively, the Export House etc. may also register themselves with an EPC concerned which accounts for major share of its exports. Then, it need not register with FIEO.
3. Any Regional Licensing Authority (Annexure having jurisdiction over the applicant firm, for the products not covered by any of the Export Promotion Councils or Commodity Boards and APEDA/MPEDA).

Product Specific Compulsory Registration

In some cases, registration with specific authorities/councils, other than Jute Manufacturers Development Authority (JMDC), is compulsory for export of specified products. For example, registration with Tribal Co-operative Marketing Federation of India Ltd (TRIFED) for export of shellac and all forms of lac, APEDA for export of grain and flour and ragi, etc. Registration with the Textile Commissioner for export of raw cotton, soft cotton, waste/ hard cotton, waste is compulsory. It will be an addition to registration with EPCs and obtaining of RCMC.

Membership/Registration

Since RCMC will be issued by an EPC or FIEO, etc. to its members only, membership or registration with them is a prerequisite.

Fee

Whereas there is no registration fee, the EPC etc., do charge membership fee. Since membership is a prerequisite for registration as an exporter and obtaining of RCMC, fee has to be compulsorily paid. The amount of feel payable may be found from the concerned Registering Authority (of EPCs/FIEO/ Commodity Boards, etc).

Regional licensing authorities do not charge any membership fee. Hence, registration with them is free.

Application

Application for Membership/Registration should be sent to the Authority concerned (Annexure) in the specified form at Annexure.

Application for membership-cum-registration should be accompanied with the following documents

1. Importer-Exporter Code (IEC) number.
2. Evidence like SSI Registration Certificate indicating that the applicant is a manufacturer, where registration is required as manufacturer exporter.
3. Bank's Certificate (Original) in support of applicant's financial soundness. It may be on the banker's letterhead.
4. (Registration-cum-Membership) RCMC form (Annexure 9), part-1 of this form should be duly filled in.
5. Cheque/Draft for membership fee, if any.
6. Any other documents required specially by the concerned Registering Authority like an undertaking at Annexure 9 for registration with Apparel Export Promotion Council (AEPC).

Appeal Against Rejection

Where the Registering Authority does not register an applicant, the appeal against its decision shall lie with the Director General Foreign Trade, Udyog Bhawan, New Delhi-110011.

Validity

The RCMC is valid for 5 year ending on 31st March of the financial year (April-March).

SALES TAX REGISTRATION

For procurement i.e. purchasing goods from manufacturers or merchants/ traders without payment of Sales Tax, the exporter needs to register himself with the Sales Tax Dept. of the State/Union Territory within whose jurisdiction he is located. He has to become a Registered Dealer under the Sales Tax Act/ Rules for which, the procedure is not very complicated, except that he has to arrange for a security/surety from another Registered Sales Tax Dealer.

Obviously, the exporter must arrange for such a security/surety before making an application for Registration under the Sales Tax Act/Rules. Alternatively, the requisite amount of security is to be deposited and FD pledged with the Sales Tax Dept.

CENTRAL EXCISE REGISTRATION/DECLARATION

Every person manufacturing excisable goods for home consumption or export or both should register himself with the Central Excise Dept., unless exempted from registration. The persons who manufacture goods specified in the Central Excise Tariff Schedule are exempt from registration, as long as the said goods are charged a nil rate of duty or remain exempt fully of the duty leviable thereon. Instead of registration, they should file a declaration. For example, SSI units i.e. manufacturers in the small sector with their total clearance and exemption for home consumption during a relevant financial year or previous financial years and utilising the full exemption, are exempt from Central Excise Registration. Instead, they should file a declaration to the Central Excise Dept. and obtain a declarant's code number.

Merchant-exporters are exempt from Central Excise Registration.

APPENDIX 1

General Instructions for Filling Appication Forms

1. Applicants are advised to read the provisions of the Export and Import Policy and Handbook of Procedures, which is amended from time to time.
2. Application should be legible and filled in capital letters.
3. All columns should be filled columns. Columns which are not relevant to the applicant should be stated as 'Not Applicable' and should not be left blank.
4. All the pages of the application should be signed.
5. An incomplete application is liable to be rejected.
6. Unless otherwise specified in the Policy and the Handbook, the application should be submitted to the licensing authority concerned in whose jurisdiction the applicant is located.
7. The following codes are to be used, wherever applicable
   (a) For unit of measurement:

Number - 01	Pair - 02
Dozen - 03	Gross - 04
Hundred in Nos. - 05	Thousand in Nos. - 06
Gram - 11	Kilogram -12
Metric Tonnes - 13	Carat - 14
Inch - 21	Foot - 22
Yard - 23	Metre - 24
Sq. Inch. - 31	Sq. Foot - 32
Sq. Yard - 33	Sq. Meter - 34
Cubic Inch. - 41	Cubic Foot - 42
Cubic Yard - 43	Cubic Meter - 44
Litre - 51	Spools - 61
Packs - 62	Set - 63

Bus - 64
Coil/Roll - 65
Boxes - 66
Cartons - 67
Kits - 68
Cans - 69

(b) For status of applicant, use the following codes:

1 - Trading House
2 - Export House
3 - Merchant-Exporter
4 - Manufacture-Exporter
5 - Star Trading House
6 - Super Star Trading House
53 - Merchant Star Trading House
54 - Manufacturer Star Trading House
7 - Service Providers
13 - Merchant Trading House
14 - Manufacturer Trading House
23 - Merchant Export House
24 - Manufacturer Export House

(c) For the nature of the concern, use the following codes:

1 - Government Co.
2 - Public Ltd. Co.
3 - Private Ltd. Co.
4 - Proprietary Firm
5 - Partnership Firm
6 - Others.

8. For Registering Authorities which are authorised to issue an RCMC, use the following codes:

1 Agricultural and Processed Food Products Export Development Authority
2 Apparel Export Promotion Council
3 Basic Chemicals, Pharmaceuticals and Cosmetics Export Promotion Council
4 The Cashew Export Promotion Council of India
5 Carpet Export Promotion Council
6 Chemicals and Allied Products Export Promotion Council
7 Coffee Board
8 Coir Board
9 The Cotton Textiles Export Promotion Council
10 Electronics and Computer Software Export Promotion Council
11 Engineering Export Promotion Council
12 Federation of Indian Export Organisations
13 The Gem and Jewellery Export Promotion Council
14 Export Promotion Council for Handicrafts
15 The Handloom Export Promotion Council
16 The Indian Silk Export Promotion Council
17 Council for Leather Exports
18 The Marine Products Export Development Authority
19 Overseas Construction Council of India
20 The Plastics and Linoleums Export Promotion Council
21 The Rubber Board
22 Shellac Export Promotion Council
23 The Sports Goods Export Promotion Council
24 Spices Board
25 The Synthetic and Rayon Textiles Export Promotion Council
26 Tea Board

27 Tobacco Board
28 Wool and Woolen Export Promotion Council
29 The Powerloom Development and Export Promotion Council and 99 Others

9. For Export Products Groups, use the following code:

61 Engineering Products
62 Chemicals and Allied Products
63 Plastics
64 Leather and Leather Products
65 Sports Goods
71 Cotton Textiles
72 Woollen Textiles
73 Natural Silk Textiles
74 Cellulosic/Non-cellulosic Mixed Blended Textile
77 Cinematograph Films (Exposed)
78 Coir Products
66 Fish and FishProducts
67 Food Products Products
68 Handicrafts
69 Cashew Kernels
70 Tobacco andTobacco Products
79 Natural Fibre Products
81 Gem and Jewellery
82 Stainless Steel Products
83 Electronics
89 Textile(For dept purpose only)
90 Miscellaneous

APPENDIX 27

List of Regional Licensing Authorities

(with their postal and telegraphic addresses) and Jurisdiction

Sl. No.	Name & Address	Telegraphic Address	Territorial Jurisdiction
1.	Director General of Foreign Trade Udyog Bhavan, New Delhi	CHIEF CONIMEX	Throughout India
2.	The Joint Director General of Foreign Trade, 4, Esplanade East, Calcutta - 700 069	CONIMPEXTRA CALCUTTA	West Bengal, Sikkim and Union Territory of Andaman and Nicobar.
3.	The Joint Director General of Foreign Trade, New Central Govt. Offices Building, S.E. Wing, New Marine Lines, Churchgate, Mumbai - 400 020.	CONIMPEXTRA MUMBAI	Maharashtra excluding the area which is under the jurisdiction of the Joint Director General of Foreign Trade, Pune and Daman, Dadra and Nagar Haveli.
4.	The Joint Director General of Foreign Trade, C' Block. Commercial Building No. 2. Pune Municipal Transport Building, Swargate, Pune,	CONIMPEXTRA PUNE	Fifteen Districts of Maharashtra vis, Pune, Ahmed nagar, Jalna, Beed, Kolahpur, Latur, Nanded, Osmanabad, Parbhani, Ratnagiri, Sangli, Satara, Solapur, Sindhu Durg and Nasik.
5.	The Joint Director General of Foreign Trade, 197, Peters Roads, Royapetah, Chennai - 600 014	CONIMPEXTRA CHENNAI	Tamil Nadu except those areas which are under the jurisdiction of Dy. Director General of Foreign Trade, Madurai, Coimbature and Pondicherry.
6.	The Joint Director General of Foreign Trade, Central Licensing Aea, B.K. Roy Court. 6-7, Asaf Ali Road. New Delhi - 110 002.	CONIMPEXTRA NEW DELHI	Delhi, two districts of Haryana, namely Faridabad and Gurgaon and four districts of Uttar Pradesh, namely, Meerut, Ghaziabad, Bulandshahar and Haradwar.
7.	The Joint Director General of Foreign Trade, 117/L/444. Kakadeo, Kanpur - 208 025	CONIMPEXTRA KANPUR	Uttar Pradesh excluding those areas which are under the jurisdiction of Jt. Director General of Foreign Trade

			(CLA). New Delhi, Varanasi and Moradabad, Deputy Director General of Foreign Trade, Panipat and Dy, DGFT, Moradabad.
8.	The Joint Director General of Foreign Trade, C&E Wing, 6th Floor Kendriya Sudan, 7th Main, 2nd Block, Koramangala Bangalore - 560 034.	CONIMPEXTRA BANGALORE	Karnataka.
9.	The Joint Director General of Foreign Trade, 'A' Block, 11th Floor, Govt. Multistoryed Building,Laldarwaja, Ahmedabad 580 001.	CONIMPEXTRA AHMEDABAD	Gujarat State excluding areas falling under the jurisdiction of Dy. Director General of Foreign Trade, Rajkot, Baroda, Surat and Development Commission KFTZ.
10.	The Joint Director General of Foreign Trade, 6-IV-C, Green Field, Near Shakti Nagar Chowk, Ludhiana.	CONIMPEXTRA LUDHIANA	Punjab excluding the districts of Amritsar and Roopnagar (Ropar)
11.	The Dy. Director General of Foreign Trade, 4th floor, Vikas Manzil, Sagar Saral, Gulzari Mal, Dharmasala Road, Moradabad	CONIMPEXTRA MORADABAD	District of Moradabad, Dehradun, Uttar-kasi Tehri Garhwal, Garhwal, Chamoli, Plthoragraph, Almora, Bijnaur, Nainital and Rampur.
12.	The Joint Director General of Foreign Trade, H.No.36/862-A Chittoor Road, (Opp. to SRVLP School) Ernakulam, Cochin - 682 001)	CONIMPEXTRA ERNAKULAM	Kerala and Union Lakshadweep.
13.	The Joint Director General of Foreign Trade, Udyog Bhavan, Tilak Marg, Jaipur - 302 005.	CONIMPEXTRA JAIPUR	Rajasthan.
14.	The Joint Director General of Foreign Trade, B-38/1-A-2, Tulsipur, Mehmoorganj, Varanasi - 221,007 (U.P.)	CONIMPEXTRA VARANASI	Districts of Varanasi, Mirzapur, Ghazipur, Azamgarh, Balia, Deoria, Gorakhpur, Basti Janpur, Sonebhadra, Mau and Sidharthnagar.
15.	The Joint Director General of Foreign Trade, Kendriya Sadan 1st Floor, V Block, Sultan Bazar, Hyderabad - 500 195.	CONIMPEXTRA HYDERABAD	Andhra Pradesh excluding area in the jurisdiction of Dy. Director General of Foreign Trade, Visakhapatnam,
16.	The Deputy Director General of Foreign Trade, R.B. Baruah Road, Guwahati - 781 024.	CONIMPEXTR GAUHATI	Assam, Arunachal Pradesh, Nagaland and Manipur
17.	The Joint Director General of Foreign Trade, III Floor, Office Bldg., 'A', Guru Bahadur Commercial Complex, T.T. Nagar, Bhopal - 462 003.	CONIMPEXTRA BHOPAL	Madhya Pradesh
18.	The Joint Director General of Foreign Trade, India Life Building (Annexe), Fourth floor) Trichy Road, Coimbatore - 641 018.	CONIMPEXTRA COIMBATORE	Four districts of Tamil Nadu viz, Coimbature, Nilgiris, Periyar and Salem.
19.	The Joint Director General of Foreign Trade, 416-L, Model Town, Panipat (Haryana).	CONIMPEXTRA PANIPAT	The whole of Haryana State (excluding Faridabad and Gurgaon) and Panchkula. and Saharanpur and Muzzaffarnagar.
20.	The Deputy Director General of Foreign Trade, Air Cargo	CONIMPEXTRA SRINAGAR	Jammu & Kashmir (Note: During winter, camp office will function at

	Complex, Sherwani Road, Srinagar.		24/C, Gandhi Nagar, Jammu).
21.	The Deputy Director General of Foreign Trade, Desai Building, Bhupindra Road, New Town Hall, Rajkot - 360 001.	CONIMPEXTRA RAJKOT	The Districts of Gujarat State known as Saurashtra (excluding Kutch) and Diu in the Union Territory of Daman and Diu.
22.	The Joint Director General of Foreign Trade, Biscomann Bhavan, Patna - 800 001.	CONIMPEXTRA PATNA	Bihar.
23.	The Joint Director General of Foreign Trade, Plot No. 9. 1st Main, II Cross Road, K.K. Nagar Madurai 625 020.	CONIMPEXTRA MADURAI	Districts of Madurai, Quidi-Milleth, Ramnad, Kamarajar, Pasum Pon Theyer. Thirumanagar, Nellai Kattabomman, Chidambaranar and Kanyakumari.
24.	The Dy. Diector General of Foreign Trade, Morello Building Shillong, Meghalaya - 790 001.	CONIMPEXTRA SHILLONG	Meghalaya, Tripura and Mizoram.
25.	The Dy. Director General of Foreign Trade, The Mall, CBR Building Amritsar.	CONIMPEXTRA AMRITSAR	Amritsar District.
26.	The Dy. Director General of Foreign Trade, Ashirwad Building, 18th June Road, Santa Inoz Panjim - 403 001 (Goa).	CONIMPEXTRA PANJIM	Goa.
27.	The Joint Director General of Foreign Trade, Sector - 35, D&CO-288. Chandigar - 160 023.	CONIMPEXTRA CHANDIGARH	Himachal Pradesh and Union Territory of Chandigarh, as well as District of Roopnagar (Ropar) and Panchkula.
28.	The Joint Director General of Foreign Trade, Maitri Vihar, Link Road, Cuttak - 753 012.	CONIMPEXTRA CUTTACK	Orissa.
29.	The Dy. Director General of Foreign Trade, P.B. No. 14, 205 Bharathi Street, Pondicherry - 605 001.	CONIMPEXTRA PONDICHERRY	Union Territory of Pondicherry, Karaikal, Mahe, Yanam and Districts of Ramaswamy Padayatchiyar and South Arcot of Tamil Nadu.
30.	The Joint Director General of Foreign Trade, Door No. 43-9-166, First Floor, T.S.N. Colony, Visakhapatnam - 503 016.	CONIMPEXTRA VISAKHAPATNAM	The district of Srikakulam Vizianagaram, Visakhapatnam, East Godavari and West Godavari of Andhra Pradesh.
31.	The Joint Director General of Foreign Trade, Kuber Bhawan, 9th Floor, E-Block, R. No. 901 & 902. Kothi Compound, Baroda - 390 001.	-	Districts of Gujarat, Vadodara; Kheda, Panchmal and Broach of Gujarat
32.	The Joint Director General of Foreign Trade, 634/636, Belgium Tower, Ring Road, Surat 395 003.	CONIMPEXTRA SURAT	Districts Gujarat of Surat Valsad and Dangs of Gujarat
33.	The Development/Joint Development/ Deputy Development/Assistant Development Commissioner, Santa Cruz EPZ, Andheri East, Mumbai	SEEPROZONE MUMBAI	Units stuated in Santa Cruz EPZ and approved 100% EOUs located in Maharashtra, Goa, Daman & Diu, Dadra and Nagar Haveli.
34.	The Development/Joint Development/ Deputy	KAFTZ GANDHIDHAM	Kutch Districts of Gujarat, Units situated in Kandla Free

	Development/Assistant Development Commissioner, Kandla Free Trade Zone, Kandla, Gandhidham.		Trade Zone and approved 100% EOUs situated in Gujarat.
35.	The Development/Joint Development/Deputy Development/Assistant Development Commissioner, Madras Export Processing zone, G.S.T. Road, N.H. 45, Tambaram, Chennai - 600 045.	MEPZ CHENNAI	Units situated in Madras Export Processing Zone and approved 100% EOUs situated in Tamil Nadu, Andaman & Nicobar Madras Export Islands. Union Territory of Pondicherry excluding Mahe and Yanam.
36.	The Development/Joint Development/Deputy Development/Assistant Development Commissioner, Kakkanad, Cochin - 682 030.	CEPZONE ERNAKULAM	Units Situated in Cochin Export Processing Zone and 100% EOUs situated in Kerala, Karnataka and Lakshadweep and Mahe.
37.	The Development/Joint Development/Deputy Development/Assistant Development Commissioner, Noida Export Processing Zone, Noida Dadri Road, Phase-II Noida District, Ghaziabad - 201 305	LIVWELL NEW DELHI	Units situated in Noida Export Processing Zone and approved 100% EOUs situated in Delhi, Uttar Pradesh, Punjab, Hariyana, Himachal Pradesh, Jammu & Kashmir Rajasthan, Madhya Pradesh and Chandigarh.
38.	The Development/Joint Development/ Deputy Development/Assistant Development Commissioner, Falta Export Processing Zone, 2nd MSO Building, Room No. 4, Nizam Place, 234/4, AJC Bose Road, Calcutta.	FEPZ CALCUTTA	Units situated in Falta Export Processing Zone and 100% EOUs situated in West Bengal, Orissa, Bihar, Assam, Arunachal pradesh, Tripura, Manipur, Meghalaya, Nagaland, Mizoram and Sikkim.
39.	The Development/Joint Development/Deputy Development/Assistant Development Commissioner, Visakhapatnam Export Processing Zone, Udyog Bhavan, Complex, Siripuram Junction, Visakhapatnam.	VEPZ	Units situated in Visakhapatnam Export Processing Zone & approved EOUssituated in Andhra Pradesh & Yanam.

APPENDIX 28

Jurisdiction of Advance Licensing Committee/HQRs EPCG Committee and Zonal Advance Licensing Committee/Zonal EPCG Committee/ Regional Advance Licensing Committee and HQRS/Zonal/Regional Licensing Committee/Regional EPCG Committee

Sl. No. (1)	*Committee (2)*	*Where Located (3)*	*Jurisdiction (4)*
1.	Advance Licensing Committee/ Special Advance Licensing Committee/HQRS EPCG Committee.	Office of the DGFT, New Delhi,	Throughout India

2.	Zonal Advance Licensing Committee/zonal EPCG Committee, Mumbai.	Office of the Jt. DGFT, Mumbai.	Districts falling under the jurisdiction of Jt. DGFT, Mumbai , Ahmedabad, Pune Mumbai, and Dy. DGFT, Baroda, Bhopal, Panjim, Rajkot and Surat as well as Development Commissioner KAFTZ as given in Appendix 27.
3.	Zonal EPCG Committee,	Office of the Jt. DGFT, Chennai.	Districts falling under the jurisdiction of Jt. DGFT, Chennai, Bangalore, Cochin, Hyderabad and Dy. DGFT, Coimbatore, Madurai, Pondicherry and Visakhapatnam as given in Appendix 27.
4.	Zonal EPCG Committee, Calcutta.	Office of the Jt. DGFT, Calcutta.	Districts falling under the jurisdiction of Jt. DGFT, Calcutta and Dy. DGFT, Cuttack Guwahati, Shillong and Patna as given in Appendix 27.
5.	Zonal EPCG Committee, New Delhi.	Office of the Jt. DGFT, New Delhi.	Districts falling under the jurisdiction of Jt. DGFT, (CLA) New Delhi, Jaipur (CLA), Kanpur, Ludhiana, Varanasi, Muradabad and Dy. DGFT, Amritsar Chandigarh, Panipat and Srinagar as given in Appendix 27.
6.	Regional EPCG Committee Bangalore	Office of the Jt. DGFT, Bangalore.	Districts falling under the jurisdiction of Jt. DGFT, Bangalore as given in Appendix 27.
7.	Regional EPCG Committee Ludhiana	Office of the Jt. DGFT, Ludhiana.	Districts falling under the jurisdiction of Jt. DGFT, Ludhiana and Dy. DGFT Amritsar and Chandigarh as given in Appendix 27.
8.	Regional EPCG Committee Ahmedabad	Office of the Jt. DGFT, Ahmedabad.	Districts falling under the jurisdiction of Jt. DGFT, Ahmedabad and Dy. DGFT, Baroda, Rajkot and Surat as well as Development Commission, KAFTZ as given in Appendix 27.

9.	Regional EPCG Committee Kanpur	Office of the Jt. DGFT, Kanpur.	Districts falling under jurisdiction of Jt. DGFT, Kanpur as given in Appendix 27.
10.	Regional EPCG Committee Cochin	Office of the Jt. DGFT Cochin.	Districts falling under the jurisdiction of Jt. DGFT, Cochin as given in Appendix 27.
11.	Regional EPCG Committee Jaipur	Office of the Jt. DGFT, Jaipur	Districts falling under the jurisdiction of of Jt. DGFT, Jaipur as given in Appendix 27.
12.	Regional EPCG Committee Varanasi	Office of Jt. DGFT, Varanasi.	District falling under the jurisdiction of Jt. DGFT, Varanasi as given in Appendix 27.
13.	Regional EPCG Committee Hyderabad	Office of Jt. DGFT, Hyderabad.	Districts falling under the jurisdiction of Jt.DGFT, Hyderabad and Dy DGFT, Visakhapatnam as given in Appendix 27.
14.	Regional EPCG Committee Pune	Office of Jt. DGFT, Pune	Districts falling under the Jt. DGFTPune, as given in Appendix 27 of the Handbook.

Note: 1. In respect of cases where the application value exceeds the financial powers of Regional EPCG Committee as given for S. No. 6 to 13 above but is within the powers of Zonal EPCG Committee, the same will be considered bythe respective Zonal EPCG Committee as per jurisdiction given from S. No. 2 to 5 above.

2. Districts/Offices not falling under the jurisdiction of Regional EPCG Committee shall fall under the jurisdiction of Zonal EPCG Committee irrespective of the fact that application value of cases falls within the jurisdiction of Regional EPCG Committee.

APPENDIX 31

Export Promotion Councils and Registration Procedure

EPCs

At present, there are following 20 Export Promotion Councils (EPCs) whose basic objective is to promote and develop the exports of the country. Each Council is responsible for the promotion of a particular group of products, projects and services.

List of Export Promotion Councils/Commodity Boards

Sl. No.	*Regional offices*	*Name of the Export Promotion Council*	*Registered Address*
1.	Apparel Export Promotion Council	NBCC Tower, 15 Bhikaji Cama Place, New Delhi - 110 066. Tel.: (91) 11-6883351/6888505 Fax: (19) 11-6168584.	New Delhi Rajasthan, Jodhpur, Ludhiana, Mumbai, Chennai, Hyderabad, Tirupur, Calcutta, Cochi.
2.	Basic Chemicals, Pharmaceuticals &	Jhansi Castle, 4th floor, 7-Cooperage Road	Calcutta, Bangalore

	Consmetics Export Promotion Council	Mumbai-400 039 Tel. : (91)22-2021288/2021330 Fax : (91)22-2026684	
3.	Cashew Export Promotion Council	P.B. No.1709, Chittor Road. Ernakulam South., Cochin-682-016 Tel. : (91)484-351973/361459 Fax : (91)484-370973	-
4.	Carpet Export Promotion Council	101-A/1, Krishna Nagar, (Behind Govt. Sr. Sec. School), Safdarjung Enclave, New Delhi - 110 029. Tel. : (91) 11-602742/601024 Fax : (91) 11-6115299.	Bhadohi (U.P.)
5.	Chemicals and Allied Products Export Promotion Council	World Trade Centre. 14/1B, Ezra Street, Calcutta-700 001 Tel. : (91) 33-267733/34/35. Fax : (91) 33-2255070.	Mumbai, Chennai, New Delhi, Calcutta
6.	Cotton Textile Export Promotion Council	Engineering Centre 5th Floor. Mumbai - 400 004 Tel. : (91) 22-2632910/11/12 Fax : (91) 22-2932914	Mumbai, Chennai, New Delhi, Ahmedabad, Calcutta, Tuticorin (TN), Cochin Coimbatore, Jaipur, North End. Kolhapur, Erode, Mumbai.
7.	Electronics and Computer Software Export Promotion Council	PHD-House, Phase-II, 3rd flr, Opp., Asian Games Village, New Delhi-110 016. Tel. : (91)11-696103/696206 Fax : (91)11-6853412 E-Mail : esc@egiasdl01.vsnl.net.in Home Page: http://www.tradeaccess.com	-
8.	Engineering Export Promotion Council	World Trade Centre. 14/IB, Ezra Street, Calcutta - 700 001. Tel. : (91)33-263080/81/82 Fax : (91)33-2258968 E-Mail : eepc-ho@ eepc.ho.eepc. ho.cmc.net.in	Mumbai, New Delhi, Chennai
9.	Gem and Jewellery Export Promotion Council	Diamond Bazar, 5th floor, 391-A, Dr. D. Bhadkamkar Marg, Mumbai-400 004 Tel. : (91)22-3871135/3888004 Fax : (91)22-3868752	New Delhi, Jaipur, Surat, Chennai
10.	Export Promotion Council for Handicrafts	6, Community Centre IInd Floor, Basant Lok. Vasant Vihar, New Delhi - 110 057. Tel. : (91)11-6875377/60087 Fax : (91)11-606144 E-Mail : secy.epch@axcess.net.in	-

11.	Handloom Export Promotion Council	18, Cathedral Garden Road, Nungambakkam, Chennai 600 034 Tel. : (91)44-8276043/8278879 Fax : (91)44-8271761	New Delhi, Hyderabad
12.	The Indian Silk Export Promotion Council	62, Mittal Chambers, 6th flr. Nariman Point, Mumbai - 400 021. Tel. : (91)22-2025866. 2027662, 2049413. Fax : (91)22-2874606	New Delhi
13.	Council for Leather Exports	Leather Centre, (3rd floor and 4th floor) 53, Sydenhams Road, Periameret, Madras-600 003 Tel. : (91)44-589098/582041 Fax : (91)44-588713/587083 E-Mail: cle@glasmdol.vsnl.net.in Home Page: http://www.leatherindia.com	Kanpur, Mumbai, New Delhi, Calcutta, Agra
14.	Overseas Construction Council of India	H-118, Himalaya House, 11th Floor, 23, Kasturba Gandhi Marg, New Delhi-110 001 Tel. : (91)11-3312936/3327550 Fax : (91)11-3312936	New Delhi
15.	Plastics Export Promotion Council	Centre-I, 11th floor, World Trade Centre, Cuffee Parade, Colaba, Mumbai-400 005. Tel. : (91)22-2184474/2184569 Fax : (91)22-2184810 E-Mail : plexcon@giasbm01.vsnl.net.in plexho@bom3.vsnl.net.in	Chennai, Calcutta.
16.	Shellac Export Promotion Council	World Trade Centre 14/IB Ezra Street, Calcutta-700 001. Tel. : (91)33-2482070 Fax : (91)33-2484046	
17.	Sports Goods Export Promotion Council	1-E/6, Swami Ram Tirth Nagar, Jhandewalan Extn. New Delhi-100 055 Tel. : (91)11-525695/529255 Fax : (91)11-7532147	Jalandhar
18.	Synthetic & Rayon Textile Export Promotion Council	Resham Bhavan, 78, Veer Nariman Point Road, Mumbai - 400 020. Tel. : (91)22-2048797/2048690 Fax : (91)22-2048358	New Delhi, Chennai, Surat.
19.	Wool & Woollens Export Promotion Council	312/714, Ashoka Estate, 24, Barakhamba Road, New Delhi - 110 001.	Mumbai, Ludhiana, Tirupur

		Tel. : (91) 11-3315512/3315205 Fax : (91) 11-3314626
20.	Powerloom Development and Export Promotion Council	Civil Court, B Wing, 4th Floor, Mahakavi Bhushan Marg, Behind Regal, Kolaba, Mumbai 400 039.

The following agencies shall also be regarded as an Export Promotion Council:

1.	Agricultural and Processed Food Products Export Development Authority	3rd Floor, Ansal Chambers II, 6, Bhikaji Kama Place, New Delhi 110 066.
2.	Coffee Board	1-Dr. Ambedkar Veedhi, Bangalore-560 001 Tel : (91) 80-257890 Fax : (91) 80-2255557
3.	Coir Board	Coir House, M.G. Road, Ernakulam South, Kochi 682 016.
4.	Federation of Indian Export Organisations (FIEO)	PHD House, 3rd Floor, Opp. Asian Games Village, New Delhi 110 016.
5.	The Marine Products Export Development Authority	P.B. No. 1663, MPEDA House, Panampilly Avenue, Cochin 682 036.
6.	Rubber Board	Shastri Road, P.B. No.280, Kottayam 686 001. Tel : (91) 481-571231 Fax : (91) 481-571380.
7.	Spices Board	Sugandha Bhavan, N.H. By Pass, Palarivattom. P.O. Cochin-682025. Tel : (91)484-333610 to 16 Fax : (91)484-331429/334429 Home Page : http:// ww.indianspices.com
8.	Tea Board	14, BTM Sarani, Brabourne Road, P.B. No. 2172, Calcutta-700 001 Tel : (91) 33-2251411 Fax : (91) 33-2251417

9. Tobacco Board

P.B. No.322.
G.T. Road,
Guntur-522 004,
Tel : (91) 863-354424/230399
Fax : (91) 863-354232.

The EPCs are non-profit organisations registered under the Companies Act or the Societies Registration Act, as the case may be. They are supported by financial assistance from the Central Government.

Role The main role of the EPCs is to project India's image abroad as a reliable supplier of high quality goods and services. In particular, the EPCs encourage and monitor the observance of international standards and specifications by exporters. The EPCs keep abreast of the trends and opportunities in international markets for goods and services and assist their members in taking advantage of such opportunities in order to expand and diversify exports.

Functions The major functions of the EPCs are as follows:

1. To provide commercially useful information and assistance to their members in developing and increasing their exports
2. To offer professional advice to their members in areas such as technology upgradation, quality and design improvement, standards and specifications, product development, innovation, etc.
3. To organise visits of delegations of its members abroad, to explore overseas market opportunities
4. To organise participation in trade fairs, exhibitions and buyer-seller meets in India and abroad
5. To promote interaction between the exporting community and the Government both at the Central and State levels
6. To build a statistical base and provide data on the exports and imports of the country, exports and imports of their members, as well as other relevant international trade data

Professional bodies In order to give a boost and an impetus to exports, it is imperative that the EPCs function as professional bodies. For this purpose, executives with a professional background in commerce, management and international marketing and having experience in government and industry are brought into the EPCs.

Autonomy The EPCs are autonomous and regulate their own affairs. They do not require the approval of the Central Government for participation in trade fairs, exhibitions etc. and for sending sales teams/delegations abroad. The Ministry of Commerce/Ministry of Textiles of the Government of India, as the case may be, interact with the managing committee of the council concerned, twice a year, once for approving their annual plans and budget and again for a mid-year appraisal and review of their performance.

Registration-cum-membership An exporter may on application, register and become member of an EPC. On being admitted to membership, the applicant shall be granted forthwith Registration-cum-Membership (RCMC) of the EPC concerned.

Procedure for issue of RCMC An application for registration may be made to the concerned registering authority in the form given in Annexure 10 along with a self certified copy of the IEC Number issued by the licensing authority concerned and Bank certificate in support of the applicant's financial soundness.

If the application for registration is granted, the concerned registering authority shall issue the RCMC indicating the status of the applicant as Merchant-exporter or Manufacturer-exporter in the form given in Annexure 10.

In case, an export desires to get registration as a manufacturer-exporter, he is required to furnish evidence to that effect.

Validity period of RCMC The RCMC shall be deemed to be valid from 1st April of the licensing year in which it was issued and shall be valid for 5 years ending 31st March of the licensing year, unless otherwise specified.

Wherever RCMC has been indicated as one of the prescribed documents against any application under Policy/Procedures, the applicant should hold a valid RCMC on the date of making such application. This RCMC may not necessarily be valid on the date of making exports, if such exports are made prior to submitting such application.

Furnishing of returns The exporter is required to furnish regular monthly returns/details of his exports of different commodities to the concerned Registering Authority in accordance with the area of his operation. This will be in addition to any other returns as prescribed by the Registering Authority. However, Export House Trading House/Star Trading House/Super Star Trading House is also required to send monthly returns to the FIEO in the format specified by the FIEO.

RCMC is a must for EXIM benefits Exports of the only registered exporters having valid RCMC will qualify for the benefits provided in the current Exim Policy. In other words exports effected by an exporter without holding any valid RCMC will not be counted for any benefits.

Intimation regarding change in constitution In case of change in ownership, constitution, name or address of an exporter, it shall be obligatory on his part to intimate such change to the Registering Authority concerned within a period of one month from the date of such change.

De-registration The Registering Authority may de-register a RCMC holder for a specified period for violation of the conditions of registration. Before such de-registration, the RCMC holder will be given a show cause notice by the Registering Authority and an adequate and reasonable opportunity to make a representation against the proposed de-registration.

APPENDIX 36

List of Offices of The Exchange Control Department of Reserve Bank of India

The Reserve Bank of India, Exchange Control Department has its Central Office at Mumbai and offices at other centres with jurisdictions as indicated below:

Office	*Address*	*Jurisdiction*
Head Office	Reserve Bank of India, Exchange Control Department, Central Office, New Office Bldg., Post Box No. 1055, Fort, Mumbai - 400 023.	
Ahmedabad	The Joint Controller, Exchange Control Dept., Reserve Bank of India, P.B. No. 1, Navjivan Post Office, Ashram Road, Near Gandhi Bridge, Ahmedabad-380014.	State of Gujarat
Bangalore	The Deputy Controller, Exchange Control Deptt., Reserve Bank of India, 10-3-8, Nrupatunga Rd., P.B. No. 6768, Bangalore-560 002.	State of karnataka
Bhopal	The Assistant Controller, Exchange Control Deptt., Reserve Bank of India, M.P. State Co-op. Bank Bldg., Malaviya Nagar, P.B. No. 312, Bhopal-462 003.	State of Madhya Pradesh
Bhubaneswar	The Assistant Controller, Exchange Control Deptt., Reserve Bank of India, New Office Bldg., Unit III, Schivalaya Marg, Bhubaneswar-751 001.	State of Orissa
Mumbai	The Joint Controller, Exchange Contol Deptt., Reserve Bank of India, Bombay Regional Office, Amar Bldg., Fort, Bombay-400 001.	State of Maharashtra, Union Territory of Dadra and Nagar Haveli and Union Territory of Daman and Diu.
Calcutta	The Joint Controller, Exchange Control Deptt., Reserve Bank of India, 15, Netaji Subhas Road. Post Bag No. 2026. Calcutta-700 001.	State of Sikkim and West Bengal and Union Territory of Andaman and Nicobar Islands
Chandigarh	The Deputy Controller, Exchange Control Deptt., Reserve Bank of India, S.C.O. 17, 18-19, Sector 17-B, Post Bag No. 2, Chandigarh-160 017.	State of Haryana (excluding the districts of Faridabad, Gurgaon and Sonepat), Himachal Pradesh and Punjab and Union Territory of chandigarh.
Cochin	The Joint Controller, Exchange Control Deptt., Reserve Bank of India, Catholic Centre, Broadway, P.B. No. 254, Cochin-682 031.	State of Kerala and Union Territory of Lakshadweep

Guwahati	The Assistant Controller, Exchange Control Deptt., Reserve Bank of India, Station Road, Pan Bazar, P.B. No. 120, Guwahati-781 001.	State of Arunachal Pradesh, Assam, Manipur, Meghalaya, Mizoram, Nagaland and Tripura.
Hyderabad	The Deputy Controller, Exchange Control Deptt., Reserve bank of India. 6-1-56, Secretariat Road, Saifabad, Hyderabad-500 004.	State of Andhra Pradesh
Jaipur	The Deputy Controller, Exchange Control Deptt., Reserve Bank of India, Tonk Road, Near Rambagh Circle, P.B. No. 12, Jaipur-302 004.	State of Rajasthan
Kanpur	The Joint Controller, Exchange Control Deptt., Reserve Bank of India, M.G. Road, Kanpur-208 001.	State of Uttar Pradesh excluding New Okhla Industrial Development Area (NOIDA) in Gaziabad District
Chennai	The Joint Controller, Exchange Control Deptt., Reserve Bank of India, Fort Glacis, South Beach Road, Madras-600 001.	State of Tamil Nadu and Union Territory of Pondicherry
New Delhi	The Joint Controller, Exchange Control Deptt., Reserve Bank of India, 6, Parliament Street, New Delhi - 110 001.	Union Territory of Delhi, The Districts of Faridabad, Gurgaon and Sonepat of State of Haryana and New Okhla Industrial Development Area (NOIDA) in Gaziabad District of State of Uttar Pradesh.
Panaji	The Deputy Controller, Exchange Control Deptt., Reserve Bank of India, Dada Vaidya Road. Panaji-403 001, Goa	State of Goa
Patna	The Assistant Controller, Exchange Control Deptt., Reserve Bank of India, South of Gandhi Maidan, Post Bag No. 162, Patna-800 001.	State of Bihar
Jammu/Srinagar	The Assistant Controller, Exchange Control Deptt., Reserve Bank of India. 'Irrum Chambers', Opp. I.G. P's Office. Balgarden, Post No. 39, Srinagar-190 010.	State of Jammu and Kashmir

Note: Arrangements have also been made at the Nagpur Office of Reserve Bank of India for dealing with applications of person, firms and Companie's resident in the districts of Akola, Amravati, Bhandara, Buldhana, Chandrapur, Gadchiroli, Nagpur, Wardha and Yeotmal of the State of Maharashtra, for travel, and for sundry remittances outlined in Annexure I to Chapter 8 of the Exchange Control Manual (1993) Edition which are beyond the powers delegated to authorised dealers.

List of Authorised Dealers in Foreign Exchange

ABN AMRO Bank N.V.
Abu Dhabi Commercial Bank Ltd.
Allahabad Bank
American Express Bank Ltd.
Andhra Bank
ANZ Grindlays Bank Ltd.
Arab Bangladesh Bank Limited
Bank International Indonesia
Bank of America National Trust and Savings Association
Bank of Bahrain and Kuwait B.S.C.
Bank of Baroda
Bank of Ceylon
Bank of India
Bank of Madura Ltd.
Bank of Maharashtra
Bank of Muscat International S.A.O.G.
Bank of Nova Scotia
Bank of Punjab Ltd.
Bank of Rajasthan Ltd.
Bank of Tokyo Mitsubishi Ltd.
Banque Indosuesz
Banque Nationale De Paris
Barclays Bank p.l.c.
Benares State Bank Ltd.
Bharat Overseas Bank Ltd.
Bombay Mercantile Cooperative Bank Ltd.
The British Bank of the Middle East
Canara Bank
Indian Bank
Indian Overseas Bank
IndusInd Bank Ltd.
Internationale Nederlanden Bank (ING Bank)
Jammu and Kashmir Bank Ltd.
Karnataka Bank Ltd.
Catholic Syrian Bank Ltd.
Central Bank of India
Centurion Bank Ltd.
The Chase Manhattan Bank
China Trust Bank A.G.
China Trust Commercial Bank
Cho Hung Bank
Citi Bank N.A.
City Union Bank Ltd.
Commerz Bank A.G.
Commercial Bank of Korea Ltd.
Corporation Bank
Credit Agricole Indosuez
Credit Lyonnais
Dena Bank
Deutsche Bank Aktiengesellschaft
The Development Bank of Singapore
Development Credit Bank Ltd.
Dhanalakshmi Bank Ltd.
Dresdner Bank A.G.
Federal Bank Ltd.
The Fuji Bank Limited
Global Trust Bank Ltd.
Hanil Bank
HDFC Bank Ltd.
Hong Kong and Shanghai Banking Corporation Ltd.
ICICI Banking Corporation Ltd.
IDBI Bank Ltd.
Societe Generale
Sonali Bank
South Indian Bank Ltd.
Standard Chartered Bank
State Bank of Bikaner and Jaipur
State Bank of Hyderabad
Karur Vysya Bank Ltd.
KBC Bank NV
Kredit Bank N.V. Belgium
Krung Thai Bank Public Company Ltd.
Lakshmi Vilas Bank Ltd.
Maharashtra State Cooperative Bank Ltd.
Mashreq Bank p.s.c.
Morgan Guarantee Trust Co. of New York, USA
Nedungadi Bank Ltd.
Oman Internationl Bank S.A.O.G

Oriental Bank of Commerce
Overseas Chinese Banking Corporation Ltd.
Punjab National Bank
Punjab and Sind Bank
Sakura Bank Ltd.
Sangli Bank Ltd.
Sanwa Bank Ltd.
Sarawsat Cooperative Bank ltd.
SBI Commercial and International Bank Ltd.
Siam Commercial Bank Ltd.
State Bank of India
State Bank of Indore
State Bank of Mauritius Ltd.
State Bank of Mysore
State Bank of Patiala
State Bank of Saurashtra
State Bank of Travancore
Suminioto Bank Ltd.
Syndicate Bank
Tamilnadu Mercantile Bank Ltd.
Thomas Cook (India) Ltd.
Times Bank Ltd.
Toronto Dominion Bank
UCO Bank
Union Bank of India
United Bank of India
United Western Bank Ltd.
UTI Bank Ltd.
Vijaya Bank
Vysya Bank Ltd.

Institutions holding restricted authorisation to deal in foreign exchange are

Export-Import Bank of India
Industrial Credit & Investment Corporation of India Ltd.
Industrial Development Bank of India
Industrial Finance Corporation of India
SBI Factors and Commercial Services Pvt. Ltd.
Small Industries Development Bank of India.

// *Chapter 11* //

Export Strategy and Export Marketing Plan

When a company decides that it is ready to export, it must formulate an export strategy. Strategy formulation is the core of any busi ness activity. It tells the firm where it is going and how it should get there. Marketing strategy is often defined as, "The selection ofa target market and the determination of the product, price promotion and distribution policies that the enterprise must implement." When a strategy has been formulated, programmes must be developed for each strategic element. A company strategy is in effect a blueprint for competing on target export markets. An explicit export strategy provides a unified sense of purpose, to w hich the staff of the enterprise can relate. In the development of such strategy, import regulations and other trade barriers must be taken into consideration, as they have a critical impact on the outcome of the export venture. To implement a strategy, an export marketing plan is required. Industrial marketing or so called 'Business to Business' marketing may differ somewhat from regular consumer marketing, but the basics remain the same. The relationship between these various steps is shown in Fig 13. 1.

MARKETING STRATEGY

This reflects an attempt to outline an overall approach to the export marketing venture. The strategy chosen should reflect the answer to the following key questions: Should the company enter the export market in a big way? Are low prices essential for success? Will product differences playa major role in competitive positioning? Will a large-scale promotional campaign be required?

The strategy chosen should reflect the management's judgement of the most effective ways of overcoming the problems and exploiting the opportunities identified by the SWOT analysis. The formulation of strategies are therefore closely linked.

Marketing strategies cover a broad range of issues, including

- The choice of export market
- Identification and choice of importers/agents/distributors
- Distribution adaptation
- Packaging, labelling, branding
- Adding value to the basic product
- Use of trade fairs/shows as promotional tools
- Export financing

- ★ Administrative procedures for exports
- ★ Negotiation of contractual terms and conditions
- ★ Export market research

Steps in Exporting

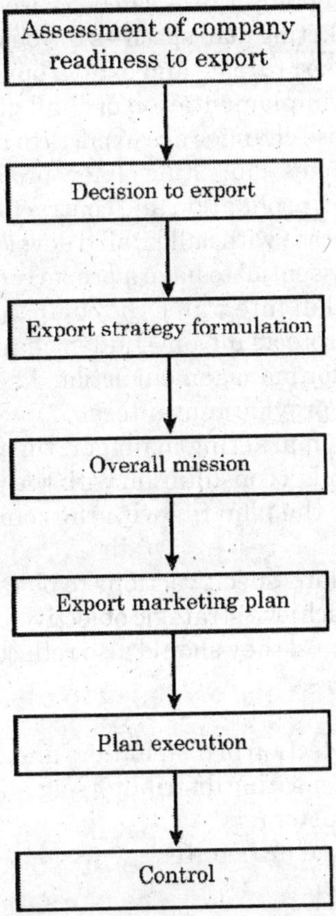

Fig 11.1 Flow chart on export marketing plan

Need for an Export Marketing Plan

To draw up an export marketing plan and a business plan (which can be combined), what will be needed most is a little time and perseverance. In addition to the steps outlined here to be followed are, to develop a plan that will be of practical aid to the company, not only in charting a course for the business, including export and keeping it under control but also in dealing with banks and other agencies who may want to know what is intend to be done with their money.

An export marketing plan is needed for one or more of the following reasons:

- ★ As part of the Business Plan The export marketing plan is an essential part of the overall business plan. I t defines w here the sales revenue will come from, and how it can be generated. The marketing plan states how much of each product can be exported. As such, it is a vital input to the production and financial planning.

* It enables reaction to changes Export markets are in constant evolution owing to change in technology, competition, imports, customer needs and the economy. These can be viewed as threats or opportunities. A good marketing plan specifies the objectives and actions which are needed to resist threats and exploit opportunities.
* It assists in the implementation of chall.ges in cOmpall.y strategy Examples of these changes are exports to new markets and expansion in existing ones; launching of new products; diversification; export expansion, consolidation and contraction.
* To Support your case with ball.ks all.d developmell.t agell.cies In such situations, it is essential to have a properly devised marketing plan.

A good marketing plan integrates the company's marketing activities into a coherent whole, protects it from sudden changes, establishes targets and acts as a focal point for management action. I t cannot however, predict, and prevent mistakes or provide guarantees.

If the company has a marketing manager, the plan should be prepared together with him/her and in consultation with the production and financial manager, to ensure that the plan fits with the company's overall business strategy.

Export marketing plans specify actions to be taken to implement marketing strategies and to achieve strategic objectives. In addition to outlining implementation procedures, they should also reflect decisions on the following matters, among others:

* Methods of sale
* Screening and selection of distributors and agent abroad
* Methods of compensating distributors/agents
* Contracts with customers
* Pricing policies and procedures
* Product adaptation

THE SUPPORT INFORMATION REQUIRED

If the export marketing plan is for an export market where the enterprise is already competing, the owner will already have much of the knowledge and experience required. If however it is for a new market, outside help will certainly be required.

If the enterprise never exported before, it should begin by documenting all that is known about the export market, using each element below as a guideline.

* Market size and trends
* Market structure
* Competitors
* Products
* Pricing
* Buyer behaviour

- Marketing channels
- Marketing communications
- Establishing a competitive advantage

THE EXPORT MARKETING PLAN

The first essential of any plan is to determine the time span it is to cover. This span could be 10 years (for a perspective plan), five years (for a strategic plan), one year (for an operational plan) or even one month (for a control plan). There are no hard rules for choosing a particular time span because it depends on the degree of uncertainty in which the company conducts its business. The higher the uncertainty, the shorter the time span should be. Even if it is difficult to prepare strategic plans for a two-to-five year span, it is advisable to do so. Break the strategic plans up into annual operational plans and further subdivide them into control charts for a monthly review.

The focal point is to establish business objectives for the company. Perhaps already an intuitive idea of what objectives are feasible in the immediate future is already there. These can however, be arrived at or improved in a more systematic way by:

- Doing a SWOT (Strengths, Weaknesses, Opportunities and Threats) analysis.
- Defining the scope of the company's business.

The next step is to decide the activities to achieve the stated objectives. This would mean preparing a capital plan, a raw material plan, a manpower plan, a financing plan. These plans are related to each other and must be complementary. In other words, the policy should not be such that while the capital plan is being carried out, the raw materials plan goes out of control, or the financing plan becomes impractical, or the marketing plan becomes irrelevant.

It follows that an export-marketing plan is a sub-plan designed to achieve the marketing objectives of the business. The combination of this plan with the other sub plans will lead to a business plan.

As already stated the export marketing plan is a step –by-step guide to stratify implementation. it specifies, targets dates and provides detailed budgets for each step. it should answer all the questions on how a strategy is to be implemented and directs the enterprise to the attainment of the strategic objective. it is obvious therefore, that the export marketing plan and the export strategy are closely interrelated and that, as the various steps are put into action,there should be a continuos interaction (modifications for instance, in the light of actual situations)between the two.

The development of export marketing plans requires decisions on the role that exporting is to play in the company's growth, the scope and nature of product lies and markets abroad, precise export performance goals and level of management commitment to the export venture.

A plan is only as good as the quality of to basic data gathered and the analysis undertaken during the planning precess.it is important to obtain the participation of all levels of management in this process and to impress upon them that, to succeed company-wide commitment to export goals is essential.

The primary puurpoe of an export marketing plan is two fold.first, it is a document that describes the basic components of the export venture.second,it is an up-to-date plan resulting from much thought and painful reflection, research, and analysis concerning what is required to start, fine-tune and carry a successful venture. The plan is not to be considered a final piece of work to be field away and forgotten .it is a dynamic working document that should be constantly reviewed and revised as the company acquires more experience, data and feedback from the market, constant attention to planning is more important than the plan itself.

The formulation of export marketing plans is a creative process. No two plans should look alike as each plan should be customized for a particular company, particular products and a particular market, nevertheless, good marketing plans share some common features. A comprehensive plan should have the following principal components:

- ★ Company background: a basic analysis of the company's mission, objectives, resources, product target markets and competition.
- ★ SWOT analysis: an analysis of company's strengths, weakness, opportunities and threats in the context of exporting.
- ★ Action programme in regard to the product distribution pricing, promotion etc.
- ★ Budget and timetable: justification and allocation of monetary and managerial resources within a time frame.

A typical export marketing plan focuses on marketing objectives, market segmentation and positioning, characteristics of the product line, distribution channels, export pricing and promotional strategies (see fig.13.2)the plan should outline the actions required in sufficient detail.it should set outsales targets, budgets and activity schedules, as well assign responsibilities for its implementation.

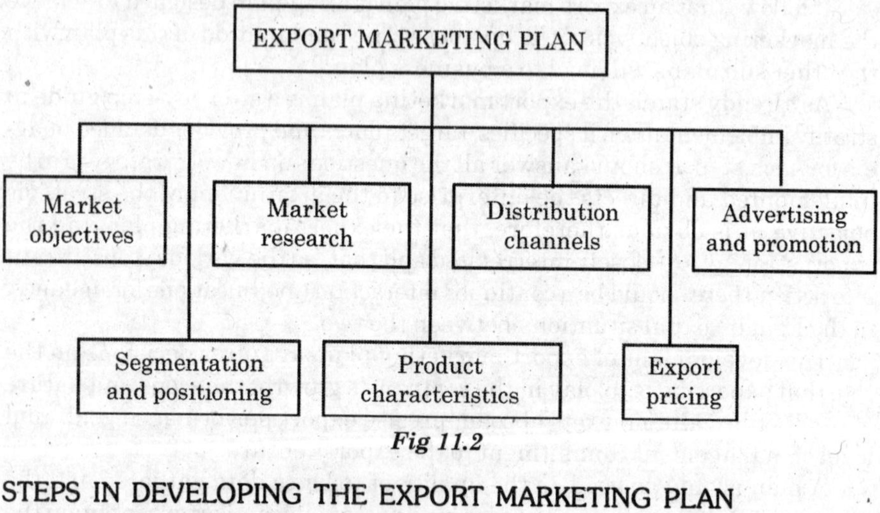

Fig 11.2

STEPS IN DEVELOPING THE EXPORT MARKETING PLAN

1. Setting of marketing objectives
2. Market segmentation

3. Market research
4. Product characteristics
5. Export pricing
6. Distribution channels
7. Promotion
8. Budget and timetable

Step 1 Marketing objectives

The first step in developing a marketing plan is to establish export marketing objectives. These objectives, which should be attainable, realistic and clear, and should be communicated throughout the company. Since they will determine the company's direction and its activities, the management will have to devote considerable time and effort to setting them. An analysis of the company's strengths, weaknesses, opportunities and threats, or a "SWOT" analysis in short, can provide a guide to management for developing effective and realistic objectives. A SWOT analysis is usually based on an evaluation of facts and assumption about the company and on market research below, the SWOT graph is presented. It is up to company to plot itself on the graph, based on several criteria.

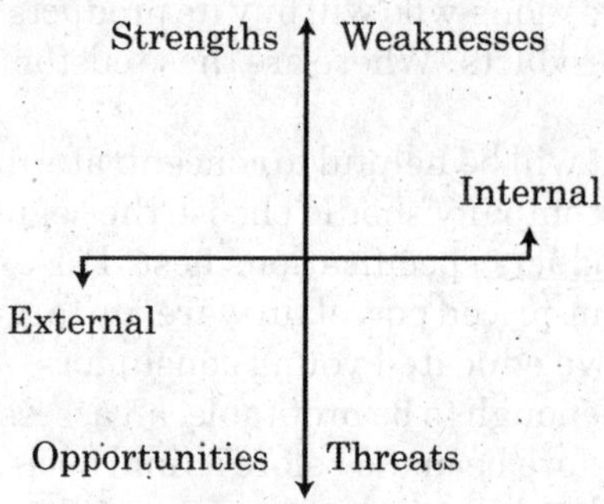

Fig 11.3 *SWOT analysis graph*

A company's strengths are its competitive advantages, that will give it an edge in the export markets. Its weaknesses are its constraints, which may inhibit marketing activities in certain directions. For example, a company lacking readily available funds, cannot undertake a large scale promotional compaign. The assessment of a company's strengths and weaknesses in relation to the competition is essential for competitive positioning. This assessment from the point of the competition should, at least consider:

★ Technology in use
★ Design, styling, trademarks
★ Product quality, quality control and the product's life cycle
★ Completeness of the product line
★ Customer service
★ Raw material supplies
★ Distribution structure and cost

The review of the opportunities and threats in the market should complement the analysis of the company's strengths and weaknesses. The aim is to identify the best business opportunities and directions of growth. A Company's opportunities on potential markets can be evaluated in terms of the firm's export customers, products, the market structure and competing suppliers. Such an evaluation may reveal the complementary relationship between the company's strengths and market opportunities.

Finally, the management should examine the so-called marketing threats on the markets being considered. These should include import rules and regulations relating to tariffs, quotas, non-tariff measures and so on. Management should also determine whether the markets under assessment are mature markets, if they are already well supplied and do not therefore provide a readily niche for the company's products.

Step 2 Market Segmentation

An export-marketing plan is not complete until the company has identified its target segment in the export market. Any large market has a variety of market segments that differ substantially. Different consumer groups exist according to income levels, age, life style, occupation and education. A crucial element of the export marketing plan is to identify the segment that the company intends to reach. In making this choice, the company should answer the following questions-who will buy its products in the export market? Why they buy these products? Where are these customers located? What are their characteristics?

In this exercise, it will be helpful to concentrate on segment similarities and differences. The company should choose the segment with the requirements that fit its products specifications best. For example, if it produces high-quality, premium-priced porcelain ware, its target segment is likely to be the high-income, we educated young consumers. A target markets segment should be large enough to be profitable. an assessment of the size of the segment should therefore be made before a final decision is taken to include it in the marketing plan.

Step 3 Market Research

To succeed in exporting, a company must identify attractive export markets for its products as accurately as possible. Market research and forecasting are therefore of great importance. Factors to be evaluated include the size of the market, the characteristics of demand in it, consumer requirement, trade channels, and the cultural and social differences that may affect the company's way of doing business with the market.

A small producer contemplating entering export trade may not be willing or able to allocate resources to expensive data collection methods. Companies in that situation can use published data to assess the market. They should, however, first evaluate the data for reliability and accuracy. One of the advantages of the European market is that it is very transparent and almost all-necessary information is available somewhere.

Step 4 Product Characteristics

The company should next consider the products that it has to offer. An analysis should be, made of any modifications required in the products, the packaging, labeling requirements, brand name and after-sales services expected. Many products must undergo significant adaptations if they are to satisfy the customer and market requirements abroad. Other products require changes at the discretion of the producer, only to improve their appeal on export markets.

Step 5 Export Pricing

In setting an export price, the company should consider the additional costs that do not enter into pricing for the domestic market. These include such items as international freight and insurance charges, product adaptation costs, import duties, commissions for import agents and foreign exchange risk coverage.

Export pricing analysis should begin with these questions – what value does the target market segment place on the company's product? How do differences in this product in this product add, to or detract from. Its market value?

In practice these are difficult questions to research, but analysing the prices and product characteristics of existing competitive products may reveal critical information. The analysis may show that it is not the cost of materials that determines the product's value, but rather the customer's perception of that value. When calculative, because you may not be willing to increase your end-user prices once you have found the right representative.

Step 6 Distribution Channels

A potential exporter should consider the following distribution options:

- ★ Exporting through a domestic exporting firm that will take over full responsibility for finding sales outlets abroad.
- ★ Setting up its own export organisation.
- ★ Selling through representatives abroad.
- ★ Using warehouses abroad.
- ★ Establishing a wholly owned sales subsidiary.

The choice of distribution channel will depend on the company's export strategy and the export market. If the company intends to export a product that has a specific feature which is likely to be a good selling point to a market segment that is already well supplied, it may need to create greater awareness of the product through an appropriate promotional strategy. In this case, it may be better to appoint an agent who does not handle many products and can allocate the time needed to promote that products.

Distribution channels should be chosen very carefully, and efforts should be made maintain good relations between the parties concerned.

Step 7 promotion

The export marketing plan should provide details on the following aspects of the promotional strategy:(1)Publicity mehtods (2) Advertising (who will be responsible for it, and how much the company can allocate to it) (3) Trae Missions (4) Buyers' visits (5) Other promotional activities (which mehtods to use), the effort will be successful as to the extent to which the company provides effective customer support.

An exporter should remember that even the best product may fil without company support to trade intermediaries and the end-users. In addition,customer support creates goodwill and loyalty to the exporter. Participation in major European trade fair is in many cases a good way to present the company's products and services to te European trade. One should not expect immediate sales, but it does show professionalism on the exported part and allows for the developing of business contacts.

Participation in exhibitions is a costly affair, but it can certainly pay off when the company has clearly defined objectives of what it wants to achieve at the exhbition and has created the conditions and methods which allow for the achieving of these objectives. Before actually participating in an exhibition, it is advisable to visit several product-related exhigbitions first. Visiting or participating in an European trade fair is also a unique opportunity to gather all sorts of information which helps in conducting proper market research (see step 3).

Step 8 Budget And Timetable

A budget must be established for the export marketing plan. This should cover such basic aspects as sources of financing, use of the financing resources and a forecast of the export venture's financial position after three to five years. A detailed timetable of activities must also be drawn up.

ANALYSING THE COMPANY'S STRENGTHS AND WEAKNESSES

As stated above, there are five straight forward steps in preparing an export marketing plan:

- Assessing the past performance of the company
- Assessing its competitors
- Looking at the export market to find opportunities and to avoid pitfalls
- Dediding on the (export marketing)objectives
- Deciding on how to achieve these strategies and action plans

The first two steps will reveal the company's strengths and weaknesses,and the third step its opportunities and threats.

Worksheets enable going through these steps one-by-one.

Assessing the past performance

Two worksheets will help in identifying the company's strong and weak points. They are aids to the analysis and will stimulate the mind to work critically.

This analysis is done to help the company and so honesty is a must it is a good idea to use other people to help with the analysis and those with some knowledge of the business would be best.

Worksheets 1 and 2 should be completed. Gaps may be left in the beginning-any entry is a start, and entries can be added later. Each step involves time and thought and things that have been forgoten initially may be remembered later.

Non-marketing strengths and weaknesses In the earlier module a fairly good picture of the reasons for the company'ssuccess and failures would have been built up. The focus was left fairly open but now some structure will be brought in to help spot areas that may have been overlooked.

While the emphasis is on marketing other factors (such as production skills and financial resources)which may be the most obvious strengths should not be forgotten.this may result in an overall advantages in serving the markets.

Exercise 1

Worksheet 1 lists some of the more important non-marketing factors. Assess the company on each point and try to take advantage if the strengths or improve the performance as appropriate.

Something brief opposite each item if possible can be written. An example might be "own my raw material source" or "contract provides for a fixed price for materials over a period of five years".

Exporter will assess the strengths and weakness in the following areas, as listed in the worksheet:production resources, management resources and financial resources.

Worksheet 1: Non –Marketing strengths and weaknesses

Factor	Strenghts	weaknesses
Production resources		
Access to raw materials, components,etc.		
Possesion of special equipement		
Specialised labour skills		
Possession of patents or licences		
Quality of packaging		
Access to new production technology		
Management resources		
Management experience		
Range of specialist management functions		
Adequacy of organisational structure		
Clarity of plans and strategy		
Incentive options		
Financial resources		
Access to aditional finance		
Level of profitability		
Availability of credit facilities		

Marketing strengths and weaknesses This worksheet looks in detail at the marketing operations to see which are the best and worst. Again, something should be written opposite to each item listed in worksheet 2.

For example, opposite "knowledge of markets", "know total market size",and a weakness "don't know breakdown by market segment" might be noted.

Exercise 2

Using worksheet 2,the marketing strengths and weaknesses can be assessed under the heading market knowledge and information: promotion and sales distribution system;products and consumer service.

Worksheet 2: Marketing strengths and weaknesses

Factor	Strengths	Weakness
Market knowledge And information		
Do you have a marketing plan?		
Knowledge of markets(e.g. market size, segments, trends)		
Knowledge of customers'image of you company		
Knowledge of how your customers make purchase decisions		
Your use of internal information, e.g.sales analysis,sales agents		
your access to external market information,e.g.trade magazines and business journals, use of State information agencies		
your dependence on:		
* A few key customers (1% of total sales to top 10 customers)		
* A few key products		
* A small geographic area		
Promotion and selling		
Your analysis of customers		
Sales incentive system used		
Use of brochures		
Use of press release		
Use of advertising		
Distribution system		
Your penetration of outlets,e.g. outlets sold to as percentage of total number of outlets.		
Incentive system for distributors		
Back-up to distributors,e.g. Displays,point-of-sale material		
Products		
Produt development record,e.g. number of new products introduced last year		
Age of present products		
Quality and function of packaging		
Specific product benefits your offer		
Customer service		
Credit facilities provided to customers		
Percentage of orders delivered on time		

Assessing the competitors

A good knowledge of the competition is required to spot opportunities. The following box provides a check list of possible ways of obtaining information about the competitors.

The main point to note in regard to the competitors is the maximum advantage should be taken of their weaknesses and efforts should be carried out to offset their strengths.

Ways of obtaining information on the competitors

1. Send for their brochures and price lists.
2. Place an order with them and examine their products and packaging.
3. Visit their premises.
4. Inquire about their delivery terms,credit terms,special capabilities, machinery, special offers to big customers.
5. Obtain copies of the century's trade promotion annual reports and check on grants given to the competitors.
6. Collect copies of their advertisements and other publicity materials from newspapers and magazines.
7. Talk to their customers.

Worksheets 3 and 4 will help in getting to know the competition. Filling in these forms may simply mean writing down all that known about the competitors and, if there are blanks,information needed to fill them in have to be obtained. If the exporter is considering entering more than one market, the worksheets for each market should be completed separetely.

The exporter need worry if he cannot fill in each line. If there are gaps,the information required should be obtained.

Exercise 3

Complete worksheets 3 and 4.

Worksheet 3: knowing your competitors

(you may wish to increase the number of columns if you have more competitors.)

Names of competitors	**A**	**B**	**C**	**D**
What equipment do they have,what special machines do they have?				
Market segments in which you complete				
Number of persons selling for them				
Do they have a prited brochure and price list?				
Do they advertise?				
Where?				
Do they get free publicity?				
Where?				
Do they have agents and/or distributors?who?				

How much of your target market do they cover?				
Are prices above,below,or equal to yours for equivalent products?				
Are their terms better or worse than yours?				

Worksheet 4: knowing your competitor's products

Names of competitors	A	B	C	D
Products				
What special features do their products have? (Take each product separately and be honest.)				
Are their products branded?				
How doesthe quality of their packaging compare with yours?				
How long has their product been on the market?				
What new products have They brought out in the Last one or two years?				
Do they offer special services With their products such as Installation,advice,guarantees, Fast delivery,etc.?				

Opportunities and Threats

Scanning the surrounding world. The preparation of an export marketing plan cannot be done in a vaccum. It should involve identifying the outside factors that will have an impact on the business in the future,either by presenting opportunities or by posing threats.

Therefore, before laying down plans, some time should be spent for systematically examining the factors beyond control that will affect the business in the future so that advantage can be taken of them,or allowances made for them.

What factors should the scan of the outside world cover and how will these factors affect the business? How can anyone know(unless he has unusual powers)what is likely to happen? The anser to the first question depends to some extent on the line of business and is discussed below. fInding the response to the second question involves keeping abreast of events and of forecasts for the future,and analysing how these are likely to affect the company.

Every business needs to look out for the following trends in the target country:

- ★ Trends in the economy
- ★ Population trends
- ★ Technological changes
- ★ Political,legislative or policy changes
- ★ General changes in society

Within each of these broad categories,there are many factors that will affect the business enterprise. But even a cursory examination of the changes likely to happen in,say the next three to five years,will reveal both opportunities and threats to the business. A plan should help prepare for these changes and keep the company may from being caught completely unawares.

Probably the exporter may not be in a position to have studies done on environmental issues. However,this does not mean that he should remain ignorant of the most important ongoing trends.

It is important to read a daily newspaper and a regular business magazine. In this way,it is possible to be informed about the most significant events as they occur. Then the possible implications of these events for the business should be studied. When these are read with the business in mind it pays off.

Worksheet 5 helps to find the world events that will affect the most. First ,a quick look at the items in the worksheet should be taken. If an entry seems obvious:it can be put in,if not then there is no need to worry. Then it is necessary to scan a quality daily paper for the last few days and circle anything that may be relevant to the SME. By using this approach over a few days,entries can be added on the worksheet.

The exporter should remember that even one good opportunity spotted may be all that is needed. Then plans can be made to take advantage of it.

Exercise 4

Taking the above suggestions into account, complete worksheet 5.

Worksheet 5: How to go about scanning

Outside influences on your company	Implications for your company Opposite each trend, know how it could affect your company and identify each as an opportunity or a threat.	
	Opportunity	**Threat**

A. Economic trends. List five trends that seem important to your company, for example, growth in service industry, lower inflation.

1.
2.
3.
4.
5.

B. Trends in technology. For example, increased applications of microchip technology.

1.
2.
3.
4.
5.

C. Political and legislative developments. For example, stricter laws on animal drugs.

1.
2.
3.
4.
5.

D. Changes in society. For example, more urbanisation, more working wives.

1.
2.
3.
4.
5.

Another way of spotting market opportunities Worksheet 5 is designed to help look at how the international market-place is changing and how it will affect the business. Now this can be looked at it in a slightly different way and to try to identify new opportunities.

The best ideas are oftern the simplest and yet good ideas are always elusive. To help spot opportunities, the simple technique shown below can be used.

This technique is called "Opportunity Boxes". It aids in finding ideas.

	PRESENT PRODUCTS	NEW PRODUCTS
PRESENT MARKETS	1. Market penetration	3. Product development
NEW MARKETS	2. Market development	4. Diversification

Box 1 Market penetration

This means marketing more of your current products to your current customers or markets.

Example: Suppose you are a soap manufacturer and you have 10%of an export market. The strategy in Box 1 calls for you to look at ways of expanding consumption of your soap by getting your present consumers to buy more of your product and by encouraging consumers currently patronising the competition to switch to your product. This may mean, for example, seeking wider product distribution. Your aim is to increase your penetration of your current market.

Box 2 Market development

This means selling your present product in new markets.

What new markets could you break into? Could someone else use your product?

Example: An SME producing men's clothing and currently supplying only the domestic market may want to try to develop an export market.

Box 3 Product development

Here the idea is to introduce new or adapted products to your present markets. This would mean developing new products, or modifying existing products, for instance by introducing quality or size variations.

Example: An engineering SME that makes locks for the construction market way want to sell building fitting to the same market.

Box 4 Diversification

This involves developing completely new products for new markets.

Example: A joinery SME making doors and windows now wants to produce office furniture.

Setting SME Objective

Objectives ar statements about what is to be achieved in the future. They are sometimes called goals or targets. Most business managers state that they are in the business probably "to make money" or becauese they want to be their own boss or something to similar effect. Such statements are, however, too vague to be useful in helping managers to decide oin future courses of action. This section helps in writing objectives that will be useful in deciding what the next moves should be:

Exercise 5

Complete worksheet 6 and see if you can use it to spot export opportunities for your company.

Worksheet 6: Opportunity boxes

Market penetration	**Product development**
Ways of selling more to your present markets:	New products you could sell to your present markets:
1.	1.
2.	2.
3.	3.
4.	4.
5.	5.
Market development	**Diversification**
New markets or segments you could sell your present products for	New products you could develop for new markets:
1.	1.
2.	2.
3.	3.
4.	4.
5.	5.

For small business, it is sometimes difficult to divorce personal from business objectives. The first thing to do therefore is to sort out one from one another.

Let us start with the personal objectives. What is needed from the business? Some of the alternatives to be considered are:

- ★ A high annual income to live very well.
- ★ A business that provides employment and keeps the family members at a reasonable standard of living (which should be defined in terms of an income figure).
- ★ An initial low income with rapid growth prospects in three years, which will enable selling of the business to start another one.
- ★ A fast-growing business leading to an annual expansion of production, workforce, capital base and profits in the foreseeable futur, to the

point where soon al big business can be run and social acceptance in the community can be gained.

These are distinctly different objectives. The objective which appeals most to a person depends on the weight he attaches to matters like:

- ★ The ability to manage a larger workforce and cope with the related problems.
- ★ The ambition level.
- ★ The readiness to work very ling hours.
- ★ The desire for free time to spend with the family.
- ★ The health and physical stamina.

So before the objectives for continued expansion or market dominance are set, it is advisable to stop and ask the above questions. There might be other reasons for working harder or working less and these should be examined before going further.

Many owners of small businesses are satisfied that their present company size ensures them an adequate standard of living and do not wish to expand because of the problems that expansion could bring. In this situation their business objectives should be geared to maintaining their lifestyle. This may mean making sure that sales continue atleast at the present levels for the foreseeable future.

However, this does not necessarily mean no new products, new markets or new competition. Planning remains essential in the ever-changing environments. Not wanting to grow does not mean not changing.

The ambitious may want to see their business develop and perhaps become a major force in their industry or expand into export markets. It depends upon the size of the mountain that a person wants to scale.

Marketing Objectives

Marketing objectives also have to be set in the context of more general business objectives such as the financial return expected on the overall investment. For example, a 20% annual return on capital invested may be wished or a growth to a certain size in terms of exployees may be wanted. The business objectives set other boundaries too.

In addition, before deciding on the specific marketing objectives, there should be a complete analysis of:

- ★ The enterprise's strengths and weaknesses.
- ★ The competitors' strenghts and weaknesses.
- ★ Opportunities and threats in the market.

Now is the time to review the analysis of these items. What is seen there? Are some things obvious?

- ★ Some examples are: The market opportunity analysis may reveal a growing market segment that had not been noticed
- ★ The analysis of the competitors may show that they have also missed this market segment but that they have become very price competitive in other areas
- ★ The analysis of the strengths and weaknesses may disclose that the product quality is fine but that the sales literature does not highlight

the product's good points. The sales staff might be untrained and that accounts are lost because of late deliveries

These findings would obviously point to what needs to be done in the long-term (develop new market segments) and in the short term (prepare new sales literature, train staff; and improve on delivery). Putting this in terms of objectives mean making statements like the following;

★ Next year, and fore each succeeding year, this SME wants to achieve an overall growht in sales and profitability of 10%.
★ During the next year, the SME will break into the following new markets (defined geographically, by customer or by market need).
★ Next year the SME will increase its market share by 2%.

Other examples could be used but these give a basic idea of how to set objectives that provide an overall direction for the SME, a measure of the change required, and a time span over whcih this change will be effected.

Exercise 6

Use worksheet 7 to state the marketing objectives.

Worksheet 7: Setting objectives

Your objectives	Quantity	When should the objective be achieved?
1. Change in profit		
2. Change in sales		
3. Change in market share		
4. Introduction of new products		
5. Other objectives (state them)		

Translating Objectives into Action

This is the final step in the planning process. If all the previous tasks of assessing the company, the competitors and the market have been carried out, and broad objectives have been set. The exporter should be well-prepared to make decisions about what is needed to do to achieve them. This involves looking at alternative strategies and deciding which one appears best.

Example: It has been decided that the long-term (say,five-year) objective is to export to Japan and the Republic of Korea while expanding the current domestic market base. To achieve this, the objectives for the next year should be set as follows:

★ Expand total sales by 10%.
★ Open up the market in Japan and sell 1% of the products there.

The alternative strategies that can be used to achieve the first objective are listed here.

★ Sell 10% more of the products to each of the present customers, that is, expand the market share in the existing market.
★ Concentrate on the fasterst-growing customers and expand sales to them.
★ Open up some new accounts in the present market
★ Add some new products to the line and sell them to existing customers.

Altenative strategies for achieving the second objective could be:

- ★ Conduct market research on th eproducts' saleability in Japan and carry out necessary product changes.
- ★ Appoint a sales agent or distributor for Japan.
- ★ Advertise in the Japanese newspapers and service customers from the home base.

The ability to think of alternative strategies dependson the knowledge of the marketing ideas that have been covered earlier.

Action Planning

A useful framework for thinking about needs to be done to put each strategy into action is the "marketing mix" concept. This consists of four items on each of which a decision has to be taken.

- ★ Product (and its presentation)
- ★ Price
- ★ Distribution (place)
- ★ Promotion

These are the four Ps which can be used to help with the action plans.

Parallel to completing the export marketing plan, other plans have to be developed, especially a production and a finance plan. Then these have to be combined in a business plan. Theere is no definite pattern for a business plan, various forms are possible. However, the model in worksheet 8 is suggested. The model is by on means exhaustive and other subjects can be added for coverage.

Marketing Action Required to Achieve Objectives (An Example)

Over all objective Increase sales by 10%	Product	Pricing and selling	Distribution	Promotion
Strategy 1				
Expand sales to present buyers this year, as follows:	Add new line. Modify the present line.	Offer a higher discount to the best buyers.	Appoint an agent	Develop a brochure.
Buyer A: + 10% Buyer B: + 20% Buyer C: + 40%	Improve packaging.	Drop prices		
Strategy 2				
Find five new in Argentina Buenos Aires:2 Cordoba:2 Mardal Plata:1	Meet new product requirements	Offer them special introduction prices.	Appoint agents in Argentina	Exhibit in a trade fair
Strategy 3				
Identify a new product line to complement existing ones and increase sales.	Find product ideas by trade fair; contacting a chamber of cmmerce: examining competing products.	Develop price strategy to penetrate the market segment.	Investigate distribution requirements	Use Public relations to introduce products

Exercise 7

Now work out your own marketing plan using worksheet 8.

Worksheet 8: Mardeting action required to achieve objectives

Overall objective	Product	Pricing	Distribution and selling	Promotion

A MODEL FOR A BUSINESS PLAN

I INTRODUCTION AND/OR SUMMARY OF THE BUSINESS PLAN

II BRIEF BACKGROUND INFORMATION ON THE COMPANY

A. Current activity
   1. Products
   2. Capacity per annum
   3. Annual sales
   4. Number of employees

B. Marketing pattern
   1. Domestic markets % of production
   Existing sales network
   2. Export markets % of production
   Export network

C. Other activities (if any)

III FEATURES OF PLANNED/PROPPOSED ACTIVITY

A. Product(s) to be manufactured
   1. Product specification(s)
   2. Annual capacity envisaged
   3. Experience in the proposed activity

B. Markets to be served
   1. Domestic markets % of production
   2. Export markets % of production

C. Type of activities to be carried out
   1. To obtain technology and marketing knowledge
   2. Marketing
      a. Domestic markets
      b. Export markets
   3. Training
   4. Management
   5. To obtain/generate capital

IV. RAW MATERIALS AND COMPONENTS

A. Available in domestic market and price

B. To be imported

1. Types required
2. Countries of origin
3. Import duty(ies)
4. Import license (required/not required)

V DOMESTIC PRODUCTION: MARKET SIZE AND PATTERN (WITH RESPECT TO PROPOSED ACTIVITY)

A. Local production

B. Market size and pattern

VI. INDUSTRIAL COSTS

A. Anticipated cost of local labour

1. Unskilled worker (minimum wage)
2. Semi-skilled
3. Skilled
4. Highly skilled
5. Supervisory
6. Engineering
7. Management
8. Allowances
9. Working time

B. Utilities

C. Cost of structure of existing production (% of sales)

1. Materials
2. Direct labour
3. Overheads
4. Utilities
5. Others

VII LOCATION, TRANSPORT AND SHIPPING

A. Location

1. Land (square meters)
2. Building (square meters)

B. Nearest port and airport

1. Containerised cargo

VIII PLANT CAPACITY

A. Existing/Utilisation

B. Installed machinery and equipment

IX ESTIMATED COST

A. Land and buildings

B. Plant land machinery

C. Provision for contingency

D. Fees for technical knowledge

X ESTIMATED REVENUE

XI ADDITIONAL INFORMATION ON LOAN FINANCING

A. Sources

B. Name of national development bank

XII PRINTED MATERIAL AVAILABLE

LESSONS EMERGING FROM THE CASE STUDIES

The case studies present the case-discussion, an opportunity for emphasising the basic principles of export marketing. The following principles have been derived from actual experiences of exporters in developing countries.

Exporters should be creative Many of the case studies suggest that developing country exporters have to carry on their business under conditions of considerable constraints. For instance, imported raw materials are often difficult to obtain, the flow of supplies is uncertain, the transport infrastructure is undeveloped. Managers must therefore fromulate creative and effective solution to these challenges. It is common knowledge that exporting is not an easy task.

Market niching may be an exporter's best optin Developing country exporters of manufactured products rarely occupy a dominant position in international markets. The exporter should therfore aim at a market niche rather than at the mass market. One advantage of market niching is that it does not require elaborate and expensive market investigations before market entry. A simple study of potential customer groups may be adequate.

Exporters should seek value-adding product strategies Another implication of market niching is that attempting to achieve price leadership may not be the exporter's best option. Product differentiation, branding distinctive styling, durable packaging, outstanding customer service, etc., could provide comparative advantages on the export market and therefore eliminate the need to compete solely on the basis of price.

Exporters should know the dey buyers in the target market Successful exporting often results from partnering a key intermediary with access to distribution channels in the export market. This intermediary may be an importer, broker, trading company, or the company's distributor/agent. Forming a business alliance with a reputable partner who can channel the export products to appropriate distribution points, is one of the most important tasks in exporting. Such a task would fall under what is termed a "push" strategy. A contrast is provided by a "pull" strategy which requires the exporter to be in direct contact with the end-users or consumers. The later is frequently a costly strategy and therefore unfeasible for the small and medium-sized enterprise.

Exporters should choose their markets carefully The choice of market can make the difference between success and failure in exporting. Exporters should carefully consider their market options and choose the market that offers the best propects. They should explore the markets where they believe they have a competitive advantage.

Exporter should clarify their motives for exporting and set their objectives at the outset They should know why they want to export and set their goals. hopefully, the export venture will contribute to both their profit-seeking and market expansion objectives.

Exporters should consider export market development as a long-term investment Managers learn the tasks of exporting gradually. Familiarity with export markets is gained over time and the business relationships evolved are strengthened over a period of time. Sustained efforts are therefore essential in export marketing.

Planning and strategy development are essential The long-term nature of export market development efforts, together with the risks assumed, implies that a planned methodical approach to exporting is imperative. To reduce uncertainty and risks, the exporter must set objectives, analyse strategic alternatives, formulate action plans, allocate resources, set time-tables and monitor performance. Without such a formal approach, the enterprise cannot sustain a profitable export effort.

Exporting requires technical expertise The cases highlight the fact that exporting requires expertise, in addition to careful planning and suitable products. Managers sometimes underestimate the complexity of exporting tasks, the risks involved and consequences of failure. A realistic understanding of the commitment required to succeed in an export venture is essential.

No enterprise should seek entry into an export market until it is ready Any attempt at exporting, without experience in domestic marketing is bound to fail. Research suggests that enterprises gain important skills, knowledge and confidence at home, which often prove beneficial in the export market as well.

The responsibility for the export effort should be assigned to a key staff member Experience suggests that an export venture is mor likely to succeed when a key person in the enterprise is assigned the export task. This person can play a combination of roles as change agent, motivator, resource person, organiser and so on. A wholehearted commitment to the effort can go a long way in terms of success.

// CHAPTER 12 //

LOCATING THE PROSPECTIVE BUYERS

Earlier attention was focussed on the organisation and the marketing tools needed to bring the products to export target countries. Ways of communication with potential buyers has also been dealt with.

This chapter deals with identification of specific markets which would be best for exporting. It also tells about how to recognise and approach them and how to establish their accessibility, in spite of competitive activities.

SELECTING THE TARGET MARKET

What is a "Market"

There are at least three definitions for the word "market".

1. A market is a group of customers or consumers who share the same needs, and who are willing and able to buy
2. A market is a place where buyers and sellers come together
3. A market is total sales (in value or in volume) of a specific product category.

Predominantly the first definition is used, as it is the purest. The old adage 'markets = people' emphasises that those people not only should be willing, but also be able to buy, which presumes purchasing power.

Market Selection Method

This chapter is about ways of finding markets for products. Some people call this market research. First, ways of identifying some potential markets have to be seen. Then a more detailed picture can be built up. Finally, how field research is needed to gather precise marketing information can be seen.

Identifying Priority Markets

It is in the country's, the company's and the individual's interest to export. It is important to market the products abroad. As customers will not come to the company, they have to be approached and persuaded to buy the products.

Clearly exporters cannot go to every country in the world to persuade people to buy their products. Even the largest international firms do not trade with the whole world, and not every country can or will buy what a particular exporter has to sell. Resources, and particularly trained marketing personnel, are scarce. Exports must be selective and marketing efforts should be concentrated on the markets, that will yield the best results.

It can be expensive in terms of trained people's time, documents and actual research effort, even to find out about the potential markets. Exporters must therefore try to identify, at minimum cost, the markets on which they should concentrate and carry out a more detailed research effort.

There are over 200 countries in the world and each could contain at least one, or probably more markets for the products. To actually find these markets several techniques are available. There are five checkpoints to be kept in mind.

The technique should be primarily systematical, secondarily effective and tertiarily based upon criteria that can be assessed and verified easily. The fourth checkpoint refers to the screening methodology, which implies the activity of selecting the countries which seem appropriate, and eliminating those show no export potential in the first analysis.

Since an exporter cannot conquer the world in one stroke, he should plan which market he would like to penetrate first.

Even the most experienced and strongest export companies rarely succeed in reaching more than one foreign market each year. The investment simply is too big to do more than that. The same applies to the risk involved in each new unfamiliar market.

Therefore, the screening method should result in a certain priority-ranking. After having applied the various screening factors to the countries of the world where it is assumed there are markets, the analysis should lead to a list, showing several countries with export-marketing potential. This is the fifth checkpoint of activity.

Screening Markets on General Criteria

Selection criteria helps in identifing potential export markets. These criteria refer to the environmental factors (formulated by Dr. Philip Kotler) that each country can be described by, e.g. for making a marketing plan.

The first and simplest way of selecting markets, is to apply the geographical criterion. For that selection method, (physical) proximity is the key word. It can be assumed that there are markets close by, which could contain potential buyers of the present product. Such markets may be found in neighbouring countries.

As a matter of fact, nations have the largest trading volume with their neighbours, crossing only one common frontier. The exporter may assume that there are opportunities in the first "circle" of neighbours around his own country.

Other Market Selection Criteria

Socio-political factors Having listed the potential markets within neighbouring countries, potential markets which are further away should be looked at. This may lead to listing the countries that have a common interest with the exporters own country, e.g. in an economic community.

Such communities are mainly based on political agreement, on the necessity of common (economic) interests. Politics have created a more or less stable trading environment for the member countries. They can be for example structured as "customs unions", having eliminated internal custom tariffs in favour of a common external system of import tariffs.

If the government has established such ties with other countries, there will probably be a potential export market there.

The same goes for countries where the social structure (relationships, family composition, age division, life styles, etc.) is similar. There are some basic requirements stemming from social situations, that run parallel worldwide. For example: blue jeans is a universal clothing of the young, young families spend more on their children than on themselves, newly-weds spend a lot on housing, furniture and interior decoration.

In fact, when selecting markets this way, socio-political factors are used as the criteria. All countries that have social and/or political environments comparable to the exporters country should be screened. Those countries that show similarities are selected for the simple reason that, fewer risks of misunderstanding may occur.

That excludes unfriendly countries. Trade only flourishes in a stable and friendly climate and not in a hostile situation. The Governments may wish to impede all influx from countries with different life styles or political systems. That will stand in the way of exports.

Economic factors When selecting the country, the potential market should be screened regarding their economic climate. That refers to their economic possibilities — can they afford to buy the product?

Of course, in such countries bartering potential may exist. But it would be wise to exclude such economics from the initial screening. The exporter may run into problems of fast devaluating currencies, of inconvertibility, of currency losses and of delay in payments.

The economic screening will limit the number of potential export countries to those with a medium or high per capita income. This information (the Gross National Product (GNP) divided by the number of inhabitants) has been calculated for all countries in the world.

Although the per capita income may prove a helpful screening factor, it can be deceptive. Firstly, it does not show the actual buying power per household. That figure is got by multiplying it by the number of persons in the average household. Secondly, even in the poor countries, there may be money to spend, for instance in certain large cities or regions. Their governments may be able to buy the goods or services. In other countries, bartering may have created an economy without money payments (like in the UK). So, treat this screening factor carefully.

A better figure may be derived from the actual productivity per head. Productivity supports the balance of payment as well as the economic stability and growth.

Cultural factors The most intangible selection criterion has to do with cultural differences. Culture, the sociologists say, is the strongest determinant of human behaviour. In cultures that differ, the exporter should have to deal with people very different from him that is, people with different ideas about what is good or appealing, consumers with different preferences and with different buying habits.

For example, an exporter of swimwear wanted to advertise his merchandise in a Saudi magazine. He found out that showing a partially

undressed women is against Arab ethics and had to withdraw from the market. A successful asian exporter had selected a potential trade partner who was an importer in the US. With utter politeness he entered the negotiations and found his counterpart far too brusque and too direct to accept him as a reliable man. So he dropped him. Later he learned that he had turned down a very attractive party, who was famous locally for his fast and sound judgement and also for his swift business successes.

Culture is evident in the life style of the consumers, in the communication with business relations, in social life, in religion, or in business ethics. It may be tempting to relate culture with the degree of civilisation. But that consideration should not interfere with the commercial purpose. It is the exporters task to recognise that there are cultural differences and to estimate their effects on the communication and commercial operations. However, it is not necessary to understand the cultures. They should merely be respected. Similarly, the trade partner too should reciprocate respecting by the exporters culture and customs. Mutual understanding is based upon respect.

Technological factors The last screening factor tries to describe the relative degree of technological advancement in export countries. That factor will be evident when comparing the "state of the art" technology in the Western target markets with the exports technology.

It can be safely assumed that some of the country's products may seem old-fashioned in industrialised countries, having been made obsolete by technological innovations. It is not possible to sell an ox-drawn plough to Western farmers who use tractors and are used to computers and robots on their farms.

Simple field research will quickly show the degree of technological development. The trade promotion official in the target country will see to that. He could also collect some trade magazines and competitors' catalogues in the interested sector.

Climate Indeed, the climate influences product preferences and can be used as a selection criterion. This need not be followed by the later. Classic examples of the opposite include, selling iceboxes to eskimos, skates to Saudis, water to the Dutch (all of which was proved possible).

Instead, conditions of climate and geography which may influence logistics (transport, storage) should be identified. Selling ice cream in the ASEAN started becoming big business only after the supplier installed a chain of open-top cooling display units. Exporting fresh produce and flowers from Kenya became a possibility after a direct airlink was established with a Dutch auction, enabling shipping whilst still fresh.

RESEARCH FOR MARKET SELECTION

Primary or Secondary Data

Market screening needs exploratory research that depends upon gathering "secondary data". These are data that have been compiled and published earlier, by someone else.

"Primary data" refers to the information that is collected by the exporter himself. This kind of information is required when secondary data falls short of the exporter's needs, e.g. when researching a specific type of consumer about the acceptance of a specific product (in the third and fourth stage of export planning).

Secondary data can usually be found in public sources, like governmental databanks and, libraries in the target country or in the exporters' country.

A surprising number of subjects have already been researched. Quantified macroeconomic data relevant to the market selection, can mostly be found for. Most importantly, the data are usually exhibited in such a manner as to enable comparison. The Eurostats (European Statistics) have been designed that way.

Secondary research is cheap and fast gathering of all the information required and is just a matter of asking for it — by letter, telephone, by computer or from behind the desk. That is why it is described as "desk research" (as opposed to "field research", which requires going out to look for primary information, e.g. by interviewing or fact-registering).

Secondary data collection works fast and costs little. The disadvantage is that the data are not tailor-made for the specific purpose and that the information is neither exclusive nor a secret. Primary research will give the answers to a specific purpose, but such research consumes a lot of time and money.

Several thousand databanks are accessible on the Internet through a computer, which by means of a modem, where one can tap information of various kinds (including the Eurostats, the European Statistics, providing many data free of any charge except for the telephone costs). Although 'surfing' (browsing) may take time, once located, the data is available with a click on the PC mouse.

Having received the data, it will be necessary to list all information about the target countries. That is tedious work but any staff member can do it. Then the selection criteria has to be applied as described above. Some criteria which has relevance to the specific industry, or the manner in which the products are used can be added.

Based on the evaluation of each and every factor, the attractiveness of the market, can be judged, for e.g. by giving them a score ("very much the same as in own country, almost similar, somewhat different, entirely different"). The larger the differences, the lower the score. The result is a tentative list of countries, offering market potential, ranked according to certain estimation.

Estimating Market Potential

Step-by-step the exporter should close in on his final customer. But can he actually be reached? And is the demand large enough to justify the effort? What competition will have to be faced?

These questions are important for deciding which market or market segment to export to. This guide will help answer the questions to enable establishing a "market potential."

Market segmentation In the countries listed in the priority ranking, export markets in which a need for your product exists will have to be found.

A market, as defined earlier, is a group of consumers, sharing a common need for a certain kind of product or service.

A sub-division can be made within that group, splitting up the group into smaller groups, which share the need for a particular product. Such a sub-divided group is called a market segment. Segments in turn, can be sub-divided into even smaller parts called 'niches'. In the present competitive times, most suppliers aim at such niches (assuming they can actually identify one) to penetrate foreign markets. Start small, is the motto.

In the early fifties, European housewives generally washed their laundry in tubs. They used solid bars of soap, sudging heavily. When the washing machines were introduced, the housewives needed a different type of soap, a low-sudging detergent, which was offered in powder form for easier administration. They formed a segment in the soap market. A new (sub) segment of market was formed.

Now-a-days, other segments still develop. For example, housewives who want strong detergents with enzymes to wash at lower temperatures (using less electricity), and housewives who want non-phosphate detergents (to protect the natural environment), or detergents to wash their modern textiles. Such segments will always come up (and eventually vanish again). The manufacturers are quick to recognise new segments, because they constitute new market potential. One of the most challenging and creative tasks for the market is to identify such segments. That is called "segmentation".

The "trick" of segmentation is finding a balance between competitiveness and profitability. This means that the segment should be:

- ★ large enough to ensure a good return on (marketing) investment,
- ★ Small enough to enable the supplier a certain domination over his competitors. In that situation he will be a trend and price-setter. If he is the first to recognise and exploit the segment, the supplier can probably obtain such a position.

So the supplier will not only be looking for markets, but will also have to identify relevant market segments and niches. "Relevant" means: fit for your specific product(s). In practice, segmenting will be combined with the identification of a possible importing buyer.

Importability

The logical question regarding market entry will be: Can the market be entered with these products? Is it possible to gain physical access?

These question should be answered easily, but in practice there may be problems.

Import regulations Most countries have an extensive set of regulations concerning products that can be imported or not. To find out if the suppliers products are included, he could start with referring to the import statistics of the countries on his priority list. They will tell if products in the interested product category have been imported before. That knowledge will give a foothold.

As pointed out, the product classification (9-12 digit) number of the product should be known, according to the official Customs Tariff Nomenclature in Europe that is the Harmonised System, also known in most developing countries). The classification number can be checked out by (any) customs.

The import statistics can be obtained at any national Embassy of Consulate or through Internet or Export Promotion Councils.

N.B. Do not put the import statistics away yet. They will be needed again soon when estimating market sizes and trends.

After having established that imports which have been registered previously, the Import Regulations of the target country should be consulted. The Import Regulations will be explicit (though complicated). They will tell whether or not a given product is allowed to be imported and under what conditions.

The conditions ("tariff barriers") can be:

★ Import is only allowed when a certain levy (import duties) is paid.
★ Import is only allowed up to a certain maximum volume ("quota").
★ Import is only allowed when originating in a certain country (e.g. as described in the Generalised System of Preferences).

These conditions should be registered carefully. May be, your TPO (Trade Promotion Office) can be of help. These may be needed for future planning, for instance when calculating the market price.

Non-tariff barriers Import duties can be very effective barriers, impeding undesired imports. So are the quota conditions, mentioned above. The GSP and similar preference systems are not meant to impede, but to promote imports (mainly from specified developing countries).

Trading will meet many other barriers, apart from duties. They are called "non-tariff barriers."

Best known are the regulations regarding the protection of the health and safety of the (European) citizens and their (natural) environment. These regulations are reflected in product norms and standards. Although their explicit goal is to protect buyers and users of the products, their effect can lead to frustration of imports. For foreign suppliers, they can pose tremendous problems, like being forced into (expensive) product adaptations and threatening the operational profit.

The CBI Green Buss database can provide valuable information on environmental aspects which might become barriers, if the supplier is not aware of the implications.

He will often be confronted with internal taxes, like "sales tax" or "value-added tax (VAT)". They increase his market prices, but since they rule all products' trade they do the same for the competitors' products too.

In some industrialised countries there are strict phytosanitary rules for import products, requiring a long quarantine period in expensive storage facilities. Sometimes the packaging and labelling should confirm to certain regulations, or the distribution of the products is limited or traditionally regulated, like in Japan.

It will prove difficult to find out which non-tariff barriers face the suppliers products. He must find out about them before deciding to enter the market. His trade representative abroad or his Embassy may be able to identify them. Organisations like the CBI usually know about them and research them frequently, sector by sector ("Environmental Quick Scan").

Having researched the tariff as well as non-tariff barriers, the exporters will be able to establish market accessibility.

Market Size

Once it has been found out whether or not the exporter can enter the market, he will now want to assess if the market is big enough to promise a return on the investment. In this case, the "market" is the consume's total demand, either evident or potential. It is necessary to estimate its size (in value and/or in volume).

At the same time, a supplier will be interested in the way the demand is growing or decreasing. So, next to size, he should assess the market trends.

Assessing market size Many markets have been researched before. There may be market surveys available.

The Export Promotion Councils/India Trade Promotion Organisation, DGCI&S surveys give relevant though condensed information on total market size (in volume, as well as in value), market trends, growth patterns, identification of buyers, frequency of purchasing, market segments, distribution channels, etc.

Such information is required when designing a personal export marketing plan.

There are two ways of assessing the market size.

a. by analysing Government statistics
b. by totalising customer demand or consumption

Governments statistics Theoretically, most markets can be quantified (in volume as well as in value of total units purchased) by adding local production to total imports per annum and deducting exports and unsold stocks.

apparent consumption = import + local production – export – unsold stocks.

However, when working through the official trade statistics, it is known that:

1) It is hard to recognize a specific product category, since the data seem too general
2) Some data are based on strange common denominators for volume or weight, that it is possible only to rely on the data indicating total value
3) Data on domestic production are very hard to obtain.

Therefore, a desk research should always include the analysis of customer demand, if only to verify an "educated guesswork."

Totalising demand All industry information found should be checked. Most industry sectors are represented by a certain organisation. These organisations usually publish production figures as well as total consumption data, mainly in value (price at wholesale level).

Occasionally, the national governments publish data on some of their markets. These could be retrieved via official channels, by asking the local TPO or commercial attache.

Specific industry sector data can be obtained from the sector organisations or found in trade or business magazines.

If a company is a supplier of industrial goods, components or if it wants to offer its production capacity on the basis of subcontracting or licensing, the prospective customer might know the market size.

Industrial suppliers know that their market potential is often based upon "demand". This means that their customers need the suppliers' products for manufacturing their own products. The demand for the latter products determine the demand for industrial goods. So if the "original demand" can be established, then the derived demand for the goods can be estimated.

Market Trends and Patterns

Trends Knowing the size of the market is a vital piece of information. However, at least another six months of lengthy preparations is needed before entering the market, so there is a need to know how large the market might be in the future. Knowing which way the trend of the market develops is vital to the planning.

Therefore, it is necessary to estimate the market size for the next three to five years. From historical data, one could try to extrapolate the future trends, i.e growth, stabilisation or decrease.

Products in western markets, particularly consumer products, tend to "grow old" quickly. The product life cycle is short. The product that is fashionable today, can become old-fashioned in a few years, sometimes even months (garments, handicraft). The product might have a tendency to grow old soon. The market may be declining too fast to be attractive. So it is better to be careful.

Industrial goods, on the other hand, tend to have longer-lived markets (unless a product is supplied to fast-developing high-tech industries, like the computer industry).

Growing markets offer potential, but they will attract strong competition, especially when the market is big. Price levels tend to decrease. Yet, there could still be room in the market when the possibilities of finding new segments are considered, by offering a competitive advantage.

Stable markets probably indicate saturated demand. Many competitors are active, though some may already have had to withdraw. Prices are under constant pressure. Promotion is heavy. Such a market is not easy to penetrate, unless a competitive price is offered.

Most markets in Europe are stable, because of saturation of the needs of a non-growing population.

Decreasing markets offer hardly any profit potential. It will cost too much to maintain a position in the market and still earn money.

This is just a generalisation. Nevertheless, it suggests that it is important to carefully assess the trend of the market, in order to make the right decision of entering a market or not.

Patterns Probably the most relevant pattern for market selection is geographical. This is directly related to the physical distribution, and the logistics of your export products.

That refers to the actual location of the demand. Is the market concentrated in a certain area with the target country? Are the customers living or buying in a specific territory well distinguishable from other areas?

In a large country like Germany there are several concentrations of buyers, mainly in the heavily populated areas (Ruhr area, Bavaria etc.). Industrial developments usually attract more people in the area. Sometimes, industrial buyers show a similar pattern, when most industries are situated in a commercially strategic area (like in Free Trade Zones, Industrial areas etc.).

The industrial and consumptive concentration zones in Europe cover part of the South East of England, the Benelux, Northern France, the French Grenoble area, Western and Southern Germany, North East Spain and Northern Italy. The recent membership of Sweden and Finland means that this industrial 'hot spot' area will extend into Scandinavia. Commercial links are being forged between the EU and associated countries in Central Europe and some Mediterranean states.

In smaller countries, like the Netherlands, it can be safely assumed that the market is spread across the entire country (with a slight preference for the western part, covering the three largest cities of Amsterdam, Rotterdam and The Hague, together forming Randstad).

The reason to focus on this geographical pattern is that it is important to know in advance what distances have to be covered by the products, to reach the customers. Geographical concentration can be advantageous for distribution. The first competitive battles in Europe will be fought with the weapons of logistics (as it is less expensive and it is easier to control timely deliveries).

Identifying the Competition

Fighting for the same customer Many other suppliers (manufacturers, traders) will be competing for the favours of the same customers.

In their efforts to restructure their economics, many Central and Eastern European countries have shifted their commercial attention to Western Europe. Their economic situation will remain tense for the years to come, industrial productivity has decreased considerably, but free enterprise inspires many business people to build trade relations with their neighbours. Countries like Poland and Hungary think about trading with the west for their growth.

Exporters from developing countries will recognise that these countries' traders will post a strong competitive threat to them, since they aim at the same markets.

Obviously, the customer can only spend his money once. So he will make a selection from the wide range of products offered in the market place. A customer's purchasing motives should be known, so as to profit from his purchase. The supplier should also be able to satisfy the customers needs and wants better than the other competitors.

The success of many suppliers to West European markets depends largely on knowing, what the competition does to win customer preference. The suppliers do not hunt for undetected 'holes in the markets,' but fight each other for their share of the market. Experience teaches them that a good competitive analysis is very effective to avoid a head-on collision with a competitor. If not avoided a showdown results in which, suppliers who enter a market after their competitors can never win.

So exporters entering a market, where competitors are already present, have to seek a different strategic position. They can try for instance, to be better or faster and more successful in winning customer preference than their competitors. Therefore, they must know who the competitor is, how strong he is and to what degree he can threaten their market position.

Competitive marketing analysis If the competitor is known, it is possible to, fight with him.

Part of the management task is to describe the competitor and his activities. This can be done by checking his marketing assets:

The products which ofter comptition can be found from any distributor or retailer. He will be able to specifically describe the present competition in his area or store. The retailer welcomes competition amongst his suppliers, as it brings prices down. But he too, has to make a choice about which product to distribute, as his selling space is physically limited. It is necessary to go to the shops or wholesalers on a regular basis (e.g. quarterly), to find out in what way the comptitors products are better. The products could be more unique or more attractive and their quality should also be noted.

It is not always commercially wise to imitate these products, as those products could even be protected by patents or trademarks, which makes imitation illegal and punishable.

In most European countries the products must carry the name of the manufacturer or importer.

The names should be noticed. Other details like, if they are small or if they belong to a multinational, are they manufacturing locally, or do they import their products (in that case, who are the potential supplying competitors) should be found. These will reveal a lot about their ability to defend their market shares. The big ones will have the knowledge, experience and money to effectively fight a new market entry or market presence.

It is very important to note the competitors' prices. Price is one of the main motives for buying - next to quality.

In most free economies in the western world, the potential buyers will force a price-fighting with the competing suppliers. Consequently, price-setting largely depends on the competitor's prices.

That goes for their (trade) discounts, their bonus or commission rates. These should be found out.

How does the competition canvass, sell, advertise or promote their products? Do they employ sales representatives? Do they have special promotional material? Are they successful? Their example should be taken but always, something special, something that no competitors can copy should be added.

Newspapers, magazines, brochures and catalogues tell a lot about the competition and about how they view their potential customers. So these should be regularly read.

The same goes for the distribution methods of the competitors. Which channels have they selected to reach their buyers? Or do they supply them directly? Sometimes, when the time or the means to find these ans-wers is not available, the competitive channel selection can be a good guideline.

The arrival of media like television, has made 'teleshopping' popular. Cable networks link households to television advertisers offering consumer goods (from consumer durables to fashion and jewellery). Direct mail or mail order has become big business.

In general, the competition, and the way in which they execute their marketing, could tell a lot about the markets in which operation has to be carried out. "Observing the competition" should be an integral part of the marketing activities. It provides valuable information and makes one prepared for any attack from their side.

The competition should not be blindly followed at all times. If an entrepreneur is convinced that he is doing the right thing, then he should go along with it, even when the competitor follows a different path. The competitor may even be beaten.

Exporter's competitive analysis Ever since Western marketers have recognised the ever-increasing changes in customers' preference, they use dynamic models to assess their own strength vis-a-vis their competitor's. The first practical model was formulated by Michael E. Porter (1980), who indicated five competitive factors which could influence competitive strength, measured by the expected decrease in profitability.

The factors are:

1. The present rivalry in the market. What would be the effect of an initiative which might distort present market shares/Is retaliation to be expected? Will that decrease profits?
2. The bargaining strength of the buyers. Are the buyers so strong that they can dictate the terms of transaction (prices, delivery conditions, etc.) to the suppliers? Or are the buyers competing amongst each other to be supplied?
3. The bargaining power of the suppliers. Same as above, but projected on the relative influence of the suppliers (of halfmaterial, component, etc.). If the supplies are few, their power is great, reducing the profits.
4. The threat of potential entrants into the market will decrease the profitability. If market entry is easy, may competitors can be expected to fight for a piece of the profits, thereby reducing the profits. But if entry barriers are high (e.g. large investments in equipment, in know-how), some protection can be had.
5. The threat of product/service substitutes is more difficult to identify. Some products can come and take over the function of other

products (e.g. desktop publishing took over the function of type setters, the manufacturers of industrial glues pushed many nuts-and-bolts producers from their markets).

Identification of substitutes requires a 'helicopter view', which is the ability to look beyond the boundaries of one's own product area.

The competitive analysis seems complicated, but has proven valuable in assessing one's own competitive strength. The organisation could analyse its' position in the near future. A discussion with key persons in the organisation ('brain storm') could provide many answers in a short time.

APPRAISAL OF MARKETS

Here the possible markets are reduced to probable or more likely markets. This process would consist of the following steps:

1. Examination of India's export statistics which are officially published in the "Monthly Statistics relating to India's Foreign Trade." This enables the potential exporter to find out where similar products are going, whether the exports are declining or increasing. If the exports are increasing, what is the rate of growth of the exports? In doing so, data for a period of three to five years should be collected as it may reveal the trend of the markets. Again, always the latest statistics should be looked for. Old statistics may not be very helpful and may at times be misleading.
2. Examination of import statistics of the selected importing countries is the next step. This gives an idea of the relative size of the various markets. How much of the product concerned is being imported in different countries? Who are the competitors in each market? Is the market expanding, static or contracting? Ideally the market to be concentrated upon should be an expanding market since this means that further sales are possible without affecting the competitors too much. This would also make the marketing task much more easy. Import statistics of foreign countries may be available in Foreign Embassies or Consulates in India and Chambers of Commerce. In addition, OECD World Trade Statistics and United Nations International Trade Statistics also provide these data.
3. Examination of India's export statistics and foreign import statistics both may give an idea of the possible unit value realisation, as also the price paid for imports in foreign countries from different sources.
4. Examination of research studies are made by the Indian Institute of Foreign Trade, India Trade Promotion Organisation and Export Promotion Councils. These reports contain useful marketing information about the various markets and products covered by them.
5. It generally pays good dividends to talk to some experienced exporters. In this respect, it would be better to approach exporters of allied items. Competitors would not necessarily be helpful. Contacting tade associations and Chambers of Commerce may also help in the process of appraising markets. In fact, it is one of the

important functions of the Export Promotion Councils to help the new exporters to find out foreign markets and give important details about each market. Freight forwarders may help the exporters to find out availability of shipping services, as also the freight charges to different countries.

6. The Economic Times, Financial Express and other financial newspapers often publish supplements covering one particular country giving a lot of informations useful to marketers.
7. Commercial banks may also provide a lot of information about the payments position and exchange control restrictions in different countries. They can also supply status reports on the commercial standing of the foreign buyers.
8. India's commercial representatives abroad may help in collecting information regarding health, sanitary and other regulations like marketing and labelling requirements and also in the selection of agents. An exporter's letter to Indian Embassies abroad seeking information, must give as much specific information as possible. For example, if the company wants to export refrigerators, it may give the following details: size of the refrigerators made, possible prices, capacity of production that could be set aside for export, description of the refrigerator line accompanied by brochures, small folders, booklets, the types of outlets that are used at home, the terms which the company is willing to offer to the possible distributors, etc.
9. 'Yellow Pages' in telephone directories of various countries contain classified list of prominent trading houses/importers of several products. The information contained in such directories is considered the most up-to-date and accurate. These directories can be referred to in various Telephone Exchanges, Embassies/High Commissions of the countries' concerned and prominent commercial libraries.
10. The various Export Promotion Councils/Commodity Boards are regularly publishing bulletins/journals, inter alia, containing information on prospective customers of the products falling within their purview. The exporter must subscribe to these bulletins.

ORGANISATIONS/INSTITUTIONS

There are various organisations — national and international — providing assistance for the location of customers abroad. While some of the organisations provide information free of charge and without any formality, a few of them may require the prospective exporters to become their members in the first instance.

International Organisations

International agencies like the ITC and UNIDO provide information on customers abroad. These organisations should be contacted with details of the product and the type of customer in which an exporter is interested.

1. International Trade Centre, Palais des Nations, Geneva (Switzerland).
2. United Nations Industrial Development Organsiation (UNIDO).

Mission of India to the Eurpean Union Trade centre, Bressels (Belgium), is the government of India centre for marketing of select products.

Import Promotion Institutions Abroad

Countries like Germany, U.K., the Netherlands, Japan, South Korea, Hong Kong, Singapore, Taiwan have set up institutions to promote imports from developing countries like India.

Chambers of Commerce

The Chambers of Commerce and other industry trade associations in different countries are the other sources of information on overseas customers.

Foreign Embassies

The embassies/mission of various countries particularly those having commercial sections and mostly located in Delhi are also helpful in locating customers in their respective countries. Their names and addresses can be had from the booklet known as "diplomatic list" issued by the Ministry of External Affiars or seen in Delhi's telephone directory.

National Organisations

The Indian organisations concerned with providing information on customers abroad are the Export Promotion Councils and Indian Embassies abroad. Export promotion bodies like the FIEO, ITPO, IIFT, etc. also provide information in this regard.

1. National Centre for Trade Information, NCTI Complex, Pragati Maidan, Gate No.3, New Delhi - 110 001.
2. Federation of Indian Export Organisations, PHD House, 4/2 Siri fort Institutional Area, Huaz Khas, New Delhi - 110 016.
3. Indian Trade Promotion Organisations, Pragati Bhawan, Pragati Maidan, New Delhi - 110 001.
4. Indian Institute of Foreign Trade, B-21, Mehrauli Institutional Area, South of IIT Campus, New Delhi - 110 016.
5. E.P. Councils.
6. Commodity Boards.
7. Small Industries Service Institute.
8. Indian Embassies/Missions Abroad.
9. Foreign Embassies/High Commission in India.
10. State Export Corporations.

The various Chambers of Commerce and Trade Associations like the FICCI, FASII and AIMO may also be contacted for information in this regard.

SELECTIVE APPROACH

Based upon the information collected from various organisations/sources detailed above, the prospective exporter would be able to compile a list of customers abroad. This list needs to be vetted and rechecked so that duplication is avoided and correct name and address can be ascertained. The best source for such vetting is the telephone directory of the city/ country concerned. Since it may not be possible to keep telephone directories of various places, the information collected should at least be compared with the information available in various market survey reports brought out by different organisations.

Since the list so complied may contain many names and writing to each of them will involve much expenditure, there is need for a selective approach to be adopted.

// CHAPTER 13 //

EXPORT MARKETING MIX

The marketing mix is one of the most fundamental concepts associated with the marketing process. It is well understood by most modern marketers and is systematically applied in many industries, especially those that deal with physical products. Yet it is easy to assume that, because most managers have heard about it and/or used it, there is no need to mention it again in a module on marketing.

A brief review of the main principles surrounding the marketing mix can help to clarify its true role in the development and execution of an effective marketing effort.

The marketing mix represents an assemblage of task and subtasks which ultimately will help to satisfy the customers' requirements in such a way, as to enable the firm to attain its objectives in a optimum fashion. The subtle part of the concept is that different companies in the same business may opt to develop different 'mixes.' In fact, it is this difference that may provide one company with a competitive advantage over its competitors.

Let us consider a simple analogy. A pastry cook is invited to prepare a cake for a given clientele, based on a number of ingredients which are placed in front of him. At the same time he is told that most of his customers are on a diet. Obviously he would use the available ingredients in such a way as to meet the dietary requirements of his customers. He would probably use less sugar but increase the use of less flattening components. If the 'mix' were right, he would satisfy the requirements of his clients and would gradually develop customer loyalty to his offering.

EXPORT MARKETING MIX

American Marketing Association has defined marketing as "the performance of business activities that direct the flow of goods from the producer to the consumer." It is in this manner that, James Culliton has described a business executive as a "decider", an "artist", a "mixer of ingredients." We may cite the example of two housewives who may go out for their shopping together and buy various articles from the same source. However, when table is laid, the same dish in the two households tastes differently. It is the way in which the two ladies mixed various ingredients vegetables, onion, garlic, spices, etc. which ultimately constituted the dish. It is the judicious blending of these ingredients which makes one dish superior to other. Similarly, we have a number of ingredients at the disposal of marketer. The way one blends these ingredients differentiates him from rest of his tribe. The success or failure of a marketing manager depends upon the judicious use of the various tools by him.

A marketing manager is faced with the task of finding the best setting of his marketing decision variables. The setting constitutes the firm's Marketing Mix.

Carthy has evolved a four factor classification of marketing decision of variables, which are called the "four Ps".

1. Product
2. Place
3. Promotion
4. Price

Each of the above variable is, in reality, a collection of instruments. For the sake of simplicity we will, however, take them here as a single variable represented by a single magnitude, e.g. rupee per unit in the case of price, total rupees in the case of promotion or place or an index of relative attractiveness in the case of product.

The firm's current marketing mix can be conveniently represented by the vector: (P,A,D,R) T

Here P represents price; A represents promotion (advertising, personal selling and sales promotion); D represents place (distribution); R represents product and T stands for a given time. If a firm is currently producing a product priced at Rs 20/- per period, distribution expense of Rs. 30,000 per period and the product quality is rated at 1.20 the company's marketing mix at time T is: (Rs 20, Rs 20,000, Rs 30,000, 1.20) T

Thus, it is evident that a company's current marketing mix is selected from a number of possibilities. To elucidate the point consider the following:

Suppose

1. The price lies between Rs. 16 and Rs. 24 (to the nearest rupee) i.e. 9 options.
2. Promotion expense lies between Rs. 1,00,000 to Rs. 50,000 (to the nearest Rs. 10,000) i.e. 5 options.
3. Distribution expense lies between Rs. 10,000 to Rs. 50,000 (to the nearest Rs. 10,000) i.e. 5 options.
4. Product quality can have two values.

This firm will have as many as 450 (9 × 5 × 5 × 2) combinations of marketing mix at that time. Had the choice not been restricted to such discrete values, the figure would have been much higher. This explains why it is difficult to find an optimal marketing mix in actual practice. In a given environment ten different managers may accept ten different solutions to the problem as optimal.

Good market planning requires that the marketing mix be under continuous study and that the individual factors be constantly altered to adjust to a changing market. This may include changed product design, promotional and selling methods, distribution channels or price adjustments. One of the biggest marketing errors in American marketing history was made by 'Ford' when they refused to alter their model 'T' in the wake of threatened changed demand pattern by General Motor's streamlined models. Before going further it may be well to have a brief overview of the four Ps. This will help appreciate the situation better.

Product

Generally speaking, the companies that are growing fast are those which spend a substantial share of expenditure on product research and development. The life of an average product is getting shorter year after year in view of increased obsolescence. The success of a company's product line depends upon decision in the following areas:

Selecting the right product, knowing when to add new products to the line, dropping products at the right time, brand and packaging, etc.

Place

In the context of marketing mix, 'place' is used to indicate the method used to get the goods to the target market. The choices are very great. Some of the questions that must be answered in solving the problems of place are:

1. What sort of wholesale and retail institutions should be used?
2. Should the goods be marketed through multiple outlets or through exclusive stores?
3. Where should the outlets be situated?
4. How should the goods be shipped and warehoused?

Promotion

It involves communicating with the target market about the product, place and price of the goods. There are many ways whereby this information can be directed to the consumer. A marketing manager must select the media that is best suited to the particular mix. Sales promotion, advertising and personal selling are the elements that must be considered in the determination of a promotion policy.

Price

In addition to product, place and promotion, the marketing manager must also select the proper price at which the goods may be sold. Some of the factors involved in this decision are competitor's actions, discounts, target profit and legal restrictions.

All four elements of the marketing mix are so closely interrelated that it is impossible to consider one to be more important than the others. The success of the programme depends upon the ease and rapidity with which the institution adjusts its marketing mix to the constantly changing market.

From the above it will appear logical that the success of a marketing mix will depend upon how a marketing manager exercises his wits in devising a mix or programme which will give a profitable business operation.

To portray this broadened concept in a visual representation requires:

1. A list of the important elements or ingredients that make up the marketing programme.
2. A list of the forces that bear on the marketing operation of a firm, to which the marketing manager must adjust in his search for a successful mix or programme.

The list of elements can be long or short depending upon how far one wishes to go in ones classification and subclassification of the marketing procedures and policies concerning the firm.

The same applies to the marketing mix. The marketer has at his or her disposal a number of components. The ability to mix them in response to an identified set of requirements, coupled with a number of other objectives, is one of the major requirements of effective marketing.

The 'four Ps model' of the marketing mix has probably gained acceptance because of its elegance rather than its validity in all situations. Regrettably, what has been gained in simplicity has been sacrificed in universal appropriateness. It is easy to find examples of marketing programmes which do not fit into the four Ps model. It is therefore important to emphasize at the outset that this model is not of universal validity. The theory underlying the four Ps concept is that, if one manages to achieve the right product at the right price with the appropriate promotion and in the right place, the marketing programme will be effective and successful. However, one must bear in mind that each of the four Ps can be broken into a number of sub-components. Table 1 lists some of these.

In other words, it is not sufficient to think in terms of the fours Ps alone. One needs to identify the significant sub-components which underlie the firm's marketing strategy. A few simple examples of the marketing mixes of various companies will help to illustrate the point.

Table 16.1 The Sub Components of the Four Ps

Product	*Price*	*Place*	*Promotion*
Brand	Credit terms	Channels	Advertising
Packaging	Payment period	Locations	Sales promotion
Warranties	Discounts	Transport	Publicity
Service	Instalments	Delivery	Selling
Features	Commissions	Stocks	
Guarantees	General cost benefit in use	/Customs clearance	

A major cosmetics company has declared that its marketing mix consists of the following components (referred to as 'the seven Ps and one A):

- ★ Product
- ★ Packaging
- ★ Price
- ★ Promotion
- ★ Personnel selling
- ★ Publicity
- ★ Physical distribution
- ★ Advertising

An international manufacturer of domestic appliances places its emphasis upon the following components:

- ★ Product
- ★ Price
- ★ Promotion
- ★ Place
- ★ Service

Automotive Components manufacturer places emphasis on the following components:

- ★ Product
- ★ Quality
- ★ Price
- ★ Place ('just-in-time')
- ★ Selling

No mention is made of promotion and/or advertising.

These are three very simple but disparate illustrations. The message is clear. What is right for a cosmetics company is not appropriate for a company manufacturing and selling automotive components to car manufacturers. The situation is probably even more complicated, as the components company may have different mixes, depending on whether it sells its products to Original Equipment Manufacturers (OEM) companies or for the replacement market. In the former case there is little point in spending resources on promotion and/or advertising, whereas in the latter case advertising may be quite relevant because one is seeking to reach a market with a large number of consumers in it.

Every situation calls for a careful analysis of the key points where marketing resources must be allocated. The marketing mix represents those key points.

ELEMENTS OF MARKETING MIX OF MANUFACTURERS

Neil H. Borden has listed the following elements of the marketing mix. This list can at best serve as a model and the marketing manager can reply upon it or can modify it as per his unique needs.

1. Product Planning

(i) Products lines to be offered their qualities, design, etc.
(ii) Market to sell - whom, were, and in what quantities.
(iii) New product policy - R&D Programme.

2. Pricing

(i) Price level to be adopted.
(ii) Specific prices to be adopted - odd, even, etc.
(iii) Price policy - one price or varying prices; price maintenance; use of list prices, etc.
(iv) Margins to be adopted for company, for trade.

3. Branding

(i) Selection of trade marks
(ii) Brand Policy - individualised or family brands
(iii) Margins to be adopted for company, for trade

4. Distribution

(i) Type of channel to be used between plant and consumer.
(ii) Degree of selectivity among wholesalers and retailers.
(iii) Efforts to gain cooperation of the trade.

5. Personal Selling

Burden to be placed on personal selling and the methods to be employed in:

(i) The manufacturer's organisation.
(ii) Wholesale segment of the trade.
(iii) Retailers level.

6. Advertising

(i) Amount to be spent.
(ii) Copy platform to adopt - product, corporate or both.
(iii) Advertising mix to the trade; through the trade; to the consumers.

7. Promotion

(i) Burden to place on special selling plans or devices directed at or through the trade.
(ii) Form of these devices for consumer promotions, for trade; promotions.

8. Packaging

Formulation of package and label policy.

9. Display

(i) Burden to be put on display to help effect sale.
(ii) Methods to adopt to secure display.

10. Servicing

Determining the type of quantum of service needed.

11. Physical Handling

Warehousing, transportation and inventories.

12. Fact Finding and Analysis

Secure, analyse and use the facts in marketing operations.

Apart from the internal elements given above, there are certain forces a marketer has to reckon with. It is therefore necessary that such forces are also enumerated and reflected in the marketing mix.

Consumer Behaviour

Motivation in purchasing, buying habits, living habits, power and numbers.

Trade BehaviourX

Wholesale's and retailer's behaviour as reflected by their motivations, their structure and procedure and portend change.

Competition

Their position and behaviour as influenced by

(a) Industry structure and firms' relation to:
  (i) Size and strength of competitors.
  (ii) No. and concentration of competition.
  (iii) Indirect competition (from other products)
(b) Relation of supply to demand.
(c) Product choices offered to consumers.
(d) Degree of competition price vs. non-price bases.
(e) Competitor likely response to the action of other firms.
(f) Social and technological trends affecting supply and demand pattern.

Governmental regulation Regarding Products, Pricing, Competitive Practices and Promotion

It is a judicious blend of internal factors, developed in the light of prevailing market forces that will determine the quality of the market mix. Since we live in a dynamic world, it is essential that the mix be constantly evaluated and necessary changes incorporated in meeting the challenge of the time. A good marketer plans on long term basis and then segments them into short-run plans, incorporating required changes as he goes along. "In short, the mix provides an ever ready checklist as to areas into which to guide thinking, when considering marketing questions of dealing with marketing problems."

Long-term and Short-term Marketing Mix

The marketing mix of a firm is mostly the result of the evaluation emanating from day-to-day marketing. It represents a programme to meet the problem posed by ever-changing, ever-challenging market. It is a continuous process. A new product, aggressive promotion, price changes, more displays, better sales force, new advertising themes, market share for a product are some of the problems which must be faced to meet the challenge of the competition. Management must arrange to obtain information on points of interest in its field of operation. The day-to-day behaviours of the consumers, competitors and the trade should be observed. These day-to-day changes affect the working of the firm and hence remedial measures have constantly to be taken. Thus we may observe that short range forces play a large part, in the fashioning of the mix to be used at any time and in determining the allocation of expenditures among the various functional accounts of the operating statement.

As against the above, the overall strategy employed in a marketing mix is the result of long range planning based on past experience and management foresight. As marketing is a dynamic process, long range planning is essential for the growth of the company. Accordingly when we think of the marketing mix, we must give proper thought to the needs of the market in the coming five to ten years. Provision of suitable measures to contain expected challenges during this period will determine, the quality of the long-range marketing mix. An example of this foresight is the entry of Hindustan Levers in the semi-processed food business. It was found that more and more housewives were seeking jobs. It evidently meant that there will be less time at the disposal of a lady for cooking family food and products like HIMA peas, etc.

In summary it can be said that the market mix is a sufficient way of keeping before all the executives of the firm, the basic facts of business. It indicates the ground rules governing the relationship between the would be seller and the free consumer. The concept of marketing mix while being very basic, does not dogmatically proclaim final answers. It is a framework within which change may be understood, initiated and managed better. It is a tool whereby a marketer can face the marketing problems effectively.

// CHAPTER 14 //

MARKETING CHANNELS

Mr. Trader began as a market stallholder but soon made progress. He became a wholesaler selling to other stallholders. Then became a factory owner employing many people. He found it better to sell his shoes to wholesalers. Mr. Trader is a long way from his market stall and he wants to expand still more. Given below is his way progress:

Mr. Trader Goes into Exports

Mr. Trader would like to do still more business. Labour and materials are plentiful but he can't increase his sales very much more in his own country. He knows that if he can increase sales, his production costs will fall. So Mr. Trader decides to explore the export possibilities for his product. He selects a suitable market abroad and visits it.

It quickly becomes plain that it would not be very economic to employ a full-time salesman in that country. So after careful search Mr. Trader appoints an agent to represent him.

Mr. Trader and his agent have only one or two direct customers who are distributors. But they have a lot of indirect customers like wholesalers, retailers and customers. Now the marketing channel for the product stretches from the factory to the retail shop in the export market where the product is bought. Our businessman has found his first venture into export markets a rewarding experience.

That is a success story from Mr. Trader. It sounds very easy. Unfortunately creating an export market is not that easy. That is what often happens.

Mr. Vague Goes into Exports

Mr. Trader has a friend called Mr. Vague who finds his home sales falling at a time when, his new factory extension is nearly ready. The cost of the oil he needs to run his machine has risen four times in the year. He realises that one way to keep his costs down and to deal with this situation is to increase production. But his salesmen are having difficulty in increasing sales in the home market. So he decides to sell his product abroad.

Mr. Vague is not as efficient as Mr. Trader and begins to hit problems. Customers complain about delivery delays. The styles of some of his products are all right for his home market but need to be adapted for the export market. Mr. Vague has also started large scale production in a colour that he discovered too late was not liked in the export market. He also has problems with his agent and his distributor.

Mr. Vague has spent a lot of money on publicity, he has also got a lot of orders that he cannot possibly fulfill.

Mr. Vague's experiences are the kind of thing that can happen when a person tries to create an export market without careful planning and foresight.

This reminder of the needs and pitfalls of export marketing is necessary, in order to understand marketing channels.

In this chapter marketing channels are discussed. The manner in which Mr. Trader is developing his marketing channels are discussed below.

Mr. Trader Finds About Marketing Channels

Mr. Trader has recently gone into exporting. In order to find outlets for his shoes, he visits some large departmental stores in Industria.

The stores take his shoes but after three months, Mr. Trade notices that the sales are poor. He decides to visit Industria to find the reasons for this.

He has make an appointment with Ruralia's trade representative in Industria, Mr. Brown. The day after his arrival in Industria he goes to see Mr. Brown to discuss the problem of his disappointing export sales.

THE ROLE OF MARKETING CHANNELS

Marketing is the process of providing the right product, in the right place, at the right time, at the right price.

Marketing seeks to maximise the profits and customer satisfaction, by getting the marketing mix right.

Each of the variables in the marketing mix can be adjusted. The aim is to achieve the most appropriate marketing mix. So, each of the segments in the marketing mix is infinitely variable.

One of the variables is 'Marketing channels'. Marketing channels are the channels through which sales are achieved and products are distributed.

Variations in Basic Marketing Channels

1. The distributor or other large buying organisation may also be the retailer. For example, a large departmental store or chain of stores may have a central buying organisation which buys the product for retail sales.
2. Industrial products usually have shorter marketing channels because, the industrial end user buys on a bigger scale; for example, a timber merchant may import directly from the exporter and sell directly to the building industry or saw mills. But a large shipbuilder may import plywood directly from the exporter without any middlemen at all.
3. All the functions may be carried out by one organisation. For example, a tea company may own plantations, process the tea, pack, ship and redistribute to its own local warehouses. It may even own its own retail outlets.

Marketing channels must be studied in order to understand, how the product flows from the exporter to the end user. One needs to understand the many influences on that flow. The important part played by middlemen in getting the product to the end user, so as to ensure that, one is paid a reasonable price. Using the proper marketing channels improves the efficiency of selling.

If marketing channels are efficient, the 'middlemen' are, provide an efficient service rather than taking a fat profit for nothing.

Push and Pull in Marketing Channels

The flow of the products is influenced by the sales made by the salesmen or agents. The sales that they make pushes the products along the marketing channels. This flow is increased by demands from the end user. Each time a consumer asks a retailer for the products, this pulls the product along the marketing channels.

This pull is encouraged by means of good publicity, which makes people to buy the product.

A satisfied customer is one who is pleased with what he has bought. It is important to know what he needs and what will please him. One also need to know when and how his needs are changing, because one must be ready to change the product in the same way.

METHODS OF ENTRY INTO FOREIGN MARKETS

Investigation for Marketing Channels

When an exporter has identified his market and his product, he must choose the appropriate marketing channel. First he must find out, what channels are used for that particular type of product in the market, and then he must decide which particular channels or set of channels are right for the product.

A person must understand the different marketing channels and must be able to select the appropriate one for the product in a particular market. Marketing channels are the routes by which orders are got and by which goods can go from the seller to the consumer. Which is the best way to do this? By selling through a sole distributor? Through a cooperative wholesale union? Through a state buying organisation or through import/export merchants?

Research into marketing channels is not easy; One must be able to find out from the published statistics that a certain company imports so many million pairs of shoes a year, and that a further quantity of shoes are manufactured and sold locally in the country itself. Before one can decide how to plan to obtain a share of this market for the company, one has to find out how these shoes reach the consumers in that country. If an exporter chooses the wrong channels, perhaps by accepting an attractive initial order, he may permanently damage his chances for long term business.

The diagram illustrates some of the possible channels through which imported shoes, for instance might reach the eventual consumer.

DISTRIBUTION CHANNELS FOR SHOES — AN EXAMPLE

Research into marketing channels This can partly be undertaken from information published by the following.

a) National statistics often show the numbers and turnover of wholesale, retail, and other types of marketing intermediaries, who are classified according to the type of product they handle.

b) Trade journals and directories give a general indication of the nature of trade in a product group.

c) The ITC and national export promotion organisations have carried out extensive research into the marketing channels for many products and countries.
d) Export Promotion Councils
e) NICEM Trade Information Services Division.

Field research On the spot field research may be necessary to obtain more details, and most important to identify the appropriate channels for the product.

a) Field surveys of consumers, or of retail or wholesale outlets, will give useful information but are expensive to undertake.
b) Visits to selected outlets identified by the country's trade representative in the market or other sources of introduction, will enable one to judge the characteristics and methods of each channel, even if they do not provide an accurate statistical data. If a potential customer realises that the exporter is evaluating him as a channel at the same time as he, the customer, is evaluating the product and its supplier, he may be more cooperative and keen to order if he is offered the chance.

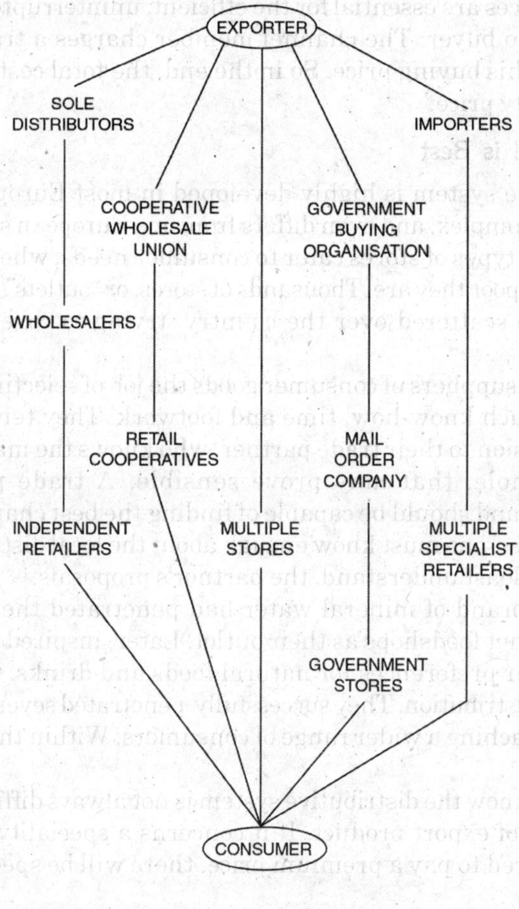

Functions of Distribution Channels

Distribution channels bring the product (close) to the buyers. They not only take care of the physical transportation, they also support selling by means of promotion or simply by making the goods available: An exporter cannot do without the help of the distribution channels, as they are the inroads to the customers.

The functions of the distribution channels are:

1. Interpreting and anticipating customer's demand.
2. Storing the required goods and distributing the goods locally to those consumers.
3. Providing low-cost storage and delivery.
4. Offering credit and capital to finance inventories.
5. Buying large quantities from the exporter and breaking them up for other intermediaries.
6. (Personal) selling to other channels.
7. Advertising promoting sales and displaying the products at the point of purchase (also called: point of sale).
8. Handling guarantees, repairs, complaints, maintenance, instructions for use, etc. on behalf of the supplier.

These services are essential for the efficient, uninterrupted flow of goods from supplier to buyer. The channel member charges a trade margin for them on top of his buying price. So in the end, the total costs add up to the final 'availability price.'

Which Channel is Best

The distributive system is highly developed in most European countries, though rather complex, and even differs from one European state to another. Many different types of stores cater to consumer needs, wherever they live, however rich or poor they are. Thousands of stores, or "outlets" as the marketer calls them, are scattered over the country, trying to cover the potential customers.

For foreign suppliers of consumer goods the job of selecting the right one involves too much know-how, time and footwork. They tend to leave that important decision to their trade partner, who knows the market better.

On the whole, that may prove sensible. A trade partner is the representative and should be capable of finding the best channels.

Nevertheless, one must know enough about the local distribution system to justify, or at least understand, the partner's proposals.

A famous brand of mineral water had penetrated the US market by selecting gourmet foodshops as their outlet. Later, inspired by the upswing in the consumer preferences for natural foods and drinks, they decided to broaden their distribution. They successfully penetrated several supermarket chains, thus reaching a wider range of consumers. Within three years, their sales tripled.

Getting to know the distributive system is not always difficult. It depends upon the kind of export product. If it concerns a speciality, for which the buyer is prepared to pay a premium price, there will be speciality stores to distribute it.

If the (consumer) product is just a normal "run-of-the-mill" product, one has to select a convenience store or a supermarket as outlet. If the low prices are the biggest asset one could consider selecting discount stores, which buy larger quantities and sell cheaply.

A TPO, a consultant or the trade partner will be able to find a list of distribution outlets and their specific function, reputation or character.

There are also specialised wholesalers, who usually supply to such outlets. Examples are in sectors such as building materials, furniture, hospital supplies, electronics, household appliances, fresh food and catering textiles/ garments, etc. Some of the larger outlets (mainly in food and garments) have their own wholesaler. The biggest of them even do their own importing or come and visit an exporter in his home country to buy directly from him.

The selection of distributive outlets of industrial suppliers is easier. The channel of distribution is shorter. That is explained by the number of buyers. There are far fewer industrial buyers than customers, so that the system can be more simple, involving fewer intermediaries.

In fact, there are no retail outlets for some industrial products. The buyers buy direct from the wholesaler type of stores. Here, "vertical integration" (channel members adopting the functions of up/down - stream distribution outlets to be able to control the supply flows better) is a common practice. Usually, most importers do their own wholesaling. In such cases their trade margins are somewhat lower.

Sell Through, Not to the Channels

The distribution channels in West-European countries have become very large and powerful. More than once, they have organised their purchasing on a cross-border basis, together with colleagues abroad. Thus, they can buy larger quantities at better prices. They know the exporter cannot do without them and they fight for their own margins - even when they have to fight the exporter.

In some countries, like The Netherlands, Belgium and Germany such distributing organisations, cater for more than 35% of the goods to be distributed. In Scandinavian countries it can be as high as 80%. The large retail outlets there virtually dominate the trade.

Wise suppliers therefore dedicate a lot of attention on the distribution channels, particularly to the large ones. They enable them to do the best possible distribution job. They adapt their own packaging and their pricing to the distributor's requirements, they plan their deliveries according to the distributor's wishes (supplying them 'JIT', Just-in-Time).

That attitude has developed into a certain kind of "trade marketing." Large manufacturers have trained special sales people as special or key account managers, whose only job is to look after such distributors.

By now, one should know, why to treat the trade channel members as the distribution partners. They have the same objectives of selling to the customers who need your product. Therefore, the agent's job is not just to sell to the distributor, but to facilitate him in selling to the customers.

In practice, that means that the exporter will be asked (by his trade partner) to prepare sales promotion instruments for the distribution. That can be either of a simple nature like, fixing special price tags or printing the UPC "bar codes" on the packs (pictorial with number of vertical narrow lines, which can be translated by computer optics into item particulars such as price, required stock level, name of supplier).

The channel members could also ask for some difficult and expensive changes like, changing the brand name into the ("private") brand of the chain store, altering the packing size, preparing a display box, providing a budget for cooperative advertising (jointly paying for such expenses).

Such requests should not be right away, even though they are expensive and seem like too much trouble for the profit. These should be discussed with trade partner and the expenditure should be evaluated against, the privilege of having a profitable position in the shops. The exporters attitude may be the decisive factor of whether the products are "to be in the market or not to be in the market."

DIRECT MARKETING

Direct marketing or DM is known to all. One only have to think of all the daily mailbox "pollution" which a consumer or secretary has to work through and it is understandable why direct marketing has acquired its negative image, it is a result of the promotional overkill of the professional marketing machines, which are active 24 hours a day in the global village. With the help of data list brokers, credit card databases, loyalty programmes, subscriptions and all the memberships that can be thought of, the direct marketer knows where and how to find the customer personally.

Neither is a person free from the direct marketing hype and the screening of mail before it reaches the boss, is part of the job description of every secretary (in direct marketing lingo called the "gatekeeper"). In this respect, it is important to keep in mind that the secretary has become an all-important decision maker.

Creativity So, is there still a future for business-to-business direct marketing? Is there still a possibility to distinguish oneself amongst the 50-100 addressed mailings a secretary has to go through, in order to present her personal selection of letter to her boss? The answer is yes, but it all depends on creativity and originality in bringing the proposal to the attention of the right decision makers.

Many Export Promotion Boards are using direct marketing mailings to approach prospective importers, but after such a mailing campaign they remain silent for the rest of the year because the budget has been spent. If these institutes had used the proper direct marketing testing technique in stimulating reactions from their prospects, their campaigns would have produced concrete results in a possible follow-up phase.

Creativity in designing a business-to-business direct marketing campaign, is the main issue of this chapter. However, like every marketing tool, direct marketing also has some basic conditions that have to be kept in mind. Otherwise, there is a risk of investing the marketing funds in vain.

The basic rules In order to know exactly what is talked about, one should select some definitions beyond the common understanding that direct marketing is relationship marketing. Actually, in the world of direct marketing there is only one internationally acclaimed guru. Bob Stone, with his classic book "Successful Direct Marketing Methods," which has already appeared in its fifth edition. Considered by many to the "bible" of direct marketing, this book is a complete, single source of information for the beginner and an up-to-date reference to the professional (ISBN 0-8442-3510-5).

Interactive

Stone defines direct marketing as "an interactive system of marketing which uses one or more advertising media to effect a measurable response and/or transaction at any location". It is interactive, so unlike other promotional communication, a person is not only sending a message, but also receiving one. Here the first golden rule is the whole direct marketing campaign should be aimed at inducing active response. By measuring and comparing the responses, one should improve the campaign continuously in order to increase the conversions (= actual orders). And that is the second golden rule!

In the case of business-to-business direct marketing, this testing sequence will reveal exactly which mailing concept did pass the secretarial filter and which did not, and for what reason. This must sound like music to the ears of every exporter, but it really is true, as long as he follows the do's and don'ts of direct marketing.

Export - special type of direct marketing Where export is concerned, one is talking about the international business-to-business direct marketing. In his book, Stone defines this as "a special type of direct marketing in which the response to value-based contacts is made by an individual on behalf of company, institution or professional organisation". This includes the individual end users, buyers, influencers, resellers, and contacts for whom information is captured in a database for the purpose of sustaining a long-term relationship and supporting all channels of distribution.

Optimal mix This is the driving force and the foundation for successful business-to-business direct marketing. In his book, Stone defines this as a "a special type of direct marketing which results in the concurrent improvement of sales productivity and customer relationships.

To achieve these objectives, a person must strive for the optimal mix of value-based contacts in an integrated campaign of mail, phone (including Internet) and field sales. The economics of these contact strategies and the monitoring of customer relations create a process that must be tested continually. This might be quite a mouthful, but it is a definition which embodies the three golden rules of direct marketing. The first two have already been mentioned, the third one is as follows:

The setting up and maintaining of a database containing potential, existing and past customers is the basic discipline of every B to B DM activity. (B to B -Business-to-Business ; DM-Direct Marketing).

The three golden rules of direct marketing

1. The whole DM campaign should be aimed at inducing active response, improving sales productivity.

2. A DM campaign should be a mandatory series of measurable tests on a long-term basis.
3. Setting up and maintaining a database of potential, existing and past customers is the basic discipline of every business-to-business DM activity.

As a conclusion, we can sum up the following features of business-to-business DM:

★ A super-ordinate focus on potential customers
★ A personal character
★ Undivided attention and empathy
★ Full creative freedom within the framework of societal and business ethics
★ Testing probabilities
★ Timing control
★ Response inducement
★ Measurability

The Cost Factors

DM is an expensive marketing tool. An experter should think about the (air) mailing costs of 1,000 large and heavy envelopes. For that reason, cost calculation should be made in order to check whether the expected costs per order are realistic. Of course, those initial costs should be in relation to the expected yield.

It is only when one manages to start working with a good curriculum, that the total DM campaign costs will be earned back by the total conversions. In order to achieve this and to show that there are ways to rationalise the decision making, one should introduce some of the most used calculation formulae for budgeting purpose.

DM Formulae	
1. **Net profit**	Net profit; Gross Profit; Relationship costs
2. **Gross profit**	Gross profit per order; Total orders obtained during a DM campaign
3. **Relationship costs**	Initiation costs of relationship; Continuation costs
4. **Intiation costs**	Total DM costs; Total number of prospects; Conversion percentage.
5. **Continuation costs**	Average costs per follow-up contact; Number of follow-up contacts
6. **Costs per order**	Variable mailing costs (the cost of 1 mailpack)

The unshakeable DM facts

★ Higher the run of the total mailing, lower the costs per mail pack.
★ Higher the run of the total mailing lower the conversion ratio.
★ Testing is the key to success for every DM campaign.
★ Forget "beautiful", focus on promising test results.
★ The ideal B-to-B DM product has a high purchase frequency, is easy to promote cheap to pack and easy to ship.

* ★ B-to-B DM is not advertising, but a selling technique.
* ★ Copy should be judged according to the four Ps; Problem statement, Promise, Product and Pay-off.
* ★ Every DM letter should start with a reader benefit, which should be repeated in the Ps.
* ★ The headline should be big and benefit-oriented.
* ★ A strong visual support relating to the headline is critical for attracting attention.
* ★ The copy should get to the point quickly and tie features and benefits together.
* ★ One should for the return of the card, requesting more information, etc. tell the prospect what one wants him to do.
* ★ When enclosing an order form, ample space has to be provided for the buyer to fill in name, address, telephone number, etc.
* ★ Print the written address or telephone/fax number clearly. Use the "place stamp here" approach; it will qualify the respondents as being interested prospects.
* ★ Always investigate the mailing density of the target group; when high, the exporter who is initiating the contact should be very creative.
* ★ Variations in the mail pack lead to renewed attention.
* ★ After sales mailing will increase customer loyalty.

DIRECT CUSTOMERS

They are those who buy the product and pay for it.

There are several kinds of direct customers in export marketing including:

* ★ Distributors
* ★ Import houses
* ★ Government departments
* ★ Central or state buying organisations
* ★ Industrial buyers
* ★ Wholesalers
* ★ Large retail stores

DISTRIBUTORS

An import house (it may be an import/export house dealing two-way trade) may buy your products as a direct customer. But they may be acting as an agent for a buyer. They may also buy on their own account as distributors or retailers.

Government Departments

In some countries government departments buy commodities, often on a long-term basis. For example a country may want the exporter to supply them with a certain quantity of rice, to be delivered at regular intervals over the next five years.

State Buying Organisations

In the planned economies, particularly of Eastern Europe, all buying from abroad, is arranged by the central or state buying organisations. The exporter must sell to them and not to private companies. Barter deals or reciprocal trading are not uncommon - for example, one may supply sugar in return for machinery.

Industrial Buyers

Large industrial companies often buy directly from producers. For example, in the ship building industry a company may place a contract for the supply of so much timber or so much furnishing material. Similar contracts may be made with industrial buyers to supply them with raw materials, foodstuffs, metals or components.

Wholesalers

Some wholesalers may be among the direct customers, though they are more likely to be indirect customers through the distributor. A wholesaler buying from the exporter does not have exclusive selling rights. But he may have a commanding position in a particular market and so, have no competition even though he has no exclusive rights.

Large Retail Stores and Supermarkets

Certain large department stores may also buy directly from the exporter. In some cases they may want exclusive rights. They can be the most important of the buyers who visit the country. Sometimes several independent stores join together voluntarily and send one buyer who buys for them all. The central buying organisations of department store or supermarket multiples, or of other types of chain stores, are among the most important direct retail buyers.

SALES AGENTS

Imagine that one has had some success in personal selling to visiting buyers or by export sales visits abroad, but now feels that the next step is to have someone selling for him in a selected export market. Or he may feel that he needs on-the-spot help in establishing the marketing channels - for example, in finding and working with distributors or wholesalers.

The exporter cannot spend a great deal of time on export selling himself because of his responsibilities to the business at home. The idea of a full-time travelling salesman may seem attractive at first. But it is probably not economic to make such an appointment as a first step into export markets. Also, if the exporter appointed one of his salesmen it would be some time before the salesman knew the export market well enough to sell successfully.

In such situations it is usual to appoint an agent. An agent is a person or firm that handles negotiations on the exporters behalf and is usually paid on a commission basis. An export agent is simply an agent who is active in the country to which it is planed to export. The word agent and the word distributor to refer to quite separate activities - they should not be confused.

- ★ He is a respectable businessman.
- ★ He is not representing a competing producer.
- ★ He has the organisation and facilities necessary to do a good job.

- ★ He has a serious long-term interest in the product-and is not representing too many other products, so as to give the exporter's product attention.
- ★ He is experienced in the product and market area and has established connections.

Finding, appointing and using an agent needs careful thought and planning. First the exporter should get a list of possible agents for his particular product. He can then write to them explaining his needs and ask if they are available to handle his products.

From the replies he can prepare a 'shortlist' of the most suitable agents. If possible he should visit each of them personally. In any case he should obtain references from other people, particularly from other firms which the agent represents.

When he has found his agent it is very important for the exporter to have a clear written agreement with him. This must cover all the points which might be potential sources of difficulty or disagreement in the future.

JOINT VENTURES AND LICENSING AGREEMENTS

So far, the process of establishing fairly conventional sales channels, perhaps with the aid of an agent, have been talked about. In recent years there has been increasing use of a rather more difficult approach, involving much closer relations between the exporter and his customer, who can actually become a partner. One example, is a customer who can actually become a partner. Another example is, cooperation in a joint venture with a company that operates in that market. An exporter might make an agreement to set up a factory to process his raw materials before exporting them, instead of the processing being done in the other country. For example, a firm in an overseas market needs cocoa butter. The firm might offer to cooperate with the exporter's country in setting up a processing facility. To take another example, a European firm may be making instant coffee in his coffee beans. The firm might offer the exporter a licence to make the instant coffee in his country. The exporter might then either sell it to them or export it in their name, paying a royalty for using their technology and trademark.

Another kind of international cooperation is when an exporter sends his raw materials to be processed and sold by another company already in the market, but with the exporter's name and trademark instead of the company's. This can be useful way of overcoming tariff barriers or of reducing packing, transport and storage costs (e.g. Coca-Cola). It is also more efficient to process and market goods in one organisation inside the export market. However, it may not be in the interest of developing country to make this kind of agreement. One of the important reasons for exporting is to stimulate employment and industrial growth in the exporting country. This would not happen if the goods were processed in the other country. It may nevertheless be better to export in this way than not to export at all.

Mr. Trader Meets a Distributor

Mr. Trader's shoes have become well established in Industria for more than a year. On a visit to Industria he meets a high pressure distributor who tries to talk Mr. Trader into granting him a sole distributorship for Industria and also for neighbouring Urbania.

The cut and thrust of the conversation between Mr. Trader and the distributor reveals the main aspects to be considered by each of them in deciding whether to sign an agreement. Mr. Trader refuses to be pressured into making an agreement, promising to phone back later with his decision.

CONSIGNMENT DISTRIBUTORS

Sometimes a distributor operates on a consignment basis. He imports a large consignment of goods but does not pay for them immediately. The exporter has to wait until part of all of the consignment has been resold by the distributor. Another disadvantage is the extra office work. The exporter may have to send a separate invoice as each part of the consignment is resold and perhaps make a separate exchange-control application as each invoice is paid.

The main advantage is the saving in cost, time and trouble that comes from dealing in large consignments. Another advantage is the better profit margin, because the distributor pays the exporter a higher price for delaying payment until they are resold. It can be useful, too, to have large stocks of the product easily available in the export market.

Distribution operating on consignment basis must be chosen very carefully. Most of them resell the goods as quickly as possible because it costs them money to keep them in the warehouse. But some of them will not work so hard to sell products that have not already been paid for.

TYPES OF IMPORTERS

Since most importers combine their function with wholesaling, they have immediate access to the market. Hence, they are capable of order-taking and delivering breaking bulk imports into smaller quantities, holding stock in (own) warehouses, invoicing, extending credit, etc. They often have their own sales force too, for canvassing the market, the buyers, the retailers or the sub-wholesalers for orders. They also provide various services like installing, instructing maintenance and repairing, in technical sectors.

As a trade partner, the exporter cannot do without an importer. Not only does he help the exporter to enter the single market by buying from him, he also gives (physical and non-physical) access to the distribution. However, as he is an independent market party, he will not have to justify his market activities to the exporter. Since he buys the goods from the exporter, he can do what he likes with the products (even reexport them or market them in disagreement with the marketing design).

Understanding the sector characteristics is essential in selecting the best importer/distributor. The main types of such trade partners are:

1. The **straight importer**, is an independent company, specialised in importing a certain range of goods from abroad. Such an organisation buys directly from the exporter and thus becomes the rightful owner

('takes title') of the goods. In turn, he will try to sell them to wholesalers or, in the case of industrial goods, to the customers.

2. The **importing wholesaler**, is a company which not only imports, but also operates facilities to forward the goods into the distribution channels by means of promotional support.
3. The **trading house**, is an independent company which specialises in trading certain range(s) of goods. Usually it covers a wide field of goods, which sometimes even compete with each other.

   A trading house or company buys and sells for its own account and risk. It decides on its own export assortment. If the product happens to be well-known and outstanding, the buyers will not wait for the supplier but will come and look him up on their own initiative. Trading houses usually have a strong commercial acumen and professionalism, though they sometimes lack a strong after-sales performance, necessary for most technical and industrial products.

   Trading companies can be located in one's own country or in the target country. Even some of the larger companies have international networks in several countries abroad.
4. The **broker**, whom the exporter can charge with the execution of his marketing plan (the broker will help design it) against a fixed fee. Brokers operate in several European markets (commodities, branded consumer goods).

Finding the right trade partner is one of the biggest headaches of any exporter. That is why it is wise to hire the services of an agent, a local person or organisation who 'sells' his/her market know-how to deal with outsiders and foreigners. He can find buyers and/or trade partners for the exporter - representing him as his ears, eyes and hands in the market. He does not buy from the exporter, buy may sell on his behalf.

The (commission) agent is an independent person or company, who only intermediates (bringing the exporter/seller and the importer/buyer together) in the form of a commission, which is percentage of the (CIF value of the goods imported.

More than half of all the exporters make use of the services of an agent, because he works fast and only has to be paid after his efforts have proven successful. However, naturally he tends to 'go after the first buck' to get a quick return for his services, and that may prove contradictory to the exporters' future market position planning. Moreover, a good agent is hard to find, as most are active for others (i.e. the competitors).

BIG OR SMALL, WIDE OR NARROW

Ambitious or not, exporters are usually realistic enough to understand their own limitations. One of them is size - in terms of time, money, output volume, sales exposure, of which is expensive and scarce, particularly for suppliers from developing countries. That has its implications in the selection of the trade partner.

Should a person aim high and find large buyers to sell to? Or should one focus on the small/medium-sized ones to get optimal effect of a customised 'narrow-focus' approach? Marketers prefer the latter, as it would give the exporter the opportunity to direct all his selling power to one prospect - and become important for him.

An exporter will find the CBI advocating the focused approach, trying to match his assortment's strengths with an importer who can fine-tune both the exporters' capabilities and his, to turn them into opportunities. Their experts tend to look for dedicated importers whose selling powers are based on specialisation rather than mass canvassing.

Indeed, that approach has its merits. If an exporter could find a smaller importer willing to push his products into the market, the exporters' position would be strong and his share of the turnover big enough to be certain of continued efforts to expand trade. As a rule, it is advisable not to shy away from the small trade partners, as they could prove effective through tailor-made marketing into their sectors. Eventually, they could grow at the same speed at which the sales increase. There are plenty examples of exporters who thank their success to finding a small, aggressive importer, preferably one who has broken away from a larger organisation and is eager to prove his skills to his peers.

Small may prove more beautiful than big, narrow more effective than a wide scope, particularly for specialised products, or for products with a distinctive competitive advantage.

Nevertheless, scores of exporters firmly believe that without the support of the very large importing wholesalers, their ventures are doomed to fail, lacking the selling power of the large outlets. Fearing lost opportunities, they try to get a foot in the door at the mega-importers, usually the procurement officers of large supermarket and department store chains (frequently with the help of CBI).

The large retail chains, fully integrating their trade functions, do their importing of food products, usually buying for their members who are operating in most European Countries. These 'buying associations' have massive purchasing power. Eight of them (AMS/EA, BIGS, CEM, Deuro, EMD, Interbuy, Eurogroup and Tengelmam) have consolidated sales of 10 to 60 billion ECU!

In practice, most exporters fall short of the needs and regulations of the large importers. Apart from the degree of export professionalism (utter reliability up to the last detail!) these suppliers may be confronted with shortcomings varying from production inadequacies, shipping delays, minute variations in product specifications, in short, to quote Murphy's Law: 'Whatever can go wrong, will go wrong'.

May be, one should start off small and narrow, profiting from market niches and specialised importers for penetrating them. In management terms, it would mean that a person would adopt a certain 'phasing-in' period in his marketing planning, allowing for learning from the experience. Only when fully confident, should a supplier consider approaching the large importers. In the meantime, the search should be limited to small and medium-sized buyers who, are also looking for means to grow gradually into their ambitions.

Advantages and Disadvantages of Indirect Marketing Strategies

In general it can be said that the above mentioned forms of indirect marketing strategies have the following advantages

- ★ less financial and political risks
- ★ less investments
- ★ the partner is already familiar with the market situation
- ★ the partner has ready access to buyers in the export market

and the following disadvantages.

- ★ dependency on the activities of the partner
- ★ a smaller profit margin
- ★ less flexibility
- ★ the partner usually lacks the product knowledge
- ★ the supplier does not have direct contact with the buyers.

SELECTING IMPORTERS, DISTRIBUTORS IN MOST EUROPEAN COUNTRIES

Selecting Importers

Isn't it any exporter's dream to be able to choose from a list of European customers who are all eager to become trade partners, and ready and willing to buy and distribute the products all over the 372 million consumer a single market? That is a dream, indeed, but even so, it pays to be well prepared when an exporter goes looking for customers. He should be able to convince the prospects in this highly competitive market that they could be dealing with a professional who knows what he wants.

Selecting the Distribution Channel

In most European countries, the distributive system, which channels the goods to the (end) customers, is highly developed and quite complex. Often that system differs from one European state to another. Many different types of stores cater to the consumers' needs, wherever they live, however rich or poor they are. Thousands of stores, or "outlets" as the marketer calls them, are scattered over each country, trying to close in on potential customers.

The job of selecting the best potential customers involves too much know-how, time and footwork for foreign suppliers of consumer goods. They tend to leave that important decision to their trade partner, who knows the market better. On the whole, that may prove sensible. This trade partner is their representative and should be capable of finding the best channels for them, and if the supplier does not have one, yet he could try to commission trade agents to find one for him. However, he must know enough about the local distribution system to justify, or at least understand, his partner's proposals.

Getting to know the distributive system is not always difficult. It depends upon the kind of export product. If it can be considered a speciality, for which the buyer is prepared to pay a premium price, there will be specially stores to distribute it.

If the (consumer) product is just a regular product (as most foodstuffs are), the supplier should select a convenience store or a supermarket as outlet. If (low) price is the supplier's the biggest asset, he could consider selecting discount stores, which buy larger quantities and sell cheaply.

A TPO, a consultant or the trade partner will be able to find a list of distribution outlets and their specific function, reputation or character. Addresses of this kind can also be found in SBI market surveys.

There are also specialised importer- wholesalers, which usually supply to such outlets. Examples are in sectors such as building materials, furniture, hospital supplies, electronics, household appliances, fresh food and catering, textiles/garments, etc. Some of the larger outlets (mainly in food and garments) have their own wholesaler. The biggest of them even handle their own importing and/or come and visit the exporter in his home country, to buy directly from him.

The selection of distributiive outlets is easier for industrial suppliers, since the channel of distribution is shorter. This can be explained by the number of buyers. There are far fewer industrial buyers than customers, so that the system becomes more simple, involving fewer intermediaries. Industrial suppliers manufacture and distribute products, which other (European) manufacturers need for their products or production. More than two-thirds of all Small and Medium Enterprises (SMEs) belong to this category.

There are in fact, no retail outlets for some industrial products and the buyers buy directly from wholesaler-type stores. Here, "vertical integration" (channel members adopting the functions of up-/down stream distribution outlets, to be able to control the supply flows better) is common practice. Usually, most importers do their own wholesaling, though in such cases their trade margins are somewhat lower.

Products can frequently be used by industrial buyers as well as by consumers; examples are building materials and power tools, PCs and their software, paints, etc. Suppliers of these products have the luxury of being able to use two types of channels, i.e. industrial as well as consumer distribution. Obviously, their marketing approach has to serve different requirements.

The best way to locate the channel which will suit the exporters purposes best, is to 'back-track' the now of goods; from his end-consumer all the way upstream to the importer(s) who may be interested in buying from him.

DISTRIBUTION AGREEMENT

An exporter who wants to do business in the EU can appoint a commercial agent, a broker or a distributor.

Distribution agreements lead, in general, to an improvement in distribution, because the manufacturer or exporter is able to concentrate his sales activities on one person/entity and does not need to maintain numerous business relations.

By dealing with only distributor, the exporter is more easily able to overcome distribution difficulties in international trade, such as those resulting from linguistic, legal and other differences. Distribution agreements facilitate the sales promotion of a product. The appointment of an (exclusive) distributor who takes over sales promotion, customer service and carrying of stocks is often the most effective way - and sometimes the only way - for a manufacturer to enter a market. This is particularly true in the case of small and medium-sized enterprises.

Own Name, Own Account

A distributor, in contrast to commercial agent, buys goods from an exporter for resale - whether or not on the basis of exclusivity - within a certain territory in his own name and for his account. There is no specific, national legislation applicable to distribution agreements. They are governed by general contract law, an important element of which is the duty of reasonableness and fairness. A distributor must be registered in the trade register of his local Chamber of Commerce.

A distributor has to respect the EU legislation on free competition. This includes no set prices, no division of markets in order to build a commercial fortress, no competition clauses and such. Exclusive distribution agreements are possible, since the EU legislation may grant exceptions.

Free and Fair Competition

Basic elements of the EU are the free movement of goods within the EU (common market) and the prohibition of agreements which restrict competition. EU legislation stipulates in principal, that neither a distribution agreement as a whole nor any single paragraph of it may contain restriction on the free traffic of goods across EU borders.

EU legislation has empowered the European Commission to apply the free competition rules by regulation to certain categories of bilateral exclusive distribution agreement (EEC regulation No. 1983/83, published in official Journal of June 30, 1983). This regulation provides an automatic exception to the EU competition rules for exclusive distribution agreements, whose anticompetitive provisions do not exceed the limits set forth in this regulation.

No Restrictions

No restrictions shall be imposed on the manufacturer, other than the obligation as not to supply the contract goods to users (i.e. users as opposed to the contracted distributor) in the contract territory. No restriction on competition shall be imposed on the exclusive distributor other than (1) the obligation to obtain the contract goods for resale only from the other party (i.e. the manufacturer/exporter) (2) the obligation not to manufacture or distribute goods which compete with the contract goods (3) the obligation to refrain - outside the contract territory and in relation to the contract goods - from seeking customers, from establishing any branch, and from maintaining any distribution depot.

Some Obligations

There are some obligations permitted. The distributor can be obligated to purchase a complete range of goods or to purchase minimum quantities. It is also possible to obligate the distributor to sell the contract goods under trademarks, or as packed and presented as specified by the manufacturer.

The distributor can be obligated to take measures for promotion of sales in particular to advertise, to maintain a sales network or stock of goods, to provide customer and guarantee services and to employ specialised staff or staff who are technically trained.

Termination and Compensation

An important aspect of a distribution agreement is its termination, including the issue of damages and goodwill. A distribution agreement which has been entered into for an indefinite period can be terminated by either party, subject to the period of notice which has been agreed upon, unless this notice period is unreasonably short, or subject to a reasonable notice period.

A distribution agreement which has been concluded for a fixed period, terminates automatically at the end of the period. If however, the parties continue to perform their obligations under the agreement after the period has expired, it will be treated as a distribution agreement for an indefinite period.

Claiming damages When a distributor has made substantial investments or incurred significant costs related to the sale of the products, which he will not be able to recover as a result of the termination, it is possible that damages will be awarded, even when a reasonable notice period has been observed.

A condition for termination of distribution agreement is that the parties have to observe a reasonable notice period. If, for example, the exporter does not give due notice, the distributor may claim damages. However, even if the parties observe a reasonable notice period, a national court can nevertheless determine damages, based on the principle of reasonableness and fairness.

Goodwill compensation On the termination of a distribution agreement, the distributor cannot in principle, claim goodwill compensation. (This is different, however, if there is an agreement with a commercial agent.) Although harmonisation is the password in the EU, differences between the individual countries do exist. Sometimes the differences give even more protection to the distributor than the EU legislation.

For example, in Belgium the distributor receives legal protection in the case of exclusive distribution. He is able to claim goodwill compensation in the case of termination of an exclusive contract and the judge will certainly grant such compensation.

Exclusivity and Territory

A distribution agreement is usually restricted to a certain territory and can be on an exclusive or non-exclusive basis within that territory. Distribution agreements will often grant the distributor some degree of exclusivity in selling goods, in the contract territory.

The manufacturer is obligated in this territory — for example. The Netherlands — to sell only to an appointed distributor and not to any other importer in that territory. However, on the other hand, the distributor still has the opportunity to resell the contract goods outside the contract territory — for example, not only in The Netherlands, but also in Germany or any other EU country.)

Commercial Agent

The rules governing commercial agents are based on an EU directive on this subject (publication by the Commission dated 24 December 1962, concerning exclusive distribution agreements with commercial agents and brokers)

The basic idea is not to provide as much protection for the agent as possible. Compensation for goodwill being recognised and granted at the termination of an agency contract is the strong point which differentiates it from the distributor contract. Many of the rules governing commercial agents are mandatory, meaning that they cannot be deviated from/by agreement.

A commercial agent is an intermediary (a natural person or a legal entity) appointed by a principal (such as the manufacturer/exporter) for a limited or unlimited duration to negotiate, or to negotiate and conclude contracts with third parties in the name and for the account, of the principal. A commercial agent who is a natural person enjoys, in some aspects, the same protection as an employee. If he acts for no more than two principals, an agency agreement cannot (except for urgent reasons) be terminated by the principal without the prior consent of the regional labour office (in most cases this would be the commercial agent's labour office).

The main obligation of the principal is to pay commission to the agent, if/when the latter concludes a sales contract with a third party. This obligation also exists if the principal does business directly with a third party established in the designated territory of the agent, unless it is explicitly stipulated that the agent does not have an exclusive right in this territory.

The principal is obliged to supply the agent with all relevant documentation and information. The principal also has to give warning to the agent, if it is envisaged that future developments will cause a structural decrease in turnover. The principal is also obliged to give timely warning to the agent whenever certain transactions cannot be accepted by the principal.

Working on Commission

A commercial agent usually works on commission, and the law sets forth numerous rules for determining when a commission is due.

The agent is obliged to look after the principal's interests with due care. For example, he shall not conclude a transaction with a third party, if the said party is in a state of insolvency. The agent is fully liable if he concludes a transaction with a third party, which is habitually insolvent. When concluding a transaction with a third party the agent is obliged to inform his principal about the solvency of the third party and about complaints, if any, by clients of the third party. The agent is also obliged to render an account of the way he executes the principal's instructions, for example, the agent has to report which agency contracts he is going to accept (with other manufacturers/exporters).

A "delcredere" clause, whereby the agent guarantees all payments by/due from clients in the market, can be used to impose some degree of liability on the commercial agent for non-performance by third parties of their contracts with the principal. EU legislation sets limits on such arrangements, in order to give protection to the agent. In spite of the EU goal of harmonisation, in the case of the "delcredere" clause, the EU countries differ from others.

Termination of Agency Agreement

Apart from termination for urgent reasons, if the agency agreement has been entered into for a definite period, it can be terminated by either party subject to the period of notice which has been agreed (*). Statutory rules specify the minimum notice period which can be agreed, as well as the notice period required in the absence of any agreed period.

As agency agreement concluded for a fixed period terminates automatically at the end of the period. If however, the parties continue to perform their obligations under the agreement after the period has expired, it will be treated as an agreement for an indefinite period under the same conditions. It will be subject to the termination rules as stated above, (*).

Goodwill compensation — agency agreement On the termination of the agency agreement, the commercial agent may be entitled to receive goodwill compensation to the extent that he has brought the principal, i.e new customers or has increased business with existing customers and the principal continues to derive substantial benefits from the business with such customers.

The amount of the compensation may not exceed a figure equivalent to the commercial agent's remuneration for one year, calculated on the basis of his remuneration in the preceding year.

Non-competition Clause

A non-competition clause must be concluded in writing and can only be valid for two years after the termination of the agency agreement. A court can, at the request of the agent, nullify or reduce the non-competition clause.

Competition Law

A commercial agent is regarded as dependent if he is acting as an "extension" of a manufacturer or an exporter. A dependent agent does not have to respect the rules of fair competition. The EU competition law is, however, applicable, if a commercial agent acts independently. The later agent will be considered as an exclusive distributor and will have to respect the legislation on fair competition.

A commercial agent will be considered as a distributor if (1) the agent carries a risk in respect to a transaction which is higher than the delcredere risk, if (2) he has to carry stock for his own account, if (3) he has to give service without charge or if (4) he is allowed to set the resale price and other resale conditions.

CHOOSING THE FORM

The choice for a certain form of export, whether direct or indirect, cannot be made until after careful consideration of the advantages of the different alternatives.

Indirect export would seem to offer the possibility to minimise certain risks when first entering an export market, after which it is always possible to decide on switching over to a direct export strategy.

CRITERIA FOR SELECTION OF IMPORTERS/DISTRIBUTORS

When searching for importers, the exporters will have a certain profile in mind sketching a wealthy buyer, who understands him as well as he understands the exporters, who will open the door to the affluent European consumers for both partners' profit. That is a good start. The profile will consist of the following:

Criteria for importer selection - an example

- ★ buyer should be creditworthy, reputable, trustworthy.
- ★ buyer should be active in the relevant industrial sector, covering at least 5% (in money terms) of the distributive trade.
- ★ importer should be experienced (a minimum of three years in business), operating a sector databank or information system and know the trends and the players in the market (and be a supplier to some important buyers).
- ★ organisation should have adequate office space, storage, technical support, all communication facilities (phone, fax, E-mail).
- ★ importer should be able to take and deliver orders, operate with up-to-date PC software, employ 3–30 sales representatives who canvas systematically, reporting regularly (also to the exporter).
- ★ importer should be willing to appoint a liaison officer (who understands marketing and export practices) to communicate with the exporter.

Trying to quantify such criteria is laudable, although it is almost impossible - and thus not always practical. Obviously, one should avoid pushing too hard, because importers are generally willing to supply the information required, provided one does does the same. If the supplier asks for the importers commercial financial performance, he should be prepared to show his in turn. If he asks about the importers organisation, he should have his corporate profile, product brochures, specifications, production standards all at the ready to answer the importers request.

In the end, the situation will achieve its own balance. That makes sense, since the confrontation is a process of building up a trade partnership, not just a one - way interview about the selling and buying. The importer must share the suppliers conviction that the product, as well as the organisation, is worth the investment of both parties time, effort and money in a commercial operation designed to be long-lasting.

THE DIRECT MARKETING (DM) JARGON

As is the case with every "discipline", the Direct Marketer also has his own professional language. We have made a small selection of the most common expressions, which will help you to find your way in Direct Marketing country:

Conversion	–	the purchase decision of a prospect
Gross-selling	–	enclosing a new proposal with the order delivery
Curriculum	–	prospect data as outcome of a survey
Curriculum test	–	survey in order to segment the target group
Direct mail	–	personally addressed commercial proposal

Dry testing	–	test mailing with an (not yet) existing offer
Hand raising	–	using mass advertising with a response possibility (coupon, telephone number), in order to obtain sales leads
Lead generation	–	sourcing of potential buyers.
List broker	–	someone who can supply a targeted mailing list
Mail pack	–	single mailing unit (envelopes, letter, brochure & incentive)
Mail density	–	the frequency with which the target group is being mailed for example, doctors
Member-get-member	–	activating customers for prospect introduction
Prospect	–	potential buyer
Response	–	direct reaction from customer or prospect
Split run	–	dividing the complete run into different tests
Test matrix	–	a matrix linking different target groups to different mailing tests
Wet testing	–	a DM offer in a small test run

The Do's and Dont's of a Business-To-Business DM Campaign

1. Primary objective: Sourcing of potential buyers (lead generation)
2. Creative:
   - ★ Copy should be shorter than business-to-business DM
   - ★ Use less elaborate formats
   - ★ Use qualifying techniques
   - ★ The creative concept must be compatible with the total sales effort
3. One must know who will follow up and how (A person should be careful not to look too promotional in B-to-B direct mail)
4. There are usually one or more buyers/decision makers whom the supplier has have to address:
   - ★ The effect of this is:
   - ★ Copy variations
   - ★ The need for multi-targeted campaigns
   - ★ "Justification" copy
5. In B-to-B marketing the exporter is addressing a more sophisticated, critical audience than in retail marketing:
   - ★ Take into consideration:
   - ★ Competitive statements
   - ★ In B-to-B DM one should avoid direct response cliches, like:Free! Buy by midnight tonight, etc.
   - ★ Avoid advertising look and tone
   - ★ Direct mail should be less overtly emotional (in copy and art)
6. The exporter is dealing with a limited market universe.
   The effect:
   - ★ He has fewer testing opportunities
   - ★ There is less risk-taking
   - ★ Opportunity for high-impact or dimensional mail
   - ★ Image/education and response function

7. The audience is often specialised or technical; one must learn new lingo/mind-set. and use the appropriate technical language.
8. Shorter attention span; action-oriented
   Effects:
   ★ Immediate cash flow
   ★ High value of personalisation (mail)
   ★ Reaction is induced
   ★ Mail and phone response
   ★ Follow-up is the key

Exercise

Study the following data on retail buying patterns in the European Union. Then suggest possible marketing channels for:

★ Textile to Belgium
★ Furniture to the United Kingdom
★ Textiles to the Netherlands

European Union: Patterns of retail buying (Percentage breakdown of sales by type of product and type of retail outlet)

	Belgium	France	Netherlands	United Kingdom
Furniture				
Large stores	25.0	13.1	15.0	40.2
Mail order	2.6	3.1	1.6	12.8
Cooperatives	0.5	2.2	0.1	7.8
Independents	71.9	81.6	83.3	39.2
Textiles				
Large stores	13.4	18.0	30.0	26.2
Mail order	2.5	7.8	2.2	12.0
Cooperatives	0.8	3.6	0.1	3.6
Independents	83.3	70.6	67.7	58.2

Answer

Textile to Belgium	Importer/distributor → whole salers → independent retailers
Furniture to the UK	Direct sates to large stores and/or importer → independents
Textiles to the Netherlands	Direct sales to large stores and/or importer → whole-saler → independents

// *Chapter 15* //

Marketing Communication Mix

Ways of selecting a target market for the product have been seen. The company now has to consider about how to hit that target surely and effectively, how to communicate with it so that the market knows about the product and is persuaded to buy it.

To achieve the objective of communicating with a market and creating a demand for the product, it is necessary to understand the various techniques that can be used.

It has already been seen how the ingredients in the marketing mix can be blended in different ways to achieve marketing objectives. In the same way, the marketing communication mix has many ingredients. It is possible to increase or decrease the relative important of each in the search for the most effective marketing communications mix to suit any particular set of circumstances.

The following diagram shows the main ones.

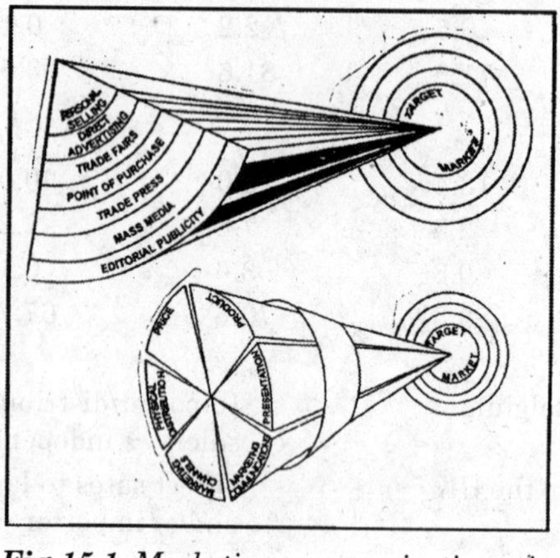

Fig 15.1 Marketing communication mix

MARKETING COMMUNICATION MIX

In this chapter the meaning and role of the promotional mix in marketing is seen. In fact, this is a process of planning and controlling a mix within a mix. Confusion is often created as a result of some textbooks referring to this mix as the 'marketing mix'. The important point to remember is that, whichever term one chooses to use, one is talking about a whole panoply of tools and not only one activity. The overall aim f the promotional mix is to communicate a range of messages to the customers and/or the channels of distribution, with the ultimate aim of ensuring that the product is sold, is consumed and creates satisfaction.

The communication process should first be explored briefly. The Fig.18.2 describes how the sender of a message has to encode it in such a way that the ultimate receiver is able to decode it. The message has to be trasmitted via a message channel, which is effective and within the receiver's sensual vicinity (ears, eyes, smell, touch). The process is completed by the sender soliciting some feedback, with a view to finding out whether the message has reached its destination in the manner that the sender hoped. Thus, the characteristics of communication process entail a number of 'players' and/or machanisms.

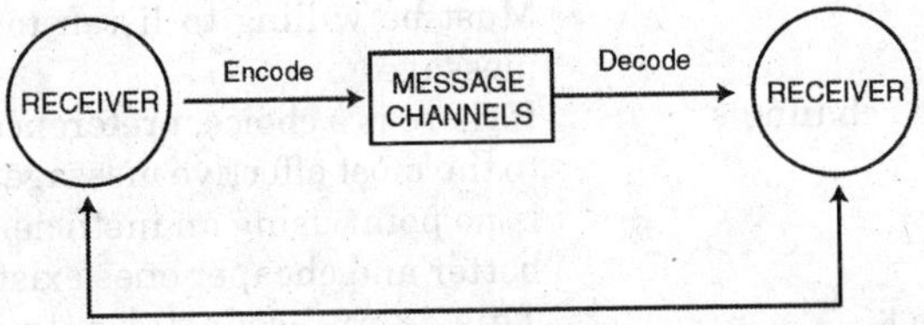

Fig 15.2

Communication takes place in all walks of life and in all areas of human endeavour. Indeed, communication takes place even throughout the animal world. Humans do not always understand animal messages because it is seldom known how to decode them. An aircraft pilot communicates with other aeroplanes or the control tower by trasmitting messages in a recognised pilots' language which he nows the receivers can easily decode, the pilot has at his disposal channels of communication which put him within communication earshot of his interlocutors. Moreover, a system of feedback is normally in operation, enabling him to judge whether the message has been received and understood.

Marketers resort to a similar pattern of communication. They send messages which they encode and transmit through the channel available to them. They attempt to ensure through a system of feedback that the encoded messages were properly decoded. This description of the communication process or the promotional mix could not be simpler. Yet there are many nuances attached to it and there is a lot that can go wrong when it is applied in practice.

The major problems associated with communication effectiveness are inherent in the process itself.

- ★ The sender is not always clear about what he or she wants to communicate.
- ★ The message is encoded into a message which the receiver is not able to decode correctly. At that point the message is likely to be misconstrued.
- ★ Interference with the transmission reduces the quality of the communication. Interference diverts the receiver's attention elsewhere. For instance, a very creative whole-page advertisement in the national press may miss its audience as a result of dramatic piece of news that attracts a lot of attention on the same day.

CHARACTERISTICS OF THE COMMUNICATION PROCESS

Parties to the Process	Points to Watch
Sender	Must have clear objective as to what he/she seeks to communicate. Must gain an insight into what the receiver is capable of understanding and decoding, and his/her willingness to listen.
Message	Must represent correctly what the sender wants to communicate and what the receiver is capable of decoding.
Receiver	Must be within 'earshot' of the communication. Must be willing to listen to or observe the message.
Message channels	If there is a choice, preference must be given to the most effective message channel. There is no point using an inefficient system when better and cheaper ones exist.
Feedback	This is an essential culmination to the communication cycle. The sender must establish that the message has been accurately received and understood.

The terms used in talking about marketing communications can be very confusing so those terms must be clarified right now.

Marketing communications means all the ways of sending sales-oriented messages to the people in the market that the company wishes to influence (the **target audience**).

PROMOTIONAL CHANNELS

Marketers have at their disposal a number of channels through which they can communicate with whomever they need to. The main channels are as follows:

- ★ Advertising
- ★ Sales promotion
- ★ Publicity and public relations
- ★ Direct marketing
- ★ Personal selling

Each one of these channels has its advantges and disadvantages, and its relevance and effectiveness have to be analysed in relation to a given set of circumstances. Indeed, in some situations all five channels can be used simultaneously with great effect.

A brief definition of the five communication channels is given below:

- ★ *Advertising* is any paid form of non-personal communication of products, services or ideas placed on one or more of the commercially available media by an identified sponsor.
- ★ *Sales promotion* also known as 'below-the-line' activities, represent non-media campaign such as demonstrations, sampling, displays, shows, exhibitions, price deals, contests and self-liquidating premiums.

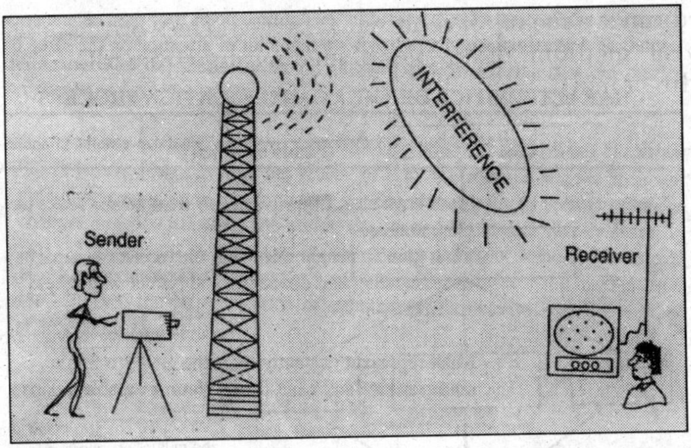

Fig 15.3 The role of 'interference' in the quality of communication

★ *Publicity* is the process of stimulating a favourable mention in the media of significance news items about the firm, its products and its activities without actually paying for it. Publicity is often achieved as a result of public relation activities.
★ *Direct marketing* is a communication through the mail, telecommunication system, or direct response advertising between the company and its customers and/or prospects based on careful targeting of individuals listed in a databank.
★ *Personal selling* is face-to-face communication with one or more prospective buyers, decoders users and/or influences with the aim of moving the prospect towards a purchase or a decision.

PREPARING THE COMMUNICATION PLAN

Although advertising, sales promotion and direct marketing are seen as separate activities, in practice they must be integrated not only with each other, but also with all the other ingredients of the mix, including sales activity. The starting point is the overall marketing plan with its objectives and strategy for a particular market segment. The process illustrated in the figure must be thoroughly pursued. Each programme of communication should provide answers to the following questions:

★ Who is the target audience?
★ What is scheduled to happen?
★ How is the activity organised?
★ When will it take place?
★ What special organisational support is required?
★ What response or results are expected?
★ How will they be measured?
★ What will it cost in relation to the anticipated benefits?

The success of any planning in the area of promotion depends upon a clear definition of one's objectives, full understanding of the customers' behaviour and their responses to the various stimuli presented to them. Without these ingredients the whole promotional programme is likely to be ill-conceived and the measurement of results will be of dubious quality.

A medium is a means of sending messages. The word "media" is simply the plural of "medium." Examples of media range from television to match boxes to direct mail.

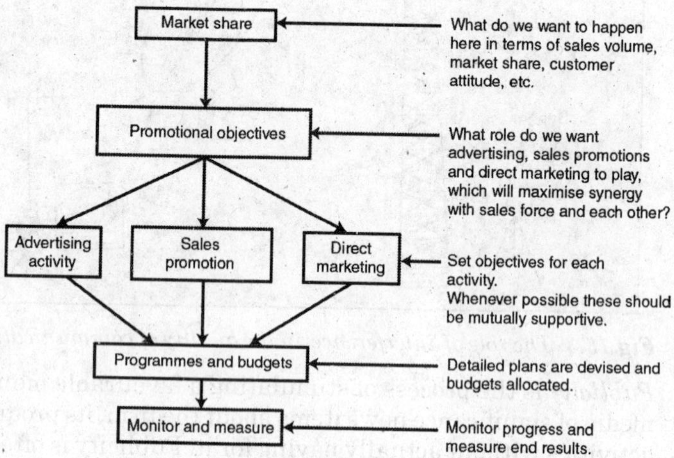

Fig 15.4

For the sake of simplicity, sometimes the word publicity is used to refer to all forms of marketing communications other than personal selling. But in the world of marketing the word "publicity" often has a more specific meaning: placing message in the media by means other than paid advertising.

CUSTOMER INFORMATION

Having adapted the product to the customer's wishes, the manufacturer should communicate with him to make sure he knows about it and will buy it and use it to his satisfaction. The communication basically serves two purposes.

1. It informs about the benefits and availability of the product, and
2. It instructs about the proper use of the product in order to ensure maximum satisfaction.

For this communication the manufacturer should know:

(a) which form the message should have
(b) which medium (message carrier) to use
(c) how to organise the communication

FORMULATION OF THE MESSAGE

The customer hardly pays attention to all the commercial messages aimed at him or her. That would be humanly impossible. Customers are virtually bombarded with all kinds of advertising. In industrialised countries, more than 2000 such messages are estimated to reach the consumer everyday.

Understandably, the consumer has become selective in what to see and what not to see. That is called **selective perception**. The product message should be so interesting and so well-tuned to what he/she wants to hear, that the consumer will inevitably pay attention.

Psychologists have simplified the mental process that is triggered by advertising. They identify the stages of perception as: arouse Attention, create Interest, stimulate Desire and provoke Action (the "AIDA" sequence). Sometimes, the S of Satisfaction is added: AIDAS.

In order to "arouse attention", the message should be striking. To "create interest," the message should be informative, giving facts. To "provoke the action" of purchasing, the message should be convincing. And to secure repeat orders, the after-sales service should be reliable.

One great advantage is to know the preferences and buying motives of the potential customers in export markets.

But the manufacturer may not know in what manner to approach him. The customers language, or his cultural and social habits are not known. A vast distance is felt between the customer and the seller, which is hard to bridge. This is, in fact, what makes international marketing so difficult.

REACHING THE TARGET AUDIENCE

Personal selling is the most direct and usually the most effective means of communication. But obviously only a limited number of people can be reached in this way. Personal selling is the method most likely to obtain sales orders from direct customers. But it is an inefficient method of creating a demand that will pull along marketing channels.

The marketing situation should be such where it is necessary to communicate only with a small number of persons to achieve the marketing objectives. For example, if a basic commodity that is in demand is marketed, then the target audience may consist of only a few important customers. Personal selling may be the sole form of marketing communications that is needed.

But usually it is needed to influence people all along the marketing channel, all the way to the end-user. This could mean reaching tens, hundred, or even millions of individuals. Personal selling obviously could not do this job. The manufacturer would have to use advertising, publicity or other means of marketing communications that can reach people in large number and if need be, over great distances.

While such forms of marketing communications can be powerful aids, they can also be a waste of money if they are badly planned or wrongly aimed. It is therefore necessary to be careful.

IDENTIFYING THE TARGET AUDIENCE

The first step in planning effective marketing communications is to identify the target audiences, who are the people who really count in achieving the goals. One cannot simply aim publicity at a vaguely defined "public" and expect orders to result. Examples of target audiences are, retailers who handle the product, whom one should encourage to stock the line; industrial buyers who use the product (not all industrial buyers); agents who are in related businesses and might be interested in handling the line; particular groups of consumers (not consumers in general), such as consumers in an area where one has just established retail distribution, or consumers of a particular sex and income group or with specific interests – if these are the type of consumer most likely to buy the product.

Once the target audience has been selected, then the best media and techniques to reach it economically and in the most suitable way should be found. The object should be to avoid waste by picking the most specialised media possible. Simultaneously, one should consider which media are most suitable in qualitative terms for the particular purpose. For example, it may be important to show the product in good colour reproduction, or to present a long, detailed story, or to make a strong impression with the brand name.

Very often, the choice of methods will be compromised between.

- ★ Reaching the target audience most precisely
- ★ Using the most effective means in physical terms
- ★ The budget

Moreover, usually a compromise will have to be made on the target audience. It is not affordable to reach all target audiences of possible use. It is far better to establish priorities and to concentrate on reaching a limited target audience effectively, than to spread the communications effort so thinly that it has no impact on anyone.

COMMUNICATION TECHNIQUES

Given below are the most important communication techniques and media available.

Direct advertising is the term which is used to describe marketing communications that can be aimed directly at named customers. The most obvious examples are direct mail, literature, and samples and gifts.

Sales Literature

Sales literature consists of printed materials containing information about the product and the company, including leaflets, catalogues and price lists.

- ★ Most companies have a price list. This gives the prices and sales terms of the product or products they are exporting, so that the prospective customers have a fair idea of the prices and costs applicable to them. Actual prices may have to vary with changes in circumstances. It is not possible to give a price list for products to be purpose-made for a customer. A price list should include weights and measurements for right calculations.
- ★ Another type of sales literature is a leaflet describing the products and pointing out their advantages and selling points. This should state how and where they can be obtained.
- ★ Sales literature comes in all shapes and sizes. It must be in the correct languages to be effective. It is best to have the translation done in the country concerned to avoid foolish mistakes. The agents will often do this. They can also have it printed locally, to prevent the mistakes caused by unfamiliarity with the language.
- ★ It may be more economical to design a multilingual leaflet so that many different leaflets need not be printed. This may also be helpful with some products as a way of stressing how widely they are used internationally.

The great advantage of sales literature is that people can read it when convenient. When personal visits to customers are made or when they visit the stand at a trade fair, one can leave something that will remind them of the visit and the product. Well-designed sales literature presented during a sales visit can also have a favourable effect on a prospective buyer, who has been difficult to persuade. It is important to face the fact that leaflets must be well designed and that money must be spent for this purpose. Very often, the customer will judge the company and its products by the quality and appearance of the sales literature.

Direct Mail

Direct mail advertising is the sending of material, including sales literature, through the mail to select or prospective customers.

It enables the supplier to reach in a low-cost way only the target audience whereas press or broadcast advertisements are seen by everyone who reads that part of the paper or is tuned into the broadcast. With direct mail there is much less "waste" in terms of delivering the message to the wrong people. Direct mail is not only a good means to communicate with customers who cannot be seen but is also effective as back-up or follow-up to personal selling or trade fairs and trade missions. A person can use his own list of contacts, or he can buy lists of every conceivable type of trader or other customer. Direct mail is a compromise between personal selling and more general publicity. The cost per contact and the impact lie between the two extremes. The following are some ways in which direct mail can be made as effective as possible:

- ★ First select the target market the types of customer one wishes to contact in this way.
- ★ A list of names and addresses will be needed. In most countries such lists can be drawn up from directories of importers or obtained from agents. Post offices sometimes provide lists and so might the chamber of commerce. Direct mail agencies in developed countries also have carefully selected lists and will undertake the direct mail work or provide the addressed labels.
- ★ Direct mail should always be sent to a named person in a company, and when lists are made, one should make sure that the person most likely to be interested is addressed by name. Most companies make their own lists as they get to know individuals and identify good customers among them. This should be done as it would increase the sales in other countries. Lists that are built from one's own experience are nearly always better then those obtained from someone else.
- ★ What to send to the persons on the mailing list should be decided - what kind of leaflet and in which language, what to say about the product and how to persuade the customer to buy it?
- ★ The leaflet will then have to be mailed; and this can be done either from one's own country or locally. The latter may be cheaper but people like receiving mail from other countries and are less likely to throw it away.

- ★ Where direct mail is used by itself it is important to include a reply form asking for more information or inviting a personal contact, so that it can be followed up.

Samples and Gifts

Gifts and samples can be used to promote exports to other countries and, in many markets, are an extremely important part of publicity.

Samples are useful because they give customers a chance to see or try the product. For example, if coffee is to be exported prospective customers can be sent free samples, on the basis of which they may decide to purchase the coffee. Sampling is often done in stores, for instance with free cups of coffee.

If an exhibit is put up at a trade fair then may give away samples to visitors at the stand, which is an excellent way of attracting people to a stand. If a supplier is on a personal sales visit abroad, he may have samples sent over to him, and offer them to his prospects, so that they can see the quality of his products.

In direct mail a sample of a product is sometimes included with the literature-for instance, a sample of wood to demonstrate quality. Another way is to offer samples to visitors when they come to the company an example, is a small packet of coffee to take away.

The samples cost money, so allowances should be made in the publicity budget.

Gifts are not quite the same thing as samples, because a gift does not have to be the product that the company is exporting. Gifts are sometimes in the form of calendars, pens, diaries and key-rings. If possible the gift should have some connection with the product or the company; for example the company name should be printed upon it. Gifts are usually given on special occasions.

If visitors come to the country, the manufacturer may like to give them a gift to take away with them so that they will remember him when they return to their country. An example is a small piece of pottery or a necktie or a scarf.

Gifts are charges on the publicity budget and have to be paid for. They help good relations, but they seldom directly result in sales.

TRADE FAIRS AND EXHIBITIONS

Personal selling usually involves going to the customer. The purpose of trade fairs and exhibitions is to attract the customer to the exporter. Trader fairs can be a very valuable marketing communication tool for exporters from developing countries. They can also be an expensive waste of time. The subject is very important and is treated in detail in another chapter.

Planning for a Trade Fair

Once it has been decided to take part in the fair, the planning process must start. This includes setting up a planning guide, a detailed timetable and a budget. Unless each of these steps is carried out properly, the participation can end in embarrassing confusion and cost for more than anticipated. Experience shows that the following basic rules help keep these projects on tract:

- ★ One person should be made responsible for the entire operation as coordinator or project manager.
- ★ Each task and responsibility should be identified at the outset. The time necessary for each should be estimated and their sequence determined.
- ★ Based on this analysis, a consolidated working plan should be drawn up as early as possible, with clear deadlines.
- ★ The persons or outside contractors to be made responsible for carrying out each task should be identified.
- ★ Ample lead times should be allowed - the longer these are, the better.
- ★ Regular revision should be scheduled to spot any problems and to compensate for delays before they disrupt preparations.

There are various ways of planning for an exhibition. Many organisations draw up network analysis diagrams, which help show the connections between the various activities and the critical deadlines. But whatever method is usd, the basic procedure is to work back from the major deadlines, starting with the fair's opening day, and including such critical dates as the deadline for applying for space and shipping dates. A suggestion for a timetable follows.

PREPARING FOR A TRADE FAIR — A SUGGESTED CHECK LIST

(Major deadlines/dates)

1. Opening day
2. Reserve space, shell stand, furnishings
3. Install stand
4. Arrival of goods in port
5. Delivery to freight forwards for sea freight
6. Order utilities, interpreter, etc.
7. Delivery to air-freight forwarder
8. Mailing of invitations.

A detailed budget should be drawn up as soon as possible after the decision is made to enter a trade fair. Although it will probably be necessary to wait for quotations and other information before all the items can be filled in with any exactness, a fairly close figure for the total costs must be obtained in time.

The planning timetable should provide for a periodic review and revision of the budget so that timely adjustment can be made in case of cost overruns. It is a good idea to add about 15% for contingencies to the estimates for the major items.

Budget Planning Guide

Item	Planned budget(s)	Actual budget(%)
Space rental		
Design and construction		
Insurance		

Shipping and handling
Stand services
Staff
Promotions
International travel:
Air fares
Hotel and living expenses
Local transportation
Exhibition recruitment
Miscellaneous
Total:

Pre-fair Promotion

Pre-fair promotion is vital and has two basic objectives:

1. To inform the target group about the product exhibition at the fair.
2. To innovative individuals in this group to come to the stand.

The techniques for achieving these objectives include: audience identification, preparation of promotional literature, direct contact through the mail, personal contact by telephone or by visits, press releases and contact with the press, advertising and receptions.

Something should be offered, that will draw the visitors' attention (e.g. play traditional music) and attract them to the stand.

During the trade fair, manning the stand is critical. The following points should be kept in mind:

- ★ The representatives should be knowledgeable about the company and its products, empowered to conduct business negotiations and are clear on the objectives in exhibiting.
- ★ The representative should never ignore a visitor to the stand; but approach visitors who seem interested in the display and do not wait for them to approach the stand.
- ★ The representative look interested and should not position himself so as to hide the products. He should not sit about chatting with his colleagues.
- ★ He should start conversation with visitors with a positive remark about the product or a question that will generate a discussion. He should identity as quickly as possible the visitor's business and specific interest and his/her importance as a prospect.
- ★ He should answer all questions as forthrightly and as factually as possible and remember to sell the company and its products and relate his remarks to the visitor's interest. The conversation should be used to elicit information about the market and reactions to the products.
- ★ The negotiations should be carried forward as far as the respresentative is empowered to, if he is convinced that the visitor represents a solid prospect.
- ★ He could use inquiry forms and supplementary notes to record details about the visitor's company, his/her interests, and follow-up action to be taken.

- ★ Time should be allowed after the fair closes, to continue important discussions and provide promised information as soon as possible.
- ★ It is necessary to observe the hours of the fair and never leave the exhibition unattended.
- ★ Slack periods can be used to make contacts with other stands, provided the representatives own is manned.

Government of developing countries often help small enterprises to prepare for trade fairs and exhibitions in foreign countries. Besides offering technical and financial assistance, they often organise such participation, thus further reducing the cost for each company. Therefore the trade association or chamber of commerce should be contacted if one wishes to participate in a fair and it should be noticed if any help can be got from them.

Types of Trade Fairs and Exhibitions

International trade fairs/exhibitions can be categorised according to the theme and aim for which they are arranged. As far as exports are concerned, they are specialised commodity trade fairs devoted to an individual or a group of selected products. These are sometimes named as Buyer-Seller Meets, mostly organised by the Indian Trade Promotion Organisation (ITPO) which aim at bringing together and establishing business contact amongst selected firms in India and abroad.

ORGANISATIONAL ASSISTANCE

To promote exports through the medium of fairs/exhibitions including BSMs, the Government of India through its various agencies help Indian exporters to participate in such activities, besides organising wholly Indian exhibitions in several countries. The various Export Promotion Council/Commodity Boards, ITPO etc. organise participation in specialised commodity trade fairs. The ITPO is the central and apex organisation for canalising participation by the industry and trade in international fairs/exhibitions, besides itself organising such activities.

Foreign exchange for participation in international fairs/exhibitions is released liberally.

Indian Trade Promotion Organisation

The ITPO, Pragati Bhawan, Pragati Maidan, Mathura Road, New Delhi - 110 001 is the central and apex authority for arranging/organising participation in international fairs/exhibitions. It draws well in advance, a programme for either organising a wholly Indian exhibition or participation in any such activity abroad. This programme is advertised through its weekly bulletin. The Export Service Bulletin and also through EPCs/Commodity Boards, State Governments, Chambers of Commerce, trade associations and even by mailing to export/trading houses and important exporters. Information in this regard can, therefore, be sought/available well in advance from/in all these organisations/publications and the ITPO itself.

Therefore, the would be participants in fairs/exhibitions should apply in the ITPO according to the schedule laid down by it. There is a participation fee for every activity. Details can be obtained from ITPO as they differ from one exhibition to another.

Direct Participation

Where the exporter wishes to participate in any fair/exhibition in which the ITPO or any other export promotion organisation like EPCs are not organising the participation, he need not approach the ITPO or the concerned organisation for not only obtaining necessary details but also getting their concurrence in advance for such participation.

FOREIGN EXCHANGE FOR FAIRS/EXHIBITIONS

The trade fairs/exhibitions are divided into two categories for the purpose of release of foreign exchange for participation therein. These are:

(i) Book fairs/exhibitions
(ii) Fairs/exhibitions other than books fairs/exhibitions

Fairs/Exhibitions

(Other than Book Fairs/Exhibitions)

For the purpose of release of foreign exchange, fairs/exhibitions (other than book fairs) are further divided into:

(i) Where expenditure in foreign exchange is upto US $20,000 or its equivalent.
(ii) Where expenditure in FE exceeds US $20,000 or its equivalent.

Where expenditure is upto US $20,000 Where expenditure in foreign exchange on participation (including expenditure on travel) in fairs/exhibitions (other than book fairs/exhibitions) is upto US $20,000 or its equivalent, foreign exchange is released by a bank (authorised dealer in foreign exchange) on an application made to it. Application on participant's letterhead can be sent to the bank, without routing it through or getting recommended by, any authority like ITPO, EPC, Chamber of Commerce, etc. Even EPCs/Commodity Boards can directly approach the banks for release of foreign exchange, where expenditure on participation (including expenditure on travel) does not exceed US $20,000 or its equivalent. The following details should be given in the letter.

(a) Space to be booked and rent payable
(b) Quantity and value of goods to be displayed
(c) Expenditure on decoration, display and labour charges
(d) Number of representatives to be sent and period of their stay abroad and daily expenses of each of them
(e) Cost of advertisement if the firm/company intends to have special advertisement, other than what will be available throughout the exhibition.

Where expenditure exceeds US $20,000 Where requirement of FE on participation (including travel) exceeds US $20,000 or its equivalent, the exporters should apply to the ITPO, New Delhi which will issue necessary authorisation for release of exchange to the firms/companies. Such applications should, inter alia, give the particulars listed above. After obtaining ITPO's recommendation, apply to the bank (AD) for FOREX.

FOREX release The AD may on receipt of application, release foreign exchange upto US $20,000 or as recommended by ITPO, subject to the condition, that the participants render proper account of the expenditure incurred.

Book Fairs/Exhibitions

Private publishers/printers etc., wishing to participate in book fairs/ exhibitions abroad, where expenditure (including expenditure on travel) does not exceed US $20,000 or its equivalent may also obtain their FE requirement from authorised dealers direct by and need not have any clearance from the Ministry of Human Resources Development, Dept. of Education. However, if their requirement exceeds US $20,000 the applicant should approach the Ministry of Human Resources Development (Dept. of Education), New Delhi - 110 001 who will make suitable recommendations to the RBI for release of FE.

Exhibits of Export Restricted Items

Items which are not subject to any export restriction, in terms of the EXIM Policy and those listed in Appendix of the Handbook of Procedures (Vol.I), can be sent abroad freely without any restriction. The items of which export is restricted, can be sent for exhibition/display abroad in terms of the EXIM Policy.

The exhibits of items export of which is totally prohibited are not allowed to be sent abroad.

MDA Grant

For participation in fairs/exhibitions, grant/assitance is available to export houses, trading houses, star trading houses and super star trading houses, under the scheme of marketing development assistance (MDA) of the Ministry of Commerce.

POINT OF PURCHASE

Point of purchase (POP) activities embrace a variety of promotional tools that are used in the retail outlet, that is, at the point of purchase. They include display materials, merchandises, special events, demonstrations and samplings.

Point of purchase can be one of the most effective marketing communications tools because it influences the consumer at the moment of choosing a product.

POP is usually combined with other marketing techniques-for example, with incentives to the retailer to persuade him to use the display material, or newspaper advertising, that alerts consumers to an in-store promotion.

TRADE PRESS

Along with the newspaper and magazines published for consumers, there are thousands of trade publications. These are magazines, newspaper(s) which cover subjects of interest to particular trades, industries, professions or vocations. Business journals covering the whole range of business activity can also be considered in this category, or at least in a category distinct from the mass media.

The trade press can be one of the most important communications media. Their number of readers is often small, so their advertising charges are relatively low. At the same time, the readership is so specialised that they can provide the most efficient way of reaching the people, the exporter wants to reach. For example, in some industrialised countries there are not only trade magazines that are read by people in the food business, but separate magazines for people at different levels of the food business processing, wholesaling and retailing.

If one has correctly analysed the marketing communications needs and has identified the target audience, he may find the trade press the best way to reach it at the lowest cost.

Mass Media

These are media which reach large numbers of the general public. Because advertising rates are based in part on the number of people who are reached by a medium, advertising in mass media is usually very expensive. The cost may be justified if the target audience is the general public (or large segments of it). Even if the target audience is not the general public but a segment of the public such as industrialists, the most effective available medium for reaching them may be one of the mass media.

The great danger in using mass media indiscriminately is that one is likely to waste money paying to reach many people, who need not be reached in order to reach the few who actually are the target audience.

Even when the target audience is the general public, one should identify the particular segment one wants to reach (middle-class women, people who like to travel, etc.) and then choose the mass media which reaches this segment most efficiently.

Media selection is a highly-refined skill, particularly in the case of the mass media; and is best left to advertising agencies or media consultants.

A quick look should be taken at the various kinds of mass media. This will give you an idea of how they can be used.

News Papers

Newspapers can reach large numbers of people at lower cost than most other mass media. Some newspapers have the further advantage of being very selective geographically-for example, one could advertise in a local newspaper to support a store promotion in the same town. One disadvantage of news paper is that each issue is thrown away quickly-and the advertisement with it.

Consumer Magazines

Using magazines can be more selective in communicating with the particular segments of the public than the newspapers. This is because many consumer magazines are aimed at particular kinds of people for example women, people with special interests for example dog owners.

Another advantage of consumer magazines is that they usually offer excellent colour reproduction, which can be important to show off a product. They are often suitable for advertisements that convey a large amount of information. Magazine readers will often take the time to study such advertisement if they are designed to attract the interest of the reader.

Television

In most industrialised countries, television is the medium that reaches the greatest number of people, and has the greatest impact. It is also one of the least selective media, and the most expensive. Moreover, TV advertising must be sustained to have an impact over a period of time. The high cost of TV advertising rules it out for companies with small advertising budgets.

Radio

The spoken word can be a valuable advertising method. Many countries have commercial radio stations which include advertisements in their broadcasting. Some have national coverage, most will offer local or regional coverage. Radio can be particularly useful where there are few newspaper readers.

Cinema

Most cities have cinemas which show advertisements between the main films. This can be very useful for local advertising. It can also be used for national advertising where the advantages of colour and sound are required. In some countries, cinema reaches mainly a young adult audience. In others, it is seen by nearly everyone.

Posters

Posters along roads, railways and in shopping areas-anywhere where large numbers of people gather are an excellent form of advertising. The effectiveness of the poster depends on its size, its presentation and the number of people who pass by and see it.

Posters are usually most effective as reminders ("Buy oranges today!") or to help build brand familiarity.

Editorial Publicity

The trade press is often interested in giving editorial publicity to a new product or to important developments in the existing products. More general media-such as news papers and radio and television-may also be interested in reporting new products but they are interested in only unusual and newsworthy, events. For example, if a person is trying to introduce an unusual or unexpected product into a new export market, then the newspapers in that country might be interested in reporting this. The company may also get useful publicity from press reports, if it is taking part in a visiting trade mission or is about to start a new export drive or open a sales office or appoint an agent.

A person should think carefully about his relation with the press and the value of editorial publicity. Public relations has been described as being a good way of getting credit for the product. Editorial publicity is a good form of public relations because someone else is giving one the credit.

It is important to have a close understanding with the press in each of the export markets. In the case of trade papers covering the exporters type of product, the exporter should visit the editor and talk with him as soon as possible after he enters the market. In this way the editor gets to know the company and feels able to refer to its products knowledgeably or even to telephone the exporter or his agent for a comment when there are developments in that industry or in the marketing. It is also advisable to take the salesman or agent along to establish good relations with editorial staff. Indeed, a good agent will almost certainly have already met the editor and be well placed to introduce the exporter to him. Another important reason for making contact with trade press editors is that they can be valuable sources of information on the state of the market.

Every opportunity of meeting journalists from the general press and from radio and television should be taken, though they will not be very interested in the technical details of the products. They will be more interested in the effect of the sales effort on the locality. For example, one may be trying to get their readers or listeners to eat a new kind of food or start to wear a new kind of clothing.

Local newspapers are likely to be particularly interested in any kind of news which has local interest. It is much easier to get editorial publicity in local newspapers than national ones.

Good relations with the press is very important when one wants editors to be interested in a particular story. It would be unrealistic to expect that by issuing press releases and holding press conferences it is possible to win space in the mass media. But the news may be worthy of mention in the trade press.

Editors of trade publications are interested in news that affects-directly or indirectly; the business interests of their readers. For example, the news that a new supplier is entering the market, that an established supplier has increased his sales,or has increased his plant capacity; or has introduced a new product, and so on. The news does not have to be earth-shaking, just of interest to the specialised readers.

Press Conferences

If there is a big and important event one can invite selected journalists to a press conference or reception to tell them about the product and the plans. A person can demonstrate or display his products and provide pleasant hospitality. One can make it an occasion to remember, for example, by providing the country's traditional hospitality. It may well be a good idea to give the journalists samples of the products to take away with them particularly if they are consumer goods such as food or handicrafts. It should be made sure that each journalist is given a printed statement of facts and information about the product to make certain the correct facts appear in the newspapers and journals. Photographs should be made available immediately. It is necessary to uncertain that there are telephones for the journalists to phone in their stories to their editorial offices.

Press Releases

A good method of giving news and information to editorial departments is through a press release. This is a simple but interestingly-presented statement about a development, which is worthy of editorial mention and will also benefit the company and the product if it appears in the editorial pages or is mentioned on radio or television. It is important that this publicity fits in with the company policy. It is no use gaining publicity for a new product and then being swamped with orders that cannot be met, as the customers would than turn to the competitors.

Editorial publicity has the attraction of being cheaper than most other forms of publicity (the space does not have to be paid for) but it requires careful planning and must be of real interest to the media. One must always be clear about objectives each time a press release is sent.

Drafting a press release Using press releases needs more skill.

The following points should be noted in drafting and distributing them.

1. The heading and presentation should be distinctive and unmistakably from the company, with its trademark featured prominently. If the release is issued by a well known PR agency on one's behalf it may be best to use the agency's own letterhead.
2. The story should have a title that clearly indicates what the release is about.
3. The text should be lively and 'newsy' straight to the point, so that journalists can immediately see the purpose of the press release.
4. A relevant quotation can be included, if possible.
5. The text should not be too long and preferably should be on a single side of paper.
6. The typing or printing should be double-spaced so that journalists have room to write alterations.
7. The text should be well written in the language of the market.
8. The press release should be with the name, address and phone number (home and office) of the agent or export salesman or whoever else can supply additional information. (It should be made sure that he will be ready to give such information.)
9. Photographs are to be included if they are relevant and if the publicity budget can afford them.
10. The timing of the press release must be planned carefully, keeping in mind the dates and times of journalists' deadlines. A press release should not be sent just before a holiday when nobody will be available to deal with any press editorial publicity. The timing of editorial

publicity should be coordinated.

11. If press releases are put out in more than one export market, their timing and content should also be coordinated.
12. If press releases are sent out too often or on subjects that are not really very important, the press may become bored with them. On the other hand, one should send out interesting releases often to keep the company and the product constantly in the minds of journalists.
13. File the press cuttings.

Given below is a sample trade press release.

Mr. Trader's Press Release (Trade Press)

Trader Shoe Company Limited
Box 4482 Ruralia Tel: 3024

News From Star Publicity
Contact: Jill Jones, Telephone 44 54 33 ext. 21

Not for release before 20 November

Novel line of desert boots from Africa to get February launch

Retailers stocking the new range of Trader's Desert Boots- the first footwear from Ruralia ever to be put on the Industria market- will get strong promotional support through an unusual personality campaign. The promotion will be launched in February with a walk across Industria by the manufacturer, former Olympics star James Trader.

In a series of dinners planned to take place in major Industrian business centres before the event, Mr trader will challenge businessmen to 'sponsor' him by contributing to the Industrian Shoe Benevolent Fund 5 cents for every kilometer he walks. He will, of course, wear his own desert boots for the 500 kilometer which will start from Easterville on February 23.

The walk is expected to receive wide media coverage, and Mr.Trader will follow it up with a two week tour to make personal appearances at major retail outlets. Retailers will also be supplied with display material featuring Mr.Trader and his walk, and brochures describing the exotic origin of this modern footwear.

Grand Department Stores already has placed a large order and will feature the new line in all its outlets.

Mr. Trader is president of Trader Shoe Co., the largest footwear producer in Ruralia. Although this is the first time his Desert Boots are being marketed in Industria, they have already won a name for themselves among tourists who brought them back.

The shoes, including the soles, are made from wild goat hide and are amazingly tough, yet supple. They are priced to retail at about US $ 10 per pair, and are available in a full range of men's and women's sizes and in three colours: Desert Tan, Hunter Brown and Forest Green. The colours are derived from tints used in traditional Ruralian textiles, and evoke the rich colours of the landscape. The dyes are made from natural pigments in plants which grow only in Ruralia.

The importer is World Wide Shoe Imports (50 Main Street, Centerville).

Notes on the Above Press Release

1. It is aimed at trade papers or magazines serving the Industrian footwear buyers. Its purpose is to interest them in stocking the new line.
2. Opening paragraph features promotional support which is of direct interest to retailers, and also highlights the novelty aspect of imports from Ruralia.
3. The Contract with the Grand Departmental Stores gives weight to the sales effort and can help arouse the interest of other retailers.
4. Facts about the manufacturer are supplied to help build confidence.
5. Details about the shoes, including price, are of direct interest to retailers.
6. The press release was sent out long in advance of the launch, to give the monthly as well as weekly journals time to run it in advance. The embargo date was also fixed early enough to permit the retailers reading the story to place orders in time to take advantage of the publicity.

Most of the different types of marketing communication which can be used to reach the target market have been looked at.

When a closer look is taken at the marketing communication mix, one can clearly see that there is a lot wrong with the famous saying:

'Build A Better Mousetrap and the World Will Beat A Path To Your Door.'

It just isn't true. Even if the mousetrap is a world-beater and has tremendous advantages over all the competitors people still have to be told that it exists. People don't just come to one. In other words a person has to go out and create a demand for his product.

// CHAPTER 16 //

LOCATING AND SELECTING OVERSEAS AGENTS

If a supplier has some success in personal selling to visiting buyers or during sales visits abroad, he may feel that the next step is to have someone selling for him in a selected export market. He may also feel that he needs on-the-spot help in establishing the marketing channels, for example, in finding and working with distributors or wholesalers.

The supplier cannot spend a great deal of time on export selling himself because of his responsibilities to the business at home. The idea of a full time travelling sales person may seem attractive at first. But it is probably not economic to make such an appointment as a first step in exporting. Furthermore, if the supplier appoints one of his sales executives to handle this, it would take this executive time before he or she gets to know the export market well enough to sell successfully.

In such situations, it is usual to appoint an agent. An agent is a person of the firm that handles negotiations on the suppliers behalf. An export agent is simply an agent who is active in the export market. Agents work on the basis of commissions and do not assume any risks. In contrast, a distributor being a direct customer, pays for the goods that are supplied and takes over the risk of further marketing. In this chapter, the word "agent" and the word "distributor" are used to refer to separate activities: one term should not be confused for the other.

The following box compares the advantages of using an agent with those of employing the company's export sales staff.

Advantages of an Agent	Advantages of the Sales Executive
Cost is variable; no expenses unless sales are achieved.	100% commitment of time.
Agent has local knowledge.	Can carry out research and other activities.
An agent's sales of an already established product can help in the introduction of a new and unknown product.	Will not fear that success will bring about his/her replacement.
Highly motivated, is paid only if he/she sells.	Staff development. Customers impressed by commitment. Knows details of production and origin.

FINDING AN AGENT

There are good agents and bad ones, and even some good ones may not be suitable for the products or for the prospective customers. When selecting, check that:

- ★ They are respectable business representatives.
- ★ They are not representing a competing producer.
- ★ They have the organisational structure and the facilities necessary to do the job.
- ★ They have serious long-term interest in the product and are not handling too many other products.
- ★ They are experienced in the type of product and market area and have established connections.

Finding, appointing and using an agent needs careful planning. First a list of the possible agents for this particular product is needed. The suppliers own embassy abroad or local chambers of commerce can probably supply that list. Then the supplier can write to these possible agents, explain his requirements and ask if they are available to handle the product.

From the replies received, a short list of the most suitable agents can be prepared. If possible, each of them can be visited personally. In any case, references should be obtained from others, particularly from other firms that the agent represents and if possible, from some customers.

It is very important that the relationship with the agents is clear. A formal agreement should cover the following points in a way that makes misunderstandings impossible.

a. A clear indication of who is the agent and who is the exporter and the purpose of the agreement.
b. A clear description of the products covered by the agreement (bearing in mind that different products might be added later on).
c. A clear definition of the territory to be covered (for example, "the whole of Kenya" or "the seaboard states of the United States").
d. The duties of the agent in terms of publicity and the publicity back-up which will be provided.
e. The duties of the agent. Will the agent be merely processing orders? Or will he/she also handle import licenses and exchange control requirements? Will the agent work on a del credere basis, e.g. guarantee that a payment will be got from the customers in return for a higher commission?
f. Payment and payment methods. For example, what is the commission? Will the commission and any other payment be made on all orders received from the sales territory, whether they are placed through the agent or directly with the supplier?
g. The duties of the exporter (for example on prices and terms of deliver).
h. The type of market information to be supplied to the agent.
i. Who will pay for operating expenses such as those for cables, telephone calls and fax messages.
j. The duration of the agreement and the way of cancelling it.

k. The law governing the agreement and the method of arbitration between them in the event of any dispute.

Methods of Paying Agents

It is usual for an agent to be paid on a commission basis. The commission is normally a percentage of the value of the goods sold and for which, payments have been received from the customer. Because of this, agents are sometime called "commission agents."

It is difficult to generalise about rates of commission. They may vary from less than 1% to more than 1% according to the nature of the market and the sales problems. For contracts covering a large volume of commodities to be delivered over a fairly long period, the agent's commission may be under 1%. At the other extreme, an agent might get a commission of 15% for small orders for handicrafts.

Sometimes there might be an agreement with the agents to pay them a commission on all orders received from customers in their territory regardless of whether orders are actually placed through them. Whatever type of agreement is there, agents should always be told about orders received direct from customers so that they can follow up and possibly obtain repeat orders. The supplier and the agent should also let each other have copies of all correspondence with customers.

Del credere agents Agents receive higher than usual payments when they act del credere. This means that they take the credit risk for the orders they obtain and are responsible for making payment to the supplier if the customer fails to do so. Del credere agents are normally paid a higher commission than ordinary agents (the extra commission may be anything from 5% to 15%), to compensate them for the credit risk they assume. Del credere agents are not very common, but where they exist they enable exporters to sell with great confidence, particularly in markets where it is difficult for them to judge the creditworthiness of prospective customers.

This exercise can be done to help the agent selection process:

Exercise 1

The letter below has been sent to potential agents, whose names have been given to the managing director of a Garments Company Limited by his country's trade attaché in Turkey.

Dear Sirs,

Our trade attaché in Turkey informs us that your company may be in a position to take up the Turkish agency for our range of leather jackets. We enclose illustrations and price lists of our products and should be grateful if you could let us have your comments.

Please let us have details of your organisation, the agencies you hold at the moment, the area you cover and the commission rate you would expect on products of this sort.

Yours faithfully,

Managing Director
Garments Company Ltd.

Here are the replies.

First reply: From the Universal Agency company

Dear sirs,

Thank you for your letter of November 1st. We are certainly interested in the agency for your most attractive range of leather garments, which we are sure would sell in Turkey, provided they are introduced by a large well-established, well-known firm of agents such as ourselves.

We have enclosed a full list of the 200 firms we represent, and you will see that they include well-known names in the field of clothing, hardware, engineering supplies and building equipment.

We employ 20 salespersons covering the whole of Turkey and 50 head office staff. We expect to receive a minimum 10% commission.

Yours faithfully,

Second reply (handwritten): From Y Evirgen

Dear sirs,

Thank you for your letter. I am very interested in becoming the agent for your impressive range of leather garments. I have already shown the illustrations to a garment shop in Izmir and I expect they will give me an order in the next day or so.

I have been an agent for the last six months and I cover Turkey using my home as my office. My wife helps with the correspondence and we currently represent the ABC Glove Company of London in Turkey. We should be happy to work for a 5% commission.

Yours faithfully,

Y. Evirgen

Third reply: From the Turkish Garment Agency

Dear sirs,

Thank you for your letter of Ist November. Your agency is of great interest to me as I specialise in leather products. I am sure I can provide you with good business.

I employ one representative to cover eastern Turkey and I cover the west myself. We employ a secretary at our office in Bursa and we are in close and continuous contact with wholesale and retail leather-garment distributions, departmental stores, mail-order houses and institutonal buyers such as the armed forces. We usually work on a 7.5% commission.

I represent the Jones Garment Company, the Ahamed Garment Company, the Fungko Brush Company and six shoe manufacturers. I feel sure that your excellent products would fit in very well with my programme.

Yours faithfully,

⇒

Fourth reply: Fax from Quickwork

TO: THE GARMENT COMPANY LIMITED

FROM: QUICK WORK REPRESENTATIVES, ISTANBUL

LETTER RECEIVED. AGENCY ACCEPTED WITH THANKS SHIP 1000 PIECES STYLE 2A, ASSORTED SIZES AT ONCE TO OUR ACCOUNT 60 DAYS CREDIT AT PRICES AS YOUR LIST PLUS CHARGES DELIVERY OUR WAREHOUSE ISTANBUL.

After studying the replies, it is necessary to reflect on the additional information required on each agent and how to obtain it. Then the four potential agents should be listed in the order of preference based on the information given in the letters and the reasons for the ranking is to be explained. These have to be written down.

Below is a discussion of additional information requirements. For all potential agents the Garment Company should:

★ Obtain the addresses of the manufacturers currently represented and write to them for independent references.

★ Obtain bank references for each agency.

★ Ask each agency to suggest a marketing plan for Turkey, for the Company's products.

★ Obtain the names of major wholesales of leather jackets from its trade attaché and ask them for their opinions of the four agents.

From the individual agents, the Garment Company should request the following information:

★ Universal Agency Company: What products are currently being sold to the leather garment trade? How many different products are sold by each of the 20 salespersons?

★ Y. Evirgen: Ask for details of present and previous connections with the leather products industry, and for call list and frequency of calls.

★ Turkish Garment Agency: Obtain full details of the five ranges of leather jackets currently sold and determine whether these will compete with or complement the Garment Companies products.

★ Quickwork: Send a cable requesting details of organisation and lines carried as asked for in your letter. Ask for cash with order, or payment on dispatch of goods ordered. Do not ship goods until payment is received and it is established that the company is qualified to be a long-term representative.

The above list of information requirements is not exhaustive. Other ideas might be just as useful.

A suggested order of preference is given below.

1. Turkish Garment Agency: If it is not selling a directly competitive line and if it is willing to guarantee a reasonable minimum volume of sales in the first six months.
2. Y.Evirgen: If he is willing to report regularly, the Garment Company can probably take advantage of Mr. Evirgen's recent entry into the trade and his weak position, to demand a full service.
3. Universal Agency Company: It is too large and is unlikely to give the Garment Company much attention. It is apparently not in the leather garment trade at all.
4. Quickwork: Appears to be seeking a "quick killing." However, it should not be rejected out of hand and should be reassessed when further information is received.

APPOINTING AN AGENT

When an agent has been found, it is important to have a clear written agreements with him or her. This must cover all the points that are potential sources of difficulty or disagreement in the future. An agency agreement is given below.

The Agreement

This agreement is between the Garment Company (the manufacturer) and Mr. Y. Evirgen of Ankara, Turkey (the agent).

1. The manufacturer hereby appoints the agent as his representative in Turkey (the territory) with effect from next January 1st.
2. The products covered are all leather garments manufactured by the manufacturer any time during the term of the agreement. Any other products that may subsequently be manufactured by the manufacturer are not covered by this agreement and would have to be the subject of a separate agreement.
3. The agreement is to run for a trial period of one year, and may be terminated on December 31st or before. Thereafter the agreement may be terminated by either partly, by written notice delivered to the other at least one year before the proposed date of termination.
4. The agent agrees to devote his best efforts to promoting the sales of the manufacturer's products, and not accept any agency or otherwise to promote the product of a competitive or potentially competitive product unless specifically permitted to do so by the manufacturer.
5. The manufacturer agrees to pay the agent a commission at the rate of 5% of the ex works value of all orders, for leather garments received and accepted during the period of his appointment, for delivery into the territory, whether or not the orders were sent direct by the agent. Such commission will be paid only when the goods have been paid for by customers, and payments are to be made in arrears quarterly. The manufacturer further agrees to inform the agent of all inquiries received and other dealings it may have with the territory.
6. The manufacturer will supply the agent free of charge with reasonable supplies of publicity material and samples. Any samples or publicity material or samples not disposed of with the agreement of the manufacturer, are to remain the property of manufacturer and are to be returned to the manufacturer at his own expense at the termination of the appointment.
7. The agent will pay for all travelling, office, stationery, postage and administrative expenditure with the territory. Any advertising will be paid for by the manufacturer at his discretion when it has been authorised by him.
8. The manufacturer shall reimburse the agent for any expenses involved in visiting the manufacturer's country if the agent is requested by the manufacturer to make such a visit. During any such visit, the agent will devote himself wholly to the business of the manufacturer unless specifically permitted to do otherwise.

9. This agreement shall be interpreted according to the laws of the manufacturer's country. In the event of any dispute, an arbitrator shall be appointed by the President of the manufacture's country Chamber of Commerce and the arbitrator's decision shall be accepted as binding on both parties.

Signed on behalf of Garment Company	Witnessed:
Peter Smith, Managing Director	Date:
	Witnessed:
Signed: Y. Evirgen, Agent	Date:

RELATIONSHIP WITH THE AGENT

It is important to regard the agent as a part of the organisation. Whichever export market he may be based in, it is important to treat him as a part of the firm and to make him feel that he really is a part of it. This is essential if he is expected to sell the products enthusiastically.

The advantages of using an agent may be summarised as follows:

- ★ There is automatic cost control if the agent is payed according to the results and orders he produces.
- ★ He is the representative and also the local salesman in the export market in which he is based.
- ★ He can provide information about his export market (too much of his time should not be used in this way because, he is there primarily to sell).

He can help with publicity and is in the best place to keep an eye on competitors' prices and to deal with enquires and complaints from customers (if he should do this effectively, he must be kept well-informed about the products and the company).

There are also certain possible disadvantages in using an agent. They include the following.

- ★ An agent may represent too many companies, this might be a temptation for him to concentrate on selling the products he finds easiest to sell - he may neglect the other products (which may include the companies products too!)
- ★ He may concentrate on short-term business and quick returns. This is less likely if he is made to feel involved in the company and its long-term interests.
- ★ If the success in the export market is not a result of his efforts, the company may be paying him more than it can afford, if it has to pay him a commission on all business.

Getting the Best from the Agent

After appointing an agent, it is in the companys' interest to get the best possible results out of him. It should be remembered that, once appointed, he becomes a part of the organisation.

- ★ He should be made to feel proud to represent the company

- ★ He should be treated as well as the company's staff.
- ★ What he can tell about his local market should be listened to.
- ★ As he will be working for other exporters as well, he cannot be expected to devote the whole of his time to this company only.

It is also worth bearing in mind the following practical do's and don'ts in developing the relationship with the agent.

Things to do

- ★ It should be remembered, even in times of stress, that he is a part of the company.
- ★ All the available information about products should be given - especially about new ones coming along - his suggestions on their potential should be found.
- ★ The company should help him to sell - especially with information about successful new ways of selling, developed by agents in other countries.
- ★ The company should put him in touch with any likely customers that it hears about.
- ★ The company should make sure that the same person corresponds with the agent or at least signs the letters, so that they get to know each other by correspondence.
- ★ He should be visited as often as possible as give him demonstrations of the product.
- ★ The manufacturer should invite him to come and see the company, and treat him like a guest.
- ★ His help should be invited in preparing marketing plans.
- ★ He should have copies of all the correspondence with customers in his market.

Things not to do

- ★ Circular letter should not be sent. He should be treated as an individual.
- ★ Too much information should not be asked for, unless he is paid you pay extra for it; an agent is there primarily to sell.
- ★ Instant success should not be expected, but of course he should not be forgotten about.
- ★ No one new in your organisation should contact him, without explaining who the new person is.

Many producing companies in developing countries do not need a marketing channel because, they work under subcontracts for companies in developed countries. The latter often supply the design, the materials and sometimes the equipment for production. Their partner companies in developing countries provide labour.

This final exercise is on distribution channels.

Exercise 2

Choose the correct answers to the following questions.

1. Which of the following products usually have shorter distribution channels?

   ❒ Consumer products ❒ Industrial products

2. Which marketing channel would you consider using to sell canned pineapples in Germany?

   ❒ Large retail stores ❒ Retail shops
   ❒ Mail-order companies ❒ Import companies
   ❒ Cooperative wholesale union ❒ Central buying organisations of food supermarket chains.

3. Suppose you were a producer of handicraft dolls and you want to market them in Chile. You have a choice between an independent agent and employing your own salesman. The agent will charge a commission of $3 for each doll sold. Contracting a salesman will cost you a fixed salary of $500 a month and a commission of $1 per doll sold.

4. Which of the two channels would you select for each of the following situations?

   ❒ You expect to sell 200 dolls a month.

   ❒ You are likely to sell 10,000 pieces a year.

// CHAPTER 17 //

ORGANISING SALES PROMOTION TRIPS

Buyers often visit other countries to buy products. The most obvious type of buyer from overseas is often overlooked. This is the tourist. Selling to tourists is the simplest form of export selling.

Selling to Buyers from Abroad

A simple way to sell to export market is by personal selling to professional visiting buyers from abroad. One might meet such people face-to-face in one's own country, or perhaps in the factory, or warehouse, showroom, or plantation. It is possible to even meet them at a reception organised by a Chamber of Commerce or a trade association, perhaps on a visiting trade mission.

Such meetings provide a very worthwhile opportunity of selling the products without spending time and money on travel.

Disadvantages in Exporting through Visiting Buyers

But there are some possible disadvantages in export selling through visiting buyers. For example, if the exporter does not visit export markets himself, he will not be able to find out about the selling opportunities there. It is also possible that he may be able to get a better price by visiting an export market, than from a buyer from that market who visits him. Another important point is that, the introduction of an unsuitable product may make it difficult to get sales later, even when the product has been made suitable for the market. It is easy to make the mistake of choosing products and unsuitable marketing channels when the only contact with the market is one buyer. Nevertheless, dealing with visiting buyers can be an important first step in export selling.

It is necessary to consider and discuss the different types of buyer from abroad, ways of making effective contact with tourists and ways of making effective contact with professional buyers.

Personal Selling by Visits Abroad

The successful exporter is the one who is oriented to the needs of the customer. The best way to find out a customer's need is to visit him in his own country. But visits abroad are expensive, so a person must plan very carefully and must always be able to satisfy himself that the cost of a visit is justified by its likely marketing value.

Gathering Market Information

The purpose of an export visit may be to obtain orders through personal selling or it may be to appoint agents or visit them and maintain a good relationship with them. Another reason for an export visit is to obtain marketing information. For example, an exporter may wish to find out about alternative marketing channels, competitors' products, trade prices, and local tastes. He can also identify the need for any future desk research or field research.

Outward trade missions are a valuable first step into export markets. At some stage an exporter will have to go out on his own and the purpose of this chapter is to get him to think about all the things that he must do to ensure a successful export visit abroad.

PERSONAL SELLING TO VISITING BUYERS

BUYERS FROM ABROAD

TOURISTS

The most obvious types of overseas buyer is sometimes overlooked. This is the tourist. People visiting the country on holiday or even on business trips are potential customers for a wide range of locally-produced goods such as clothing, handicrafts and souvenirs.

Selling to tourists is the simplest form of export selling. Often the tourist comes to the stall or shop to buy. But one may go and seek him out to sell.

Whichever way the exporter chooses he must discover something about his likes and dislikes, the things he wants to buy.

PROFESSIONAL

- Inward trade missions
- Department stores
  - Independent retailers
  - Industrial buyers
  - wholesale distributors
- Import houses
- Central buying organi-sations
  - State buying organi-sations (planned economics)

Ways of Making Effective Contact Contact with Tourists	*Ways of Making Effective Contact with Professional Buyers*
Display the product where tourists stay, where they visit - hotels, airports and main shopping centres.	To make sure, one always knows, when visitor from buying organisations are due to arrive, one must keep in touch with your government officials.
Make it easy for them to pay in any currency. But first check the bank the exchange rate and transferability of the chosen currency.	Be ready to see buyers when it is convenient for them.

Arrange to have goods sent to the airport or to their homes, especially when they are heavy or bulky. Leave at least a few words of the common tourist language in the country and certainly the numbers and currencies.	If when meetings are arranged, one has to be punctual and should not missing the appointment. Have all the details about the products, for example prices and terms of payment. Because deliveries and process must vary, it is better to let the buyer have a written offer with samples or photographs of the product. Keep up correspondence with the buyer after he returns to his country. If there is a government trade promotion organisation, one must make full use of it. It is necessary to have an interpreter if the exporter does not speak the buyer's language and he vice-versa.

PLANNING EXPORT VISITS

Given below is a description of a successful export visit. While going through the case study one should write down a checklist of all the things that should be done in planning a sales trip abroad.

MR. TRADER'S WELL PLANNED TRIP

Mr. Trader makes thorough preparation for his sales visit abroad to Industria. First, he sets out his objectives and makes arrangements with his secretary to travel at a time suitable from his own point of view and that of his prospective customers. He writes to prospective agents and also checks that the EPO has sent information on distributors and that the language-learning tapes and phrase books he needs have arrived. Mr. Trader also makes arrangements for the samples and leaflets he will need.

Mr. Trader checks various aspects of the forthcoming trip with his accounts office, his export sales office and his dispatch department. Then he arranges his itinerary in detail with a travel agent and also has a word with the bank about finance.

Once he arrives in Industria, he arranges further details with his country's trade attaché.

It is useful to draw up the checklist under four headings: (a) planning the selling; (b) planning sales promotion literature; (c) planning the travelling and (d) making the visits.

A badly planned visit abroad wastes time and money. But a well planned visit has a good chance of leading to profitable business. The exporter can make a success of his export sales visit, by checking the following points during the planning stage.

Planning the Selling

1. Decide which country or countries to visit by balancing cost against likely marketing value. Also decide which parts of a country to visit.
2. Take care to avoid public holidays in countries to be visited.
3. Tell the most important people about the visit and try to make appointments in advance so that the visit is not spoilt by missing important customers.
4. Learn about each country before the visit, so that time is not wasted during the visit.
5. If language will be a problem, make sure to take a good phrase book and arrange for an interpreter in each place.
6. If there is need for samples or sales literature that cannot be take because they are too heavy, have a supply sent to in advance at each place that is to be visited. But make sure they are in the appropriate language and measurements. Remember that you will have to arrange documentation to ensure getting the samples and sales literature through customs.
7. Make sure to have plenty of business cards ready to be taken, perhaps in more than one language.
8. Find out whether anyone else in the company has problems in the countries to be visited and see whether there might be any way in which to assist them.
9. Make sure to know what accounts and receipts will have to bring back to justify the money thus spent on the visit.
10. Let the company know where one would be at each stag in the journey, so that contacted can be made quickly if need be.

Planning Sales Promotion Literature

For a small company, with a very limited product line, a single piece of sales promotion literature may be sufficient. In most cases this should be accompanied by an up-to-date price list. But many companies should really have a variety of pieces, each designed for different functions. The following are the types of literature that a small company would probably find most useful and practical.

The company brochure or leaflet A simple brochure or leaflet describing the company is very helpful in creating a good initial impression and setting the stage for business talks. Such a publication should of course, describe the company's products or product lines in fairly broad terms. It can be enclosed with letters introducing the company, requesting meetings or inviting people to visit the company's trade fair exhibit, or used in answering inquiries. It can also be used as a handout at trade fairs or on missions and sales calls.

Product leaflets and date sheets These describe specific products, models or lines. They can be used to solicit sales by mail, answer inquiries, inform sales representatives of new products, hand out at trade fairs and so on. They can also be supplied to agents and importers for distribution to their own customers. Such literature will vary greatly in detail and presentation, depending mainly on the nature of the product.

Catalogues A catalogue contains a full listing and basic descriptions of a company's products. Catalogues often include prices and illustrations. While they can be very useful, often even essential sales tools, catalogues can also be complicated to prepare and costly to print and mail.

Instead of producing a full catalogue, many companies find it more economical and flexible to produce a series of product sheets or leaflets, which can contain more detailed product information and can be distributed individually or in various combinations, as required by the particular situation. They an be enclosed in a printed folder along with a current price list and perhaps a company information sheet or leaflet. Basic company information can also be printed on the folder itself.

Price lists As already noted, rather than printing prices in product literature, it is often more economical to distribute separate price lists, which can be updated more frequently and cheaply. This also makes it easier to quote different prices to different types of customers or in different markets.

Design and production European business people are used to sale literature of a high standard, in terms of design, illustrations, printing and paper. Anything of a lesser standard is likely to create negative impressions. So it is worth spending as much money as is needed to obtain the quality appropriate to the particular type of literature.

This does not mean that one should be extravagant. Every piece of sales literature does not have to be a highly elaborate production, printed in full colour on luxury paper. Particularly when the supplier is selling ordinary products to the trade or industrial customers, the most important element is the information and how clearly it is presented. A straight forward, simple piece, printed correctly but not elaborately, can do the job. It is better to produce a simple, well printed piece than an elaborate but shoddy one.

Unfortunately in some countries, it is difficult to obtain printing and paper that are up to European commercial standards. Getting good-quality photographs and colour printing can be especially difficult. It may be feasible to have the material printed and even mailed in Europe, perhaps with the assistance of an agent. If the literature is to be used mainly for distribution in Europe, this may actually save on costs.

The writing and design of sales promotion material is a job for specialists. If possible, it should be assigned to a good advertising agency or creative studio, perhaps one in Europe. The techniques of designing sales literature are beyond the scope of the discussion, but the following tips may be helpful:

- ★ Try to standardise the use of the company logo and colour on the letterheads and all sale literature. Use consistent styles of typefaces.
- ★ To the extent possible, stick to the paper sizes of the International Organisation for Standardisation (ISO), which are widely used in Europe. The most common is size A4 (210 mm × 297 mm), unfolded or folded.
- ★ Use photographs only if they contribute to the needed information and are of excellent quality. If one cannot get colour photographs printed well in the country, it may be better to send prospects, actual photographic prints, neatly mounted and captioned.

- ★ Use short paragraphs, organise the material logically, and indicate each subject with headings.
- ★ If possible, print sales literature in the language of the target readers, and have the translation done in their country. If this is not possible, and one is trying to sell throughout Europe, print the literature in English.
- ★ When on a visit or when exhibiting at trade fairs in Europe, collect examples of the sale literature distributed by European companies and study them. This will give a better idea of what European customers expect.

Distributing sales literature No matter how good a piece of sales literature is, it will not help unless it reaches the target audience. As already noted, literature is often handed directly to such people during sale visits and trade fairs, or enclosed in letters to established contacts or in response to inquiries.

But the exporter may also want to seek new customers or representatives by mailing literature to a wider audience. This can become an expensive and highly wasteful operation unless he has targeted and updated mailing lists.

It is possible to purchase such lists from companies that specialise in this business. But minimum quantities have to be bought and hence the cost may be too high.

Mailing lists can be built up using a variety of sources. These could include the following:

- ★ Lists of registered visitors to trade fairs can be had from some fair organiser who will supply these to exhibitors on request.
- ★ Own record of visitors to the trade fair stands and to trade inquiries sent to the company.
- ★ Listings and advertisements in trade fair catalogues.
- ★ Import promotion organisations in the target markets.
- ★ Chambers of commerce in those markets.
- ★ ITC market studies.
- ★ Own country's trade promotion organisation and/or trade information service.

Planning the Travelling

1. Plan carefully the method of travel at each stage of the journey and book tickets. Air is the most usual form of business travel. Remember that rail travel is best in some countries for journeys of up to 200 miles. A hired car may also be useful in markets such as Europe.
2. Decide who to see during the travels and calculate how much travelling this will involve. For example, one cannot afford to make a big detour except for an important customer.
3. Plan which hotels to stay in and remember that they can get booked up well in advance. A good travel agent can help in this.
4. Ensure that the passport is in order and that one has all the necessary visas.

5. Get an International Health Certificate in good time and check that the health requirements of the countries to be visited are met. Allow plenty of time for the necessary vaccinations.
6. Find out what clothes will be needed. This will depend on the climate and time of year.
7. Remember that the upper weight limit for the luggage allowed on airliner is 20 kg, which on average means a large suitcase plus a brief case.
8. Work out how much money will be needed for hotels, meals, fares and so on. Probably, a minimum of $60 per day plus travel will be needed. Decide the form in which to take the money. Travellers cheques are the most common method. But credit cards are often very useful. Make the necessary banking arrangements. Remember to take some currency in case, immediate cash cannot be obtained on arrival (for example the banks may be closed).

Making the Visits

It is important to make the best possible use of the time during a visit to export markets. The following are some of the points to watch.

1. Make sure to have all the possible information about each prospect before calling on him.
2. To spend the first working day making appointments may be a waste of time. So make appointments in advance, add to them as time goes by.
3. Plan how to get to meetings without wasting working time - a street map may be useful.
4. As much cannot be seen from a taxi - be prepared to walk, and look around.
5. Time and punctuality can be important. Some people are time conscious and appreciate punctuality for appointments, while in other countries time is often meaningless. Notice varying office hours; some countries start early and finish early - and some later and finish later as in Britain. In hot countries sometimes businessmen start early, say 6 a.m., and finish at midday.
6. Don't judge a prospective customer purely by what his office looks like. In some countries business is often done in cafes, so be prepared.
7. Doing business with 'foreigners' requires great understanding, some being keen to try new ideas, while other are less willing to do so.
8. Entertainment in business varies - nationals of some countries enjoy it, but others often have just a sandwich and a glass of milk for lunch and do not entertain visiting businessmen much.
9. Always record names accurately, and learn the local customs in how they are said and what titles are used.
10. Remember to keep a record a things done during visit. The best time to do this is in the evening, so that the impressions are fresh and up-to-date, ready for the next day. Important points may be forgotten if one waits to get back home.

TRAVELLING ABROAD FOR EXPORT

Foreign travel can be grouped under

1. Business visits by individuals
2. Business Delegations

Business Visits

Business visits can be further grouped under:

1. Participation in trade fairs/exhibitions
2. Visits to trade fairs/exhibitions by non-participating exporters
3. Visits for business against
   (a) foreign hospitality and
   (b) one's own expenditure i.e. non-hospitality visits

Business visits on non-hospitality for any purpose, other than participation charges for fairs/exhibitions, are allowed almost freely.

Foreign exchange in non-hospitality visits US $350 per day for all, other than the Chief/Senior Executives like Chairman, Managing Director, Director who are allowed US $500 per day, is given by any AD, i.e. authorised dealers in foreign exchange which comprise of banks and other dealers, bank on application made to it. It is given for a maximum period of 45 days per person in a single trip. However, a FE of up to US $5000 per visit regardless of the duration of the visit and without applying the appropriate per dime rate may be released. This would be inclusive of exchange under any other head, viz. entertainment expenses, secretarial services and no separate exchange for these purposes would be permissible.

Entertainment expenses FE towards entertainment expenses may be released not exceeding US $2000 per trip to Chief Executives and others per person and US $5000 to Chief Executive of export/trading/star trading houses.

EEPC account holders The EEFC Account holders can also utilise the funds therein for travel abroad only for business visits themselves or by their representatives including supporting manufacturers in connection with export promotion including participation in trade fairs. Similarly, FC Accounts may also be utilised for this purpose.

Application Application by letter (in duplicate) may be sent to the AD (bank) by the sponsoring firm/company/organisation indicating the traveller's-

(i) name and address
(ii) nationally
(iii) passport number
(iv) nature of visit in each country
(v) FE required
(vi) Exporter's Code No. allotted by RBI
or
IEC-O-Import-Export Code No. allotted by licensing authority
or
RCMC issued by an EPC, etc.

In fact, the RBI has stated that bankers and authorised dealers in foreign exchange may insist upon either of the three registration certificates as at (vi) above before releasing foreign exchange.

Certificate The sponsors should also certify that the expenses are being borne by them.

Undertaking An undertaking that the FE will be utilised only for the purposes stated in the application is also to be given.

Foreign hospitality business visits FE may be released up to a maximum of US $500 per person if the visit is up to a period of 10 days or US $50 per day up to a maximum period of 45 days. Application by a letter (in duplicate) may be sent to the AD by the applicant giving full name, address, passport number and date, nationality of the traveller, country of visit, period of stay, name and address of the host, purpose of visit, etc.

Business Delegations

Foreign Exchange is also released to travel abroad to members of business delegations sponsored by trade bodies like Chambers of Commerce, FIEO, etc., at a rate not exceeding US $350 ($500 to Chief Executives/Senior Executives) or its equivalent per day, for a period not exceeding 45 days, or US $5000 per member regardless of the duration of visit and per dime rate.

SUMMARY

Below are suggestions for making the most of sales promotion trips:

Establish specific objectives for the visit
An exporter should have specific aims not only for the trips as a whole but also for each market. His primary objective might be to negotiate sales, find new customers, find an agent, introduce a new line, clear up some problems or find out what is happening in the market. Probably his objectives will include several of these aims. If he is clear about his objectives and puts them in order of priority, he will be able to decide better, on the types of contacts to make, and the time that he should spend on each.

Identify specific prospects or other people that one should see, in advance
The exporter may already have some of these names through previous contacts or from files of inquiries received. Other sources of names could be the import opportunity offices or import promotion offices of the countries he is planning to visit, his country's articles and advertisements in trade journals, trade association and perhaps even trade directories.

Write in advance for appointments, and confirm them
When the exporter writes asking for an appointment, it is necessary to explain who he is and his company are, and his purpose in visiting. He should try to suggest what benefit the host might gain from the visit, and should include some company and product literature. The exporter should find out as much as possible about the business of the people he plans to visit. This will not only help him to make the most of the visit, but will also help him to write a more convincing letter of introduction.

Bring samples along on each visit, if appropriate
The exporter may have to ship these ahead to each hotel, along with extra sales literature. He should also bring a sufficient supply of business cards.

Contact in advance one's own governments commercial office or embassy in each country that one plans to visit, if they exist

These offices, and perhaps import promotion offices, can often be helpful not only in making suggestions on whom to see, but also in arranging appointments and obtaining interpreters if necessary. Commercial representatives should also be able to give you useful briefings on the local business situation, so plan to visit their offices.

Do not try to cover too much territory

By limiting the number of cities needed to visit, one could have a better chance of spending enough time in each to achieve the objectives. If a person tries to visit too many cities, he risks spending too little time in each while increasing his expenses, and the whole trip many produce little in the way of results.

Allow enough open time for unforeseen meetings

A person may need this time to follow up on his original appointments, and to meet with the people he hears about during the course of the trip. In large cities, he should plan on being able to have a maximum of four meetings a day, unless he already knows people well enough to able to schedule luncheon or dinner meetings with them.

Avoid visiting during public and school holidays

The July to August, Christmas and New Year, and Easter periods are especially bad for arranging appointments in many European countries. School holiday times (when business people often vacation with their families) vary from country to country, and even within countries such as Germany. So it is advisable to check on local holiday times when planning the trip.

Work out the itinerary to economise on costs

A local travel agent may be helpful, but check with airline sales offices as well. Look into special train fares for foreign visitors to Europe. Trains are often cheaper and more convenient than airplane for travelling within Europe, especially for shorter distances.

Take along sufficient funds

Allowing an average of US $200 a day for living expenses in Europe is far from extravagant. Calculate more if one plans to stay in first-class hotels or to entertain. Carry some US dollars traveller's cheques and at least one major credit card (and make sure that the credit line is open).

Try to arrange the hotel in advance

This will enable the exporter to advise his home office and his contacts about how to reach him. However, this may not always be possible. If minimising costs is an important concern, he may wish to stay in budget hotels or rooming houses. These are often difficult to find from the home country, but one can generally count on finding such lodgings through the accommodation desks at almost any large airport or train station in Europe.

Check visa and health certificate requirements several weeks in advance of the departure

Consider using publish transportation in cities

Public transpiration is good in many European cities. It is often faster, and always cheaper, than taxis. Obtain a local street and public transportation map from the tourist information desk or news-stand on arrival in each city.

Call ahead to reconfirm appoinments

As the exporter progresses on his trip, it is a good idea to telephone the contacts in the next city on the schedule, to be sure that they will still be available. This can save a great deal of time.

Be punctual for appointments

In most parts of Europe, business executives expect appointments to be kept, on time. It is a good idea to plan the routes and means of local transport each evening for the following day. If the exporter cannot locate an office or figure out how to reach it, he should call the day before to find out. He must also telephone if he thinks that he is going to be late for an appointment.

Write up notes on each visit as soon as possible

The best time to do this is immediately after each visit. If this is not possible, write up the notes every evening. Highlight any follow-up actions which have been promised or those which one wishes to take. Keep all of the business cards collected in good order; later it can be very helpful to have written the date of each meeting on the cards.

Write to the contacts when one returns home

This is not only a matter of courtesy; it may also help to progress the business that has been started. Through letters, confirm any agreements that have been made and sent any information that has been promised. If one is unable to provide such information immediately, inform the contact as to when it will be sent.

PERSONAL SELLING SKILLS

The Role of Personal Selling

It is not enough to have the right product, and to have selected the right marketing channels. One will often have to 'sell' the company to a prospective agent or distributor, and convince him of the worth of the products and once a person has established the channels, people have to be persuaded to order the goods before the channels can be of use. This all involves personal selling face-to-face.

Personal selling, the face-to-face contact between salesman and prospective customer, is the most concentrated form of selling. It is the situation most likely to produce sales orders directly, if the salesman has prepared thoroughly for the meeting and presents the case of his product effectively.

Trust Between Salesman and Prospect

There are two people involved in a direct sale. One of them is the prospect who must be persuaded to buy or sign a contract. The other is the businessman who wants to close the deal.

Success in personal selling depends on more things than just the price and the quality of the goods. It also depends on whether the customer believes and trusts the salesman, whether he thinks the company is reliable, and even how much he likes the salesman as a person. To the customer, the salesman IS the exporter, and what he thinks and feels about the salesman is what he will think and feel about the exporter.

In any face-to-face business transaction, a person should remember that he is the salesman for the company, whether he is talking to a customer, an agent or anyone sale.

In the case study at the end of this chapter an exaggerated version of a salesman, a really bad salesman at that, in action. One should try to identify and note some of the more obvious errors.

Mr. Vague Drops a Brick
(Refer Case Study - Towards the End of This)

Mr. Vague is a salesman for the Ruralian Cloth Company and Mr. Helpful is a buyer for the Brussels Wholesale Fabric Supply and Import Company.

Mr. Vague call on Mr. Helpful to try to make a sale. He is a bad salesman and makes a succession of typical salesman mistakes - mistakes that could be even more serious if Mr. Helpful were not an exceptionally tolerant buyer.

Discussion

One should identify the following errors made by Mr. Vague in this very exaggerated but not wholly unrealistic transcript.

1. Mr. Vague arrived late.
2. He criticised about the city and the country.
3. He did not know the nature of the business of the customer.
4. He had not brought any samples.
5. He had not converted the measurements or the price into the locally accepted metric system and currency.
6. He quoted too high a price and was immediately prepared to make large concessions.
7. He did not know his product and the colours available.
8. He offered absurd delivery which, it was obvious, could not be fulfilled.
9. He insisted on a specific shipping line.
10. He insisted on letter of credit terms without any regard for the customer's wishes, or credit rating.
11. He forgot even to make a note of the customer's name.

After hearing and discussing Mr. Vague's unfortunate experience, one may wish to hear more about a successful sales call:

Mr. Trader's Salesman Meets a Californian Buyer

Going through the conversation in the case study, one can and see what happens when a good salesman with a good product meets a prospect for the first time. Mr. Smith of Trader Shoe Company wishes to introduce the new range of 'desert boot' suede leather men's shoes to California. One can see how the salesman meets his prospect, the footwear buyer for California Sales by Mail? who is interested in indulging a range of such shoes in his mail-order catalogue, but at the right price and on the right terms.

The ensuing dialogue records the conversation between Mr. Smith and the California buyer leading to a large order for 18000 pairs of desert boots.

Discussion

Discuss the performances of The Trader Shoe Company salesman and the California Sales by Main Buyer, which of them made a success of the 'sales call'? Did they both success?

PERSONAL SELLING CHECKLIST

Preparing to Meet the Prospect

In addition to briefing himself with information on the export market in general, it is most important that a salesman should prepare very carefully before meeting with his prospect. The salesman must be clear about the objective of each call he makes. There are several points to be checked out:

What are the needs of the customer and how can the product satisfy these needs and benefit the customer?

Has the firm done business with the salesman's firm before?

Does the firm also deal with the other exporters?

Does it operate in many different places or concentrate in one place?

What exactly is to be achieved in this call? How can one do it?

Is it necessary to have an interpreter?

All this is useful information will help a salesman to sell effectively when he meets his prospect.

A salesman should also make sure that he has the necessary information, samples, photographs and drawing. He must know about his firm's method of doing business, about deliveries, transport, prices, payments and all the other things that are part of an export transaction.

Before the meeting it is useful to imagine oneself as the prospective customer. In that way one can imagine the sort of questions and objectives that the prospect might ask.

Having made all these preparations, make sure to arrive at the meeting on time.

Face-to-face with the Prospect

First the objective of the meeting has to be remembered. Usually of course this will be to obtain an order from the customer. Open the meeting briefly and pleasantly and find out how one can help the customer by, asking questions that produce a positive response from him. Make sure that the sales talk and demonstration of the product is concise and to the point, so that the prospect does not think that one is wasting his time. Above all, explain how he will benefit from the product and how it is related to his needs.

Invite him to ask questions and to comment on the product. Do not contradict his view if it is contrary to the interests, but show him that there is another point of view. Make it clear that an order is expected by asking 'How much will you buy'? instead of 'Will you buy'?

Avoid allowing the prospect to give only a promise to send an order later (it is easy for him to forget or even change his mind once he is no longer under the pressure to buy).

Finally, try to leave the meeting on a cheerful and pleasant note - preferably with an order but otherwise with a promise to do something which will produce an order soon.

The Follow-up After the Meeting

After the meeting it is important to make notes on it, both as a reminder for oneself and for the information of other members of the company. Reports on sales visits are an important part of an effective marketing operation. Note any special likes or dislikes of the prospect and see that these are also recorded in his file.

Above all, if he has placed an order see that it is dealt with quickly and efficiently.

EXPORT SALESMAN

When is an Export Salesman Economic

As the export selling expands, or if there is an opportunity for a greatly expanded export sales effort, the idea of a full-time salesman becomes a more economic proposition. Indeed, in a dynamic export situation there comes a time when an exporting company decides to sent its own sales force, large or small, into the field as one way of having complete control over its own export operations and making certain of accurate, factual information.

It is a big decision to send salesmen abroad and also very expensive. Generally speaking, an organisation sends its own salesman when it seems that an agent can no longer offer the best service. For example, the move into a new export market or the expansion of a share of a market may require more selling and resources, than an agent could supply.

At the beginning the company would probably send only one salesman to an export market. As business develops it may decide to build up an export sales force. As the sales force become more complex it will have to decide how it should be organised, whether by product or market area or some other way.

Selecting a Salesman

Choosing the right salesman to operate in an export market is even more important than for the home market. He will often be working at great distances from home base, so the cost of his travel expenses and accommodation abroad is likely to be heavy. The export salesman will need all the normal skills of a good salesman. He will need a lot of knowledge about the product and must be able to make a good presentation to a potential buyer. He will also need to be a man of initiative and be able to operate without constantly asking for instructions and guidance. He should have the following qualities:

1. Know about the general economic and social situation and be aware of religious and political attitudes.
2. Be able to speak the language.
3. Know about the modern financial techniques and control of trade and investment abroad.
4. Have background knowledge of export documentation, procedures, methods of payment and the currency regulations in different countries.
5. Have knowledge of transport methods.
6. Know something about trademarks, patents, licensing procedures, health requirements and quality standards.
7. Be very healthy.

It is unlikely in the early stages that sales to any one market will cover the cost of a salesman. It may however be possible to appoint a man to cover several markets. In some, he could supervise agents and in others, he would do the selling himself.

// CHAPTER 18 //

SENDING EXPORT SAMPLES TO PROSPECTIVE BUYERS

Samples should normally be sent by post (airmail) than airlifted, to minimise costs. Samples of goods not otherwise prohibited to export, are allowed to be exported to all permissible destinations, by any mode including post. Practically, there is not much formality to export samples.

Export (purchase) orders by foreign buyers are placed on exporters (sellers) only when the former are satisfied with the size, specification, look (appearance) or design, price, etc. of the product, besides being satisfied with the 'terms of delivery', payment methods, etc. While most of the requirements are/can be settled through correspondence or on personal contact, design or look of the product needs to be seen by the buyer and so he must be presented with the product, i.e. a sample.

Hence, samples are invariably sent to foreign buyers. When the buyers ask for the same. In the first instance, negotiations are carried on, inter alia, through product brochures, catalogues, leaflets, simple photographs or other descriptive literature. When the buyer is satisfied with the broad terms conveyed by the seller and evinces interest in the product, he normally asks for its sample, if he has not seen it yet. On receipt of such communication, the exporter should arrange to send the sample to foreign buyer by post (airmail) or air. The postal channel being comparatively cheaper than sending goods by air (as distinguished from airmail), exporters may normally adopt the former system. However, there are certain restrictions with regard to weight and dimension on the post parcels. Hence, sample may have to be sent by air, if they cannot be exported by post. Moreover, the samples should have certain properties like attraction, information, retention and reminder value as detailed below.

Sample Properties

Attraction value The sample must be able to provoke a detailed assessment from the recipient.

Information value The sample should contain full technical/commercial information in order to elicit a purchase decision.

Retention value The sample must lend itself to easy storage and retain its values for future use in decision making.

Reminder value The sample must remind the importer of the name of the exporter and his previous association with the sample. In other words, it must have recall value.

Other properties The other properties which a sample must possess are-

- ★ low bulk, as transportation costs are high, but sufficient enough to exhibit the full properties of the product or to lend itself for necessary testing as the case may be.
- ★ ease of packing, transportation, storage and retrieval.
- ★ durability - sample must not be cut or packed in such a way that any kind of distortion/spoilage could occur during transit/storage.
- ★ amenable to testing - in some cases,
- ★ a 'true representation' of the merchandise intended to be marketed. In the case of made-ups, if it is final packed by exporter, it is worthwhile showing the final package of a unit in the sample.
- ★ must not contain colours which are considered as taboo in a particular market.

TRADE SAMPLES/GIFT PARCELS

Export of sample for trade (commercial) purposes are to be distinguished from gift parcels. Gift parcels, the contents of which do not exceed Rs 10,000 in value are allowed to be exported, provided that the item is not prohibited/restricted for export. However, commercial sample of any value can be exported for business (export) purposes if the exporter fulfills the prescribed conditions and sends through the authorised channels and to permissible destinations as detailed in this chapter.

The policy and procedure for export of samples can be divided into three categories, namely-

(i) items subject to export control listed in Negative List of Exports contained in Export-Import Policy
(ii) items listed in Public Notices issued by the Government from time to time.
(iii) items which are not subject to export trade control under EXIM Policy.

EXPORT CONTROL ITEMS

Export Policy (other than Garments and Jewellery) The EXIM Policy, 1997-2002 contains the Negative List of Export Items. It has three parts as follows:

Part I – Prohibited items
Part II – Restricted items i.e. exports permitted subject to licensing
Part III – Export permitted through specified canalising agencies

The Public Notices as amended, contain the list of items, export of which shall be permitted as per the terms and conditions specified against each. An export licence may or may not be required.

Samples Export Policy

The policy for export of samples of items in the negative list of the Exim Policy and the Public Notices above, is as follows:

Prohibited items

(i) Export as samples of products listed in Part I of the Exim Policy are totally prohibited.

(ii) Export of samples of certain items of the Exim Policy can also not be made, except with specific permission/licence of the DGFT and/or the agency authorised for the purpose.

No export licence Samples of items, export of which requires a licence, other than those prohibited/restricted for export as mentioned above can be exported without licence if their value does not exceed Rs 25,000 in any licensing year (April-March).

Export licence Where the vale of samples of items which requires an export licence, exceeds Rs 25,000 in a licensing year, their export will be allowed against a licence issued by DGFT. However, export of samples of specified items requires a licence irrespective of the value of samples.

Garment Samples

Sample shipments will be allowed to be made only by exporters who are registered with the Apparel EPC (or the Wool and Woollens EPC for woollen knitwears). The limits are as follows:

(i) *Fast moving items* Not more than 25 pieces in one category/country once in 10 days. Certification on shipping bills will be valid for a period of 10 days. More than one certification together not exceeding 25 pieces can be obtained within 10 days, with all certifications expiring on 10th day from the date of first certification.

(ii) *Slow moving items* 100 pieces in the relevant country/category every day. However, if there are no balances available under the FCFS systems, then certifications for sample consignments shall be restricted as for fast moving items.

For USA and Canada, the limits are as follows:

Canada Consignments valued at less than Canadian $500 are not debited to restrained level and no restriction will be applied to sample shipments which are not above the prescribed value limits.

US Samples properly marked as "Commercial Samples" or "Mutilated Samples" valued at US $250 or less, are not debited to restraint levels and no visa/exemption certificate is required for export of such samples. However, samples not properly marked will be debited to restraint levels and Circular Visae are required for export of these samples, even if their value is US $250 or less.

Note: A sample consignment in the case of US/Canada should not be clubbed with another sample consignment or commercial consignment.

Excess number/value If the sample consignments are in excess of the limits specified above, exporter should use their own Past Performance Entitlement (PPE)/Manufacturer-Exporter's Entitlement/Non Quota Exporters Entitlement.

No EMD/council charges It is not necessary to furnish EMD or AEPC charges for sample consignments within the limits specified above. No proof of shipment is also to be given for such samples.

Floor Price Sample shipments will be subject to floor prices, as applicable to the relevant country/category.

Jewellery Samples

Jewellery/precious stones of over specified value to be sent as sample or export, require valuation/sealing of packets, by or in the presence of customs and counter signature on relevant form.

Application furnishing particulars like the present market value of each item to be sent and mode of despatch including personal carriage if desired, should be sent to the RBI for necessary permission.

After obtaining RBI's permission, submit the packet to the Customs for valuation and sealing and/or for issue of export certificate and stamping of invoice. The sample parcel after valuation/sealing will be handed over to the concerned airlines or the exporter for personal carriage or despatch by post.

De-controlled items

Samples of de-controlled items i.e. the items of which export is not subject to export control, and also of items like precious jewellery, are allowed without any limitation and permission. Hence, there is no need of any permission for sending any quantity of samples or of any amount by the exporters for items which are not listed in the negative List of Export. However, the export of samples shall be governed by any other law for the time being in force. In such cases, samples can be sent on obtaining a certificate of 'non-involvement of foreign exchange' from an authorised dealer (i.e. Bank) in foreign exchange.

EXPORT PROCEDURE

(i) Export of Free Samples by Post of De-controlled Items

Export of samples to be sent by post are further sub-divided into following categories, namely:-

(a) articles sent as gift upto a value of Rs 10,000

(b) articles of value more than Rs 10,000, but less than Rs 25,000

(c) jewellery/garment samples, as discussed above.

Where the value of the article is less than Rs 10,000/-, the exporter should file a simple declaration that the sample does not involve foreign exchange and its value is less than Rs 10,000.

The articles of value in excess of Rs 10,000 can be exported as gift parcels by air freight [and not post (including air mail under certificate issued by an Authorised Dealer (AD)] in Foreign Exchange saying that-

(i) the export does not involve any transaction in foreign exchange, and

(ii) give a notation to the effect that the value of shipment shall be subject to acceptance by Customs.

For jewellery items, the authorised dealers certify on the PP form

The export procedure of export control items, all seen in the following pages.

(ii) Limits on Weight

Whereas there is no limit on the weight of a parcel to be sent by air or sea, the weight of post parcels should not exceed the specific limits as given below.

Surface mail 10 kgs to all countries except those which don't admit parcels of more than 10 kgs/15 kgs, but upto a maximum of 20 kgs. Information on such countries should be obtained from post offices in India.

Air mail 20 kgs for all countries except Lebanon, Marshal Island, Nepal and Pureto Rico for which the limit is five (5) kgs. Parcels for Taiwan can be sent upto 3 kgs.

(iii) Limits on Dimensions

Information in respect of parcels to be air freighted in regard to their volume may be obtained from any clearing and forwarding agent/airlines concerned. The limits put on parcels to be sent by post is as follows:

Minimum A parcel should have surface measuring not less than 90 mm × 140 mm.

Maximum Length of a parcel should not exceed one meter. The sum of the length and greatest circumference measured in all directions other than the length, should not exceed two meters.

Packing Do take care of special packing conditions in case of products like precious metals, glass or other fragile objects, liquids and substances, dry colouring powders, etc.

Booking at post offices Parcels packed and addressed in the manner prescribed by the postal authorities and conforming to the dimensions and the weight instructions stated above can be booked to any permissible destination at any post office in India.

(iv) Documents

Post parcels should be accompanied with the following documents while booking at Post Office.

(a) Customs declaration form (CDF) is to be submitted in duplicate (one copy having been pasted on the parcels) with goods whose value do not exceed Rs 10,000. These forms should contain as accurate and detailed description of the contents of parcel as possible. The net weight of contents and value of the parcels should be expressed in Indian rupees.

In case of parcels addressed to importers in US, instructions regarding their disposal in the event of non-delivery, should also be recorded on the CDF.

(b) Despatch note contains instructions regarding disposal of parcels in case of their non-delivery to the addressee. This note is to be filled in for all parcels sent to permissible countries other than US. (For US, these instructions are to be given on CDF as explained above.)

In practice however, parcels are accepted even if not accompanied by the Despatch Note, provided disposal instructions are given on the CDF itself in case of parcels addressed to any destination including US.

Since all parcels which remain undelivered on account of any reason whatsoever, are redirected to the sender who is liable to pay the return charges, don't forget to record instructions for disposal. Also do write on the parcel "NE PAS nexpeder" i.e. "Do not redirect" where parcel is not required to be delivered back.

(c) A certificate from an authorised dealer in foreign exchange-normally scheduled Bank-to the effect that the articles contained in the parcels are being supplied free of charge and that no transaction in foreign exchange is involved. As explained above, this "Certificate" is applicable in case of parcels containing articles of value more than Rs 200, but less than Rs 15,000. It is given by the Bank on the commercial invoice itself, submitted by the exporter.

(d) Export licence, including AEPC/W&WEPC certification, for readymade garments, in respect of export control items.

(e) Customs clearance of jewellery items.

(v) Export of Free Samples by Air/Sea But Other Than by Post of De-controlled Items

Export of trade samples, (and not exhibits to be displayed in a trade fair or exhibition) supplied free of payment is allowed by sea/air (and not sea/air mail) without any value restriction, provided the Customs Authorities are satisfied about the bonafide of the goods, that these are trade samples for promotion of exports, and not falling in Export Control or accompanied with an Export Licence/AEPC Certification and Customs permission for jewellery items. The Customs may ask for such paper i.e. correspondence, etc. between the exporters and overseas buyers which shows that samples are being sent to generate export business. No permission or certification from the RBI or authorised dealer in foreign exchange (Bank) is necessary. Samples of any value can be sent freely by air or sea, if the Customs Authorities are satisfied.

(vi) Documents

Accordingly, samples properly marked with regard to value, to be sent by air or sea require the following documents:-

(a) A Free Shipping Bill in duplicate (or in triplicate if transhipment is involved) is to be filled in, since the samples neither attract any export duty nor are entitled to Duty Drawback,

(b) A copy of the export's commercial invoice declaring the value of the parcel(s).

(c) Packing List (one copy), if more than one packet.

(d) Any proof showing the need for sending the sample. Usually, foreign buyer's letter asking for the same should be sent in original.

(e) GR form duly attested by an authorised dealer in case of jewellery exports.

Parcels packed and addressed in the prescribed manner may be sent along with the above mentioned documents to the Clearing and Forwarding Agents. After their shipment by sea or air, one will get a Bill of Lading or Air Way Bill a copy of which should be sent to the addressee by the exporter, for enabling the former to take its delivery.

(vii) Trade Samples against Payment — Samples which involve Foreign Exchange

The samples of goods against which the foreign buyer agrees to make payment can be exported in the same manner in which normal exports are effected.

Procedure For export of such samples, procedure has been detailed in separate Module for export by sea, air and post. The usual declarations on the foreign exchange forms i.e.the GR and PP forms have also to be made by the exporter.

Samples for testing abroad Samples of items for testing abroad can also be sent in accordance with the policy and procedures for sending samples as gifts or trade samples as explained above. Authorised Dealers in FE have been delegated powers to issue a Certificate about non-involvement of foreign exchange, etc., to enable their constituents to send samples for testing abroad.

The Authorised Dealers should however follow up such cases, to ensure re-import of samples after testing or submission of a destruction certificate from the overseas laboratory in case the sample is destroyed during the test/ re-import of the goods, after repairs.

Hence, the Authorised Dealers may probably ask for an undertaking to re-import such articles.

Details about remittance of testing charges are given in the chapter on FE for Exporters.

Personal carriage of samples An exporter traveller can also personally carry the samples of any product, whether under export control or not personally, provided these are otherwise permissible or cleared for export as explained above.

In case of precious jewellery/stones items however, the exporter should declare personal carriage of samples to the Customs while leaving the country and obtain necessary endorsement on the Export Certificate issued by Jewellery Appraiser of the Customs.

In case of re-import at the time of the exporter's return to India, the samples earlier carried and now brought back, shall be verified along with the export documents. The samples would thereafter be sealed by Customs. The sealed parcels will be handed over to the exporter for presenting to the Jewellery Appraiser of the Customs for necessary appraisal.

GOVERNMENT AMENDMENTS

> In an amendment, the Government has issued Notification No.2(RE 98)/ 1997-2002 of 13.4.1998, whereby samples exports has been liberalised. Plant and Plant Portions, their derivatives and extracts export restricted. The condition relating to Wheat and Wheat products, Bajra, Ragi and Jowar, Grain and Flour of Barley, Maize has been deleted.

The entries appearing at following serial numbers of Schedule 2 Appendix 1 of the book titled "ITC (HS) Classifications of Export and Import Items 1997-2002" shall be amended as under:

(a) The entry appearing at sl.no. 3 relating to Black Pepper (Asta Quality MG-1) shall be deleted;

(b) The word "DGFT" appearing in condition no.(1) against the entry at s.no. 6 relating to Cotton Yarn shall be amended to read as "Government";

(c) The condition no.(ii) against the entry no. 12 (i) and (ii) relating to wheat and wheat products and grain and flour of Barley, Maize, Bajra, Ragi and Jowar (excluding Hybrid Jowar grown as Kharif crop) shall be deleted;

(d) The condition against the entry at S. no. 21 relating to Samples shall be amended to read as:

"Samples of goods including those in Parts II and III of the Negative List of Exports and this Appendix, except items as sl. no.1 Beddomes cycad (Cycas beddomel), 2 Blue vanda (Vanda coerulea). 17 Taxus Wallichiana (common Yew or Birmi leaves) and 19 (Aconitum species) of this Appendix and items at sl. no.2, 5, 24, 28, 30 and 31 of Part II of the Negative list of Exports, may be exported without a licence if the value of the samples so exported, taken together does not exceed US $2000 (two thousand) in any licensing year. However, export of physician samples not for sale/free samples of medicines or pharmaceutical formulations by a firm, whether accompanying the commercial quantity or being exported separately, shall be permitted upto 1% of their medicines/pharmaceutical formulations in the preceding licensing year. DGFT shall be the licensing authority in this behalf".

(e) The condition No. (I) against the entry at sl. no. 30 relating to export of Tea to Russia under the rupee Debt Repayment Mechanism shall be deleted; and

(f) The entry at sl. 33 relating to Sandalwood Oil shall be amended to read as under:

"Sandalwood Oil Quantitative ceiling as may be notified by the Director General of Foreign Trade from time to time.

The Schedule 2 appendix 2 of the book titled "ITC (HC) Classifications of export and items 1997-2002" relating to Export of plants, plant portions and their derivatives and extracts obtained from the wild shall be amended as under:

"The export of Plants, Plant portions and their derivatives and extracts obtained from the wild is prohibited (Item Nos. 1 to 29).

Plant and Plant portions, derivatives and extracts (including value added herbal formulations) of the cultivated varieties of the above species [excluding sl. no.16 viz. Pterocarpus santalinus (Redsanders)] will be allowed for export subject to production of a Certificate of Cultivation from the Regional Deputy Director (Wildlife) or Chief Conservator of Forests of Divisional Forest Offices of the State concerned from where these plants and plant portions have been procured.

The value added herbal formulations made out of imported species of plants and plant portions as specified will be allowed freely without any restriction subject to furnishing of an affidavit to the Customs Authorities at the time of export that only the imported plant species as above have been used for the manufacture of value added herbal formulation being exported in the event of affidavit proving to be false, on the basis of random sample tests, action would be initiated against the firm under the Foreign Trade (Development and Regulation) Act, 1992.

Exports are allowed only through the ports of Mumbai, Calcutta, Cochin, Delhi, Chennai and Tuticorin.

// CHAPTER 19 //

EXPORT TERMS OF PAYMENT

International trade thrives on credit. Where there is a little to choose from the quality of goods, from one producer or the other, it is often inducement of credit terms offered by a seller which clinches the contract with the buyer.

THE FINANCIAL PACKAGE

The main points for consideration in any financial package include the length of credit, the rate of interest and the currency of payment. Trade credit, the granting of time to pay by suppliers is the most natural form of credit a buyer could wish for. It usually does not cost more than what can be passed on in the final sales price, does not tie up the buyer's bank lines, and is normally easy to administer. Unfortunately, trade credit carries a risk to the granter of the credit, and is generally accorded only in well-established relationships, most buyers and seller therefore have to resort to some form of financial package.

It is obvious that the buyer and seller have conflicting interests in the financial package, but there must be some compromise before a deal can be concluded. Banks can provide a solution acceptable to both parties, by providing credit to either the buyer or the seller. In many countries export credit insurance assumes the risk of non-payment – for a premium – and this can be assigned to the funding bank. Bank and insurers agree that the level of credit need not be linked to the size of the customer's balance sheet and may be based on their ability to perform the contract from which the repayment will be made. So, balance sheet weakness may be compensated by strong performance capability. The bank could also repurchase an exporter's receivable, thereby refinancing any supplier's credit (i.e. the credit granted by the exporter to the buyer); the bank thus becomes the lender. The exporter's receivable could be in the form of letters of credit with deferred payments or incorporated in bills of exchange and promissory notes.

Additionally, the bank may (for a fee) absorb the *country risk* element in a deal where for example, there may be a risk of non-performance for political or economic reasons, such as blocked foreign exchange in the buyer's country or an embargo on exports from the seller's country. Usually the seller's bank undertakes to guarantee payment to the buyer's bank (assuming that the later bank has given its own undertaking). For buyers, their bank will guarantee that the seller's bank will honour its obligation under any performance bond it has given on behalf of the seller. The level of risk depends on the relationship between the two banks, and whether the guaranteeing bank can recover monies it may have to pay out under a claim.

If sellers have to wait for their money beyond the normal credit terms because of a foreign exchange restriction in the buyer's country, this delay could soon wipe away the profit hoped for. If buyers do not receive the expected raw materials because of an export embargo in the seller's country, it could cause the buyers to stop production or cost them more to buy it from elsewhere.

Once a financial package is agreed and a contract concluded, how do sellers collect their money, and how buyers obtain their goods? They use the banking system.

TERMS OF PAYMENT

Payment and financing arrangements for exporting are more difficult than for merely selling in the home market because the customer lives in another country. Not only does this mean that a great distance separates the exporter and his customer, but the customer probably deals in a different currency, works under different regulations, communicates in another language, uses other customs, and is less easily subject to legal recourse should this be necessary. All these things can be obstacles to the exporter, unless he is aware of the correct procedures and knows when and how to use them.

The Export Invoice

The first step in getting paid for an order is the preparation of an invoice for the goods.

The *export invoice* is a basic document in exporting. It is basically the same as any other sales invoice. It is the bill for the goods. It is the document in which the customer is told in detail how much money he has to pay for the products. But the export invoice has wider uses than an ordinary invoice, and there are different kinds for different purposes.

The *pro-forma invoice* is used by the customer in an export market to make arrangements for import licenses or exchange control clearance. The *commercial invoice* is used by the customer to secure customs clearance of products once they reach his country, and for making insurance claims. To fulfill requirements of the importing country the exporter may also have to supply a *certified invoice*, which is a commercial invoice certified by a chamber of commerce or other specified institution, or a *consular invoice*, which must be prepared on an official form and can be quite costly.

Period of Credit

Whenever goods are sold, the seller must agree with the customer on the period of time that will be allowed before the goods must be paid for – the period of credit.

Deciding on this question of credit is difficult. If the credit period extended to a customer is shorter than what competitors are offering, or if the methods of payments are more demanding, business can easily be lost. On the other hand, it is useless for an exporter to sell abroad if he has to wait too long for his money or has too many bad debts.

The creditworthiness of a customer, and in some cases of his country, are often difficult to assess. The ordinary *credit report*, which may be sufficient for home sales, is usually not sufficient when considering credit terms in an export market. Even the most willing and credit-worthy customer cannot complete payment if his country runs into foreign exchange difficulties and imposes restrictions upon payment abroad. In these circumstances there can be delays in settlement or even a complete loss. So the economic, financial and political situation in the country that is importing the goods must be taken into account before credit is extended abroad. This type of risk is known as 'country risk.' The longer the period of credit, the more important 'country risk' becomes, because the more time there is for changes in government policy.

DOCUMENTARY COLLECTION

Documentary collection is a means of ensuring that the goods are only handed over to the buyer when the amount shown on a *bill of exchange* is paid or when the customer accepts the bill as a contract to pay by a specified date. A bill of exchange is *accepted* by the customer putting his signature across it.

A bill of exchange is simply a written order to pay to someone on demand or at a *fixed time in the future* a certain sum of money. A bill is addressed by the exporter to the customer.

How it works In *documentary collection* the bank acts on the instructions of the exporter and the exchange of the documents to title, takes place at the customer's place of business.

Once the exporter has dispatched his goods to the customer, the exporter collects the shipping documents, which give title to the goods. He 'draws a bill of exchange on the buyer'. This merely means that he fills in a bill of exchange with all the relevant details relating to the particular shipment. This is made out to be payable either on sight (on demand) or within a specified time (for example 90 days).

The exporter sends the bills of exchange and the shipping documents to his bank, which forwards them to an advising bank in the customer's country.

This bank, or the exporter's agents in the country concerned, takes the documents to the customer. If it is a sight bill the customer pays the amount directly. If it is a time bill he signs the bills, which means he 'accepts' it for payment within a certain specified time (a time bill is sometimes called a term bill or usance bill). In return for either payment or acceptance, the customer is handed the shipping documents.

The customer now has authority to collect the goods, which may already have arrived at the port of destination. The customer's bank pays the exporter for the goods.

If the bill of exchange is a sight bill and the money is actually paid when the bill is presented, this arrangement is known as document against payment (D/P). It is known as document against acceptance (D/A) when the bill of exchange is a time bill and the money is to be paid within a specified time.

Dishonoured Bills

An exporter takes a risk when he sells on the basis of documents against payment (D/P) or documents against acceptance (D/A). The customer can 'dishonour' the bill, that is refuse to pay or to sign the bill. Although the exporter keeps title to the goods, he has the problem of what to do with them.

Very little business is completely safe, and an exporter may have to take calculated risks. Even though the stability of a particular country may be doubtful, an exporter may decide to export to a customer in that country because of good long-term prospects or because of the need to penetrate a market quickly. These reasons could make certain risks worthwhile.

Credit Policy

In establishing a credit and payments policy, the following vital matters should be considered:

- ★ the political stability of the customer's country
- ★ the currency exchange or import regulations in the customer's country
- ★ foreign exchange or import regulations in the customer's country
- ★ the amount of money involved in a transaction
- ★ credit status of the individual customer
- ★ the nature of the products traded. Do they require special design or manufacture that would make them difficult to sell elsewhere if the customer fails to pay? Are they durable or capital goods, or are they perishable and must therefore be sold quickly?
- ★ prevailing interest rates and cost of money
- ★ terms currently granted by competitors
- ★ the custom of the particular trade
- ★ financial position of the country which is the export country
- ★ any regulations in force in the customer's country which prescribe certain methods of payment and credit terms
- ★ the ability to give credit
- ★ the company's financial position
- ★ the availability and cost of credit insurance
- ★ the likely effect of total loss on the company
- ★ the potential of this particular customer, and the likelihood that more or less credit will be needed if the business develops.

Creditworthiness of Customers

The checking of an individual customer's credit status can be done through the following types of person or institution:

1. The bank, which can consult its correspondent bank in the customer's country.
2. The agent in the customer's country, if there is one.
3. A fellow exporter or manufacturer with some experience in the customer's country. This can be a valuable but unofficial method of obtaining information.
4. A credit-rating organisation.
5. Export credit insurance organisation, including government ones, which often include provision in their policies for vetting the customer's credit status land for setting limits on the credit.

Checklist for Customer Credit Rating

1. How long will the debt be outstanding?
2. What else could we do with the money for that period?
3. What is the risk of total loss?
4. Can we insure against loss?
5. Can we finance the credit?
6. What will the customer do if we say 'no'?
7. How important is this order to us?
8. What is the future potential of the customer?
9. How else could we satisfy the customer at no lower risk or cost to us?
10. Will this debt prevent us from extending credit to other customers?

In order to establish his customer's credit rating, an exporter can approach:

* Firms which investigates all major companies' financial situation and publish their ratings in a directory and also makes individuals reports to subscribers,
* banks,
* possibly his own country's trade attaché.

In this way an exporter can minimise the risk he has to take.

METHODS OF PAYMENT

Having decided on a credit policy, the next step is to decide on a means of payment that will bring together the credit and financing aspects. Basically there are **six methods** of obtaining payment for export shipments:

* **Cash payment** – Either on confirmation of order or when the goods are ready for shipment.
* **Open account** – Payment after goods are delivered.
* **Shipment of consignment** – Payment after goods have been sold.
* **Documentary credit** – Using of letter of credit.
* **Documentary collection** – Using paid bill of exchange or sight draft.
* **Documentary collection** – Using accepted bill of exchange or time draft.

Cash payment

The ideal form of payment for any exporter is to receive cash with the order. With this method of payment, money is received before the goods are delivered and no risk is involved. But it is unlikely that this method can be used, unless the product being sold is in heavy demand. There may be also cases where specialised goods are custom-made. In such circumstances, the exporter will probably ask for cash with the order.

In practice a compromise is often sought. For example, cash payment may be required when the goods are *ready for shipment*. Another type of compromise is when a percentage of the price is paid wit the order, a further percentage at a certain stage of manufacture, and the remainder on delivery of the goods.

Open Account

The open account procedure is when the exporter dispatches the goods, prepares the invoice, sends them to the customer and then waits for payment. The exporter should get his money as specified in the *terms of payment*. But there is a very real risk of total loss.

There is no special procedure or documentation. All that has to be agreed upon is the period of credit. Typical credit arrangements are: net monthly account; cash within seven days; 2½ % discount for payment within 30 days.

Open account is generally restricted to transaction where the exporter and the customer have a close relationship or understanding, and where there are no exchange restrictions to complicate settlement. Sales on this basis are usually paid for by periodic payments, such as monthly statements by bank, mail or cable facilities. Obviously the exporter must have sufficient financial strength to carry the cost of the goods until he receives payment.

It may well be decided that open account terms are the ones to use when selling in competitive, sophisticated and demanding markets and the customers are very well known.

Shipment on Consignment

In a shipment on consignment deal, the exporter retains title to the goods and agrees to wait for payment until the goods have been sold in the customer's country. This method means that the goods are placed in the foreign market, but the risks involved are considerable. Until the goods are sold, the customer or consignee may return them at ay time, without liability. There might be difficulty in ensuring that the consignee observes the terms of the agreement faithfully. The exporter's stock may be built up and abroad to a dangerously high degree, outside his control, and subject to political change and climatic risks.

Shipment on consignment should therefore only be made, with a full understanding of the credit and other risks that are involved, and should probably be limited to stable countries where the exporter has proved and trusted agents to keep an eye on the market and where the customers are well known and committed to the exporter.

Documentary Credit and Documentary Collection

The above methods are all used in exporting and all have their drawbacks. But by far the most common ways of getting paid are by:

- ★ documentary credit using a letter of credit (L/C), and
- ★ documentary collection using a bill of exchange (DA/DP).

DOCUMENTARY CREDIT

When an exporter has an order for his goods, he also has a problem. He has to dispatch the goods to some distant land without some assurance that he will receive payment.

In the home market this is not such a difficult problem. But great care must be taken when little is known about a customer who lives thousands of miles away.

If, for example, the customer is unwilling or unable to pay for the goods once they had been shipped, an exporter could spend a good deal of time and money trying to recoup his loss.

By the same token, the customer does not want to pay any money until he has the goods or is sure that they are on their way to him.

Documentary credit is a method of payment which can ensure that an exporter gets his money *when he dispatches his goods* and not when they are *received* by the customer. It also ensures that the customer is assured of title to the *goods before he pays for them*.

The problems of the exporter and his customer are solved by the intervention of a third party. That third party is a bank. A documentary credit is merely a credit opened with a bank in the exporter's favour. The word 'documentary' indicates that the whole negotiation is linked with the shipping documents – the invoices, bills of lading, insurance certificates, etc. A documentary credit is often called a 'letter of credit' (L/C).

How it Works

In *documentary credit* the instructions come from the *customer* and the exchange of documents and payment take place at the exporter's place of business. The customer opens a credit account at his bank for a certain sum of money, in favour of a certain exporter. The money is only to be paid under certain conditions. Normally these are that:

★ the goods will be as specified on the order
★ the price of the goods will be as specified
★ the delivery or dispatch will be by a certain date
★ charges for freight, insurance, etc. will be as specified.

Two banks are actually involved in the documentary credit process:

★ The customer's bank, which opens the credit, is known as the *opening or issuing bank*.
★ The money is actually paid to the exporter by another bank, located in his own country. This bank is known as the *advising or corresponding bank*.

Example Industria Import Ltd. have ordered goods worth \$3000 from Ruralian Exports Ltd. Industria Imports Ltd go to their bank and open an account for \$3000 in favour of Ruralian Exports Ltd, payable under specific conditions.

The exporter arranges for the delivery of the goods, according to the terms of delivery stipulated in the contract and collects the necessary documents.

He presents the shipping documents to his advising bank, whereupon he is paid his \$3000, since the bank now knows that the goods have been shipped as specified, and since the exporter has passed over his title to the goods, in the form of shipping documents in general and the bill of lading in particular.

The advising bank then forwards the shipping documents to the issuing bank. This bank hands over the documents to the customer who can then collect the goods from the port of destination.

Type of Payment	*When You Get Your Money*	*Extent of Risk(*)*
Cash payment	With the order	No risk.
Open account	Specified time after delivery to the customer	Risk of total loss if customer fails to pay.
Shipment on consignment	After customer has resold the goods	Risk of loss if customer fails to sell the goods.
Documentary credit using letter of credit	At the time of shipment	Risk limited to cost of bringing back goods from the port which may have been specially made.
Documentary coll-ection using paid bill of exchange or sight draft	On arrival at port of destination	Risk of having to bring back goods or dispose them at a loss.
Documentary collec-tion using accepted bill of exchange or time draft	Specified time after delivery	Risk of total loss if customer dishonours bill of exchange with the bank.

(*) Less risk if one has an export credit guarantee arrangement with one's government agency

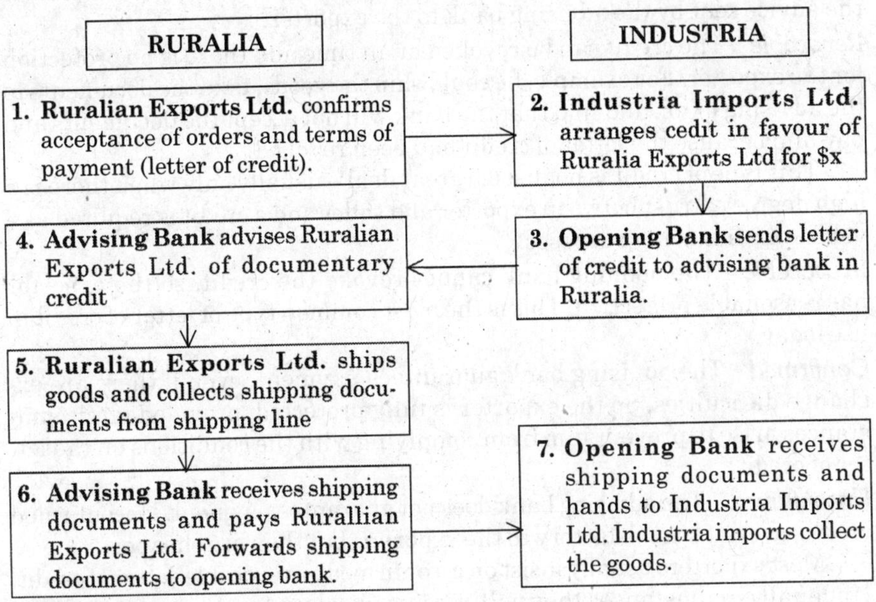

EXERCISE

The following summary gives the main stages involved in a documentary credit transaction:

1. The exporter and the customer agree in their contract that payment shall be made by documentary credit.

2. The customer instructs his bank (opening bank) to open a documentary credit for the exporter on certain terms.
3. The opening bank arranges with a bank in the exporter's country (advancing bank) to negotiate, accept or pay the exporter's draft upon delivery of the shipping documents by the exporter.
4. The advising bank advises the exporter that it will negotiate, accept or pay his draft upon delivery of the shipping documents.
5. The exporter ships the goods, presents the documents to the advising bank, and is paid.
6. The advising bank forwards the documents to the opening bank in the customer's country.
7. The opening bank gives the documents to the customer, who presents them at the port and receives the goods.

Types of Documentary Credit

There are four kinds of letter of credit:

- ★ revocable
- ★ irrevocable
- ★ confirmed
- ★ unconfirmed.

The terms *revocable* and *irrevocable* refer to instructions received by the advising bank form the opening bank. *Confirmed* and *Unconfirmed* refer to the advice sent by the advising bank to the exporter.

Revocable The credit can be revoked at an time and there is no protection for the exporter. For example, he could ship the goods, take the documents to the advising bank, and find that the bank will not accept the documents and pay him because the letter of credit had been revoked.

This type of credit is not used a great deal – usually only when there is a high degree of trust between exporter and seller and a credit is required as a vehicle for financing purposes.

Irrevocable The opening bank cannot revoke the credit, so the exporter has reasonable protection. This is the most common type of letter of credit in use today.

Confirmed The advising bank guarantees payment, even if there are exchange difficulties. So the exporter is fully protected, provided no circumstances arise to prevent him from complying with the conditions on the letter of credit.

Unconfirmed The advising bank does not guarantee payment. Unconfirmed credits are not so satisfactory to the exporter, but they are cheaper.

Most exporters usually insist on a 'confirmed', irrevocable' letter of credit. Under all circumstances they will receive payment for their goods, as long as they keep to the conditions stipulated in the letter of credit.

Revolving Credits

A buyer may regularly purchase goods form an exporter and may not wish to make an application for documentary credit for each separate shipment. So the buyer gives the bank standing instructions to arrange in favour of the exporter, a credit which at no time shall exceed a fixed maximum. This is known as revolving credit.

The documentary credit system is the safest method of payment. It is also the most expensive because of bank charges, etc. The exporter must decide if the increased charges are worth the added security. Often they are.

DOCUMENTARY COLLECTION

Documentary collection is a means of ensuring that the goods are only handed over to the buyer when the amount shown on a *bill of exchange* is paid or when the customer accepts the bill as contract to pay by a specified date. A bill of exchange is *accepted* by the customer putting his signature across it.

A bill of exchange is simply a written order to a bank to pay to someone *on demand or at a fixed time in the future,* a certain sum of money. A bill is addressed by the exporter to the customer and can be used as money.

There are three parties to a bill of exchange:

★ the drawer
★ the drawee
★ the payee

The **drawer** is the person (the exporter) who makes out the bill to a certain person (the customer) demanding a certain sum of money.

The **drawee** is the customer. He must sign the bill to indicate that he has accepted the bill and its terms. Only then he will be handed the shipping documents, which give him ownership of the goods.

The **payee** is the third party – the bank.

So the drawee (the customer) pays the money to the payee (the bank) who forwards it to the drawer (the exporter).

How it Works

In *Documentary Collection* the bank acts on the instructions of the *exporter* and the exchange of the documents to title takes place at the customer's place of business.

Once the exporter has dispatched his goods to the customer, the exporter collects the shipping documents, which give title to the goods. He 'draws a bill of exchange on the buyer'. This merely means that he fills in a bill of exchange with all the relevant details relating to the particular shipment. This means that he *fills in a bill of exchange* with all the relevant details relating to the on *sight* (on demand) or within a specified time (for example, 90 days).

The sum of money to be paid by the customer includes:

★ the cost of goods,
★ the freight
★ insurance
★ any other charges, such as packing.

The exporter sends the bill of exchange and the shipping documents to his bank, which forwards them to an advising bank in the customer's country.

This bank, or the exporters' agents in the country concerned, takes the documents to the customer. If it is a *sight bill* the customer pays the amount directly. If it is a *time bill* he signs the bill, which means he 'accepts' it for payment within a certain time (a time bill is sometimes called a *term bill*). In return for either payment or acceptance of payment, the customer is handed the shipping documents.

The shipping documents include:

- ★ commercial and customs invoices
- ★ marine insurance policy or certificate
- ★ bills of lading.

Certificates of origin and packing lists may also be required. The customer now has authority to collect the goods, which may already have arrived at the port of destination. The customer's bank forwards the money when it is received, to the exporter's bank, which pays the exporter for the goods.

If the bill of exchange is a sight bill and the money is actually paid when the bill is presented, this arrangement is known as *document against payment* (D/P). It is known as *document against* (D/A) when the bill of exchange is a time bill and money is paid within a specified time.

The exporter must signify:

- ★ Whether the documents are to be handed to a referee if required.
- ★ Whether the buyer shall be allowed a rebate for early payment.
- ★ What to do if documents are not taken up.

If bill is not accepted by the drawee when it is offered to him for acceptance, it is known as *dishonoured bill.*

When a bill is dishonoured, the bank refuses to give the customer the bill of lading giving title to the goods. The bank seeks instructions from the exporter on how it should act. Basically the exporter can then give one of the following four types of instruction, each of which involves expense.

- ★ Dump the goods in the sea. In this case the loss is at best the value of the goods. Import duty may also be payable.
- ★ Put the goods into store and try to persuade the customer to pay for them. At best this will incur extra storage costs.
- ★ Sell the goods to any taker, perhaps through the bank. The exporter is likely to have to sell at less than the original price. As well as making a loss on the particular transaction, there is a danger of spoiling the market with low-cost goods.
- ★ Instruct the bank to return the goods. This will incur further freight costs as well as, perhaps duties. The goods may also be difficult to sell to another customer if they have been custom-made for the original customer or designed for the particular export market.

Another kind of problem occurs when a time bill is accepted by the customer but he is then unable to pay at the due time, either through his own default or through a change in his government's import restriction or exchange control. When this happens the exporter is no better off than under open account terms, unless he has been able to cover himself against this kind of risk through an export credit guaranteed scheme run by his government.

The greatest safeguard against a term bill being dishonoured is probably the fact that the advising bank is unlikely to release the bill of lading and other shipping documents to the customer unless it is confident that he will be able to pay when the bill falls due.

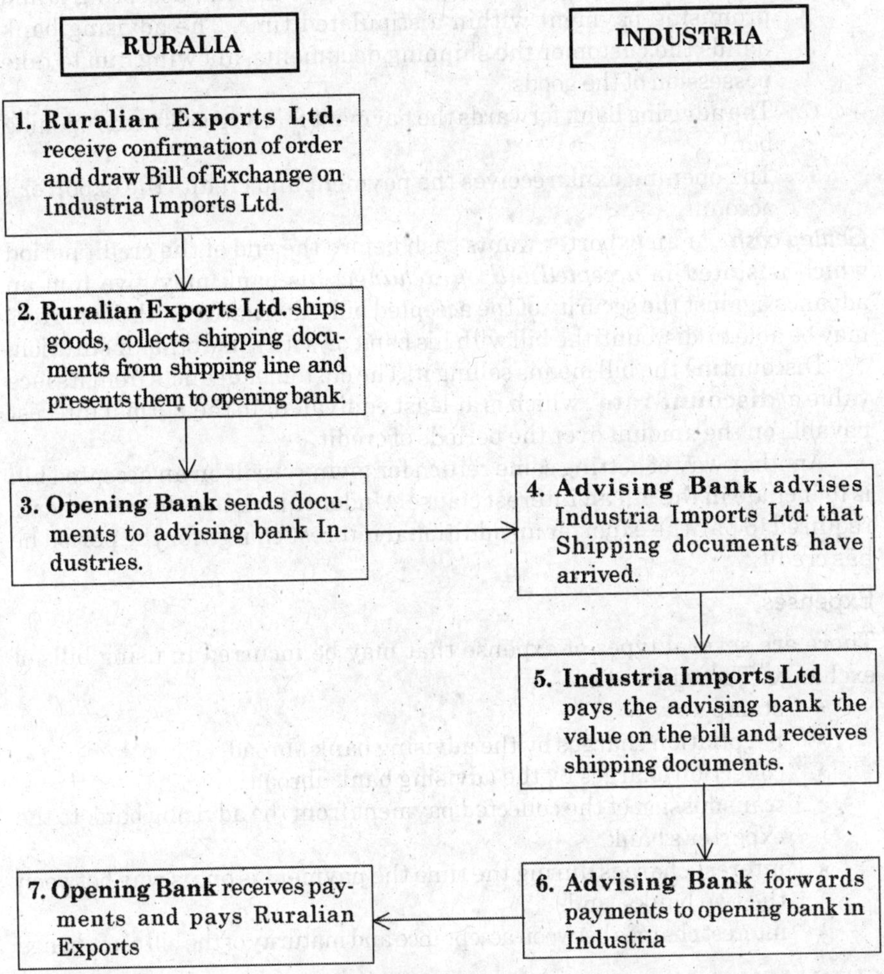

EXERCISE

The various stages in the collection process should be written down inorder to go through its various stages, to find out if any errors are there.

The following summary gives the main stages in the documentary collection transaction:

1. The exporter and customer agree in the contract that payment shall be made using documentary collection. The exporter draws a bill of exchange on the customer.
2. The exporter ships his goods to the customer, collecting the shipping documents from the shipping line and presenting them to his bank.
3. The exporter's bank (opening bank) sends the documents and the bill to the customer's bank (advising bank).

4. The advising bank advises the customer that the shipping documents have arrived.
5. The customer pays for the goods or signs the bill, accepting it and promising payment within a stipulated time. The advising bank hands the customer the shipping documents, allowing him to take possession of the goods.
6. The advising bank forwards the payment for the goods to the opening bank.
7. The opening bank receives the payment and credits the exporter's account.

Getting cash If an exporter wants cash before the end of the credit period which is stated in *accepted bill of exchange*, his bank may give him an advance against the security of the accepted bill. Alternatively, the exporters may be able to 'discount' the bill with his bank or with some other institution.

Discounting the bill means selling it. The customer deducts from its face value a **'discount-rate',** which is at least equivalent to the normal interest payable on the amount over the periods of credit.

Another way of getting some return for giving credit on an accepted bill is to include in the bill an interest clause. Under this clause the customer is required to pay the exporter an additional interest charge for the period he has credit.

Expenses

There are several types of expense that may be incurred in using bills of exchange. These include:

★ stamp duty
★ negotiation charges by the advising bank abroad
★ collection charges by the advising bank abroad
★ transmission of the collected payment from the advising bank to the exporter's bank
★ interest charges during the time the payment is on its way between the two banks, and
★ interest charges between acceptance and maturity of the bill of exchange

SUMMARY

By using documentary collection, the exporter can ship the goods with some safety before receiving payment, because he retains title to them until they are paid for, or until the customer binds himself to pay. But as has seen, this safety is far from complete.

IMPORTANT CHECKS TO BE MADE BY AN EXPORTER ON RECEIPT OF AN L/C

Key Checks

1. Is the L/C of the type agreed to? In particular, do check if it is revocable or irrevocable, and also whether it is confirmed or unconfirmed.
2. Are the amount and unit price given in the L/C the same as in the sales contract?

3. Expiry date and place of presentation of documents? Is the expiry date ahead? Would one be able to meet the expiry date? Does it give any mention about the last shipping date? What is the place at which documents have to be presented and if the place is not in the exporters' own country, would he in that case be able to adhere to the expiry date?
4. Terms of Delivery? Any deviations from the INCOTERMS?
5. Documents called for? Would one be able to procure each and every document indicated in the L/C? What about the number of copies of each document?
6. Spellings in the L/C. Do check carefully and if any one of them needs corrections, do approach the importer to get it suitably amended.
7. Are there obvious inconsistencies in the L/C?
8. Where and when is the credit available and payable?
9. Is there any indication in the L/C that it is subject to terms and conditions as per ICC Document dealing with Uniform Customs and Practice For Documentary Credits ICC Public 500, 1993?
10. Does the L/C require the furnishing of any declarations and if so their nature and format?
11. Check the name and address as given in the L/C? Also do check the name and address of importing unit.
12. In the case of an L/C confirmed by a foreign bank, one has to consider whether such a bank does have a measure of reliability and strength? What about conditions in the country of the confirming bank?
13. If some documents require attestation and authentication, one has to consider carefully whether he will be able to get all the required work done within the time frame indicated by the expiry date.
14. Does the L/C require the exporter to furnish some documents which, for some reason or the other, cannot be obtained?
15. Does the L/C prohibit part shipment? If part shipment is permitted, what is the schedule?
16. What is the suggestion in the L/C regarding the nature of draft? Had the exporter agreed to it earlier?
17. Does the description of goods in the invoice tally in all respects with that indicated in the L/C?
18. Any particular conditions indicated in the L/C regarding shipping, e.g. place and date of shipment, port of destination, whether B/L is to be issued to order of the importer or is to be made out in importer's name, etc.
19. Is the correct type of shipping document called for? CTD or B/L?
20. Does the L/C permit loading of merchandise on deck or for that matter its loading on a sailing ship?
21. Does the L/C call for Insurance certificate or Insurance Policy?
22. Does the L/C mention in specific terms, risks that have to be covered by insurance company?
23. Does the L/C call for any import or export licences?
24. Does the L/C insist upon some kind of specific standards in regard to rules of origin?
25. Is any special type of certificate of origin called for?

26. If documents require 'legislation' one has to ascertain whether consulate of the importing country is indeed fully equipped to undertake the necessary attestation? What are the terms and conditions of legalisation? Can the legalisation be effected in time?
27. Does the L/C mention in specific terms, names of agencies that alone can give quality certification?
28. What kind of transport document does the L/C ask a person to procure-precise position in regard to mode of transport on one hand and also whether the document has to be in the nature of 'on-board' or 'accepted for carriage' or 'taking charge' document on the other?
29. Does the L/C require one to arrange for insurance?
30. Are the risks to be covered, properly defined in the L/C?

Common Discrepancies and Lapses Leading to Rejection

1. Exporter fails to present the document before the expiry date.
2. L/C had mentioned both expiry date of L/C and last shipping date, but the exporter fails to meet either both of them or any one of them.
3. L/C had prescribed both expiry date and last shipping date. Exporter got the expiry date extended, but did not ask for extension of the shipping date and failed to stick to the original shipping date.
4. Between the date of actual shipment and the presentation of documents to bank, more than 21 days have elapsed

   or

   In the L/C it was specifically stated that the exporter should present the documents to the bank so many days (not exceeding 21 days) after the shipment date, but the party failed to comply with this requirement.
5. Shipping document is not 'clean' but 'claused'.
6. Shipping document is not of a type prescribed in the L/C.
7. Shipping document does not give adequate evidence of its being an 'on-board' document whereas the L/C had prescribed 'on-board'.
8. Shipping document shows that goods have been shipped on deck, without any authority for such a course having been specifically mentioned in the L/C.
9. A charter party B/L is furnished to the bank without specific authorisation.
10. Commercial invoice presented to the bank does not on its face appear to be issued by the exporter and or it is not made out in the name of the importer.
11. The currency and the amount stated in the invoice do not correspond to those given in the L/C.
12. Description of goods as given in the invoice is not the same as given in the L/C.
13. Invoice lists some goods or costs which are not stipulated in the L/C.
14. Insurance document does not appear, to have been issued and signed by an insurance company or an underwriter or an agent of any one of them.
15. Insurance Document has been issued in more than one original, but all the originals are not presented to bank.
16. Insurance cover has been issued by brokers.
17. Insurance document bears a date of insurance later than the 'date of loading on board' or 'date of dispatch' or 'date of taking in charge'.
18. Insurance cover is not in specified currency.

19. The Insurance amount mentioned in the relevant document is not in conformity with the stipulation that it should be plus 10% of the amount mentioned in L/C or amount mentioned in Invoice.
20. Packing list does not contain necessary details such as, number of units in each package, container breakdown, etc.
21. Marks given in the packing list are not consistent with those on the B/L.
22. The certificate of origin has not been attested/authenticated by the required organisation.
23. Results of analysis as given in the certificate of analysis do not agree with those given in L/C or with data in other accompanying documents.
24. The data given in various documents do not appear to be consistent with each other.
25. Some of the documents are not complete.
26. Some documents presented to the bank are not in prescribed form or in prescribed number.
27. Shipment is short and thus invoice amount and L/C amount do not tally and partial drawings have not been agreed to.
28. Bill of Exchange has been drawn on a wrong party.
29. Bill of Exchange is payable on an indeterminate date.
30. L/C had asked for some important declaration, e.g. a declaration to this effect that shipment advice has already been sent to importer and no document giving that declaration is presented to the bank.

Presentation of Documents to Bank

- ★ Present all the documents enumerated in the L/C, in exactly the same number as indicated in the L/C.
- ★ Without delay
- ★ Within expiry date
- ★ Within specified period after shipment
- ★ Documents should be complete, in conformity with the terms of L/C and consistent with each other.
- ★ There should be no discrepancies in the documents.

// CHAPTER 20 //

EXPORT COSTING AND PRICING

Price is one of the key variables in the export marketing mix – the mix that aims to provide the right product, in the right place, at the right time and at the right price. What is the "right" export price? This is an easy question to ask but a difficult one to answer because so many factors enter into the establishment of an export price. Some of these factors are controllable by the export company, but others are not. Export pricing is an art – it is not simply reducible to a set of rules or cost calculations. Flexibility is essential in any export pricing operation.

Many firms that are just starting to export assume that setting an export price for their products merely involves calculating production and marketing costs, and then addition on an amount of profits. Export pricing is much more complex than this. It includes of course, an evaluation of a firm's costs of producing the product and bringing it to the market, but it also entails an assessment of the marketing situation for the product. The market, and the company's objectives in that market, should be the starting point for pricing decisions. Cost information should be used only to determine whether that market can be satisfied at a profit. This duel assessment – looking at the market as well as the costs, is central to successful export pricing.

The dual assessment of market and costs does not make it any easier to establish the "right" price, which is the basis for laying down the appropriate approach to export pricing.

In export marketing the exporter often has to accept a price for his product, that is lower than the price he can get in the home market. This is why business people are often reluctant to go into exporting. They overlook the fact that exporting can be profitable, even if prices sometimes do have to be lower.

To understand how to market at a lower price and still make a profit, one must examine the whole question of costing and pricing.

A decision on what price to set for your product(s) will have to be taken:

★ The costs
★ The market
★ The intended profit margin

What are the Costs

First we have to define the **cost**.

A cost is the amount of expenditure incurred on, or attributable to a specified thing or activity.

The cost of production and the marketing and delivery costs can be major cost items. There are also overhead costs.

Overhead costs, also called indirect costs, are costs that cannot be directly attributed to a product. This is seen in the simplified example given below.

A factory has three different products (A, B, and C) and three workers. Each worker works on one product only. One foreman supervises them. In this case, the direct cost for each product is clear, the salary being paid to a worker working on one specific product. But what about the foreman's salary? He supervises all the workers and hence covers all products. As his costs are not directly attributable to one product only, they are overhead costs. One appropriate way of taking into account these costs would be to charge each product with a third of the foreman's salary, as he spends almost the same amount of time on each product.

How Much will it Cost to Produce

The cost of production varies with the quantity produced. For example, 5000 pairs of shoes cost more to produce than 500 pairs. However, the cost per pair is less. In other words, the unit cost decreases as the quantity increases. There are fixed costs to be paid, no matter what quantity is produced. Examples are the factory rent, the cost of machinery, the wages of the factory manager. The more units produced, the more these fixed costs can be spread, reducing the fixed cost per unit.

On top of these fixed costs are the variable costs, which rise as the quantity produced rises. Examples are the cost of materials, direct labour, fuel and power.

Marketing and Delivery Costs

Production costs are sometimes regarded as the only important items when costing and pricing a product. However, marketing, and delivery costs can be just as significant, particularly in export marketing. For example, the exporter has to take into account the costs of holding stocks (capital and physical storage costs), packing and transport, commissions, advertising, sales trips, etc.

Marketing and delivery costs can also be divided into fixed and variable costs. For example, a salesman's salary is a fixed cost, while his commission is a variable cost. It is not always easy to distinguish the fixed and variable costs of marketing and delivery, but it is important to try to differentiate them when pricing the product.

Break-even Price

When the supplier has determined the total cost for producing and marketing any given quantity of product, he should divide this total cost by the number of units. This unit cost is his break-even price. If he markets above this price he makes a profit. If he sells less than this price, he incurs a loss.

The darkest section of the graph given below represents the fixed costs; one can see that these do not vary with the quantity of goods produced.

They are the same, regardless of whether none or 50 units of output are produced. The lighter triangle immediately above represents the variable costs. Variable costs added to the fixed costs make up the total cost.

The line representing the total costs shows the break-even prices at any given level of production. It can be seen that the unit cost goes down as the number of items produced goes up. For example, at a level of production of 100 units, the unit cost is $2.00; at a level of production of 200 units, the unit cost is only $1.50.

Remember that the unit cost of production is also the break-even price. Therefore, by increasing the number of units produced one can increase the profit on every unit sold, assuming that the same price is maintained. Thus, as exporting will call for increased total production, it can lower the unit costs.

Maximising the Profit

The exporter will have to pay fixed costs regardless of the quantity he produces. These costs include the factory rent, the cost of basic machinery, the wages of the factory manager, and the costs of the sales office.

On top of these fixed costs are the variable costs, which rise as the quantity produced increases. Examples are the cost of materials and direct labour, the cost of oil and electricity to run the machines, transport, the agent's commission and so on.

Getting the highest price for the product or marketing the maximum number of units are not necessarily the ways to earn the largest profit. The trouble with trying to increase the profit by raising the price is that, higher prices usually mean fewer sales. On the other hand, marketing more units by lowering the price could simply mean lower revenue from sales. The successful marketer is one who sets his or her price at the level, revenue from sales exceeds total costs by the largest margin. Finding this point is what pricing policy is all about.

Given below is an exercise on maximising profits:

Exercise 1

(on maximising profits)

Study the figure and the table below. Then compete the missing figures in the table for expected sales revenue, total costs and profit. Refer to the graph and see which of the different price options can be choosen.

	Option A	Option B	Option C
Unit price	($) 3.0	($) 2.50	($) 2.0
Expected number of units sold	100	200	250
Expected sales revenue	($)____	($)____	($)____
Total costs	($)____	($)____	($)____
Profit	($)____	($)____	($)____

Will the Customer Pay the Price

The easiest way to set prices for the export products is to start at the "Ex-works" price level, add a certain percentage for profit and offer it on "FOB" basis* to an importer abroad. This method, called the cost-plus method, is a common practice. This may be the easiest method, but is far from the best.

Reason 1: The price into the target market may be too low, enabling the importer to make a huge profit without sharing it with the exporter.

Reason 2: The price may be too high, which prevents the exporter from obtaining a market share since nobody wants to buy his product.

The cost-plus method is not suited as an instrument for export marketing, because one cannot influence the customer to buy the product and one depends too much upon others (e.g. the importer). It is better to find out ourselves what the customer is willing to pay for the product. It is an important **buying motive** as it represents the sacrifices (paying money) he/she is willing to make in order to obtain satisfaction (the function of the product).

All customers constantly make buying decisions, comparing the sacrifice with the expected satisfaction. He/she compares prices of competitive products (e.g. different kinds of bread), but also their different qualities (which product brand gives best value). Thirdly, the customer compares products which can substitute each (e.g. rice and bread). The main criterion used is **price**.

SETTING PRICE

Exporters in developing countries will usually be **price-followers**, not price-setters. Their products will rarely be so unique in the target markets, that they can actually dictate the price level in that market.

For **price-followers** the pricing decisions, to be taken by management are:

1. Establish the current market pricing for comparative and/or substitutive products in the target market.
2. Establish all the elements of the market price, like VAT, margins for the trade and the importers, import duties, freight and insurance costs, etc.
3. Make top-down calculation, deducting all the elements of the expected market price of the products(s) in order to arrive at the price "Ex-works" or "Ex-factory/Warehouse."
4. See if this price can be met.
5. If not, recalculate the costs price, by finding ways to decrease costs in the own factory or organisation. Or decrease the marketing budget, which also burdens the export-market price.
6. Estimate total sales over a three-year period, add total planned expenses, including those of the export department, travelling and canvassing efforts.

* FOB stands for Free on Board, which implies that the importer will pay for transport, insurance, import duties, etc. This is a Term of Delivery, universally accepted in the Incoterms 1990.

7. Make a bottom-up calculation per product item, dividing the supporting budgets over the total number of items to be sold.
8. Set the final market prices.
9. Test the price (through market research).

These are the nine steps for selling the final price in the market. It will prove a lengthy and difficult process, but it is an essential one. Here are two examples:

1. A "top-down" calculation, enabling one to establish if he can meet competitors' market prices at cost-price level.
2. A "bottom-up" calculation to help one in setting the final price in the target market.

Example 1 Top-Down Calculation

Calculation			
Consumer price:	1180		
VAT*:	180	+	18%**
Market price minus VAT:	1000		
Margin retailer:	250	+	25%**
Price to retailer:	750		
Margin wholesaler:	90	+	12%**
Price to wholesaler:	600		
Margin importer:	33	+	5%**
Landed-cost Price:	627		
Import duties:	188	+	30%**
Other costs (storage, banking):	15	**	
CIF (port of destination):	424		
Transportation costs:	120	**	
Insurance costs:	4	**	
FOB (port shipment):	300		
Transportation costs factory to port:	5	**	
Export price ex-works (EXW):	295		
Factory cost price:	255	**	
Export profit (per unit):	40		

* Note that VAT is calculated as a percentage of the price without VAT. Trade margins are usually calculated as percentage of the trade selling prices (see example 2). The trade margin for some sectors are calculated as a percentage of trade buying prices.

** assumptions.

This 'multiplier' is a calculation aid, cutting short lengthy calculations when price alternatives are to be considered. When using the multiplier, keep in mind that it may cause slight calculation deviations.

Example 2 Bottom-up Calculation

1. Estimate total sales in the plan year in number of units.
2. Set factory cost price* per unit and multiply with total number of units to be sold.

* Do not forget the costs of currency and credit and agent's commission.

3. Gives total cost price for planned sales volume.
4. Add: targeted profit (or feasible profit indicated by top-down calculation); also
   add: total budget for export marketing support, or export promotion.
5. Add: total transportation costs, factory to port of shipment (plus possible costs in port).
6. Gives total (planned) turnover at FOB level.
7. Add: total transportation costs to port of destination, also add insurance costs.
8. Gives total turnover at CIF destination level.
9. Add: import duties and handling costs in port of destination.
10. Gives total (planned) value of sales at LCP level (Landed Cost Price). From here on, the calculations are done on unit basis, i.e. broken down into smaller sales units: boxes for the distributive trade, or items for the consumer price setting.
11. Calculate sales price of the importer (assume his margin as 5% of his sales price).
12. Calculate sales price of wholesaler (assume his margin as 12% of his sales price).
13. Calculate net sales-price (excl. VAT) of the retailer (assume VAT is 25%).
14. Calculate consumer price, or retail price including VAT (assume VAT is 18%) unit.
15. Compare with general market pricing. Adjust (sales target, profit target or promotion budget) if necessary.

Calculation

Steps	Results (units)	Methods
1.	1000	
2.	255	× (unit currency)
3.	255,000	= turnover (T/O)
4.	40,000	16% of T/O
	55,000	estimate
5.	5,000	1,000 × 5
6.	3,55,000	added-up
7.	1,24,000	1,000 × 124
8.	479,000	added-up
9.	143,700	assumption : 30% of CIF
	8,000	assumed handling charges
10.	6,30,700	added-up
	6,307	Box assumed: 10 units/box
11.	6,639	(100:95) × 6,307
12.	7,544	(100:88) × 6,639
13.	10,059	(100:75) × 7,544
		Package assumed: 10 units/box
14.	1,187	(1,18 × 10,059):10
15. If market price = 1,100, then deduct (255:1,187) × 255 = 54.78 from factory (Cost price, bringing it to 200)		

The feasibility calculations are also executed according to the top-down/bottom-up method. In this case, the period is usually longer (up to 3 years), since the exporter will have to invest in a market position.

The calculations for industrial goods are less complicated, since there are fewer intermediate levels between supplier and customer. Also, VAT can be left out.

The Permanent Pressure on the Cost Price

Competition is ever-increasing in industrialised markets. In order to survive, the suppliers to such markets should dedicate a lot of attention to decreasing costs and price. In the single market, prices are expected to show an overall decrease of 6% before the change of the millennium.

The level of the cost price is very important to the market price. Addition of $1 to the cost price; means that the market price (in the calculation example) will increase by $4. The multiplying factor can be established via the "top-down calculation."

Therefore, one should always try to keep the cost price as low as possible. Managements should continuously look for ways to decrease their costs. Just claiming low labour costs, is usually not sufficient for price-matching. In industrialised countries, labour has largely been replaced by automation, so in that respect their production costs are as low as in the developing countries.

METHODS FOR MARKET PRICING

a. The exporters primary aim in the target market is to offer his products at a price level which does not exceed that of his competitors. The importer will be the first one to tell him that.
   Actually, one should try to price slightly lower, particularly when entering the market. This is called **Penetration Pricing** trying to gain the customer's preference, because the price is irresistibly low compared to the product quality.
   The reverse policy is called **Skimming**, but that will not only be used when offering a unique product with obvious customer benefits – and unfortunately only few exporters can offer that.
b. An exporter will probably try to apply the Penetration Pricing method. Be careful: do not price it too low, as not to create suspicion in the minds of the prospective buyers.
   The Japanese car manufacturers successfully used Penetration Pricing when entering Western Markets in the early sixties. Now, their prices are virtually at their competitors' level. In another case, a Hong Kong watch manufacturer entered the market offering his Rolex-look-alike products at 150% of current prices. He failed. The consumers reasoned: That watch is priced so low, it cannot be good quality."
   Try to find a **balance between the quality and the price** of the product. In fact an exporter should try to price it at the "perceived value level." Market research will tell us how consumers perceive that level to be. A penetration price will probably lie somewhere between 5 and 20% below the current price.

c. Having bagged a certain foothold in the target market, the exporter may gradually want to increase his profit – by increasing the price. That is logical, as long as the customer accepts it. That goes for the trading partner too. He has a vital task in the price-setting policy. How does one know if the customer will accept that price increase? That depends upon the **price elasticity of the demand**.
Essentially, **price elasticity** describes how much the price can be changed before the customers begin to react: i.e. by buying less when the price is increased, by buying more if the price is decreased.
Convenience goods (like many packaged foodstuffs) do not meet much reaction when prices increase moderately. Consumers will buy anyway. Shopping goods (more expensive consumer items) receive a stronger reaction, because the buyers start comparing with other brands or substitutes to satisfy their needs. Industrial goods meet even fewer reactions, unless the buyers can choose from a multitude of suppliers.
The exporter can actually calculate the price elasticity of the demand by using the following formula:

$$\text{When } \frac{\%\text{ change in the quantity demanded}}{\%\text{ change in price}} > 1, \text{ then demand is elastic.}$$

Example In a split-run research (simultaneous survey on comparable target groups) it has been found out that, a price increase of 5% resulted in 10% less sales, while a decrease of 10% resulted in 20% higher sales. The quotient in both cases is 2, which implies that the products meet an elastic demand. If so, one must avoid drastic price increases, or use price decreases only when (temporary) turnover targets are set higher.

REACT TO CHANGES IN MARKET PRICING

Pricing is one of the strongest instruments in the marketing mix. It certainly is the best instrument to evoke swift market reaction. So one must constantly 'play' with this instrument, like an angler keeping a tight one to the fish.

There are many reasons which may induce the exporter to change his price, having gained market presence. Most of these reasons are usually external forces which make the market prices go up or down.

Market Prices Go Down

Reasons

★ Supply increases (any dumping?)
★ Effects of currency fluctuations
★ Price leader decreases price (= more competitive)
★ Distribution channel decreases price (policy)
★ Product range becomes old-fashioned
★ New competitors enter the market with penetration pricing

React by

★ Following decrease
★ Add new product

- ★ Sleeping status or withdrawal from the market
- ★ Change quality, contents
- ★ Increase % margins for the trade
- ★ Appeal to buyers via promotional campaign
- ★ Appeal to government (price control)

Market Prices Go Up

Reasons

- ★ General cost increased
- ★ Supply decreases
- ★ Effects of currency fluctuations
- ★ Price leader increases prices
- ★ Some supplier is 'skimming'

React by

- ★ Following increase
- ★ Same price, but with temporary decrease (discount)
- ★ Promoting ones' 'low price'
- ★ Increase supply
- ★ Appeal to consumeristic organisation
- ★ Appeal to Government

Whatever the (forced or voluntary) changes in the prices may be, always make sure that the customer and trade partner understand the reason for it. Those reasons should be made acceptable, and justifiable in their minds.

CURRENCY DECISIONS

The choice of currency in which the exporter wants to be paid eventually will prove more academic than realistic.

The advantages when invoicing and getting paid in ones' own currency.

- ★ you know what you get in terms of value for money.
- ★ you do not have to organise complicated and expensive currency transactions (usually with the bank).

The **disadvantages**, which could be remedied by invoicing in **European currency** are:

- ★ the buyer may refuse to pay in the exporters' currency or at least charge him with the costs of currency exchange;
- ★ the desired currency may not be available on the money markets in Europe;
- ★ during the transaction period the exporters' currency may lose value quicker than the (hard) European currencies. The buyer will profit from that more than him.
- ★ one will have to pay twice for currency exchange if/when materials and machines for production are about Europe.

On the whole, it may seem sensible to quote in European currency, particularly if the exports become substantial. As the "Europe" money will grow into the hardest and easiest exchange currency in the future, the exporting should profit from that instrument.

QUOTING A PRICE

In previous units the following have been examined:

★ The different models of transport forgetting the product to the export market.
★ The various factors that have to be taken into account when selecting transportation
★ The importance of the terms of delivery.

An exporter must have a thorough understanding of these things before he begins exporting, because when quoting a price for his product, he must take into account all the potential costs. There are many traps for the unwary exporter – and many 'hidden' costs.

Things can go wrong if account is not taken of transportation costs and terms of delivery are not taken into account.

ENQUIRIES INTO ORDERS

It is not good having the right product at the right price, if no one knows about it. And it is no use getting enquiries from prospective customers if the exporter does not manage to convert any of those enquiries into firm orders.

But changing enquiries into orders can be a long process with several very important stages. An exporter must know these stages well so that he can respond quickly and efficienty to any enquiries he receives.

His knowledge and ability may make all the difference between getting an order or not getting one. It may also make the difference between a satisfied and an unsatisfied customer. An unsatisfied customer is unlikely to approach him again.

MAKING A QUOTATION

When an enquiry is received, some exporters send back quotations on special forms. These forms may include acceptance slips which the customer has to fill in and return if he accepts the price and wishes to place an order.

This means that a quotation may be interpreted as a definite *offer to supply*.

It may be advisable for the exporter to stress on his quotation, or in a covering letter included with it, that the quotation is subject to materials being available or, to the production, freight and insurance rates remaining at current levels.

Very often a *pro forma invoice* is used as a form of quotation. This looks very much like a normal commercial invoice but it does not go through the normal book-keeping system until an order is forthcoming. Pro formas are often required by the customer's government when issuing import licenses or currency permits.

There may be delay if the customer has to submit the pro-forma invoice to a government department – another reason why an efficient exporter will usually indicate the length of time the quotation will remain firm. The customer might obtain an import license and then find the price has increased and therefore that the license value was not sufficient.

Export quotation/pro forma invoice	**Fisons Scientific Apparatus**
E1-Salam Trading and Contracting Establishment, Scientific Division Box 21140 Kuwait	Bishop Meadow Road, Lougbouough Leicestershire, LE11 ORG England telephone Loughborough 31166 telex 34110 telegram fisxience-Loughborough-Telex your ref. Exp/FACT/70148/REB our ref. date: 4th April, 1998

As per attached Schedule

Total F.O.B. UK Port	£ 5965.36
Less 12 ½% Quantity Discount	£ 745.67
	£ 5219.69

We regret we are unable to quote accurate freight charges at this stage.
We regret we are unable to quote for the items omitted.
*Net Price Quoted
With reference to Item 11, please see attached literature, these water stills are available from our distributor in Kuwait, Al-Shutani Chemical And Servicing Contracting Co., PO Box 61220 Kuwait.

Deliver : Available Shipment UK Port approx 8 weeks from receipt or order.
Terms: FOB UK Port
Period: Valid 2 months from above date
Package: Included
Payment: Irrevocable Letter of Credit

This quotation is subject to the for general condition of sale overleaf E & O.E. and is valid for 2 months.

FISONS SCIENTIFIC APPARATUS

Res Bennett (Mrs.)

There are three vital aspect of efficiency in handling enquiries, quotations and orders:

Speed A quick response to an enquiry will show the customer that the supplier is keen and efficient. But the customer has probably sent a similar enquiry to other companies as well and they maybe nearer to the customer. Speed is essential if one wants to get the order. If there will be some delay in sending the quotation, the supplier should immediately acknowledge the enquiry.

Clarity When the exporter sends a quotation, he should make sure it is made out in the manner requested by the customer. Query the details of the customer's needs that are not clearly stated in his order. Check whether there could be an import licence problem, and be quite clear about the packing that the customer wants. The exporter should also check that he can meet the delivery date required by the customer. If he is unable to do so, the customer should be informed immediately.

Keeping in contact If the exporter does not receive a reply to a quotation, he must contact the customer after a reasonable time to find out whether he is place an order or not.

Points to be Remembered

The following points should be made clear:

★ The enquiry to which it refers is not specified. The customer may, deliberately or otherwise, order more expensive goods which may have been described in a different enquiry from that referred to by the exporter.

★ There is no specification in the enquiry of material, sizes, colours, etc., of the shirts. Even if the original specification was known, this still leaves opportunity for misunderstanding, with possible loss for the exporter.

★ Maximum and minimum quantities are not specified. The customer might order an economically small quantity or a large quantity quite beyond the capacity of the supplier.

★ The packaging is not described. The customer might expect export packaging to be available without further cost and he may assume individual cartons or other refinements which are in fact not included.

★ No information is given as to the terms of delivery, so that the customer might expect the shirts to be delivered CIF his own port, for instance, when the price only cover ex-works or FOB.

★ There is no information of the term of payment required. The customer might expect open account or documentary sight draft when cash with order of letter of credit is expected.

★ The type of currency is not specified. The customer might pay in Ruralian dollars or others, which are less valuable than those intended by the exporter.

★ There is no indication as to how long it will take for the goods to be ready for delivery. The customer may have expected immediate dispatch when in fact it requires some months for the shirts to be made.

All the problems highlighted in the above points would lead to misunderstanding. They might even lead to law suits and considerable loss and expense.

A good quotation Using the above list as a'guide and reversing its comments, this comprehensive quotation which covers all the necessary information is made. But is not negative or restrictive in tone. In fact, because it is comprehensive it serves the interest of the customer, since he is unlikely to have further questions and can place an order knowing what he will receive and how. He can pay for it.

A Good Quotation

Dear Sirs

Many thanks for the enquiry of 4 March 1982, reference MH/CH. We have pleasure in quoting as follows:

Write 50/50 polyester/cotton mixture men's shirts as per sample, label no. 203 in assorted size between 35 and 44, individually packed in plastic bags and boxed in

> *100's, no less than 50 of each size, packed in export crates of 1000 shirts...*
> *US $ 5 per shirt.*
> *Ex-works*
> *Payment by confirmed irrevocable letter of credit opened in our favour, with the commercial bank of Ruralia, Industrial Area Branch.*
> *Quantity minimum 1000 shirts, maximum present capacity 10000 shirts per month.*
> *Delivery: with 3 months of notification of receipt of letter of credit.*
> *Validity: This quotation is firm for orders dispatched before 1 August 1982.*
> *We hope that this meets with your approval. Please let us know if your require any further information or samples.*
> *Yours faithfully*

A bad quotation Consider this example of a bad quotation and note wrong presentation.

> **A Bad Quotation**
>
> *Dear Sirs,*
> *Many thanks for your enquiry.*
> *The shirts you mentioned can be supplied for $5 each according to your specification.*
> *We look forward to receiving your order in due course.*
> *Yours faithfully*

Export Costing Sheet

The export costing sheet presented in the following figure will give an idea of the type of costs an enterprise owner must consider when making an export quotation:

> **Export Costing Sheet**
>
> Date: ______
>
> Quoted : ______
>
> Unit: ______
>
> Gross weight: ______ Cubic measurement: ______
>
> 1. a. Cost of unit ______
>   b. Cost of 1 freight ton ______
> 2. Profit: % and amount ______
> 3. Agent's and/or exporter's commission ______
> 4. Special labels, labelling, containers ______
> 5. Packing ______
> 6. Making ______
> 7. Strapping or bundling ______
> 8. Hauling to goods yard, wharf or other ______
> 9. Freight to wharf, route land courier ______
>   Freight to wharf per freight ton ______
> 10. Unloading charge: ______ per ______
> 11. Demurrage, cold storage
>   Charge per freight ton
>   Amount per freight ton

12. Terminal fees: Weight______ Measure ______
13. Long-load or heavy-load charge ______________
14. Other charges (list) ______________
15. Consular invoices ______________
16. Ocean freight: Weight______Measure______On deck__________
    Under deck____Ventilated____Rate per freight ton__________
    Currency________Amount:
17. Shipping agent's fee
18. Total in local currency
19. Marine insurance:
    a. Value/ton (item 18)________
    b. + 10% of value___________
    c. Amount to be insured______
    Type______Rate_____Premium in local currency______
20. Financing charge (for credit sales)
21. CIF in local currency (add up costs for items 18,19,20)
22. Convert to $ US or invoicing currency

Terms of Delivery

The terms of delivery that the exporter offers in his quotation may make all the difference between profit land loss. So being able to select the right terms is vital. When buyer and seller agree on terms of delivery, they are legally binding themselves together to these vital aspects of the transactions

- ★ which costs are paid by the buyer, which by the seller
- ★ which documents the exporter will obtain and at whose expense
- ★ when the title to the goods – and the responsibility for them – passes from the seller to the buyer
- ★ when and where the goods are delivered.

The transportation of goods is a complex procedure involving a great deal of documentation. While this may seem unnecessary at first, the paperwork is in fact vital to the efficiency of the whole procedure. The different stages in the transport of goods from the exporter's factory to the customer's warehouse abroad should be noted.

INCOTERMS

Terms of delivery such as 'ex-works' and 'free on board' have been developed over many years to fit particular circumstances. But because the terms could be interpreted in differently ways, misunderstandings were frequent.

In order to clear up the confusion that existed in international trade, the International Chamber of Commerce drew up a set of standard terms and definitions on 1 July, 1990. These are called **Incoterms 1990** and indicate the division of costs and administrative responsibility between the exporter and his customer.

Although internationally accepted, the terms are still sometimes interpreted differently in different countries. So care and clarification are necessary when using them. For example, a French customer may use the term CAF (cout, assurance, fret) instead of CIF, although both mean the same thing.

Given below in detail are the obvious Incoterms and what they mean.

Listing the Incoterms

The most recent version of the universal Incoterms 1990 are grouped in four categories. The first group (E) has only one trade term: EXW. The second F group indicates the obligation of the seller to hand over the goods to a carrier Free of risk and expense to the buyer. The third C group includes terms that indicate the seller's obligation to bear certain Costs after the critical point for the division of the risks has been reached, i.e. after main carriage. The fourth D group includes the terms which prescribe that the goods must have arrived at a certain destination.

Incoterms 1990		
Group E Departure	EXW	Ex-works
Group F Main Carriage unpaid	FCA	Free Carrier
	FAS	Free alongside Ship
	FOB	Free on board
Group C Main carriage paid	CFR	Cost and Freight
	CIF	Cost, Insurance, Freight
	CPT	Carriage Paid to
	CIP	Carriage and Insurance Paid to
Group D Arrival	DAF	Delivered at Frontier
	DES	Delivered Ex-ship
	DEQ	Delivered Ex-quay
	DDU	Delivered Duty Unpaid
	DDP	Delivered Duty Paid

(Note that when the Incoterms indicate a certain point or "...", the point of destination or origin must be mentioned.)

The Incoterms Divide Cost and Risks

The Incoterms of trade have been designed to clarify obligation of both parties, buyer and seller.

Principally, these are:

Seller must:	**Buyer must:**
★ provide the goods according to contract	★ pay the price agreed upon.

In order to finalise the transaction, both parties will have to perform certain tasks, like:

★ arrange for licences	★ arrange for licences
★ authorisation and formalities	★ authorisation and formalities
★ arrange for shipment	★ arrange for shipment
★ arrange for delivery	★ accept delivery
★ bear the risks in his activities	★ bear the risks involved in his contractual activities

As such, the actions and the risks and costs involved in their contractual obligation can be divided between the partners. The Incoterms 1990 give iron-clad descriptions of which risks and costs should be borne.

The 13 Incoterms (As Revised on 1 July 1990)

Definition		*International code*
Ex-works (...named place)	"Ex-works" means that the seller fulfills his obligation to deliver the goods which he has made available at his premises (i.e. works, factory, warehouse etc.) to the buyer. In particular, he is not buyer or for clearing the goods for export, unless otherwise agreed. The buyer bears all costs and risks involved in taking the goods from the seller's premises to the desired destination. This term thus represents the minimum obligation for the seller. This term should not be used when the buyer cannot carry out directly or indirectly the export formalities. In such circumstances, the FCA term should be used.	EXW
Free Carrier (...named place)	"Free Carrier" means that the seller fulfils his obligation to deliver, when he has handed over the goods, cleared for export, into the charge of the carrier named by the buyer at the named place or point. If no precise point is indicated by the buyer, the seller may choose within the place or range stipulated where the carrier shall take goods into his charge. When, according to commercial practice, the seller's assistance is required in making the contract with the carrier (such as in rail or air transport) the seller may act at the buyer's risk and expense. This term may be used for any mode of transport, including multimodal transport. "Carrier" means any person who, in contract of carriage, undertakes to perform or to perform or to procedure the performance of carriage by rail, road, sea, air, inland waterway or by a combination of such modes. If the buyer instructs the seller to deliver the cargo to a person, e.g. a freight forwarder who is not a "carrier," the seller is deemed to have fulfilled his obligation to deliver the goods when they are in the custody of that person.	FCA

	"Transport terminal" means a railway terminal, freight station, a container terminal or yard, a multi-purpose cargo terminal or any similar receiving point. "Container" includes any equipment used to unitise cargo, e.g. all types of containers and/or flats, whether ISO accepted or not, trailers, swap bodies, ro-ro equipment, igloos, and applies to all modes of transport.	
Free Along-Side Ship (... named Port of shipment)	"Free Alongside Ship" means that the seller fulfills his obligation to deliver when the goods have been placed alongside the vessel on the quay or in lighters at the named port of shipment. This means that the buyer has to bear all costs and risk of loss of or damage to the goods from that moment. The FAS term requires the buyer to clear the goods for export. It should not be used when the buyer cannot carry out directly or indirectly the export formalities. This term can only be used for sea or inland waterway transport.	FAS
Free on Board (... named Port of shipment)	"Free on Board" Means that the seller fulfils his obligation to deliver when the goods have passed over the ship's rail at the named port of shipment. This means that the buyer has to bear all costs and risks of loss of or damage to the goods from that point. The FOB term, requires the seller to clear the goods for export. This term can only be used for sea or inland waterway transport when the ship's rail serves no practical purpose, such as in the case of roll-on/roll-off or container traffic, the FCA term is more appropriate to use.	FOB
Cost and freight (... named port of destination)	"Cost and Freight" means that the seller must pay the costs and freight necessary to bring the goods to the named port of destination but the risk of loss of or damage to the goods, as well as any additional costs due to events occurring after the time the goods have been delivered on board the vessel is transferred from the	CFR

seller to the buyer when the goods pass the ship's rail in the port of shipment.

The CFR term requires the seller to clear the goods for export.

This term can only be used for sea and inland water-way transport. When the ship's rail serves no practical purpose, such as in the case of roll-on/roll-off or container traffic the CPT term is more appropriate to use.

Cost insurance and freight (... named place of destination) — CIF

"Cost, Insurance and Freight" means that the seller has the same obligation as under CFR obligation as under CFR but with the addition that he has to procure marine insurance against the buyer's risk of loss of or damage to the goods during the carriage. The seller contracts for insurance and pays the insurance premium.

The buyer should note that under the CIF term the seller is only required to obtain insurance on minimum coverage.

The term can only be used for sea and inland waterway transport.

When the ship's rail serves no practical purposes such as in the case of roll-on/roll-off or container traffic, the CIP term is more appropriate to use.

Carriage paid to (... named place of destination) — CPT

"Carriage paid to..." means that the seller pays the freight for the carriage of the goods to the named destination. The risk of loss of or of damage to the goods, as well as any additional costs delivered to the carrier, is transferred from the seller to the buyer when been delivered into the custody of the carrier.

"Carrier" means any person who, in a contract of carriage, undertakes to perform or to procure the performance of carriage, by rail, road, sea, air, inland waterway or by a combination of such modes.

If subsequent carriers are used for the carriage to the agreed destination, the risk passes when the goods have been delivered to the first carrier.

	The CPT term requires the seller to clear the goods for export.	
Carriage and insurance paid (... named place of destination)	This term may be used for any mode of transport including multimodal transport. "Carriage and insurance paid to.." means that the seller has the same obligation as under CPT but with the addition that the seller has to procure cargo insurance against buyer's risk of loss of or damage to the goods during the carriage. The seller contracts for insurance and pays the insurance premium The buyer should note that under the CIP term the seller is only required to obtain insurance on minimum coverage. The CIP term requires the seller to clear the goods of export. This term may be used for any mode of transport including multimodal transport.	CIP
Delivered at frontier (...named place)	"Delivered at Frontier" means that the seller fulfills his obligation to deliver when the goods have been made available, cleared for export, at the named point and place at the frontier, but before the customs border of the adjoining country. The term "frontier" may be used for any frontier including that of the country of export. Therefore, it is of vital importance that the frontier in question be defined precisely by always naming the point and place in the term. The term is primarily intended to be used when the goods are to be carried by rail or road, but it may be used for any mode of transport.	DAF
Delivered Ex-ship (... named port of destination)	"Delivered Ex-ship means that the seller fulfils his obligation to deliver when the goods have been made available to the buyer on board the ship unclear for import at the named port of destination.The seller has to bear all the costs and risk involved in bringing the goods to the named port of destination. This term can only be used for sea or inland waterway transport.	DES
Delivered Ex-quay (duty paid) (... Named port of destination)	"Delivered Ex-quay (duty paid)" means that the seller fulfills his obligation to deliver when he has made goods available to the buyer on the quay (wharf) at the named port of	DEQ

destination, cleared for importation. The seller has to bear all the risk and costs including duties, taxes and other charges of delivering the goods thereto.

This term should not be used if the seller is unable directly or indirectly to obtain the import licence. If the parties wish the buyer to clear the goods for importation and pay the duty the words "duty unpaid" should be used instead of "duty paid".

If the parties wish to exclude from the seller's obligations some of the costs payable upon importation of the goods (such as value added tax (VAT), this should be made clear by adding words to this effect: "Delivered ex-quay, VAT unpaid (... named port of destination)".

This term can only used for sea or inland water way transport.

Delivered Duty Unpaid (...Named Place of Destination

DDU

"Delivered duty unpaid" means that the seller fulfills his obligation to deliver when the goods have been made available at the named place in the country of importation. The seller has to bear the costs and risks involved in bringing the goods thereto (excluding duties, taxes and other official charges payable upon importation as well as the costs and risks of carrying out customs formalities). The buyer has to pay any additional costs and to bear any risks caused by his failure to clear the goods for import in time.

If the parties wish the seller to carry out customs formalities and bear the costs and risks resulting therefrom, this has to be made clear by adding words to this effect.

If the parties wish to include in the seller's obligations some of the costs payable upon importation of the goods (such as value added tax (VAT), this should be made clear by adding words to this effect: "Delivered duty unpaid, VAT paid, (... named place of destination.)"

This term may be used irrespective of the mode of transport.

Delivered Duty paid (... Named place of destination)	"Delivered duty paid" means that the seller fufills his obligation to deliver when the goods have been made available at the named place in the country of importation. The seller has to bear the risks and costs, including duties, taxes and other charges of delivering the goods thereto, cleared for importation. Whilst the EXW term represents the minimum obligation for the seller, DDP represents the maximum obligation. This term should not be used if the seller is unable directly or indirectly to obtain the import licence. If the parties wish the buyer to clear the goods for importation and to pay the duty, the term DDU should be used. If the parties wish to exclude from the seller's obligations some of the costs payable upon importation of the goods (such as the value added tax (VAT), this should be made clear by adding words to this effect: "Delivered duty paid, VAT unpaid (...named place of destination)". This term may be used irrespective of the mode of transport.	DDP

// CHAPTER 21 //

PROCESSING AN EXPORT ORDER

Export orders must conform to the terms of sent contract which is sent to the foreign buyer. Before its confirmation, it must be scrutinised with regard to the products and their specifications, terms of payment, price, delivery schedule, etc.

The immediate task of the exporter is to acknowledge the export order which is different from its acceptance. Then he should proceed to examine the export order carefully with respect to the item, specification, preshipment inspection, payment conditions, special packaging, labelling and marking requirements, shipment and delivery date, marine insurance, documentation, etc. If the exporter is satisfied on these aspects, a formal confirmation of the export order should be sent to the buyer and the exporter should proceed to enter into a formal contract with the overseas buyer. The various aspects relating to processing of an export order are discussed as under:

Nature

Export order is a document, communicating the decision of foreign buyer to purchase items from the exporter. It would clearly indicate the exporter's pro forma invoice/quotation number and its date, including item, quantity, price, delivery date, shipping marks, insurance, payment terms, documents required, etc. Before acceptance, the export order should he scrutinised in all aspects.

Acknowledgement

The exporter should write a simple letter to the overseas buyer thanking him for the export order and stating that the confirmation of the same would be sent soon. It may be mentioned here that acknowledgement is different from confirmation. Details of this are given in the chapters on "Export Business Correspondence", "Internet", etc.

Scrutiny

The export purchase order should be examined carefully and its contents scrutinised, in terms of the pro forma invoice/contract sent to the foreign buyer, on the following aspects.

(i) The order has been received for the product for which quotation/offer was sent and the exporter is still in a position to supply the product.

(ii) Size and specifications should be same as per offer/quotation. Even slightest variation could create problems for the purchaser and the supplier at a later stage.

(iii) Pre-shipment inspection should be either by exporter himself or an agency which is easily available. If the buyer desires the inspection to be done by an agent/agency of his choice, financial and physical aspects of the inspection should be examined and communicated to the buyer. If compulsory pre-shipment inspection by an Indian Export Inspection Agency is required, the buyer should be informed about the applicable scheme. In fact this should be done at the stage of sending an offer/quotation.

(iv) Payment conditions are same as stipulated. An irrevocable Letter of Credit (L/C) should be opened, where required.

(v) Special packaging, labelling and marking requirements, if any, should be noted for compliance. Particular attention should be paid to the individual packaging of consumer goods required for direct sale to the consumers. In such a case, labels, price tags, poly pack/skin packing, etc., would be required and their supply should be assured.

(vi) Shipment and delivery date is in conformity with the exporters production plans and whether:
  (a) Part shipment is allowed
  (b) Transhipment is permissible or not
  (c) Port of shipment/destination is same or changed

(vii) Documents, particularly those which are required with the Bill of Exchange are:
  (a) Commercial invoice as usual or any specific notation if required thereon.
  (b) Certification by an authority on the commercial invoice. For instance, it may require certification by Embassy-Consulate of the foreign country.
  (c) Bill of Lading 'straight' or 'to order', 'shipped' or 'received for shipment', direct or 'through,' etc.
  (d) Certificate of Origin whether the usual one issued by a Trade Association or Chamber of Commerce or special ones like that required for availing of GSP concessions or other preferences. Also whether necessary certification on commercial invoice would suffice or a separate Certification of Origin is required.
  (e) Packing list
  (f) Insurance Policy or Certificate.

Confirmation

If the exporter is satisfied on various aspects referred above, a formal confirmation of the exporter should be sent to the buyer.

Clarification

If the exporter is not completely satisfied with the terms of the export order, clarification should be sought from the buyer before its confirmation.

The clarification could be in terms of quantity, delivery schedule, terms of payment, etc. The delivery period should be specific and not a value like "immediate delivery" or "as soon as possible". Similarly, the payment should be made in the country of the exporter if a foreign bank is involved.

RESERVATION OF SHIPPING SPACE

Reservation

If the exporter has accepted/confirmed the export order, his immediate task is to get shipping space reserved in accordance with the delivery schedule set out therein. Reservation of shipping space commences generally 6 to 8 weeks before the ship's arrival at port. Information on shipping services/sailings can be obtained from the Clearing and Forwarding Agents.

In case the goods are exported by Air, there need not be a reservation of space as it is generally at short notice. However, the exporter must confirm this fact from his Clearing and Forwarding Agent.

Clearing and Forwarding Agent

The exporter must appoint an agent to help him in the shipment/air freighting of goods. The clearing and Forwarding Agent should be a firm of repute experienced in handling export/import cargo. If the goods are to be exported by sea, the Clearing and Forwarding Agent should have branches in the major ports like Bombay, Calcutta, Chennai and Cochin.

DELIVERY NOTE/PURCHASE ORDER

Simultaneously with the confirmation of the export order, a delivery note may be issued to the production department or the factory in case the exporter has his own manufacturing facility. When the goods are to be procured from other manufacturers/suppliers, a purchase order should be issued by the suppliers.

Contents

The Delivery Note/Purchase Order must contain the following details:–

(i) Details of the product in terms of –
   (a) sizes, specifications, standards, etc.
   (b) quantity required.

(ii) Delivery schedule. The delivery schedule to be indicated to the Production Dept./factory or the supplier must be much before the date on which goods are to be shipped, depending upon the time which is spent on transporting the goods from the factory to the port of shipment.

(iii) Any special requirement with regard to the components including raw materials to be used in the product.

(iv) Packaging/packing stipulations.

(v) Labelling requirements.

Forward Exchange Contracts, Export Licence/Quota, Importer-Exporter Code (IEC) Number, Sales Tax Registration, etc.

Soon after the receipt of export order, the exporters may obtain the Forward Exchange Contract and apply for Export Licence, if necessary. He should also obtain an Importer's-Exporter's Code Number from the Regional Licensing Authority, in case the same has not been obtained earlier. Also apply for export licence/quota allocation, etc., wherever necessary. The steps required to be initiated after the receipt of export order are explained below:

Forward Exchange Contract

The exporter should also obtain a Forward Exchange Contract from the banks to cover the risks involved as a result of fluctuation in exchange rate. For obtaining this contract, the exporter should approach his bank along with a (i) application on plain paper for obtaining the Forward Exchange Contract and (ii) L/C and/or the Confirmed Export Order (in original).

The application for the Forward Exchange Contract should clearly indicate the definite period (not the exact date but period say between such date to such date) in which the export documents would be submitted to the bank. An important condition is that the L/C covering the particular export contract should not be restricted to any bank(s). It must be rather restricted to the exporter(s) Bank. In case of confirmed export order, the exporters should ask their overseas customers (importers) to open the L/Cs on their banks.

Export Licences/Quota

In case the product to be exported is subject to the Export Trade Control, the exporter should apply for an Export Licence to the concerned Licensing Authority.

Central Excise Declaration

File a declaration with the concerned Central Excise Authority, in case the export goods are subject to Excise Duty and obtain a declarant's Code Number, in case the exporter has no Central Excise Registration.

Importer-Exporter Code No. (IEC)

Also obtain the Importer-Exporter Code No. from the Regional Licensing Authority concerned.

Sales Tax Registration

Get registered with the Sales Tax Department and become a Registered Dealer, for obtaining goods without payment of Sales Tax from other manufacturers/ merchants.

THE INTERNATIONAL SALES CONTRACT – CENTRAL TO TRADE TRANSACTIONS

> A contract is the basis for every foreign trade transaction. The main features of such contracts and some new developments relating to them.

The contract to buy and sell goods is the starting point of international trade. Around the sales contract revolves a series of connected but distinct relationships, including the transport arrangements, cargo insurance, Customs formalities and payment procedures. Although the contract is central to an international trade transaction, the rules and practice concerning such contracts may vary considerably from one export situation to another, depending not only on the legal system involved but also the type of agreement concluded between the trading partners. Some of these differences, as well as new developments at the international level to harmonise rules on International Trade Contracts, are discussed in the following sections.

Offer and Acceptance

An international sales contract comes into being when one party – the exporter – makes an offer and the other – the importer – accepts it. The offer and the acceptance have to match, for the agreement to be formalised.

The principle of offer and acceptance is simple, but in practice it may be more complex. Suppose for instance, the exporter sends out his quotation on a standard form incorporating his general conditions. The importer then possibly accepts the offer, but sends his reply on a form referring to his own standard purchasing conditions. The two sets of conditions – those of the exporter and those of the importer – probably differ on various points.

Under most legal systems it will be considered that no enforceable agreement has come into being in a case such as this. The condition "acceptance" in this example (the importer's reply on his own form) is merely a counter-offer that the other party may accept or refuse. But if the exporter reacts by sending the goods without mentioning the conditions, he has probably implicitly agreed to the importer's terms.

Form of the Contract

In general, Export Agreements do not have to follow any particular form, although the precise requirements vary from one country to another. In many countries a legally binding contract arises from an agreement between the exporters and the importers and can be manifested in many different ways – their agreement may be a formal document, a series of telexes, an exchange of messages between computers, a telephone conversation or simply an oral agreement during contact at a trade fair. In certain other countries however, for instance in the East European countries, contracts must normally be written documents.

Format and Contents of an Export Contract

What is indeed important is not so much the format as the contents of a contract spelling out terms and conditions on which the contract is based. In particular:

- ★ Specific terms and conditions pertaining to the product/products that are the subject matter of sale/purchase
- ★ General terms and conditions.

In the first group, quality and specifications of the product are to be included. These would naturally differ from product to product. What is essential is that in the contract, detailed and careful description is given about the characteristics, design and specifications of the product. As far as general conditions are concerned, the standardised position can be a good guide, but it is essential that both the exporter and importer do understand the implications of each of the standardised conditions and agree to them in the standardised form after duly considering pros and cons of each one of the conditions.

Some important general terms and conditions, which usually get incorporated into Export Contract/Orders – either explicitly or implicitly – and which would be desirable for the parties to deliberate upon with a view to arriving at agreed positions on each one of them are discussed below:

i. ***Formation or conclusion of a contract*** In the case of a written agreement, a contract would be deemed to have reached the formation/ conclusion stage when both the parties have affixed their signature on it. In the case of a 'construed contract', if one party has sent a telex, telephone or any other kind of message, saying that terms and conditions as referred to in such and such telexes are acceptable, then the contract would be deemed to have been formed. It is desirable that finally parties exchange reconfirmation messages, for this would avoid all kinds of ambiguities.

ii. ***Assignment*** In case the intention of any one of the parties is to assign one's own rights and obligations set out in the contract to some other party, the best course then would be to indicate such arrangement in the contract itself. Unless it is specifically done, there would be difficulties at a later stage.

iii. ***Pre-shipment inspection*** It is in the interest of both the parties in a contract, that arrangements for Preshipment Inspection of goods for quality, quantity and/or price are mutually agreed upon and incorporated into the contract. This would be helpful at various stages, in particular, in securing payment or making claims on carrier or insurance company.

Once the arrangements have been agreed upon and the Inspection Agency identified, it is the duty of the exporter, unless a contrary position has been mutually agreed upon by the parties, to inform the agency concerned some days in advance of the date of shipment to take up inspection work. The exporter has to provide all necessary facilities and cooperation to the Inspection Agency. The contract should clearly indicate as to which party is going to bear the cost of inspection – the exporter or importer.

iv. ***Product description and specifications*** It is the duty of the exporter to ensure that the product is in conformity with the standards and specifications agreed upon. If a sample has been approved by the importer, then the items supplied should match the sample.

v. ***Quantity*** The contract should indicate in specific terms. If the quantity of goods delivered by exporter is less than the quantity indicated in the contract, the importer then has the right to refuse to take the delivery. However, if the importer does accept short consignment, then he/she is bound to pay for the actual quantity delivered to him/her.

If the consignment is larger than the quantity indicated in the contract, the importer may accept only the quantity contracted and may refuse to accept the excess. However if the importer does accept the excess, then he/she is bound to pay for the excess.

vi. ***Quality***: The goods delivered by exporter should be in conformity with the contract.

Unless the contract specifically mentions that goods to be supplied may be second hand ones, all supplies have to be of new and of unused goods only.

If the quality of goods is at variance with the contracted quality, the importer can reject the goods and claim damages. Alternatively importer can negotiate with exporter that he would accept goods only if price is reduced by such and such margin.

In situation where exporter is to supply goods in instalments and if more than one instalment is of defective goods, importer has the right to repudiate the whole contract.

vii. ***Packing, marking and labelling*** An export Contract should indicate clearly requirements specially insisted upon by the importer in regard to packing, marking and labelling. All the items entail costs, which have to be borne by the exporter who would like to load them on to the quoted price and that is why the entire position in regard to special requirements should be clear from the very beginning.

The usual understanding in regard to 'reasonable' packing, in contrast to special stipulations set out by importer, is that the exporter shall provide such packing as is required to prevent damage or deterioration of goods during transit to their final destination and that it would be strong and protective enough to withstand, without limitation, rough handling during transit and exposure to vagaries of temperatures, salt and precipitation during transit and open storage.

All packages have to be clearly marked and labelled as required in the contract. In the case of marking, information that has to be indicated on each package should be in easily readable ink, giving the name of the consignee, contents of the package including name of the product, net and sometimes also goods weight, country of origin, etc.

viii. ***Incoterms, price and total value*** The contract should indicate clearly the price and total value. Price would of course, depend upon terms of delivery and for this purpose Incoterms are usually used.

ix. ***Taxes, duties and other charges*** Who would bear which tax depends very much on how the prices are quoted and herein Incoterms become relevant.

x. ***Delivery period*** It is important that contracts do clearly indicate stipulations with regard to the delivery period. There should be no vagueness on this issue. Expressions such as 'immediate', 'prompt', etc., should as far as possible be avoided to describe the delivery period, as they give rise to ambiguities.

In the case of payment of Letter of Credit (L/C), if the expiry period is expressed in terms of months and not precise dates, the expiry date is determined by taking into account the date on which the exporter received first notification of the L/C either from the issuing or advising bank.

In the case of late deliveries (not involving L/C mechanism of payment), the importer can insist upon payment to be made by exporter by way of liquidated damages, a sum equivalent to a certain percentage of the contract price for every week of delay.

However, acceptance or non-acceptance of late delivery is an option of which only the importer can take advantage. It is perfectly open to the importer not to accept late deliveries at all and exercise the option of rejecting the contract.

xi. ***Acceptance*** In transactions other than those involving payment by L/C, the importer would be deemed to have accepted goods only when he/she has had reasonable time and opportunity to examine them to determine whether they are in conformity with the contract.

xii. ***Transfer of risk*** Incoterms define the point at which risk passes on from the exporter to the importer. Unless otherwise agreed between the parties, the risk passes on to the exporter when the goods are handed over to the first carrier for transmission to the importer.

xiii. ***Mode of payment*** The contract should clearly indicate the mode of payment – whether it is L/C or Documentary Collection (D/C) or Document on Acceptance (D/A) – and other precise details, in particular terms, currency, amount etc. in each case.

xiv. ***Documents*** It is important that exporter supplies to importer all essential documents pertaining to a contract and its execution. Some important documents being:

- ★ Shipping Advice
- ★ All other essential negotiable and non-negotiable documents, in particular
- ★ Bill of Lading
- ★ Commercial invoice and its other variations
- ★ Packing list
- ★ Insurance documents
- ★ Certificate of Origin

These documents should be supplied expeditiously. In fact a sound percept is that documents must travel faster than goods.

xv. ***Guarantees and warranties*** This clause in the contract should clearly provide details of guarantees and warranties and the period over which they will be operative. This clause is usually on the following lines.

"The contractor warrants that everything to be furnished hereunder shall be free from all defects and faults in material, workmanship and manufacture and is consistent with the established and generally accepted standards for material of the type ordered and in full conformity with the specifications, drawing or samples, if any, shall, if operable operate properly. The warranty shall apply to inspection of payment for and acceptance of the goods, but shall expire except in respect of complaints notified to the contractor prior to such date, months after their delivery or months after their arrival at the ultimate destination, whichever shall be sooner."

xvi. ***Redress and liquidated damages*** The contract should provide for specific remedies with respect to different contractual defaults, in particular with regard to the quantum and manner of calculations of liquidated damages.

xvii. ***'Force Majeure' and frustration*** Sometimes performance of a contract becomes impossible because of occurrence of certain unforeseen and uncontrollable events – e.g. war, civil disturbance, natural calamity, economic upheavals, etc. Such situations are called "Act of God", "Frustrating Events", "Failure of presupposed Conditions" or "Force Majeure".

It is important that Export Contracts contain a clause providing for such eventualities, specifying clearly the *type of events* that would be covered by the term and if necessary the *manner of recognition* of such eventualities including, if necessary, *remedies and procedures*.

International Chambers of Commerce has prepared model contract clauses on "force majeure and hardship". If the intention of the parties of a contract is that ICC model clauses should be applicable to a given contract, then they should specifically mention this by using the following wording.

"The Force Majeure (Exemption, Clause of the International Chambers of Commerce (ICC Publication No. 421) is hereby incorporated in this contract.

ICC Publication mentioned above has enumerated the following impediments as the one in respect of which the "Force Majeure", clause will be applicable

a. war, whether declared or not, civil war, riots and revolutions, acts of piracy, acts of sabotage;
b. natural disasters such as violent storms, cyclones, earthquakes, tidal waves, floods, destruction by lightning;
c. explosions, fires, destruction of machines of factories and of any kind of installations;
d. boycotts, strikes and lockouts of all kinds, go-slows, occupation of factories and premises and work stoppages which occur in the enterprise of the party seeking relief;
e. acts of authority, whether lawful or unlawful, apart from acts for which the party seeking relief has assumed the risk by virtue of other provisions of the contract;
f. unless otherwise provided in the contract, impediment does not include lack of authorisations, of licence, of entry of residence permits, or of approvals necessary for the performance of the contract and to be issued by a Public Authority of any kind whatsoever in the country of the party seeking relief.

xviii. ***Third party claims and indemnities*** If an exporter is supplying some goods or items in which intellectual property rights in the nature of 'patent' or 'copyright' do exist, then that fact must not only be disclosed to importer but indeed a suitable clause should be incorporated in the contract. In the absence of such disclosure or clause, the importer would be exempt from any liability or claim made by any third party, in case the importer is required to indemnify the former of all such expenses.

xix. ***Settlement of disputes and applicable law*** There is indeed no single, uniform, well-integrated and comprehensive International Law which can be applicable to all aspects of international sales contracts. On some specific aspects, however, there are as mentioned earlier, standard practices and codes developed by International Chambers of Commerce, examples being Incoterms, Uniform Customs and Practices for Documentary Credits, etc. If an export contract specifically refers to those standard codes, then provisions as set out in those codes apply. However, if the contracts do not refer to standard codes, nor do they have specific clauses on issues discussed above, then the possibility of difference of opinion leading to dispute may crop up. How are the disputes to be resolved?

For settling disputes one can either go to the Courts of Law, or may choose to resort to Arbitration. It is important that Export Contracts include appropriate clauses indicating how the disputes are going to be resolved.

If any one of the parties decides to go to a Court of Law, then the question arises whether it is the Courts of Law of the exporter's country or those of the importer's country, that have this jurisdiction. The general practice has so far been that, unless in the contract itself the jurisdiction aspect has been clearly spelt out, the law of that country with which the agreement is most closely connected will apply. In the case of an export contract, it is the country of the exporter which is most closely connected with the agreement because it is in that country that the goods are to be assembled and put on board ship and therefore the jurisdiction will be with the exporting country's Courts of Law.

In international trading transactions, parties normally do not like to go to courts and instead decide to go to Arbitration. The fact that disputes are to be settled by resorting to Arbitration should be clearly stated in the contract, inter alia indicting whether Arbitration in accordance with International Chambers of Commerce rules or the rules set out by UN Commission on International Trade Law will be applicable.

// CHAPTER 22 //

LABELLING, PACKAGING, PACKING AND MARKING OF EXPORT CONSIGNMENTS

The manner in which a product is packaged often helps to sell it. However, preferences for certain numbers, colours, shapes or phrases used in label and packing a product are as varied as the cultures from which they spring. This may mean different types of packaging for the same product for different countries, besides ensuring safe arrival of the goods at their destinations.

Proper marking, including handling instructions of packs for export help their quick and safe transportation.

Facilities to import labels, price tags, labelling, marking equipment exist in the current policy.

Having produced/procured the goods and after getting them inspected for export, the next stage is to put labels on them and pack them in the containers/boxes, etc., desired by the buyers. Necessary markings have to be affixed on the export packages according to shipping requirements.

Packing, marking and labelling is not unknown in domestic marketing. Added importance is attached to them on account of the different types of hazards faced in international shipment of goods and the special marking and eco-friendly labelling requirements of export goods urged upon by special countries. For example, Oman has made it obligatory for all imported goods to be labelled in the Arab language on packages with regard to the contents. The use of adhesive label is forbidden. The indications must be printed on the original label or else on the package itself.

A good export packing helps in avoiding excess costs on freight and delivery of the goods in proper shape, besides eliminating the possibility of the insurance company's refusing to pay a claim because of the "inherent vice" in the manner the consignment was packed. The main purpose of marking of export package is identification of cargo, and that of labelling is to tell the consumer the quality and quantity of products.

LABELLING

Sometimes the foreign buyers insist on the attachment of particular types of labels, price tags, etc., specifically made out by them. **The import of such articles may be allowed without Import Trade Control (ITC) restrictions, provided the Customs authorities are satisfied** on the basis of evidence produced to them that the articles, in question, are **required for bonafide use in connection with a confirmed export order**.

Supplies made by foreign buyers of labels, price tags and like articles, to be attached to the goods against specific orders placed by them on Indian exporters, may be allowed clearance, provided the Customs Authorities are satisfied with the bonafides of the case.

Registered exporters of garments, knitwears and made-ups coming from abroad may be allowed to import labels as part of their baggage without any value restriction.

Supplies made by foreign buyers, of labels, price tags and trimming materials like buttons and belts to be attached to the goods against specific order placed by them on Indian exporters may be allowed clearance without a licence. This will also cover import of "hangers" supplied free of charge to be re-exported with the garments.

Various countries have prescribed, under their laws, the requirements as regards labelling of products for sale and distribution in their countries. Generally, every country has prescribed that the label on the product must indicate the country of its origin. Thus, for exporters from India, it is essential to ensure that each item carriers a label indicating 'Made in India'. Besides, there may be certain other requirements as detailed below, for example:

In some cases the foreign buyers may though not insist on the attachment of the labels supplied by them, these labels may have to indicate the information required by the regulations of their trade/country. For example, German Government has passed a law making compulsory that all textile articles containing 100% cotton should be marked as "100% Baumolle". Certain items manufactured in India for Japanese market must bear labels. In Canada, each package must carry a label, printed in both English and French. The label should contain the following information:

a. Name and address of Exporter and Importer
b. Product name and its type
c. Country of Origin
d. Specifications of the products (size, weight etc.)
e. Lot no. of consignment

The textile products under regulation by category includes-knitted fabrics, pants, skirts, sweaters, shirts, raincoats, neckties and table clothes. Exporters must, therefore, take care of all labelling requirements of their overseas buyers which should be ascertained from them.

A few symbols recommended for labelling textiles are given later in this chapter.

Colour, Shapes and Sizes

While putting the label on a product, take care to make it of the shape, size and colour preferred by the buyer.

Colours, shapes, sizes and numbers influence significantly the design of the labels. For example, buyers from Italy do not prefer purple colour; buyers from Japan do not like Budha shaped bottles or Jars which are round, triangular or hexagonal in shape; and buyers of Germany consider number 13 as a symbol of bad luck. On the other hand, colours red and white or gold and silver are preferred by people in Japan, colours with soft tones are preferred in Italy; red, white and blue are preferred in the Czech Republic and Denmark and so on. The exporters should not use colours, shapes and numbers which are not preferred by the customers. This will help in ensuring that the customers do not shy away from such products. It may also be clearly understood that use of colours, shapes and numbers having positive effects on the minds of the people, will however not push up the sales.

PACKING

Natural Packing of Excisable Goods

Under Rule 185 of the Central Excise Rules, 1944, the exporters are required to indicate the manufacturer's name/place of manufacture, etc., on the excisable goods intended to be exported. However, the foreign buyer sometimes insists that the Indian goods be supplied without markings. In such cases, the Govt. of India (CBEC) has allowed all Commissioners of Central Excise to relax such markings. On receipt of applications from the Central Excise assesses, the Commissioners may allow natural packing on goods (all commodities) which are meant for actual export out of India.

Green Logo

According to the new packaging law in Germany, retailers in that country have agreed that they will only buy products bearing the Green Logo. Although this Logo concerns only consumer packaging and not transportation material, some retailers are demanding that their supplier affixes it on all packaging. To use the Green Logo, German and foreign companies must follow strict guidelines.

Packing vis-à-vis Packaging

Packing or bulk packaging as some prefer to call it, as distinguished from (consumer) packing, refers to the protective covering used for transportation and shipment of goods; packaging being concerned with the containers in which the products reach the ultimate consumer. Though the subject of both packing and packaging is closely related, packing is of prime significance as no product (consumer) package can be exported without some sort of outer packing. Most of the exportable products require an outer container of some kind. However well a product is packaged, if it is not adequately packed, will reach its destination in indifferent condition which may result in its undervaluation or rejection. While standards for suitable packing of several important export products have been laid down, and enforced by the Export Inspection Council under the Export (Quality Control and Inspection) Act, there are hardly any such national specifications for packaging. Because of the importance attached to packing for developing and sustaining exports, this chapter is restricted to this aspect only.

Shipping Hazards

An ideal packing is one which ensures safe arrival of goods at destination. It must be strong enough to protect its contents against the physical hazards of transportation, especially during a voyage by sea. It should stand against hazards like dampness, rough handling, stacking, improper storage and pilferage. 'Protection is required against spillage, dirt, ingress and egress of moisture, insect infestation, contamination by foreign material, tampering and pilferage.' The 'contents need to be preserved by ensuring freedom from bacteriological attack, enzymatic reaction, oxidation, etc.'

If the goods are not properly packed, and there is danger of their being damaged or damaging other products, they may not be either accepted for shipment or the Bill of Lading is endorsed as "packing is unsatisfactory." Such an "unclean" Bill of Lading may not, then, be accepted by the banks.

Proper export packing can guard against most of these hazards. However, packing should not be such as to add unnecessarily to freight expenses or to import duties in countries where these are levied on the basis of weight of goods imported therein. Extreme care has to be taken in the matter of packing material, size and design of the special requirements, national as well as international, for packing export products.

Types of Packs

The selection of the type of pack and its material for a given product, is determined by the product itself depending upon its physical and physico-chemical properties, the distance to be shipped to, transhipment(s) involved, etc. While in some cases, the importer himself specifies the types of packing, standards have been laid down in several cases by the Export Inspection Council (EIC) and the Bureau of Indian Standards. The Indian Institute of Packaging (IIP) is a specialised institute set up to help and guide the exporters in the matter of suitable packing for different products for export to different markets. The exporter should therefore, consult these organisations before deciding upon the type of packing, in case the same has not been specified by his overseas customer. Nevertheless, an attempt is made here to suggest the types of packs and materials utilised in general, by Indian exporters.

INTERNATIONAL SYMBOLS FOR TEXTILE CARE

A group of 13 countries called Ginetex had evolved international symbols for the care of textile items in December, 1985. These symbols have been introduced in the member countries of Gintex with effect from January 1, 1986. These countries are Austria, Finland, Israel, Germany, U.K., France, Spain, Belgium/Luxembourg, Portugal, The Netherlands, Italy, New Zealand and Switzerland. Today, these symbols have been accepted all over the world. These symbols are given at the end.

Forms of Label

- ★ Strip of cloth
- ★ Card label
- ★ Sticker

Check List of Information on a Label

- ★ Legal requirements
- ★ Care of the product

- ★ Size of the product
- ★ Material used
- ★ Country of origin
- ★ How to use the product
- ★ Information about the product and the people who made it. It is very useful if the product is a classic art piece, is of cultural/historical background, in brief, about importance of the product is also welcome. It adds to the promotional value of the product.

How to Make Good Quality Label

A good quality label can be prepared if the following aspects are kept in mind.

- ★ Include only relevant information.
- ★ Use the language of importer's country, if possible.
- ★ Check spellings of information given on the label. An error can lead to the conclusion that the exporter is careless.
- ★ Use appropriate labels. For example, one should not use adhesive labels on leather/handicraft items as these would leave marks on leather, wood and stone handicrafts.

EXPORT PACKAGING AND PACKING

Today packaging is considered as one of the most important constituents for marketing any product. Nobody can underscore the need for good packaging when he decides to export his product. Packaging means packing of the product in some container to reach the ultimate consumer and packing means protective covering used for transportation and shipment of goods. Packaging fulfills a vital role in helping to get the export products to the market in the best condition, as well as in presenting goods to overseas buyer in an attractive way. In other words, packaging of a product performs the role of silent salesman as it

- ★ Improves presentation of the product
- ★ Protects the product during distribution
- ★ Makes handling and retail display of the product easier

While packaging, quality should not be compromised merely to cut down the costs. Saving or cost reduction in packing costs can usually be made in any packing operation by studying the entire packaging process carefully.

Exporter should select a large supplier for supply of packing material. Reputed firms can offer alternative packages, sizes and designs. Marginal advantages in price are offset by delay in delivery, inferior or inconsistent quality and the like in the case of a small supplier. Substantial savings can be achieved by ordering the suppliers standard products, sizes and shapes. Any particular package can easily be personalised through distinctive, promotional labelling. In most cases the delivery period for the standard items are shorter, usually ex-stock and the quality better due to faster quality control for longer production run.

TYPES OF PACKAGING AND PACKING

Packaging

An exporter can use the following containers for packaging of the product:

- ★ Polythene bags

- ★ Box made of card paper or cardboard
- ★ Box made of fibre board/plastic/acrylic sheets
- ★ Tin-box

Packing

The following types of boxes can be used for packing of the package meant for exports:

- ★ Wooden boxes
- ★ Fibre or corrugated board boxes
- ★ Steel drums

Wooden boxes The wooden boxes are the most useful forms of packing as these are strong enough to withstand the loads placed on the top of it without crushing or causing damage. One should use soft wood amenable to nailing. Unless it is unavoidable the weight of a standard box should not exceed 100 kgs. This helps in minimising the freight handling charges and the freight of the shipment. A cube shaped wooden box has the maximum protective strength. Fragile goods should be packed in wooden boxes.

Fibre board or corrugated board boxes These boxes are useful for the shipment of non-fragile goods. Its use is very common in developed countries. The boxes should be, as far as possible, cube-shaped and each box should not exceed 20–25 kgs in weight. These boxes are light weight which saves in shipping cost, and also they have a good deal of strength and fair resistance to moisture, compression, etc.

The exporters should use cushioning material like rubberised animal hair, plastic material, polyurethane foam sheets, straw, saw dust, wood dust, wood, wool and paper cuttings. This helps in protecting the packages from damage caused by bumping, rubbing or tossing about in the boxes during rough weather, at sea or because of vibrations within an aircraft.

Steel drums Steel drums are used for sending liquids in bulk. A drum should normally not exceed more than 250kg. (50 gallons). Second hand drums should be used only if the buyer has agreed to their use.

PACK NOTE AND PACKING LIST

Once packaging has been completed, the exporter should prepare

a. Pack Note
b. Packing List

Pack note is a detailed listing of the packages placed in a box. It gives complete description of the items in the box. Such notes are very useful reference points whenever part of the cargo is misplaced, damaged or stranded and the exporter is required to replace them.

Packing list is a statement of various boxes with description of the goods packed in each box. Thus, it is the boxwise statement of the shipment as against Pack note which is the itemwise description of the shipments. Pack note is used by the exporter for his in-house management and packing list is one of the pre-shipment export documents.

MARKING

The main purpose of marking on export consignments is identification of cargo. Proper markings including handling instructions on boxes for export help in their quick and safe transportation. Markings are of two kinds.

(i) Leading marks
(ii) Subsidiary Marks

Leading marks include the following information:

★ Shipper (Exporter's) Mark
★ Importer's mark as mentioned in Letter of Credit
★ Destination
★ Order No.
★ Destination and Port of Entry

Subsidiary marks include the following information:

★ Country of origin
★ Port of shipment and place of despatch
★ Gross/Net Weight – Tare Weight
★ Handling instructions including symbols

The following points must be observed carefully while marking export boxes:

★ Old marks on the boxes should be completely erased/obliterated
★ Black pigment type ink should be used
★ Markings should be
  a. neat and legible
  b. printed or stencilled in letters of adequate size
  c. as per shipping documents, particularly Bill of Lading, Packing Lists, Consular and Customs invoice
  d. water proof, weather proof, smear proof and permanent
★ If stencils are used for marking, ensure that letters and figures do not lead to any confusion.

Specimens of marking on an export case and international freight marking symbols are given at the end.

NEW PACKAGING RULES IN GERMANY

Germany has introduced an ordinance under which packaging of all products imported into the country has to be eco-friendly, and also made of material that can be recycled. Manufacturers/Exporters of other lands are required to take back packaging material for recycling under this ordinance.

Taking-back and Recyling Obligation

Manufacturers and distributors have an obligation to take back packaging materials once it has fulfilled its purpose and direct it material recycling outside the public waste disposal system.

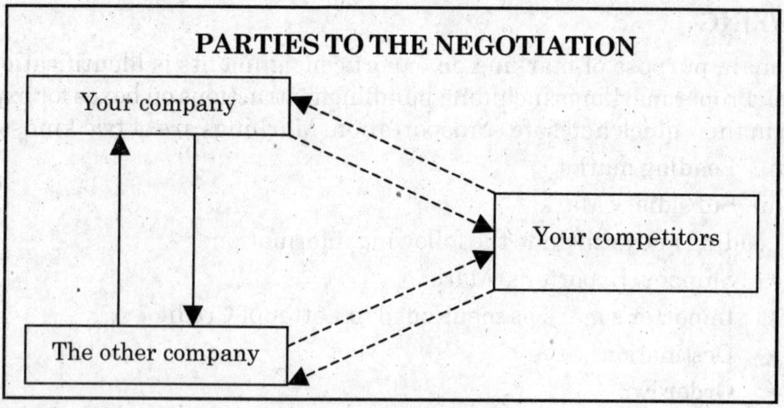

NEW INTERNAL CARE LABELLING CODE FOR TEXTILES INTERNATIONAL SYMBOLS

New care labelling has been unanimously decided by Ginetex, an organisation responsible for care labelling of textile items in December, 1985. This new code has been introduced since 1st January, 1986 in 13 member countries of Ginetex, viz. Austria, Belgium/Luxembourg, Finland, France, Great Britain, Italy, Israel, New Zealand, Portugal, Spain, Switzerland, The Netherlands and Germany.

EUROPEAN ECO LABEL FOR CLOTHING AND TEXTILES

EU Label Objectives

The objective of the European Union's eco label are:

★ To promote the design, production, marketing, and use of products which have a reduced environmental impact during their entire life cycle, by awarding an eco label to these products.

★ To inform consumers about the impact of these products on the environment. The International Cargo Handling Coordination Association has set these out for the use of exporters and carries a number of recommendations for the marking of goods carried by ocean-going vessels. Many of these are equally useful for the marking of goods being forwarded by other modes of transport. These are the following:

i) The marks should appear in a certain order. Essential data should be placed in oblong frames with lines 1.5 centimetres thick, and subsidiary information should be placed in another type of frame.

ii) Declaration on large packages should be placed on two continuous sides, and for consignments bound together on a pallet, also on the top. Handling instructions should be placed on all four sides. Similar packages, such as goods in sacks, should be marked on two opposite sides.

iii) Lettering should be at least 7.5 centimeters high for essential data, and at least 3.5 centimeters for subsidiary data.

If the package is too small for such letter, other sizes may be used, but in the same ratio. The sizes of the symbols should also be in proportion to the size of the package and of the other markings.

INTERNATIONAL CARE LABELLING SYMBOLS

Chlorine based bleaching (hypochlorite)	
CHLORINE-BASED BEACHING ALLOWED	CHLORINE-BASED BEACHING ALLOWED
(only cold and in dilute solution) 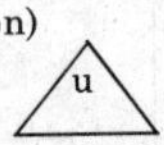	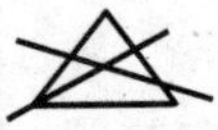

Dry Cleaning			
ALL SOLVENTS Used in Dry Cleaning Allowed	ALL SOLVENTS Except Trichlo-Ride Ethylene	ONLY SOLVENTS Allowed White Spirit and Solvent (1)	DO NOT DRY Also no Spotting with solvents
	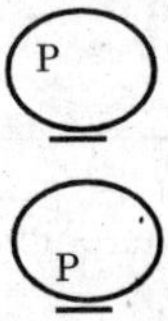	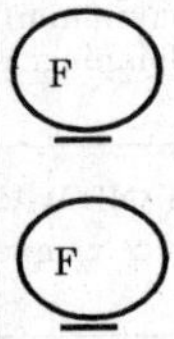	
(1) Self-service cleaning only in machines using solvent R 113			
(2) The bar under the circle indicates that certain limitations in the dry cleaning process are required. These may concern mechanical action and/or water addition in the solvent.			
(No self-service cleaning allowed.)			

Ironing (1)

IRONING TEMPERATURE			DO NOT IRON (2)
HIGH (200°C max.)	HIGH (150°C max.)	LOW (1) (110°C max.)	
			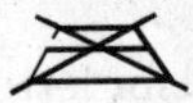
(1) Steaming and steam treatments could be risky			
(2) Steaming and steam treatments are not allowed			

	WASHING
	NORMAL PROCESS AT 95°C Mechanical action: normal Spinning: normal
	MILD PROCESS AT 95°C Mechanical action: reduced (1) Rinsing at gradually decreasing temperature (cool down) Spinning: with care
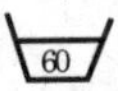	NORMAL PROCESS AT 60°C Mechanical action: normal Spinning: normal
	MILD PROCESS AT 60°C Mechanical action: reduced (1) Rinsing at gradually decreasing temperature (cool down) Spinning: with care

SYMBOLS IN USE IN SOME COUNTRIES ONLY	
	MILD PROCESS AT 30°C Mechanical action: reduced (1) Rinsing at gradually decreasing temperature (cool down)
	VERY MILD PROCESS AT 30°C Mechanical action: very reduced (minimum) (2) Spinning: with care
(1) For these articles a reduced loading of the machine and a higher liquor level are recommended.	
(2) Apart from the precautions under (1) the mechanical action of the machine must be reduced considerably: short washing and rinsing cycles, longer standstill period of slower rotation speed.	

	NORMAL PROCESS AT 40°C Mechanical action: normal Spinning : normal
	MILD PROCESS AT 40°C Mechanical action: reduced (1) Rinsing at gradually decreasing temperature (cool down) Spinning: with care
	VERY MILD PROCESS AT 30°C Mechanical action: very reduced (minimum) (2) Spinning: with care
	HAND WASH max. temperature: 40°C
	DO NOT WASH

Tumble drying (after washing (1))		
TUMBLE DRYING ALLOWED		DO NOT TUMBLE DRY
No limitations on temperature	Drying at a lower temperature setting	
		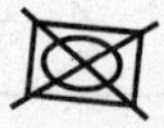

(1) This symbol is optional

iv) Only fast dyes should be used for lettering. Essential data should be in black and subsidiary data in a less conscpicuous colour; red and orange lettering should be reserved for dangerous goods only. For foods packed in sacks, only harmless dyes should be employed, and the dye should not come through the packing in such a way as to affect the goods.

v) Stick-on labels should only be used on individual package or parcel and all old labels should be removed.

vi) Marking should be made by stencil or by branding or by pencil or brush without a stencil. If stencils are used, care should be taken that the letters and figures are perfectly legible to prevent confusion. This is especially true of the letters and figures – B.R.P,O,G–G–D–C, H–N; 3–8: 6–9 and 1–7.

vii) The surface to be marked should be smooth and clean. If packages are to be banded, they can be marked before this is done; the hoops should not however, cover the markings.

viii) The figure should indicate the total number of packages making up the consignment and the consecutive number of the individual package. For example, 1520/15/1 identifies the first packages of a total number of 15 and 1520/15/15 the last one.

ix) The name of the ship and the bill of lading number should be shown when this is possible. Handling instructions must appear in the language of the exporter and the importer, and also if possible, in the language of the countries where goods are to be handled ***en route*** or transhipped.

MARKING ON AN EXPORT CASE

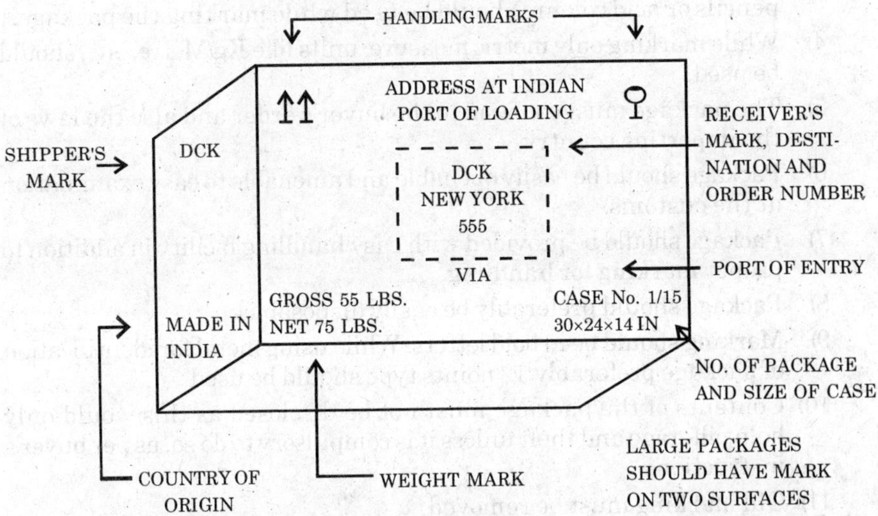

Symbols of Important Handling Instructions on Export Packs used Internationally are the following:

INTERNATIONAL FREIGHT MARKING SYMBOLS

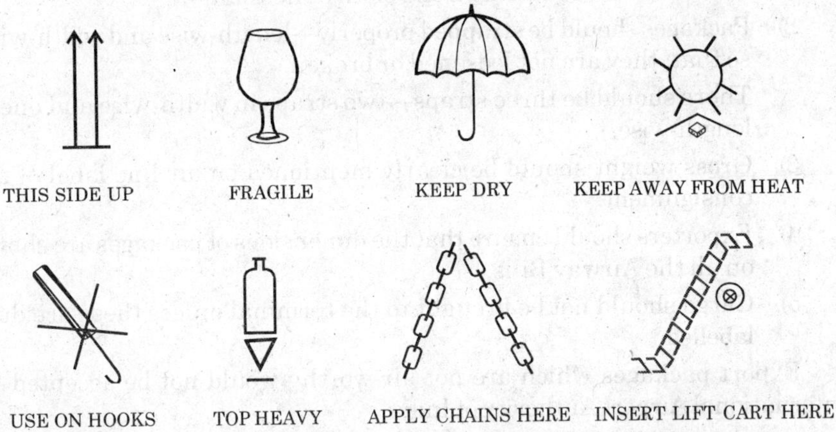

While large packages should have marks on two surfaces, drums are marked on top and side. Size of the marks in capital letters, should be of largest practical dimensions to fit the marking area on the package. Sub-marks should be approximately half the size of the leading marks (2 inch to 3 inch high).

Some important points in respect of marking, packaging and packing are given below:

1) Package must be made in conformity with the trend in the country for which it is meant, as otherwise wrong handling/treatment is possible in the importing countries. For details see Part II of this book.
2) Legible marking and use of stencils must be made.

3) Only permanent colours, preferably pigments and not chalk or colour pencils or acid colours should be used while marking the packages.
4) While marking only metric measure, units like Kg/Metre, etc., should be used.
5) The package must conform to the buyer's order and also the laws of the importing country.
6) Package should be easily openable and amenable to easy examination at the customs.
7) Package should be provided with easy handling facility in addition to proper marking for handling.
8) Package should preferably be easily disposable.
9) Marking should be in bold letters. While using metal for identification of package preferably 12 points type should be used.
10) Contents of the package must not be disclosed as this would only help pilferage and theft unless it is compulsory to do so, as per buyer's instructions.
11) Old marking must be removed.

Further, Standard Facilitation Committee for Cargo (CAFAC) have suggested the following points for cargo exported by air:

1) The expensive consignments like consignments of silk goods, etc., should be covered with strong cloth or hessian.
2) Packages should be strapped properly—length-wise and width-wise, so that, they are not loosened or broken.

   There should be three straps—two straps in width-wise and one in length-wise.
3) Gross weight should be clearly mentioned on air line label of the consignment.
4) Exporters should ensure that the dimensions of packages are shown on all the Airway Bills.
5) Cargo should not be brought to the terminal unless these are duly labelled.

Export packages which are not air-worthy would not be accepted by International Airport Authority of India.

ANNEXURE 1 SOME MARKETING AND TECHNICAL REQUIREMENTS FOR GOOD PACKAGING

1. **Physical protection**
   ★ resistance against damages (shock, puncture, drop, crush)
   ★ dimensions
2. **Quality protection**
   ★ required shelf life
   ★ fitness packaging material for product
   ★ barriers against light, oxygen, microbes, water, moisture
   ★ protection of flavour, colour, etc.

3. **Product promotion**
   - ★ quality image
   - ★ display value, visibility
   - ★ brand name promotion
   - ★ quality of decoration, printing, varnishing
4. **Product information**
   - ★ production recognition
   - ★ readability of text
   - ★ instructions for use, warnings, CE-marking
   - ★ information on weight, contents, keepability (legal)
   - ★ name of manufacturer, seller, importer, origin.
5. **Efficiency in use**
   - ★ ease to handle, to empty, to open, to dispense
   - ★ pack stability, firmness
   - ★ environmental acceptability, disposability
   - ★ child-proof
6. **Convenience in use**
7. **Storage before handling**
8. **Processability**
   - ★ temperature resistance
   - ★ attitude of filling area
   - ★ stress/crack stability
   - ★ performance, quality assurance
9. **Machinability**
   - ★ machine stop sensitivity
   - ★ pack (shape) stability before, during, after use
   - ★ ease of capping, labelling, printing
   - ★ filling speed, temperature, opening, level
   - ★ volume inspection
   - ★ surface smoothness, abrasion properties, glue compatibility
   - ★ in-line coding
10. **Storage**
    - ★ primary pack protection, buffer
    - ★ fitness for palletisation
    - ★ stacking weight, strength
    - ★ fitness for internal transport
11. **Transport**
    - ★ weight/volume ratio, maximum weight
    - ★ transport distance
    - ★ pallet dimensions (truck load), stability
12. **Trade appeal**
    - ★ weight, stacking performance, stability
    - ★ identification of product, brand, markings, code
    - ★ shelf-space efficiency, display visibility
    - ★ handling outer pack

- ★ disposability
- ★ anti-pilfering devices
- ★ guarantee closure
- ★ ease of refilling racks, shelves

13. Recyclability

- ★ weight minimisation/reduction
- ★ no PVC, plastics; only natural materials (carton, paper, wood, etc)
- ★ returnable (glass, pallets)
- ★ contract with waste packaging destructor (Germany's Green Dot)

// CHAPTER 23 //

QUALITY CONTROL AND PRE-SHIPMENT INSPECTION

The Export Inspection Council of India was set up by the Government of India under Section 3 of the Export (Quality Control and Inspection) Act, 1963 to provide for the sound development of export trade through quality control and pre-shipment inspection. Suitable amendments were incorporated in the act in July, 1984 in order to provide the power to search and seize commodities, initiate adjustification proceedings against erring manufacturers and exporters, cancellation or withholding of the certificate to inspection issued by the Inspection Agencies, etc.

The Export Inspection Council (EIC) consists of a Chairman appointed by the Central Government, 4 ex-office members and 15 members nominated by the Central Government. The EIC is an apex body for controlling the activities of the quality control and pre-shipment inspection of the commodities meant for export. The main functions of the EIC as assigned in the Act are:

(i) To advise the Central Government regarding measures for enforcement of quality control and inspection in relation to commodities intended for export and to draw up programmes therefore, and

(ii) To arrange pre-shipment inspection of notified commodities for export.

With a view of inculcating quality consciousness among the manufacturers and to motivate them to adopt quality discipline, the EIC has been engaged in quality development and export promotional activities by way of arranging training on various quality control techniques to the personnel at all levels in the industry. In addition, the EIC also arranged seminars and workshops designed to educate the manufacturers and exporters on the methods of maintaining quality including packaging.

During the year 1995–96, 12 seminars/workshops in different disciplines were arranged by the EIAs at different places to propagate the adoption of quality systems in the units in tune with ISO 9000 Standards requirements. During the period 1.4.1996–30.9.1996, 5 such programmes/workshops were arranged.

In addition to conducting seminars/workshops in the context of ISO–9000 Standards requirements, the EIAs also arranged training programmes with a view of enabling the trade/industry to upgrade the quality of products intended for export, matching with international quality parameters. During 1.4.1996–30.9.1996, the EIAs carried out 21 such programmes.

COMMODITIES COVERED UNDER THE QUALITY CONTROL AND PRE-SHIPMENT INSPECTION

The Export (Quality Control and Inspection) Act, 1963, inter alia empowers the Government to notify the commodities which shall be subjected to quality control and inspection, specifies the type of quality control and inspection which will be applied to such commodities and prohibits the export of notified commodities unless it is accompanied by a certificate of export worthiness from the Inspection Agencies recognised under the Act.

997 items under product group heads of engineering, chemicals and allied products, food and agricultural products, jute and jute products, coir and coir products, footwear and footwear components, cashew, fish and fishery products etc., are under the aegis of the Compulsory Quality Control Inspection System.

Government of India has issued a notification on 21.8.1995 relating to the export of fish and fishery products where the EIAs have been authorised as Competent Authority, to ensure compliance with the specified conditions given in the EEC directive No. 91/493 dated 22.7.1991 with specific reference to introduction and adoption of HACCP Plan by the Units to avoid safety and health hazards of fish and fishery Products.

With a view to create better demand for Indian goods in the overseas markets, the quality standards of the notified items are periodically reviewed and upgraded.

MACHINERY FOR QUALITY CONTROL AND INSPECTION

Export Inspection Agencies

For carrying out pre-shipment inspection of export goods, the Government of India has established five Export Inspection Agencies (EIAs) one each at Calcutta, Chennai, Cochin, Delhi and Mumbai under the technical and administrative control of the EIC. In addition to their headquarter offices at Calcutta, Chennai, Cochin, Delhi and Mumbai, the EIAs have a network of 61 sub-offices located at important industrial centres and ports of shipment. These EIAs have well equipped laboratory facilities for the testing of export products. During the year 1995–96, export consignments worth Rs 1,770.03 crores were certified under Consignment-wise Inspection (CWI) and In-process Quality Control (IPQC) Systems. During the period 1.4.1996 – 30.9.1996, the value of consignments certified comes upto Rs 477.55 corers. The EIAs also undertake inspection on a voluntary basis, when desired by the foreign buyers. To ensure that the export cargo meet the specific conditions prescribed in the Export Trade Policy, the EIAs also carry out inspection of products such as meat and meat products, Indian made foreign liquor, stainless steel products, etc., as required under the Trade Policy.

The EIAs have also been authorised by the Government of India to issue certificates of origin under the Generalised System of Preferences (GSP) for exports to Japan, EEC, USA, Canada and East European countries. During the year 1995–96 and the period 1.4.1996 – 30.9.1996, as many as 4,59,091 and 2,00,652 GSP certificates were issued by the EIAs, respectively.

Other Recognised Agencies

Government has also recognised 21 private inspection agencies and 7 government inspection agencies to supplement the work of quality certification under the Act 15. Agencies have also been recognised for fumigation of export cargo.

QUALITY STANDARDS FOR EXPORTS

For all commodities notified under the act, quality standards are prescribed by the government. While in a large number of cases, buyers' requirements have been recognised as the basis of inspection, for products involving safety or health hazards, minimum standards have been prescribed. Commodities for which minimum standards have been prescribed are not allowed for export unless the minimum standards are attained, though the foreign buyers may be inclined to accept the product below such minimum standards. In a phased manner, minimum standards are being prescribed for more and more products. The standards are reviewed periodically in consultation with the trade and industry and also keeping in view the latest technological changes and the changing needs of the overseas buyers.

SYSTEMS OF INSPECTION

Three systems of inspection are in operation at present. They are:

(i) Consignment-wise Inspection (CWI)
(ii) In-process Quality Control (IPQC)
(iii) Self-certification (SC)

Consignment-wise Inspection (CWI)

Under Consignment-Wise Inspection, each export consignment is inspected and tested by the recognised inspection agencies, by selecting consignments on the basis of statistical sampling plan to satisfy conformity of the products with the prescribed standards.

In-process Quality Control (IPQC)

The IPQC system lays emphasis on the responsibility of manufacturers and processors in ensuring consistent quality during each state of production by exercising checks on raw material and bought-out components through process control, product control, metrological control and packaging control by the manufacturers and processors themselves. The certificates of inspection in favour of the units approved under the Scheme are issued by the EIAs. These units are then kept under surveillance by the EIAs and random spot checks of the consignments are carried out by the EIAs from time to time. During 1995–96, 26 new units were brought under the IPQC system and 81 units were taken away from the system.

Self-certification (SC)

Under the Self-certification system, the manufacturing units fulfilling the stringent norms prescribed for design and development, raw materials and bought-out components, process control, product control, metrological control, packaging, after sales service, quality audit house keeping and maintenance are authorised by the Central Government to issue certificates of inspection under the act themselves for their products. There were 16 units approved under Self-Certification as on 31.3.1996. During the period 1.4.1996 to 30.9.1996, 1 unit was deleted from the Self-certification Scheme, leaving 15 units approved under the Self-certification Scheme.

SIMPLIFICATION AND STREAMLINING OF COMPULSORY PRE-SHIPMENT INSPECTION PROCEDURE

With a view to enabling the manufacturers and exporters to take up the responsibility of ensuring quality of export products rather than depending upon EIA inspection, the machinery for enforcement of compulsory quality control and pre-shipment inspection was simplified and streamlined in 1990 and 1991 by taking the following steps:

(i) Star Trading Houses, Trading Houses and Export Houses have been exempted from the purview of compulsory pre-shipment inspection of all products, notified under the Export (Quality Control and Inspection) Act, 1963.

(ii) Units approved by the EIAs under the system of IPQC have been authorised to issue statutory certificates by themselves instead of the EIAs.

(iii) Industrial units set up in EPZ, FTZ and 100% EOUs have been exempted from the purview of compulsory pre-shipment inspection.

(iv) Items notified under the Export (Quality Control and Inspection) Act, 1963, have been exempted from compulsory pre-shipment inspection, provided the exporters have a firm letter from the overseas buyers stating that the overseas buyers do not want pre-shipment inspection from any official Indian Inspection Agency, which shall be filed by the exporters before the Customs authorities at the ports of shipments.

(v) Manufacturers/exporters of engineering products who have attained the export of these products on an average level of Rs 1.5 crores during the last 3 years and have not received any quality complaint from foreign buyers and are competent to carry out pre-shipment inspection, will be recognised as inspection agencies for their own products.

(vi) To provide quick and efficient professional service to the trade and industry, in addition to the EIAs, Governmental and Private Inspection Agencies having competence in carrying out pre-shipment inspection and testing of engineering products and fish and fishery products, will also be approved inspection agencies under Section 7(1) of the Export (Quality Control and Inspection) Act, 1963.

PROCEDURE FOR PRE-SHIPMENT INSPECTION

Application and Documents

All manufacturers/exporters not falling within the provision relating to in-process quality control and also not having ISI/Agmark and also merchant exporters of products falling within the purview of the pre-shipment inspection should apply in the prescribed form to the concerned inspection agency well before the expected date of shipment with the following documents:

(i) Invoice (5 copies)

(ii) A crossed cheque/demand draft/PO or bank passbook showing the deposit of necessary fee in favour of EIA

(iii) Declaration regarding importer's technical specification of quality and/or a sample approved by the importer in support of the declaration of his (importer's) specifications.

Inspection certificate If a consignment is found to satisfy the required standards and specifications, the exporter is given an inspection certificate in triplicate. In case the consignment is not approved, "Rejection Note" is issued.

While original (white) copy is to be submitted to the Customs, the duplicate is for the overseas buyers and the triplicate for the exporter.

Appeal against rejection If the exporter is not satisfied with the Rejection Note, he may file within ten days of the receipt of this note, an appeal to the Export Inspection Agency to convene a meeting of the Appellate Panel. On such appeal, the Appellate Panel will review the inspection report, hear the exporter and inspect the consignment concerned, if necessary. Its decision is final and binding on both the parties, i.e. the EIA and the exporter.

TEXTILE GOODS INSPECTION

The pre-shipment inspection of textile goods are carried out under a number of regulations and schemes. These regulations have been laid down for different items, either for compulsory inspection or voluntary inspection.

Since there are different schemes for the inspection of various items of textiles, exporters should seek necessary information from the Textile Committee and/or concerned inspection agency.

In regard to items for which inspection is not compulsory, but which are eligible for duty drawback and other export benefits, inspection is carried out on a voluntary basis, by the Textile Committee, 79, Dr. Annie Besant Road, Worli, Mumbai – 400 018.

It is also conducted in respect of goods for which special certification to get tariff concessions and quota free treatment at the importing end, as detailed later, are required.

Applications

Application for pre-shipment inspection of textile goods are, by and large, to be made to the Textile Committee in the following manner –

(i) Application in the prescribed form (there are different forms for different categories of textiles)

(ii) Invoice (one copy)

(iii) Export Order/Contract (one copy) along with original.

(iv) Packing list

The applicant should also mention the category number and the NIMEXE Code No. (TSUS No in case of US) along with the description of the garment. The necessary combination form, GSP form, etc., as applicable to the particular category by which export is to be made, should also be enclosed along with the necessary service charges.

Applications are to be sent at least one day in advance of the date when inspection is required. However, small consignments can be brought to the office of the Textile Committee before noon any day.

Procedure for Handling of Quality Complaints

Procedures have been evolved for assessment and evaluation and settlement of complaints on quality received from foreign buyers, by the Regional Standing Committees set up at Ahmedabad, Bangalore, Calcutta, Chennai, Cochin, Delhi, Hyderabad, Kanpur, Ludhiana and Mumbai.

Training Facilities

For providing training to the Inspection Officers on a regular basis, a Quality Development Centre (QDC) has been set up by the EIC at Chennai. Through the curriculum of training, Officers of the EIC and the EIAs are given training on the methodology and techniques of quality assurance including the latest techniques in inspection and quality control prevalent in other countries.

// CHAPTER 24 //

CENTRAL EXCISE CLEARANCE OF GOODS FOR EXPORT

Recently there have been drastic changes in the Central Excise Rules and Procedures covering export of Excised goods. New Rules 12, 13, 185, 187, 187A, 187B and 189 have substituted the old rules as a measure of simplification and rationalisation. Form AR 4A has been merged with the new Form AR 4. The highlights of the new procedure for Excised goods are as under:

(i) Now there is only one new Rule 12 for exports under claim of rebate of Duty. New Rule 12 is for granting rebate of duty for end-stage, i.e. finished stage Duty as well as input stage Duties. Hence, it integrates the provisions of superseded Rules 12, 12A and 191A.

(ii) There is one new Rule 13 for export of goods in bond as well as utilisation of raw materials, etc., without payment of duty for manufacture and export of exciseable goods. Prior approval of manufacturing formula for export goods (under the old rules), has also been dispensed with.

(iii) The term 'manufacture' for the purpose of export has been enlarged to include any kind of processing of blending of any goods or making alternations or any other operations thereon.

(iv) (a) No intimation is required to be given to Central Excise Officers by an exporter if he desired that examination will take place only at the point of shipment, i.e. at ports, airports or land customs stations only. If the exporter desires examination of export goods in a factory of warehouse or other point of storage and not at the point of export, then prior intimation is to be given to Central Excise Officers, who will examine and seal the goods. Hence, self-removal procedure for export of goods where no examination is required in factory/warehouse has been introduced;

(b) Rebate claim can be lodged either with Maritime Commissioner at the Port of shipment or the Assistant Commissioner having jurisdiction over the factory or warehouse of the exporter.

(c) With regard to marking and numbering on export packages, the Commissioner has been empowered to relax any of the conditions of Rule 185 of the Central Excise Rules.

(v) Chapter X - Procedure of Central Excise Rules has been made applicable to movement of non-duty paid inputs from the place of their manufacture to the place of manufacture of export goods.

(vi) In case of export of Duty-paid goods under claim of rebate of Duty, facility which was hereto available only to some of the goods, notified on a case to case basis, has been extended to all items permitted for export.

(vii) Earlier minimum limit of rebate of Rs 50 has, however been enhanced to Rs 500/- with a view to rationalise the system.

(viii) The facility of manufacture under bond of export goods has been extended to all goods including intermediate goods, even if they are manufactured by a job worker.

(ix) The distinction between Forms AR4, AR4 (land) and AR4A has been removed. These forms were replaced by a single modified (and further revised in March '95) form AR 4 which can be utilised for export in Bond of all Exciseable goods by any mode, i.e. sea, air, post, land. When manufacturers desire to clear Excise goods for export without examination under Rule 187, they will issue the AR4 by themselves without the countersignature of the Inspector of Central Excise. When they desire the examination done at the factory to waive examination at the port by the Customs, they will use the same form AR4 for examination in the factory as is being done previously in AR4s. In form AR4, they will also indicate from whom they will claim the rebate or by whom proof of export is to be admitted on the basis of the Bond executed for such exports. Moreover, AR4 form is now both export in Bond and under claim of rebate of Duty on finished goods.

(x) The procedure for export in Bond to Nepal/Bhutan and under the procedure of payment of Excise Duty to His Majesty's Government of Nepal has been completely revised.

(xi) The procedure for export of ship stores in Bond has also been modified.

New Central Excise Clearance Procedure

Every exporter must obtain clearance of the Central Excise Authorities in respect of shipment of goods subject to the levy of Excise Duty. The basic form used for this purpose is called AR-4 (Application for removal of Excisable goods for export by Air/Sea/Post/Land). This form is required to be filled by the exporter in all cases viz.

i. Export clearance of their own without examination by the Central Excise Officer whether under claim for rebate or under Bond.
ii. Export clearance under Central Excise Seal under claim for rebate or under bond.

// CHAPTER 25 //

TRANSPORTATION AND SHIPMENT OF GOODS FOR EXPORT

When an exporter wishes to send his goods to another country he may have a choice of transportation. Goods can be shipped by surface (road, rail or sea) or by air. By far the most important method is sea, with air freight as an occasional option.

OCEAN FREIGHT

Ocean freight is the most widely used form of transportation in international trade. It still has the attraction of being a cheap mode of transport for delivering large quantities of goods over long distances.

The procedures for arranging a shipment of goods can be complex. Before goods can be shipped by Sea the exporter or his Shipping or Forwarding Agent must:

- ★ find out freight rates
- ★ select a shipping line and a particular vessel.
- ★ book shipping space
- ★ register cargo on a shipping note and send shipping note to Shipping company
- ★ register details on Custom entries forms and send to Customs
- ★ arrange adequate packing, including shipping marks
- ★ receive calling forward notice from Shipping company
- ★ send goods to port with consignment note
- ★ receive Bill of Lading from Shipping company
- ★ pay freight bill
- ★ enclose bill of lading and send copies to shipping line and customer, or to the Bank acting as intermediary

Shipping and Forwarding Agents

In practice only the largest companies try to handle all the shipping and despatch of their goods overseas themselves. With large quantities of goods to export they can afford to employ their own export staff.

Small exporters find it easier to use the services of Shipping and Forwarding Agents, or freight as they are sometimes called. They are experts on the availability of the different modes of transport for different markets, on the cost, and on the suitability of each mode. Their job involves booking space, arranging documentation and in many cases, collecting the goods from the factory and transporting them to the Docks, Airport, Railway station or Road collection point.

Shipping and Forwarding Agents deal with Customs entries and other formalities. They arrange payment of freight charges and insurance, if necessary and handle collection of necessary documents. They may also help by consolidating or grouping together a number of consignments to make transportation more economic.

Types of Shipping

The freight rates that have to be paid to send goods by Ocean freight depend to some extent on which type of shipping is used. The four basic types of shipping are:

Conference line vessels These are ships operated by a line, which is a member of a shipping conference. Conferences are groups of shipping line. They establish common freight rates, regular scheduled departures and common shipping conditions. They provide international liner services for the carriage of Cargo on a specified route or routes.

Non-conference vessels They are ships operated by shipping companies giving scheduled services but quoting freight rates independently.

Tramp ships These are ships operated by shipping companies giving scheduled services but quoting freight rates independently.

Charter ships These ships do not follow regular routes but travel as and where cargoes are available.

Of these types of shipping, the most commonly used are Conference Line Vessels, which make regular journeys and offer special discounts to exporters who use them regularly. The exporter or his Freight Forwarder may make such special arrangements with Conference Lines.

The Shipping company will charge either by weight (W) or measure (M), whichever is greater.

In the case of particularly valuable cargo, the shipping company may charge an *ad valorem* freight rate. That is, an extra charge because the goods are so valuable, such as might be the case with a consignment of furs.

A minimum charge may apply to freight charges if the goods are too small for a Shipping company to handle them strictly by volume or weight.

Freight rates may also be increased by a special surcharge in special situations, such as local unrest or disaster or the need for a longer journey than necessary, as for example, when the Suez Canal was closed. Another possible form of surcharge is after a major devaluation of currency. Or there may be a 'congestion surcharge' which may be as high as 75%.

It is important that these possible 'extras' are taken into account when freight rates are estimated.

AIR FREIGHT

Air freight is the most recent form of transportation for the exporter. It has many advantages over other modes of transport and its use is increasing. Generally, Air freight is most practical for goods which have a high unit value- that is, a high ratio of price to weight. But there are no hard and fast rules.

The most obvious advantage of Air freight is of course the speed of delivery. For many items, such as fresh flowers and fruits, it is the only logical mode of transport if the customers are far away. Air transport may also be vital for carrying fashionable goods that have a short selling life, or for seasonal goods. But the other advantages of Air transport should not be forgotten.

The speed of delivery means that because the customer receives his goods more quickly, the exporter receives his payment faster. This can be very important for small exporters who may not be able to afford having their capital tied up for three months which is the time a ship takes to completes its voyage.

An exporter may find that Air Freight can save him storage costs because he may have to maintain a small inventory of raw materials or finished goods, particularly in the export market.

Cost savings also stem from

- ★ Greater security in transit
- ★ Less jostling in transit
- ★ Lower insurance costs

The greater security of Air transport means that insurance premiums on shipments by air are usually lower than for Sea transport, because the risk of pilferage and damage is much smaller. The smoother ride and gentler handling of Air freight means that the packing needed for shipment by Air is much lighter than for shipment by Sea. Indeed, 'domestic' packing is often sufficient. Lighter packing can be a big advantage in countries where Custom Duties are based on the weight of the consignment.

For each product that an exporter considers shipping abroad, he should consider the possibility of using Air freight. Below is an example of how Air freight packing can save money.

Example: A Swiss firm ships ceramic heating tubes made up in consignments of 24 tubes of different diameters with an average weight of 300g each. Total net weight on one such consignment is 7.2 kg. When the company shipped by surface, it had to pack the consignment in five small wooden crates, which in turn went into a wooden crate. Together with the packing material (shredded wood) the packing weighed 64.5 kg.

Eventually the firm switched to Air freight and devised new packing. It consists of one corrugated cardboard box, expanded polystyrene and foam rubber for cushioning, and two wooden boards for stiffening.

Total weight of the new packing is only 6.9 kg - a saving of 54.4 kg.

Of course certain goods are unsuited to carriage by Air, including many bulky goods and raw materials, where the high cost outweighs other advantages. Hazardous cargoes are subject to strict regulations for Air freight. As a general rule, the longer the journey for an export shipment, the less favourable the Air Cargo rate becomes, compared with Ocean freight.

Procedures for Shipping Ocean Freight have been developed over centuries and are therefore complex. Air freight procedures are newer and simpler. All the same, the procedures may take up too much of an exporter's time and he may wish to use the services of an Air Cargo Agent.

Air Freight Rates

Air freight rates vary more than shipping rates, but the basis of calculation is usually a price per kilogram (or 427 cubic inches) with certain minimum charges.

Because bulky cargoes present problems to Airlines, rates are sometimes charged by volume rather than weight. That occurs if 1 kg of air freight exceeds a volume of 7 cubic decimeters. Other costs which may be incurred include:

- ★ Terminal charges for Customs clearance
- ★ Sorting, pick-up and delivery
- ★ Transit charges at the Airport
- ★ Over-flying tax now charged by some states and which Airlines add to the freight costs

Air Way Bill

The documentation for Air freight is far simpler than for Ocean freight. If exporting by Air freight, the exporter normally begins by completing an Air-consignment note, or letter of instruction to the Airline. This note gives basic details of the cargo, the customer's name and address and the services the exporter requires, such as COD or special insurance arrangements.

From these instructions the airline prepares the **Air Waybill.** This document is

- ★ A receipt from the Airline acknowledging that it has received the consignment from the Shipper
- ★ A contract between the Shipper and the Airline for moving the goods
- ★ An instruction sheet
- ★ A customs declaration
- ★ A bill for the freight
- ★ A certificate of insurance, if the amount and extent of insurance are included in it.

The Air Waybill is an internationally standardised document, printed in English and in the language of the Air carrier. Unlike the Bill of Lading, the Air Waybill does not give title to the goods.

As the goods go forward, an Air Waybill goes automatically to the consignee or customer to enable him to collect the goods without further formality, unless there is a COD arrangement. Such an arrangement is a major protection when using Air freight, if payment is required before the goods are collected by the customer.

Choosing the right transport In the great majority of cases, geography, availability of services and the physical characteristics of the product will leave the exporter little choice as to which mode of transport he chooses. But an exporter should not assume he is using the best mode until he has really analysed his choices. The obvious choice is not always the best.

The major choice is likely to lie between Sea and Air transport. Road and rail may be used for exports to countries in the same continent. But for most exporters in developing countries, Road and Rail transport are primarily a means of moving goods to and from Docks or Airports.

It has already been considered how freight rates are calculated. But the actual freight rate is not only the cost but it is the total cost of transportation. **What are these other costs?** The additional main costs are:

- ★ **Packing cost** Extra packing may be required for Ocean freight, and this costs money.
- ★ **Time value** The travel time, which can be weeks or months for Ocean freight, means that the exporter may have his money tied up in the product if he cannot receive payment until delivery.

In addition to these two additional costs we must bear in mind some other costs:

- ★ Cost of preparing Shipping documents
- ★ Handling fees and Port dues
- ★ Insurance (dependent on the value of the goods and the risk of damage or loss)

TRANSPORTATION AND SHIPMENT

Always reserve the shipping space, ensure proper Shipping/Port Documents, give required declaration thereon, fill in the correct classifications, etc. Despatch the documents to the agent in time, to keep to the delivery schedule.

The process of shipment involves various stages right from the reservation of shipping space to transportation of goods from the exporter's place to the Port of shipment, preparation of Shipping documents and actual shipment.

Clearing and Forwarding Agent

For smooth and timely shipment of cargo, the exporter should appoint a suitable Clearing & Forwarding Agent. Nevertheless, he should prepare the shipping documents himself as there are many intricacies and technicalities which he alone would know properly. He should not depend too much on the C&F Agent, who should be entrusted with getting the documents processed and shipment only.

Export cargo can be despatched to the overseas buyer by Sea, Air, Post, Land, River, etc. Shipment by sea is however, the most popular and generally resorted to as it is comparatively cheaper besides the ship's capacity is unlimited and can carry any quantity of cargo. Nevertheless the other modes of conveyance, particularly air are being increasingly utilised as they are quicker and safer though expensive. But export by land or river is limited to neighbouring countries like Nepal, Bangladesh, Pakistan, Bhutan or even Afghanistan.

For smooth and timely shipment of goods, the exporter must appoint a suitable Clearing and Forwarding Agent who is able to, *inter alia*, provide the following services:

Essential

(i) Warehousing facilities before the goods are transported to docks.

(ii) Transportation of goods to docks and arrangement of warehousing at port.

(iii) Booking of shipping space or air freighting, and advice on relative cost of sending goods by Sea and Air.

(iv) Arrangement for shipment to be on board.
(v) Equipped with/can provide information on shipping lines and freight to different destinations, and various charges payable by exporters.
(vi) Obtaining Marine Insurance Policies.
(vii) Preparation and processing of shipping documents, Bills of Lading, Dock Receipt, Export Declarations, Consular Invoices, Certificate of Origin, etc.
(viii) Forwarding of Banking collection papers.
(ix) Storage facilities abroad, at least in major international markets, to warehouse the goods, in case the importer refuses to take delivery on any account.
(x) Can trace the goods, if shipment goes astray, through his international connections.
(xi) Arrangement for assessing the damage to shipment en route.

Reservation of Shipping Space

Booking memos/note Reservation can be done either through a formal letter or even by conveying necessary information on phone. A formal letter known as Booking Memo/Note should contain the following information:

(i) Name and address of the shipper (exporter)
(ii) Details of cargo i.e. the product, weight/volume, number of cases, etc.
(iii) Port of loading and destination
(iv) Date of loading

Shipping Order

On reservation of shipping space, the concerned company issues a document known as Shipping Order. While its original copy is sent to the exporter, its duplicate is meant for the Commanding Officer of the ship for receiving on board the ship and the cargo specified therein. It contains details regarding the cargo, name of the broker if any, and shipper, expected date of loading and freight rate.

Transport to Port

On getting the shipping space reserved, exporter should take steps to transport the goods from factory/warehouse to the port of loading either by road transport or rail. Normally rail transportation may be resorted to on account of the priority given in cargo movement.

I. TRANSPORT BY RAIL

> Transportation of goods by rail can also be done in full wagon or in small lots as the case may be. The goods can be booked at any Railway Station for the port of loading.

However, the exporter may like to obtain priority in movement, in accordance with the procedure detailed below:

Procedure

For obtaining rail priority, the exporter should apply to the Station Master of the Railway Station concerned, with the following documents:

(i) Copy of shipping order or a letter from the shipping company stating that shipping space has been reserved for a particular date.

(ii) A letter stating the date by which the cargo should be moved in order to catch the sailing.

A shipping company's certificate as at (i) above is however, not necessary in case of cotton textiles, power alcohol and raw tobacco, deoiled cake from solvent extraction plants, etc.

Indent for Wagons

The exporter should send a forwarding note duly filled in along with the prescribed fee for indenting a wagon. The type of wagon, open or covered should also be indicated.

Railway Receipt

On booking the cargo, the Railways issue to the consignors a Railway Receipt (RR). It may either be 'Freight Paid' or 'Freight-to-Pay'. It can be endorsed in favour of the consignee who may be the exporter's Agent/Branch at the Port of loading. With such endorsements, the endorsee is enabled to take delivery of the goods at the destination.

Shipping Documents

Any export shipment whether by Sea, Air or Post and Land route involves several documents. The format of some of these documents/forms although common for all ports, differ at some. Contact your clearing and Forwarding Agent for proper knowledge and guidance.

For shipment of cargo, several documents are required to be presented to the Customs/Port Authorities. It is on the basis of these documents/statements, etc. that necessary permission is granted to export goods. Therefore, a deeper knowledge about these documents is necessary for quicker clearance of goods at the Customs and Port Offices. Some of the important documents have been explained in the foregoing paragraphs.

Shipping Instructions

The Railway Receipt (RR) [or the Goods Receipt (GR) in case the export consignment is by road to the port of shipment] along with other documents (particularly and usually the Invoice and Packing list) should be sent to the Clearing and Forwarding Agent retained by the exporter. Such documents should be sent under the cover of Shipping Instructions, detailing:

(i) Cargo details
(ii) Name of the Vessel
(iii) Date of sailing or flight No.
(iv) Shipping company/Airlines
(v) List of Documents being sent

II PROCEDURE FOR EXPORT BY SEA

> The procedure for export at different sea ports is different. Although the Documents for Customs are the same, the documents for Port Authorities differ.

The Shipping Documents can broadly be divided into two categories, namely, (i) Principal Documents and (ii) Additional Documents. More or less all the documents have already been explained.

The Principal Documents for Port Authorities are different for different Ports, but the documents to be submitted to the Customs Authorities at all the ports are the same. The additional documents are common and have to be submitted to the Customs Authorities at all the ports. The documents for shipments are usually prepared by the Customs House Agent, and hence is not dealt with here.

Process of Shipment

There are different stages involved in the shipment of goods. These are:-

(i) Customs verification of Shipping Bills
(ii) Carting and Receipt of Cargo of/in transit Sheds
(iii) Cargo examination at Docks
(iv) Loading of cargo
(v) Issue of Mate Receipt

The procedure adopted at different ports relating to different stages is different. Since all these formalities are, by and large, to be completed by the Clearing and Forwarding Agents, these are not discussed here.

Mate Receipt

After the loading of cargo, the Master of the Vessel issues a document known as the Mate Receipt. It contains details regarding the name of the vessel, berth, date of shipment, description of packages, marks and numbers, conditions of cargo at the time of its receipt on board.

Qualified Mate Receipt

The Qualified Mate Receipt shows that the cargo at the time of its receipt on Board was not in perfect condition. Hence, it should not be accepted from the vessel unless it is so desired and endorsed on the Dock Challan by the exporter.

Endorsement by Customs Preventive Officer (CPO)

After obtaining the Mate Receipt, the exporter should submit the receipt and all copies of Shipping Bill including Export Promotion copy, to the Customs Preventive Officer (on duty). The CPO puts the stamp of shipment and his signature on the Shipping Bill and makes an endorsement on Export Licence/ Certificate regarding shipment of export cargo on the AR4/5 Form, Invoice and on such other documents wherever required.

Bill of Lading

It is issued by the Shipping Company or its agent usually after the cargo is loaded on the ship and Mate Receipt has been obtained. Its style and layout may be different but contents are almost the same. Normally, it is made out in sets, a set consisting of certain number of originals (two or three) and a few copies, depending upon the requirement of buyer. The number of copies in original are known as 'Full Set B/L'. The originals signed by the company are negotiable, copies being non negotiable.

The Bill of Lading is a document of:

(i) Title of goods shipped,
(ii) The receipt for the goods shipped and admission of their apparent conditions and quality at the time of shipment,
(iii) An evidence of the contract of affreightment
(iv) It is transferable by endorsement and delivery.

Kinds of bill of lading The kinds of B/L are explained in Chapter 39.

Shut-out Advice

No Shut-out Notice is to be filed. Where the ship does not accept the Cargo in full, a Shut Out Advice is issued showing the goods/packages not accepted. In case such cargo is desired to be shipped by a subsequent vessel, a fresh Shipping Bill has to be filed and Carting Permit obtained from the Ship's Agent and the superintendent of the shed where the cargo is to be loaded.

Shipment Advice

On the receipt of Bill of Lading, the exporter should send a shipping or Shipment Advice along with the following documents to his overseas buyer.

(i) Bill of Lading (non-negotiable copy)
(ii) Commercial Invoice or invoice (copy)
(iii) Customs/Consular Invoice (copy), if any
(iv) Packing List

IIA. SHIPMENT THROUGH INLAND CONTAINER DEPOTS AND CONTAINER DEPOTS AND CONTAINER FREIGHT STATIONS

A scheme to accept containerised cargo for export by Sea at selected places like Delhi, Panipat, Ludiana, Jalandhar, Jaipur, Morabad, Ahmedabad, Hyderabad, Bangalore, Guntur, etc., has been introduced. This chapter explains the details of the scheme of ICDs including the process for the cargo/ documents. Contact the concerned ICD for further information before sending the consignment there for export.

Presentation of the Shipping Bill (S/B)

The exporter will file Shipping Bills at the export section of the Inland Container Depot (ICD), in case the cargo comprises of a Full Container Load (FCL) and at the Container Freight Station (CFS) in case the cargo comprises of Less than Container Load (LCL). In case of Duty Free, Dutiable and Ex-bond Shipping Bills, 5 copies are filed comprising of Original, Duplicate, Triplicate (Export Promotion) and two Transference copies and in case of Drawback Shipping Bills, 6 copies are filed, the Drawback copy being extra compared to other Shipping Bills. The export section will allot a serial number to the Shipping Bill and affix the date of filing on the Shipping Bill.

Port of exit In addition to the usual information given on the Shipping Bill, the exporter should maintain the Port of exit and the serial number of the containers. Such container must have different marks and number details, which may be settled by the Collector in consultation with the Railways and Steamer Agents.

Documents to be Sent with Shipping Bill

Following documents are to be sent with the Shipping Bill

(1) Invoice – 3 copies plus 2 copies showing excise clearance
(2) Packing-cum-weight list – 2 copies
(3) GR Form in duplicate
(4) Buyer's order
(5) Copy of Letter of credit
(6) Export Licence/Permit if applicable on the export produced
(7) Inspection Certificate or a letter from the buyer that they do not want any inspection to be carried out by any agency in India
(8) AR-4 Form of Central Excise – 2 copies
(9) Any other document

Scrutiny of Shipping Bills

After noting all the documents sent along with the shipping bill, the proper officer scrutinises the Shipping Bill with respect to the following -

(i) To check the forms used
(ii) To check whether all the columns of Shipping Bill, GR Form, Invoice, etc., have been duly filled.
(iii) To check that each S/Bill submitted at the Customs House has been signed by an authorised representative of the exporter. In case the documents have been presented by a licensed Customs House Agent (CHA), to check whether, in addition to the signature of the exporter, the S/Bill has been signed by an authorised representative of the CHA.
(iv) To check that the Harmonised Indian Trade Classification Code Number i.e. ITC(HS) Code of the export commodity has been shown on the Shipping Bill for the purpose of the Statistical Department.
(v) To check that G.R. Forms or GR Waiver from Reserve Bank of India are attached with Shipping Bills where no payment is involved.
(vi) To compare the original and duplicate Shipping Bill.
(vii) To see that all the copies of S/Bills show clearly the GR Number and all the columns of G.R. Form are duly filled in. The R.B.I. Code Number allotted to individual exporters on G.R.Forms should also be shown in the Shipping Bills.
(viii) To see that all particulars, viz. classification, description, quantity (in w.t. and/or in number), value, port of exit, marks and number of the container(s), Duty Drawback Rates and other particulars required in all the columns of the Shipping Bills are correct and complete, that the number of packages, weight and value are declared both in figures and in words.
(ix) To return the S/Bill which are lacking in requirements or under objection and to accept them again on furnishing the requisite particulars for which they were returned.

The Drawback S/Bills where FOB value is more than Rs 50,000/- and all Shipping Bills under DEEC Scheme, are sent to the Assistant Collector for final scrutiny.

After scrutiny of papers, the original copies of Shipping Bill, G.R. Form and copies of Invoice, Packing List are detained and retained by Customs Department and a "Customs Detach Number" is allotted on the duplicate and triplicate copies of the S/Bill.

Carting of Goods Inside ICD/CFS

After processing of the S/Bill, the goods are brought inside the ICD/CFS, as the case may be, and stocked in the proper sheds. An acknowledgement of the godown clerk is obtained certifying that the goods have been received in the godown.

Examination

All the Shipping Bills against which goods have been brought inside, are sent to the Assistant Collector and he/she decides as to which material/goods he/she would personally likely to examine and marks those Shipping Bills. Now all the S/Bills are taken to the Custom Superintendent who further marks them for physical examination of the goods by the concerned examining officers. The examination is conducted in accordance with the procedure prescribed for the same. Normally random examination is carried out and in general only 10% examination of goods are examined. But in case the proper officer thinks fit, he can always conduct 100% physical check. The Inspector writes the examination report on duplicate (also on triplicate copy in case of a Drawback S/Bill) and superintendent signs the "LET EXPORT" order on the S/Bill. The goods are now stuffed into the containers and are sealed.

The quantity of goods loaded/shut out should be recorded on the duplicate copy of the G.R., in the space provided for the same. The duplicate copy of the S/Bill, Invoice, Packing List are also retained by the Customs.

The triplicate copy of S/Bill, Drawback copy of S/Bill, copy of G.R. Form, AR-4/AR-4A form, GP1/GP2, all duly signed and endorsed by Customs are returned to the exporter or his authorised CHA. After showing the EP copy of the shipping line, the exporter gets the Bill of Lading from them.

Transit to the Gateway Port

The sealed containers are carried by rail to the Gateway Port. The two Transference copies of the S/Bills should be placed in a sealed envelope and handed over to the carrier (Railways) who will be responsible for its being carried along with the container and its production to the Customs Officer at the port of exit.

GR formalities Same as given in the earlier chapter.

Procedure at the Exit Port

At the exit port, the containers will be allowed to be exported under preventive supervision on checking of the seals without any further examination (Examination will only be done if the seals of the containers are found to have been tampered with or on the basis of any information, doubt, etc.). The Preventive Officer who will be inspecting the containers will suitably endorse the two 'Transference Copies of the S/Bills', regarding the fact of shipment in the following manner.

(i) Inspected and found intact the containers bearing the following marks and number:- (1), (2), (3), (4), etc.

(ii) The Customs seals on the above have been shipped under my supervision.

At the port of shipment, the steamer Agent will also file the export manifest in duplicate regarding the containerised cargo, in the container unit of the export department of the Custom House.

The container unit of the export dept. will, within 24 hours of the receipt of the S/Bills, telex that portion regarding the fact of the shipment to the concerned ICD giving reference of the S/Bill number to which it pertains. The 'container unit', with reference to the date of filing of the S/Bill at the ICD/CFS and the date of entry outwards of the vessel by which it has been shipped and in case there has been any change in the rate of Duty/Cess in between the two dates, immediately issue a telex pointing out the same with reference to the particular S/Bill Number. The 'container unit' shall then despatch one copy of the 'Transference S/Bill' and one copy of the export manifest under registered A.D. to the ICD/CFS Collectorate within 48 hours of their receipt. A statement containing the following particulars shall be submitted to the Assistant Collector in-charge of the container unit on a weekly basis:

(i) Shipping Bill Number, date of filing of S/Bill at the ICD, date of entry outwards of the vessel whether any change in rate of duty has taken place, if so whether any telex has been issued,

(ii) date of loading of the container,

(iii) date of receipt of the S/Bills in the container unit of the Export Department,

(iv) date of filing of the Export Manifest,

(v) date of despatch of the documents referred to above, to the ICD Collectorate,

(vi) date of telex regarding GR forms issued to the ICD Collectorate.

The Assistant Collector will check the statement to ensure that all the Shipping Bills and manifest have been duly despatched to the ICD/CFS Collectorate and that telexes regarding shipment certificates and change of Duty (if any) have been duly despatched. A copy of the statement may also be forwarded to the ICD/CFS Collectorate each week so that proper correlation can be kept at the end.

The second copy of the Transference Shipment Bill will be retained by the Custom House for publication of export statistics.

Procedure at the ICD Collectorate

The Export Manifest, Transference copies of S/Bill and the weekly statement received from the Custom House will be correlated for finalisation of drawback claims, closure of export manifest and for redeeming of bonds if any, for export of import containers within six months of the date of importation.

Transference copies of the S/Bill should also be scrutinised from the point of view of entry outwards of the vessel, to ensure that no change in export Duty/Cess has taken place in between initial assessment made in the ICD and final export. If any change is there, the duty Cess should be collected or refunded as per Section 27 and 28 of the Customs Act, 1962.

III EXPORT BY AIR

Air freighting of cargo of "Trade goods" and "Trade Sample" is a little different. The basic distinction between a 'Sample' and 'Trade goods' is that the former is free of payment and the latter is sent against payment only.

The procedure for air freighting of cargo is by and large, similar to the shipment of goods by sea as detailed in the previous paragraphs. But, the procedure of filling documents and their processing, etc., is different in airports which has been computerised.

Air Freighting of Samples

Samples to be exported by air are divided into three categories depending upon their value. The documents required for Air freighting are as given below:

For sample, where the value is not more than Rs 10,000

(i) Free Shipping Bill
(ii) Invoice
(iii) Simple declaration that the value of the sample does not exceed Rs 10,000
(iv) Any other document.

For samples of value of more than Rs 10,000

(i) Free Shipping Bill
(ii) Invoice
(iii) A Certificate from the Bank (AD in FOREX) saying that:
   1. the export does not involve any transaction in Foreign Exchange, and
   2. give a notation to the effect that the value of shipment shall be subjected to acceptance by Customs.

Having completed these documents, the exporter may submit the samples to the Airlines concerned.

Air Freighting of Trade Goods

For exporting goods by air, the consignment should in the first instance, be cleared/passed by the concerned Authorities/Export Inspection Agencies, if the same are Excisable/covered by Preshipment Inspection Rules. The manner of such clearance has been detailed in Module No. 35.

Customs Clearance of Exports by Air

The phases involved in the Customs Clearance of export cargo by air are the same as for Customs Clearance of export cargo going by ship, which has already been discussed in the preceding paragraphs.

However, suitable adjustments have been made in these phases to suit the requirements of expeditious movement of cargo by air. These are mentioned below:

(i) Actual booking of the flight concerned is done in advance. Even Airway Bill is obtained before arrival of the flight.

(ii) All the documents required for customs clearance i.e. the Shipping Bill, the appropriate type, and all the supporting documents as required in connection with the shipment by a vessel are to be brought along with the cargo for which booking has already been done. The documents are first submitted to the section meant for checking them at the Air Cargo Complex. After the documents have been checked and physical examination order has been given, physical examination is conducted in quick succession.

(iii) Physical examination is conducted on a much larger scale in respect of export by air, as compared to export by vessel i.e. 50 to 25 per cent of the total in respect of air cargo, as against 1 to 2 per cent of the total in respect of cargo moving by vessel. Each packet is to be passed for shipment—whether examined and passed for shipment or passed for shipment.

(iv) The export cargo examined and passed for shipment is kept under the charge of Customs in the control of Ground Handling Authorities. Usually some cooling period is observed, 24 to 48 hrs. before the cargo is to be loaded on board the aircraft.

(v) Before arrival of the flight Export General Manifest (EGM) whether provisional or final, is to be prepared by the Airline concerned and is to be handed over to the Customs Authority.

(vi) With the help of EGM, goods are to be moved from the storage under Customs charge to the place wherefrom they are to be moved alongside the aircraft for being loaded on board.

(vii) In the case of air flights, no Entry Inward Permit is required for each flight. There is standing facility granted to the Airline concerned for landing and taking off specified flight. Hence, Non-Rotation Number is allotted in advance. This number is allotted by the Station-Officer on duty when the flight has landed.

(viii) The Customs Officer who has to supervise the loading operation with reference to the EGM has to write the Rotation Number on the Shipping Bill—the copies available at that stage and the EGM.

(ix) Unlike the practice followed in the case of export by ship, there is no arrangement for associating a Preventive Officer right from the stage when Entry Inward Permit is granted. The Customs Officer in-charge of the duty routine for the period when the flights are scheduled to land, assigns the task of supervision unloading and loading operation to Customs Officials on duty.

(x) After the loading of the cargo on board the aircraft, the Captain does not issue Mate's Receipt. He signs the duplicate and triplicate copy of the Shipping Bill against contents received. He may have the initial copy of the Shipping Bill. This flexibility is provided in keeping with requirement of air cargo's expeditious movement.

Air Way Bill

The airlines concerned issues the Air Way Bill or Air consignment Note relating to the Consignment. It is a document similar to the Bill of Lading discussed earlier, the major difference being that is "not negotiable".

After the export of cargo, the Customs Authorities will return the Shipping Bill (export promotion copy) duly authenticated by them along with all the documents except the original copy of GR and AR4/5 Form, Invoice and Packing List.

Where the goods are not loaded on account of non-availability of space, the Customs authenticated copy of the Shipping Bill is returned to the exporter or his agent after the actual loading of the Cargo.

SHIPMENT ADVICE

After sending the goods by air, send by courier or fax a shipment or shipping advice along with the following documents to the overseas buyer:

(i) Air Way Bill
(ii) Invoice
(iii) Customs/Consular Invoice
(iv) Packing List

IV EXPORT BY POST

> Exports of articles by post can be grouped under two heads, namely, (i) Gift parcels and trade samples not involving Foreign exchange and (ii) Trade goods i.e. the articles which involve foreign exchange.

Trade Samples/Gift Parcels

The Regulations and Procedure for sending Trade Samples abroad has been dealt with in Module No.24.

Trade Goods

Trade goods i.e. products involving foreign exchange are also allowed to be exported by Post. These are divided into three categories, namely:

(i) Jewellery items
(ii) Goods other than jewellery, not entitled to Customs Duty Drawback
(iii) Goods which are entitled to Customs Duty Drawback.

There is a little different procedure for exporting jewellery items and goods entitled to Customs Duty Drawback or Excise rebate.

Drawback Articles

All parcels or articles proposed to be exported under the scheme of drawback or excise rebate may or may not be examined by Central Excise authorities before clearance from a factory or warehouse. Where examination is required, the articles should be presented to the jurisdictional excise office along with the Form AR4/AR5 and Form for Claim of Drawback.

Drawback Form

This form is required to be filled in the case of articles entitled to Customs Duty drawback known as Drawback Parcels. The exporter should fill in part 1 of this form (in quadruplicate) which is in five parts. The sealed Parcels and Drawback Form duly filled in will be returned to the exporter for presentation at the booking counter of the Post Office.

Form AR4/AR5

These Forms are to be filled in quadruplicate in case of goods to be exported by Post under Excise rebate. The duplicate copy of this duly processed Form should be affixed with sufficient Postage Stamps before presenting them at the Post Office.

Before or simultaneous with presenting the trade goods entitled to Customs Duty Drawback to the Post Office, the exporters should send separately to the Customs Office which is attached with the foreign Post Office, the following documents:

(i) Commercial Invoice for "canalised items" - the Invoice must be endorsed by the Canalising Agency,
(ii) Packing List in case there is more than one parcel in one consignment,
(iii) Quality Control and Pre-shipment Inspection Certificate, if required.

Documents

In addition to the documents stated above, which are to be submitted to the Customs Office attached with the foreign Post Office, the exporter is required to prepare the following documents to be submitted to the booking Post Office along with the Parcel.

These documents are by and large, common for all kinds of trade goods i.e. (i) Jewellery items (ii) goods other than jewellery not entitled to Customs Duty Drawback and (iii) Drawback articles.

Small Pouch

For speedy clearance of the Parcel, the exporter should stitch one small pouch on one of the packets (where there is more than one Packet) and keep therein:

(i) PP Form (2nd copy)
(ii) Invoice (one copy)
(iii) Packing List (one copy)
(iv) Self-addressed envelope with sufficient postage stamps for registration.

After keeping the above mentioned documents in the pouch, stitch it and write on the parcel in block letters "Documents Enclosed."

Documents Needed in Export of Trade Goods

For exporting Products involving foreign exchange i.e. trade goods by Post, the following documents are required to be filled in:

(i) The PP Form (in duplicate, with original copy duly countersigned) should be presented to the Bank for counter-signatures. However, the PP Form covering parcels containing articles of jewellery or precious stones must first be produced for valuation to the Customs who will seal the parcel and stamp the invoice. The Bank will countersign the PP Form only after the completion of customs formalities. All parcels would moreover be addressed to the Bank's Branch or correspondent in the country of importation, except where (1) advance payment has been received for export, (2) where the irrevocable Letter of Credit has been opened in favour of the exporter and advised through the Bank concerned and (3) where the exporter has obtained prior approval of the RBI for addressing the parcel direct to the consignee.
(ii) Export Licence, if applicable.
(iii) Drawback Form in quadruplicate for goods entitled to Customs Duty Drawback duly processed in the manner described earlier.

(iv) AR4/5 Form (in sixtuplicate) for goods entitled to excise rebate processed in the manner described earlier.
(v) Insurance Cover Note issued by Post Offices for articles like jewellery and precious stones for which insurance is obligatory.
(vi) Duty Exemption Entitlement Certificate, if applicable.
(vii) Commercial Invoice (in duplicate).
(viii) Packing List (one copy).

Make Up and Packing of Parcels

All post parcels whether of trade samples or trade goods are required to be packed in the prescribed manner in terms of the dimensions and the weight. The Foreign/Head Post Offices have to be contacted for details.

Customs Clearance of Post Parcel

Post parcels can be sent from any part of the country even without completing Customs Clearance before the booking of the parcel. As such, employment of Customs House Agent can be easily dispensed with. However, it should not be construed that the post parcel can be despatched to foreign destinations without Customs check. In fact the booking Post Office cannot prepare the final bag for destination. The parcel has to be routed through the foreign Post Office having the destination within its jurisdiction, where Customs check and Clearance are arranged. At each foreign Post Office there are two wings - Customs Wing and Postal Wing. The latter has to get Customs examined Parcels received from different Post Offices of the country for despatch to foreign destinations.

In the case of post parcel there is no Shipping Bill required instead a Customs Declaration Form, prescribed by the Universal Postal Union (UPU)—an international Apex body coordinating the activities of national Postal Administration to facilitate movement of Postal articles among different countries of the world is required. This document, popularly known by its code number CP2/CP3 has to be prepared in quadruplicate duly signed by the sender. One copy is to be pasted on the parcel and two copies are to be placed inside the parcel along with two copies of the Invoice. One copy is to be retained by the sender for record and future reference.

Another document prescribed by the Universal Postal Union (UPU) is the Despatch Note, popularly known by its code number, CP2. It has to be filled in by the sender to specify the action to be taken by the postal authority at the destination if the address is not traceable or if the importer refuses to accept the parcel. It has to be safely tagged to the parcel.

The other prescriptions of the Universal Postal Union (UP) are regarding the minimum and maximum sizes of the parcel and its maximum weight.

Minimum size: Total surface area not to be less than 140 mm × 90 mm.

Maximum size: Lengthwise not more than 1.05 M Measurement of any other side of circumference 0.9M/2.00M

The two taken together

Maximum Weight: 10 kg for most destinations
20 kg for some destinations

SHIPPING ADVICE

Soon after the export of goods whether by Sea, Air or Post and receipt of Bill of Lading/Air Way Bill and other documents, the exporter should send a "Shipping Advice" to his importer abroad. It is a sort of intimation given to the importer so that he starts making arrangements for taking delivery of the consignments. There is no particular form of the Shipping Advice. It contains information regarding the number of Invoice, Bill of Lading/Air Way Bill, name of vessel/flight number, name of port, description of goods and quantity and date of export. It should be sent along with the following documents:

(i) Bill of lading (non-negotiable copy)
(ii) Invoice
(iii) Customs Invoice/Consular Invoice
(iv) Packing list

COMPUTERISED PROCESSING OF EXPORT DOCUMENTS

In order to ensure increased automation in the processing of import and export documentation for expeditious clearance of cargo through the Air Cargo Unit at the IGI Airport, Delhi, Customs has introduced electronic processing of export documents relating to export of goods w.e.f. 1.11.1996. After its success, the Indian Customs EDI systems has been extended to Mumbai and ICD Tughlakabad (New Delhi) and will be implemented in a phased manner to cover other Customs Houses.

OCEAN/AIR/DECISIONS EXERCISE

A Shipping Manager must decide between air and sea shipment for the following consignments. The Company pays 12% per annum for its working capital requirements, and all the consignments are due to be paid for on Documentary Sight Terms on arrival at final destination.

Air freight takes 24 hours to reach the final destination. Sea transportation with the necessary land links takes two months on an average.

Calculate the total cost of sea transport. Compare this with the air freight cost. Which method of transport can be recommended for each consignment? What additional information might be needed in each case to assist in making a decision? All these points have to be thought about.

Item	*Value (Rs)*	*Ocean Freight Cost (Rs)*	*Extra Packing for Ocean Freight (Rs)*	*Air Freight Cost (Rs)*
Shoes	50,000	2,000	1,000	10,000
Transistor Radios	5,00,000	2,000	1,000	12,000
Tractor	1,00,000	6,000	500	40,000
Fresh-cut flowers	5,000	2,000	500	6,000
Tinned Mangoes	1,000	1,000	None	2,000
Publicity Material	5,000	1,000	None	5,000
Hand-made Jewellery	1,00,000	1,000	750	3,500
Hammers	80,000	20,000	None	2,00,000

// CHAPTER 26 //

MARINE AND AIR CARGO INSURANCE

A marine or cargo insurance policy has an international character and therefore, a policy taken in one country is acceptable in the other country. This is because of the adoption of universally acceptable uniform rules governing insurance in different countries.

CARGO INSURANCE

Cargo or Marine insurance in India is subjected to the following legislations:

- ★ The Insurance Act, 1938; and Insurance Rules, 1939
- ★ Marine Insurance Act, 1963

In India, cargo insurance cover is provided only by the nationalised insurance companies i.e. General Insurance Corporation of India or its four subsidiaries in India. These companies operate within the standard rules and regulations including those which are provided in the 'All India Marine Cargo Tariff' in India.

Marine Insurance Contract

Article 3 of the Indian Marine Insurance Act, 1963 defines marine insurance contract as follows:

"It is an agreement whereby the insurer undertakes to indemnify the assured in the manner and to the extent thereby agreed, against marine losses, that is to say, the losses incidental to marine adventure."

Before different aspects of the marine insurance contract are explained, it should be clearly understood that the word "marine" used in the definition does not have any specific connotation. Despite the usage of this word, cargo insurance principles as stated in the definition are equally applicable to all modes of transport used in the carriage of goods.

Parties to the Contract

There are two parties to the agreement-insurer and insured. The insurer is the insurance company, also known as underwriters, which assumes the liability when the loss takes place. On the other hand, the insured is the one who either procures an insurance policy or becomes a beneficiary through it.

The Need for Insurance

All experienced exporters are aware of the risks to their cargo while it is in transit. These include fire, storm, collision, pilferage, leakage and explosions. Goods travelling from the country must be insured against loss or damage at each stage of their journey, so that whatever mode of transport is being used, neither the exporter nor the customer suffers any loss.

In insurance language the shipment of goods is called an 'adventure' or 'venture' - terms used long ago when the shipment of goods was far more hazardous than it is today. Goods should be insured if a person has a financial stake (an 'insurable interest') in the arrival of the goods at their destination. Under the law, a person may purchase marine insurance in a venture only if he has insurable interest in it.

Either the exporter or his customer will be liable for the goods at any one point in the journey. The liability laid down in terms of delivery normally conform to when the title of ownership to the goods passes from the exporter to the customer. This is known as the *passing of risk*.

For example, in an FOB contract the transfer of ownership is at the point where the goods pass over the ship's rail. In theory the exporter insures the goods upto that point and the customer takes responsibility from then on. (In practice, the customer normally buys insurance to cover the whole journey in FOB, FAS and C and F contracts, from the exporter's warehouse to the final destination.)

Under a CIF contract, the exporter takes out ocean insurance even though his ownership and responsibility for loss or damage and when the goods have been placed on the vessel. He takes out cover against the risks customarily covered in his particular trade. He is not required to do more unless both parties have agreed to it. These rules are of course subject to local usage. Whatever allocation of responsibility is agreed on, it must be absolutely clear and cover any emergency.

Even when an exporter's responsibility ends when he leaves the consignment at the dock (FAS), it may be wise in many cases for him to take an insurance for the whole voyage, because his financial stake in the 'venture' continues up until he is actually paid for the goods. If the goods are damaged in transit the customer may be unwilling, or unable even, to pay for them.

To avoid any such risks, the exporter should make it a general policy that his conditions of sale make him responsible for providing marine insurance - even in FOB contracts. If this is not possible due to local customs, an exporter can purchase special contingency insurance which will make up any shortage in claims paid by the customer's insurance. It should be noted that *marine insurance is a misleading term and can be extended to cover transportation over land or on inland waterways.*

How to Insure

Insurance can be arranged by an insurance broker or an insurance company. An insurance policy is issued when the goods are insured, but it is also usual to use a 'certificate of insurance' which is used as an evidence of insurance. A policy is a contract, a legal document, and principally it serves as an evidence of the agreement between the insurer and the person taking insurance. The marine insurance policy or certificate forms part of the shipping documents. A policy is also used as collateral security when an exporter gets an advance against his bank credit.

Individual policies for a single shipment are seldom used by companies regularly engaged in foreign trade. Exporters normally insure under long term policies, known as 'Open Cover'. These contracts may run for a fixed time or indefinitely until cancellation. As evidence of insurance of each shipment, the insured or his insurance broker can issue a certificate of insurance, which gives all the information contained in an insurance policy. The open cover gives the exporter automatic, continuous coverage. It also saves him the trouble of having to arrange for protection every time he makes a shipment, and he always knows his exact insurance costs. This makes it easier for him to quote a landed sales price.

On a CIF contract the exporter sends the certificate of insurance to the customer, for him to claim at the port of destination if the goods have been damaged on the ship.

It is a common practice to insure for 10% above the CIF value of the goods, in order to allow for problems involved in replacing the goods, waiting for the money etc. The goods may be insured for even higher amounts - for example, to cover loss of import duty paid on products which have subsequently disappeared.

Kinds of Coverage

In buying insurance, the object is to buy as much protection as is necessary or prudent, at as low a cost as possible. To do this, one has to know what risks can be covered, and to decide how much coverage is needed.

An insurance policy defines its coverage in terms of the nature of the loss or damage, the extent of the loss or damage, and the conditions under which it occurred.

For example, sea-water damage is a major risk and is covered to some extent by all marine policies. But one policy may pay for sea-water damage only if the loss is total or if the vessel has been stranded, sunk, burnt, or in a collision. Another policy may be more inclusive, and pay for partial sea-water damage caused not only by such calamities, but even by heavy weather (a storm, etc.).

Generally, the specific risks or perils covered by a policy are not consolidated in a single paragraph, they are listed in several clauses set into various places in the policy. In the case of raw materials, policies sometimes do not fully define the coverage, and claims are settled according to prevailing customs in the trade.

Kinds of Perils

The events which lead to loss or damage to the cargo are the perils against which insurance cover can be obtained. These perils may be categorised into four groups:

- ★ Marine Perils (Act of God - natural calamity)
- ★ Extraneous Perils (Faults in loading, unloading, breakage, leakage, etc.)
- ★ War Perils (War, civil war, revolution, rebellion, etc.)
- ★ Strike Perils (Strike, lockouts, etc.)

Kinds of Losses

Losses are of two types. These are

- ★ Total loss
- ★ Partial loss (also known as Average)

Total loss, in turn, can be of two types. These are

- ★ Actual total loss
- ★ Constructive total loss

Partial loss or Average is also of two types. These are

- ★ General Average
- ★ Particular Average

Average terms To a great extent, the protection that a marine insurance policy gives is defined by its 'average' terms.

The word 'average' has a special meaning in insurance. It means partial loss. 'Partial loss' in turn can mean the total loss of part of the insured cargo, or simply damage to all or part of it.

Particular average, is a partial loss suffered by part of the cargo.

General average, is a loss that affects all cargo interests on the ship, and the ship itself. General average has been defined as 'a partial and deliberate sacrifice of the ship, freight, or goods, undertaken for the common safety of the adventure in time of peril and/or extraordinary expenditure with the like object.'

The idea of general average liability is to spread the losses suffered by only some individuals involved in a voyage, so that all interested parties assume their fair share. If for example, a ship founders in a storm and some of the cargo is thrown overboard to save it, the resulting loss is considered 'in general average'. The value of the lost goods is contributed to proportionately by the parties interested in the voyage - all of the cargo owners and the shipowners. Each of them is required to pay a share of the damage, even though his own cargo may not have been lost or damaged at all.

Accidents often result in both general average and particular average losses. Take the example of a fire in a cargo hold. The ship's crew puts out the fire with water. Some of the cargo in the hold is damaged by the fire itself. This is a particular average loss. If the owners of the fire-damaged cargo are insured against this kind of peril, they will be paid for the loss by their insurance company. But cargo in the hold has also been damaged by water used to put the fire out. This is a general average loss. Whether or not the owners of the damaged cargo are insured for this kind of damage, they will be largely reimbursed for the loss by contributions from all the other cargo owners, even if their own group was not damaged, and also from the shipowners.

Types of Insurance

The extent of possible insurance coverage that may be purchased varies; there is a wide variety of standard types of coverage.

Three important ones are Free of Particular Average, With Particular Average, and All Risks.

FPA (free of particular average) This is the minimum coverage in general use. It covers losses due to a ship or aircraft being totally lost. Partial loss is not covered, except to a limited extent and in particular circumstances. Which partial losses are covered and under what conditions vary according to national practice.

WPA (with particular average) Insures against the goods being damaged in transit, but not because the ship was in danger. Partial loss is normally covered with a percentage franchise. That is, losses above a stated percentage of the value of the insured cargo are paid for, in practical terms. The additional coverage one gets with WPA terms, compared with FPA, is protection against damage from sea water caused by 'heavy weather'.

All risks Insures against most risks **except risk of *force majeur* (war)** unless the exporter has specifically asked for this to be included.

Additional specific risks may be covered by additions to the FPA and WPA Clauses. These include not only maritime perils, but such risks as damage from hooks, oil, rain, bilge or fresh water, theft, shortage or non-delivery, sweat, contact with other cargo, leakage or breakage.

A variety of clauses are used to cover certain goods against special risks, such as the Institute Provisional Value Clause for grain covers, the Institute Replacement Clause for machinery, the Skimmings Clause for coffee and cocoa, the Labels Clause for canned goods, etc.

'All Risks' coverage is the broadest kind of standard coverage. But it does not, as its name suggests, really cover 'all risks'. The 'All Risks' clause excludes coverage against damage caused by war, strikes, riots, etc. (These perils can be covered by a separate clause.) It covers only physical loss or damage from external causes.

Types of Policies

The contract of cargo insurance in international trade transactions takes *three forms*. It comes into being when either a *Specific Voyage (and Time) Policy or an Open Cover, an Open Policy is procured.*

Specific voyage policy A voyage policy covers the risks that may rise during a journey from one specific place to another.

The terms and conditions of the insurance are set out in the appropriate ILU (Institute of London Underwriters) and other clauses. These clauses cover mainly the perils covered under the policy as well as conditions related to the insurable value and claims according to the Indian Stamp Act. Each policy must be stamped. The stamp duty is recoverable from the insured. For creating transferability, the policy is required to be assigned by blank endorsement by writing 'for and on behalf of' followed by the name of the insured (e.g exporting firm and the signature of the director or partner).

The insurance policy comprises of the "MAR" Policy form, which contains no insurance conditions and the Institute Clauses (A, B or C and War and Strike Clauses) which contain insurance conditions. It must be noted that Duration Clauses, which provide warehouse to warehouse cover, are part of the Institute Cargo Clauses. Hence, unless specifically deleted, the warehouse-to-warehouse cover is deemed to be effective. In this way a Voyage Policy also becomes a Time Policy.

Open cover Open Cover is an insurance arrangement designed specifically to meet the needs of those firms which have substantial import/export turnover and frequent transactions. Such firms are spared the inconvenience of negotiating insurance contracts every time the transaction is to be made. Main features of an Open Cover arrangement are as follows:

i) Unlike an insurance policy, Open Cover is not an enforceable contract. Instead it is an agreement under which the insurance company would honour and accept declarations of shipment of cargoes and issue stamped specific certificates of insurance against each declaration.
ii) Under an Open Cover arrangement, agreement between the insured and the insurer is reached about the subject matter (e.g. goods) insured, packing conditions, voyages, risks covered, rates and other conditions of the cover. The insured can obtain insurance cover within these agreed conditions.
iii) No premium is charged when an Open Cover is issued, but the insurance companies unusually require the insured to furnish either a bank guarantee or cash deposit towards payment of premium against each declaration, as the declarations are made.
iv) The validity period of an Open Cover is twelve months.
v) It is customary to make an Open Cover agreement subject to two limitation clauses, Per Bottom and Per Place Clauses. The effect of these clauses is to limit the liability of the insurance company to an agreed amount. Thus, if the loss in an accident is more than this amount, the loss will be partly recoverable upto this agreed amount. For example, in an Open cover, if the limitation clause is for Rs 10 lakh and the loss is Rs 20 lakh, the insurance company will pay only Rs 10 lakh.

   These two limitations are imposed to reduce the risk of the insurance company. In the case of the Per Bottom Clause, cargo of the value exceeding the agreed amount should not be carried in one carrier. Similarly, under a Per Place clause (also known as Location Clause), cargo exceedng the agreed amount should not be accumulated at one place. It must be understood that according to Indian insurance practice, the effect of the Per Place Clause is not confined only to pre-shipment accumulation of risk; it applies also to similar accumulations at the destination
vi) An Open Cover may be cancelled by either party by giving 30 days notice in writing. This stipulation does not cover War and Strikes risks for ocean voyage. For ocean voyages other than from/to US the notice period for cancellation of War and Strike risks is seven days and for shipments from/to US it is 48 hours.
vii) When the loss takes place, claim will be awarded with reference to insurable value calculated on the basis of CIF plus ten per cent
viii) The duty of the insured is to declare each and every shipment as soon as known. Unintentional failure to export shipment will be condoned by the insurance company. However, if the insured does

not wilfully report shipments, the insurance company may hold the Open Cover null and void for all subsequent shipments.

Open policy Also known as Floating Policy, it has much in common with the Open Cover. This policy benefits clients with a substantial turnover and a large number of dispatches. Thus, it covers a series of consignments with all stipulations of the Open Cover, except that:

i) Open Policy is an enforceable contract of insurance and is hence duly stamped.
ii) Open Policy is for an agreed amount, against which a series of consignments may be dispatched and declared as a result of which the sum insured will gradually diminish by the amount of each declaration until it is finally exhausted.
iii) Even through the open Policy ceases on expiry of one year from the date of its issue, the sum insured is of paramount importance. Therefore, the sum insured may exhaust prior to the expiry of the policy.
iv) Open Policy is subject to cancellation by either party after giving 15 days' notice of cancellation in writing.

What is Not Insured

To have a clear idea of what 'all risks' really means, one must understand the meaning of 'risks' and 'external' as these terms are used in insurance. A 'risk' is something that may happen, but not something that must happen. It is in other words, a possibility that may arise as a fortuity, an accident, and not an inevitability.

This means that marine insurance does not cover the kind of damage that can be expected to occur under normal conditions because of the nature of the goods themselves i.e. their 'inherent vice'. For example, if butter turns rancid during a voyage that is not interrupted by an accident, this damage would be considered a result of its inherent vice, and would not be covered by the policy. Another case of inherent vice would be fragile glassware inadequately packed. Breakage would be due to its inherent vice-in other words, due to internal rather than external causes, even if the packages were handled roughly.

Inherent vice is specifically excluded from coverage in the All Risk Clause, and it is an implied exclusion in all insurance policies, whether or not it is specifically mentioned.

Delay is another exclusion that is usually specifically stated, and it is implied in all policies in any case. This means that if goods are delayed in transit and there is a loss because the delay causes them to spoil or lose market value, this loss is not covered in the case of especially sensitive products, such as meat or butter, it is possible to have the policy changed to pay for physical damage caused by delay, but even then the delay usually must be the result of fortuitous named perils.

Other Exclusions

Clearly, it is as important to understand what marine insurance does not cover as to understand what it does. All insurance is written within a frame of basic conditions, or implied warranties, which do not appear in the policy, but which have been backed up over the years by court decisions. If these conditions are violated, the insurance may be invalidated, and the underwriter would have the option of rejecting claims.

Perhaps the most important principle of insurance is Utmost Good Faith. This means that the insured is obligated to disclose to the insurer all facts relevant to the risk when applying for the insurance. If, for example, an exporter misrepresents the kind of packing used and breakage occurs, the insurance company may well refuse to pay for the damage.

All insurance policies also carry the implied conditions that the assured must follow the generally established trade usages for the particular product, and that he will not contribute to the loss through wilful fault or negligence. Another implied warranty is that the venture must be legal.

Insurance contracts may explicitly limit the coverage for particular goods or circumstances. Thus, the following losses could be excluded in a contract: leakage or hook losses on goods packed in bags; spontaneous combustion fires in cotton; solidification of palm and coconut oil, unless heated storage is provided.

Choosing the Right Coverage

Most exporters will probably want to have the widest form of coverage they can get such as an 'All Risks' coverage. But because of the nature of their goods, underwriters may agree to provide only a more limited form of cover.

Moreover, even though an exporter can get All Risks coverage, he may decide that it is uneconomical. An experienced exporter will come to know the losses he can expect, and may find it cheaper to write them off as trade losses rather than to pay the relatively high All Risks premium.

Products should be insured in the appropriate category. A good rule of thumb is that an exporter should insure for the coverage accepted in his particular trade. The following exercise should help understand which type of insurance to use for particular products.

Claims Procedure

The cardinal point about claim adjustments is that the insured has clearly defined responsibilities when there is a loss. If he does not fulfill these responsibilities, the insurer can refuse to pay.

In the event of loss or damage it is important to claim quickly, usually within one month. All relevant documents must be held by the person claiming, and insurance company procedures must be followed. The Insurance companies themselves will advise.

Generally, the exporter endorses the Insurance policy or certificate on a shipment over to the buyer at the same time he endorses the bill of lading – before the ocean voyage starts. Then the customer becomes the insured party, and if loss or damage occurs from then on it is his responsibility to file the claim. However, the exporter does have a real financial interest in the shipment until he has been paid. Payment may not be forthcoming until the voyage is completed, so the exporter may cover the shipment with his own contingency insurance and then claim if there is a loss.

Procedure and Documentation when a Loss Arises

(a) Give immediate notice of loss to the Insurance company and/or their agents mentioned in the policy, giving the details of loss.

(b) Ensure that all rights against carriers, bailees or other third parties are properly preserved and exercised.

(c) If the packages show any outward sign of loss or damage, the insured and/or their agents must call for a detailed survey by ship surveyors on such packages and also lodge a proper monetary claim on the shipping company for loss or damage found.

(d) If the ship survey is time barred then the insured and/or their agents must call for an insurance survey on such packages before effecting delivery. If the packages are found in apparently sound condition but on unpacking any loss or damage is found, the insured and/or their agents must immediately inform the insurance company and obtain an insurance survey. Insured should keep the goods as well as the contents with its packing materials intact for inspection by the surveyors for proper assessment of loss or damage.

(e) In case of packages which are found to be missing, the insured must lodge a proper monetary claim for the full value of the missing packages, with the shipping company and also with the bailees, and obtain a proper acknowlegement from them.

(f) In terms of Carriage of Goods by Sea Act, 1925, the time limit for filing suits against shipping companies is one year from the date of discharge.

Documents to be accompanied The claims on the insurers should be submitted duly supported by the following documents:

i) Original insurance policy or certificate of insurance duly endorsed by the insured;

ii) Full set of Bill of Lading in respect of total loss claims. Otherwise non-negotiable copy of the Bill of Lading, Airway Bill, Railway Receipt, etc. as applicable;

iii) Copy of invoice with packing/weight list;

iv) Insurance Survey Report or other documentary evidence to substantiate cause and extent of loss;

v) Joint Ship Survey/Discrepancy Certificate issued by the carriers;

vi) Port Authority Landing remarks certificate;

vii) Casual Report when a vessel is missing or lost;

viii) Ship Master's Protest or an authenticated copy of extract from ship's Log Book, in case the vessel encountered heavy weather or other casualty during the voyage;

ix) In case of short landing claims, a Short Landing Certificate issued by the carrier or Port authority;

x) A landed but Missing Certificate from the Port Authority in case the package had landed but is missing;

xi) In the event of General Average claim for refund of GA Deposit, the GA Deposit Receipt and Bank Counter Guarantees;
xii) Triplicate copy of Bill of Entry (in case of India);
xiii) Copies of letters lodging claims on the carriers, Port Authority etc.;
xiv) Letter of Subrogation duly stamped and signed; and
xv) Any other document as may be asked for by the insurers.

Documents needed under rail/road policies The following documents, as applicable, are required to be submitted to insurers in support of claims under Rail/Road Policies:

1. Original Policy or Certificate of insurance duly endorsed
2. Original Railway Receipt (Non-delivery cases)
4. A copy of the Railway Receipt (damage claim)
5. Original Consignment Note (Non-delivery cases - Road Transit Claim)
6. A copy of the Consignment Note (damage claim - Road Transit)
7. Invoice (Original or copy)/packing list/weight specification
8. 'Non Delivery' or 'Partial Delivery' certificate from the Railways/ Road Transport Operators.
9. Open Delivery/Assessment Delivery Certificates (Rail/Road)
10. Certified copy of the Remarks in the Railway Delivery Book (Damage Claims)
11. Certified copy of the Remarks in the Delivery Challan (Road Transit Claims)
12. Independent Surveyor's Report, if any.
13. Copy of (a) Notice of claim lodged on the carriers (Rail/Road)
    (b) Relative Postal Registration Receipts and A.D. Cards
    (c) Subsequent correspondence with the carriers
14. Letter of Subrogation
15. Special Power of Attorney (Rail Transit Claims)
16. Letter of Authority (Rail Transit Claims)

The insured will file claim with the insurance company after meeting the aforementioned requirements. The insurance company is generally contacted immediately on discovery of loss to the cargo, which will assist the insured in carrying out the responsibilities.

It is quite natural that there is disagreement between the insured and the insurers regarding insurance claims. In such a case, the insured can take legal recourse against the insurers and file a legal suit. However, under the Indian Limitation Act, no suit can be filed against the insurer in respect of a claim under an insurance policy after a lapse of three years from-

(a) the date of occurence causing the loss; or
(b) the date when the claim is repudiated either partly or wholly

It is clear that if liability is not denied for three years, the claim of the insured would become time barred under the law. If the claimants want to keep their claim right open, they will have to file-suit against the insurer before the expiry of the period of three years. The claim would also remain open, if the insurers belatedly repudiate the claim.

Duties of the Insured (Preservation of Recovery Rights)

In the case of a claim it has to be ensured by the claimants that the right of recovery against the carrier is properly preserved. In the absence of the same, recovery action against the carrier becomes prejudiced. This will adversely affect the right of the insured to claim under the policy. This has been incorporated as a specific provision in the Institute Cargo Clauses (A), (B) and (C) under the heading 'Duty of Insured'.

Insured should insist on a carrier's survey, if they observe any damage to the goods while taking delivery. They should demand an open delivery certificate indicating the condition of the goods before delivery is taken. No clean receipt should be issued to the carrier, when the goods are in an apparently damaged condition. The carrier may refuse to give a Damage Certificate/Open delivery Certificate. Then the insured or his representatives, should send a letter stating that he is arranging for a survey to be conducted. If the carrier does not join with the surveyor, insured/claimant should serve a notice on him that the findings of such a survey will be binding on him (carrier). When damage is noticed in the case of an inland transit, the insured must give only a qualified receipt or he can write about the damage upon the delivery challan. Underwriters must also inform the insured of the period within which they have to issue notice of claim against the carrier.

Claims Against Marine Policies

Claims against marine insurance policy when payable to exporters in India will be paid only in rupees by GIC and its subsidiaries, irrespective of the currency of the relative policy. When a claimant is not a resident of India, claims may be settled in foreign currency provided the GIC and its subsidiaries are satisfied that ownership of the goods lost, damaged, etc., vests in such claimant.

GIC will settle claims in rupees in favour of Indian exporters even in cases where the title of goods has passed on to a foreign buyer, if a request to the effect has been made by the non-resident claimant. In such cases a certificate indicating full particulars of the transaction including number of relative GR/PP form and amount paid in settlement of claim will be issued to the exporter to enable him to obtain the necessary approval of RBI for making replacement shipments.

Marine Insurance Contract

Marine Insurance contract is an arrangement by which the insurance company (insurer) agrees to indemnify the owner (insured) of a ship or cargo against risks which are incidental to marine adventure. Such contracts are based on the following principles:

i) Principle of utmost good faith i.e. the insured must disclose to the insurer all the material facts or circumstances which are known to him or which ought to be known to him in the ordinary course of business.

ii) Principle of insurable interest i.e. no person can enter into a valid contract of insurance, unless he had insurable interest in the object

The Statutory Time Limits for Lodging Notice of Claim and Filing Suits

	Time Limit for Lodging Claim	*Time Limit for Filing Suit*
Steamer	Within the period of 3 days from the date of discharge of cargo from overseas vessel.	Within one year from the date of discharge from overseas vessel.
Port Trust Authorities	For "short landing" and "landed but missing." Within 5/7 days from the General Landing date (Bombay Port within 7 days of landing). (Calcutta and Madras Ports within 5 days of landing).	Within 6 months from the date of discharge, 6 months from the date of accrual of the cause (Bombay and Madras Ports). 3 months from the date of accrual of the cause (Calcutta port).
In all cases, one month's notice of intention to file suit must be given. Notice against the Port Authorities Customs/Carriers must be Registered [Post (A.D.)] copies sent to the insurers, to enable them to decide on questions of eventual recovery. The above are as per provisions of the Indian Carriage of Goods by Sea Act, 1925 and provisions of the Major Port Trust Act.		
Rail Carriers	6 months from date of booking (as per Sec.78B of the Indian Railway Act).	3 years from date of delivery or date when consignment ought to have been delivered.
Motor Lorry Carriers	6 months from the time the loss or damage came to knowledge (Sec 10 of the Carriers Act).	-do-
Air International	14 days from the date of delivery of cargo	2 years from the date of arrival at destination or the date on which aircraft ought to have arrived (as per Indian Carriage by Air Act)
Domestic	7 days from the date of delivery of cargo	-do-
Non-delivery International	21 days from the date of booking of cargo	-do-
Domestic	14 days from the date of booking of cargo	-do-
Postal Authorities	Immediately	3 years from the date of postal receipts

or the life insured. Insurable interest is understood as an interest in the preservation of a thing or continuance of a life, as recognised by law. Thus, one can have an insurable interest only when one would stand to benefit financially by the continuance of the life or object insured, otherwise financial loss would result. Thus, a person can take a policy on his ship, an owner of the goods can take policy on cargo and a person entitled to receive freight can take policy on freight. All such persons have insurable interest in the subject manner. Without insurable interest such contracts are merely wagering agreements, which are not valid contracts.

iii) Principle of indemnity i.e. the contracts of insurance only indemnify (make good) a loss resulting from risk covered under the policy. However, the cargo owners are usually allowed a reasonable anticipated profit. In other words, we can say that the marine insurance policy provides a commercial indemnity rather than indemnity in a strict legal sense.

DOS AND DON'TS FOR SAFEGUARDING CARGO FROM DAMAGE OR LOSS

The primary objective of the marine cargo insurance policy is to provide financial protection against unforeseen damage to cargo. Exporters should keep in mind that the insurance will cover only specific types of losses. Situations like loss of business reputation and losses consequential to cargo damage/loss cannot be compensated. It is therefore essential that all organisations do the utmost to minimise cargo losses through risk management. This was the message given to the participants of a workshop on Marine Cargo Insurance held on 23rd June 1977, at Calcutta, organised by FIEO with technical support from the National Insurance Company Ltd.

A prudent approach towards risk management starts from loss control, where good packaging and care through the transit is considered and ensured to minimise the chances of loss itself. Merchandise exported or imported is subject to many hazards, both physical and environmental which can cause loss or damage. Cargo losses are mainly attributed to poor handling, storage, stowage, fire, explosion, sinking, collision, theft, pilferage, non-delivery and weather damage. It is estimated that about 70% of cargo loss is preventable. The following measures can be considered and implemented when planning cargo loss control.

Packaging

Statistics show that nearly 40% of damages occur during handling, storage and transit, and can be prevented by improving the packaging.

Loss Control in Ports

Packaging can play a significant role in reducing pilferage. Choosing an appropriate clearing and forwarding agent and carrier wil ensure that adequate supervision is available during the handling. Proper warehousing and prompt clearing of goods from the port can ensure that the cargo is within control.

Generally, the policy cover is only for the voyage, and is effective from warehouse to warehouse. The policy terminates 60 days after discharge.

The types of loss which are covered include the following:

Actual total loss This occurs when the goods are totally destroyed, or when the goods are so damaged, that they cease to be of the kind insured.

Constructive total loss This is a commercial total loss and arises, when cargo is damaged and the cost of repairing the damage and forwarding the goods to their destination exceeds their value on arrival at the destination.

General average During voyage, a situation sometimes arises where the entire venture may appear to be in danger. In such circumstances, the Captain of the vessel will declare General Average and may take certain extraordinary steps in order to save the entire volume. It may result in an extraordinary sacrifice or expenditure, voluntarily and reasonably made at the time of common peril. As per international practice, all interests have to contribute to make good the losses incurred in the General Average Act. In case the cargo is sacrificed, the owners of the cargo can make their claim directly to their insurers. In case cargo is saved, the owners of the cargo can claim directly to their insurers for their liability to contribute for General Average losses.

Particular average or partial loss, occurs where part of the cargo is totally lost, e.g. non-delivery, theft, loss during loading/unloading and goods arriving in damaged condition.

Documents Required for Processing Cargo Claims

1. Policy certificate of insurance in original
2. Invoice
3. Packing slip
4. Carriers Receipt
5. Certificate of Loss/Damage from Carriers/Port Trust
6. Survey Report
7. Claim Form with Bill
8. Copy of claim on carriers with their reply, if any

The above are requirements in general and they may vary from case to case.

Do's and Don'ts

★ Arrange earliest clearance of goods from carriers.
★ Clear the goods only after carefully examining the packages.
★ Claim on carriers for missing packages, if any.
★ Do not give clean receipt to carrier of goods if they are in a doubtful condition.
★ Clear the imported goods externally damaged, only after joint survey by Steamer Agents/Air Carriers/Customs Authorities and Insurers is done within the statutory time.
★ Clear inland consignments externally damaged only after taking open delivery certificate from Rail/Road transporters.
★ Recondition and repack the damaged goods, making them fit for further transit.
★ Preserve the packing materials intact for inspection by surveyor.
★ Give prompt notice of loss/damage to the insurers with estimate of loss/damage, and to the carriers involved.

★ Assist insurance surveyors to the maximum possible extent.
★ Send notice of claims only under Registered Post with A.D.
★ Preserve the salvage safe till disposal of claim.
★ Extend time limit for filing suit pending finalisation of the claim.
★ Seek refund of duty wherever due.
★ Extend period of insurance, if necessary.

With the advent of the Multimodel Transportation of Goods Act, 1993, it is essential for every exporter to acquaint himself with the provisions of the enactment to ensure compliance with the statutory pre-requisites for fastening liability on the multimodel transport operators. This aspect is especially important for those exporters who mobilise export cargo by different modes of transportation from the hinterland.

THE REMOVAL OF GOODS UNDER CLAIM OF REBATE FROM FACTORY OR WAREHOUSE WITHOUT EXAMINATION BY THE CENTRAL EXCISE OFFICERS

The exporters are allowed to remove the goods for export on their own without getting the goods examined by the Central Excise Officers. The AR4 in such cases would be prepared in sixtuplicate, giving all particulars and declarations. The exporters shall deliver triplicate, quadruplicate, quintuplicate and sixtuplicate copies of AR4, to the Superintendent of Central Excise having jurisdiction over the factory or the warehouse, within twenty-four hours of the removal of the consignment and would retain the original and duplicate copies for presenting along with the consignment to the Customs Officer at the point of export.

The jurisdictional Superintendent of Central Excise shall examine the information contained in AR4 and verify the facts of payment of Duty and other Certificates/Declarations made by the exporter. After he is satisfied that the information contained in the AR4 is true, he will sign at appropriate places in the four copies of AR4 submitted to him and put his stamp with his name and designation below his signature. He would then dispose of the triplicate, quadruplicate, quintuplicate and sixtuplicate copies of AR4 as under:

i) **Triplicate** To the rebate sanctioning authority viz. Maritime Collector of Central Excise or the Assistant Collector of Central Excise declared by the exporter on the AR4. This copy on the request of the exporter may be sealed and handed over to the exporter/his authorised agent for presenting to the rebate sanctioning authority.
ii) **Quadruplicate** To the Chief Accounts Officer in the Collectorate Headquaters.
iii) **Quintuplicate** Office copy to be retained by the Central Excise Officer.
iv) **Sixtuplicate** To be given to the exporter.

The Customs Officer should not withhold such export Shipments for want of triplicate copy of the AR-4 from the Range Superintendent.

(a) The exporters should not clear such goods unless they execute necessary Bond in terms of Rule 13 or Rule 14 as the case may be and they should also indicate the Bond number and the authority before whom the Bond is executed in the relevant column provided in Form AR4

(b) Rule 13 and Rule 14 provide for execution of a Bond with surety or Bond without Surety/Security. **Exporters of the following categories can execute the Bond without Surety/Security.**

- ★ Super Star Trading House
- ★ Star Trading House
- ★ Export House
- ★ Registered exporters (Registered with relevant Export Promotion Council)
- ★ Manufacturers registered with Central Excise Department.

A Unit, whose value of clearance for home consumption is less than Rs 30 lakhs in the preceding financial year or during the current financial year will not be required to take Central Excise Registration.

The above relaxation is subject to the condition that

i) The exporters have not come to the adverse notice of the Department in the last three years.

ii) All the formalities required under Central Excise Acts and Rules related to exports are regularly complied with by exporters.

iii) A copy of the Registration-cum-Membership Certificate (RCMC), duly attested by the exporter is submitted.

This facility can be withdrawn without prior notice to any exporter if he comes to the adverse notice of the Department.

PROCEDURE FOR EXPORTS UNDER CENTRAL EXCISE SEAL

When the exporter desire the sealing of the goods by the Central Excise Officers so that the export goods may not be examined by the Customs Officers at the Port/Airport of shipment, he should present an AR4 Application in sixtuplicate to the Superintendent of Central Excise having jurisdiction over the factory/warehouse. However, where, exporter is unable to give 24 hours advance notice to the Superintendent of Central Excise, his request for shorter notice is normally accepted. All such relaxations are then reported to the Assistant Collector of Central Excise for post facto approval.

The Superintendent of Central Excise may depute an Inspector of Central Excise or may himself go for sealing and examination of the export consignment. Where the AR4 indicates that the export is in discharge of an export obligation under a Quantity-based Advance Licence issued under the Duty Exemption Scheme, the consignment is invariably examined and sealed by the Superintendent of Central Excise himself.

The Central Excise Officer examining the consignment would draw samples wherever necessary in triplicate. He would handover two sets of samples, duly sealed, to the exporter or his authorised agent for delivering to the Customs Officers at the point of export. He would retain the third set for his records.

The export consignment is examined vis-à-vis the description of goods, their value and other particulars/declarations of the AR4. The Central Excise Officer shall verify the facts of payment of Duty and other Certificates/ Declarations made by the exporter. After he is satisfied that the information contained in the AR4 is true he would allow the clearance of export consignment and also sign all the six copies of AR4 at appropriate places.

The copies of AR4 would be disposed of as under:

i) Original/Duplicate: To the exporter for presenting to Customs Officer at the point of Export alongwith the export consignment.
ii) Triplicate: To the rebate sanctioning authority i.e. Maritime Collector of Central Excise or the jurisdictional Assistant Collector of Central Excise, as declared by the exporter on the AR4. The Central Excise Officer may handover this copy under a sealed cover on the exporter's request.
iii) Quadruplicate: To the Chief Accounts Officer at his Collectorate Head Quarters.
iv) Quintuplicate: To be retained for records.

Markings The package in which the goods are to be exported would be legibly marked in ink or in oil colour or in such other durable manner with progressive number commencing with No.1 for each calendar year and with the exporter's name.

AR4 FORM – DIFFERENT COLOURS

The different copies of AR4 forms are of different colours indicated below:-

i)	Original	–	White
ii)	Duplicate	–	Buff
iii)	Triplicate	–	Pink
iv)	Quadruplicate	–	Green
v)	Quintuplicate	–	Blue
vi)	Sixtuplicate	–	Yellow

Exporters should take adequate care in filling up the AR4 pro forma. The Rebate Sanctioning Authority, alongwith its complete postal address should be clearly mentioned at the appropriate place in the AR4. The applicable portions should be carefully retained and inapplicable portions struck off. The exporters are now required to give the following Certificates/ Declarations:

"We hereby certify that the above mentioned goods have been manufactured-

(a) availing facility/without availing facility of Modvat credit under Rule 57A of the Central Excise Rules, 1944.
(b) availing facility/without availing facility under Rule 12(1)(b) of Central Excise Rules, 1944.
(c) availing facility/without availing facility under Rule 13(1)(b) of Central Excise Rules, 1944.

We hereby delcare that the export is in discharge of the export obligation under a Quantity based Advance Licence/Under Claim of Duty Drawback under Customs and Central Excise Duties Drawback Rule, 1971."

Processing of AR4 by the Customs Officer at the Port of Export

The original, duplicate and sixtuplicate copies of the AR4 shall be presented by the exporter/his authorised agent to the Customs Officer at the point of export along with the goods, Shipping Bill/Bill of Export and samples sealed by the Central Excise Officer. The export consignment shall be checked by the Customs Officer to see whether the seals are intact, whether the marks and the number tally are proper and if found in order he may allow exports after ensuring that the No. of the AR4 has been indicated in the Shipping Bill or the Bill of Export, as the case may be. After the goods have been shipped the proper Officer of Customs would make necessary endorsements in the Original, Duplicate and Sixtuplicate copies of the AR4 at appropriate places and put his stamp with his name and designation below his signature. The copies of AR4 shall be disposed off by him in the following manner:

Original and sixtuplicate To be handed over to the Exporter. Original shall be used for filing rebate claim. Sixtuplicate copy shall be used for Drawback/DEEC endorsement.

Duplicate To be sent to the Rebate Sanctioning authority declared on AR4. This copy on a request by the exporter may be sealed and handed over to the exporter/his authorised agent for presenting to the rebate sanctioning authority.

CLAIMING REBATE

Where the export is from any of the Port, Airport or Post Office falling with the jurisdiction of Maritime Collector of Central Excise, option is available to file claim of rebate before Maritime Collector of Central Excise or the Jurisdictional Assistant Collector of Central Excise. For this purpose, Exporters are required to clearly indicate their option on AR4 along with complete postal address of the Authority from whom the rebate shall be claimed.

Filing and Sanction of Rebate Claim

i) With maritime collector of central excise Where the export of goods is from any of the Ports, Airports or Post Office falling within the jurisdiction of Maritime Collector of Central Excise of Bombay, Calcutta, Madras, Paradeep, Visakhapatnam, Cochin, Kandla, the exporter can opt to claim rebate. The rebate can be claimed from exportation within time limit prescribed under sec 11B of the Central Excise and Salt Act, 1944 i.e. six months from the date of export. This should be done in prescribed form alongwith the original copy of the AR4 duly endorsed by the triplicate copy of the AR4 received from the Central Excise Officer and the duplicate AR4 received from the Customs Officer. The Maritime Collector after due scrutiny and verification of the said AR4s, will sanction the rebate claim in whole or in part.

ii) With assistant collector, central excise having jurisdiction of the factory Where the exporter wishes to claim rebate of excise duty from the Assistant Collector having jurisdiction over the factory or warehouse from where the goods were removed for export, he will file the claim of rebate within six months from the date of export. This should be done in prescribed form along with the original copy of AR4, duly endorsed by the Customs Officer certifying export of the consignment (and the duplicate copy handed over to him by the Customs Officer in a sealed cover). The Assistant Collector of Central Excise, would verify and compare the original copy of AR4 with the duplicate copy of AR4 received from the Customs Officer and with the triplicate copy of AR4, received from Superintendent, Central Excise Range and after satisfying himself that the claim is in order will sanction the rebate either in whole or in part.

Documents to be Filed for Claiming Rebate

Following documents should be filed for claiming rebate:-

- ★ Application in prescribed form
- ★ Original copy of AR4
- ★ Duplicate copy of AR4 in sealed cover received from Customs Officer (optional)
- ★ Duly attested copy of Bill of lading
- ★ Duly attested copy of Shipping Bill (Export Promotion copy)
- ★ Disclaimer Certificate (in case where claimant is other than exporter)

Time Limit for Disposal

The rebate sanctioning authority should point out deficiency (all at the same time), if any, in the claim within 15 days of filing the same and ask the exporter to rectify the same within 15 days. The claim of rebate of duty on export of goods should be disposed off within a period of two months.

EXCISE CLEARANCE FOR EXPORT

> Excisable goods can be exported either by making payment of Excise Duty and claiming its refund after export or by executing a Bond. There is still another system 'manufacture-in-bond' where Excise/Customs Duty is not to be paid even on raw materials, components, etc, used in export products. Excise Duty paid on raw materials, components, etc, used in export products is also refunded to the exporters of such goods (and not to their manufacturer/producers) in the form of "Draw Back."

Export goods subject to Central Excise Duty can be exported either under claim for rebate of Excise Duty or under Bond. While under the former system, the Excise Duty is to be paid first and its refund claimed after effecting exports, in the latter case the goods are allowed to be exported outside the country without payment of Duty.

Simplified Procedure for SSI Units

No AR4 procedure The CBEC has vide its Circular No.212/46/95-Cx dt. 20/5/96, introduced a simplified procedure for SSI units having value of clearances for home consumption within exemption limit during the relevant financial year, and who are availing full exemption. Hence, the units which though eligible for full exemption, are not availing themselves of the exemption, are not covered by the simplified export procedure.

No registration declaration The SSI Units availing full excise exemption and exporting their products need not register themselves with the Central Excise Dept. Instead they shall file a declaration and obtain a **declarant's code number.**

Regular AR4/5 procedure In the case of manufacturers who need clearance for the consumption and for export, who do not furnish proof of export within 6 months, and whose value of clearance exceeds the exemption limit, should take Central Excise Registration and follow the regular AR-4/AR-5 procedure.

Export in Bond of Finished Excisable Goods to All Destinations other than Nepal

The Units manufacturing dutiable (excisable) goods and desiring to export the same without payment of Excise Duty, can do so after execution of the requisite Bond with the competent Central Excise Authority. The Bond is to be filed and requires AR4 procedure to be followed even in case of SSI units whose clearance in the domestic market exceed Rs 30 lakhs a year. The exemption from following the required AR4 procedure is explained under item 1 above.

The procedure to export in Bond is a little different for (I) export by Sea or Air or Post and (ii) by Surface i.e. Land route. However, before clearing goods from the factory, the exporter may get the goods examined by the Central Excise Authorities or can remove without such examination. They are also required to prepare certain documents which are explained below:

Documents Form AR4/5 is an application for removal of excisable goods in Bond or under claim of rebate on export from India by any mode i.e. Sea, Air, Post, Land (surface), etc.

Invoice Assessee's invoice is to be used as transport document for clearance of goods from the factory.

For in-bond exports of excisable goods to Nepal for which payment is received in freely convertible currency, there is a special form of invoice. It is also different from Nepal Invoice.

Bonds For export of excisable goods without payment of Duty, there are six types of Bonds from which exporters have to choose the appropriate one. These forms are B.1 (Surety), B.1 (Security), B.1 (General Surety) and B.1 (General Security), B. 16 (General Surety) and B.16 (General Security).

Bond B.1 is to be executed for one particular consignment and B.1 (General) to cover a series of exports from factory. The manufacturer exporters who have executed B.16 bond are not required to execute a separate bond to cover Duty on the goods exported without payment of Duty.

Bank certificate This is a special type of certificate to be used in the case of excisable goods for which payment is received under freely convertible currency for export to Nepal.

Application for refund of rebate on duty There is an Application for claim of Rebate on Duty for excisable goods exported by Sea/Air, Post of Land (surface).

Export by Sea/Air or Port

Packing/marking of case Packing export case or package or bale should be marked in ink or oil colours with Central Excise mark, date and numbers.

Documents Prepare the necessary documents i.e. AR4/5 and Invoice and fill in by giving necessary information/declaration.

Filing of proof and discharge of bond After having exported the goods, the exporter should file the following documents as proof of exportation, with the Central Excise Authority having jurisdiction over the factory/ godown:

1. Original Copy of AR4 Form.
2. Duplicate Copy of AR4 form in sealed cover received from the Customs Officer Optional.
3. Attested copy of Bill of Lading.
4. Attested copy of Shipping Bill (Export Promotion Copy).

Partial export If the scrutiny of AR4 Form reveals that only part of consignment removed **in Bond** for export has actually been exported out of India, the Excise Authority concerned shall call upon the **Bonder** to pay within 10 days the Duty leviable on the quantity short shipped, in terms of the Bond.

Export of Finished Excise Paid Goods under Claim for Refund of Duty

Refund (rebate) of duty is granted under Rule 12 of the Central Excise Rules and Notifications Nos. 41 to 44/94-CE (NT) all dated 22/9/94, 46/94-CE(NT) dt 22.8.94 and 50/94 CE (NT) dt. 22/9/94, paid on-

a) All excisable goods except mineral oil products exported as stores for consumption on board an aircraft on foreign run and goods exported as ship stores for consumption on board a vessel bound for any foreign Port.
b) Materials used in the manufacture of goods.

The rebate of Duty on goods exported to Nepal is made to the Nepal Government and hence, explained separately.

The claim authority The claim for refund of any Duty of Central Excise is to be made to Assistant Commissioner of Central Excise having jurisdiction over the factory of manufacture.

Time limit The claim is to be filed before the expiry of six months from the date on which the ship or aircraft in which such goods are loaded, leaves India or the date on which such goods pass the frontier in case export is made by land or the date of despatch of goods by the Post Office in case of postal exports.

Application form The Application for refund is to be filed in prescribed form in duplicate. This form is to be used for refund against all goods.

Documents The following Documents should be enclosed with the application form:

i) AR4 form (original) duly endorsed by the Customs
ii) Duplicate copy of AR4 in sealed cover, if obtained from Customs

iii) Bill of Lading (non-negotiable copy)/airway bill or air consignment note/Postal receipt, duly attested
iv) Attested copy of Shipping Bill/Bill of Export
v) Duplicate copy of Invoice under which Central Excise duty was paid on goods cleared for export
vi) Disclaimer Certificate, where claimer is other than an exporter
vii) Detailed worksheet indicating the amount of rebate claimed

SALES TAX EXEMPTION ON EXPORTS

No Sales Tax

There is no tax on sales made for export purpose. It implies that the exporter need not pay Sales Tax either on the goods purchased from manufacturers or traders i.e, other merchants.

The only condition imposed is that the exporter must be a registered dealer with the Sales Tax Department. If he is not a registered dealer, he cannot utilise the facility provided for export of good without payment of Sales Tax under Form H.

The condition of the exporter being a registered dealer therefore implies that, if the exporter is engaged in selling products in the country which is not otherwise subjected to Sales Tax, and hence has not got himself registered with the Sales Tax Department, he cannot utilise the Form 'H' facilities, i.e. exporting goods without payment of Sales Tax.

Registration Procedure

Therefore, the exporter should get himself registered with the Sales Tax Department for utilising the facility. Apply to the Sales Tax Officer under whose jurisdiction the Head/Registered Office is located. Therefore, a Sales Tax Inspector may visit the Office to check

i) Account books showing sales/purchase transactions
ii) House rent/tax receipt
iii) Partnership deed, or other relevant documents
iv) Ration card, etc.

Then, he will send a report to the STO for registration or otherwise. On receipt of the report, the STO may call for the exporter for further clarifications, if any. If satisfied, he will permit Registration.

Security

The STO usually asks the exporter to file a security bond from another firm(s) registered under the Sales Tax law.

Form

Having got registered, the under mentioned procedure should be followed:-

i) Apply to the concerned STO for obtaining Form 'H' with:-
   a. copy of the L/C, or
   b. copy of the confirmed export order,
   c. copy of the export invoice, where the goods have already been purchased

ii) Put prescribed Court fee Stamp for each form according to the number of forms sanctioned.

iii) The STO will put the name stamp of the company in the Form 'H'.

Hence, the exporter should approach the STO for obtaining the Form 'H' alongwith the Company's name stamp to be put in the body of the form.

Filling in the Form 'H'

After exporting the goods, Form 'H' (in triplicate) obtained from the STO is filled in the manner described above, and given to the party from which the goods for export have been purchased. It may be **reiterated** that the goods can be purchased from the manufacturer as well as from merchants.

The Form 'H' is to be filled in triplicate. While one copy is retained by the exporter himself, the remaining two copies will be given to the seller of the goods i.e. the manufacturer or trader from whom the goods have been purchased by the exporter. The seller will then send one copy of the Form 'H' given to him by exporter to the STO concerned, alongwith his Return of Sales Tax. Its third copy will be retained by him.

No document is required to be attached with Form 'H' while submitting it to the STO, alongwith the Sales Tax Return.

No further endorsement Form 'H' cannot be endorsed to any other party than the one to whom it is issued in the first instance.

// CHAPTER 27 //

IS/ISO 9000 AND NEW ISO 14000 SERIES INTERNATIONAL STANDARDS FOR QUALITY SYSTEMS

Quality awareness is catching up with the consumer the world over and the textile industry is no exception. ISO 9000 provides a kind of integrated but flexible quality management information system, which can fit into an overall management information system, which can also accommodate comfortably with the production management system of varying complexity. ISO 9000 series is essentially a quality assurance system, the legal aspect of which has been accepted by all the national standard bodies, on standards such as the harmonised standards for implementation.

The Bureau of Indian Standards is the national standards body of India and is a member body of the International Organisation for Standardisation (ISO). Bureau of Indian Standards (BIS) is operating the Quality Systems Certification Scheme (QSCS) under the Bureau of Indian Standards Act, 1986. Under the Scheme, BIS is certifying the Quality Systems of industrial organisations including service sector as per IS/ISO 9000 series of standards. The Bureau has so far certified Quality Systems of over 350 organisations. BISQSCS is accredited for 10 major economic activities by Raad voor Accreditatie (RvA) (previously known as Raad voor de Certificate), the Dutch Council for Accreditation.

The new ISO 14000 series of standards are identical to the internationally accepted ISO 9000 series of standards of quality.

In simple terms, the ISO 9000 quality system can be described as follows:

Say what you do	–	Describe your quality system
Do what you say	–	Make your system work
Prove it	–	Have your system certified by an independent third party

The methodology for establishing an ISO 9000 quality system depends on a number of factors such as the nature of business, current status of quality control and market requirements. Unless a company's management sincerely believes that ISO 9000 is good for its business, it will not put in the genuine effort required to implement it. It is commonly believed that ISO 9000 can be implemented only by large companies as it involves elaborate documentation not practicable in small firms. This is a misapprehension. It is also much easier to effect the attitudinal changes required for the ISO quality system in firms with a smaller number of employees than in larger firms.

Before starting the implementation process, it is necessary to decide on the type of quality system to be put in place. One approach is to determine which elements of ISO 9004 apply to the particular business and then to choose the appropriate assessment standard. ISO 9000-1 can be consulted for the purpose. The most common approach is to start by meeting the minimum requirements of ISO 9001 or ISO 9002 or ISO 9003 as applicable to the nature of the business and to the needs of the customers.

Given the state of quality control in small and medium-sized companies in developing countries, the implementation of ISO 9000 has to be taken up as a major project, for which a sequence of steps are suggested in this chapter.

In order to produce quality products, suppliers must have a customer/market orientation, must establish an adequate product quality-price relationship, must have a well-trained and motivated work force and a firmly established quality management system. Furthermore, the market now increasingly requires the adoption of internationally recognised quality management systems and the demonstration of this fact through certification or registration by independent accredited bodies. Such certification is considered a factor in competitiveness since it adds value, and increases the buyers confidence and facilitates access to national and international markets.

"The customer is king" is more true today than ever before. As the quality of life improves, demand for better quality services and products also increases. Customers all over the world, at all times demand that they be assured (and later satisfied) that the product or service for which they are paying will meet their specifications (expectations) and will perform as anticipated. Buyers have traditionally relied on inspection and certification before accepting goods. However, inspection is not a satisfactory way of giving assurance that the product will perform as desired during its life. It is generally agreed that the required level of quality can be built into the product only through the use of a proper quality management system. Fortunately, with the advent of the ISO 9000 series of standards, it is now possible to measure tangibly the effectiveness of quality management in an enterprise. The objective of the ISO 9000 series is to provide a mechanism for determining and fulfilling customer needs, preventing errors wherever possible and correcting them in such a way that, the process if improved will meet customer's needs consistently at a lower cost.

This chapter deals with basic concepts of quality and quality management and explains briefly the structure and content of the ISO 9000 standards. It also covers establishment, implementation, auditing and third-party certificate of quality management systems as relevant to small and medium-sized export oriented enterprises.

In the wake of international trends and competitiveness taking new dimensions, the Bureau of Indian Standards (BIS) has introduced the Quality system Certification Scheme according to IS/ISO 9000 family of standards.

These standards are identical to the internationally accepted ISO 9000 family of standards on quality management system.

These guidelines contain useful information on processing of an application, procedure for grant of licence, obligations and responsibilities of the firms interested in obtaining licenses to relevant model, according to IS/ISO 9000 family of standards.

These guidelines are in the nature of extracted information from the applicable regulations. For complete details, reference is to be made to BIS (Certification) Regulations, 1988 - Amended up to 1991.

This scheme envisages grant of Quality Systems Certification License to firms according to three Quality Systems Models, as under:

MODEL I - IS/ISO 9001

Quality Systems – Model for Quality Assurance in Design, Development, Production, Installation and Servicing

IS/ISO 9001 should be selected and used when the need is to demonstrate the supplier's capability to control the processes for design, as well as production of conforming product. The requirements specified are aimed primarily at achieving customer satisfaction by preventing non-conformity at all stages, from design to servicing. IS/ISO 9001 specifies a quality assurance model for this purpose.

MODEL II - IS/ISO 9002

Quality Systems - Model for Quality Assurance in Production, Installation and Servicing

IS/ISO 9002 should be selected and used when the need is to demonstrate the supplier's capability to control the processes for production of the conforming product. IS/ISO 9002 specifies a quality assurance model for this purpose.

MODEL III - IS/ISO 9003

Quality Systems - Model for Quality Assurance in Final Inspection and Test

IS/ISO 9003 should be selected and used when conformity to specified requirements is to be assured by the supplier, solely at the final inspection and test. IS/ISO 9003 specifies a quality assurance model for this purpose.

HOW TO OBTAIN A LICENSE

Application and its Processing

Firms interested in obtaining license for quality systems as per the IS/ISO 9000 family of standards, should ensure that they are operating quality system in accordance with the relevant standard. They should apply on the prescribed proforma in triplicate at the nearest Regional Office of BIS along with the prescribed application fee as applicable. The application fee is non-refundable.

The application is to be signed by the proprietor, partner or the Chief Executive Officer (CEO) of the firm or any other person authorised to sign any declaration on behalf of the firm. The name and designation of the person signing the application must be recorded legibly in a space set apart for the purpose in the application form.

Each application must be accompanied by a supplimentary questionnaire duly filled in alongwith the documented quality system (such as quality manual, quality plan, etc) prepared by the firm. The documented quality system shall be in line with the requirements of the relevant quality system standard.

If necessary, BIS shall provide to the applicant, further information about the scheme and also ask for further information from the applicant.

BIS reserves the right to reject an application which is incomplete and does not fulfil one or more of the following requirements –

i) Application fee not accompanying the application;
ii) Application form is incomplete
iii) Annexures to the application are not clear

The reason for rejection of the application shall be communicated to the applicant by BIS.

BIS will acknowledge the receipt of the application and application fee. Every application will be given a serial number known as the 'Application Number'. In all future correspondence, reference must be made to the 'Application Number'.

Adequacy Audit

After the application has been accepted, the documented quality system (Quality Manual/Quality Plan, etc) shall be examined by the BIS for verifying the conformity to relevant standard. Any significant omissions or deviations from the prescribed requirements intimated by BIS, will have to be corrected by the applicant and BIS will advise accordingly to process the application further.

Preliminary Visit

BIS official(s) may make a visit to the premises of the applicant to acquaint himself/themselves of the size, nature of the operation and firm's readiness for the audit. The number of the auditors for audit and its duration will vary according to the size and nature of operation of the firm being assessed.

Assessment Fee

Assessment fee will be payable in advance, estimate of which will be provided by BIS, depending upon the man-days expected to be spent on the audit of the firm and the anticipated expenses for travel/stay, etc.

Assessment

An Audit team from BIS will visit the firm for assessment of the firm's compliance to the procedures and activities enumerated in the documented quality system and relevant quality systems standard.

The Assessment will comprise the following sequence:

a) Opening Meeting – This meeting will be conducted by the leader of the audit team in which the Chief Executive Officer (CEO) of the company, the management representative and heads of all the departments being audited are expected to be present. During this meeting, the leader will explain the scope and extent of the audit and the important terms used in the assessment.

b) Conduct of Assessment – Each auditor should be accompanied by a guide who is conversant with the activities of the department(s) the audit team is auditing. Observations recorded by the auditors must be signed by the guide as a token of acceptance.

c) Closing meeting and report
   i) All the members present in the opening meeting should preferably be present in the closing meeting as well when the audit team present their findings to the firm.
   ii) The non-conformities observed by the audit team will be handed over to the firms at the end of each day for necessary corrective action.
   iii) Time frame for the corrective action(s) will be decided by the firm.
   iv) The non-conformity reports will be signed by the Management Representative or authorised signatory as a token of acceptance.

Responsibilities of Applicant During the Audit

The firm is expected to provide the following assistance to the audit team during the audits:

a) Arrangements of stay, local guidance and travel arrangements, etc.
b) The CEO and the Management Representative of the company must be present during the opening and closing meetings. As far as possible, all responsible personnel of the company whose departments are being audited should be present in these meetings
c) In the interest of the firm, all efforts should be made to ensure that the time of the audit team is not wasted on account of non-availability of relevant personnel, documents, records, shut down of unit(s) being audited, etc.
d) The firm will arrange a place/room where members of the audit team can meet and discuss during the day and at the end of the day to exchange their notes and findings.

Before the grant of license to the firm is considered, corrective actions taken by the firm on the non-confirmities observed during the audit will have to be verified by BIS. This may call for a follow up audit, full or partial, as the case may be.

Before a license is granted to the applicant, they shall give the following undertaking:

"We shall make no claim direct or implied that the license to be granted relates to any products or processes other than those that will be sent out in the license and the schedule."

Based on the findings of the audit team and a satisfactory report, the firm will be granted a license by BIS.

Grant of License

The license shall be granted for a period of three years. Grant of license will be followed by surveillance visits once in six months by the auditor(s) of BIS to verify the effective implementation and maintenance of the quality system established by the firm.

During the operation of license, when a licensee fails to observe the conditions of the Quality Systems Certification Scheme or where there have been significant changes in the organisation of the licensee, license of the firm is liable to be suspended and may call for special visits, for which the firm is liable to pay special visit charges, as set out in schedule of fees.

Renewal, Deferment, Expiry and Cancellation of License

Any license granted automatically expires at the end of the period for which it is granted. A renewal notice will be issued to the licensee by the concerned regional office of BIS about four months before the expiry of the current operative period. The licensee is required to submit the renewal application along with the original copy of the license atleast three months in advance before the expiry of the license which will be followed by a complete audit of the quality system of the firm.

If some discrepancies are found during the audit, the licensee will be asked to take corrective action. After the licensee has taken the necessary action to remove discrepancies, the Quality System Certification license will be renewed for a period of three years.

Obligations of Licensee

A licensee on grant of certification for quality system will:

a) Only claim that he is holding a license in respect of the capability which is the subject of the license and which relates to the products or processes in accordance with the license requirements.
b) Not use the license in any manner to which the BIS may object and shall not make any statement concerning the authority of the licensee's use of the license which in the opinion of the BIS may be misleading.
c) Submit to the BIS for approval of the way in which he proposes to use the license or proposes to make references to the license.
d) Not make any change to the Quality System which forms the basis for the grant of the license and which prevents its compliance with the scheme without prior approval of the BIS.
e) Upon suspension or termination of the license, however determined, discontinue its use and withdraw all promotional and advertising matter which contains any reference thereto.
f) Submit to the BIS any amendments to the Quality Manual and/or Quality Plan.
g) Document all changes made to the Quality System and make records of such changes available to Bureau's designated officers on request. A change in key personnel in relation to quality assurance, key technological functions or senior management shall be notified to the BIS by the licensee.

h) Permit access to BIS officer(s)/team(s) appointed by the BIS for purposes of assessment, audit or surveillance. Licensee shall give full details of all actions taken in response to field problems arising from allegations of defects in products or processes covered in the license and allow BIS officers' access to all relevant records and documents for the purpose of verifying such details.

i) Be required to produce evidence of continuing operations for the products or processes covered by the license. Licensee shall notify the BIS in writing of discontinuance in such operations exceeding three months. Discontinuance of operations in excess of six months or more may lead to cancellation of the license. In such cases, a fresh application shall be lodged with the BIS.

j) Pay all financial dues to the Bureau as prescribed, even for the period during which the operation of the license remains discontinued by him or suspended by the BIS.

k) Operate and maintain procedures for handling and recording of complaints and shall report any complaints against the quality system operated and/or license to BISQSCS. Cooperate and assist BISQSCS on the investigation and resolution of such complaints.

l) Operate within the provisions of the BIS Act, 1986 Rules, 1987 BIS (Certification) Regulations, 1988 amended upto 1991 and Certification Scheme Procedure for grant of license.

Privileges of Licensee

The privileges enjoyed by BIS licensees include:

a) Original Quality System Certification license which can be demonstrated by the licensees to anyone concerned. If needed it can be photocopied and displayed at various locations.

b) A very attractive plaque containing details of certification is presented as a compliment at the time of award of certificate. Additional plaques can also be provided by BIS on actual cost payment basis.

c) Use of Quality System Certification Mark on letter-heads, in advertisements, brochures, complimentaries and for other promotional purposes. However, Standard Mark shall not be directly applied on the product and its packaging so as to imply that the product itself is certified by BIS.

d) Each licensee shall be listed in the register of licensees maintained by BIS.

CERTIFICATE OF CONFORMITY TO ISO 9000

Certification of conformity to ISO 9000 is another universal phenomenon. This was demonstrated by the 100,000 certificates issued in about 86 countries by the end of 1995. Almost 75% of the certificates were given in Europe (about 50% in the United Kingdom), 8% in the United States of America and Canada, 7% in Austria and New Zealand, 6.5% in Japan and other Far Eastern Countries and only about 4% in developing countries. This is a clear disadvantage for developing countries, which for financial, technological and other reasons lag behind the rest of the world in introducing ISO 9000. Since purchasers, importers and retailers in industrialised countries tend to prefer suppliers that are ISO 9000 certified, this may become a technical barrier to the developing countries trade.

One of the main advantage of the ISO 9000 system is its universality: it is recognised world wide. Certification of conformity to ISO 9000, while it is a voluntary, market-based requirement, will give enterprises wishing to penetrate new markets, a clear advantage.

The other benefits of having an ISO 9000 quality management system include improved quality awareness throughout the organisation, clarity in the distribution of responsibilities, increased involvement of employees in quality goals, full customer confidence, higher internal efficiency, a better company image, and consistency in the performance of tasks and in product quality.

As explained in this chapter, a company to organisation wishing to introduce an ISO 9000 system should be ready to carry out a preparatory phase of about 12 to 18 months. Activities during this phase will include training at all levels; preparation of quality manual and related documentation (procedures, methods, work instructions); formulation and dissemination of the quality policy, plans and objectives; quality system implementation, internal auditing and management reviews. Frequently, the assistance of an experienced consultant will be essential. After successful completion of this phase, the company will be ready for external auditing and certification by a component, duly accredited third-party certification body.

The certificate will have a validity of two to three years. During this period, the certification body will conduct surprise visits (audits) to ascertain that the system is operating as planned and as approved. Internal audits and management review exercises should also take place (two or three times a year as needed) to give management the confidence that the system is well established and is operating on a continuous basis.

ISO 9000 is also applicable to service organisations such as banks, hospitals, laboratories, hotels and transportation companies, independent of size, capital, ownership and other factors.

The public and private sectors in developing countries should carry out a joint effort to enable export-oriented enterprises to adopt and to obtain certification for ISO 9000 systems. Programmes and incentives in this area should cover such aspects as training, consultancy, testing, inspection, certification and accreditation services. Failure to do this efficiently and in good time will put their exporters at a competitive disadvantage in the international market place.

The use of ISO 9000 quality systems in export-oriented enterprises in developing countries will facilitate their access to, and increase their competitiveness in, international markets.

SCHEDULE OF FEES FOR QUALITY SYSTEMS CERTIFICATION

Quality Systems Models: IS/ISO 9001
IS/ISO 9002
IS/ISO 9003

Application Fee

Application fee shall be Rs 15,000 (Rs 10,000 for small scale industries) which includes the adequacy audit of documented Quality System and preliminary visit fee. However, expenses for travel/stay of auditor(s) for preliminary visit will be charged at cost.

Assessment Fee and Reassessment Fee

Rs 3,000 per auditor(s) per day towards assessment fee plus expenses for travel/stay of auditors which will be charged at cost. Normally assessment time would be six to nine man-days (for example three auditors for three days). However, this is flexible and would depend upon the quality system model and the size and nature of operation of the company.

License Fee

For all the three models, the license fee for a period of three years shall be Rs 60,000 (Rs 40,000 for small scale industries). The fee is payable at the time of grant of license. However, charges for surveillance audits will be extra towards man-days spent (Rs.3,000 per monday) plus expenses for travel/stay of auditors, which will be charged at cost.

Reassessment Fee for Renewal

The fee is payable once in three years and an amount of Rs 3,000/- per auditor per day towards assessment fee plus expenses for travel/stay of auditors will be charged at cost.

Special Visit Fees

Any other audit or special visit will be charged at Rs 3,000/- per auditor per day towards fee plus expenses for travel/stay of auditors, which will be charged at cost. The above charges will be leviable for any other visit covering additional requirement which can be assessed during these routine visits.

THE QUALITY MANUAL

One of the most common misapprehensions about the ISO 9000 quality system is that it involves a massive increase in documentation and paperwork. This is not in fact the case. The standard (ISO 9001, ISO 9002, or ISO 9003) requires documentation in areas where its absence would have an adverse efect on quality. The most important document is the quality manual. This chapter explains how this manual is prepared and how to document procedures for implementing quality system elements. Other documents, viz. quality plans, external documents and verification records required for the system, are also discussed.

Purpose of the Quality Manual

The primary purpose of the quality manual is to provide an adequate description of the quality system and to serve as a permanent guide for the implementation and maintenance of that system. The quality manual can become a repository of the knowledge of an organisation. In many organisations, a great deal of useful information is locked away in people's heads. Putting this information in writing will reduce the management's dependence on the continued presence of key persons.

The quality manual also serves the following purposes:

★ It improves communication between departments, sections and individuals

★ It provides an invaluable training aid by defining how quality is managed within the company.

★ It assists staff to do their job more effectively by removing ambiguities, defining the system, designating responsibilites and identifying those responsible, so that everyone knows what is going on.

★ It provides a basis for periodic audit and review to determine, first "Are we doing what we say we are doing?" and, second, "Does the system still meet our needs?"

★ It demonstrates to the company's customers, certification agencies and even shareholders that the quality system has been systematically planned.

★ It can be used as a marketing tool as it demonstrates the company's efforts to meet international business requirements.

IMPLICATIONS OF IS/ISO 9000 STANDARDS IN INDIA'S FUTURE EXPORTS

The European Community at present consists of 15 member states - Belgium, France, Germany, Italy, Luxembourg, Netherlands, Denmark, Ireland, United Kingdom, Greece, Portugal, Spain, Sweden, Austria and Finland. A large number of companies in the European Union buying goods and services demand from their suppliers adherence to the ISO-9000 series. The United Kingdom has already taken initiative in this direction and more than 15,000 U.K. companies have already been assessed and certified adhering to ISO 9000.

It should be clearly understood that the purchase power of the European Union is tremendous and India cannot afford to keep silent at the changing scenario in the European Union Market. In fact, E.U. is the leader in the world trade followed by US and Japan. Over the years, the European Union has emerged as India's largest trading partner. We can sustain this position only if the Indian industry could adopt IS/ISO 9000 standards. Our ability to carve out a better share of EC Market will also help us in establishing our products and services in other developed countries of the world outside E.U., on the strength of improved quality reputation and competitive edge of our products and services by adhering to ISO 9000 standards.

List of Products where compulsory ISO 9000 certification is required in Euro:

1. Toys
2. Simple pressure vessels
3. Electromagnetic compatibility
4. Gas appliances
5. Personal protective equipment
6. Machinery

7. Medical devices (active and non-active)
8. Active implantable medical devices
9. Non-automatic weighing instruments
10. Telecommunication terminal equipment
11. Upholstered furniture
12. Recreational craft
13. Pressure vessels
14. Lifting equipment e.g. Ski-lifts
15. Marine equipment
16. Equipment in explosive atmosphere
17. Temporary structures e.g. Scaffolding fairground equipment
18. Children's playground equipment
19. Medical diagnostic kits

ISO 14000 AND ENVIRONMENTAL MANAGEMENT STANDARDS 14001 AND 14004

What is ISO 14000 and Which Standards Does it Contain So Far

The ISO 14000 series, developed by the International Organisation for Standardisation (ISO), is a voluntary set of standards in the areas of environmental management, auditing, performance evaluation, labelling, and Life Cycle Assessment (LCA), designed to ensure compliance with environmental law and regulations. ISO 14000—which consists of guidelines on principles, systems, and supporting techniques—has two primary components:

- ★ the establishment of an environmental management system (EMS)
- ★ the practice of environmental auditing

It establishes general principles concerning EMSs and is the "umbrella" for several subcategories that contain more specific guidelines for related environmental programmes. ISO 14001 contains the specifications for the establishment of EMSs; ISO 14004 sets forth general EMS principles and supporting techniques; ISO 14010-12 addresses environmental auditing; and ISO 14031 contains criteria for environmental performance evaluations. Other sub-categories are being developed. These focus on product standards, such as environmental labelling, in ISO 14020, 14021 and 14024 and Life Cycle Assessment in ISO 14040.2.

Approval of Drafts

Delegates from more than 50 nations approved drafts of the first two standards in the ISO 14000 series on June 29, 1995. ISO 14000 which later became ISO 14004; and ISO 14001. ISO 14001 and 14004 now apply to more than 100 nations which are members of ISO. Final draft standards concerning other sub-categories of ISO 14000 pertaining to environmental product labelling, Life-Cycle Assessment, and environmental performance tools are still forthcoming.

The ISO 14000 series set no discharge/emission limits or performance requirements but instead targets the means by which companies run business.

(International) Pressure to Comply

Like the other standards established by ISO, such as ISO 9000 on quality management systems, ISO 14000 is a system which can be implemented voluntarily.

However, (specialised) manufacturing and service sector companies will most certainly feel the strong market pressure to comply with ISO 14000, in order to do business in the international market place. This pressure will come from direct and indirect sources. Consumers will provide direct pressure to comply, as the public increasingly demands products with ecologically sound designs, produced by companies with environmental management systems. Companies which do not sell their products internationally, will feel similar market forces indirectly from international companies which will require their suppliers to meet the ISO criteria.

Benefits of ISO 14000 Compliance

Meeting direct consumer preferences and other market forces is the primary reason for achieving compliance with ISO 14000, but advantages are likely to arise in the financial and efficiency/performance fields.

Market advantages

- ★ Meeting customers' environmental expectations.
- ★ Maintaining positive public relations.
- ★ Enhancing image and market share (leadership).
- ★ Meeting supplier certification criteria (primarily for small and medium-sized companies).

Financial benefits

- ★ Satisfying investor criteria and improving access to capital.
- ★ Obtaining insurance at a reasonable cost.
- ★ Liability limitation.
- ★ Cost control.

Efficiency and performance benefits

- ★ Ability to dispose of waste effectively, pollution prevention.
- ★ Conservation of input materials and energy.
- ★ Technology development and transfer.
- ★ Improved industry-government relations.

Applicability of ISO 14000

Given the fact that the ISO 14000 series of standards is voluntary, any business organisation may pursue compliance. The ISO 14000 standards are devised to be, in theory, applicable to all types and sizes of organisations. ISO 14000 does not itself establish any specific environmental performance criteria, but requires a business organisation to study its operations and the significant environmental impacts resulting from that operation, and thereafter to implement an environmental policy and EMS that addresses those impacts.

Environmental Audits/Certification

Environmental auditing is the formalised method by which the effectiveness of a company's EMS may be evaluated to assess its performance and continual improvement. The audit should be based on objectives defined by the client, and the scope of the audit should be determined by consultation between the auditor and client.

ISO 14010 reinforces the point that the audits may be conducted by external or internal auditors, provided that the auditor is not directly accountable to those individuals directly responsible for the subject matter of the audit. This serves to avoid conflict of interest/bias concerns. The standard also establishes general principles, such as professional care, confidentiality and discretion, which highlight the relationship between the auditor and client. ISO 14011 outlines the specific and correct audit procedures while ISO 14012 establishes qualification criteria for environmental auditors.

While striving for third-party certification, an accredited "registrar" company will have certified auditors to review a company's EMS and verify its conformity with ISO 14001. The duration of an ISO 14001 registration is expected to be three years.

Costs

The costs of achieving compliance with the ISO 14000 series will of course, vary with the size of the company and extent of its environmental impacts. Considering the complexity of the process to devleop and implement an EMS, together with third-party audit/registration fees, total costs of around US $100,000 should not be surprising for many businesses.

Developing Countries

The ISO 14000 standards of series now define 'good environmental practice for businesses'. Although it is too early to judge the effect of ISO 14000, it is likely that companies in the 'heavy' industries such as the chemical industry may require ISO 14000 certificates from the suppliers (combined, or not, with an ISO 9000 certificate).

ISO has stated that for the time being, it will not develop specific guidelines for assisting SMEs and companies in developing countries in implementing ISO 14000. The representative normalisation institutes in developing countries have not protested against this.

There is however a chance, that the International Network for Environmental Management (INEM) will start working on such guidelines shortly. As with ISO 9000, certification costs for ISO 14000 may well prove to be an obstacle. Using ISO 14000 as a guideline to streamline business processes however, is a good start in this direction.

// CHAPTER 28 //

GENERAL SYSTEM OF PREFERENCE (GSP) SCHEME – CERTIFICATE OF ORIGIN

What is GSP? Under the auspices of GATT (General Agreement on Tariff and Trade) Agreement, the developed countries will extend preferential tariff on imports of certain products from developing countries. In other words, developing countries will enjoy duty free or duty concessional entry on their certain export products into the developed countries. GSP has thus been formulated as early as in 1971.

Our country is a developing country and hence goods exported from India are eligible for duty rebate in importing countries. This duty rebate can be claimed by the importers only by producing GSP certificate/Certificate of Origin to their Customs. It is, therefore, an essential document which must accompany air consignments unlike other export documents which are routed through normal banking channels. The Government of India has authorised the Export Inspection Council of India and its various agencies to issue the Certificate of Origin. The Export Promotion Offices at Bombay, Calcutta, Madras and Cochin and the head of the licensing offices in the rest of the places have also been authorised to issue the Certificate of Origin. In case of textile items, the Textile Committee, in case of silk, Silk Board; in case of handicrafts, All India Handicrafts Board; in respect of coir items, the Coir Board have been empowered to issue the Certificate of Origin. The following important matters relating to issue of GSP should be noted.

Necessity

Certificate of Origin is required by the importer either for taking advantage of a preferential tariff granted to exports from India in a particular country or to ensure that particular goods from India are not banned for import in the country concerned. Sometimes, it ensures that goods have not been reshipped by a seller who has brought them into his own country from some other place of origin, not enjoying the preference.

Production of True Copy of AWB/BL

Certificates will be issued only on production of a true copy of one Air-way Bill or Bill of Lading, with non-negotiable copy for verification, indicating direct transport within the meaning of the provisions of Article 6 of the Rules of Origin and no undertaking to produce this later will be accepted.

However, in case of issue of certificates at the airport at the time of customs examination, if the Airway Bill or Bill of Lading is not available, the certificate will be issued on the basis of the verification of shipping documents showing direct transport.

Issue of Certificates "Restrospectively"

Certificates should be obtained within three days from the date of shipment. In exceptional cases, a certificate may be issued after the actual exportation of the products to which it relates, if it was not issued at the time of exportation as a result of errors involuntarily made or omissions or other special circumstances. However, to facilitate a smooth certificate, exporters should adjust their programme of shipping documentation in such a way that the application for GSP certificates are filed well in advance.

Validity Period

According to Article 8 of the Rules of Origin, the validity period of the Certificate of Origin is 10 months from the date of issue. There is no need to revalidate any certificate after the expiry period because the importer can use the certificate after the expiry of the validity period by invoking the provisions in article 8(2) governing the force majeure.

Postal Consignment

Postal consignments upon the values prescribed for each country do not need the GSP certificate in Form A and instead APR Form should be furnished by the exporter at the time of export and not subsequent to export.

Types of Certificates of Origin

The Certificate of Origin is generally of the following three types, namely:–

(1) Certificate required in general by all countries for clearance of goods by the importer,

(2) Certificate required for availing of concession under Generalised System of Preference (GSP),

(3) Certificate for availing of concession under any other kind of preference.

PRESCRIBED FORMS

General Certificate of Origin

All the three types of 'Certificates' are to be obtained on prescribed forms which has now been standardised. The Certificate is issued by a Chamber of Commerce/Trade Association, etc. It is issued on the prescribed formats.

Handloom Certificate/Garment Certificate

It is issued by:-

(a) Chamber of Commerce like PHD, as may be required in general by any country which does not specify the issuing authority and/or the format.

(b) In the case of export all "handloom garments" corresponding to restrained i.e. quota items, other than Category I (tailored collar shirts) to Canada, Cotton Handloom, Manmade Fibres, Handloom

Blouses, Garments to Austria and special quantities reserved for Handloom garments in some of the restrained categories of EEC, Norway and Finland, the Textile Committee issues the certificate as prescribed in the Bilateral Agreements for such products.

(c) For exports of handloom garments in Category I (tailored collar shirts) to Canada and special quantities reserved for handloom garments in some of the restrained categories to US, the Apparel Export Promotion Council issues Export Certificate/Certificate of Origin/Visa as stipulated in the Bilateral Agreement. It will issue this certificate for garments subject to restraint to Austria.

(d) In case of United Arab Republic and Yugoslavia, Certificate of Origin of goods required for tariff concession in customs duties for clearance of eligible garments, AEPC issues the Certificate of Origin.

GSP Certificate

It is used in connection with tariff concession under GSP by the importer abroad, and obtained (in triplicate) on Forms 'A' and 'B' from specified agencies, namely.

(i) Export Inspection Agencies established at various centres.
(ii) Director General of Foreign Trade, New Delhi and Officers Incharge (Export Promotion) in offices of Joint Director General of Foreign Trade in Delhi (CLA), Bombay, Calcutta and Madras.
(iii) Central Silk Board, Bangalore.
(iv) Coir Board, Cochin.
(v) Development Commissioner, Handicrafts, New Delhi.
(vi) Textile Committee.

While the agencies at Nos. (i) and (ii) above are authorised to issue the 'Certificates' in respect of any item, the remaining agencies at Nos. (iii) to (vi) generally issue the same for the products falling within their purview.

The GSP certificate on form A is used for goods exported by any mode except post. For postal articles, form APR is required.

Form 'A' is a combined declaration and certificate of origin, containing columns for details regarding exporter, consignee, means of transport and route, description of goods, declaration by the exporter and certification by the certifying authority.

Form 'B' is given on the reverse of the triplicate copy of Form 'A'. This constitute the application for Certificate of Origin. The exporter has also to mention in this Form, the documents which he is submitting in support of his declaration. Such documents may be import documents, invoices, etc. relating to the materials or components used in the production of goods exported. On the reverse of the Form, fill-in its various columns. The forms are available from the concerned certifying agency against payment of a small fee.

APR Form (Only for Postal Consignments) for GSP Concession

A postal consignment containing originating products may be granted preferential treatment on presentation of Form APR if the value of the consignments does not exceed a specified amount. The Form APR, which must conform to the prescribed specimen should be completed by the exporter and need not be endorsed by any authority. It must be made out in English or French. If it is handwritten, it must be completed in ink and in block capitals. Form APR shall be 210 × 148 mm. A tolerance of upto plus 8mm or 5mm in the length is permitted. The paper used shall be white writing paper, sized, not containing mechanical pulp and weighing not less than 64 GSM. The Form APR must be completed for each postal consignment.

Combined Certificate of Origin and Value

The Certificate of Origin for the purpose of Commonwealth Preference is also known as the 'Combined Certificate of Original and Value'. It is required by Canada and New Zealand and is given by the grower/producer/supplier and exporter on special printed forms obtainable from the High Commission of the country concerned. The forms may be/are sometimes different for different types of goods mainly divided into goods grown/produced and manufactured. The exporters should therefore, ascertain the particular form which satisfies the requirements of the port of destination as well as the particular goods go be exported. This form is also termed as an invoice.

Special Tariff Concession Forms

Our country has entered into bilateral agreements for economic cooperation and trade expansion with some countries. Such agreements envisage grants of tariff concession on the products of each country on presentation of a Certificate of Origin issued by an authorised agency.

India Item Certificate

Indian items which are traditional folklore, handicraft, textile products, are termed as "India items". There are 39 items/group of items in this list. They are allowed duty free entry in importing countries comprising EEC, U.S.A, Finland, Australia, Sweden, Canada and Norway on the basis of appropriate certificate issued by the office of Development Commissioner (Handicraft) or the Textile Commissioner, which may be contacted for this purpose.

Issue of Certificate of Origin by FIEO

FIEO is authorised to issue a Certificate of Origin to member Export Houses, Trading Houses, Star Trading Houses and Super Star Trading Houses.

SALIENT FEATURES OF NEW GSP SCHEME

The new GSP scheme of the European Union came into force on 1st January, 1995. The scheme was valid for a period of four years, i.e. from 1st January, 1995 to 31st December, 1998. The scheme applied to most products falling within Chapters 25 to 97 of the Harmonised System.

The salient features of the new GSP Scheme are:

(a) Unlike the erstwhile GSP scheme for industrial products, which provided for zero rate of preferential duty, but with access circumscribed by NTMs such as quotas (fixed duty-free amounts) and ceilings, the new scheme has no provisions for quotas and ceilings. They have been replaced by tariff modulation reflecting the sensitivity of different sectors (products or groups of products). The admissible products have been brought under four lists and they are now subject to different rates of preferential duty. The "very sensitive" products attract a GSP duty rate of 85% of the MFN tariff. Products in the "sensitive" list attract a duty of 70% of the MFN tariff while the "semi-sensitive" products attract 35% of the MFN tariff. For "non-sensitive" industrial products, the GSP duty rate remains at zero per cent. Textiles and clothing are among the highly sensitive goods.

(b) In order to be eligible for preferential arrangements under GSP, products must comply with the Rules of Origin in force in EU.

(c) The new scheme seeks to spread the benefit of GSP to those countries which have not gained enough through it so far. The EU intends to ensure this by a "graduation" mechanism. EU feels that some developing countries are no longer in need of GSP benefits, and the graduation mechanism will help transfer preferential margins gradually from relatively advanced to less-developed countries.

Under the new graduation policy, countries with a per capita GNP of over US $6000 in 1991 (Hong Kong, Singapore, South Korea, Saudi Arabia, Oman, Brunei, Qatar, United Arab Emirates, Kuwait, Bahrain, Libya and Nauru) would get only 50% of GSP benefits w.e.f. 1st April, 1995 and would be excluded from GSP altogether w.e.f 1st - January, 1996. Countries with per capita GNP of less than US $6000 would have a 50% reduction of benefits w.e.f. 1st January, 1997. In sectors where they have achieved a high degree of trade specialisation, GSP benefits were withdrawn altogether for these sectors w.e.f. 1st January, 1998.

The sectors/country graduation system is supplemented by a "solidarity mechanism" which applies to beneficiary countries whose exports of products covered by GSP in a given sector exceed 25% of all beneficiaries exports to the Community in that sector. The graduation mechanism will not apply to countries whose exports to the Community of products covered by the scheme in a given sector do not exceed 2% of beneficiary countries' exports to the Community in that sector.

The most advanced of the beneficiary countries will be excluded from EU's GSP scheme w.e.f. 1st January, 1998 on the basis of objective and clearly defined criteria, for which the commission has been invited to present proposals to the Council prior to 1st January 1997.

(d) Under the new GSP scheme, preferences will not be granted in respect of products subject to anti-dumping or anti-subsidy measures, unless it can be shown that the said duties were based on a price reflecting the preferential tariff arrangements granted to the country, concerned.

(e) Transitional arrangements have been provided for any good for which contracts have been concluded already in 1994 and shipped (have left the country of origin) before 1st January, 1995 and are released in the Community market before 15th March 1995. This, however, only applies to the existing GSP scheme valid from July-December, 1994 and would not be admissible for products under quota and ceiling for which the MFN duties have already been re-introduced.

// CHAPTER 29 //

EXPORT DOCUMENTATION FRAMEWORK

Any export shipment involves a number of documents required mainly by the Customs/Port Authorities. Mostly the format of these documents is common in most of cases, but may differ in respect to Documents used at different ports. Hence, a reference to the Clearing and Forwarding Agent and/or the Customs/Port Authorities is suggested.

Legal Provision

According to the Customs Act (Section 40), the person incharge of a Conveyance-vessel, vehicle, Aircraft, etc., cannot permit loading of export Cargo at the Customs Station unless and until the formal permission to export given by the proper Customs Officer, is presented. Before granting the permission, the Customs Officer, however ensures that the goods being exported are in accordance with the different regulations, particularly in terms of the following:

(i) The goods are of the same type, sort and value as have been declared by the exporter,

(ii) The Duty or Cess leviable thereon has been properly determined and paid,

(iii) Provisions of Export (Control) Order, Export (Quality Control and Inspection) Act and Foreign Exchange (Regulation) Act are complied with.

The Customs Act (Section 50) further states that the exporter, in case of goods to be exported in a vessel or aircraft, has to present the **Shipment Bill** and other connected documents to the proper officer. Any export shipment therefore, involves the preparation of several document declarations and certificates, on the basis of which the Customs Authorities grant necessary permission. There are also several documents required for submission to the Port Authorities. In addition, a few more documents are required if the export product(s) fall(s) within the purview of the Export Assistance Schemes and Facilities.

Export Documentation

Some of the procedures that must be followed when an exporter has marketed his goods and received an order are now considered. These procedures often involves a good deal of documentation. This documentation is one of the major differences between trading in the home country and trading with a foreign country.

A number of documents must accompany every export shipment. They must be the correct documents and this is not a simple matter, because the requirements differ from country to country. If the documents are not the correct ones, or if they are not filled in correctly - down to the last detail, the importer cannot obtain the goods from his port when they arrive. He may even have to pay a fine and/or storage charges while the correct documentation is obtained. Additional charges may have to be made by the exporter. Obviously, a customer will think twice about future dealings with an exporter if he has experienced unnecessary delays.

Some exporters are worried by export documentation because they think it is very complicated. But it can be learnt, and Institutions such as the local Ministry of Commerce, Chamber of Commerce or Trade Associations will help the perplexed exporter. Furthermore, instead of handling documentation themselves, exporters often use Shipping and Forwarding Agents, who obtain and fill out documents, arrange transportation, etc.

But whether or not the exporter uses a Shipping and Forwarding Agent, he should know something about documentation because it plays such an extensive role in export procedures.

One major purpose of documentation is to provide a specific and complete description of the goods, so that they can be correctly assessed for Import Duty. This assumes that the customer has obtained an Import Licence if necessary.

But documentation also plays an important role in transport arrangements, in payment and credit procedures and in relation to cargo insurance and claims. In this chapter the documents which must accompany an Ocean Shipment, or those that are required before the shipment leaves the country in which it originates are looked at.

The Major Documents

The major documents that any exporter must be familiar with include the following:

- ★ Bill of Lading
- ★ Export Licence
- ★ Customs Entry Form
- ★ Commercial Invoice
- ★ Customs Invoice
- ★ Legalised/Visaed Invoice
- ★ Consular Invoice
- ★ Bill of Exchange
- ★ Certificate of Origin and GSP Certificate
- ★ Certificate of Value
- ★ Certificate of Health/Sanitary Certificate
- ★ Certificate of Inspection, Analysis or Weight
- ★ Packing List
- ★ Certification of Inspection
- ★ Black List Certificate
- ★ Weight Note
- ★ Manufacturer's/Supplier's Quality Inspection
- ★ Certificate/Languages Certificate
- ★ Manufacturer's Certificate

- ★ Certificate of Chemical Analysis
- ★ Certificate of Conditioning
- ★ Certificate of Insurance
- ★ Shut Out Advice
- ★ Short Shipment Form
- ★ Shipping Advice
- ★ Antiquity Certificate
- ★ Certificate of Measurement
- ★ Certificate of Exports
- ★ Shipping Bill/Bill of Export
- ★ Transhipment Bill
- ★ Transhipment Permit
- ★ Shipping Order
- ★ Car/Lorry Ticket

Not all the above documents are required by all countries, and not for all goods. The exporter must find out which ones are necessary in each case. He must know what these documents are needed for.

EXPORT DOCUMENTATION

Once the goods are ready, an exporter has to prepare and execute various documents at different tages of sending the shipment of goods to the importer. These documents are important for two reasons:

(a) as an evidence of shipment and title of goods and

(b) for obtaining payment

The various documents are therefore, of vital interest to the exporter and the Bank which is the usual media of payment. The documentary requirements are both regulatory and operational in nature and have to comply with the Rules and Regulations of the Indian Government as well as the importing country for different types of products. These requirements are different for different types of products. When exporting for the first time, exporters should, always find out from their buyers the documents required for the product concerned.

Accuracy and completeness are a prime necessity in documents covering export shipments. Whether two or twenty copies of the Invoice are required by the buyer, the same should be supplied as, the buyer probably has some reasons for it. Minor discrepancies of any kind either in the date itself or in the typing in the documents, which look harmless sometimes assume a menacing form. Erasures and strike over in typing or changes or additions made in ink must never be indulged as these only arouse the suspicion that the documents have been tampered with. Any alteration or addition made by an Authority issuing the documents must be endorsed properly, with the signatures of the person issuing the documents only. If the documents are not the correct ones or if they are not filled in correctly to the last, the importer may not be able to get the goods when the ship carrying them arrives. This may seem obvious but it bears emphasis since both the requirements and penalties are greater beyond comparison in export than in domestic trade.

The main purpose of the documents accompanying a shipment is to provide a specific and complete description of the goods so that they can be assessed correctly for Duty purpose and meet the Import Licensing requirements or Import Quota Restrictions imposed on the goods for clearance purpose. If there are any discrepancies in the documents and/ or if the required documents are not produced, the shipment may not be allowed for import or may even be confiscated by the Customs of the importing country. There is a plethora of documents in export trade - different forms, applications and documents are required to be filled in for obtaining Export Licences, completing Pre-shipment Inspection, for Customs Clearance and shipping, for obtaining payment and export finance and for claiming export benefits like Duty Drawback, etc.

The experienced exporter, because of the complexity of documentation, will find it a good idea to have the various documents prepared for him by a Shipping and Forwarding Agent or should take advice from a fellow exporter. The Exporter should also develop a habit of thoroughly scrutinising the documents for any possible errors or discrepancies and if any errors or discrepancies are found, must rectify them immediately before despatching them to the Bank of buyer.

STANDARDISED PRE-SHIPMENT EXPORT DOCUMENTS

The Government of India has made it mandatory for every exporter to use standardised preshipment export documents w.e.f. September 1, 1991. This is popularly known as Aligned Documentation System (ADS), based on UN Layout Key. The ADS Methodology involves the preparation of documents on a uniform and standard A4 size of paper. The documents are aligned to one another in such a way that, the common items of information are given the same relative slots in each of the documents included in the System. This makes it possible to prepare one Master document embodying the information common to all the documents included in the aligned series and to run off all the aligned documents from the same Master document with the help of suitable marking reproduction techniques. The Pre-shipment documents on a Standard Layout were first introduced by Sweden in 1956 followed by Denmark, Finland and Norway. It was later that most of the European countries, USA, Australia, etc, have adopted this ADS system.

Advantages The ADS system offers the following advantages:

1. Dispenses with the conventional documentation practices.
2. Brings in uniformity in documentation.
3. Ensures economy, speed, accuracy and convenience.
4. Facilitates expeditious checking and processing of documents at different stages.
5. Generates as many copies as required of Commercial and Regulatory Documents from their respective Master Copies through Photocopying Machines.

DOCUMENTATION PRACTICES IN INDIA

In India, on an average, about 25 documents are associated with the Preshipment stage to export transaction. These documents are classified into two categories namely, Commercial and Regulatory. The Commercial documents are those which, by Customs of Trade, are required for effecting physical transfer of goods and their 'title' from the exporter to the importer. Regulatory Preshipment documents are those which have been prescribed by different Government Departments/Bodies in compliance of the requirements of various Rules and Regulations under relevant laws like Exchange Control Regulations, Export Trade Control, Customs, etc.

On an average, there are 16 Commercial documents and 9 Regulatory documents. The following are the 16 Commercial documents generally involved at the pre-shipment stage:

Commercial documents

1. Pro-forma Invoice
2. Commercial Invoice
3. Packing List
4. Shipping Instruction
5. Intimation of Inspection
6. Certificate of Inspection/Quality Control
7. Insurance Declaration
8. Certificate of Insurance
9. Shipping Order
10. Mate's Receipt
11. Bill of Lading/Combined Transport Document
12. Application for Certificate of Origin
13. Certificate of Origin
14. Bill of Exchange
15. Shipment Advice
16. Letter to the Bank for Collection/Negotiation of Documents

Out of the above 16 Commercial documents, 14 have been standardised and aligned to one another. Two documents, namely Shipping Order and Bill of Exchange could not be standardised for the reason that they have different data elements and very little commonality when compared with other commercial documents. The Regulatory documents associated with the pre-shipment stage of an Export transaction are given below:

Regulatory documents

1. Gate Pass-I/Gate Pass-II (now deleted)
2. AR-4 Form
3. Shipping Bill/Bill of Export
4. Export Application/Dock Challan/Port Trust Copy of Shipping Bill
5. Receipt for Payment of Port charges
6. Vehicle Chit
7. Exchange Control Declaration (GR/PP) Forms
8. Freight Payment Certificate
9. Insurance Premium Payment Certificate

Out of the above 9 Regulatory documents, four have been standardised. In fact, these four documents have been reduced to only three. The receipt for payment of Port Charges has been incorporated in the Export Application/ Dock Challan/Port Trust Copy of Shipping Bill, thus one document has been completely eliminated.

MASTER DOCUMENTS

Under ADS, two Master documents - Master document I and Master document II are prepared to develop various Commercial and Regulatory documents. Master document I is used to develop Commercial document and Master document II is used for the Regulator documents.

Guidelines for Commercial Documents and Master Document 1

Paper size and specifications The ADS, as discussed earlier, involves the use of standardised trade documents aligned to one another. All the documents under the system are to be prepared on A4 size of paper, measuring 297mm * 210mm with standard margins - 10mm top, 20mm left, 6mm width and 180mm in length. The size of the individual boxes should be strictly as per specifications. Maximum tolerance is 1mm. The captions inside boxes should be printed in 6 points, sans-serif face and should be located as near to the top left of the boxes as possible. As the documents are to be generated mechanically, it is important for the paper to be of a consistent specification, with grammage of 70 to 85 gm, by all users. The paper should be stable in conditions of 50 to 60% relative humidity. Needless to emphasise that accuracy in layout and printing is an essential requirement.

Master document I The Master document will be typed on a sheet of paper in light blue ink. The mask for the photocopier may be made of a transparent polyester film (of 0.004 in. or 0.005 in. thickness) with white opaque patches to blank out unwanted information from the Master document or it may also be cut from an opaque white plastic sheet. After the desired information is typed on Master document - I, the relevant mask is laid over it. Both the Master document and the mask over it are then fed to the photocopying machine. The desired information is then automatically reproduced on the relevant document through transparent or open portion of the mask. Any additional information, which is specially required to be given in any particular documents, can be either pre-printed or inserted in the relevant box as and when required.

Guidelines for Regulatory Documents and Master Document II

Paper size and specification As against the Commercial documents which are designed on A4 size of paper, Regulatory documents are to be prepared on foolscap size of paper measuring 34.5 cms * 21.5 cms, The margins are, top 1.5cms, bottom 1.5 cms, left 1.8 cms and right 0.5 cms. The inside measurement are 31.5 cms * 19.2 cms. The measurements of individual boxes, as indicated in the Master document - II, should be strictly adhered to. The paper to be used for these documents should be of consistent specifications.

Reproduction technique The three Regulatory documents under reference have been so aligned that their respective common data requirements have been accommodated on the front side of each of these documents. This makes it possible to prepare a single Master document (as illustrated in Master document - II) from which the front side of all the three documents can be run off at one go without/using any mask. The caption Master document - II would, however need to be blanked out to prevent its reproduction on the blank forms of the Regulatory documents with pre-printed titles. The blank forms of shipping Bills/Bills of Export, GR Forms and the Port Trust documents will have a common pre-printed Declaration, as to the correctness of the particulars furnished in these documents. Besides, the exporters will also attach other relevant Declaration(s) with the Shipping Bill/Bills of Export, as per the printed statement to this effect on these documents.

The Master document in respect of the Standardised Forms of Shipping Bill/Bill of Export, Exchange Control Declaration (GR) Form and the Port Trust document is a sort of three-in-one, as it seeks to present the common requirements on the front side of each of these documents. The form of Shipping Bill, however, does incorporate several pieces of information which are not required by the Customs but are required by the Reserve Bank of India under the Foreign Exchange Regulations Act.

Conversely, these are some details which are required by the Customs Authorities but not required by the RBI. Similarly, the Port Trust document may also have on its face some information with which Port Authorities are hardly concerned. In the interest of alleviating the burden of the Exporter in the preparation of these documents individually and to facilitate preparation of these three documents from a single Master document, this minor concession on the part of each of these authorisation is not only desirable but also necessary. While the front side of these three Regulatory documents can be prepared from Master Document - I, necessary provision has been made on the reverse side of these documents. It will be useful if the following points are kept in view while completing the Master Document-II from which the Regulatory documents are to be generated:

i) All the columns in Master document-II should be completed and necessary information typed within the relevant boxes or columns without any overlapping. The Caption Master document-II should be suitably covered to prevent its impression on the documents to be generated through the Master.
ii) With a view to achieving total legibility, and having due regard to the layout of the documents, it is necessary that typewriter and not a fountain pen should be used by the exporters.
iii) As the Master document-II embodies all the information which is common to the front side of the three Regulatory Documents it would need to be prepared separately. The three documents with the requisite number of copies may be photocopies from the Master Document-II on Bank forms of the documents with pre-printed captions. No masks need to be used.
iv) Each copy of the three documents should be signed in ink by the exporter Forwarding Agent, as the case may be, so that it becomes a legally valid document.
v) Six versions of Master document-II have been designed and Forwarding Agents/Exporters should use the relevant Master document-II, depending upon the type of Shipping Bill/Bill of Export required to be filled.

Master Document-II (A)	:	For shipping Bill for Export of Dutiable goods and Shipping Bills of Export goods under Claim for Duty Drawback.
Master Document-II (B)	:	For Shipping Bills for Export of Duty Free Goods.
Master Document-II (C)	:	For Shipping Bills for export of Goods Ex-bond.
Master Document-II (E)	:	For Bills of Export of Duty Free Goods
Master Document-II (F)	:	For Bills of Export of Goods Ex-bond.

vi) As regards Shipping Bills, different forms have been designed for different types of Shipping Bills, namely, Shipping Bills for Duty Free goods, Shipping Bill for Duty Free goods Ex-bond, Shipping Bill for Dutiable goods and Shipping Bill for goods under Claim for Duty Drawback. A separate Form exists for Bill of Export. Appropriate Form should be used depending upon the type of goods to be exported.

vii) As the Port Trust document incorporated the receipt for payment of port charges (called Export Application at Bombay Port), it may be necessary for the Exporters/Forwarding Agents to prepare this document in triplicate. While the original of the Port Trust document is meant for keeping record of receipt and shipment of goods, the duplicate copy is to be used as the receipt for payment of Port charges. The triplicate copy of this document will serve the purpose of the Shipper's copy as record of shipment and payment of Port charges in respect to the goods handled by the Port Trust.

viii) On the reverse of the Port Trust document Export Application/Dock Challan/Port Trust copy of Shipping Bill - space has been provided for completion of carting permission and Customs formalities. Particulars have also been made for acknowledgement of goods 'on Board' by the Master of Vessel. This seeks to do away with the practice for Kacha Notes of any interim document required to be issued by the Master of Vessel prior to the issue of 'Mate's Receipt' in respect of consignments shipped on-board.

With the adoption of the Aligned Documentation System involving the use of two Master documents, it will be possible for the exporters and other concerned agencies/bodies to avail the advantages of 'System approach' to Export documentation.

NEED FOR PREPARING EXPORT DOCUMENTS

Export documents have to be prepared for various purposes, viz.

1. Declaration of Exports as per Exchange Control Regulations of the country.
2. Transportation of the goods.
3. Customs clearance of the goods.
4. Other purposes.

Some of the forms for preparing documents have been standardised under the Aligned Documentation System introduced w.e.f. 1.10.1991.

Documents for Declaration of Goods under Foreign Exchange Regulations

The statutory control Notification No.F1/67/EC/73-1 dated 1st January, 1974, as amended, deals with export otherwise than by Post and prohibits the export of all goods, either directly or indirectly to any place outside India, other than Nepal and Bhutan, unless the exporter furnishes a Declaration in the prescribed Form and affirms in the said Declaration that the full export values of the goods has been or will be paid in the prescribed period and manner.

The Notification further provides, that the above prohibition shall not apply *inter alia* to the export of –

(a) Trade Samples supplied free of payment;
(b) Personal effects of travellers, whether accompanied or unaccompanied;
(c) Goods despatched by Air freight and accompanied by a Declaration by the sender that they are not more than ten thousand rupees in value and that their despatch does not involve any transaction in Foreign Exchange;
(d) Goods despatched by Air freight covered by a certificate issued by an Authorised Dealer that their export does not involve any transaction in Foreign Exchange;
(e) Goods, the export of which in the opinion of Reserve Bank do not involve any transaction in Foreign Exchange, and which the Reserve Bank has, by a general or special order, permitted to be exported without furnishing a Declaration as provided for herein.

Declaration forms There are four main declaration forms which are prescribed. These are called GR, PP, VP/COD and Softex Forms. All exports to which the requirement of declaration applies must be declared on appropriate forms as indicated below:

GR Form : Used for exports to all countries made otherwise than by Post.

PP Form : Used for exports to all countries by Parcel Post, except when made on "Value Payble" or "Cash on Delivery" basis.

VP COD Form : Used for exports to all countries by Parcel Post under arrangements to realise proceeds through Postal channels on "Value Payable" or "Cash on Delivery" basis.

SOFTEX : Used for export of Computer Software in non-physical form.

While Export Declaration are to be made in a set of two copies (original and duplicate) of GR or PP form, VP/COD forms are to be submitted in a single copy.

GR/PP forms are printed in distinctive colours and each set bears a printed number which appears on both copies of the Form. They are available for sale with Reserve Bank of India. However, exporters can get these forms through Authorised Dealers also. VP/COD Forms are sold directly to exporters by Reserve Bank of India.

Export Declaration Forms have utmost importance and are binding on the exporter. It is therefore necessary, that enough care is taken while declaring exports on these forms with special reference on the following points:

(i) Name and address of Authorised Dealer through whom proceeds of exports have been or will be realised should be specified in the relevant column of the form.

(ii) Details of commission and discount due to foreign agent or buyer should be correctly declared otherwise difficulties may arise at the time of remittance of such commission.

(iii) It should be clearly indicated in the form whether the export is on 'Outright sale basis' or 'on Consignment basis' and irrelevant clauses must be struck out.

(iv) Under the item 'Analysis of Full Export value', a break up of the full export value of goods under FOB value, freight and insurance should be furnished in all cases, irrespective of the terms of the contract.

Disposal of copies of export documentation form

(i) GR Forms covering export of goods other than jewellery should be completed by the exporter in duplicate and both the copies should be submitted to Customs at the Port of Shipment. Customs will give their running Serial number on both the copies of the GR Forms after verifying the particulars and admitting the corresponding Shipping Bill. The value declared by exporter will also be verified by Customs and they will also record the assessed value. Duplicate copy of GR Form will again be presented to Customs at the time of actual shipment. After examination of goods and certifying the quantity passed for shipment, the duplicate copy will again be returned to exporter for submission to an Authorised Dealer. However, an exception to submission of GR forms to the Customs Authorities has been made in case of deep Sea fishing.

(ii) (a) PP Forms are to be first presented to an Authorised Dealer for counter signature. The Form will be countersigned by the Authorised Dealer only if the Post Parcel is addressed to his Branch or Correspondent Bank in the country of import. The concerned Overseas Branch or Correspondent Bank is to be instructed to deliver the Post Parcel against payment or acceptance of relevant Bill, as the case may be.

(b) For Post Parcel addressed directly to the consignee, the Authorised Dealer will countersign the Form, provided -

(1) an irrevocable Letter of Credit for the full value of export has been opened in favour of exporter and has been advised through Authorised Dealer concerned; or

(2) the full value of the shipment has been received in advance by the exporter through an Authorised Dealer, or

(3) the Authorised Dealer is satisfied on the basis of standing and track record of the exporter and arrangements made for realisation of the export proceeds that he could do so. If the Authorised Dealer is not satisfied about the standing, etc., of

the exporter, the application is rejected. No reference is entertained by the Reserve Bank in such cases.

(iii) In the case of VP/COD Forms only one copy is required to be completed and submitted to Post Office along with the relative parcel at the time of despatch.

The export of computer software may be undertaken in physical form i.e. software prepared on magnetic tape and paper media as well as in non-physical form by direct data transmission through dedicated earth stations/satellite links. The export of computer software in physical form is subject to normal declaration on GR/PP Form and regulations applicable thereto will also be applicable to such exports. However, export of software in non-physical form is fraught with many risks and special guidelines have been framed for handling such exports.

Documents for Transportation of Goods

The following documents are connected with transportation of the goods:-

Airway bill/air consignment note The receipt issued by an Airline Company or its Agent for carriage of goods is called Airway Bill or Air Consignment Note. It is not a document of title and it is not issued on a negotiable form. The goods are delivered to the Consignee mentioned in the AWB after he identifies himself as the party named in the Airway Bill as Consignee/Receiver, against payment of charges if any. It is therefore desirable, to consign the goods in the name of a foreign correspondent Bank, as it will enable the exporter to retain the control over goods until the payment is made/documents are accepted for payment.

The Airway Bill consists of three originals and six to eleven copies. It is a Non-negotiable document. Original 1 (Green) is retained by the Carrier issuing the AWB for accounting purposes. Original 2 (Pink) accompanies the consignment to its final destination. Original 3 (Blue) is given to shipper as proof of receipt of the goods for shipment.

Bill of lading The Bill of Lading is a document issued by the Shipping Company or its Agent acknowledging the receipt of goods mentioned in the Bill for Shipment on Board the Vessel and undertaking to deliver the goods in the like order and condition as received, to the Consignee or his order, provided the freight and other charges specified in the Bill of Lading have been duly paid. Bill of Lading is issued in the Standardised Aligned document Format.

For preparation of Bill of Lading the exporter should submit the complete sets of Bill of Lading together with Mate Receipt in the Standardised Aligned Form to the Shipping Company, which will calculate the freight amount on the basis of measurement or weight as certified by the recognised Chamber of Commerce. On payment of the freight, the Shipping Company returns the Bill of Lading duly signed and supported by the required adhesive stamps.

A Bill of Lading is generally made out in sets of two or three originals. All originals are duly signed by the Master of the Ship or the Agent of the Steamship Company and all the originals are equally valid for taking the delivery of the goods and once one original is utilised, the other originals become null and void. Utmost care is therefore required to ensure that the full set of original B/L is obtained by the exporter from the Shipping Company and no original copy goes in the wrong hand. Few extra copies of B/L are also issued generally marked as 'Non negotiable Copy', which cannot be utilised for taking the delivery of the goods.

The type of Bill of Lading required will depend upon the terms of the Letter of Credit (L/C). The following are the various types of Bills of Lading, some of which are not acceptable under L/C unless specifically permitted.

(a) Received for Shipment B/L, certifying only receipt of goods - not acceptable under L/C unless specifically permitted.
(b) On Deck B/L, containing a remark that goods are shipped on Deck - not acceptable unless specifically permitted.
(c) On Board B/L, certifying goods received on board the ship.
(d) Combined B/L, covering several modes of Transport.
(e) Custody B/L, issued by American Warehouses pending arrival of carrying vessel in Port-acceptable.
(f) Forwarding Agent B/L, issued by Forwarding Agent not accepted unless specifically authorised - a single B/L covering a group of several consignments meant for different consignees - delivery achieved by issuing Delivery Orders relating to specified portions of the whole consignment.
(g) House B/L, unacceptable as either evidence of title or Contract of Carriage.
(h) B/L - one on which the detailed conditions of transportation are not printed - not acceptable unless specifically permitted.
(i) Through B/L, covering goods being transhipped *enroute*. It covers the whole voyage and is acceptable if transhipment is permitted.
(j) Charter Party B/L, covering Shipment on Chartered Ship - issued subject to Charter Party Agreements which supersede the usual Memorandum of Conditions of Carriage appearing on the reverse of B/L, not acceptable unless specifically authorised.
(k) Ocean/Linear B/L, covering shipment by Sea from Port of shipment to destination port usually covering Shipment made under Letter of Credit.
(l) Third party B/L, acceptable if third party Shipper endorses it in favour of the beneficiary (seller) who in turn either endorses it in blank or as stipulated in Letter of Credit.

A clause B/L is a B/L containing additional clauses limiting the responsibility of the Shipping Company and indicating defective conditions of the goods. Such a B/L is not acceptable under L/C unless specifically authorised. A clean B/L is one which does not bear any superimposed clause or annotation, which expressly declares a defective condition of the goods and/or the Packaging. A stale B/L is one which is tendered to the paying Bank at so late a date, that though within validity of Letter of Credit it is impossible for it to be despatched to the consignee in time to reach him before the goods themselves arrive at the destination Port.

Example An exporter sent off his goods but forgot to send the Bill of Lading to the customer. Without this document the customer was unable to obtain the goods at the Port of destination, so the goods had to be stored at the docks until the Bill arrived. The customer sent the storage charges to the exporter, maintaining that because the exporter's fault, the charges had been incurred. He sued the exporter for the costs of the storage, and won.

Mate's receipt It is issued by the Chief of Vessel after Cargo is loaded and it contains the name of Shipper, place of receipt and Voyage No., Port of loading, Port of discharge, place of delivery, Marks and Nos., Container No., description of goods, gross weight and other details as per the Standardised Aligned document Format. The receipt is of transferable nature and must be presented at the Shipping Company's Office to be exchanged into Bill of Lading.

Combined transport document Inland Container Depots have been set up at various centres in the country. These dry ports have made it possible to cover the entire movement of goods from ICD to destination under the Transport document called Combined Transport document.

Documents for Customs Clearance of Goods

Shipping bill/bill of export Shipping Bill is the main document required by the Customs Authority for allowing shipment. Basically, Shipping Bills are of four types. The major distinction between one type and another lies with regard to the goods being exported (a) Export Duty/Cess, (b) Free of Duty/Cess, (c) Entitlement to Duty Drawback and (d) Re-export of imported goods.

Free Shipping Bill is used for export of goods which neither attracts any Duty/Cess nor is entitled to Duty Drawback on their exportation. Dutiable Shipping bill is used in case of goods subject to Export Duty/Cess but may or may not be entitled to Duty Drawback. Drawback Shipping Bill or Bill of Exports is used in the case of goods which are entitled to Drawback. Shipping Bill for Shipment Ex-bond is for use in case of imported goods for Re-exports and which are kept in Bond.

Following documents are required for the processing of a Shipping Bill:

(a) GR Forms in duplicate for shipments to all countries.
(b) Four copies of Packing list giving contents, quantity, gross and net weight of each Package.
(c) Four copies of Invoices indicating all relevant particulars such as no. of packages, quantity, unit rate, total FOB/CIF value, correct and full description of goods, etc. (One copy of this Invoice is to be pasted on the duplicate copy of Shipping Bill).
(d) Contract, Letter of Credit, Purchase Order.
(e) Inspection/Examination Certificate.

The Formats presented for the Shipping Bill are as under:

1. White Shipping Bill for export of Duty Free goods prepared in triplicate in the Standardised Format.
2. Green Shipping Bill for export of goods under claim for Duty Drawback prepared in quadruplicate in the prescribed Form.
3. Yellow Shipping Bill for export of Dutiable goods prepared in triplicate in the prescribed Form.
4. Pink Shipping Bill for export of Duty Free goods ex-Bond prepared in triplicate in the prescribed Form.

Where the goods are to be cleared by the Land Customs, Bill of export is prepared instead of Shipping Bill. Bill of Exports are also of four types i.e. white, green, yellow and pink for the purpose stated above. Standardised Formats of the Bill of Export are also available with the booksellers who deal with Exim publications.

Appraisal by the custom authorities The Customs Appraiser/Examiner examines the Shipping documents and appraises the value with regard to the following considerations.

1. That the value and quantity declared in the Shipping Bill is the same as in the Export Order/Letter of Credit.
2. That the formalities regarding Exchange Control, Pre-shipment Quality Control Inspection, etc., have been duly completed. After examination of documents and appraisement of value, the Customs Examiner/Appraiser makes an endorsement on the duplicate copy of the Shipping Bill giving direction to the Dock Appraiser about the extent of physical examination of the cargo to be conducted at the docks. All the documents, except GR (original) Form, the original Shipping Bill and a copy of the Commercial Invoice are returned to the Forwarding Agent to be presented to the Dock Appraiser.

After taking delivery of documents from the Export Department, Forwarding Agent presents the Port Trust documents to the Shed Superintendent of the Port and obtains Carting order for bringing the export cargo to the Transit shed for physical examination by the Dock Appraiser and for the shipment. After bringing the cargo into the shed he presents the following documents to the Dock Appriaser for conducting physical examination of the cargo:

1. Duplicate, triplicate and export promotion copies of the Shipping Bill
2. Commercial Invoice
3. Packing List
4. AR4 (original and duplicate) and Invoice
5. Inspection Certificate (original)
6. GR Form (duplicate)

The Dock Appriaser after conducting physical examination, records the examination report and makes "Let Export" endorsement on the duplicate copy of the Shipping Bill and hands it over to the Forwarding Agent along with all other documents to be presented to the Preventive Officer of the Customs Department who supervises the loading of cargo on board the vessels.

The Preventive Officer makes an endorsement "Let Ship" on the duplicate copy of the Shipping Bill. The duplicate copy of the Shipping Bill is then handed over to the Agent of the shipping company. This constitutes an authorisation by the Customs to the shipping company to accept the cargo on board the vessel.

After the goods are loaded on Board the vessel the Captain of the ship issues a receipt called "Mate Receipt" to the Shed Superintendent of the Port.

The Forwarding Agent then makes a payment of the Port charges and takes delivery of the Mate Receipt. He presents the Mate Receipt first to the

Preventive Officer who records the Certificate of Shipment on all copies of Shipping Bill, original and duplicate copies of the AR-4 Form and returns the Export Promotion copy, a copy of Drawback Shipping Bill and duplicate AR-4 Form to the Forwarding Agent. The latter then presents the Mate Receipt to the Shipping Company and requests it to issue the Bill of Lading (2/3 negotiable and few non-negotiable copies are required).

Exports by land/river are effected either by lorry, rail or in boats usually to three countries, i.e. Bangladesh, Pakistan and Nepal. Exports to Bhutan and Nepal though made by land route are not considered as exports except in specified circumstances. The procedure to export by land/river is by and large the same as outlined for shipment by sea or air except that the goods must pass through the specified Border (Customs) Check Posts. Instead of Shipping Bill, Bill of Export is used which is also of four types like the Shipping Bill.

Separate procedure is prescribed for export of containerised freight from the Container Freight Stations/Internal Container Depots.

Other Documents

Other important documents used in Export business are briefly explained as under:

Commercial invoice It is one of the most important documents issued by the seller in the Standardised Format. The Invoice is usually made out for the full realisable amount of goods as per Trader term, the exception being the undrawn balance which is shown as a deduction from the full amount.

If the export documents are drawn under L/C, unless otherwise stated in L/C, Commercial Invoice must be made out in the name of the applicant for the credit and the description of the goods in the Commercial Invoice must correspond with the description in the credit. Similarly, it should be noted that unless otherwise stipulated in the credit, Banks may refuse Commercial Invoice issued for amount in excess of the amount permitted by the credit.

The Invoice should be strictly according to the Contract of Sale and should be on the paper of the seller and must be signed by him or by the person acting on his behalf.

Consular invoice Consular Invoice is a document required mainly by the Latin American countries and countries like, Kenya, Uganda, Tanzania, Mauritius, New Zealand, Burma, Iraq, Australia, Fiji, Cyprus, Nigeria, Ghana, Zanzibar, etc. This Invoice is the most important document which needs to be submitted for certification to the Embassy of the country concerned. The exporter has to pay to the Embassy concerned, some fees for the certification of this invoice.

A Consular Invoice is required to be prepared in a prescribed format and it should be signed/certified by the Consul of the importing country located in the country of export. The main purpose of the Consular Invoice is to enable the importer's country to collect accurate and authenticated information about the value, volume, quality, source, etc., of the import for assessing Import Duties and for other statistical purposes. It helps the importer to get cleared the goods through the Customs without any undue delay. The Consular Invoice Forms are generally available at the importing country's Consuls and is certified against payment of some fees.

Consular Invoices should be made in multiple copies as per the buyer's requirements.

Customs invoice Countries like U.S.A., Canada, etc., need Customs's Invoice. It is generally made out on a special form prescribed by the Customs Authorities of the importing country and helps for allowing entry of goods in the importing country at preferential tariff rates. The Invoice Forms are generally available at the Consular Officer of the importing country and are required to be signed and witnessed after duly filling out the same.

Legalised/visaed invoice These are the Invoices sworn for their genuineness by the seller as being correct, before the appropriate Consulate/Chamber of Commerce/Embassy as the case may be, and they bear the stamp and authentication of the Consulate/Chamber of Commerce/Embassy as being in order. A nominal charge is collected by them from the seller for doing this. These Invoices are required by some of the Latin American Countries. There is no prescribed form of this Invoice.

Certified invoice At times the exporter is called upon to certify on the Invoice, that the goods are of particular origin or manufactured/packed at a particular place and in accordance with specific contract. When Certificates as such appear on the Invoice, it is called as a Certified Invoice.

Bill of exchange/draft A Bill of Exchange also known as Draft contains an order from the credit to the debtor to pay a specified amount to a person mentioned therein. The maker of a Bill is called the "Drawer", the person who is directed to pay is called the "Drawee" and the person who is entitled to receive payment is called the "Payee."

When it is drawn on a foreign firm it is termed as a Foreign Draft or Bill of Exchange. It is prepared either in an international currency or Indian Rupees depending on the terms of the contract. Accordingly, the Bill is known by the name of currency in which it is drawn. For example, a Bill drawn in US dollars is known as 'Dollar Bill' and when prepared in rupees, being termed as 'Rupees Bill'.

When the goods are shipped by Sea, the bills are drawn in sets and two sets of documents, including drafts are mailed to the foreign correspondent through an authorised dealer for presentation to the Drawee (importer). Each one bears a reference to the other.

A Bill of Exchange or Draft is of two types: (I) 'Sight Draft' or 'Draft at Sight' and (ii) "Usance Draft" or "Usance Bill".

When the Drawer i.e. exporter expects the Drawee i.e. importer to make payment immediately after the Draft is presented to him, it is called a 'Sight Draft'. Unless and until the Draft is received, the Negotiating/Collecting Bank does not hand over the Shipping documents and the buyer cannot take delivery of goods.

As there is no Aligned document for Draft, the same can be prepared by the Exporter in the usual format.

Packing list It is a List showing details of goods contained in each Parcel/Shipment. It shows item-by-item the contents of the Containers or Parcels shipped to enable the buyer/receiver of the shipment to check the shipment. Packing List has to be prepared in the Aligned document Form.

Certificate of inspection Inspection Certificate, indicating that goods have been inspected before shipment, is needed under some contracts or by some countries. This Certificate is generally required to be issued by one of the authorised independent Inspection Agencies/Surveyors in the exporter's country. The Certificate is issued in the Aligned document Form.

Black list certificate This is to certify that the ship/aircraft carrying the goods has not touched a particular country on its journey or that the goods are not of a particular country. This certificate is usually called for when countries have strained political relations with another.

Weight note This document is used to confirm that the Packets/Bales, etc., are of a particular weight and not more than the stipulated weight as per contract. It may at times give gross weight and net weight of the whole consignment.

Manufacturer's/supplier's quality/inspection certificate This is a Certificate to the effect that the goods which have been manufactured/supplied are as per the requirement of the Contract of Sale.

GSP certificate/certificate of origin The EEC member countries have adopted the Generalised System of Preferences. Under GSP, manufacturers and semi-manufacturers from developing countries, including India, will be entitled to a concessional rate of Import Duty in these countries.

The Govt. of India has authorised the Export Inspection Council of India and its various agencies to issue the Certificate of Origin. The Export Promotion Offices at Bombay, Calcutta, Madras and Cochin, FIEO, Chambers of Commerce and the Heads of Licensing Offices have also been authorised to issue the Certificate of Origin.

Languages certificate Importers in the European Economic Community Countries require Languages Certificate along with the GSP Certificate in respect of handloom cotton fabrics classifiable under NEMEX Code 55.09. Indian exporters should apply for this certificate simultaneously or separately. The Language Certificate is issued in quadruplicate, three copies of which are given to the exporter. He should transit one copy to his overseas importer, along with other documents, for realisation of export proceeds.

The Languages Certificate is issued by the Textile Committee against a small fee.

Manufacturer's certificate In addition to the Certificate of Origin, some countries require a Manufacturer's Certificate to the effect that goods shipped have actually been manufactured and are available.

Certificate of chemical analysis To ensure that the quality and grade of items like metallic ores, pigments, etc., is the same as specified in the Sale Contract, importers may require the exporter to send a Certificate of Chemical Analysis from a recognised analyst.

Certificate of shipment This Certificate is issued by the Shipping Agent and ensures that a certain lot of goods have been shipped.

Health/veterinary/sanitary certificates When the goods that are exported are foodstuffs, marine products, hides, livestocks, etc., usually depending upon the goods which are being imported, a certificate from the Health/Veterinary/ Sanitary Authorities is called for by the overseas buyers. This is because the importer desires to know if the goods are fit for human consumption.

Certificate of conditioning Certificate issued by a Competent Office in which, on the basis of the ascertained humidity factor, the dry weight of wool or silk is reckoned and certified.

Antiquity certificate This Certificate is required in the case of export of antiques. It is issued by the Archaeological Survey of India.

Certificate of measurement Freight can be charged either on the basis of weight or measurement. When it is charged on weight basis, the weight declared by exporter is accepted. However, Certificate of measurement from the Indian Chamber of Commerce or any other approved organisation may be obtained by the exporter and given to the shipping company for calculation of necessary freight. This Certificate contains the name of vessel, the Port of destination, description of goods, quantity, length, breadth, depth, etc. of packages.

Transhipment bill This document is used for goods imported into a Customs Port/Airport intended for transhipment.

Transhipment permit The Transhipment Permit is the permission for transhipment of goods from the Vessel on which the same are booked originally to another for export.

Shipping order Shipping Order is issued by the Shipping (Conference) Line intimating the exporter about the reservation of space of shipment of cargo through a particular vessel from a specified port and on a specified date.

Car/Lorry ticket This Ticket is prepared for admittance of cargo through the Port gate. This is also known as 'Vehicle Ticket or Gate Pass'. This includes the details of export cargo, i.e. shipper's name, car/lorry numbers, marks on packages, quantity and description.

Shut out advice It is a statement of packages shut out by a ship and is prepared by the shed concerned and sent to the exporter showing the particulars of packages, for disposal arrangement.

Short shipment form Short Shipment Form is an application to the Customs Authorities at Port advising the short shipment of goods and for claiming the return of the Duty and/or Cess paid on such short shipping goods.

Shipping advice A Shipping Advice is used to inform the overseas customer about the shipment of goods. The Shipping Advice is prepared in Aligned document. The Exporter only advises his importer about the Invoice number, Bill of Lading/Airway Bill number and date, name of the vessel with date, the port of export, description of goods and quantity and the date of sailing of the vessel.

Guidance/Clarifications

For any further clarifications/guidance on the issue of the Standardised Pre-shipment Export documents readers may approach–

(1) The Export Commissioner, O/o the DGFT, Udyog Bhavan, New Delhi – 110 011.

(2) The Indian Institute of Foreign Trade, B-20, Institutional Area, South of IIT Campus, New Delhi - 110 016.

(3) The Federation of Indian Export Organisations, PHD House, Hauz Khas, New Delhi - 110 016.

The Export Promotion Councils (EPC) and Indian Trade Promotion Organisation (ITPO) can also be contacted.

// CHAPTER 30 //

FOREIGN EXCHANGE CONTROL REGULATIONS FOR EXPORT

As one is aware, the policy regarding exports from the country is formulated by the Director General of Foreign Trade, Government of India, Ministry of Commerce, New Delhi. While the physical movement of goods exported is regulated by the Customs Authorities, the Reserve Bank of India, Exchange Control Department, in terms of the relevant provision of the Foreign Exchange Regulation Act, it is concerned about the realisation and repatriation of export proceeds to India within the prescribed period and in the prescribed manner. For further details and clarifications, exporters are advised to refer to the Exchange Control Manual (1993 Edition) as amended from time to time and/or approach any Office of the Reserve Bank or Authorised Dealers (Banks).

EXPORT DECLARATION FORMS

In terms of Sec. 18 of the Foreign Exchange Regulation Act (FERA) 1973 and Rule 5 of the Foreign Exchange Regulation Rules, 1974, every exporter must declare to the prescribed authority in the prescribed form the full export value of the goods that are exported to any place outside India other than Nepal and Bhutan. The forms contain an Undertaking that the exporter will deliver tot he Bank named in the form, the Foreign Exchange representing the full export value of the goods on or before the due data for payment or six months from the date of shipment whichever is earlier in the manner prescribed in Rule 9 of the Foreign Rules, 1974. This is a legally binding one and failure to fulfil it would attract the penal provisions of FERA, 1973. The Export Declaration Forms act as a vital link between the agencies (Customs/ Post Offices) under whose supervision goods leave India and the agencies (Authorised Dealers and the Reserve Bank of India) which monitor the realisation of Foreign Exchange proceeds of the exported goods.

Types of Export Declaration Forms

At present there are four types of Export Declaration Forms in use. All exports, other than the ones exempt from declaration, must be declared on an appropriate form as indicated below:

(a) GR Form is used for export to all countries made otherwise than by Post.

(b) PP Form is used for exports to all countries by Parcel Post

(c) VP/COD Form is used for exports to all countries by Parcel Post under arrangements to realise proceeds through Postal channels on a 'value payable' or 'cash on delivery' basis.

(d) SOFTEX Form is used in the place of GR Form when computer software is exported in the non-physical Form

The Export Declaration Forms are printed by the RBI. The forms bear printed serial numbers.

Exempted Exports

Certain categories of exports are exempt from declaration in the above manner. Two such exemptions that are of interest to the general public are:

(i) Goods despatched by Air freight or Post Parcels, provide the packet is accompanied by a Declaration by the sender that the value of the goods is not more than Rs. 10,000 and the export does not involve any transaction in Foreign Exchange.

(ii) Goods despatched by Air Freight or Post Parcel, where the Parcel is accompanied by a Certificate issued by an Authorised Dealer (AD) that the export of goods does not involve any transaction in Foreign Exchange. The AD will issue his Certificate provided inter alia the following conditions are fulfilled.

(a) The sender is a regular customer of the AD and the customer makes an Application for the Certificate.

(b) The AD is satisfied that the export does not involve any transaction in Foreign Exchange and

(c) The value of the shipment does not exceed Rs 25,000.

The Certificate issued by the AD will also carry a notation to the effect that the value of the Shipment should be subject to acceptance by Customs.

PROCESSING AND DISPOSAL OF SHIPPING DOCUMENTS

(i) CG Forms are completed by the exporter in duplicate and submitted to the Customs Authorities along with the Shipping Bill filed with them. The Shipping Bill is the Customs Document, based on which the goods mentioned therein are accepted by Customs for export. After admitting the Shipping Bill, Customs will give a running serial number on both copies of the GR Form. This number comprises of ten digits, denoting the Code Number of the Port, the calendar year and a six digit running serial number. Customs will certify the value declared by the exporter in both copies of the GR Form and also record the assessed value. They will return the duplicate GR From to the exporter and retain the original for transmission to the RBI. The exporter submits the duplicate GR Form again to customs along with the cargo to be shipped. After examination of the goods and certifying the quantity passed for shipment on the duplicate, Customs will return it to the exporter. The exporter then submits the duplicate GR Form to his Bank along with the export Bill for negotiation/collection.

(ii) PP Form will not be accepted by Post Offices unless they are countersigned by an AD. The exporter should present the PP Form in duplicated to an AD. The AD will countersign the form only if he is satisfied that current Exchange/Trade Control Provisions for sending the goods by Post/Parcel Post are complied with. The AD will return the original to the exporter, retaining the duplicate with him. The exporter tenders the original PP Form to the Post Office along with the parcel. The original PP Form will be forwarded to the RBI by the Post Office. The exporter submits the relative export Bill for collection/ negotiation to the AD who countersigned the PP Form.

(iii) In the case of VP/COD Form, only one copy is required to be completed by the exporter and submitted to the Post Office along with the relative parcel at the time of despatch.

(iv) Export of computer software in non/physical form should be declared on the SOFTEX Form. Each set of the SOFTEX Form comprises three copies marked original, duplicate and triplicate, each carrying an identical pre-printed number. The completed SOFTEX Forms are submitted to the Department of Electronics (DoE) of the Central Government. Authorised Officials of the DoE will verify the form and certify that the software declared in the form has been actually transmitted and the export value declared is found to be in order and accepted. The original will be forwarded to the RBI, duplicate will be returned to the exporter and the triplicate retained by the DoE. Each exporter will have to designate a single Branch of an Authorised Dealer to whom the duplicate SOFTEX Form and export Documents in respect of all software exports in non-physical form will be submitted for negotiation/collection.

(v) The Importer exporter Code number of the exporter is to be mentioned on all Export Declaration forms. While completing the forms, the exporters must ensure that all columns are properly completed. If any Agent's commission is payable, discount allowed or other deductions are to be made from the gross invoice value, such deductions with appropriate rate must be indicated. The duplicate GR Form and the like together with relative Shipping Documents and an extra copy of the Invoice should be lodged with the AD named in the form within 21 days from shipment of goods. In all correspondence with the RBI, exporters should mention the printed number of the relative Declaration Form. In respect of GR Form the ten digit Number affixed by Customs should also be mentioned.

(vi) The Ads to whom the duplicate copies of export Control Forms are handed over, retain the duplicate with them till the proceeds have been realised. Thereafter, the duplicate copies of export Control Forms are handed over, retain the duplicate with them till the proceeds have been realised. Thereafter, the duplicate is submitted to the RBI by the AD, duly certified.

ADs may accept from their customers for negotiation or collection, Shipping Documents covering exports even where the original declaration on the GR Form had been signed by some other party, provided the customer tendering the bill, countersigns on the duplicate copy of the GR Form undertaking to deliver to the AD the Foreign Exchange proceeds of the shipment, within the prescribed period.

If the exporter fails to realise the proceeds and fails to seek extension of time from the RBI, the AD is expected to report the matter to the RBI in addition to individual default Reports, Ads will also furnish tot he RBI a half-yearly consolidated statement of all export Bills outstanding beyond the period prescribed for realisation as at the end of June and December on Form XOS. Based on the individual Reports and the details in the XOS Return, the RBI takes action against the defaulting exporters.

Exporters are liable to be questioned by the RBI till the duplicate export Control Form is forwarded by the AD to the RBI either with a Realisation Certificate or in the event of non-realisation/short realisation, with an acceptable explanation. In their own interest, exporters should seriously follow up with their foreign buyers the matter of unpaid bills. In case they are not able to realise the full value, they may agree for reduction in value with the prior approval of the RBI. In the extreme case of non-realisation, they must seek permission to write off the bill amount from the RBI. All such requests should be routed through the AD who handled the export Documents. Of late, Ads themselves have been vested with delegated powers to approve reduction in value or to write off unpaid bills. The powers delegated to Ads are subject to fulfilment of certain conditions and subject to value limitations.

EXPORT OF GOODS LEASE, HIRE

Machinery, equipment, etc. are sometimes exported on lease basis, hire basis, etc., under agreement with the Overseas lessee against collection of the higher charges and ultimate re-import of the goods exported. Exporters who wish to export goods on these terms, should approach with full particulars, through an Authorised Dealer, the Office of the Reserve Bank of India under whose jurisdiction the exporter is situated.

EXPORTS BY AIR

Exporters sending goods by air run the risk of losing value of goods if the negotiable Shipping Documents are absent or if they are countersigned directly to the Overseas Buyer/Consignee and not to the Overseas Branch/correspondent of an Authorised Dealer, or if they are not covered by an irrevocable Letter of Credit opened by the Buyer for the full value of the goods in advance. Exporters are therefore, well advised to consign the goods in such cases to the concerned Overseas Branch/correspondent of the Authorised Dealer through whom Shipping Documents will be forwarded for collection. This is done to enable the Authorised Dealer through whom Shipping Documents will be forwarded for collection to instruct the Overseas Branch/correspondent of the Authorised Dealer to arrange for issue of Delivery Order in favour of the buyer on payment or acceptance of bill drawn by the exporter.

CONSIGNMENT EXPORTS

When goods are exported on consignment basis, at the risk of the exporter for sale and eventual remittance of sale proceeds to him by the Agent/Consignee abroad, the Authorised Dealer, while forwarding Shipping Documents to his Overseas Branch/correspondent, will instruct them to deliver the Consignment only against trust receipt, undertaking to deliver the sale proceeds by a specified data. The specified date should be within the period prescribed for realisation of proceeds of the export. In case of goods exported on consignment basis, Freight and Marine Insurance must be arranged in India.

FOREIGN EXCHANGE FACILITIES

The following Foreign Exchange facilities are available to the exporters as per RBI's new Exchange Control Manual, 1993 Edition (as amended up-to-date).

The Agents/Consignees may deduct from sale proceeds of the goods, expense normally incurred towards receipt, storage and sale of the goods, such as landing charges, warehouse rent, handling charges etc., and remit the net proceeds tot he exporter. Foreign Exchange is released/remitted abroad freely for various activities connected with exports. Even exporters can open Foreign Currency Accounts known as EEFC accounts and FCA in India and/ or abroad even. Foreign Exchange facilities thus cover:

1. Foreign Currency Accounts
2. Foreign Travel
3. Agency Commission
4. Export Claims
5. Reduction in Export Invoice Value
6. Expenses on Dishonoured Export Bills
7. Arbitration Fee
8. Publicity and Advertisement
9. Newspapers and Magazines/Journals Subscription
10. Membership fee for Trade Associations
11. Testing Charges
12. Overseas Branches/Offices
13. Tender Documents
14. Export Information
15. Trade Samples
16. Exploration of Foreign Markets
17. Fairs/Exhibitions Abroad
18. Hospitality to Non-resident-Visitors
19. Engagement of Foreign Technician(s)
20. Patent, Trade Mark Fees
21. Registration Fee for Conferences
22. Maintenance/Annual Service Charges for Machinery/Software
23. Replacement of Parts/articles
24. Freight Payment in Foreign Currency
25. Electronic Database Costs
26. Legal Expenses Connected with exports
27. Consultancy Fees
28. Feasibility/Pre-feasibility Studies for Projects in India
29. Miscellaneous Remittances and
30. Miscellaneous Purposes

FOREIGN CURRENCY ACCOUNTS BY EXPORTERS

Reserve Bank may consider selectively application from exporters having a good track record for opening Foreign Currency Accounts with Banks abroad for crediting the proceeds of export shipment made (except to countries which are members of Asian Clearing Union), subject to certain terms and conditions. The facility will generally be extended to export/Trading/Star Trading/ Super Star Trading House and other exporters whose net Foreign Exchange earning during the preceding year from exports and imports are not less than RS. 4 crores. A designated branch of an Authorised Dealer in India will monitor the operations in the account abroad. Applications for this purpose may be submitted through the designated branch of an Authorised Dealer on the prescribed Form EFC to the concerned Office of the Exchange Control Department under whose jurisdiction the exporter is functioning.

FOREIGN CURRENCY ACCOUNTS

Foreign Currency Accounts which can be maintained by exporters are:

1. Foreign Currency Accounts
2. Exchange Earners Foreign Currency
3. Escrow Accounts
4. Other Foreign Currency Accounts

PARTICIPATION IN TRADE FAIRS ABROAD

(i) Firms and Companies wishing to participate in Trade Fairs and Exhibitions (other than Book Fairs and Exhibitions), should apply to an Authorised Dealer with necessary particulars if the expenditure (including expenditure on travel) does not exceed US $20,000. Authorised Dealers may, on receipt of application, release Exchange upto the equivalent of US $20,000 subject to the condition that the participant Firm/Company will render proper account of the expenditure incurred. If the expenditure exceeds US $20,000, the exporters should approach the India Trade Promotion Organisation (ITPO) which will issue necessary authorisation for release of Exchange to the Firms/Companies. Authorised Dealers may release Exchange on the strength of such authorisation subject to such condition as are indicated therein.

(ii) Private publishers, printers, etc., wishing to participate in Book Fairs/ Exhibitions abroad should apply to Authorised Dealers with necessary particulars if the expenditure (including expenditure on travel) does not exceed US $20,000, or its equivalent. If the expenditure does exceed US $20,000 or its equivalent, the applicant should approach the Ministry of Human Resources Development (Department of Education), Government of India, who will issue necessary authorisation for release of Exchange. Authorised Dealers may release Exchange on the Strength of such authorisation subject to such conditions as are indicate therein.

No prior ITPO or RBI clearance is required for direct participation in Fairs/Exhibitions (other than Book Fairs and Exhibitions) abroad by Firms/

Companies who are having Exchange Earners Foreign Currency accounts, as such accounts can be utilised towards expenditure on participation without any limit for specified purposes.

EXPORT DISCIPLINE REALISATION OF EXPORT PROCEEDS

Normally, the exporters should realise the export proceeds through normal banking channel. However, exporters may also receive payment directly from the overseas buyers in the form of Bank Draft, Payment Order, Banker's Cheque, personal Cheque in Foreign Currency, Traveller's Cheques, Foreign Currency Notes, etc. Export proceed can be realised from the overseas buyers' NRE/FCNR accounts in India. Payment of upto Rs. 50,000 per transaction is also permitted from a Rupee account held in the name of an Exchange House with an Authorised Dealer in India. An exporter must realise the value of exports on the due date for payment or within six months from the date of shipment, whichever is earlier. In case, for some reason, export proceeds are not realised within this prescribed period, an application should be made in Form ETX through the Bankers, to the Reserve Bank, for obtaining suitable extension of time limit.

The prescribed period of realisation of proceeds of export consignments, to any Indian owned warehouse established abroad with the permission of the Reserve Bank, has been fixed at 15 months from the date of shipment. This period has been prescribed considering various stages in the cycle of despatch of merchandise to an overseas warehouse for eventual sale to buyers from different parts.

The reserve Bank will permit on application, exporters with satisfactory tract record a longer period of upto 12 months, for realisation of export proceeds for exports on consignment basis made to CIS countries and East European countries financed in any permitted currency.

Pure Supply Contracts

Export of goods (pure supply contracts), where at least 90 per cent of the export value will be realised within the prescribed period of 180 days and the balance amount within a maximum period of two years the date of shipment, will not be subjected to the discipline prescribed for Project Exports, provided the exporter does not require/avail of any funded or non-funded facility for such exports from any Authorised Dealer, and ECG's prior approval for appropriate cover is taken.

The exporter should however, obtain approval for payment terms from the concerned Office of the Exchange Control Department of Reserve Bank of India.

Project Exports and Service Exports

Export of engineering goods on deferred payment terms and execution of turnkey projects and civil construction contracts abroad are collectively referred to as Project exports. Project exports contracts are generally of high value and exporters undertaking them require competitive credit terms to be able to secure order from foreign buyers, in the face of stiff international competition. Indian exporters offering deferred payment terms to Overseas buyers in respect of export of goods and those participating in global tenders for undertaking turnkey/civil construction contracts abroad require specific prior approval of Reserve Bank for credit terms to be offered, third country imports and opening of a Liaison Office.

Export on Elongated Credit Terms

Normally, proceeds of export of goods, other than those for which exporters have been permitted to offer commercial credit, have to be realised on the due date for payment or within 6 months from the date of shipment whichever is earlier (or 15 months from the date of shipment in respect of exports to Indian-owned warehouse established abroad with the permission of the Reserve Bank). In some cases, however, the overseas buyers may be seeking longer period for payment of proceeds of commodities which are normally exported from India on "cash" terms, generally on the ground that remittances of proceeds are not permitted within 6 months or earlier by the buyer's country in view of its difficult Balance of Payments position. Exporters intending to export goods on such terms may submit their proposals in the prescribed From ECT through their Banks to the concerned Regional Office of the Reserve Bank, for consideration.

Transfer of Documents

Authorised Dealers may accept from their constituents for negotiation or collection, shipping documents covering exports even where the original declaration on GR, forms which had been signed by some other party provided the constituent drawing the bill countersigns on the duplicate copy of GR and From, the undertaking to deliver tot he Authorised Dealer the Foreign Exchange proceeds of the shipment within the prescribed period. In case the constituent exporter is one who is placed on exporters, caution list by Reserve Bank, Authorised Dealer may negotiate the documents provided the shipment is covered by advance remittance or by irrevocable Letter of Credit where the documents conform strictly tot he terms of the Letter of Credit.

TRADE DISCOUNT

(i) Bills in respect of exports by sea or air which fall short of the value declared on FR Forms on account of trade discount, may be accepted for negotiation or collection by Authorised Dealers only if the discount has been declared by the exporter on the relative GR Form at the time of shipment and accepted by Customs.

(ii) In case of exports by Post Parcel against declaration on PP Form, Post Offices will not undertake scrutiny of trade discount deductions if any, if declared on the forms. Authorised Dealers may accept deductions towards trade discount in such cases, provided the discount declared is in conformity with the normal level of discount usually offered in the particular line of export trde.

ADVANCE REMITTANCE

(i) Where part/full invoice value of goods exported has been received in advance, Authorised Dealer may certify the GR/PP form provided he is satisfied about the receipt and no interest is involved. In cases where Invoices indicate that the advance remittance received by exporter involves payment of interest to overseas remitter, Authorised Dealers should obtain prior approval of RBI before undertaking negotiation/collection of documents. Where, however, exporters have obtained Reserve Bank's permission for receiving interest bearing advances and shown such interest as deduction in the Invoice, Authorised Dealers may certify the deduction on the reverse of the relative duplicate copy of the GR From citing the number and date of RBI's approval. The appropriations made against every shipment must be endorsed on the original certificate of inward remittance of advance payment.

(ii) Authorised Dealers may freely grant Pre-shipment advances against 'Red clause' Letter of Credit in favour of their export-constituents. Advance made by the Letter of Credit opening Bank, will however be treated as advance remittances against exports.

PART DRAWINGS

In certain lines of export trade, it is the practice of exporters not to draw Bills for the full Invoice value of the goods but to leave a small part undrawn for payment after adjustment due to difference in weight, quality, etc., ascertained after arrival and inspection, weight or analysis of the goods. In such cases, Authorised Dealers may negotiate bills, provided:

(a) undrawn balance is in conformity with the normal level of balance left undrawn in the particular line of export trade, subject to a maximum of 10 per cent of the full export value; and

(b) an undertaking is obtained from exporter that he will surrender/ account for the balance proceeds of the shipment within the period/ prescribed for realisation.

Authorised Dealers should obtain the above undertaking from the exporter on the duplicate copy of GR/PP Form and should vigorously follow up such undertakings.

Note: In cases where the exporter has not been able to arrange for repatriation of the undrawn balance inspite of best efforts, Authorised Dealers on being satisfied with the bonafides of the case, may submit duplicate copies of GR/PP Forms to the RBI, duly certified for the amount actually realised. This is done provided the exporter has realised at undrawn balances or 90% of the value declared on GR/PP Form, whichever is more and a period of one year has elased from the date of shipment.

REDUCTION IN VALUE

If after a Bill has been negotiated or sent for collection and an amout thereof is desired to be reduced for some reason, the authorised Dealer may approve such reduction on submission of an application by a letter with full particulars of shipment and attested copy of Invoice and documentary evidence in support of the reduction sought for, provided:

(a) the reduction does not exceed 10% of Invoice value

(b) it does not relate to an export of

(i) Gold or silver jewellery or articles made out of cut polished diamonds;

(ii) the exporter is not on the exporters' caution list of RBI ; and

(ii) the exporter should surrender proportionate export incentives availed, if any.

In the case of exporters who have been in the export business for more than three years, reduction in Invoice value may be allowed without any percentage ceiling, subject to the above conditions as also subject to their track record being satisfactory, i.e. the export outstanding does not exceed 5% of the average annual export realisations during the preceding three calendar years. For this purpose, the exporter's declaration, duly certified by his Auditor or by a Chartered Accountant indicating the total export realisations during each of the preceding three calendar years and the exportbills outstanding beyond the prescribed period for realisation of export proceeds and average outstanding absolute and percentage terms would be outstanding export bills to average the export realisations during the preceding three calendar years, outstanding export bills in respect of exports made to countries facing externalisation problems may be ignored, provided the payments have been made by the buyers in the local currency. Authorised Dealers should obtain the above Declaration duly certified, as on January and every year.

WRITE-OFF OF UNREALISED EXPORT BILLS

In case where the exporter has not been able to realise the outstanding export dues despite his best efforts, he may approach the Authorised Dealer, who had handled the relevant shipping documents with appropriate supporting documentary evidence with a request for write off of the unrealised portion. Authorised Dealers may accede to such requests (the Branch concerned should obtain the approval of its Controlling Office) subject to the undernoted conditions:

(a) The relevant amount has remained outstanding for 360 days or more.

(b) The aggregate amount of write off allowed by the Branch of the Authorised Dealer during a calendar year should not exceed 5% of the toatl export proceeds realised by the concerned exporter through its medium during the provious calendar year.

(c) Satisfactory documentary exidence has been furnished in support of the exporter having made all efforts to realise the dues but has been unsuccessful due to reasond beyond his control.

(d) The case falls under any of the undernoted categories:

i) The Overseas buyer has been declared insolvent and a Certificate from the offcial liquidator indicating that there is no possibility of recovery of export proceeds has been produced. (Names, addresses and other relevant particulars of the overseas buyers wo\ho have been declared insolvent may be intimated to ECGC for updating their files on buyers).

ii) The overseas buyer has not been traceable over a reasonably long period of time and suitable supporting documentary evidence to that effect has been produced. (His name, original address and other relevant particulars may be reported to ECGC for updating their files).

iii) The goods exported have been auctioned or destroyed by the Port/ Customs/Health Authorities in the emporting country and a Certificate issued by the said authorities or the Indian Mission or Chamber of Commerce in the country of destination indicating that the goods have been auctioned or distroyed, has been produced.

iv) The unrealised amount represents the balance due in case settled through the intervention of the Indian Embassy, foreign Chamber of Commerce or similar organisations.

v) The unrealised amount represents the undrawn balance of an export bill (not exceeding 10 per cent of the invoice value) and has remained outstanding and truned out to be unrealisable despite all efforts made by the exporter. The Authorised Dealer should take into consideration the track record of the exporter, documentary evidence/correspondence showing that there is nopossibility of recovery of the undrawn balance, frequency of similar cases considered in the past and the past history of the overseas buyer, if available, before allowing the closure.

vi) The cost of resorting to legal action would be disproportionate to the unrealised amount of the export bill or where the exporter even after winning the court case against the overseas buyer could not excute the court decree due to reasons produced to fully satisfy the Authorised Dealer.

vii) Bills wee drawn for the difference between the Letter of Credit value and actual export value or between the provisional and the actual freight charges but the amount has remained unrealised consequent on dishonour of the bills by the overseas buyer and documentary evidence is roduced to show that there are no prospects of realisation.

(e) The case is not the subject-matter of any Civil or Criminal Suit which is pending.

(f) The exporter has not come to the adverse notice of the Enforcement Directorate or the Central Bureau of Investigation or such other law enforcement agency.

(g) The exporter has surrendered proportionate export incentives if any, availed in respect of the relative shipments.

CHANGE OF BUYER/CONSIGNEE

Prior approval of RBI is not required if after goods have been shipped they are to be transferred to a party other than the orignal buyer in the event of default by latter, provided the reduction in value, if any involved, does not exceed of

10% and the realisation of export proceeds is not delayed beyond the period of 6 months from the date of shipment. Where the reduction in value exceeds 10%, the conditions stipulated for reduction in value should also be satisfied.

EXTENSION OF TIME LIMIT

In case where an exporter has not been able to realise proceeds of a shipment made by him within the period prescribed (i.e. the due date for payment which has to fall within 6 months from the date of shipment, vide rule 8 of Foreign Exchange Regulation Rules, 1974) for reasons beyond his control, but will be able to realise proceeds if extension of the period is allowed to him; necessary application (in duplicate) for the purpose should be made to the RBI in the prescribed Form ETX together with appropriate documentary evidence. Extension will not ordinarily be granted unless the RBI is satisfied that the exporter is in no way directly or indirectly responsible for the delay in realisation of proceeds and that by grant of a short extension the exporter will be able to realise proceeds.

EXTENSION CONTROL REGULATIONS

RBI Circular No. 17A.D.(M.A. Series) Dated 6th June, 1998.

Amendments to the Exchange Control Manual (ECM)

1. Intersest in Import Bills
2. Import throuth Courier – submission of evidence of import
3. Payment of royalty on Computer Software
4. Remittance facilities for holding international Conferences/Seminars/ Training programmes in India
5. Loans/Overdrafts to Residents against secrity of Fixed Deposits in NRE accounts Credit to NRE Accounts
6. Credit to NRE Accounts

It has been decided to amend/modify the Exchange Control Regulations as set out in the following paragraphs.

Interest in Import Bills

In terms of paragraph 7A 12 of ECM [as amended vide AD (MA Series) Circular No. 7 dated 3rd February 1998] Authorised Dealers are permitted to allow remittance of interest accrued on usance Import bills under normal interest clause of overdue interest paid on Sight Import Bills for a period not exceeding six months from the date of Shipment. Authorised dealers were also advised that where such interest does not form part of invoice value and is being remitted separately, they should advise the concerned importer to declare the interest to the Customs Authorities and produce Exchange Control Copy of revised or supplementary Bill of Entry, incorporating therein the amount of interest before effecting the remittance.

The matter has since been reviewed and it has been decided that Authorised Dealers need not insist on importers declaring the Interest amount, where it does not form part of the Invoice value, to Customes Authorities and submitting their revised or supplementary Bill of Entry.

Import Through Courier – Submission of Evidence of Import

In terms of Paragraph 7A 20 (I) of ECM, importers are required to submit Courier wrappers as evidence of import in respect of goods imported through Courier Services. Under the provisions of the Courier Imports (Clearance) Regulations, 1995 with the Courier Imports (Clearance) Amendment Regulations, 1997 issued by the Government of India, Department of Revenue, Central Board of Excise and Customs (CBEC), New Delhi, importers are required to file a separte Bill of Entry where the value of such import is Rupee One lakh or more. Accordingly, in respect of import made through Courier services where the CIF value of the consignment is Rupees one lakh or more, Authorised Dealers should insist on submission of Exchange Control Copy of Bill of Entry for home consumption by the importer as in the case of other imports. Where however, the value of the import is less than Rupees one lakh, Authorised Dealers may obtain from the importers a certified copy of Bill of Entry in the prescribed form issued by the Customs in the name of the registered Courier Company, duly certified by the Authorised Dealer of the Company indicating the particulars of consignment for which the remittance was/is sought to be made.

Payment of Royalty on Computer Software

In terms of items IV of Part B of Annexure 1 to Chapter 8 of ECM Authorised Dealers have been permitted to allow remittances of royalty by Indian Software reproducers to overseas copyright holders for reproduction of Computer Softview, for upto 30% of the Indian published price. Where the royalty exceeds 30%, the applicant is required to obtain specific approval from the Government of India. It is clarified that in such cases also Authorised Dealer concerned may allow the remittance in accordance with the terms of approval issued by the Government of India, Department of Electronics.

Remittance Facilities for Holding International Conferences/Seminars/Training Programmes in India

At present Applications for payment of Honoraria to persons invited as guest speakers,etc, in connection with International Conferences/Seminars/Training Programmes of Scientific, Technical or Educational nature organised in India are required to be referred to the Reserve Bank. Similarly, remittances of fees to the concerned International Organisations abroad, by Indian organisers for holding such Seminars/Conferences in India also requires the approval of Reserve Bank. It has now been decided that Authorised Dealers may permit remittances of Honoraria to overseas invitees visiting India as best speakers, remittances of Honoraria to overseas invitees visiting India as best speakers, etc., as also towards fees, if any, payable to the concerned International Organisations in connection with such Conferences/Seminars/Training Programmes, etc., organised in India, provided the Indian organisers have obtained prior approval of the concerned Administrative Ministry of the Government of Indiafor holding such Conferences/Seminars/Training Programmes in India. Approval from the Ministry of Hme Affairs and Ministry of External Affairs of the Government of India is also necessary in case of participation of foreign delegates. remittances towards fees, remuneration, etc., in such cased may be allowed by the Authorised Dealers after verification of appropriate documentary evidence indicating details of payment, name of the Conference/Seminar etc. A certified copy of approval obtained by the applicant from the concerned Administrative Ministry of the Government of India, as also of the permission obtained from the Ministry of Home Affairs and Ministry of External Affairs, as the case may be should verified and kept on record by Authorised Dealers for verification by their Internal Auditors/ Reserve Bank. Further, the remittance may be effected on production of among other things, an undertaking relating to payment of Income-tax together with an Accountan's Certificate in the prescribed form, regarding payment of Income-tax for onward transmission to the Income-tax authorities.

Loans/Overdrafts to Residents Against Security of Fiexed Deposits in NRE Accounts

In terms of paragraph 13B.9 (ii)(b), 13B 9 (iii) (a) and 13B, 10(b) of ECM, Authorised Dealers have been permitted to grant loans/overdrafts to NRE account holders and to resident individuals/firms/companies in India against collateral security of fixed deposits held in NRE accounts subject, inter alia, to the condition that the period of the loan should not exceed the unexpired period of maturity of the fixed deposit accepted as security. It is clarified that there is no objection to Authorised Dealers renewing such deposit as also the loan granted there against on specific request from the NRI depositor and resident borrower, provided the interest rate directives issued by Reserve Bank are complied with. The other terms and conditions mentioned in the above Paragraphs of ECM remain unchanged.

Credit to NRE Accounts

In terms of item (I) of paragraph 13B 22 of ECM [as amended vide AD (MA Series) Circular No.11 dated 3rd March, 1988], Authorised Dealers have been permitted to credit to NRE/FCNR Account interest, if any, paid by the House Building Agency on the application money for allotment of flat/earnest money, provided the original payment was made by debit to the NRE/FCNR Account or by direct remittance from the concerned NRI. It is clarified that only the net amount (i.e after payment of tax, if any) of the interest received should be credited to the NRE/FCNR Account. Other conditions stipulated in item (I) of paragraph 13B 22 remain unchanged.

EXPORT FINANCE AND FOREX

Time limit for disposal of appications received in Exchange Control Department.

Type of Application	Maximum No. of Working Days for Disposal of Applications
Travel	
References relating to release of exchange for travel abroad for various purposes.	3
Exports	
1. Approval/Countersignature of GR/PP forms in respect of caution-listed exporters.	3
2. General permission for waiving GR form formalities for exports.	5
3. Extension of time limit for realisation of export proceeds.	5
4. Approval for direct despatch of shipping documents to the consignees/their agents (in case where powers are not delegated to authorised dealers).	5
5. Export of goods for display in exhibitions/trade fairs abroad.	3
6. Export on Elongated Credit Terms.	3
7. Approval for payment terms in respect of Project exports	3
Imports	
1. Hiring/leasing of aircrafts/ships.	7
2. Advance remittance for imports.	3
3. Issue of code number for opening of diplomatic bond store account.	3
4. Application for permission for facility for import into bond.	3
5. Hiring of transponders.	3
Miscellaneous	
1. Release of exchange against inward remittances.	1
2. Release of exchange on repatriation basis.	3
3. Issue of Money-changer's licence.	5
4. Remittance of retirement benefits to expatriate staff.	4
Foreign Investment in India	
1. NRI Investment.	15
2. Foreign Technical Collaboration.	15
3. Disinvestment of shares by foreign investors.	
External Commercial Borrowings	
1. Short term.	7
2. US $3 Million Scheme.	7

Indian Investment Abroad	
1. Investment in overseas Joint Ventures & Wholly Owned Subsidiaries under fast track route.	21
2. Investment in overseas joint ventures/wholly owned subsidiaries (not covered by automatic route).	60
3. GR approval for exports to Indian Joint Ventures abroad against equity participation	3
4. Issue of licences to Indian companies holding shares in Joint Ventures/Subsidiaries abroad.	3
5. Issue of licence for export of share certificates.	3
6. Disivestments of shares in overseas Joint Ventures/Subsidiaries.	15

Notes:

i. The number of days mentioned above exclude the day of submission of application.

ii. The maximum number of days for disposal of cases indicated above are applicable provided the applications are complete in all respects.

iii. The above time schedule is not applicable in cases which require reference to Government and other agencies.

// CHAPTER 31 //

ARRANGING FINANCE FOR EXPORT - PRE-SHIPMENT AND POST-SHIPMENT

International trade thrives on credit. Where there is little to choose from between the quality of goods from one producer or the other, it is often the inducement of credit terms offered by a seller which clinches the contract with the buyer.

The main points for consideration in any package include the *length of credit, the rate of interest and the currency of payment.* Trade credit, the granting of time to pay by suppliers is the most natural form of credit a buyer could wish for. It usually does not cost more than what can be passed on in the final sales price, does not tie up the buyer's bank lines, and is normally easy to administer. Unfortunately, trade credit carries a risk to the granter of the credit, and is generally accorded only in well-established relationships. Most buyers and sellers therefore have to resort to some form of financial package.

It is obvious that the buyer and seller have conflicting interests in the financial package, but there must be some compromise before a deal can be concluded. Banks can provide a solution acceptable to both parties, by providing credit to either the buyer or the seller. In many countries, export credit insurance assumes the risk of non-payment - for a premium - and this can be assigned to the funding bank. Bank and insurers agree that the level of credit need not be linked to the size of the customers' balance sheet and may be based on their ability to perform the contract from which the repayment will be made. So balance sheet weakness may be compensated for by strong performance capability. The bank could also repurchase an exporter's receivables, thereby refinancing any supplier's credit (i.e. the credit granted by the exporter to the buyer); the bank thus becomes the lender. The exporter's receivables could be in the form of letters of credit with deferred payments or incorporated in bills of exchange and promissory notes.

Additionally, the bank may (for a fee) absorb the *country risk* element in a deal where for example, there may be a risk of non-performance for political economic reasons, such as a block in foreign exchange in the buyer's country or an embargo on exports from the seller's country. Usually the seller's bank undertakes to guarantee payment to the buyer's bank (assuming that the latter bank has given its own undertaking). Or, for buyers, their bank will guarantee that the seller's bank will honour its obligation under any performance bond it has given on behalf of the seller. The level of risk depends on the relationship between the two banks, and whether the guaranteeing bank can recover any money it may have to pay out under a claim.

If sellers have to wait for their money beyond the normal credit terms because of a foreign exchange restriction in the buyer's country, this delay could soon wipe away the profit hoped for. If buyers do not receive the expected raw materials because of an export embargo in the seller's country, it could cause the buyers to stop production or cost them more to buy from elsewhere.

Once a financial package is agreed and a contract concluded, how do sellers collect their money, and how do buyers obtain their goods?

They use the banking system.

Export Finance

As was seen in the previous chapters, the exporter is running a risk when he ships his goods to the customer. An exporter, like any other businessman, needs money to continue operating in business. So he wants a speedy payment for his goods. He also wants protection against any default on the customer. The customer however, requires credit. An exporter can maximise his chances of getting orders by offering the right credit terms.

Export credit insurance can protect against default, but the timing of the exporters cash inflows will depend on the *terms of payment* or on his access to export financing.

There are six different terms of payment:

- ★ open account
- ★ cash with order
- ★ consignment terms
- ★ documentary collection, using a sight bill of exchange (D/P)
- ★ documentary collection, using a time bill of exchange (D/A)
- ★ documentary credit, using a letter of credit, (L/C)

and five stages at which payment can be expected:

- ★ payment when work is started on the goods,
- ★ payment at an agreed time after the goods have reached the customer.

The customer is unlikely to want to pay for the goods in advance of shipment and will be interested in those terms of payment that give him the most credit.

But the exporter's ability to provide credit to his customer from his own resources is limited. An exporter will need to obtain adequate financing from other sources.

In the first place he needs to be able to cover his production costs. This is particularly important if many months and heavy investment are required between the receipt of an order and the dispatch of the goods. In order to obtain working capital for this period the exporter may need recourse to *pre-shipment financing*.

Nature of export finance

- ★ Export Finance = Working capital finance
- ★ Treated as high priority. No export effort should suffer for want of finance.

The two distinct stages of export finance are

1. Pre-shipment Export finance
2. Post-shipment Export finance

Some special aspects

- ★ Made available at concessional rates of interest and for this purpose RBI provides refinance.
- ★ Credit guarantee coverage by ECGC
- ★ Purpose oriented and need based
- ★ Linkage between pre-shipment and post-shipment stages and desirability of treating the two as single package
- ★ Liberal approach in regard to margin requirements
- ★ No margin requirement against export receivables
- ★ Export credit over and above MPBF
- ★ Exemption for application of loan delivery system

Pre-shipment Credit

Form and purpose of shipment credit

- ★ Pre-shipment credit to be liquidated from the proceeds of export bills
- ★ Forms of Pre-shipment credit
  - ★ Packing credit
  - ★ Advance against incentives receivables
  - ★ Advance against cheques/drafts received as advance payment
- ★ Purposes for which granted
  - ★ Purchase of raw materials and other inputs
  - ★ Processing
  - ★ Manufacturing
  - ★ Merchant exporters acquiring products for export
  - ★ Packing
  - ★ Transportation
  - ★ Warehousing

Eligible parties

- ★ An exporter with an export order or an L/C in his own name who would actually perform the act of exporting.
- ★ Supporting manufacturer, provided the exporter gives a letter stating the particulars of an export order or L/C and states that he is not going to avail of export finance.
- ★ Order or L/C or running a/c facility.

Submission of the export order or L/C to bank

- ★ Either a firm order or an L/C or some other communication containing at least some minimum details such as (a) Name and details of the overseas buyer (b) Particulars of goods: quantity, specifications, unit price, value (c) date of shipment (d) terms and conditions of sales and payment terms (e) an undertaking by the exporter that he shall submit fuller details within a reasonable period.
- ★ Lodgement of the order with the bank or endorsement on the order indicating involvement of the concerned bank.

Grant of running account facility

- Good track record of the exporter
- Need for the exporter to satisfy the bank that there is justification for establishing running account facility.
- The exporter has to produce within a reasonable period a confirmed order or an L/C for items covered by the "elective credit controls", the period for this purpose being one month.

Crucial aspects that banks take into account while considering proposals for export finance

- Viability of the proposal and integrity of the exporter.
- Capability and capacity of the exporter to execute the order under consideration
- Track record of the exporter
- IEC Code No.
- Export Licence or quota requirements
- If exporter plans to import some inputs for executing the export order, his chances of getting an import licence
- If the order is covered by L/C then the status of the opening bank as also status of the importing country, including aspects such as political and financial conditions.

Quantum

- Need based
- Normally not to exceed FOB value - exceptions.
    - HPS groundnuts: deoiled and defatted cakes, rice bran, etc.
    - If goods are covered by the export production finance guarantee of ECGC.
- Margin requirement, banks to assess carefully keeping in mind such aspects as capability of exporter and desirability of exporter, having a stake, viability of proposal, integrity of the borrower, etc.
- Bank finance not to cover exporter's profit margin.

Period of finance

- Logically it should be determined in the light of duration of production cycle of the product to be exported and adding to it the time taken in making the shipment after the production/acquisition stage.
- Period to be counted from the date of first disbursement till the last date of shipment as indicated in contract or L/C.
- Normally the rule of 180 days applies. However, further extension by 90 days (making a total of 270 days) may be permitted depending upon the merits of the case. However, the rate of interest for the extended period of 90 days goes up. Banks are authorised to grant a period of 270 days *ab initio* also, if there are special reasons for taking this step. If for some reason shipment is delayed beyond 360 days, then banks are authorised to levy a rate of interest as decided by them and in any case in which, there would be no element of concessionality. Also the rate of interest imposed would become applicable from the original date of advance.

Rates of interest and other levies, if any

(i) Pre-shipment advance for up to 180 days at a concessional rate

(ii) Pre-shipment advance for further period of 90 days

(iii) For advance beyond 270 days and upto 360 days the banks are free to determine the rate

(iv) If the export is not completed banks can determine the rate which would become leviable from the first day itself. If for some period interest at concessional rate has been charged, then the difference between the total interest determined by the bank for 360 days and beyond the period and the amount already recovered at concessional rate would be recovered from the exporter.

- ★ Apart from interest, no other service charges are payable by the exporter. Also banks are not required to pay income tax on interest earned by the bank on export profit and therefore they do not have to recover anything from the exporter on that account. However, banks are required to pay a guarantee fee to ECGC and they recover the amount so paid from the exporter.

Pre-shipment credit in foreign currency (PCFC)

- ★ Under PCFC, the exporter can approach the bank and request for export finance in any of the convertible currencies which can be used for acquiring domestic and/or imported inputs.
- ★ For providing this facility, banks may in turn source funds from any one of the undermentioned devices.
  (i) Balances available with the financing bank in the exchange earners foreign currency accounts (EEFC).
  (ii) Balances available in foreign currency (Non-resident) banks scheme (FCNR(B)).
  (iii) Lines of credit arranged by the financing bank itself.
  (iv) Lines of credit arranged by the Export-Import Bank of India and out of that refinance in foreign currency is provided to financing bank.
  (v) Cost of funds under PCFC lower than that on rupee credit = libor + 2 or 2.5% (for those banks that have no overseas branches).
  (vi) PCFC drawal is liquidated by discounting of bills under "the rediscounting of export bills abroad scheme."
  (vii) PCFC is self liquidating in nature.
  (viii) Credit period is normally for 180 days. If it extends beyond 180 days then the rate prevailing at the time of extension is applied. If within 360 days there are no exports, the PCFC is then adjusted at the selling rate for the currency concerned.

Other miscellaneous aspects

- ★ Security goods meant for export form the primary security initially at the time of first disbursement the credit may be clean but as raw materials etc. are acquired, hypothecation charge over them may be established.

- ★ ECGC cover: "packing credit guarantee" and "export production finance guarantee" of ECGC.
- ★ Disbursal of funds in stages.
- ★ Follow up and monitoring.

POST-SHIPMENT CREDIT

Purchase of Finance

- ★ Basically for financing export sales receivables after the date of shipment of goods to the date of realisation of export proceeds.

It can be classified as follows:

- ★ Negotiation/payment/acceptance of export documents under Letter of Credit
- ★ Purchase/discount of export documents under confirmed orders/export contracts, etc.
- ★ Advances against export bills sent on collection basis
- ★ Advances against exports on consignment basis
- ★ Advances against undrawn balance on exports
- ★ Advances against receivables from Govt. of India
- ★ Advances against retention money relating to exports
- ★ Advances against approved deemed exports

Quantum

It can be extended upto 100% of invoice value of goods.

Rates of interest

(a) Demand bills for transit period as specified by FEDAI

(b) Usance bills for total period comprising usance period of export bills, transit period as specified by FEDAI and grace period wherever applicable.

(i) Upto 90 days

(ii) Beyond 90 days and upto six months

(iii) Beyond six months from the date of shipment

(iv) Against incentives receivables from Government covered by ECGC guarantee (upto 90 days)

Concepts

- ★ Normal transit period = NTP
- ★ Direct and indirect bill
- ★ Notional due date for arriving at this following components have to be taken into account:
  - (i) Normal transit period as fixed by FEDAI
  - (ii) Usance period of the bill
  - (iii) Grace period if applicable in the country in which the bill is drawn
- ★ Value Gate
- ★ Sight Bills
- ★ Usance Bills
- ★ D/P
- ★ D/A

Problems of Credit

There are many reasons why companies may hesitate about deciding to export. One of the most important reasons is credit. Companies need more finance for export business than for home sales, if only because transit times are longer and thus payments tend to be delayed unless payment is made before shipment.

Also, the risk of bad debts is greater in the case of export business than home trade. This is true for several reasons:

- ★ Greater distance means longer credit, which increases the chances of changes in circumstances.
- ★ It is more difficult to discover the credit worthiness of foreign customers.
- ★ Amounts owed by one customer are often very large because of sole distributors covering a whole country, etc.
- ★ Misunderstandings are more frequent, and more difficult to settle, at a great distance.
- ★ Currency exchange rates may change.
- ★ Foreign Governments may introduce new foreign exchange regulations prohibiting payment, even if the customer wishes to pay.
- ★ Financial intermediaries such as banks may be involved.
- ★ Political difficulties may prevent payment.

Need for Export Credit Insurance

There is a need for exporters to be able to insure against credit risks. Credit insurance has an important bearing on the provision of finance, since banks may be willing to lend money to exporters only if their credit risks are covered. In some countries a credit insurance policy is a valuable key to obtaining loan finance. But some exporters don't seem to want to use it.

So if the exporter decides that export credit guarantees are worthwhile what can he do about it? Commercial insurance companies are usually not equipped to take on this business, which is generally on a larger scale and requires extensive knowledge of foreign customers and conditions. It must be done by the Government, but if it is correctly organised there is no need for a credit insurance operation to lose money. The aim is to *spread* the risks and not to subsidise exporters.

In many credit insurance schemes, there are two main types of policies:

Comprehensive policies This is the cheapest form of credit insurance. To get a comprehensive policy a firm has to agree to cover all its export business in all markets (or in a fair range of its markets) for all risks, for a period of perhaps one year. Comprehensive policies are designed for steady trade, often with regular buyers.

Credit terms accepted for insurance typically vary from upto six months for consumer goods and raw materials, and upto five years for heavy machinery.

Comprehensive policies may cover up to 90 or 95% (in some circumstances up to 100%) of any loss incurred.

Specific policies These cover large, single transactions overseas, such as power station equipment, for which payment terms may extend to five years from shipment or in exceptional cases, even longer. Premium rates are calculated for each case and because there is no spread of credit-worthiness and market risks, they are higher than for comprehensive policies.

FOREIGN EXCHANGE

We all have our own currency, whether it is rupees, dollars, sterling, francs or whatever. This is what we use when we buy and sell within our own national boundaries.

When we sell to other countries we are involved with their currencies, because they use their own currency to pay for our goods even though we get paid in our currency. Hence, exporters must know the major currencies in the world, and in particular the currencies of the countries to which they export. Any bank will provide this information.

Currencies will be quoted in terms of the exporters' own currency - the dollar, for example, is worth so many French Francs, or German Marks or Indian Rupees. And the different currencies can be exchanged at the rate which is being offered at the particular time.

There are two basic rates: one when a person buys foreign currency and one when he sells it. The difference between the rates is the commission made by the dealers in these currencies.

There are spot rates - prices applying only at the time they are quoted, and forward rates, which the bank will quote for dealings upto say six months in the future. These forward rates are quoted either at a 'premium' (meaning that the value of the foreign currency is expected to be higher than it is now) or at a 'discount' (when a fall in value is expected).

How foreign exchange works If an exporter sells to a customer in West Germany in his currency, the customer will ask his bank to buy that amount of the exporters' currency with his German Marks and then send the exporter his currency to pay for the goods he has sent the customer.

But the customer may ask to be quoted in his currency, German Marks. In either case the bank will do the exchange, but the difference in the two cases is that in the first the exporter will know what amount he will receive, because he gets paid in his currency, whereas in the second he will not know exactly what he will get because it will depend on the value of his currency when the customer pays in his German Marks.

Thus, foreign exchange rates affect both the method of quoting and how a person actually receives his money. The less the exporters' currency costs the customer to buy with his own currency, the cheaper are the exports (this is what happens when there is devaluation of currencies). The more the exporters' currency is worth, the more expensive are his exports. So foreign exchange rates affect the prices quoted to your export customer.

To guard against losing money through changes in the rate of exchange, the exporter may sell his foreign currency 'forward' from his bank (if one is importing, of course, one will buy the currency forward). This means that the exporter will arrange with the bank that on a certain day it will deliver his currency to him at a certain rate (the forward rate), so that he is certain of his money at an agreed rate.

Forward exchange is of great advantage to traders. An industrial importer who has a payment to make in Ruralian dollars in three months time is able, by buying 'three months forward dollars', to make certain how much the payment will cost him in his dollars. Similarly, if an exporter is due to receive dollars in three months time, he can ascertain exactly how much he will receive by selling forward.

There is an alternative to quoting the customer in either his currency or the exporters currency. This is to quote him in the currency of a third country, usually one of the major trading nations. A person might, for example, quote in US Dollars, UK Sterling, the Japanese Yen or the French Franc. A quotation in one of these currencies might be better understood by the customer than if the exporter quotes in his own currency, particularly, if it is a little known currency for which there is not a regular trade in the customers' country. Thus, the exporter might stand a much better chance of getting an order by quoting in a well-known third currency. Moreover, quoting in a third currency might reduce the risk of exchange rate changes. In many parts of the world it is a tradition to trade in the US Dollars.

USING THE SERVICES OF BANKS

The bulk of international settlement is settled through the account which banks maintain with their correspondent banks abroad.

It is necessary for an exporter to know the services he can get from his bank. Through its correspondent banks abroad, his bank can help find out for him his export customers' financial soundness. It can also advise on any special procedures or documents required when dealing with a customer in another country.

The bank will deal with money received from a customer who is paying cash in advance, by crediting it to the exporters' account. The bank will also handle collection of money from a customer paying an open account against an ordinary commercial invoice and sending the money at the end of the month.

As has been seen, the bank will also handle letters of credit, prepare bills of exchange and, through its correspondent bank in the customer's country, arrange to collect money in exchange for handing over the documents which enable the customer to collect the goods. Banks will also advise on and arrange foreign currency exchange. It has been seen that they can also be of service in helping to guard against credit risks.

So a close relationship must be established with the bank if the exporter is to be well advised on all these important matters. Remember too, that banks provide these services at a price. An exporter would be well advised to shop around the banks to make sure that he is getting value for his money.

CASE STUDIES

Case Study I

An exporter of hand tools received an enquiry for 300 hammers from a new customer in a distant market, where only isolated sales had been made in the past. The exporter quoted CIF the customer's port as recommended and asked for an irrevocable Letter of Credit to cover the full cost, namely:

Hammers at $1 each	$300
Export packing	30

Freight and charges	120
Insurance	50
Total	$500

The exporter's bank soon reported that the documentary credit had been opened as requested and the goods were shipped without further incident. A further order for 200 hammers followed and was delivered as the first. The customer then asked for a quotation for 5000 hammers, delivered CIF as before, but asked to be allowed to pay on collection of the bills rather than by documentary credit. The exporter reasoned that the customer would not obtain title to the goods until the bill was paid and the hammers were therefore shipped as requested. The costs paid by the exporter were as follows:

Hammers at $1 each	$5000
Export packing	500
Freight and charges	2000
Insurance	500
Total	$8000

Shipment took two months, after three months the exporter's bank reported that the customer had refused the bills. They requested instructions as to disposal of the hammers which were accumulating storage charges and were deteriorating in the humid conditions. The exporter obtained no reply from the customer when he wrote and cabled asking for an explanation, the exporter asked the other two customers in the country if they could take the goods but none of them were able to help. Two months later the bank reported that the storage charges now amounted to $1000 and that a scrap metal dealer had offered to pay the charges and a further $3000 for the hammers. The exporter made the following calculations:

- ★ Accept offer, net receipts $3000.
- ★ Bring back goods to the factory, cost of freight and insurance $2500, cost of storage $1000, total costs $2500, value of hammers received $5000 (less deterioration). Net receipts $1500 or less.

He therefore accepted the scrap dealer's offer as the least expensive solution.

The exporter later discovered that several exporters had experienced such losses and it finally came to light that the customer had deliberately engineered this on a large scale. The 'scrap dealer' was actually the original customer's brother and they had in this way obtained large quantities of goods for half the price or less. What should the exporter had done to avoid this loss?

Case Study 2

A Ruralian exporter of fabrics received an enquiry from Industria for 4000 metres of printed cotton. He quoted FOB as requested and offered payment 120 days after acceptance of the bills. This decision was based on favourable credit reports and the agreement of his credit insurance underwriter. The price was quoted as follows:

'4000 metres of printed cotton at In $1 per metre. The cost In $4000 FOB Ruralian port'.

At the time when; the exporter made the quote, the exchange rate was In $1 = Ru $2.50, which meant that the order was worth Ru $100000. However, the value of the Industrian dollar began to weaken against the Ruralian dollar, and on the date the Industrian buyer's payment became due, the value of the Industrian dollar had fallen to In $1.00 = Ru $2.00. When the exporter converted the In $4000 payment at his bank, he received only Ru $8000, instead of the Ru $10000 he had expected, and as a result lost money on the order. How could the exporter have avoided this unexpected loss?

BANKS FREE TO FIX INTEREST RATES ON DEPOSITS

Reserve Bank of India's Governor, Bimal Jalan on 29th April, 1998 unveiled his maiden monetary policy, cutting bank rate by one per cent to signal reductions in lending rates and granting banks greater freedom in deposit and lending operations.

The policy gives banks freedom to offer different interest rates according to the size of the domestic term deposits and reduce the minimum period of maturity of term deposits from 30 days to 15 days.

HIGHLIGHTS

- ★ Bank rate cut from 10 % to 9 %.
- ★ Minimum period maturity of term deposits halved to 15 days.
- ★ Banks to offer different interest rates on deposits of same maturity as per the size of the deposits.
- ★ Interest rate ceiling on FCNR(B) deposits of one year and above is up.
- ★ Banks to fix their own overdue interest rates in respect of FCNR(B) and NRE deposits.
- ★ Banks to determine penal interest rates for premature deposit withdrawal.
- ★ FIIs can purchase/sell treasury bills.

In order to remove the disincentive flow of credit to small borrowers borrowing less than Rs 2 lakh, the RBI has stipulated that henceforth interest rates on loans below Rs 2 lakh should not exceed the prime lending rate which is available to blue chip borrowers.

Effectively, this measure would increase the cost of finance for small borrowers but it would help increase credit flow.

The central bank has also increased the ceiling on advances against shares and debentures to individuals from Rs 10 Lakh to Rs 20 lakh and has reduced the margin for such advances from 40 to 25 per cent. But these loans would be available only for shares which are dematerialised.

FCNR DEPOSITS

There is an increase in interest rate ceiling on Foreign Currency Non-resident Accounts of one year and above by 50 basis points and reduction of 25 basis points on deposits of one year and less.

Banks have been permitted to determine their own penal interest-rates for premature withdrawal of domestic term deposits as well as non-resident (external) deposits, as in the case of FCNR (B) deposits.

With effect from May 9, export credit refinance would be restored to 100 per cent of the increase in outstanding export credit over the level of such credit as on February 16, 1996. The interest rate on pre-shipment export credit upto 180 days has been cut from 12 to 11 per cent.

THREE MAJOR COMMERCIAL BANKS CUT INTEREST RATES

Major commercial banks have decided to revise their prime lending rates and deposit rates following the announcement of the credit policy by the Reserve Bank of India (RBI), State Bank of India (SBI), Oriental Bank of Commerce (OBC) and Dena Bank are among those who have effected the reduction with immediate effect.

SBI has reduced the prime lending rate from 13.5 per cent to 13 per cent. The new rate will be exclusive of interest tax. The bank has also reduced the medium-term lending rate that is charged on term loans for 3 years and above, anchored to bank rate, from 13.25 per cent to 17.75 per cent which is 3.75 over the bank rate.

The maximum interest spread continues to remain at 3.50 per cent. Thus effectively, the maximum interest for working capital requirements will be 16.5 per cent and that on medium-term loans, 16.25 per cent.

OBC has also reduced the prime lending rate from 14 to 13 per cent. In fact, OBC was the first to declare reduction in PLR almost immediately after the credit policy was released. Normally, SBI and foreign banks take the lead in announcing the new interest rates. But this time, Oriental Bank scored one over the others.

Hong Kong Bank also has declared a new rate of seven per cent for deposits of 15 to 29 day maturities, while deposits for a period of 30 days and above would attract interest of 10 per cent. The board of directors of State Bank have also finalised the new deposit rates. A new slab of 15 days to 45 days maturity which will carry an interest of 5 per cent. For deposits between 46 days and 179 days the interest will be 6 per cent, 180 days upto one year will be 8 per cent, for one year and two years 10 per cent, two and three years 10.5 per cent and deposits above three years will be 11.5 per cent. For NRE deposits of between 6 months and one years, the new rate will be eight per cent, for deposits of between one and three year, the interest will be 10.5 per cent while for deposits of three years and above, the interest will be 11.5 per cent. For NRE scheme, the interest will be 11 per cent for deposits between six months and one year, while for deposits of maturity between one and three years, the interest will be 12 per cent.

FORFEITING — A NEW FINANCING OPTION FOR INDIAN EXPORTERS

1. Forfeiting is discounting of export receivables on non-recourse basis, i.e. without recourse to the exporter. It is an alternative to post shipment credits as it enables the exporter to receive the full amount of the export

bills without any liability in the event of the payment not forthcoming from the buyer for some reason. Forfeiting is derived from the French word 'a forfeit' which means the surrender of rights.

2. Under forfeiting, the forfeiter, usually a finance company operating in an international financial centre such as London, Singapore, New York, discounts bills of exchange or promissory notes drawn by an exporter on an overseas buyer which are 'availised' i.e., co-accepted' by a bank overseas, generally the buyer's bank. For exchange of the co-accepted bills of exchange, the exporter receives cash. The discounting is without recourse to the exporter. Thus forfeiting is feasible if the co-accepting bank or availising bank is acceptable to the forfeiter. Generally, forfeiting is used for exports on medium and long-term credit basis i.e., from six months to seven years.
3. Advantages
   (i) Forfeiting converts an export of credit term into a cash transaction, improving the liquidity and cash flow of the project. No export credit insurance is necessary as payment is received upfront, thus saving on credit insurance.
   (ii) It is a form of off balance sheet finance, as no contingent liability is assumed by the exporter.
   (iii) It provides finance up to 100% value of the export bill unlike in normal bill discounting by banks, where a margin of 10-15% is sometimes retained particularly in deferred payment exports. In terms of RBI Guidelines on deferred payment credit, minimum 10% advance/down payment is required to be obtained from the overseas buyer, thus restricting post-shipment credit to 90% of the contract value.
   (iv) It does not have an impact on the exporter's borrowing limits with his bankers and thus provides an additional source of funding, supplementing the post-shipment credit limits from the banks. It is particularly advantageous if the exporter is exporting to a reputed buyer, as the cost of forfeiting is related to the buyer's creditworthiness. Thus forfeiting may be cost competitive as compared with normal discounting by banks, whose rates depend upon the creditworthiness of the exporter.
   (v) As forfeiting results in export proceeds being realised soon after shipment, it is a desirable form of financing from the national point of view.
   (vi) The usual export incentives are available to the exporter who uses forfeiting as would be applicable to post-shipment credit from banks.
4. Cost: There are three types of costs in forfeiting:
   (i) Discount which is usually addressed as in terms of US Dollar Libor + a spread which depends upon the creditworthiness of the overseas buyer/the availising bank, the country of import, the period of credit etc.
   (ii) Commitment fee payable by the exporter which is computed on the unutilised portion of the commitment given by the forfeiter during the availability period of the facility.

(iii) Documentation fee which is applicable for complicated transactions and not for simple transactions.

5. Regulatory position. In India, RBI has permitted forfeiting as an approved method of export financing vide AD (GP Series) circular no.3 dated February 13, 1992. Exim Bank was designated as the Nodal Agency to operate forfeiting. In the October 1997 RBI Credit Policy, commercial banks have been authorised to undertake forfeiting. The role of Exim Bank or other commercial banks as regards forfeiting in India is essentially to act as an intermediary between Indian exporters and overseas forfeiting agencies. The actual forfeiting or discounting and payment is undertaken by the overseas forfeiting agencies. Exim Bank issues the necessary certificates to enable exporters to remit the fees payable to the forfeiter.
6. Conclusion. To sum up, forfeiting is an alternative export financing mechanism at the post-shipment stage which is now available to the Indian exporter. It enables exporters to access international finance at rates reflecting the credit risk perception of the buyers than the sellers. It is particularly well suited for exports on medium and long-term credit basis. Export credit insurance is done away with. All necessary regulatory approvals are in place. The Indian exporter does not need to obtain any regulatory approval or adopt different procedures other than those currently being undertaken in the case of normal discounting banks. Forfeiting can thus be used to supplement the post-shipment credit available from banks.

RBI'S BANKING OMBUDSMEN REGARDING EXPORTER'S COMPLAINTS/GRIEVANCES ON BANKING SERVICE

In view of the frequent complaints from exporters against banks regarding delays in sanctioning of credit limits, non-observance of prescribed time schedule for disposal of credit proposals, non-observance of RBI's directives/ instructions, etc., the Reserve Bank has drawn attention to the fact that Banking Ombudsmen have been appointed in various States and Union Territories under the Banking Ombudsman Scheme 1995, for redressal of grievances against deficiency in various types of banking services. The ambit of the Banking Ombudsman's authority has been specified in Chapter III, paragraph 13 of the Scheme. As advised by RBI, the names and addresses of the Ombudsmen have been published so that exporters can straightaway lodge their complaints with them for redressal of their grievances falling within the specific ambit of their authority.

Name and address of Banking Ombudsman and Area of operation:

Shri B. N. Shetye
C/o Reserve Bank of India
Garment House, Ground Floor
Dr. Annie Besant Road, Worli
Mumbai - 400 018
Tel: 4924607/4960893
Fax: 022-4960912
Delhi, Haryana, Jammu & Kashmir and Ghaziabad District of Uttar Pradesh

Shri. B. L. Chadha
Jeevan Bharti Bldg., Tower
No. I, 7th Floor, 124
Connaught Circus
New Delhi - 110 011
Tel: 372 5445/372 5219
Fax: 011-3725218
Delhi, Haryana, Jammu & Kashmir and Ghaziabad District of Uttar Pradesh

Shri. A. K. Pandya
C/o Reserve Bank of India
Hoshangabad Rd, P B No. 32
Bhopal - 462 011
Tel: 573772/573776
Fax: 0755-573779
Madhya Pradesh

Shri. J.C. Lynn
C/o Reserve Bank of India
10/3/8, Nrupatunga Road
Post Box No.6768
Bangalore - 560 002
Tel: 227 5629/227 5020
Fax; 080-224 4047
Karnataka

Shri. R.C. Kapoor
C/o Reserve Bank of India
New Office Bldg, Sector 17
Central Vista
Opp. Telephone Bhavan
Chandigarh- 160 017
Tel: 709 589/773 011
Fax: 0172-771 880
Himachal Pradesh, Punjab, Union Territory of Chandigarh

Shri. R. K. Ragala
C/o Reserve Bank of India
6-1-50, Secretariat Road
Saifabad, Post Bag No.31
Hyderabad - 500 004
Tel: 210013/210248
Fax: 040 210014
Andhra Pradesh

Shri. J. P. Sharma
C/o Reserve Bank of India
South of Gandhi Maidan
Post Box No.182
Patna - 800 001
Tel: 654 160/655 767
Fax: 0612-655407
Bihar

Shri. O. P. Sodhani
C/o Reserve Bank of India
Ram Bagh Circle, Tank Rd.
P B No.12, Jaipur - 302 004
Tel: 570357/570392/564661
Fax: 0141-562 220
Rajasthan

Shri. G. C. Agarwal
C/o Reserve Bank of India
M. G. Road, P B No.82
Kanpur- 208 001
Tel:361191/310593
Fax: 0512-362553
Uttar Pradesh excluding District Ghaziabad

Shri. H. N. Das
C/o Reserve Bank of India
Manipur, Meghalaya, Mizoram
Station Road, Pan Bazar
Nagaland and Tripura
P B No.120, Guwahati-781001
Tel: 540445/510054
Fax: 0381-540033
Assam, Arunachal Pradesh, Manipur, Meghalaya, Mizoram, Nagaland and Tripura.

Dr. Sitakant Mahapatra
Reserve Bank of India, Pandit
Jawaharlal Nehru Marg
P B No.16,
Bhubaneswar-751 001
Tel: 418007/8, Fax: 418006
Orissa

Shri. R. Ramalingam
C/o Reserve Bank of India
Of Pondicherry and Andaman
Fort Glasis, South Beach Road
Chennai - 600 001
Tel: 561923/563 443,
Fax: 4321801
Tamil Nadu, Union Territories of Pondicherry and Andaman & Nicobar Islands

Shri. S.L. Bose
C/o Reserve Bank of India
15, Netaji Subhash Road
Calcutta - 700 001
Tel: 220622,
Fax: 033-220 5899
West Bengal and Sikkim

Shri. S.A. Kamath
C/o Reserve Bank of India
La Gajjar Chambers,
Ashram Road
Ahmedabad - 380 009
Tel: 6582357, Fax: 079-6583325
Gujarat, Union Territories of Dadra and Nagar Haveli, Daman & Diu

Shri. S.A. Rahman
C/o Reserve Bank of India
Bakery Junction
Thiruvanathapuram - 695 033
Tel: 332723, Fax: 0471-321625
Kerala and Union Territory of Lakshadweep

// CHAPTER 32 //

THE ROLE OF THE EXPORT CREDIT GUARANTEE CORPORATION OF INDIA

Payments for exports are open to risks even at the best of times. The risks have assumed large proportions today due to the far-reaching political and economic changes that are sweeping the world. An outbreak of war or civil war may block or delay payment for the goods supplied. A coup or an insurrection may also bring about the same result. Economic difficulties or balance of payment problems may lead a country to impose restrictions on either import of certain goods, or on transfer of payments for goods imported. In addition, one has to contend with the usual commercial risks of the foreign buyer going bankrupt, or losing his capacity to pay. Conducting export business in such conditions of uncertainty is fraught with danger.

The loss of a large payment may spell disaster for any exporter, whatever his prudence and competence. On the other hand, too cautious an attitude in evaluating risks and selecting buyers may result in loss of hard-to-get business opportunities. Export credit insurance is designed to protect exporters from the consequences of payment default on account of both adverse political and commercial developments, and to enable them to expand their business without fear of loss.

Export credit insurance also seeks to create a favourable climate in which exporters can hope to get timely and liberal credit facilities from banks at home. For this purpose, export credit insurance provides guarantees to banks to protect them from the risk of loss inherent in granting various types of finance facilities to exporters.

In order to provide export credit insurance support to Indian exporters, the Government of India set up the Export Risks Insurance Corporation (ERIC) in July, 1957 which was transformed into the Export Credit and Guarantee Corporation (ECGC) in 1964. To bring it into sharper focus, the Corporation's name was once again changed to the present Export Credit Guarantee Corporation of India in 1983. ECGC is a company wholly owned by the Government of India. It functions under the administrative control of the Ministry of Commerce, and is managed by a Board of Directors representing Government, Banking, Insurance, Trade and Industry, etc.

The cover provided by ECGC is of four types:

i) Standard policy issued to exporters to protect them against payment risks involved in exports on short term credit and Small Exporter's policy issued for the same purpose to exporters with small exports;

ii) Specific policies designed to protect Indian firms against payment risks involved in (a) exports on deferred terms of payment (b) services rendered to foreign parties and (c) construction works and turnkey projects undertaken abroad,

iii) Financial guarantees issued to banks in India to protect them from risks of loss involved in their extending financial support to exporters at the pre-shipment as well as post-shipment stages; and

iv) Special schemes, viz, Transfer Guarantee meant to protect banks which add confirmation to a Letter of Credit opened by foreign banks, insurance cover for Buyer's Credit, Line of Credit, Overseas investment Insurance and Exchange Fluctuation Risk insurance.

STANDARD POLICY

Shipments (comprehensive risks) Policy, which is commonly known as the Standard Policy, is ideally suited to cover risks in respect of goods exported on short-term credit, i.e. credit not exceeding 180 days. This policy covers both commercial and political risks from the date of shipment. It is issued to exporters whose anticipated export turnover for the next 12 months is more than Rs 25 lakhs. The appropriate policy for exporters with an anticipated turnover of less than Rs 25 lakhs is the Small Exporter's Policy.

Risks Covered Under the Policy

Under the Shipments (Comprehensive Risks) Policy, the Corporation covers, from the date of shipment, the following risks:

Commercial risks

- ★ Insolvency of the buyer,
- ★ Failure of the buyer to make the payment due within a specified period, normally 4 months from the due date,
- ★ Buyer's failure to accept the goods, subject to certain conditions.

Political risks

- ★ Imposition of restrictions by the Government of the buyer's country, or any Government action which may block or delay the transfer of payment made by the buyer,
- ★ War, civil war, revolution or civil disturbances in the buyer's country, new import restrictions or cancellation of a valid import licence,
- ★ Interruption or diversion of voyage outside India resulting in payment of additional freight or insurance charges which cannot be recovered from the buyer.

Any other cause of loss occurring outside India, not normally insured in general by insurers, and beyond the control of both the exporter and the buyer.

Risks Not Covered

The policy does not cover losses due to the following risks:

- ★ Commercial disputes including quality disputes raised by the buyers, unless the exporter obtains a decree from a competent court of law in the buyer's country in his favour;

- ★ Causes inherent in the nature of the goods;
- ★ Buyer's failure to obtain necessary import or exchange authorisation from authorities in his country;
- ★ Insolvency or default of any agent of the exporter or of the collecting bank;
- ★ Loss or damage to goods which can be covered by general insurers;
- ★ Exchange rate fluctuation;
- ★ Failure of the exporter to fulfil the terms of the export contract or negligence on his part.

SHIPMENTS COVERED

The Shipments (Comprehensive Risks) Policy is meant to cover all the shipments that may be made by an exporter on credit terms during a period of 24 months ahead. In other words, an exporter is required to get the insurance provided by the Policy for each and every shipment that may be made by him in the next 24 months on DP, DA or Open Delivery terms to all buyers other than his own associates. The policy cannot be issued for selected shipments, selected buyers or selected markets.

Exclusion

An exporter may of course, exclude shipments made against advance payment, or those which are supported by irrevocable Letters of Credit, which carry the confirmation of banks in India, since he faces no risk in respect of such transactions. Where an exporter is dealing with several distinct items, ECGC may agree to exclude all shipments of certain agreed items, provided that what is offered for insurance consists of all items of allied nature and offers the Corporation a reasonable portion of the exporter's total business with a fair spread of risks.

SHIPMENTS AGAINST LETTERS OF CREDIT

Unless they are confirmed by banks in India, payments under irrevocable Letters of Credit are subject to political risks. Exporters, therefore, will be well advised to get them also covered under the Policy. Such shipments, which are excluded from the scope of the Policy can be covered under it if an exporter so desires. Lower premium rates are applied to them because they do not involve commercial risk and only the political risks have to be covered.

For shipments made against irrevocable Letters of Credit, an exporter has option to obtain either political risks cover only or cover for comprehensive risks, i.e., for all political risks and the risk of insolvency or default of the bank opening the irrevocable Letter of Credit. In either case, cover will be provided by the Corporation only if the exporter agrees to get all the shipments made against irrevocable Letters of Credit covered under the Policy. Cover will not be available for selected transactions.

SHIPMENTS TO ASSOCIATES

Shipments to associates i.e. foreign buyers in whose business the exporter has a financial interest, are normally excluded from the policy. They can however, be covered against political risks under the Policy if an exporter so desires. Where the associate is a public limited company in which the exporter's share holding does not exceed 40%, cover can be provided against insolvency risks in addition to all the political risks.

SHIPMENTS MADE BY AIR

Where shipments are made by air, the buyers are often able to obtain delivery of the goods from the airlines before making payment of the bills or accepting them for payment, as the case may be. If the buyer fails to make the payment subsequently as per the contract, the risk of loss will not be covered under the Policy if premium has been paid on the shipment for DP or DA terms of payment. An exporter can however, get cover for such contingencies also if he obtains Credit Limit on such buyers on Open Delivery terms, and also pays premium at rates applicable to Open Delivery terms.

SHIPMENTS MADE ON CREDIT EXCEEDING 180 DAYS

The Policy is meant to provide cover for shipments involving a credit period not exceeding 180 days. In exceptional cases however, cover may be granted for shipments with longer credit period, provided that such longer credits are justifiable for the export items concerned.

SHIPMENTS TO ASSOCIATES

Shipments which are made to an overseas agent under an agreement that he will receive the goods as agent of the exporter and remit the proceeds on their being sold by him are excluded from the scope of the Policy. However, if an exporter wants it, the Corporation can get them included under the Policy. Cover will be provided only against political risks, since the agent acts for the exporter. If, however, goods are sold to ultimate buyers on credit terms, comprehensive risks cover can be provided for sales to such ultimate buyers if the exporter wants such cover.

ECGC — HOW THE RISKS ARE COVERED

Maximum Liability

As the Policy is intended to cover all the shipments that may be made by an exporter in a period of 24 months ahead, the Corporation will fix its maximum liability under each Policy. The maximum liability is the limit upto which ECGC would accept liability for shipments made in each of the policy-years, for both commercial and political risks. It will be advisable for exporters to estimate the maximum outstanding payments due from overseas buyers at any one time during the policy period, and to obtain the policy with maximum liability for such a value. The maximum liability fixed under the Policy can be enhanced subsequently, if necessary.

Credit Limits on Buyers

Commercial risks covered are subjected to a Credit Limit approved by the Corporation on each buyer to whom shipments are made on credit terms. The exporter has therefore, to apply for a suitable Credit Limit on each buyer. On the basis of its own judgement of the credit worthiness of the buyer, as ascertained from credit reports obtained from banks and specialised agencies abroad, the Corporation will approve a Credit Limit which is the limit upto which it will pay claim on account of losses arising from commercial risks. The Credit Limit is a revolving limit and once approved it will hold good for all shipments to the buyers as long as there is no gap of more than 12 months between two shipments. Credit limit is a limit on the Corporation's exposure on the buyer for commercial risks, and not a limit on the value of shipment that may be made to him. Premium has therefore, to be paid on the full value of each shipment even where the value of the shipment of the total value of the bills outstanding for payment is in excess of the Credit Limit.

As the Credit Limit is indicative of the safe limit of credit that can be extended to the buyer, it will be advisable for exporters to see that the total value of the bills outstanding with the buyer at any one time is not out of proportion to the Credit Limit. In cases where the Credit Limit that the Corporation is prepared to grant is far lower than the value of outstandings, exporters should discuss the problem with the Corporation.

Credit limits need not be obtained if a shipment is made on DP or CAD terms, and if the value of the shipment does not exceed Rs 5 lakhs. Political as well as commercial risks will stand automatically covered for such shipments, the only qualification being that the claims will not be paid on more than two buyers during the Policy period under this provision.

Restricted Cover Countries

For a large majority of countries, the Corporation places no limit for covering political risks. However, in the case of certain countries where the political risks are very high, which are around 57 at present, cover for political as well as commercial risk is granted on a restricted basis. Policy holders intending to export to such countries are required to obtain specific approval of the Corporation for each shipment or contract in advance, preferably before concluding the contract.

Where Specific Approval is granted, it may be subjected to certain special conditions and in some cases, subjected to payment of a Specific Approval Fee in the range of 0.5% to 2% of the contract value. Specific Approval Fee is payable in addition to the premium on the shipments. A portion of the Specific Approval Fee is refundable in the event of shipments not taking place, or if the payments are received before the expiry of the waiting period for claims.

Time for Payment of Claim

A claim will arise when any of the risks insured under the Policy materialises. If an overseas buyer becomes insolvent, the exporter becomes eligible for a claim one month after his loss is admitted to rank against the insolvent's estate, or after four months from the due date, whichever is earlier. In case of protracted default, the claim is payable after four months from the due date. Claims in respect of additional handling, transport or insurance charges incurred by the exporter because of interruption or diversion of voyage outside India are payable after proof of loss is furnished. In all other cases, claim is payable after four months from the date of the event causing loss.

However, in case of exports to countries where long transfer delays are experienced, ECGC may extend the waiting period and claim for such shipments are payable after the expiry of such an extended period.

Where the buyer does not accept goods or pay for them because of disputes over fulfilment of the terms of contract by the exporter, counter claims or set-off, ECGC will consider claims after the dispute between the parties is resolved and the amount payable is established, by obtaining a decree in a court of law in the country of the buyer. This condition is waived in cases where the Corporation is satisfied that the exporter is not at fault and that no useful purpose would be served by proceeding against the buyer.

SMALL EXPORTERS' POLICY

The Small Exporters' Policy is basically the Standard Policy, incorporating certain improvements in terms of cover, in order to encourage small exporters to obtain and operate the policy. It is issued to exporters whose anticipated export turnover for the next 12 months does not exceed Rs 25 lakhs.

The Small Exporters' Policy differs from the Standard Policy in the following respect:

Period of Policy

Small Exporter's Policy is issued for a period of 12 months, as against 24 months in the case of Standard Policy.

Minimum Premium

The Minimum premium payable for a Small Exporters' Policy is an amount equal to 0.30% of the anticipated turnover on D/P and D/A terms of payment plus where the exporter seeks cover also for L/C shipments, 0.10% of the anticipated turnover on L/C terms or Rs 1000, whichever is higher.

Declaration of Shipments

Shipments need to be declared only twice: in the seventh month for shipments made in the first six months of the policy period, and in the 13th month for shipments made in the last six months of the Policy period.

Declaration of Overdue Payments

Small Exporters are required to submit monthly declarations of all payments remaining overdue by more than 60 days from the due date, as against 30 days in the case of exporters holding the Standard Policy.

Percentage of Cover

For shipments covered under the Small Exporters' Policy, the Corporation will pay claims to the extent of 95% where the loss is due to commercial risks, and 100% if the loss is caused by any of the political risks. Under the Standard Policy, the extent of cover is 90% for both commercial and political risks.

Waiting Period for Claims

The normal waiting period of 4 months under the Standard Policy has been halved in the case of claims arising under the Small Exporters Policy.

Change in Terms of Payment or Extension in Credit Card

In order to enable small exporters to deal with their buyers in a flexible manner, the following facilities are allowed:

(a) A small exporter may, without the prior approval of the Corporation, convert a D/P bill into a D/A bill, provided that he has already obtained suitable Credit Limit on the buyer on D/A terms.

(b) Where the value of the bill is not more than Rs 3 lakhs, conversion of D/P bills into D/A bills is permitted even if Credit Limit on the buyer has been obtained on D/P terms only. But not more than one claim can be considered during the policy period, on account of losses arising following such conversions.

(c) A small exporter may, without the prior approval of the Corporation, extend the due date of payment of a D/A bill provided that a Credit Limit on the buyer on D/A terms is in force at the time of such extension.

Resale of Unaccepted Goods

If upon non-acceptance of goods by a buyer, the exporter sells the goods to an alternative buyer without obtaining prior approval of the Corporation as required under the Policy, the Corporation may consider payment of claims upto an amount considered reasonable by it, provided that the Corporation is satisfied that the exporter did his best under the circumstances to minimise the loss.

Claims Due to Loss or Damage to Goods

The Corporation may also consider payment of claims upto an amount considered by it as reasonable where loss is due to loss of or damage to the goods due to certain risks which are not normally included in general/marine insurance policies. The exporters should in such cases, have exercised normal care in obtaining the general/marine insurance policies.

In all other respects, the Small Exporter's Policy is the same as the Standard Policy.

GUARANTEE TO BANKS

Timely and adequate credit facilities, at the pre-shipment as well as post-shipment stage, are essential for exporters to realise their full export potential. Exporters may not however, be able to obtain such facilities from their bankers for several reasons, e.g. the exporter may be relatively new to export business, the extent of facilities needed by him may be out of proportion to the equity of the firm or the value of collaterals offered by the exporter may be inadequate. ECGC has designed a scheme of Guarantees to Banks with a view to enhancing the credit worthiness of the exporters so that they would be able to secure better and larger facilities from their bankers. The Guarantees seek to achieve this objective by assuring the banks, that, in the event of an exporter failing to discharge his liabilities to the bank, and thereby making the bank incur a loss, ECGC would make good a major portion of the bank's loss. The bank is required to be a co-insurer to the extent of the remaining loss. Any amount recovered from the exporter subsequent to payment of claims will be shared between the Corporation and the bank in the same ratio in which the loss was borne by them at the time of settlement of claim. Recovery expenses will be the first charge on the amounts recovered.

To meet the varying needs of exporters, the Corporation has evolved the following types of Guarantees:

1. Packing Credit Guarantee;
2. Export Production Finance Guarantee;
3. Post-shipment Export Credit Guarantee;
4. Export Finance Guarantee;
5. Export Performance Guarantee; and
6. Export Finance (overseas lending) Guarantee.

ECGC'S ADVICE ON FOREIGN CREDIT INFORMATION AGENCIES

Export credit risk insurance organisations throughout the world cover commercial risks like insolvency of overseas buyers, and protracted default mainly on the basis of the credit/status report received on the Overseas Buyer from various credit information agencies and commercial banks. Needless to say, before negotiating a contract, or making shipments to an overseas buyer on credit terms like DP, CAD, DA, consignments basis, etc., an exporter must know the standing and creditworthiness of the overseas buyer. It is thus essential for the exporter to obtain a report on his buyers from the credit information agencies or banks and also undertake a systematic appraisal of the buyer before extending credit. It should be noted that even exporters in developed countries deal with their buyers on credit terms only after ascertaining their credit ratings from reputed credit information agencies.

ECGC is playing a vital role in underwriting risks on the overseas buyers under the policies issued to exporters by obtaining status reports on the buyers from credit information agencies, commercial banks, etc. At present, ECGC has an arrangement with 28 such agencies throughout the world which are providing credit reports to it on overseas buyers from all over the world.

The ECGC experience shows that often exporters approach it for approval of credit limit at the last moment, or just before the date of shipment. The exporter-clients want credit limit on the buyer immediately, and they sometimes even approach the Corporation after the shipment is effected. It has been observed that exporters do not give ECGC reasonable time to obtain a report on the buyers and assess their rating. In the absence of a report, it is difficult for the Corporation to underwrite commercial risk, though it has given certain powers to approve provisional limit on DA/DP basis within certain financial limits to its branch/regional offices on the basis of the exporter's track record.

In view of this situation, ECGC urges exporters in their own interest to obtain a report on the buyers from one of the agencies with which ECGC has an understanding, and then apply for credit limit on the buyers to the concerned Branch Office, along with a copy of the said report.

Offices of Export Credit Guarantee Corporation of India Ltd.

Registered Office
Express Towers, 10th Floor
P O Box 373, Nariman Point
Mumbai - 400 021
Tel: 2845452/2845463/2845471
to 73, 3845537 2846049
Tlx: 011-83231
Fax. 022-2045253/2023267

Western Regional Office
The "Metropolitan", 7th Floor
Plot No.2-26 /27, 'E' Block
Bandra Kurla Complex
Bandra (E), Mumbai - 400 051
Tel: 6452637 to 6452643
Fax: 022-6452646

Branch Offices
Nagindas Chambers, Ist Floor
Opp. NTC Showroom
Usmanpura, Ashram Road
Ahmedabad - 380 014
Tel: 408499/466932/6426394
Tlx: 01216566, Cable: ERICBAY
Fax: 079-6426394

Vastu Chambers, Ist Floor
1202/39, Shivaji Nagar
Post Box No.880, Shirole Road
Pune - 411 004
Tel: 321998/321388
Tlx: 0145-7147,
Cable: ERICBAY
Fax: 0212-321388

Eastern Regional Office
Appejay House, 4th Flr, Block A
15th Park Street
Calcutta - 700 016
Tel: 292452/53,292444
Tlx: 021-7725, Cable: ERICBAY
Fax: 033-290386

Branch Offices
S-20/56 D Kennedy Road
The Mall Cantonment
Varanasi - 221 002
Tel: 46278, Fax: 348492
Tlx: 0545-283, Cable: ERICBAY

A-77, Shaheed Nagar
Bhubaneshwar - 751007
Tel: 412837, 410398
Tlx: 0675-6428,
Cable: ERICBAY
Fax: 0674-412837

North Eastern Regional
Inustrial Estate,
Bamuni Maidan
Guwahati - 781 021

Southern Regional Office
Spencer Towers, 7th Floor
770A, Anna Salai
Post Box No.325,
Chennai-600002
Tlx: 041-7170,
Fax: 044-8522537
Tel: 8522616/8522998/
8523146/8524550
Cable: ERICBAY

Branch Offices
Raheja Tower, 11th Floor
West Wing, 26 M.G. Road
Bangalore - 560 001
Tlx: 0845-2730,
Fax: 080-5589779
Tel: 5589775, 5589779
Cable: ERICBAY

HDFC House, 2nd Floor
Ravipuram Junction
M.G. Road Ernakulam,
Cochin - 682 016
Tlx: 0885-6517,
Fax:0484-374016
Tel: 367824/374273, 35447

Tulsi Chambers, 1st Floor
195, West Tiruvenkataswamy
Rd., R.S. Puram,
Coimbatore-641002
Tlx: 0855-570,
Fax:0422-439284
Tel: 446961, 449416
Cable: ERICBAY

HACA Bhavan 2nd Floor
Opp. Public Gardens
Near Police Control Room
Hyderabad- 500 004
Tlx:0425-6954,
Fax:0842-231346
Tel:234334,231346,
Cable:ERICBAY

Rajah Muthiah Mandram
2nd Floor, Dr. Ambedkar Road
Madurai - 625 020
Tel: 45856, Cable: ERICBAY
Fax: 0452-41220

Northern Regional Office
Antariksh Bhawan, 8th Floor
22, Kasturba Gandhi Marg
Connaught Place
New Delhi - 110 001
Tlx: 031-65831.
Fax:011 -3317708
Tel: 3317505,3319125,
3320853 3711078
Cable: ERICBAY

Branch Offices
Suryakiran Complex.
2nd Floor
92, The Mall, Post Box No.281
Ludhiana - 141 001
Tel: 403078/38007,
Tlx:0386-313
Fax:0161-403078,
Cable:ERICBAY

15/46. Ist Floor, Civil Lines
Opp. Miur Mills Ltd.,
P O Box 116
Kanpur - 208 0() 1
Tel: 311249, Fax: 311249
Tlx:0325-250, Cable: ERICKAN

Vikas Manzil, 3rd Floor
Hall No.3, GMD Road
Moradabad- 244 001 U.P.
Tel: 315476
Fax: 0591-310244, Tlx:0591-332
Cable: ERICMOR
O.S.D. Air Cargo Complex
M Sheerwani Road
Srinagar- 190 001
Cable: ERICBAY

N-17/B Chomu House, Ist Floor
Sardar Patel Marg, 'C' Scheme
Jaipur - 302 001
Tel: 380 015
Fax: 01412-380015
Tlx: 0365-2594
Cable: ERICJAI

9/4, Sanjay Place
BLC Building, Ground Floor
Agra - 282 002 (U.P)
Tel: 54948/350136
Tlx: 0565-328
Cable: ERICAGRA
Fax: 0562-350136

To help exporters in this regard, a list of credit information agencies which should be approached by them for obtaining a status report on the buyers with whom they wish to deal on credit terms, is given below:

S. No.	Country Code	Agency Code	Name of the Agency and Address	Tel./Fax/Tlx. No.
1	406	AGN-1	Afro Asian Trading Office P O Box 587, Jeddah 21421, Saudi Arabia	Tel. 6606303 Fax: 6658062
2	473	AGN-2	Alpha MI SA 15 Neratziotissis Street 15124 Manoussi-Athens, Greece	Tel: 01-6125400 Fax: 06-6125931
3	385	AGN-3	AMA Research 13th Floor, Chiao Shang Building, 92-104 Queen's Rd. Central, Hong Kong	Tel: 2522 7078 Fax: 2868 1401 Tlx: 83195AMAH HK
4	472	AGN-4	Burgel Wiltschaftsinfor- mationen Gmbh and Co. Kg, GasstraBe 18, 22761 Hamburg, Postfach 50 01 66 22701 Hamburg, Germany	Tel: 040-899651 Fax: 040-8905348
5	514	AGN-5	Canadian Credit Reporting Limited 0200 Consumers Road Suite 406 Willowdale, Ontario M2J 4R4, Canada	Tel:416-4999936 Fax:416-4999703
6	344	AGN-6	Credit Guarantee Insurance Corporation of Africa Ltd. 31 Dover St. Randburg P O Box 125, Randburg 2125 Johanesburg South Africa	Tel:011-8997000 Fax:011-8861027 Tlx:4-20508 SA
7	467	AGN-7	Dansk Kaution 14, Gl. Torv. P O Box 2168 DK 1016, Copenhagen, Denmark	Tel: 45 33480200 Fax: 45 33480360
8	417	AGN-8	Dun and Bradstreet India Pvt. Limited 106 Free Press House, Free Press Marg Narirnan Point Mumbai - 400 021	Tel: 2841898 Fax: 2872640
9	469	AGN-9	Dun and Bradstreet Soliditet AS, Stralfjaera 20, NO903 OSLO Norway	Tel: 22897300 Fax: 2287303
10	478	AGN-10	Eurocredit SRL 80055 Portici (NA) Via-B-Cellini 8/A, Italy	Tel: 2498000 Fax: 081-486910 Tlx: 722323
11	469	AGN-11	Finska Soumen Asiakastieto	Tel:358-0-613711 Tlx:123197

			OY, P O Box 386 Fax:358-0-513707 00101, Helsinki, Finland	CREDO FI
12	473	AGN-12	ICAP 64, Queen Sophia Avenue, Athens 11528 Greece	Tel: 7250601 Fax: 7220255
13	398	AGN-13	Industrial and Management Consultants Lot 3.30 2nd Floor, Wisma Central, Jalan	603-2637345 603-2637344
14	407	AGN-14	Ampang, 50450 Kuala Lumpur, Malaysia International Credit and Trade Information Agency Pvt. Ltd. 06-07 Katong Shopping Centre 0865 Mountbatten Road, Singapore - 1543	
15	390	AGN-15	International Report Inc. 502, 1-4-1 Haruno Ohmiya 330, Japan	
16	490	AGN-16	Informes Servicosa S.L. San Enrique, 4,2	
17	463	AGN-17	10 Netherlands B V Goudesesingel 102 3011 KD Rotterdam, Postbus 1369 3000 BJ Rotterdam, Holland (Netherland)	
18	425	AGN-18	Kemps Group of Companies P O Box 151, Rundle Mall South Australia 5000, Australia	
19	394	AGN-19	Korea Credit Guarantee Fund 254-5, Kongdok Dong, Mapogu 121-744, Seoul, Korea	
20	321	AGN-20	Kutz Corporation Ltd. P O Box 40756, Gathani House Homa Bay Road, Nairobi, Kenya	

21	392	AGN-21	Mecico-Kuwait P O Box 5618, 13057 Safat, Kuwait	
22	533	AGN-22	Owens On-Line Inc. Airport Business Centre, Free Trade Zone 4707 140th Avenue, Suit 208 Clearwater, Florida 34622, U S A	
23	492	AGN-23	Turk Eximbank Export Credit BK of Turkey Inc. Information Services Dept. Mudaffaa CAD-20, 06100 Ankara, Turkey	
24	488	AGN-24	UC AB International Upplysningrcentralen UC AB, S-114 96 Stockholm, Sweden	
25	489	AGN-25	WYS Muller Reniseignements Commerciaux SA Avenue Henri-Dunant 8, CH-1205 Geneva Switzerland	
26		AGN-26	Middle East Business Consultants Limited 2, Ambleside Crescent, Enfield Middlesex, EN3 7LZ, London, UK	
27	493	AGN-27	Mira Inform Pvt Ltd. 102, G'Neelambuj, Shankar Lane Kandivli (W), Mumbai - 400 067	
28		AGN-28	ABC Group Companies Inc. 1100 Main Street Buffalo New York 14209-2356, US	

// CHAPTER 33 //

EXPORT IMPORT BANK OF INDIA (EXIM BANK)

Export Import Bank of India, set up in 1982, for the purpose of financing, facilitating, and promoting foreign trade of India, is the principal financial institution in the country for co-ordinating working of institutions engaged in financing exports and imports.

OPERATIONS

Finance

The present focus of Exim Bank is on export finance. The Bank finances export of Indian machinery, manufactured goods, consultancy and technology services on deferred payment terms. Exim Bank finance is also available at export production stages. Exim Bank undertakes co-financing with global and regional development agencies and assists Indian exporters in their efforts to participate in such overseas projects. The Bank has diversified into all stages preceding export of goods, on credit terms.

Services

Exim Bank provides information, advisory services to enable exporters to evaluate the international risks, export opportunities and competitiveness. These include country studies, merchant banking services, advice on international marketing and data to enable effective participation in opportunities offered by projects of multilateral institutions.

Exim Bank through its wide network of alliances with financial institutions, trade promotion agencies, information providers across the globe assists externally oriented Indian companies in their quest for excellence and globalisation. Services include search for overseas partners, identification of technology suppliers, negotiating an alliance and consummating a joint venture.

Research and Analysis

Research and Analysis is carried out on specific industry subsectors with export potential, and international trade related subjects. These are widely disseminated amongst exporters, academicians, industry and trade organisations and the Government. Exim Bank thus follows a three pronged strategy to promote Indian exports. More than export finance, the Bank is engaged in export capability creation.

Resources

As on March 31, 1997, the Bank had paid-up capital of Rs 5 billion, equivalent to US $139.08 million. Networth of the Bank stood at Rs 10.44 billion, equivalent to US $290.51 million. The Bank raised loan resources from domestic and international markets.

A Variety of Programmes

Exim Bank promotes exports through a variety and a range of lending and service programmes. These programmes are tailored to meet the needs of different customer groups, viz. Indian exporters, overseas entities and commercial banks.

Exim Bank offers competitive finance at various stages of the export cycle, viz. export product development, export production, export marketing and export credit at pre and post-shipment stages.

More than Export Finance, Exim Bank Creates Export Capabilities

Does the exporter sell a product that has met the test of domestic competition? Does he wish to sell his product to developed countries? Does he possess the will to withstand the rigours of international competition?

If the exporter is an Indian manufacturer, and his answers to the above questions are affirmative, the following are offered to him:

Export marketing finance Loan finance for modernisation, capacity creation, quality upgradation, product development and marketing.

Eximius club Services aimed at promoting globalisation.

Eximius centre Disseminating skills/knowledge to match the best in the world.

ORGANISATION

Exim Bank is fully owned by the Government of India and is managed by a Board of directors with representation from Government, financial institutions, banks, and business community. The operations are grouped into Project Finance, Trade Finance, Overseas Investment Finance supported by Planning and Coordination Groups.

A Variety of Lending and Service Programmes

Programme	*Use*
For Indian Entities	
Export (Supplier's) Credit	Enables Indian exporters to extend term credit to overseas importers, of eligible Indian goods.
Finance for Consultancy and Technology Services	Enables Indian exporters of consultancy and technology services to extend term credit to overseas importers.
Pre-shipment Credit	Enables Indian exporters to buy raw material and other inputs for export contracts involving cycle time exceeding six months.
Finance for Deemed Exports	Enables Indian Companies to meet cash flow deficits of contracts secured in India and financed by multilateral funding agencies.

Finance for Rupee Expenditure for Project Export Contracts	Enables Indian project exporters to meet Rupee expenditure incurred/required to be incurred for execution of overseas project export contracts.
Foreign Currency Pre-shipment Credit	Enables eligible exporters to access finance for import of raw materials and other inputs needed for export production.
Finance for EOUs and Units in EPZs	Enables Indian companies to acquire indigenous and imported machinery and other assets for export production.
Foreign Currency Lines of Credit for Imports	Enables eligible export-oriented units to acquire imported machinery for export production.
Export Vendor Development Finance	Enables Indian firms to undertake product development, R&D for exports.
Export Product Development Finance	Enables Indian firms undertake product development, R&D for exports.
Overseas Investment Finance	Enables Indian promoters to finance equity contribution in joint ventures/WOS set up abroad.
Software Training Institutes	Enables setting up of institutes for software training.
Export Marketing Finance	Enables exporters to implement market development programmes and finance p productive capabilities through loan financing.
Production Equipment Finance	Enables eligible export-oriented units to acquire equipment.
Programme for Export Facilitation: Port Development	Enables Indian companies undertaking projects/equipment suppliers in projects involving port development and associated activities.
Programme for financing Product/Process Quality Certification	Facilitates corporates to obtain product/ process quality certification by reimbursing 50% of eligible expenditure as grant.
Services	
Underwriting	Enables Indian exporters to raise finance from capital markets through public/rights issues of equity shares/debentures with the backing of Exim Bank's underwriting commitment.
Forfeiting	Enables Indian exporter to convert credit sale to cash sale without recourse basis.
Guarantee Facility	Enables Indian companies to provide requisite guarantees to facilitate execution of export contracts and import transactions.
L/C confirmation	Confirmation of L/Cs covering import of capital goods.

Project Preparatory Services Overseas	Enables Indian consultancy firms to undertake project preparatory studies in developing countries by grant/loan financing.
Business Advisory and Technical Assistance Services Overseas	Enables Indian consultancy firms undertake specific assignments in select countries through grant financing.
Cooperation Arrangement with African with African Management Services Co (AMSCO) Amsterdam	Enables Indian consultants secure assignments in various projects that are managed by AMSCO in different parts of Sub-Saharan Africa, through grant financing.
Executive Services Overseas Programme	Enables senior Indian experts to share their experiences with beneficiaries overseas, through provision of a variety of technical assistance.
Africa Enterprise Fund	Enables Indian consultancy firms to undertake specific assignments to assist small and medium entrepreneurs in Sub-Saharan Africa.
Africa Project Development Facility	Enables Indian consultancy firms undertake specific assignments in Sub-Saharan Africa through grant financing.
EC Investment Partners Facility (ECIP)	Enables setting up of joint ventures in India between Indian companies and enterprises in the European Community.
Asian Countries Investment Partners Programme (ACIP)	Aims at promoting joint ventures in India with companies in East Asian countries, through four facilities that address different stages of a joint venture project cycle viz. Sector study, project identification, feasibility study, prototype development, technical, and managerial assistance.
For Commercial Banks	
Refinance of Export (Supplier's) Credit	Enables banks to offer credit to Indian exporters of eligible goods, who extend term credit over 180 days to importers overseas.
Small Scale Industry (SSI) Export Bills Rediscounting	Enables banks to rediscount export bills of their SSI customers with usance not exceeding 90 days.
Relending facility	Enables banks overseas to make available term finance to their clients, for import of eligible Indian goods.
Refinance of Term Loans to EOUs	Enables banks to offer credit to eligible export-oriented units to acquire indigenous and imported machinery and other assets for export production.

Bulk Import Finance	Enables banks to offer finance to importers for bulk import of consumable inputs.
Guarantee cum Refinance Supplier's Credit	Enables banks to protect their own cash flow as also its exporter client's cash flow on account of default by overseas buyer. Protects the Bank by not treating the advance as a Non Performing Asset for provisioning purposes.
Programme for Confirmation of Letters of Credit	Enhances the ability of commercial Banks in India to open Letters of Credit on behalf of their importer customers for import of raw materials and other items.
For overseas entities	
Lines of Credit	Enables overseas financial institutions, foreign governments, their agencies to lend term loans to finance import of eligible goods from India.
Buyer's Credit	Enables overseas buyer to import eligible goods from India on deferred credit terms.

EXPORT-IMPORT BANK OF INDIA

HEADQUARTERS

Centre One, Floor 21,
World Trade Centre,
Cuffe Parade, Mumbai 400 005.
Phone: (022) 2185272 Extn. 2217/2218
Fax: (022) 2182572
Email: eximind@giasbm01.vsnl.net.in

OFFICES	
NEW DELHI	CHENNAI
Tower 1, Floor 8, Jeevan Bharati Building, 124, Connaught Circus, New Delhi 110 001. Phone: (011) 3326375/6625 Fax: 011-3322758/3321719 Email: eximnd@del2gems.vsnl.net.in	UTI House, Floor 1, 29, Rajaji Salai, Chennai 600 001. Phone: (044) 5224714/49 Fax: 044-5224082 Email: bank.eximimd@gems.vsnl.net.in
CALCUTTA	MUMBAI
5A&5B Park Plaza 71, Park street, Calcutta 700 016. Phone: (033) 292467/2454630 Fax: 033-2269357 Email:bank.eximca@gems.vsnl.net.in.	Maker Chambers IV, Floor 8, 222, Nariman Point, Mumbai 400 021. Phone: (022) 2830761/2823320 Fax: 022-2022132 Email:bank.eximbm2@gems.vsnl.net.in

BANGALORE	BUDAPEST
Ramanashree Arcade, Floor 4, 18 M.G. Road, Bangalore 560 001. Phone: (080) 5585755/5589101-04 Fax: 080-5589107 Email: bank.eximbg@gems.vsnl.net.in	Floor 3, Unit 308, ECE City Centre, Bajcsy-Zsilinzky UT. 12, 1051 Budapest, Hungary. Phone: (361) 1382833/1176699 Fax: 361-1178354 Email: eximindia@mail.matav.hu
AHMEDABAD	ROME
Sakar II, Floor 1, Next to Ellisbridge Shopping Centre, Ellisbridge P.O., Ahmedabad 380 006. Phone: (079) 6576852/6843 Fax: 079-6578271 Email: eximind@ad1.vsnl.net.in	Via Boncompagni - 79, Scala "A", Int. 3A, 2°Piano, I-00187 Rome, Italy. Phone: (396) 420 83 808 Fax: 396-420 83 471 Email: exim.bank.of.india@Agro.stm.it
WASHINGTON D.C.	JOHANNESBURG
1750 Pennsylvania Avenue N.W., Suite 320 Washington D.C. 20006 U.S.A. Phone: (202) 223-3238/3239 Fax: 202-785 8487 Email: indexim@worldnet.att.net	158, Jan Smuts, Ground Floor, 9, Walters Avenue, Rosebank, Johannesburg 2196 P.O. Box 2018, Saxonwold 2132, Johannesburg, South Africa. Phone: (2711) 4428010/4422053 Fax: 2711-4428022 Email: eximindia@icon.co.za
SINGAPORE	
10, Collyer Quay, # 15-06 Ocean Building, Singapore 049315. Phone: (65) 532 6464 Fax: 65-535 2131 Email: eximbank@singnet.com.sg.	

INDEX